CIVIL HUMAN RIGHTS IN RUSSIA

CIVIL HUMAN RIGHTS IN RUSSIA

MODERN PROBLEMS OF THEORY AND PRACTICE

F. M. RUDINSKY
EDITOR

TRANSACTION PUBLISHERS
NEW BRUNSWICK (U.S.A.) AND LONDON (U.K.)

Library of Congress Catalog Number: 2007027440
ISBN: 978-0-7658-0391-7
Printed in the United States of America

Library of Congress Cataloging-in-Publication Data

Rudinsky, F. M.
   Civil human rights in Russia : modern problems of theory and practice / [compiled by] F.M. Rudinsky.
       p. cm.
   Includes bibliographical references and index.
   ISBN 978-0-7658-0391-7 (alk. paper)
       1. Civil rights--Russia (Federation) 2. Human rights--Russia (Federation) 3. Russia (Federation)--Politics and government--1991- I. Title.

JC599.R9R83 2007
323.0947--dc22

                                                                    2007027440

CONTENTS

To the Foreign Reader

This volume was written by the group of Russian authors — researchers, judges, lawyers, legal experts. It was initially written in Russian and published in Volgograd (former Stalingrad) by the Russian Academy of the Ministry of Internal Affairs in 2004. In this institution from as early as in 1989 one of the first faculties of human rights in the USSR was created headed by the scientific editor of this volume.

The theme selected by the authors of this volume is no way casual. Civil rights is a groups of human rights called to ensure the provision of individual personal freedom, guarantees of privacy and personal security. This group differs from other human rights guaranteed by the international Bill of Rights: political, economic, social and cultural. The rights of victims of the crimes as well as those accused and condemned and others relate to civil human rights such as a right to life, dignity, personal freedom, personal immunity, freedom from tortures, freedom of movement and freedom of residence.

The challenge of civil rights' enforcement has always been very acute all over world. In Russia we have always experienced and continue to experience significant difficulties in their realization (A fact that the reader will become very well acquainted with after reading this book), but this is especially true with regards to civil rights.

However, in the theoretical literature, in particular in Russian, such questions concerning legal features of civil rights, forms of their realization, typical infringements and means of their protection, have been researched quite insufficiently.

This book is an attempt to give answers to the specific problem of civil rights' enforcement. Certainly, we do not claim to provide absolute truth but we would like to emphasize that this book rep resents the objective scientific research of the problem based on revealing the established facts stated in the materials of the United Nations, the Council of Europe, reports of Ombudsman of the Russian Federation, and the official statistical data from different Russian offices of state.

However, as Mark Twain noted, ''there are three kinds of the lie: a lie, a bald lie and statistics''. Therefore, we have aspired to compare data presented by the state authorities with the facts ascertained by the international and Russian nongovernmental public organizations. We also have based our research on personal experience as a number of our authors are engaged in legal practice.

In this book the analysis of regulations of international law, the Russian legislation, decisions of the European Court on human rights, of the Constitutional Court of Russia and other materials of law enforcement practice is given.

The gravity of the research level is provided by professional skills of those who carry it out. It is necessary to say that informed enough experts having the modern technique of scientific research have been involved in the work on this book.

The author of each section of the book is the expert who has written and has successfully defended the scientific dissertation on the given question, or has a significant practical experience connected with the subject. In particular, Professor F.M. Rudinsky and Professor P.V. Anisimov are the members of Russian Federation Ombudsman Expert Council. They have writ ten theses for a doctor's degree on topics which had been included into the book as its sections. The Volgograd professor I.V. Rostovschikov has written/wrote the section about the mechanism of human rights' guarantees. S.A. Burjanov, the legal expert, the President of the Moscow Public Institute of Freedom of Worship, has written the corresponding section of the book. E.L. Menshutina, the Moscow judge, has written the part about human right on fair, impartial and lawful proceeding. The lawyer A.G. Manafov is the author of the chapter about the right to legal protection, and the lawyer S.V. Mamicheva has written about protection of the rights of victims of crimes and abuse of authority. The authors of the chapter about the rights of suspected and accused are experts on criminal trial and senior lecturers of the Volgograd Academy of the Ministry of Internal Affairs of the Russian Federation S.A. Kolosovich, V.G. Glebov and the lawyer from Rostov-on-Don S.I. Ponomarenko. They have not only characterized the specified rights, but have given the characteristic of the modern state of Russian criminal procedure.

Rather original is the section of the book about the right to privacy, written by the young researcher from Arkhangelsk the university senior lecturer G.B. Romanovsky. The author of the dissertation about freedom of movement in the country O.V. Rostovschikova has written the corresponding section of the book.

E.M. Pavlenko, the lawyer, is the author of the section about formation of culture of human rights. She is a trainer of the Council of Europe on education in the sphere of human rights, the graduate of the Helsinki High International Fund on Human Rights (Poland).

The senior lecturer of the Moscow academy of the Ministry of Internal Affairs of the Russian Federation N.B. Hutorskaya is a prominent expert on penal law and the author of the section about the rights of condemned. The head of the department of constitutional law of the Volgograd Academy of Public Service, senior lecturer V.D. Goncharenko is the author of the first dissertation in Russia devoted to the problem of realization of the right to freedom from tortures and other kinds of the inhuman treatment and punishment. A young researcher R.J. Shulga for the first time to Russia has written the dissertation about forms and methods of nongovernmental public organizations' activity in protection of human rights.

An absolutely young postgraduate student I.V. Shishenina has done a very difficult job: she has written the sections about lawful restriction of civil rights and freedoms and about guarantees of the right to honour and dignity of a person.

Thus, in the group of authors there are researchers from Moscow and from some northern and southern regions of Russia.

One of features of the book (as it follows from its name) is the analysis of modern problems of human rights. It is only possible to perceive the essence of certain phenomena only when it is being researched in the period of its occurrence and development.

On the other hand, quite often it happens so that the passion of the author for historical plots is in essence the flight from the reality. We have aspired to concentrate on the situation existing in the end of the 20th — the beginning of the 21st centuries, avoiding unjustified digressions to history.

Another feature of the book is its humanistic essence. The authors represent different age groups, different occupations, and have various visions and original approaches to certain legal phenomena, however, are in agreement in one: of the necessity to protect civil human rights, to expand and develop their guarantees in Russia as well as all over world. In the authors' opinion, the unique criterion of legitimacy of civil human rights realization is their exact conformity to general Declaration and to international pacts and conventions on human rights.

Finally, the third feature of the book is that it represents the point of view on the problem of civil human rights from a Russian perspective.

Written by Russian researchers it concerns international aspects of the problem but the main attention of the authors is concentrated on our domestic problems. Here again we would like the foreign reader to understand us. And we hope that the book will be able to dispel (even partially) some erroneous stereo typical thinking about Russia and the destiny of human rights in this country which are widespread in the West.

In western society the popular belief is that Russia is a huge Eurasian, low civilized country described by A. Solzhenitsyn in his book "Archipelago Gulag", a country where the overwhelming majority of citizens do not know about human rights and human dignity. These representations require some serious corrective amendments.

In the middle of the 20th century on the basis of world culture in world community there was a universal concept of human rights based on that was embodied in the International Bill of Rights. If we study closely the Universal Declaration of Human Rights of the United Nations (1948) and international acts accepted on its basis, it is possible to come to the conclusion that the essence of this concept consists in the following: 1) recognition of human dignity and human rights as a highest absolute values; 2) non derivativeness of human rights from commands of the state and their inalienability; 3) equality of people in dignity and human rights; 4) incompatibility of human rights with tyranny, exploitation and oppression, fear and need, arbitrariness and criminality; 5) recognition of all systems of interconnected civil, political, economic, social and cultural rights, and their connection with duties; 6) recognition of values of democracy and justice; 7) maintenance of the system of international and interstate guarantees of human rights.

In western Europe and America there is a tendency to identify human rights with values of western Atlantic civilization, but it is an erroneous representation. ''Human rights are the things that make us people, — Kofi Annan said, — truly understood and fairly interpreted human rights are not alien to any culture and close to all people''.

Certainly, it is impossible to deny the fundamental value of the British Magna Carta (1215) Declarations of Independence (1776) first ten amendments to the Constitution of the USA (1791) the French Declaration of Human and Civil Rights (1789) in the formation of the first generation of human rights, among which there are those that we now call civil rights. However, each country and each continent have contributed to the strengthening of the universal concept of human rights. And it is not casual that in addition to the accepted UN instruments of human rights in Europe, in America, Africa, and in the Islamic world, the corresponding regional documents reflecting civilized features of each continent in understanding of human rights and means of their protection are accepted.

Russia has contributed to the formation and recognition of the above-stated universal concept of human rights. First of all, we should note the spiritual and moral influence of the great Russian culture based on the propagation of humanity, good and justice on world culture. As is it well-known, during the Second World War the USSR played a significant role in the crushing defeat of German fascism and Japanese militarism.

The USSR was one of founders of the United Nations, and its representatives actively participated in preparation of general Declaration of Human Rights and international covenants on human rights.

Natural, geopolitical, historical, ecological, ethnic, spiritual, and psychological features inherent to Russia render serious influence on the process of realizing human rights. If we look back at the history of our country, then here over centuries (including the Soviet and post Soviet periods) two opposite tendencies have existed: liberation movements, i.e. movements for freedom and personal rights, and on the other hand, reactionary movements, i.e. autocratic, totalitarian, bureaucratic, interfering the strengthening of human rights and freedoms.

It is necessary to remind the reader that Russia down to the beginning of the 20th century was an absolute monarchy, a semi feudal state. French Marquis de Custine, who visited Russia in 1839 wrote, "This empire... is just a prison, a key to which is located with the emperor... The Russian commoner receives not beating in his life, than the emperor does... Whether Providence keeps these people, the very heart of human race under oppression? When will liberation come?"[1]

According to the pre-revolutionary Russian criminalist professor N.S. Tagantsev in the 19th century the number of exiled to Siberia reached 900,000 people. The condemned were forced to go on foot, in fetters, a lot of them were chained to carts[2] (the number of people in prisons was not given).

In no circumstances it is possible to justify the cruelty and the lawlessness that occurred in the USSR in 1930s to 1950s, but readers of the book "Archipelago Gulag" should know that the Stalin prison system had not arisen out of nowhere. Over certain stages of Russian history were dominated with an emancipating tendency. Therefore, in 1861 the Emperor Alexander II abolished serfdom, releasing millions of Russian peasants from it. Or another example: in the 1950s of the 20th century following Stalin's death hundreds of thousands of illegally condemned people were released from prisons, the rights of wrongfully repressed people were restored, and 50 million of citizens received free apartments in houses built at the expense of the state.

It is necessary to bear in mind certain features of Russian public consciousness: domination of moral values, belittling of the role of law and low level of trust in justice of officials and citizens. In Russia there has never existed western cult of cold validity, humanism in the spirit of the Renaissance, concepts of freedom as characterized by legal propositions. In the country of Tolstoy and Dostoevsky the understanding of humanism as a rule, was based on humanity, compassion, pity to the abandoned, degraded and offended. Centuries of unlimited authority of autocrats, general secretaries, and absence of parliamentary traditions have hardened political culture based on canonizing of sovereigns. Absence of stable law and order, reliable guarantees of personal rights, corruption of the state machinery, lawlessness and arbitrariness of officials have generated mistrust on the part of citizens towards the law, court proceedings as to means of protection of personal interests.

If in western society the concept of human rights as a rule, is connected with the procedure of their judicial protection, then in consciousness of Russian citizens they were considered as an embodiment of personal dignity as a moral category. And even during the gravest times a Russian person understood his human value. The first words which were written by illiterate peasants in mass schools for liquidation of illiteracy created after revolution of 1917 were words in the textbook: "We are not slaves". In 1941 when Hitlerite Germany attacked the USSR, in the country general free education and health care had already been introduced.

In 1992 a document taken from archives of the Hitlerite Gestapo was published in Berlin. During the Second World War German propaganda distributed among the population of Germany claimed that Russian was just a stupid half-starved mass of people used to corporal punishments practiced by the political police — the GPU. However, tens of thousands of workers and prisoners of war taken to Germany confuted these conceptions. The Gestapo marked out in a confidential service document that, in fact, the workers from the East amazed Germans with " their technical ingenuity", and the fact that Russian agricultural workers were more educated than German counterparts, and that "these people did not know corporal punishments", had high morals of behaviour, and a lot of them wore Christian crosses on their necks[3].

Some of the features of Russia include huge distances, absence of normal roads in the countryside (especially in the Urals, in Siberia), and a severe climate. It is difficult to survive here alone. The environment creates a necessity for joint collective work. Therefore community, collectivism of the Russian consciousness is opposed to western individualism. Naturally, Marxist theses (Marxism (Leninism) is the German theory transferred to the Russian ground) about social equality, about the necessity to protect the rights of workers are so popular among many citizens. These factors render significant influence on formation of culture of human rights.

At the same time, during the last fifteen years in the country certain changes have appeared in public consciousness. Development of market relations has led to such a rise in court proceedings that judges no longer have time to consider them in statutory terms. The prestige of judicial education has also increased. The number of law faculties and entrants, wishing to become lawyers, increases from year to year.

However, the public remains skeptical towards the role of courts in protection of human rights. And these are not just groundless doubts of sober minded people. It is possible to read about it in more detail on pages of this book.

As for Russian jurisprudence, it has deep traditions and serious development has contributed considerably to the on problems of human rights. The Russian intelligentsia (and legal scientists belong to it) has always treated the achievements of western philosophy, political science and jurisprudence very attentively.

Studying this book will allow the reader to familiarize them selves with the names of the scientists who developed the remedial theme in the past and are dealing with it today.

Thus it is necessary to bear in mind that Russia is a country included into the world family of Romance-Germanic law. Unlike Anglo-Saxon legal system where judicial precedent has special value, in Russia the main role in the dispute resolution is played by legal provisions fixed in law or legal code. Therefore, the so called normative trend in jurisprudence has always been a determining factor. The law was always considered as a system of obligatory legal regulations fixed in legal acts, accepted by the government. The personal rights (sometimes called legal or subjective rights belong to separate people) were considered as legal concepts resulting due to realization of legal provisions. And as ay are established by the state the personal rights depend on the state will. However, recently there has been an approximation of the Romance-Germanic and

Anglo-Saxon legal systems. Decisions of the European Court of Human Rights, the Constitutional Court of the Russian Federation in effect are precedents and become sources of Russian law.

During the last 15 years another legal concept called the "revival school of natural law" has been increasingly recognized in Russia. Its main point is that human rights, as specified in Article 1 of the General Declaration of Human Rights, are inborn (i.e. appear from the moment of birth) and integral with the person. The state, with the help of legal regulations, is obliged to recognize and to protect them. This book has been written from this point of view.

There is one more circumstance which has created significant difficulties in writing of this book. We live in an extremely dynamic and quickly changing world. The situation with civil human rights is also constantly varying. This is especially true in Russia.

In the end of the 19th century Oscar Wilde noted, "There is nothing impossible in Russia, except for reforms". The 20th century has proved this judgement of the brilliant English writer to be wrong. The country which has survived two world wars and one civil war, three revolutions in the beginning of the 20th century and one counterrevolution at the end, till now has been in the constant state of reforms. A well-known Russian poet A. Tvardovsky characterized such situation as, "Committee of the infinite alteration of affairs".

The parliament accepts hundreds of laws, and infinite amendments are made to recently accepted acts. Instability of the legislation leads to instability of personal rights. For example, in 2001 a new Code of Criminal Procedure was accepted, in 2002 it was published in a new edition, and then other numerous amendments have followed. The reader will read on the pages of this book that introduction by this Code of the judicial control of arrests has resulted by 2003 in reducing the number of suspected and accused people in custody. But the life takes its own course. According to the Ministry of Justice in 2005 the number of imprisoned persons of this category has again increased. Legal proceedings of arrests have appeared an insufficient guarantee of personal immunity for the accused in minor offenses. The accusatory bias dominates the consciousness of many public prosecutors and judges and appears to be stronger than the technical procedures provided by the new law.

In such a difficult, at times even confusing situation, the authors of this volume have tried to reveal the most essential features of the problem of civil rights realization. One of the main ideas which illustrates it is a recognition and development of a new science of human rights which aimed at integrating the achievements of various public and natural sciences concerning a person and their opportunities of free development. The French scientist of the 20th century K. Vasak put forward the idea of formation of such science, but it has yet not received sufficient recognition in Russia as well as in other countries of the world.

Another new idea put forward by the authors of this book consists in the special value of the right to legal protection of a person. In conditions of mass infringement of human rights in many countries, the science is aimed at paying special attention to the forms and ways of their protection. The term "human rights activity" has a rather narrow meaning in Russia. The activity of non governmental public organizations is mostly characterized in this way. It seems that human rights should be actions of all structures: state as well as public.

This book consists of three parts. The first part covers the general theoretical problems of civil human rights. The second part is devoted to separate civil rights. And, finally, in the third part the guarantees of all civil human rights are discussed. In the end of the book the reader can take a closer look at the list of modern Russian scientific works on the problems of civil rights.

We hope that this book will help the reader to understand the deep essence of civil human rights, to estimate the situation with their realization in Russia and all over the world and to reveal the reasons of their infringement and ways of their protection.

Professor F.M. Rudinsky
January, 2006
Moscow

Notes

[1] Marquis de Custine. Russia in 1839. Moscow, 1990. pp. 123,173, 220.
[2] See: N.S. Tagantsev. Russian Criminal Law. St. Petersburg. 1902. p. 996.
[3] See: Service circular SD "Messages from the Reich" about the image of Russian population. 4/15/1943 - War of Germany against Soviet Union 1941-1945. Documentary exposition edited by Reinhardt Rurop. Berlin. 1992. P. 183-184.

Introduction

Human rights relate to legal rights of a person. In the modern sense, human rights represent the most essential opportunities of a person's development, the integral properties defining freedom of a person.

These rights have been internationalized as a result of adopting the Universal Declaration of Human Rights and international treaties of human rights in the second half of the 20th century. They have been legally recognized by the majority of states in world, and an international mechanism for their protection has been generated. Mankind has gradually entered a new phase of its development called globalization. It is characterized by transition from industrial to information-oriented society, from national economy to world economy, by the strengthening of the transnational corporations' power that exceeds the might of a lot of states, and by the creation of a new system of mass media. On the one hand, mankind has created mass life support facilities that may provide necessary living conditions for people. On the other hand, weaponry capable of killing all life on our planet has also appeared.

The collapse of the USSR and emergence of the post-Soviet states in the territory of CIS and in Eastern Europe, the strengthening of the political influence of the USA, the expansion of NATO, the strengthening of European Union, the economic successes of China, India and some other countries have created an absolutely new international situation. Contradictions between the North and the South have become extremely aggravated. There have arisen new conflicts connected with the struggle for repartition of world and getting control over energy resources. All these circumstances have led to serious difficulties and contradictions in human rights enforcement.

During the last decades human rights recorded in international legal provisions and constitutions of many countries have been recognized by public conscience. International organizations and their structures (Human Rights Commission, United Nations High Commissioner for Human Rights (UNHCHR), Human Rights Committee (HRC), Committee Against Tortures (CAT), Committee on the Rights of the Child (CRC) and others, European Court of Human Rights, etc.) have accumulated significant advocacy experience. In many countries the interstate mechanism of human rights protection, including not only the branched system of tribunals, justice institutions, Offices of Public Prosecutor, but also ombudsmen, advocacy organizations, has been created. Legal procedures providing protection of rights are recorded and practiced in the legal provisions. In many states of world the legal status of a person corresponding to international legal standards has been already recognized at the official level.

The institute of legal (international and interstate) responsibility for dangerous encroachments on human rights has been further developed during recent years. Criminal liability for genocide and other crimes against humanity, war crimes and assaultive offences/crimes is stipulated not only by the rules of international law/international legal regulations, but is also included in the criminal codes of many countries. The coming into force of the Roman Statute of the International Criminal Court in July, 2002 is also of great importance. During the last decades there have been law proceedings on criminal cases of dictators accused of severe atrocities against citizens in different countries (Chile, Argentina, the Philippines, etc.). Antidemocratic regimes have collapsed in a great number of countries of world. The activity of human rights organizations, trade unions, and political parties supporting human rights has become more comprehensive.

At the same time a great deal of negative phenomena creating new obstacles in enforcement of these rights is integrally inherent to the globalization epoch achievements.

The UN Secretary General's Report "Globalization and Its influence on Human Rights Enforcement", presented in 2000 on the 55th session of the General Assembly of the United Nations stated the following: "the internet enables representatives of various regions and cultures to communicate quickly, being on significant distance from each other, and to have online access to the information … it can substantially stimulate the progress in the field of public health and education. The internet provides connection between representatives of the civil society that renders direct influence on encouragement and protection of human rights"[1]. The Secretary General of the United Nations continued: "Maldistribution of new technologies can lead to marginalizing of people. In the countries with a high level of the income there are on average 311 personal computers owners per 1000 people, in the countries of Latin America and Caribbean basin there are only 34 people per 1000, and in the countries of Southern Asia there are only 2.9 people per 1000 having computers"[2].

The internet is used for violation of human rights, including kindling hatred, propagation of racism, child pornography, religious intolerance, and scornful attitudes toward women. The internet turns into a "rather effective means of freedom of speech abusing and discrimination encouragement"[3].

The report states that trade and financial flow liberalization in the globalization environment has caused a sharp increase in global export of goods and services. In 2000 "almost one fifth of all industrial goods and services was sold in international markets"[4]. Trade makes an important contribution to economic development and can lead to reducing the level of poverty. However, capital flows are, as a rule, still concentrated in the developed countries, and the economic development inequality between the North and the South is gradually increasing. The research of nine countries carried out by the United Nations has shown that liberalization of trade was accompanied by salary reduction, growth of partial employment, the emerging of anti-women discrimination[5]. Globalization has facilitated international arms traffic that, in turn, has created conditions for confrontations, has strengthened the scales of waste disposal polluting the environment in developing countries. It is accompanied by increase in international turnover of drugs, trade in people, including children, and the development of the sex industry[6].

Globalization has considerably strengthened the threats to human rights, including the following: increasing risk of nuclear catastrophe, international conflicts and wars; famine and poverty of scores of millions people, deepening of the abyss between the developed and developing countries; aggravation of violence, in particular terrorism and international criminality/delinquency; aggravation of environment pollution; spreading of AIDS and other dangerous diseases; complication of problems of population; kindling of conflicts on racial, ethnic, religious grounds; display of totalitarianism, authoritarianism and suppression of human rights by bureaucracy. These are global threats to the whole system of human rights. This book will focus on typical violation of civil human rights. It also would be necessary to talk about encroachments on economic and social rights, first of all on the right to an adequate standard of living.

International organization United Nations Development Program (UNDP) prepares annual reports on human development in world. According to this organization, in 2003 more than 1.2 billion out of 6.5 billion of world's population, i.e. one fifth of the population is living on less than 1 dollar a day. By UN parameters this is the sign of extreme poverty.

In the 1990s, the share of the population suffering from extreme poverty decreased from 30 to 23%, but due to world population growth, the actual number of the people living in such conditions has increased by 28 million. The number of starving people has also risen. Every sixth adult in the world is illiterate. Every day 30,000 children, i.e. more than 10 million a year, die of diseases that could have been prevented. More than 1 billion people have no access to safe water, and 2.4 billion have no access to the modern sanitary facilities. More than 500,000 women die every year during pregnancy and in childbirth. 42 million people in world are infected by HIV/AIDS, and 39 million of them live in developing countries[7]. UNDP cites the following data concerning the property inequality in world: the richest 1% of world population has received the income equal to the income of 57% of the population[8].

One of the serious problems arisen during recent years is belittling of the UN role in human rights enforcement. It was dramatically revealed during wars in Yugoslavia and in Iraq when the USA and the NATO states were making decisions on military operations, just ignoring the UN system. In international practice there have occurred new interpretations of the categories standard in law, which are aimed, as air authors consider, at ensuring the human rights enforcement, though, in fact, they have some other purposes. It is a special question of such categories as "state sovereignty", and "humanitarian intervention". "Particularly traditional concept of the sovereignty cannot justify hopes of all people for gaining basic freedom any more", the UN Secretary General Kofi Annan has declared[9]. International Commission of intervention and State Sovereignty aimed at defining the criteria and procedures of "humanitarian intervention" into the state matters accused of mass violations of human rights has been created. Virtually, it is a question of revision or even full rejection of the principle of the state sovereignty which is one of basic principles of the United Nations Charter. As considered, such actions can lead to intervention legalization of the powerful states against the weak states, accompanied by mass violation of human rights. Anyway, this question requires very serious scientific studying. These are the basic features of world state of human rights.

All these tendencies have also become apparent in Russia, which entered the global world in the beginning of the 1990s. Our country has made certain steps to the creation of the mechanism of human rights' guarantees. International standards of human rights have been recognized, first of all, in the Constitution of the Russian Federation, in the current legislation, in particular, in new Civil Code, Criminal Code, Code of Criminal Procedure, Code of Procedure and other codes.

The state structures, aimed at providing guarantees of these rights, have the necessary human rights competence (president, judges, law machinery, including Office of Public Prosecutor, Ministry of Internal Affairs, etc.). Some of these structures (Human Rights Commissioners in the Federation and its constituents) have been introduced for the first time in Russian history, and they have already proved their efficiency in practice. It is necessary to note, that such measures as transfer of criminal penal organizations from Ministry of internal Affairs' jurisdiction into the system of Ministry of Justice, and judicial reform are focused on achievement of the humanitarian purposes. New legal procedures (e.g., the procedure of the judicial appeal of wrong acts of officials, the procedure of the judicial control over arrests) have been introduced in the country as legal guarantees of human rights. The judiciary practice focused on enforcement of human rights is being developed in Russia. In particular, it includes some decisions of the Constitutional Court of the Russian Federation, and other courts.

It is possible to rank the strengthening of principles of political and ideological pluralism, periodic elections of the state authorities among the achievements of the last decade. All this has salutarily affected the enforcement of political human rights. In 2002-2004 arrears of wages of workers and employees were reduced that contributed for the economic and social rights enforcement, though the most difficult problems in this sphere have remained and have even become more serious. The last decade has witnessed some actions in the field of education of human rights.

However, as a whole, the state of human rights is unsatisfactory, that is confirmed by the reports of the Human Rights Commissioner in the Russian Federation in 1998-2003, independent human rights organizations, and scientific researchers. The most serious failures took place in enforcement of the right to life (the subsequent chapters of this book are devoted to this problem), the right to an adequate standard of living, and other economic and social rights. As the president of the Russian Federation has admitted, poverty of the significant part of the population is one of the most complicated problems. The amount of the people being in the state of extreme poverty is estimated ambiguously.

According to data of the Director of Institute of Social and Economic Problems of the Population, today Russia has the lowest salary in Europe—30% of workers receive a salary that is below the cost of living[10].

According to Vice Premier G.N. Karelova, in the end of October, 2003 the number of Russians living below the poverty line, was 33 million people[11].

According to communiques of the Russian State Statistics Committee (Goskomstat), in 2003 the amount of the poor people living below the poverty line was 29 million, i.e., 20.3% of the population. In January, 2004, the debt for state employees was 2.3 billion roubles, and number of unemployed was 6.3 million, 1.6 million of them were registered on labour exchange[12].

Based on the official data, the amount of the poor and jobless people has been decreasing during recent 57 years. However, the level of poverty and unemployment is rather high. According to the Human Development index (HDI) determined by UNDP, in 1999 Russia ranked 77th place, in 2002 it ranked 62nd, in 2001 it ranked 55th, and in 2002 Russia ranked 60th place in the list of 162 countries[13]. This advance has occurred due to the parameters/activities on education. Russia is among the countries of the "average level of development" according to the HDI which is considered on three levels: longevity, education and adequate living standard. However, it is necessary to note that during the last 25 years HDI for Russia has considerably decreased. Other parameters of economic and social rights enforcement in Russia are also of great interest.

Thus, according to international organization World Economic Forum (WEF), in 2003-2004 Russia in the information development rating ranks 63rd place in the list of 102 countries[14]. The experts based their conclusion on such parameters as population, the quantity of telephone numbers, TVs, internet users, etc. It is interesting, that the place of Russia in this list almost coincides with its place in the list of UNDP according to HDI. In conditions of globalization there is an absolute connection between the level of information development of the country and the level of human rights enforcement. The research held by the company Vision international People Group, has shown, that by rights of financing Russian Public Health Service occupies 185th place out of 188 countries participating in the research[15]. According to President of this company, D. Buryak, "the overwhelming majority of our compatriots is not provided with qualitative medical care"[16].

Former Minister of Health of the Russian Federation, the academician of Russian Academy of Medical Science, Y. Shevchenko, has provided the following data: not more than 20% of our population is still healthy. Life expectancy of Russians is 10-14 years less than in Japan, USA, England and France[17].

Russia is in demographic crisis: every year the population of the country decreases by 900,000 to 1 million people. According to the Russian

State Statistics Committee, in 2002 the natural loss in population was 6.5 per 1000 people and in 2003—6.2[18].

· The well known expert demographer, Doctor of Medicine I.A. Gundarov investigating the problems of quality of life, has offered certain digital parameters of this phenomenon. Having studied them he has come to the following conclusions. If we take 1998 for 100%, then in 2003 the death rate in Russia was 122%, murders—132%, suicides—106%, the number of divorces to the number of marriages—176%[19].

Let us cite also data of the American institute SATO carrying out the research "Economic Freedom in world". According to the level of economic freedom (the right to free competition, protection of the people and the property, the amount and level of taxes, etc.) Russia has got 112th place in the list of 125 states[20].

The inequality in income distribution should also be added to this list. According to the official data, in 2001 10% of the most wealthy population had 33.3% of the total amount of cash income, and 10% of the least wealthy population had 2.4% of it[21]. Considering "shadow" receipts, the rich in Russia have the income that is 30 times bigger than the poor. In western countries this gap is 4-5 times smaller[22]. These are the basic estimations of economic and social rights in Russia.

During recent last 4 to 5 years there have arisen new difficulties concerning political human rights. A new law about political parties, changes in the suffrage, new Federal Constitutional Law "Referendum in the Russian Federation" has limited the rights of citizens to participate in the government and have complicated/hampered the activity of political parties. Strengthening of the influence of the state structures and the large private companies on mass media is currently observed that negatively affects the enforcement of citizens' right on information, freedom of thought and speech. International organizations have given rather a critical estimation to the State Duma election in December, 2003.

There are serious problems in the cultural rights enforcement, first of all, the right to education. Among them there are insufficient financing of educational institutions, gap in computerization, low salary of teachers, and high cost of the textbooks. Contrary to Article 13 of international Pact of Economic, Social and Cultural Rights, free education, especially the high education, is gradually disappearing. Commercialization of scientific work leads to turning of academic/scientific degrees into objects of sale and purchase.

As we have specified above, this book is devoted to one of the types of human rights, namely, to the civil rights and freedom of a person.

There is a great amount of the scientific literature dedicated to the problem of individual freedom and civil (individual) human rights. It was in the focus of the special attention of such outstanding thinkers of the 17th to 20th centuries, as J. Locke, Voltaire, J.-J. Rousseau, Ch.L. Montesquieu, I. Kant, L. Feuerbach, K. Marx, J.-P. Sartre, A. Schweitzer.

As for Russia, these questions were studied in the works of A.N. Radishchev, S.E. Desnitsky, E.N. Trubetskoy, B.N. Tchitcherin, etc. They were reflected in the constitutional projects of Decembrists, in Speransky's work, in Alexander's II legislation, program documents of oppositional and revolutionary parties of pre-revolutionary Russia.

During the Soviet period the essential contribution to the development of problem of a person's rights was made by the scientists and lawyers N.N. Poljansky, M.M. Grodzinsky, M.S. Strogovich, E.A. Elistratov, E.A. Flejshits, L.D. Voevodin, V.A. Patjulin, I.E. Farber.

The first master's thesis about person's constitutional rights belonged to A.P. Gorshenev (1972). The first doctor's thesis belonged to F.M. Rudinsky (1980).

The modern literature concerning these problems is characterized by certain essential features. Firstly, the number of articles, books, and dissertations/thesis has considerably increased. Secondly, a lot of young researchers have appeared.

From the methodological point of view it is necessary that a lot of the authors have rather successfully used the comparative-legal, historical-legal, concrete-sociological methods of researches. Many of them have provided rather valuable suggestions on the legislation development. The advantage of these works is that they consider international standards of human rights as a reference point, criterion of democratic character of Russian legislation and law enforcement policy/practice. However, from the ideological point of view, the overwhelming majority of studies from Marxism-Leninism (of the Soviet type of 30-80th) have turned to liberalism in its out-of-date form of the end of the 19th-the beginning of the 20th centuries. The rejection of ideological variety, in our opinion, appears to be the essential flaw/drawback of many authors.

It is impossible to enumerate all researchers dealing with the problems of civil human rights. Thus, we should mention only some of them.

Within the framework of the forming science of human rights the essential role was played by the following authors of monographs and textbooks of "Human Rights" course: B.L. Nazarov, E.A. Lukasheva, M.M. Utyashev, A.G. Berezhnov, O.O. Mironov, V.V. and L.V. Boitsovy,

L.I. Gluhareva, S.I. Glushkova, V.M. Kapitsyn, V.S. Ustinov, A.J. Azarov, A.Y. Sungurov.

The significant contribution to the development of these questions in the sphere of general legal and state theory has been made by N.I. Matuzov, G.V. Maltsev, A.S. Mordovets, I.V. Rostovschikov, A.V. Stremouhov, P.V. Anisimov. In the field of constitutional law it is necessary to note the works of N.S. Bondarj, B.S. Ebzeev, M.V. Baglay, S.A. Glotov, N.J. Hamaneva, N. Komkova. A great number of works has also been written in the field of international law. Among them it is necessary to mention the works of R.A. Mullerson, V.A. Kartashkin, V.A. Tumanov, O.I. Tiunov, A.H. Saidov, B.G. Manov, S.V. Chernichenko, M.L. Entin, T.D. Matveeva.

In the above-stated works devoted to general problems of human rights and their guarantees, the questions of the civil rights are also been developed.

At the same time there has appeared a great deal of research focused on the whole system of the civil (personal) rights and the separate civil rights (works of N.I. Petruhin, J.I. Stetsovsky, B. Romanovsky, L.O. Krasavchikova, A.P. Rasskazov and I.V. Uporov, M.P. Avdeenkova and Y.A. Dmitriev).

We would like to note especially the works of the young researchers of this subject: G.V. Antipova, V.N. Blagodarnaya, I.I. Larinbaeva, T.V. Kochukov, N.V. Kuzjminych, A.P. Morozov and many others.

In our country the works of such foreign researchers as K. Vasak, M. Janis, R. Kay and E. Bradley, D. Gomien, D. Harris and L. Zvaak, F. Lusher, Z. Piktet, E. Lentovska, K. Ekshtein, etc. are rather popular.

In recent years a new branch of scientific knowledge, called the science of human rights, has being formed in the system of social studies. It focuses on: the basic laws of occurrence and development of categories of dignity and freedom of a person, their rights and guarantees; the legal regulations fixing human rights (the right to human rights); economic, social, political, cultural conditions of existence of the indicated social rights and also factors preventing their realization, the ways of overcoming of these factors (the right to protection of human rights); political, legal, philosophical, ethical doctrines about human rights.

The science of human rights does not relate to the field of jurisprudence. It is a complex social study integrating the achievements of philosophy, ethics, jurisprudence, political science, history, sociology, psychology and other liberal arts and natural sciences about the person and their rights.

In this science human rights are considered not from the specialized scientific angle but as an integral humanitarian phenomenon.

In this book the problems of civil human rights are considered within the framework of this new science. It has become possible thanks to the fact that the composite authors include representatives of different specialties, not only legal (legal and state theory, constitutional law, criminal trial, etc.) but also culturologists and teachers. Among the authors there are not only theorists but also experts like: the judge, lawyers, and legal experts.

There are skilled and young researchers among the composite authors headed by Professor F.M. Rudinsky. The study of this subject has begun still in 60-80 of the last century when the scientific adviser of this collective/group prepared a number of theses/dissertations dedicated to the problems of freedom of conscience and personal constitutional rights of citizens. After formation in Volgograd High School (ВСШ) of the Ministry of Internal Affairs of the USSR (today the Volgograd law Academy of the Ministry of Internal Affairs of Russia) of the Human Rights Department in 1989 the development of problems of civil rights and the role of law enforcement bodies in their protection (the right to life, freedom from tortures, freedom of movement, etc.) has begun. The works of the authors from Volgograd have made the basis of this book. Besides, the researchers from Moscow, Severodvinsk, Rostov-on-Don have also participated in it.

Notes

[1] United Nations Organization. General Assembly. 55th Session UN Secretary General's Preliminary Report "Globalization and Its influence on Human Rights Enforcement" August, 31. Geneva, 2000. P.8. / Организация Объединенный Наций. Генеральная Ассамблея. 55-я сессия. Пункт 116 в предварительной повестки дня. Вопросы прав человека. Глобализация и ее воздействие на осуществление в полном объеме всех прав человека: Предварительный Доклад Генерального секретаря. 31 августа 2000. Женева, 2000. С. 8.

[2] Ibidem. P 9.

[3] Ibidem.

[4] Ibidem.

[5] See: Ibidem. P. 11.

[6] See: Ibidem. P. 12.

[7] See: Summary // Human Development Report, 2003. New York, 2003. P. 5, 6, 8, 9. / Резюме // Доклад о развитии человека за 2003 г. Нью-Йорк, 2003. С. 5, 6, 8, 9.

[8] See: Human Development Report, 2001. Use of New Technologies. New York. 2001. P.19 / Доклад о развитии человека за 2001 г. Использование новых технологий. Нью-Йорк, 2001. С. 19.

[9] *Kofi Annan,* The Problem of interference. Reports of UN Secretary General. New York, 1999. P.40 / Кофи Аннан. Проблема вмешательства. Выступления Генерального секретаря ООН. Нью-Йорк, 1999. С. 40.

[10] See: *Romashevskaya N.* Expertise. Those Who Work Do Not Eat// Civil Dialogue. 2003, # 4./Ромашевская Н. Экспертиза. Кто работает – тот не ест // Гражданский диалог. 2003. № 4.

[11] See: *Karelova G.N.* Poverty Has a Village Face. // Rossiskaya Gaseta. 2003, October 28/ Карелова Г. Н. У бедности деревенское лицо // Российская газета. 2003. 28 окт.

[12] See: *Sokolin V.L.* Vice in the Motherland// Rossiskaya Gaseta. 2004. January, 27/ Соколин В. Л. Порок в своем отечестве // Российская газета. 2004. 27 янв.

[13] See: *Dymarsky V.* Are We Doing Well?// Rossiskaya Gaseta. 2001. July, 12/ Дымарский В. Хорошо живем?// Российская газета. 2001. 12 июля; *Rusanova O.* Russia Borders on Malaysia and Dominican Republic// Nezavisimaya Gazeta. 2002. July, 25/ Русанова О. Россия граничит с Малайзией и Доминиканской Республикой // Независимая газета. 2002. 25 июля.

[14] See: *Saprykin I.* information Development Rating// Nezavisimaya Gazeta. 2003. December, 24/ Сапрыкин И. Рейтинг информационного развития // Независимая газета. 2003. 24 дек.

[15] See: *Rozhin A.* There Can't Be Too Much Health// Rossiskaya Gaseta. 2003. May, 27/ Рожин А. Здоровья много не бывает // Российская газета. 2003. 27 мая.

[16] Ibidem.

[17] See: *Shevchenko Y.* Ministry of Health is the Department of Diseases and Health? // Rossiskaya Gaseta. 2003. August, 5 / Шевченко Ю. Минздрав – ведомство болезней и здоровья? // Российская газета. 2003. 5 авг.

[18] See: Basic Activities of Social and Economic State of the Russian Regions in 2002 // Rossiskaya Gaseta. 2003. March, 15, Basic Activities of Social and Economic State of the Russian Regions in 2003. Rossiskaya Gaseta. 2004. March, 6 / Основные показатели социально-экономического положения российских регионов в 2002 году // Российская газета. 2003. 15 марта; Основные показатели социально-экономического положения российских регионов в 2003 году // Российская газета. 2004. 6 марта.

[19] See: *Gundarov I.A.* Quality of Life in Russia // Economicheskaya I filosofskaya Gazeta. 2004. # 10 (490), / Гундаров И. А. Качество жизни в России // Экономическая и философская газета. 2004. №10 (490); Why Do People Die in Russia? How Can We Survive (facts and arguments), Moscow, 1995. / Он же. Почему умирают в России, как нам выжить (факты и аргументы). М., 1995.

[20] See: *Orehin P.V.* Economic Liberty Is Not Enough For Russia/ Орехин П. В. России мало экономической свободы // Независимая газета. 2003. 11 авг.

[21] See: Russian State Statistics Committee. Social and Economic State of Russia, Moscow, 2001. P. 191 / Госкомстат РФ. Социально-экономическое положение России. М., 2001. С. 191.

[22] See: *Primakov E.* Power And Business: Mutual Responsibility // Rossiiskaya Gazeta. 2003. December, 26 / Примаков Е. Власть и бизнес: ответственность друг перед другом // Российская газета. 2003. 26 дек.

PART I

CIVIL HUMAN RIGHTS:
(GENERAL THEORETICAL QUESTIONS)

Chapter 1. INDIVIDUAL FREEDOM AND CIVIL RIGHTS

§ 1. Individual Freedom as the Essential Part of Personal Liberty

Personal freedom being the major institution of democracy has a complicated/compound structure. It consists of individual, political, economic, social and cultural freedom. Each of the stated sides of personal freedom has its specificity and is realized in certain sphere of human life.

Certain attributes characterizing its nature, qualitative originality are inherent in individual freedom. First of all, it is realized in the sphere of some isolation and self-determination of a person.

From the time of Aristotle it is known that a person is a public being. On the one hand, comprehension of their personality, personal interests are peculiar to a person/them/her, on the other hand, sociability, interaction with other people, participation in social life are also inherent in a person.

As K. Marx noted, a man is in the most literal sense a public animal, "not only an animal to whom communication is peculiar but an animal that can stand apart only in a society"[1]. It suggests that characteristics of an individual as a public being and an individual aspiring to isolation are interconnected.

That is general philosophical interpretation of this question. At the same time, the formation of notions about individual freedom is the important step in human civilization development.

The problem of isolation has special significance in answering the question of freedom. The traditional western understanding of freedom put forward by progressive thinkers as early as in the 17th-19th centuries was connected with alienation of a person from a society, non-interference of the state to private business of citizens. In such interpretation

31

the demand of cancelling of personal dependence of the worker from the proprietor of instruments and means of production was expressed, that had the antifeudal orientation and saved progressive importance during the long historical period.

Communication and isolation are historically arisen and constantly improved forms of social relations' existence that are inseparably linked between each other, they are forms of self-affirmation and functioning of a person in a society.

A.I. Gertsen, having analyzed this problem, came to the conclusion, that "egoism[2] and community ... are basic elements of human life. If you destroy community in a person you will get a furious orangutan; if you destroy egoism in them/her you will get a quiet/meek gray parrot. Slaves have the least of egoism".[3] He considered that it was expedient "to harmoniously freely combine these two integral principles of human life".[4] Further he wrote, that "harmony between world and the society is not achieved once and forever, it is stated by each period, almost by each country and changes under circumstances".[5]

It seems that the 20th century with its newest technical means of intervention into the sphere of individual freedom (interception, police shadowing people, information suppression of a person, etc.) has confirmed this fair judgement.

The essential feature of individual freedom is in the fact that it is the sphere of the state non-interference, the area that is free from legal regulation.

Back in 17th century B. Spinosa acutely noted that: "The one who wishes to regulate everything by laws will more likely provoke vices, rather than correct them"[6]. It is clear that in this sphere there are also moral principles, customs, religious doctrines but legal regulation of private life, tastes, ideas, believes in a democratic state is inadmissible.

The right to personal privacy is one of the civil rights but it also influences the efficiency of democratic institutions functioning and has a direct attitude to other rights.[7] It, in particular, means that citizens have the right to receive unopened mail, to conduct telephone conversations which are tapped by nobody, to freely express the religious or atheistic ideas, etc.

As European Commission of Human Rights in one of its resolutions has noted that the right of privacy is not only "the right to live how it would be desirable, avoiding publicity of private life details" but also the right to establishing and maintaining of relations with other people, especially in the emotional sphere for development and realization of people's personality".[8]

Thus, the doctrine of privacy is interpreted by the European Court of Human Rights also in the sense that the state is responsible not only for providing of non-control of citizens' private life but also to create effective mechanisms to protect this right. So, in the case of X and Y against the Netherlands (1985) the mentally disabled Dutch girl and her father claimed that in this country there were no legal provisions which would allow them to initiate a criminal case against the person who had conducted sexual violation to her. The court admitted the claim of the declarants.[9]

Individual freedom also presupposes the self-determination of a person at decision-making in the sphere of private life and personal relations.

J. Locke identified "freedom of a person to have and dispose of one's personality, actions and property" with freedom in general.[10]

As B. Spinosa wrote, "Everyone by the greatest right of nature is a master of their own ideas". Therefore "the laws ordained apropos of speculative subjects are absolutely useless"[11].

I. Kant believed that there was only one absolute law, namely, freedom, i.e. "independence from compelling arbitrariness of another person". Virtue of a person "to be their own master"[12] he considered as one of basic properties of an individual.

These humanistic ideas as early as in the 20th century formed the basis of international Bill of Human Rights and legislations of many countries of world.

The sphere of individual freedom makes a part of the all interpersonal relations set of the civil society that is beyond the scope of a state.

Virtually, a civil society is a society of market, private-capitalist relations in the basis of which basis a legally free person. The structure of a civil society is formed by various public institutions, including:

1) relations of production/production relations (private enterprises, trade unions, etc.);

2) political relations (parties, movements, lobbyists, etc.);

3) social, cultural and religious relations (family, creative unions, church, etc.)

It is obvious, that the sphere of individual freedom covers (not completely) the third type institutions and social relations.

Hegel used he term "a civil society", thus defining the sphere of a social life where an individual can express them/herself in the own identity.

Writing about a civil society, the authors speak about the category that expresses the correlation between a society and a state. Regarding the correlation between a society and a person, all social relations can be classified as concerning the social life and the sphere of individual interests and personal needs.

Forms of individual freedom display are complex and diverse. They cover a great number of social bonds conveying such important values inherent to a person as life, name, honour, dignity, conscience, personal safety of a citizen. There a subject acts as a bearer of moral qualities, individual features and characteristic properties.

At the same time it is necessary to note that the sphere of isolation can become an area of "alienation" if individuality and person's originality turns into egoistical reflection of public interests.

Individual freedom in its reasonable interpretation does not resist but naturally supplements other aspects of personal freedom. This sphere is connected by thousand strings with surrounding social environment. In this environment material, political and cultural preconditions of private life are created. And the aspect of a person, who is the participant of moral and everyday/common, personal relations, is characterized by certain social status, political views and psychological features. Finally, the society carries out the social control over its members. For this reason we speak about certain isolation of a person from a society as a full and absolute self-determination is just impossible.

Freedom is a necessary condition of full and comprehensive prime of a person, thus, the various sides and aspects of freedom act as different forms of expression and means of perfection of many-sided qualities, properties and needs of an individual.

Specific features are inherent in each person. They are determined by a person's social status, conditions of education and upbringing, an environment, national, professional and other attributes.

At the same time each person has unique features reflecting their specific life, private circumstances of family and private life, and certain natural and specifically typological features. The specific feature of individual freedom is that it acts as a condition and means of expression and development of individually unique features and abilities of a person. The existence of private life sphere guarantees the individual's education and comprehension of own social value and allows them/her to develop the correct attitude to a society. However, the absolutization of the sphere of isolation and self-determination of a person in private life does not correspond to the scientific understanding of this problem.

On the other hand, the denying of the sphere of private life isolation and a tendency to unify it actually conduct to destruction of personal freedom.

Social value of individual freedom is determined by the fact that it is one of the forms of human dignity display, i.e. recognition of a person as a supreme incomparable value. Not accidentally the list of the rights of person in the Universal Declaration of Human Rights begins with declaration of the first civil rights, namely, the right to life, liberty and security of person (Article 3). 3). Enjoying the individual freedom that is one of the major human values, is one of indispensable conditions of democracy functioning. Without its protection/securing the real realization of authority/power of people is rather problematic.

But the value of personal freedom for realization of people's authority is not limited to it. In fact, private life is not only the sphere of moral, family-everyday relations, the sphere of private life, restoration of cultural and physical strengths after work but also in a sense the preparation, accumulation of forces for the subsequent activity. Individual freedom guarantees an opportunity to form will as a precondition of free participation of a citizen in social and political life of a society. The opportunity of self-determination is a necessary condition for realization of political freedom. That is why it is impossible to imagine real democracy without observance of civil rights of citizens.

It is necessary to note, that individual freedom and rights of person, independently are not capable to guarantee genuine freedom but it is possible to say about any aspect of personal freedom. Indeed, freedom presupposes real liberation of a person in all spheres of social being: social and economic, political, cultural and individual.

As in the Resolution 41/117 of General Assembly of the United Nations of December, 4, 1986, "Indivisibility and interdependence of Economic, Social, Cultural, Civil and Political Rights" is stated; the development and protection of one category of rights never can serve as a pretext for release of the state from the development and protection of other rights".

Personal freedom and personal immunity, originated in the epoch of bourgeois revolutions, have found the legal embodiment in British Habeas Corpus Act 1679, in the French Declaration of Human and Civil Rights (1789), in the American Bill of Rights, (1791) and in other constitutional instruments.

Civil and political rights, fixed in these documents, were called the first generation of human rights. In the 19th-the 20th centuries the second and third generations of human rights were formed and received legal recognition. In the end of the 20th and the beginning of the 21st century the question of the fourth generation of human rights is being discussed which should protect from the threats connected with experiments in the sphere of genetic heredity of a person.

However, the importance of individual freedom is not decreasing today. In present many countries are dominated by extreme individualism, whereas such values of cultural life of people as honour, conscience, dignity, turn into an object of shameless trade. That creates the conditions interfering with the really free development of an individual.

Such heavy encroachment on the rights as extrajudicial executions, executions without appropriate proceeding, massacre during confrontations, violent kidnapping of people, terrorism, hostage taking, and traffic in children, women, human organs, racism and xenophobia are extending.

Growth of militarism, criminality, and totalitarian tendencies affects personal freedom of citizens in the most pernicious way.

The well-known English political scientist Erskine May in due time wrote, "Guarantees from suspicious and biased supervision are valued immediately after personal freedom. It is possible not to limit freedom of people, they can go where they like; but if each their step is under supervision of spies and intelligencers if their words are written down to serve as charge against them if their friends are watched as conspirators, who will dare say that they are free? It is possible to measure the freedom of the country by a degree of freedom from this disastrous practice"[13].

Freedom and personal immunity today still have not lost their social value and continue to remain the scene/sphere of fierce political and world outlook confrontation. Certainly, their antifeudal contents has become a thing of the past (though not worldwide) and at present the struggle against arbitrariness, personal violence, the struggle for the protection of rights of person is one of the burning political questions.

Genuine individual freedom presupposes impossibility of unlawful violent interference of the state into the private sides of human life and also guarantees protection of life, honour, dignity, conscience and personal safety of each member of a society. Real individual freedom means liberation from totalitarianism that transforms a citizen into a victim of suspiciousness, constant police supervision and denunciations of intelligencers; overcoming of conformist and individualistic tendencies; struggle against the organized crime that nullifies life, freedom and personal immunity and other rights of citizens.

The problem of individual freedom can be viewed from different aspects. Firstly, it acts as set of legal, political, moral rules and principles regulating behaviour of citizens in the sphere of moral relations, every-day private life, i.e. as a sociopolitical and legal institution. In this case it makes a part of a much wider social institution of personal freedom. Secondly, when we speak about freedom we mean socially wide histori-cal practice of this freedom, its implementation, i.e. individual freedom as an actual status.

§ 2. Features of Legal Regulation of the Social Relations Arising in the Sphere of Individual Freedom

The legal provisions guaranteeing individual freedom are, first of all, international-legal, constitutional propositions which establish the right to life, freedom and personal immunity and other civil rights. Besides, some civil (the right on name, the right to honour and dignity, etc.), criminal (for example, the right of necessary defense) and other propositions of other branches of the law.

Social relations, in which individual freedom of citizens displays, have a complex structure.

Firstly, among them it is possible to single out the social relations that directly express an opportunity of an individual to freely self-de-termine, to protect honour and dignity, to have freedom of conscience, life privacy, etc. This group of social relations has a main value as social relations are connected with direct enjoyment of a citizen of the values of personal freedom. Secondly, there are social relations in which con-ditions of legitimacy are expressed, borders of the sphere of individual freedom as it is not boundless and its realization cannot be interfaced to encroachment on interests of a society, a state and other persons. Thirdly, it is necessary to single out social relations appearing in connection with limitation (lawful or illegal) of personal freedom.

Specificity of the mechanism of legal regulation in the sphere of indi-vidual freedom lies in the fact that first of the mentioned groups of social relations basically is not subject to legal regulation. For example, the law does not regulate particularly personal tastes and desires: a choice of a friend, specific features of life, etc.

"It is necessary to see the limits of legal influence; the law is a mighty, valid and highly effective but not the almighty instrument of social de-velopment. By means of the right and the law it is impossible to make "everything" … The law regulates not all social relations but only those which can be subjected to the external control and are guaranteed by the state regulation"[14].

In the modern literature it is noted that "limits of legal regulation are caused by extralegal facts. They lie in the nature of human activity, predetermined by their general culture and civilization, determined by existing system of relations, economic, historical, religious, national and other circumstances"[15].

The state of modern culture, level of civilization allows making a conclusion that the sphere of individual freedom is basically not subject to legal regulation.

The first group of reviewed relations as a rule is not exposed to the state control. The second and third groups of social relations are subject to legal regulation. State recognition of legal rights and assignment of legal duties on their participants is caused by objective necessity. In fact, this sphere of social life exists not in vacuum and not on a desert island but in territory where the sovereign government power works. Leadership as a major part of the state sovereignty, in particular, presupposes that it is the government that determines the whole structure of legal relationships establishes general law and order and legal capacity of all interstate unions and persons and also has monopoly of known compulsion inside of borders of the given state.

However, the limits of the state-legal regulation are determined by existence of human rights as said in Article 2 of the Constitution of the Russian Federation, their recognition, observance and protection are the state's duty. One of the definitions of human rights is that they act as limits of realization of the government. At the same time during realization of individual freedom interests of a person can become an object of illegal actions of separate citizens or officials. In this connection there is a necessity for legal warranting of individual freedom.

On the other hand, abuse of rights of person integrated with infringement of rights of other citizens from legal subjects is not inconceivable. Thus, it entails the necessity of legal determination of exact borders/limits of individual freedom. Finally, there are objective conditions which inevitably lead in some cases to its lawful limitation in the form of a detention, an imprisonment, a search, and limitations in personal correspondence of the condemned, in the movement of citizens because of a quarantine, etc.

Specificity of the state-legal regulation of social relations in the sphere of individual freedom is substantially revealed by means of the constitutional terms "inviolability" (personal immunity, inviolability of dwelling) and "secrecy" (privacy of correspondence, advocate secrets as one of elements of the right of defence).

In our opinion, the concept "inviolability" has a much wider meaning than it is usually thought. Not only a person but also their dwelling is inviolable. The privacy of correspondence means inviolability of personal information, the right of defence means inviolability of rights of the accused, the freedom of conscience in its essential aspects is inviolability of conscience of a person.

The constitutional term "inviolability" (of a person, a dwelling) is filled by the deep humanistic contents and expresses inadmissibility of illegal personal violence in a democratic state. in their new work/book "Inviolability in the constitutional law of the Russian Federation" (Moscow, 2004) O.E. Kutafin for the first time is absolutely fairly examining the concept of "inviolability" as one of the major categories of the constitutional law describing a degree of democratic character of a state. He is characterizing the inviolability of territory of the state, of rights of person, authorities, foreigners and stateless persons in detail. We consider this category with reference to the contents of civil human rights.

At first sight, the concepts of "personal immunity", "inviolability of dwelling" mean that a person cannot be subjected to coercive actions, whence they proceeded. But here it is necessary to make two remarks. First, the compulsory authority is in any human conduct and compulsion is the integral attribute of any social community, even of non-state one. There are different kinds of compulsion. For example, educational measures connected with the well-known compulsory moments used by parents to their children are also kind of compulsion but it does not restrain the rights of security of person (certainly, it is a question of lawful realization of the parental rights).

Speaking about personal immunity and inviolability of dwelling we mean freedom from the coercive actions representing threat of personal safety of an individual, to their life, health, corporal inviolability, an opportunity of privacy and private life.

Secondly, the need of use of state-coercive actions is dictated by necessity of human rights protection, protection of the law and order, maintenance of legality. In some cases the limitation of rights of personal immunity and inviolability of dwelling is connected with protection of interests of a person and people surrounding them/her (for example, compulsory treatment of an infectious patient).

Thus, the essence of rights of personal immunity and inviolability of dwelling is that, basically, any compulsion of a citizen is forbidden but it can be used in the exclusive cases that are strictly regulated by the law by the state bodies, officials or separate citizens. Any coercive action is a compelled/forced, necessary and legal deviation from the constitutional principle of personal immunity and their rights. Compulsion is the compelled reaction to illegal behaviour. It is necessary for protection of interests of a society and its citizens and is regulated by the law.

In the strict sense of the word the concepts of "personal immunity", "inviolability of dwelling" should mean that illegal use of coercive actions to a citizen is forbidden or inadmissible. But in the science of criminal trial these concepts are considered in a narrower plan, i.e. as certain legal guarantees in case of imprisonment or search of a citizen.

The right of privacy of correspondence is the right of a citizen to keep in a secret, to intentionally hide from others what is written in the sent or received letter. The element of secret is inherent also in other personal constitutional rights: the right of inviolability of dwelling is called to ensure the provision of, in particular and secret of private life, secret of privacy of a person, their family; the right of defence as an opportunity to not inform the court and the investigation of data, which the accused prefers to save as fiduciary or to entrust only to the defender, who is obliged to keep it in a secret (advocate secrets), etc. The constitutional term "secret" expresses inadmissibility of illegal and unreasonable penetration into the sphere of individual freedom with a view of illegal acquirement of personal information of a citizen against their will. Virtually, here again there is a question of illegal compulsion and in this sense the term "secret" is a development, logic continuation of the idea of personal immunity. in the propositions of the administrative and family law by means of the concept "secret" the interdiction on distribution of personal information (for example, medical secrecy, secrecy of adoption) is expressed.

Features of international-legal and constitutionally-legal regulation of social relations in the sphere of individual freedom are the following. Firstly, the standards of international law and the Constitution regulate the most important, essential sides of these relations expressing an opportunity of a unobstructed choice of various variants of behaviour in the sphere of moral relations, everyday life and individual life of people if this behaviour does not contradict legal propositions and principles of moral and does not infringe upon the rights of other persons; secondly, these propositions formulate on the whole the civil human rights and their most essential guarantees. The detailed regulation and concrete definition of these rights are included in the current legislation.

§ 3.   Civil Human Rights and Personal Constitutional Rights of a Citizen (Concepts Relation)

The system of civil human rights is recorded in Articles 3-16 of the Universal Declaration of Human Rights, in Articles 6-17, 23, 26 of international Covenant on Civil and Political Rights, in two optional protocols to this legal instrument and also in many other things is internationally-legal documents. in particular, in UN Declarations it is said about elimination of all forms of intolerance and discrimination on the basis of religion or belief, about protection of all persons against violent disappearances, about principles of justice for victims of crime and abuse of power; in international conventions on slavery, international Convention on the Elimination of Racial Discrimination (ICERD), Convention against torture and other cruel, inhuman or degrading treatment or punishment, Convention on the Elimination of all Forms of Discrimination Against Women, Convention Un relating to the Status of Refugees. On the European continent the civil rights are recorded in the European Convention on Human Rights and Basic Freedoms and in other international-legal regulations of the Council of Europe, OSCE and the CIS. The indicated rights are implemented in the legislation of many states of world (in particular, in Ch. I of Constitution of the Italian Republic, in section I of the constitutional charter of Germany, in Ch. II of the Constitution of Spain).

In the Constitution of the Russian Federation of 1993 the civil (personal constitutional) rights are recorded in Article 20–28, 47–54. The indicated rights are indicated and legally guaranteed in the propositions of the criminal, civil, family law, etc.

The term "civil rights" is ambiguous. It is used in the legislation, judiciary practice and scientific literature, being filled in each concrete case by the special contents. In particular, in international Covenant on Civil and Political Rights it is a question of versions/varieties of human rights. In Article 6 of the European Convention for the Protection of Human Rights and Basic Freedoms it is a question of human rights to lawful proceeding at definition of their civil rights and duties. Here it is a question of wider understanding of this term. Judiciary practice of the European court in Strasbourg considers the concept of "civil rights" very widely, distributing it on all questions of private law[16], distinguishing in some cases "civil rights" from "public rights". In the Civil Code of the Russian Federation the term "civil rights" is considered as a synonym of the legal rights of a citizen arising on the basis of propositions of civil law (Article 8).

In the scientific literature on international public law the civil rights are considered as a version of the human rights, recorded by international-legal provisions. in the domestic literature on constitutional law the rights recorded in constitutions regulating individual freedom, some authors call "personal", "personal constitutional" rights, while some other authors call "personal (civil) rights"[17].

Even authors of special researches on the problems of human rights identify the term "civil rights" with the concept of "rights of person" or replace the first concept by the second one.[18]

In the English literature the term "civil freedoms" (civil liberties)[19] is used and they are considered as a right of everyone to do everything, that he/she wants if it does not contradict the law.

In the USA the terms "civil rights" and "Constitutional rights" often are used as synonyms. Another specifically American meaning of the term "civil rights" is the ideal propositions symbolizing the requirements of consecutive realization of equality[20].

In the French literature there are various approaches to this problem. In F. Lusher opinion, individual freedom (alongside with public freedom and freedom of local and territorial collectives) makes one of aspects of freedom.

It is necessary to remark that in works of domestic authors on this question the tendencies such to the American understanding of civil human rights are observed. It was most brightly showed in L.D. Voevodin's last book which has been devoted to the legal status of a person as he wrote; the term "person" has universal character ... expresses the essence of two terms that are "a person and a citizen".[21] Therefore the term of "right of a person" is considered by them as a concept uniting human rights and the rights of a citizen.

Authors of the textbook "Human rights" edited by E.A. Lukasheva also consider constitutional rights as a version of human rights. As they write, basic rights of an individual are constitutional rights.[22] In this case it is a question not only of terminology (though the question of terms is also important) but about the essence of the problem. It is difficult to agree with such identification of human rights and the rights of a citizen. Firstly, the term "basic rights of a person" contains in a preamble of the Universal Declaration of Human Rights where it is a question of them, rather than constitutional rights of a citizen.

Secondly, in the Article 17 of the Constitution of the Russian Federation referred by the authors of the abovementioned textbook, distinguishes human rights and rights of a citizen. Besides, in the same Constitution human rights (Article 20-30) clearly differ from the rights of a citizen (Article 31–33). The same it is possible to say about constitutions of other states (Spain, Greece). Whether it is possible to say that human rights, implemented in the text of constitutions, do not change their legal nature, while basic rights of a person are constitutional rights?

It is well-known, that human rights differ from the rights of a citizen by origin: the first arise from the moment of a birth of an individual, the second appear from the moment of occurrence of citizenship. Another distinction is on the normative basis. Human rights are realized on the basis of legal provisions, moral principles, political requirements, religious doctrines; the rights of a citizen are realized on the basis of legal provisions. They differ by the forms of realization as human rights are realized within the limits of legal, moral, political and other social relations and the rights of a citizen are realized only within the limits of legal relationships. And finally, the essential distinction lies in forms of defence. Protection of human rights is realized by interstate as well as internationally-legal means, whereas protection of rights of a citizen can be only interstate.

It is also necessary to note, that the correlation between categories of "human rights" and "right of a citizen" varied during the 19th-the 20th centuries.

In conformity with the meaning of the Declaration of Human Rights (1789) human rights are the rights realized in private life, in civil society; while rights of a citizen are the rights realized in the sphere of the state life. In the modern Constitution of France and the French literature this division into individual and public freedom (and also freedom of local and territorial collectives) has been saved.[23]

As for the Universal Declaration of Human Rights (1948) it ascribes to human rights the right to freedom of assembly and associations and the right to participation in management and equal access to public service and suffrages.

Thus, those political rights, which under the Constitution of the Russian Federation are the rights of a citizen (Article 31-33, 36), appear as human rights in are international-legal documents.

In the modern world the human rights recorded in international Bill of Rights, represent international standards below which the level of guarantees of these rights in the separate states is inadmissible. The rights of a citizen are those real opportunities of satisfaction of the interests and needs which the state can provide to individuals. They can correspond to or mismatch international standards.

Implementing human rights in the Constitution and the legislation, the state specifies them with the reference to conditions of the given country, distributes their legal action concerning all persons (citizens, foreigners, stateless persons), present on its territory. Such implementation testifies that the given state is guided by the requirements fixed in international instruments about human rights and aspires to realize them. In this case human rights and constitutional rights of a citizen are certainly very close but nevertheless they are not always identical. It is possible to illustrate it on the example of civil human rights, especially the right to life.

As it is known, Article 6 of international Covenant on Civil and Political Rights and the Second optional protocol to international Covenant on Civil and Political Rights aimed at abolition of death penalty, provide the basic international standards with reference to the right to life. The majority of the states of world recognize the right to life as a first and foremost human right. However, the attitude to this institution in the different countries is different. In some states the death penalty is used, in others it is either cancelled or not used.[24] Hence, the scope a right to life as a human right recorded in international law and scope of this right, implemented in the constitution of certain state are various. in the state constitutional and other human rights as well as human rights implemented by the legislation are realized. A person is a holder of both of them.

Democratic is a state in which the rights given to individuals present in its territory correspond to international standards of human rights.

Thereupon there is also a question of personal constitutional rights. The concept "personal constitutional rights of citizens" developed in the literature on state law in the end of 40th - the beginning of 50th years and now is conventional. The only objection against this term was stated by L.D. Voevodin: "Why, for example, it is necessary to call only one group of the rights and freedom the "personal" rights and freedoms? Unless all the others are not "personal", i.e. belonging to a person? It is easy to prove, that all without exception rights, freedoms and duties of citizens written down in the Constitution are "personal".[25]

However, the concept of "rights of person" expresses not the fact of their belonging to a person but something different: that these rights individualize a personality of a citizen and are realized in the sphere of personal freedom. One of the meanings of the word "personal" is "expressing specific features of a person or a subject".[26] In such meaning within the limits of the science of constitutional law the term "rights of person" has a right to existence.

The term "personal non-property rights" for a long time have been used in civil law as a concept distinguishing them from property rights (though the last also relate to a person). The term "rights of person" is used in the legislation, for example in the Family Code of the Russian Federation (Ch. 6) and here again the legislator separates rights of person from property and other rights and interests.

L.D. Voevodin has offered another name for this group of rights (which he considers together with duties): the rights and duties in the field of personal safety.[27] In our opinion, both private life and personal safety are social values that are components of individual freedom. Therefore, is quite admissible to speak about constitutional rights of citizens in the sphere of individual freedom as about equivalent to personal constitutional rights. In use these terms are synonymous.

As we have already mentioned, social relations in which individual freedom displays are complex and diverse. As settled legal propositions, these relations get the legal character legal participants of which are marked out by personal legal rights and duties: civil, administrative and others (the right of defence of life and health, a copyright, the right to freedom of residence, the right to freedom of movement in the country, etc.).

Among the indicated rights the special place is occupied with those which are recorded in propositions of international and constitutional law.

Personal constitutional rights are civil human rights implemented in Russian constitutional propositions. In many cases their contents is identical to the civil rights but in some cases they cannot be recognized as identical.

§ 4. Civil Human Rights:
Contents, System and Legal Nature

Civil human rights are a group of rights embodying their individual freedom.

Unlike other human rights where a person represents them/herself as a politician (political rights), the worker and the proprietor (the economic rights), the participant of a social and cultural life (the social and cultural rights), in the civil rights the interests of a person as individualities, i.e. a person having unique and original features are embodied. These rights individualize a person; promote the best display of cultural interests, inclinations, personal abilities. They guarantee an opportunity of an unobstructed choice of various variants of behaviour in the sphere of individual freedom. Their contents is determined by the fact that they are called to ensure the provision of such essential values of this freedom as inviolability of life, honour and personal dignity, personal safety, the values of private and family life.

The indicated rights are called to guarantee autonomy of an individual in the sphere of a civil society, in the personal and family life, to ensure the provision of their legal protection from illegal intervention. They are aimed at maintenance of a priority of individual, internal reference points of development of each person.[28] These rights have non-property character; they directly are not connected with using material benefits and are realized in the sphere of moral relations embodying cultural and moral values. In these rights the major bases of legality and law and order (personal immunity, the right of judicial defence, etc.) are also recorded.

Unlike other human rights (for example, political) the collective way of realization rather than individual is inherent in the civil rights.

It is necessary to note, that realization of some of the civil rights (personal immunity, inviolability of dwelling, freedom of conscience) has more general character than realization of other basic rights, for example, political. In fact, each citizen has personal safety, practices some religion or does not practice any and, hence, realizes the rights of personal immunity and freedom of conscience. As if we such political right as freedom of press, though it relates to each citizen it is realized in less mass scale (not all citizens necessarily express their opinion in press).

As it is well-known, the Universal Declaration of Human Rights, 1948 begins with enumeration of civil human rights. And it is not accidentally. The primary place of civil rights among the whole catalogue of human rights is explained not only by the fact that historically they have been recognized before all others but also by their social importance. In fact without life, dignity, freedom and personal safety all other rights and freedoms of a person become senseless. Certainly, this circumstance cannot be interpreted as means of belittling, limitation or elimination of other human rights. Unity and interdependence of the whole system of human rights is a condition of original and all-round realization of each of them.

The problem of the system of civil human rights deserves special attention.

Let's say a few words about the history of the question. Russian pre-revolutionary lawyer B.A. Kistjakovsky classifying the rights depending on the attitude of a person to the state, marked out a special group of rights ("personal freedom from the state") where he ascribed to personal immunity and inviolability of dwelling, mail, freedom of movement, freedom of conscience, freedom of speech, press assemblies, unions,[29] i.e. not only personal but also political freedoms.

The question about the system of rights in the sphere of individual freedom is considered in domestic and in foreign literature. Thus, French political scientist A. Esmen has divided all freedoms into two groups: a) material and b) moral rights and interests. He puts personal freedom in the narrow sense (i.e. personal safety), personal property, inviolability of dwelling to the first group; freedom of conscience and religious freedom he puts into the second group.[30]

In France the rights in the sphere of individual freedom as a rule are called freedoms of a physical person. G. Burdeau allots three types of the rights: freedom of movement and freedom of residence, personal safety, right to privacy (liberte de l`intimite), consisting in inviolability of dwelling and privacy of correspondence.[31]

In the modern American literature there are various classifications. in particular, A. Mason and W. Beany see three groups of rights in first eight amendments to the Constitution: the first group of rights is recorded in Amendment I (freedom of religion is among them); the second group is in Amendments II and III (they as authors claim, "were not important in our constitutional history"); and, finally, the third group of the rights is Amendments IV-VIII (they are intended "to protect citizens against any police action and to ensure the provision of fair legal trial at any official action by means of which a person can lose freedom or property").[32] Usually in this group of rights there are a number of remedial rules, including guaranteeing the right not to be subject to unreasonable imprisonments and searches, the right to public and fast trial, the right to have a defender and also the right of property.

For western classifications of rights in the sphere of individual freedom inclusion in the structure of this group of the right of private property is characteristic and it is not casual, because as K. Marx remarked, the bourgeois "considers himself an individual only so far as he is the bourgeois".[33]

In the domestic literature there have been also a number of attempts to classify these rights. Thus, M.A. Nikiforova subdivides them into two groups:

1) the right to life, to freedom and physical inviolability;
2) other civil rights specifying the first group of rights.[34]

L.D. Voevodin has distinguished three groups of rights:

1) the right to life, to personal immunity, to honour and dignity;
2) the rights providing privacy of individual family life;

3) freedom of thought, speech, conscience.[35]

At the present stage of jurisprudence development this problem can be solved with the help of the system analysis.

One of properties of the system is its relativity. The matter is that the given system can be considered as an element of another one being of higher rank. The initial system, in its turn, includes some elements of the systems of the lower rank.[36] Hence, civil rights need to be considered as an element of the system of basic rights and duties and this latter as an element of a wider system of legal rights and legal duties of a person. At the same time civil (personal constitutional) rights have properties of a kind of independent system which in its turn consists of elements of the lower rank, namely separate rights. Each separate civil (personal constitutional) right is a core of a complex legal institution.

The group of the indicated rights has properties of community and integrity. The meaning and purpose of certain rights is providing citizens with the values of individual freedom from different aspects. The sphere of individual freedom is that core which is the basis of the whole system, its main axis.

The civil rights are organized in the system in such a manner that each of them is directly connected on the other one and follows from it (for example, the right of inviolability of dwelling is logic continuation of the right to personal immunity). From the point of view of development social systems are usually subdivided into stationary and non-stationary.

Besides, among social systems they distinguish dynamic and static. Between the elements of static system (unlike dynamic) the feedback is poorly expressed. For example, changes in one of the human rights making static the system can cause changes in the other but changes of the second are not necessarily reflected in the first one. The group of civil (personal constitutional) rights is, certainly, a stationary (marked by sufficient stability) and static socially-legal system.

In these rights the most important forms of individual freedom display find the legal embodiment: life, personal safety of a citizen, right to privacy and private life, protection of honour, personal dignity, and freedom of conscience.

These forms of individual freedom display are the important personal values and are fixed by propositions of international and constitutional law. So, some of the mentioned propositions guarantee one personal value (for example, Article 18 of international Covenant on Civil and Political Rights, Article 9 of the European Convention for the Protection of Human Rights and Basic Freedoms, Article 28 of the Constitution of the Russian Federation is freedom of thought, conscience and religion), others guarantee a number of personal values. So, the right to privacy of correspondence, telephone conversations and other messages provides honour and dignity, the intimate sides of cultural life, an opportunity to control the distribution of personal information.

If we consider the values of individual freedom as criterion of civil (personal constitutional) rights classification it is possible to emphasize the following six groups:

I. The right to life and the right to dignity which provide such absolute values as inviolability of life and the highest value of a human being.

II. The right to freedom, abolition of slavery and slave trade, freedom of movement in the country and freedom of residence, the right to leave and come back to the country. This group of civil rights provides the values of personal freedom, the freedom of self-determination.

III. The right to security of person, the right to freedom from tortures, severe and inhuman treatment and punishment; freedom from any imprisonment and detention. This group of rights guarantees personal safety.

IV. The right of guarantees of privacy, freedom of thought, conscience, religion, the right of inviolability of dwelling, privacy of correspondence, telephone conversations and other correspondence, the right of protection of marriage and family. The given rights provide the values of personal (private) and family life, guarantee non-interference to the sphere of private life and cultural freedom.

V. The right to acknowledgement of legal personality; equal protection of the law/right to equal protection and trial; the right to equal protection of the law; equality of women and men; freedom from discrimination based on race, nationality, sex, religious and political convictions; the right to citizenship; the right of foreigners and stateless persons. The indicated group of rights provides an opportunity of recognition of a person as a holder of the right and a guarantee of equality.

Finally, there is also the sixth group of civil rights. Their originality is that they serve as conditions and means of effective legal protection of civil and other human rights. Virtually, they are rights-guarantees providing the reality of many human rights. However, we relate them to civil rights as some of them guarantee personal safety of a person. We relate to them the following: the right to fair and impartial proceeding; presumption of innocence; the right of the accused and condemned; the rights of a victim of a crime and abuse of power; interdiction of condemnation for doing something which according to the law had not been/was not criminal in the moment of that action; interdiction of imposing a more grave punishment, than what could have been imposed in the moment of committing of a crime.

The question of the legal nature of civil human rights and personal constitutional rights of a citizen deserves the special attention. It seems that both the first and the second are versions of the legal rights of a person.

It is reputed, that the legal right is a kind and a measure of possible behaviour of an authorized person. Besides, the legal right is always the right to something, to any object representing certain value in material, moral, political or another respect. M.S. Strogovich considered the legal right of a person as an opportunity to use certain social values; an authority to act and to demand corresponding actions from other persons; freedom of behaviour and actions in the limits established by legal proposition.[37] This point of view has found support in the legal literature and it seems to us rather convincing. It allows giving the all-round characteristic to civil (personal, constitutional) rights. Using the social values is the purpose which justifies the existence of the very category of legal rights, filing it with real public contents.

The social values are material, cultural and other values, possession o which is connected with satisfaction of needs of people and development of their abilities. "At that using the social values should be understood in a broad meaning of word. It can consist not only in having/possessing of certain objects (values) but first of all, in freedom of behaviour, in freedom of making (within the law) certain actions, that in itself is already a value (non-material)".[38]

The question of the correlation of civil (personal constitutional) right and the social values provided by it deserves special consideration. R.O. Halfina considered that the Constitution provides "not the right on inviolability, honour, dignity but these social values".[39] Meanwhile, the rights are guaranteed with the help of which the social values are provided to citizens. Denying of the fact that a citizen has constitutional rights is equivalent to the statement, that the state is not obliged to ensure the provision of these values as are no legal means of their protection.

It is necessary to stress the inseparable connection between the real opportunity of having the social values and the scope of the legal right guaranteed by propositions. The scope of the legal right during its realization can be legally limited. V.A. Patulin considered this question in a different way. "Even a criminal is not deprived (and not restricted) of the right of personal immunity. He can on the basis of and according to the law be deprived of an opportunity to freely self-determine (detention, imprisonment, imprisonment according to a verdict of court); their personal security as an actual status will be legally limited but in this situation a citizen does not lose the right guaranteed by the state to protection from illegal encroachments".[40] This point of view was supported by M.F. Orzih.[41]

Certainly, all citizens have the right to personal immunity, including infringers. However, it would be erroneous to assume, that the scope of this right (each legal right is a measure of possible behaviour and as any measure it has certain scope) is identical both to a free citizen and to a person who serve one's sentence in a colony.

The legal responsibility is a kind and a measure of compulsory deprivation of the offender from the values directly belonging to them. Realization of the legal responsibility in the form of imprisonment also means that a person loses the opportunity to use such personal values as inviolability of dwelling and privacy of correspondence and, hence, does not have the corresponding legal rights at all. A condemned has a right to personal immunity but in a narrowed scope.

For example, a free citizen cannot be imprisoned without a verdict of the court and a condemned is already imprisoned, their physical inviolability is legally limited. It is obvious that freedom from illegal imprisonment as an element of the right to personal immunity has unequal scope for a free person and a condemned. The same it is possible to say about the constitutional freedom of conscience as being in institution of confinement, the condemned cannot realize a number of the rights of a member of religious association. As for personal constitutional rights the right to life, dignity, protection of the suspected and accused, presumption of innocence, etc. does not undergo changes.

The meaning of the legal right is having/possessing the social values. If the opportunity of using of this value is legally limited, the legal right also should undergo certain changes. Otherwise that will remain from the legal right if authorized person cannot use the guaranteed social values?

The legal right has a complex internal structure. In the legal literature of 60-80th of the 20th century the deep and all-round characteristic of it (works of N.G. Alexandrov, N.S. Bratus, S.S. Alekseev, N.I. Matuzov, V.A. Patulin, N.V. Vitruk, etc.).

For us regulations about concept of categories of the contents and structure of the legal right, consisting of certain legal opportunities and competences given to citizens, their interrelation has the special value. "If the legal right can be called a "molecule" in a tissue of legal relationships, and competences will be "atoms" of them".[42]

Each legal right consists of certain elements-competences. In general plan of the legal right offered by N.I. Matuzov, there are four such competences: the right-behaviour (i.e. the opportunity of certain behaviour of the authorized person), the right-requirement (i.e. the opportunity to require certain behaviour from the responsible person), the right-using (i.e. the opportunity to use certain social values) and the right-claim (i.e. the opportunity to protect these rights). The unity of all competences determines the contents and structure of the legal right.[43] With reference to the sphere of individual freedom the right-behaviour acts as an opportunity of having personal values.

Thus, general plan of civil (personal constitutional) rights is represented to us in a following way:

1) right to use certain values of individual freedom;

2) the right to demand from the responsible persons not to interfere with using of these values;

3) the right to resort in case of necessity to measures of the state compulsion for protection of opportunities to use the indicated values.

As it is known, according to the first optional protocol to international Covenant on Civil and Political Rights, the European Convention on protection of rights and basic freedoms, Article 46 part 3 of the Constitution of the Russian Federation everyone has a right to address international bodies for protection of their rights. Therefore this plan can be added by the fourth competence: the right to resort in case of need to means of international-legal protection.

This general plan has specific forms of display in certain civil (personal, constitutional) right. If, for example, in general plan there are three elements-competences, than in certain right there can be more of them.

As each civil law has rather high community, competences included in it also have this feature. Each basic competence (or a basic element) of the constitutional law is indicated in many branch legal rights. So, freedom of religious worships as one of competences of religious freedom is indicated in the right to be a member of religious association, the right to participate in prayerful assemblies, etc. The problem is to determine features of the contents of each civil law based on general plan of legal right.

The legal nature of civil rights is characterized, firstly, by general properties of all human rights; secondly, by specific qualities which only they have. First of all, human rights differ from other legal rights by the increased value, the special importance of the social values at which they are aimed.

These rights provide an opportunity to use the social values determining certain conditions of human life in a society and a state. They fix the most essential, basic connections and relations between the state and a person and they are realized in the most important spheres of social life, providing granting to citizens the values, inalienable from a person. In comparison with the branch legal rights the human rights are characterized by high community and significant stability. These absolute laws exist constantly and are not cancelled by numerous realizations. Their feature is that they mediate relations and connections of citizens not with each other or with separate state bodies but with world community, the state as a whole. A person in the indicated relations acts as an individual, an associate bearer of the sovereignty of people, a participant of economic, social and cultural life.

These are the most essential general legal features of all human rights including personal.

At the same time the civil rights are also characterized by some specific features. First of all, they guarantee such values inseparable from a person as life, health, honour, dignity, freedom of conscience, personal safety. The indicated values have no economic value and use to them of cost criteria and estimations is excluded. As a rule, they arise with birth and stop by death and cannot be gifted to another person. Civil human rights (similarly to non-property civil rights) personify individuality of a person and the appropriate estimation of this individuality from a society.

Originality of these rights lies in ways of their guarantee from the state. The state has no right to interfere with the sphere of private life of citizens which lies beyond the framework of their duties before the state. Simultaneously, it incurs obligations in case of need to ensure the provision of protection of personal freedom of citizens from illegal encroachments from the state bodies, officials and citizens.

That is why there are a lot of such rights which are called negative ("freedom from …") among the civil rights. For example, the right to life means inadmissibility of any deprivation of life, the right to private life means inadmissibility of intrusion into the sphere of private life. But there are also positive rights ("the right to …"). There are such rights as a right to freedom of residence, freedom of conscience and religious freedom, etc.

Similarly to all human rights the civil rights are natural and integral as ay relate to persons as individuals.

The question of natural character of civil rights deserves special consideration.

Theory of natural human rights arisen as early as in the ancient world, affirmed in 17th-18th centuries and revived in the 20th century, certainly, has progressive value. The modern science has found deeper substantiation of this theory.

A person as a species has certain genetic abilities of behaviour, specific reactions to acts of violence and these human properties exist in different civilizations and cannot be explained only by cultural-historical factors and connections for such connections just do not exist. The mildest of people reacts by an attack, having seen, that a child is being beaten or a woman is being raped. Obviously, there are genetic preconditions of human rights which root in natural aspiration of mankind to survive. But the fact that these preconditions can become the integral properties of a person only under certain historical circumstances is also essential. Thus, at early stages of a primitive society different tribes had a custom of killing of old people as severe conditions of life did not give an opportunity to support/feed them. The right to life was finally formed only in the middle of the 20th century. The mankind not at once has come to idea of the French Declaration of Human Rights (1789) about equal and inalienable rights. The British Magna Carta (1213) or Letter of grant of Ekaterina II (the Great) to nobility (1785) gave the rights (privileges, to be exact) only to one social group: "free people" or noblemen.

Thus, the natural character of human rights becomes obvious and could be realized when objective political, social, economic and cultural conditions were formed.

It seems that thesis formulated in Article 1 of the Universal Declaration of Human Rights: "all human beings are born free and equal in dignity and rights" relates to all human rights but not just to the civil. The judgement about specific features of civil human rights as natural rights is today rather widespread. In particular, it is written that they are not connected directly with belonging to citizenship, do not follow from it and relate to everyone from birth.[44]

Meanwhile, the meaning of Article 1 of the Universal Declaration of Human Rights contradicts this point of view. Besides, Article 21 of this document testifies that the rights to take part in the government, to have equal access to public service which, certainly are connected with citizenship of the state, are also considered as human rights. On the other hand, the state of a person in citizenship strengthens the reality of civil rights as it allows them to use means of their protection more effectively.

There is also another extreme in interpretation of natural character of human rights. The UN special speaker Hose Bentoa spoke about it at the session of one of subcommittees of the Commission of Human rights on June, 9th, 1998. It was a question that according to newest western concepts the economic, social and cultural rights are not the high-grade rights but only objects of aspirations of the state. Supporting the recognition of these rights as integral, the speaker declared, that they make "the ethical-legal code", "ethical border between life in a human society and life beyond a human society".[45]

The aspiration to approve civil human rights by means of denying natural and integral character of other human rights, at first sight, seems a positive phenomenon as it increases their prestigiousness. Actually, it contradicts spirit and the letter of international Bill of Rights and represents an attempt to destroy a principle of unity and interdependence of all human rights. A person deprived of such rights as a right to food, clothes, dwelling, work; freedom from famine cannot normally realize their civil rights. Last years in the resolutions of the UN Commission on Human Rights the right to adequate standard of living is considered as an element of the right to life.

Civil (personal, constitutional) rights have some general features with personal non-property rights fixed by civil-legal provisions (the right on name, the right to image, etc.) but these rights are not identical. In particular, civil personal non-property rights are absolute and civil (personal, constitutional) rights cannot be called absolute, for there are embodied not the connections of authorized persons with surrounding persons but their mutual relations with a world community, the state as a whole. At the same time the branch legal rights arising during the process of definition of these rights can be absolute.

The problem of the legal nature of the indicated rights is part and parcel of the question of forms of their realization and implementation. In the legal literature there are two Paragraphs of view on this question. Whereas some authors thought that constitutional rights exist and were realized beyond of legal relationships (P.E. Nedbailo, M.S. Strogovich, L.S. Yavich), others considered rights of person as elements of legal relationships (S.S. Alekseev, M.N. Matuzov, V.S. Osnovin, V.A. Patulin).

For example, M.S. Strogovich thought that the legal right of personal immunity exists in the structure of legal relationships only in case of occurrence of the legal facts connected with certain criminally-remedial legal relationships. Before the indicated subjective decision does not depend on any legal relationships.[46] It seems to us to be incorrect. In fact, the duty of the state to ensure the provision of personal safety of a citizen corresponds to the constitutional law of personal immunity of a citizen. Thus, certain public relations settled by legal propositions assuming, on the one hand, the legal right and on the other - the legal duty, i.e. legal relationship. If we consider that the legal right exists in itself and nothing is opposed to it, it comes to naught.

Thus, civil (personal, constitutional) rights exist and are realized in legal relationships but types of these legal relationships are different. The indicated rights exist not in administratively-legal, civil-legal and other branch legal relationships having strictly individualized character (such relations can arise during realization of these rights or at infringement or illegal use of the given rights), within the limits of relations "a state – a citizen". These are constitutional-legal and international-legal relationships.

It is necessary to say, that the civil rights as well as all human rights are realized in moral, cultural, religious relations but their realization in legal relationships at that is absolute.

It is necessary to note, that for a long time the legal literature was dominated with the point of view that the individuals cannot be holders of international law. "Formation of international-legal provisions on human rights started by the decision of the Nuremberg tribunal and the Universal Declaration of Human Rights, - as a experts on international law M. Ganis, R.Kay and E.Bredly wrote, - has been characterized as a most radical event for the whole history of international law as it so quickly has made not only the state but also individuals holders/subjects of international law".[47] It is necessary to assume, that it is a really progressive event which has strengthened the guarantees of human rights.

However, we can't forget that the universal concept of human rights cannot be opposed to a principle of the state sovereignty on the basis of which UN has been created. Intervention in internal affairs of the state under the covering of the slogan "protection of human rights" leads as events in Yugoslavia, in Iraq show, to mass encroachments on the right to life and other civil rights.

In the legal literature they distinguish three kinds of the legal status of a citizen:

1) general for all citizens;

2) status for certain category of people (for example, a legal status (modus) of students, workers of the Ministry of internal Affairs, pensioners);

3) for individuals.

Civil (personal, constitutional) rights as a rule are the indispensable element of all kinds of the legal status of a citizen but the given rights can be narrowed in the scope or be modified for imprisoned persons.

For all kinds of the rights including personal, the following stages of existence and realization are characteristic: the stage of occurrence and existence of a personal right; the stage of its direct realization.[48]

At the first stage these rights exist within the limits of general legal relationships of the type "a state – a citizen". At the second and the third stages they are concretized in the branch legal rights and are realized within the limits of branch legal relationships.

It is difficult to agree with L.D. Voevodin who considered that the right to personal immunity could be realized beyond certain legal relationships. Process of realization of this right leads to appearing of certain constitutionally-legal, administratively-legal, criminally-remedial and others legal relationships which presuppose not only the presence of legal duties of everyone who contacts the holder of the right, not encroaching on their personal safety but also calling the guilty to account.

The originality of such civil rights as personal immunity and inviolability of dwelling, freedom of conscience lies in the fact that they are being constantly, continuously realizing, at that all stages of their existence and realization are merging and consequently it is difficult to differentiate them. As for the right of privacy of correspondence and the rights of an accused on protection, citizens always have them but realize them sporadically, from time to time.

Features of realization of personal constitutional rights lie also in that some of them are realized by personal actions (the right of defence, the right of privacy of correspondence). As for the rights of personal immunity and dwelling, their realization can't be determined only by the terms "action" or "inaction" as a indicated inviolability consists in certain actual status subjects of which continuously use the values of personal safety, honour, dignity and this using is not connected directly with its action or inaction. And, finally, unlike social and economic the process of realization of rights of person has no property-material character.

The problem of civil rights guarantees is very important. In the literature there are various ways of classification of civil rights guarantees into general and special, objective and subjective, state and public, direct and indirect. We won't consider them in detail as this question falls outside the limits of the present research. In this connection the problems of classification of guarantees into general and special are meaningful. N.V. Vitruk puts to the number of general such guarantees as economic, political and ideological and to special – legal guarantees. Another point of view seems to be more convincing, according to which "the whole set of rights and duties guarantees can be subdivided into general guarantees (for all rights and duties) and special guarantees of each right and each duty".[49]

Any human right is provided by general economic, political, cultural and legal as well as special economic, political and other guarantees. Each right has original, specific conditions and means of providing its reality which are inherent only to it. But it is necessary to emphasize that the system of special guarantees of one right on its structure, set of conditions and means of warranting is not identical to such system of another, because in each case there is a special kind of the social relations subject to state-legal regulation. The problem of the researcher also consists in finding out, firstly that connection between general guarantees and the given right is and, secondly, which special guarantees it is provided by.

To start with, we are going to investigate the system of guarantees of personal constitutional rights general for everybody, the special guarantees will be subjected to studying in the subsequent chapters of the book. This system consists of legal, political, material, cultural guarantees.

Special importance for realization of civil rights should be given to legal guarantees, in particular to those that are fixed in international-legal documents and the Constitution. We call their rights-guarantees (see above).[50]

§ 5.   The Problem of Lawful Limitation of Civil Human Rights

One of the definitions of human rights is that they act as limits of realization of the government. At the same time during realization of individual freedom interests of a person can become an object of illegal actions of separate citizens or officials. In this connection there is a necessity for legal warranting of individual freedom. Characterizing freedom, Ch.-L. Montesquieu emphasized that "in a state, i.e. in a society where there are laws, freedom can consist only in having an opportunity to do what one should not want to do... Freedom is a right to do what one should want to do and not to be forced to do what one should not want to do".[51]

On the other hand, abuse of rights of person integrated with infringement of rights of other citizens from holders of the identified rights/legal subjects is not inconceivable. Thus, it entails the necessity of legal determination of exact limits of individual freedom. Finally, there are objective conditions which inevitably lead in some cases to its lawful limitation in the form of detention, imprisonment, search, etc.

L.I. Gluhareva calls the limitation of rights, on the one hand, an establishment of limits (borders) of the legal contents of the right, on the other - the withdrawal (reduction, narrowing) of the scope of the contents of the right established by the law before. Reducing the contents of the right is possible when it is dictated, firstly, by the special reasons of the high public or private importance and, secondly, when established restrictive measures are not excessive and are adequate to circumstances demanding their limitation. Thus it is necessary to remember that limitation can be positive, undertaken in the name of public dignity and negative, qualified as infringement of human rights.[52] Negative limitations of the rights can be connected also with the mistakes, indented reasons of the legislator, non-inclusion of international obligations of the state into the national instruments, etc. However, in this case, only the first situation, i.e. the positive limitation of the rights is considered.

An interesting definition of limits of realization of constitutional rights and freedom is given by A.A. Astrahan. He understands it as meeting the requirements of the social justice, corresponding to interests of a society and the state, the system of criteria and reference points of lawful behaviour, observance of which is an obligatory condition of appropriate using the rights.[53] Here it is possible to emphasize the following important points: firstly, it is the system of criteria and reference points of lawful behaviour (the behaviour corresponding to the instructions of legal provisions); secondly, these criteria should meet the requirements of social justice (the society should proceed from the interests of citizens, society or a state); thirdly, they are an obligatory condition of appropriate using of the rights.

Legal limits of realization of constitutional rights and freedoms can be characterized also as set of the legal means establishing the scope and limits of the constitutional law and freedom. Overrunning these limits leads to use of measures of the legal responsibility to the offender.[54] We support this point of view. Limitations of civil human rights can be realized at the levels of normative regulation (in constitutions, laws), individually-legal regulation (verdicts and decisions of courts, etc.) and also in actual actions of law enforcement bodies, citizens (delivery and detention of a suspect, etc.). All the above-mentioned limitations of the rights can be lawful and illegal.

Lawful limitations of civil human rights can consist in lawful detention, imprisonment, custodial placement, imprisonment, recognizance not to leave, search, seizure, suspension of religious organizations' activity, their elimination, etc.

The strongest limitation of human rights is death penalty. Here it would be necessary to speak not about limitations but about liquidation of the indicated rights as air subject is destroyed. Arbitrary and extrajudicial executions are among the most serious crimes against a person and mass actions of such type relate to international crimes against humanity. In the states that have kept death penalty as sentence, it is admitted as lawful in case it is realized within the limits of Article 6 of international Covenant on Civil and Political Rights. However, world tendency is observed: the number of the countries which have refused from this severe and archaic sentence is increasing every year.

International standards of human rights provide criteria and conditions of lawful limitation of civil human rights.

The Universal Declaration of Human Rights (1948) (part 2 Article 29) establishes three conditions of lawful limitation of human rights: if they are established by the law; if they provide a due recognition of and respect of the rights of other persons; if they are aimed at satisfaction of fair requirements of morals, public order and a general well-being in a democratic society.

The conditions of lawful limitation of civil rights are also fixed in international Covenant on Civil and Political Rights, 1966 and the European Convention for the Protection of Human Rights and Basic Freedoms, 1950.

Let's trace it on the example of the fundamental law of a person, namely, the right to life. This right is the logic precondition of other rights. It is fixed in Article 3 of the Universal Declaration of Human Rights where it is said, that "everyone has a right to life, liberty and security of person". However, in the Universal Declaration there is no article, concerning the abolition of death penalty. international Covenant on Civil and Political Rights does not provide an obligatory cancelling of death penalty but Article 6 of the Covenant contains a number of limitations on pronouncement of sentence, for example an interdiction on passing a death sentence to persons under 18 years and execution of such sentences towards pregnant women.

Clause 2 of the European Convention on Human Rights and Basic Free-doms protects the right to life. In this respect Article 2 provides directly protection from actions from the states, rather than from individuals. The major principle of this clause consists in protecting an individual from any deprivation of life by the state.

Protocol 6 to the European Convention does not suppose use of death penalty in the states - members of the Council of Europe.

Clause 2 of the European Convention limits circumstances at which the state has a right to deprive an individual of life: for protection of any person against illegal violence; for realization of lawful imprisonment or prevention of runaway of a person detained on the lawful bases; in case of the actions stipulated by the law, for suppression of revolt or mutiny/rebellion. The majority of legal controversy arises in the connection with this provision.

At consideration of one of few interstate affairs under the Convention (Cyprus versus Turkey) the Commission of Human Rights has found out that at least in 12 documentary confirmed cases the Turkish army killed civilians in infringement of Article 2. The Commission has also found out that proofs lead to the conclusion that Turkey is guilty of a plenty of illegal murders.[55]

Paragraph 2 of Article 15 of the European Convention also provides an opportunity of deprivation of life as a result of lawful military actions or the death penalties connected with war. Thus, the European Convention in detail regulates the bases of lawful limitation of the right to life and law enforcement practice of the Council of Europe precisely differentiates lawful limitations of this right from illegal ones.

One more of the major civil human rights is the right to physical inviolability. Clause 3 of the European Convention says the following: "No one can be subjected torture and inhuman or degrading treatment or punishment". The same right is fixed in Article 5 of the Universal Declaration and in Article 7 of international Covenant on Civil and Political Rights.

The right to be free from torture and the right to be free from the inhuman or degrading treatment are some of the most important human rights as ay are coordinated to security of person and human dignity of an individual. The extremely high position of these rights in international hierarchy of human rights reflects their special status in this respect. For example, Paragraph 2 of Article 15 of the European Convention on Human Rights which allows the states to deviate/recede from the obligations under the Convention in case of force majeure, emphasizing value of the rights according to Article 3, fixes that under no circumstances the state cannot recede from the obligations under given clause.

So, in the case of Ireland versus the United Kingdom the forms and methods of interrogation (usually called five methods) which the government of the United Kingdom had used to suspected in Northern Ireland were prejudiced. These are the following five ways: to make suspected to stand at a wall during many hours in an extremely inconvenient position; to make suspected to put on a head a hood during interrogations; to deprive suspected from sleep; to subject suspected to noise nuisance; to deprive suspected from necessary food and drink.

The European Commission has come to the conclusion that these five methods represent torture and inhuman treatment according to Article 3 of the European Convention,[56] having recorded the indicated actions as illegal ways of limitation of human rights.

Let's turn to Article 5 of the European Convention which fixes the right to freedom and security of person. Here freedom from any imprisonment and detention is mainly envisaged. An individual is not accountable to the state or a society for their daily residence; he has a right to be in any place. It is freedom in personal or physical terms. However, the European Commission of Human Rights and the European Court on Human Rights distinguish between general limitations of this right for the population as a whole (for example, all inhabitants register their usual residence at authorities) and lawful limitations for certain individual established by court or other bodies authorized by the law (imprisonment of an individual in the limited physical space). And though such limitations can represent imprisonment according to the European Convention, the Commission and Court estimate the legality of such detention in view of the admissible bases and the remedial actions listed in the clause. In some cases the Commission considered that an individualized limitation of personal freedom, for example the order to stay in a certain place or to report in a police station once a week, is not equivalent to the forbidden imprisonment.[57] However, in other cases the Court considered that the compulsory keeping on an island where the freedom of movement is limited at night to a building and in the afternoon to the small area of island, is equivalent to the forbidden imprisonment.[58]

It is necessary to note, that in the report on the case of Arrowsmith the Commission has balanced the rights to freedom and inviolability, having noted, that "the right to security of person includes a guarantee of that individuals will be imprisoned and detained only on the bases and according to the procedure prescribed by the law".[59] This formulation is conformable with the formulation of Article 9 of international Covenant on Civil and Political Rights where it is emphasized: "No one should be subjected to arbitrary arrest or detention. No one can be deprived of their liberty except on such grounds and in accordance with such procedure as are established by law". We should note that in the European Convention those bases on which an individual can be detained that is legally more exact in comparison with general interdiction of arbitrary imprisonment stipulated by the Covenant are particularly listed.

The European Convention fixes six kinds of lawful imprisonment, whether it be imprisonment, detention, internment or something else. They are considered as exceptions of the principle of right to personal freedom and inviolability. Among them there are: lawful detention of a person on the basis of their conviction by competent court; lawful imprisonment or detention of a person for contempt of the lawful decision of court or with the purpose of providing the meeting of any obligation prescribed by law; lawful imprisonment or detention of a person made with a view of their passing to competent judicial body on proved suspicion in committing an offence or in case when there are sufficient bases to believe, that detention is necessary for prevention of committing an offence by them or to prevent them from hiding after committing. Detention of a minor person on the basis of the lawful decision for educational supervision or their lawful detention for passing to competent body; lawful detention of persons aimed at prevention of infectious diseases distribution and also detention of insane persons, alcoholics, addicts or tramps; lawful imprisonment or detention of a person aimed at prevention of their illegal entrance to the country or a person against whom the measures on their deportation or extradition are taken.

Each of the categories of admissible imprisonment is interesting and deserves special attention. However, we should stop in detail only on Paragraph 1 and 3 of Article 5 of the European Convention.

Paragraph 1 of Article 5 of the European Convention on Human Rights resolves imprisonment and detention of someone "on the proved suspicion" in committing an offence when there are enough bases to believe that detention is necessary for prevention of their committing an offence to prevent them from hiding after the committing. However, these three bases coordinate with the corresponding obligation of the state in relation to an imprisoned or detained person to pass them to competent judicial body. This obligation of the state is further developed and supplemented in Paragraph 3 of Article 5: "Every imprisoned or detained person according to provision of Article (c) 1 of given clause should be immediately taken to the judge or to another official authorized by the law to carry out judicial functions and has a right to proceeding during reasonable term or right on release pending trial. Release can depend on granting guarantees of appearance in court". From the conditions of this provision it appears that Paragraph 3 of Article 5 is not used to detention pending the performance of decision on deportation or extradition.

Many countries establish exact term during which the imprisoned person should stand before corresponding judicial body. The requirement "On immediacy" can frequently mean that judges should be on their place in weekends or on holidays but it does not mean that they should be accessible on a twenty-four hour basis. Though in the interstate legislation of the European countries the usual term is from 24 up to 48 hours, the Commission and Court do not establish rigid timetable concerning Paragraph 3 of Article 5. Type of fences of which certain person is suspected can play the role at definition of cases when the requirement of "immediacy" was fulfilled. in case of Brogan and others where it was a question of investigation of terrorist crimes, the European Commission agreed with reasons of the government that longer terms of detention were admissible than at investigation of usual crimes. Though the European Court on Human Rights has expressed sympathy in connection with complexity of investigation of crimes of terrorism, nevertheless, it has found out infringement of Paragraph 3 of Article 5 concerning these applicants. According to the Court: "Giving of such value to the features of this case to justify the long term of detention without taking to a judge or another official in court would mean an unacceptable wide interpretation of a simple word "immediately". Such interpretation will introduce into Paragraph 3 of Article 5 serious easing of a remedial guarantee to the detriment of an individual and will cause the consequences weakening the essence of the right, protected by this provision".[60]

Preparation for such immediate hearing in court is, certainly, limited and here again impossible to demand any detailed certificates or charges. At the same time, though in the majority of the countries imprisoned persons have the right to a legal aid at this stage; it is not stipulated in the Convention. The defender can be in court together with them but their desire to have one can detain the hearing.

The concept "a judge or another official authorized by the law to carry out judicial functions", means that is this person not only is authorized but also actually carries out judicial powers.

In Schisser's case the Court has noted, "According to Paragraph 3 of the clause 5 there are both remedial requirements and requirements in essence. The remedial requirement imposes on "the official" the obligation to listen to an individual brought to them…the requirement in essence imposes on them the obligation to consider the circumstances speaking for or against of detention, to solve referring to judicial criteria, whether there are reasons to justify the detention and to make a decision on clearing if such reasons are not present".[61]

In some countries legal propositions concerning criminal cases are those, that imprisonment or detention are impossible to make if the judge hasn't made a decision about it in advance and has not approved it, except for extreme situations. The Convention doesn't go so far.

A body making a detention should bring an individual to the judge. independence of the judge and personal meeting with imprisoned persons are the basic guarantees for anyone who comes within provisions of Paragraph 1 of Article 5 and, hence, Paragraph 3 of Article 5. For the defender and other representatives of the imprisoned person it is not enough to be present at this meeting.

Having considered opportunities of lawful limitation of the civil rights in international instruments, we should address to the national legislation of Russia on the given question. First, it is necessary to dwell on ways of limitation of individual freedom at the constitutional level and then to pass to consideration on certain examples of the branch legislation.

The Constitution of the Russian Federation in Article 55 and 56 has established the bases of limitation of the human rights, concerning those included into civil rights. However, a number of conditions of lawful limitation of limits of individual freedom have been stipulated also by the authors of the project of the Constitution of the Russian Federation, prepared by the constitutional commission during the constitutional reform of Russia 1990-1993. Let's trace the influence of this project in the given context on the final text of the operating Constitution of the Russian Federation, 1993.

In the project of the constitutional commission it was fixed that "basic rights and freedoms of a person are inalienable and relate to them from birth" (part 1 Article 13). However, in the same clause the principle of limitation of the rights but only by the Constitution and the law with a view of protection of the constitutional system of the Russian Federation, public morals, the rights and freedom of other citizens is fixed (part 3 Article 13). In turn, part 1 of Article 15 says that realization of the rights and freedoms a person and a citizen should not outrage the rights and freedoms of other persons. However, the proclaimed constitutional rights and freedoms are not absolute. Almost every one of them has exceptions supposed in special cases, under special conditions, in exceptional circumstances. These exceptions in relation to any of the rights, to any of freedoms are specific. So, the right to life is limited to an opportunity of necessary defense, execution by military men of lawful battle-orders, abortions. Another rights and freedoms have other possible limitations but frequently they are also specific.

The project of the constitutional commission alongside with fixing of the right (in some cases) spoke about an opportunity of its limitation. Thus, fixing in Article 21 the right to freedom and security of person, the project spoke about limitation of these rights. Limitation of freedom can be limited to imprisonment only by a court decision and the bases of limitation of security of person can be established by the Federal law. The project of the constitutional commission in this part in many respects has repeated Russian Declaration of Rights and Freedoms of a Person and a Citizen, 1991. Thus, the right to personal privacy, privacy of correspondence, negotiations, post, telephone and other messages (Article 21) was limited on the basis of the law and only by a court decision. In Article 23 of the projects it was said that the Federal law can establish withdrawals from the right to inviolability of dwelling but only in interests of protection of life and health of people, prevention of significant damage to dwelling and property in it. Further, part 2 of the same clauses continued that a search and other actions made with penetration into a dwelling are permitted only on the basis of the Federal law and by a court decision. But in urgent cases there can be another order established by the Federal law providing obligatory subsequent judicial check of legality of these actions. Thus, judicial check of legality and validity of these actions was fixed.

Such rights as freedom of movement (Article 24) could be limited only by the Federal law. The part 2 of Article 20 of the project of the constitutional commission has fixed death penalty which should be used as an exclusive sentence for especially grave crimes and be passed only by a verdict of court. Thus, the project of the constitutional commission provided that human rights could be limited under the following conditions: firstly, only by the law; secondly, in some cases by a court decision; thirdly, for protection of bases constitutional system, moral, health, rights and legitimate interests of other persons, safety of the state and public order; fourthly, at introduction of state of emergency.

The Constitution of the Russian Federation, in turn, has accepted these provisions of the project. Their formulations in a greater degree corresponded to international standards and Russian Declaration of Rights and Freedoms of a Person and a Citizen, 1991.

In part 3 of Article 56 of the Constitution the principle of inadmissibility of limitation of such civil rights as a right to life, dignity, personal privacy, personal and family secrecy, protection of honour and reputation, the right to distribution of the information on private life, freedom of conscience and freedom of creeds and also legal guarantees of the civil rights stipulated by the Constitution (Article 46-54) is established.

The Constitution stipulates that enumerating of basic rights and freedoms in it should not be interpreted as denying or belittling of the conventional rights and freedoms (part 1 Article 55). The prohibition of the legislator to publish laws cancelling or belittling human rights (part 2 Article 55) is also fixed there. Then the Constitution of the Russian Federation reproduces, basically, the formula of Article 29 of the Universal Declaration of Human Rights but specifies it with reference to Russian reality.

Human and civil rights can be limited:

1) only by the Federal law (rather than laws of subjects of the Federation);

2) for protection of bases of the constitutional system, moral, health, rights and legitimate interests of other persons, guarantee of defense and safety of the state (part 3 Article 55).

Thus, the protection of bases of the constitutional system (not protection of the rights of other persons as it is written down in the Universal Declaration of Human Rights) is brought here in the forefront.

The special clause of the Constitution is devoted to an opportunity of "separate limitations of the rights and freedoms with the indication of limits of their action" (part 1 Article 56) in conditions of state of emergency. However, as it appears from Article 88, introduction of state of emergency relates to the exclusive competence of the President which he declares on the basis of the special Federal constitutional law and the head of the state only informs the parliament about it. It seems that such procedure can be hardly called democratic as it allows limitations of the civil rights without the mechanism of control and counterbalance.[62]

The substantive provisions connected with lawful limitation of the civil rights find a certain definition and reflection in the branch legislation of the Russian Federation. Thus, the Administrative Code of the Russian Federation and the Code of Criminal Procedure of the Russian Federation provide certain procedures of civil human rights limitation. In particular, administrative punishments relate to such limitations (part 1 Article 3.1 of the Administrative Code of the Russian Federation). The same clause contains a humanistic ascertainment that administrative punishment cannot have the purpose to humiliate human dignity of a natural person who has committed an offence, or causing to them physical sufferings and also making harm to business reputation of a legal person.

One of the kinds of administrative punishment is administrative imprisonment that is isolation of an infringer from a society and is set by the judge. It is specially stipulated that administrative imprisonment is established and set only in exceptional case for certain kinds of administrative offences. The given kind of punishment is not used to pregnant women, women having children under 14 years, minors and also to invalids of I and II groups. The Administrative Code of the Russian Federation has established the important provision according to which the term of administrative detention is included into the term of administrative imprisonment. Thus, the legislator has established the limits of opportunities of the state in limitation of human rights.

In turn, the Code of Criminal Procedure of the Russian Federation provides wider spectrum of procedures of limitations of individual freedom unlike the Administrative Code.

Let's dwell on opportunities of lawful limitation of civil human rights at detention.

One of measures of remedial compulsion is detention of the suspected (Ch. 12 of the Code of Criminal Procedure of the Russian Federation). Here the following order of proceedings is established: body of inquiry, the investigator, the inspector or the public prosecutor (i.e. definite circle of subjects) has a right to detain a person on suspicion in committing of a crime at presence of the following circumstances: firstly, for this crime punishment in the form of imprisonment can be set, secondly, at presence of one of the circumstances indicated in the Code of Criminal Procedure of the Russian Federation (part 1 of Article 91 Code of Criminal Procedure of the Russian Federation).

After taking a suspected into the place of inquiry to the inspector or the public prosecutor the report of detention should be made during a strictly certain term, no more than three hours. In the report the mark that the rights of the suspected have been explained to them should necessarily be put. In the report the bases, grounds and other circumstances of detention are indicated. The report of detention is signed by a person who wrote it and a suspected. It is possible to emphasize the following guarantees of observance of conditions of lawful limitation of the rights suspected at their detention:

1) obligatory notifying the public prosecutor in writing about detention within 12 hours from the moment of detention;

2) a suspected prior to the beginning of interrogation a confidential meeting with the defender is given on their request;

3) After 48 hours from the moment of detention a suspected is subject to discharge if no preventive punishment in the form of the detention has been selected or the court has not prolonged the term of detention.

4) a suspected is subject to immediate discharge if the decision of the judge about punishment in the form of detention or prolongation of the term of detention will not appear during 48 hours from the moment of detention.

The analysis of practice of the European Commission and the European Court on Human Rights given above allows drawing a conclusion that de jure many Russian legal regulations, basically, correspond to international standards in the field of lawful limitation of civil human rights.

But not all legal regulations. Thus, in the Code of Criminal Procedure of the Russian Federation the rights of victims (in comparison with the rights of accused) are limited. The Federal law on struggle against extremism contains the formulations creating conditions for arbitrariness from law enforcement bodies. The term "extremism" is too wide and vague that it hardly can be considered as a strict legal category. The law on freedom of conscience and religious associations contains unreasonable limitations for some religious organizations and puts atheists in unequal position in comparison with believers. As to law enforcement practice (let alone criminals the scope of activity of whom is increasing) it abounds with illegal encroachments on civil rights. Other chapters of this book are devoted to this question.

Notes

1. *Marx K., Engels F.* Compilation of works. Vol. 12. P. 710/ Маркс К., Энгельс Ф. Сочинения. Т.12. С. 710.

2. A. Gertsen distinguished between "narrow, brutal, filthy egoism" and "egoism as aspiration to be oneself". (*Gertsen A.I.* Comp. in 2 vol. Vol.2. P. 100) / А. Герцен различал "эгоизм узкий, животный, грязный" и эгоизм как "стремление быть самим собою" (Герцен А. И. Соч.: В 2 т. Т. 2. С. 100).

3. Ibidem. P. 105.

4. Ibidem.

5. Ibidem. P. 107

6. *Spinoza B.* Selected works. Vol. 2. Moscow, 1957. P. 263 /Спиноза Б. Избранные произведения. Т. 2. М., 1957. С. 263.

7. See: *Gomien D., Harris D., Zvaak L.* European Convention on Human Rights and European Social Charter: Law and Practice. Moscow, 1998. P. 290. / См.: Гомьен Д., Харрис Д., Зваак Л. Европейская конвенция о правах человека и Европейская социальная хартия: право и практика. М., 1998. С. 290.

8. Ibidem. P. 295.

9. See: Ibidem. P. 294.

10. See: *Locke J.* Selected philosophic works. Moscow, 1960. P. 24 / См.: Локк Дж. Избранные философские произведения. М., 1960. С. 24.

11. *Spinoza B.* Specified work. P. 206, 267. Спиноза Б. Указ. соч. С. 206, 267.

12. *Kant I.* Compilation of works: in 6 vol. Vol. 4. P. 2. Moscow, 1965. P. 147 / Кант И. Сочинения: В 6 т. Т 4. Ч. 2. М., 1965. С. 147.

13. *Pritt D.* Spies and Intelligencers as Witnesses. Moscow, 1960. P. 23. / ритт Д. Шпионы и осведомители на скамье свидетелей. М., 1960. С. 23.

14. Alekseev S.S. Problems of Law Theory. Vol. 1. Sverdlovsk, 1972. P. 91. / Алексеев С. С. Проблемы теории права. Т. 1. Свердловск, 1972. С. 91.

15. General Theory of Law and State / Edited by Lasarev V.V. Moscow, 1999. P. 147. / Общая теория права и государства / Под ред. В. В. Лазарева. М., 1999. С. 147.

16. See: Gomien D., Harris D., Zvaak L. Specified works. P. 227, 228; Ganis M., Kay P., Bradley A. European Law in Human Rights. Practice and Commentary. Moscow, 1997. P. 452, 453. / См.: Гомьен Д., Харрис Д., Зваак Л. Указ. соч. С. 227, 228; Дженис М., Кэй Р., Брэдли Э. Европейское право в области прав человека. Практика и комментарии. М., 1997. С. 452, 453.

17. Constitutional Law / Edited by A.E. Kozlov. Moscow, 1997. P. 72. Конституционное право / Под ред. А. Е. Козлова. М., 1997. С. 72.

18. See: Human Rights. History, Theory and Practice / Edited by B.L. Nazarov. Moscow, 1995. P. 224; Human Rights / Edited by E.A. Lukasheva. Moscow, 1999. P. 142. / См.: Права человека. История, теория, практика / Под ред. Б. Л. Назарова. М., 1995. С. 224; Права человека / Под ред. Е. А. Лукашевой. М., 1999. С. 142.

19. See: lder J. Constitutional and administrative Law. L., 1994. P. 319, 328.

20. See: Nikiforova M.A. Civil Rights and Freedoms in the USA: Legal Doctrine and Practice. Moscow, 1991. P. 3. / См.: Никифорова М. А. Гражданские права и свободы в США: судебная доктрина и практика. М., 1991. С. 3.

21. Voevodin L.D. Legal Status of a Person in Russia. Moscow, 1997. / Воеводин Л. Д. Юридический статус личности в России. М., 1997.

22. See: Human Rights / Edited by E.A. Lukasheva. Moscow, 1999. P. 133, 135. / См.: Права человека / Под ред. Е. А. Лукашевой. М., 1999. С. 133, 135.

23. See: Lusher F. Constitutional Protection of Human Rights and Freedoms. Moscow, 1993. p. 84. / См.: Люшер Ф. Конституционная защита прав и свобод личности. М., 1993. С. 84.

24. See: UN Economic and Social Council. Main session 1995. Crime Prevention and Criminal Sentence in the World. Death Penalty and Realization of Measures for Protection of Rights of those Facing the Death Penalty. Secretary General Report. Geneva, 1995. P. 45. / См.: ООН. Экономический и Социальный Совет. Основная сессия 1995 г. Предупреждение преступности и уголовное наказание в мире. Смертная казнь и осуществление мер, гарантирующих защиту прав тех, кому грозит смертная казнь. Доклад Генерального секретаря. Женева, 1995. С. 45.

25. Voevodin L.D. Constitutional Rights and Duties of the Soviet Citizens. Moscow, 1972. P. 254. / Воеводин Л. Д. Конституционные права и обязанности советских граждан. М., 1972. С. 254.

26. Contemporary Dictionary of the Russian Literature Language. Vol. 6. Moscow, Leningrad, 1957. P. 295. / Словарь современного русского литературного языка. Т. 6. М.; Л., 1957. С. 295.

27. See: Voevodin L.D. Specified work. P. 190. / См.: Воеводин Л. Д. Указ. соч. С. 190.

28. See: Human Rights / Edited by E.A. Lukasheva. Moscow, 1999. P. 142. / См.: Права человека / Под ред. Е. А. Лукашевой. М., 1999. С. 142.

29. See: Kistyakovsky B.A. State Law (General and Russian). Moscow, 1908-1909. P. 311. / См.: Кистяковский Б. А. Государственное право (общее и русское). М., 1908–1909. С. 311.

30. See: Esmen A. Basics of Constitutional Law. Saint-Petersburg, 1909. p. 396. / См.: Эсмен А. Общие основания конституционного права. СПб., 1909. С. 396.

31. See: Burdeau Georges. Les libertes publiques. Paris, 1961. P. 89.

32. Mason A.T., Beany W.M. American Constitution Law. Second Edition. N.-Y. P. 516.

33. Marx K., Engels F. Compilation of works. Vol. 3. P. 217. / Маркс К., Энгельс Ф. Сочинения. Т. 3. С. 217.

34. See: Comparative Constitutional Law. Moscow, 1996. P. 282. / См.: Сравнительное конституционное право. М., 1996. С. 282.

35. See: Voevodin L.D. Specified work. P. 192. / См.: Воеводин Л. Д. Указ. соч. С. 192.

36. See: Sadovsky V.N. Systems and Structures as Specific Subjects of Contemporary Science // Problems of Systems and Structures' investigation. Moscow, 1965. p. 43. / См.: Садовский В. Н. Системы и структуры как специфические предметы современного научного знания // Проблемы исследования систем и структур. М., 1965. С. 43.

37. See: Strogovich M.S. Basic Questions of Soviet Socialist Law. Moscow, 1966. P. 168. / См.: Строгович М. С. Основные вопросы советской социалистической законности. М., 1966. С. 168.

38. Matuzov N.I. Legal Rights of USSR Citizens. Saratov, 1966. P. 42. / Матузов Н. И. Субъективные права граждан СССР. Саратов, 1966. С. 42.

39. Halfina R.O. General Study of Legal Relations. Moscow, 1974. P. 124. / Халфина Р. О. Общее учение о правоотношении. М., 1974. С. 124.

40. Patulin V.A. inviolability of a Person as a Legal institution // Soviet State and Law/ 1973. #11. P. 16 / Патюлин В. А. Неприкосновенность личности как правовой институт // Советское государство и право. 1973. № 11. С. 16.

41. See: Orzih M.F. Person and Law. Moscow, 1975. P. 96. / См.: Орзих М. Ф. Личность и право. М., 1975. С. 96.

42. Alekseev S.S. Problem of Law Theory: Course of lectures. Vol. 1. Sverdlovsk, 1972. P. 308. Алексеев С. С. Проблема теории права: Курс лекций. Т.1. Свердловск, 1972. С. 308.

43. See: Matusov N.I. Person. Rights. Democracy. Saratov, 1972. P. 100 / См.: Матузов Н. И. Личность. Права. Демократия. Саратов, 1972. С. 100.

44. See Kozlova E.I., Kutafin O.E. Russian Constitutional Law. Moscow, 1995. P. 198. / См.: Козлова Е. И., Кутафин О. Е. Конституционное право России. М., 1995. С. 198.

45. Komkova G.N., Shudra O.V. et al. institution of Human Rights in Russia. Saratov, 1998. P. 86. / Комкова Г. Н., Шудра О. В. и др. Институт прав человека в России. Саратов, 1998. С. 86.

46. See Strogovich M.S. Basic Questions of Soviet Socialistic Law. Moscow, 1966. P. 177-178. / См.: Строгович М. С. Основные вопросы советской социалистической законности. М., 1966. С. 177–178.

47. Ganis M., Kay R., Bradley A. Specified works. P. 21. / Дженис М., Кэй Р., Брэдли Э. Указ. соч. С. 21.

48. See: Patulin V.A. State and a Person in USSR. Moscow, 1974. P. 186-203. / См.: Патюлин В. А. Государство и личность в СССР. М., 1974. С. 186–203.

49. Denisov A.I. Soviet State Law. Moscow, 1974. P. 322. / Денисов А. И. Советское государственное право. М., 1974. С. 322.

50. This problem is considered in more detail in Part II of this book.

51. Montesquieu Ch.-L. Selected works. Moscow, 1955. P. 289. / Монтескье Ш. Избранные произведения. М., 1955. С. 289.

52. See: Gluhareva L.I. Mechanism of Human Right's Guarantees // Law and Life. 2000. #27. P. 90-91. / См.: Глухарева Л. И. Механизм гарантий прав человека // Право и жизнь. 2000. № 27. С. 90–91.

53. See Astrahan A.A. Guarantees and Limits of Constitutional Rights and Freedoms Realization of Soviet People. Abstract of the dissertation … Candidate of Jurisprudence. Moscow, 1986. p. 8. / См.: Астрахань А. А. Гарантии и пределы осуществления конституционных прав и свобод советских граждан: Автореф. дис. … канд. юрид. наук. М., 1986. С. 8.

54. See: Astrahan A.A. Specified work. P. 9. / См.: Астрахань А. А. Указ. соч. С. 9.

55   See: Cyprus versus Turkey / См.: Кипр против Турции. Comm. Report 10.7.76, par. 352–355 (unpublished).

56. See: Ireland versus the Great Britain. Comm. Report 25.1.76, para. B, Eur. Court H.R., Series B. No. 23-1. P. 496.

57. No. 7690/77, Dec. 16.7.77 (unpublished).

58. See: Court decision on Goodzardy of November, 6, 1980/ См.: Судебное решение по делу Гудзарди от 6 ноября 1980 г. Series A. No. 39. P. 32–35, par. 90–95.

59. Arrowsmith versus the UK. Comm. Report 12.10.78, par. 64. D.R. 19. P. 5 (18).

60. Court decision on Brogan case et al. of November, 29, 1988. / Судебное решение по делу Броган и другие от 29 ноября 1988 г. Series A. No. 145-D. P. 33-34, par. 62.

61. Court decision on Schisser's case of December, 1979. / Судебное решение по делу Шиссер от 4 декабря 1979 г. Series A. No. 34. P. 13–14, par. 31.

62. On the Question of Human Rights Limitation see: Ustinov V.V., Volkov A.P., Stukalova T.V. Enforcement of Human Constitutional Rights and Freedoms. Nizhny Novgorod, 1998. P. 94-111. По вопросу об ограничениях прав человека см.: Устинов В. В., Волков А. П., Стукалова Т. В. Обеспечение конституционных прав и свобод личности. Н. Новгород, 1998. С. 94-111.

Chapter 2 THE STATE OF CIVIL HUMAN RIGHTS
IN THE MODERN WORLD

§ 1. Problems of Civil Human Rights
Realization in Globalization

World civilization being at a stage of globalization creates serious contradictions in realization of all human rights (as we speak about in the foreword), including the civil rights. On the one hand, internationalization of social life was showed in acceptance by international organizations of significant number of the legal regulations fixing the civil rights and their guarantees. Thus, in last quarter of the 20th century the United Nations passed Declarations on the Right of Peoples to Peace, Declaration on the Elimination of All Forms of intolerance and of Discrimination Based on Religion or Belief, protection of all persons against violent disappearances, main principles of justice for victims of crimes and abuse of power, etc.

In these years the Second Optional Protocol to international Covenant on Civil and Political Rights (1989), the Convention against Torture and Other Cruel, inhuman or Degrading Treatment or Punishment (1984), the Body of Principles for the Protection of All Persons under Any Form of Detention or Imprisonment (1988), the Convention on the Rights of the Child and Optional Protocols to it on the involvement of children in armed conflict, on the sale of children, child prostitution and child pornography (2000) have been passed. During this period the Protocols to the Convention on Protection of Human Rights and Basic Freedoms and among them the Protocol 6 concerning the abolition of the death penalty (1983), the Convention on Human Rights in Biomedicine (1998) have been accepted in Europe.

International mechanism of protection of civil human rights was improved. In particular, the activity of the Commission of Human Rights was developed. At all its sessions the special attention was paid to this group of the rights. In 2002 the indicated Commission formed nine working groups and among them the groups: on preparation of an optional protocol for the Convention against tortures; arbitrary detention;

violent disappearances; effective realization of the Durban Declaration on Struggle Against Racism and Racial Discrimination. The committees on human rights, against tortures, on the rights of the child and other international bodies created for the control over observance of agreements, considered a significant number of the complaints connected with infringement of civil rights.

In last decades the procedure of consideration of complaints of citizens of the European states connected with infringement of their civil rights has been created in the European Court on Human Rights.

In the decisions of international organizations, in public opinion new ideas connected with the further development of the system of civil rights are being formed. Thus, in Article 10 of the Universal Declaration on the Human Genome and Human Rights, adopted by UNESCO (1997) and approved by UN General Assembly (1998), it is stated that no research or research use concerning the human genome, in particular in the fields of biology, genetics and medicine, should prevail over respect for the human rights, fundamental freedoms and human dignity of individuals.

Thus, in the end of the 20th - the beginning of the 21st century the contents of human dignity is enriched.

One of the positive phenomena in the sphere of civil rights realization shown during the last decades is world tendency to abolition of the death penalty. If we compare the reports of the Secretary-General of the United Nations on this question, presented in ECOSOC and in the Commission of Human Rights in 1995 and 2004, the following situation comes to light: in May, 1995 the death penalty was used in 91 countries of world, legally the death penalty has been cancelled completely in 56 countries, cancelled de facto - in 28 and the whole number of the states using the was 84. In 14 countries this sentence has been cancelled partially (only for general crime).[1] In 2004 the amount of the states which have saved the death penalty, was reduced to 71, i.e. it has decreased on 20. But the amount of the countries which are not using the death penalty has increased up to 110. Among them 77 countries have completely cancelled it, 33 have cancelled it de facto and 15 use it only for general crime.[2] The following parameters are characteristic: if from 1980 up to 1995, i.e. during 15 years, 33 countries have refused from the death penalty, from 1995 up to 2004, almost 10 years, there have been 20 such countries. In total during the quarter of a century 53 states of world have refused from criminal sentence, that according to the Resolution 2003/67 of the Commission of Human Rights accepted on April, 26th, 2003, "promotes increase of the importance of human dignity and progressive development of a person".[3] However, it is necessary to say that in a number of the large states in which territory the significant part of mankind lives (the USA, India, Pakistan, China, Iran, etc.) the death penalty is used till now. in the indicated Resolution the Commission of Human Rights has noted that in some countries the death sentence is passed after proceeding which mismatches international standards of validity and this severe sentence concerning persons belonging to national or ethnic, religious and language minority, has been passed disproportionately often. Quite often women are exposed to death penalty on the basis of the discrimination to them.[4]

Human rights organization "International Amnesty" which has been carrying out researches of practice of use of death penalty for many years, results in a number of positive facts when in some countries saving the death penalty, people wrongly condemned to death penalty (Philippines, Malaysia, China, Pakistan, Turkey, and Japan) have been released. However, as authors of the "International Amnesty" report published in 1998, declare, "authorities of the USA have never directly recognized executions of an innocent person in this century".[5] The investigation of the case of Sacco and Vanzetti, executed in 1927, carried out in 1977 show the innocence of the condemned. However, they have not been rehabilitated till now. According to incomplete data of this organization, in the USA up to 1984 there were innocently executed 23 persons.[6] In the same report data about execution in Russia of the maniac A. Chikatilo in 1994 is cited. On this case it was officially recognized that before this execution innocent A. Kravchenko had been executed and another unreasonably accused citizen, had committed suicide. According to the United Nations, contrary to Article 6 of international Covenant on Civil and Political Rights in a number of the countries the death penalty of the minor (the USA, Yemen, Iran, Pakistan, and Saudi Arabia) is used till now.[7]

It is necessary to note that objective materials of international organizations testify that the epoch globalism is accompanied by strengthening of negative tendencies in the sphere of civil rights. Such mass encroachments on these rights become the integral component of a world policy and practice of many states of world. And some new rather dangerous attributes of these criminal acts are outlined. Among them first of all it is necessary to note encroachments on the major human right to peace. Military conflicts in Yugoslavia (1999), in Iraq (2003) have killed thousands of people and have put world community on a verge of a catastrophe. Thus it is necessary to note that the USA, NATO used new kinds of firearms of mass destruction. It was declared on November, 6th, 2002 by the Secretary-General of the United Nations. This question was discussed in 2003 at the session of the Subcommittee on Encouragement and Protection of Human Rights of the Commission of Human Rights of the United Nations. According to the UN Environment Program (UNEP), in Yugoslavia, Afghanistan the firearms included depleted uranium was used. The members of the above-stated Subcommittee have mentioned the facts, testifying that new kinds of firearms relate to the number forbidden by propositions of the humanitarian law. The special trouble was caused by the approval on May, 9th, 2003 of the bill of so-called "mini-nuclear charges" development. New technologies connected with manufacturing and use of firearms of mass destruction or not selective action or the firearms, capable to cause excessive damages or unnecessary sufferings, contradict human rights. The statement of the governmental figures of some countries concerning their readiness to use the nuclear firearms as means of making the "first" or even anticipatory blow are especially dangerous.[8]

In modern conditions there was a special danger to the right to life. After events of September, 11th, 2001 in the USA and massacre by terrorists in Spain and in Russia (2004) the terrorism is considered by international community as huge threat to mankind.[9] in the Resolution of the Commission of Human Rights 2003/37 from April, 23rd, 2003 the more and more becoming stronger connection between terrorist groups and other criminal organizations, engaged illegal circulation of firearms and drugs and also the fulfillment of murders connected with it, extortions, kidnappings, armed attacks, captures of hostages and robberies is noted. On December, 9th, 1999 general Assembly of the United Nations has accepted international convention on struggle against financing terrorism. The Security Council of the United Nations accepted the Declaration on global efforts on struggle against terrorism on November, 12th, 2001.

There was a serious danger of use of new technologies by terrorists. In this connection in the United Nations international convention on struggle against acts of nuclear terrorism is developed.

The Commission of Human Rights in 2003 has revealed especially dangerous kinds of attempts at the right to life. Murders, in particular are included to their number: made on any discrimination grounds, including sexual orientation; acts of violence over racial promptings, leaders to death of the victim; murders of representatives of national, ethnic, religious or language minority; murders of refugees, internally displaced persons, homeless children or members of radical communities; murders of the people connected with their activity (legal experts, lawyers, journalists, demonstrators, etc.).

Last years international organizations repeatedly noted that such dangerous kinds of infringements of civil human rights as extrajudicial executions, executions without appropriate proceeding, violent and not voluntary disappearances, any detention and imprisonments, racism and xenophobia, trade in people and human bodies extend. Modern forms of slavery have not been eradicated: trade in girls and women, sexual exploitation of children and child labour, regular rapes of women and sexual slavery during military actions, compulsion to prostitution, compulsory sterilization, and debt servitude.

The Commission of Human Rights at 59th session in 2003 expressed extreme concern in scale and mass character of moving of people in many areas of world and also sufferings of refugees and displaced persons, the big share among which are women and children.

It is well-known that according to international-legal regulations about human rights, states and nongovernmental organizations are called to play the important role in encouragement of tolerance and protection of freedom of religion and belief.

Accepted in 1995 the Declaration of principles of tolerance has by general Conference of UNESCO proclaimed respect, acceptance and correct understanding of a rich variety of cultures of our world, forms of self-expression and human individuality display. However, the end the 20th - the beginnings of the 21st century is characterized by strengthening of religious intolerance, formation of a negative stereotypic image of religions and discrimination people on religious grounds in some regions of world. The extremist organizations and groups are becoming more active, campaigns on religion defamation are organized. Events on September, 11th, 2001 have led to that the Islam in opinion of many people in different states has become wrongly associated with infringement of human rights and terrorism. Thus, there have appeared new negative tendencies in the sphere of realization of freedom of conscience and religion.

Last years the tendencies to limitation of legal guarantees of civil human rights have increased. In particular, the encroachments on independence of judges, lawyers and other judicial workers have become more frequent. The Commission of Human Rights has noted the close connection between weakening of the guarantees, given to figures of justice and prevalence and weight of infringements of human rights.[10] As a rule, the victims of discrimination in the sphere of criminal justice are the representatives of racial, national minorities, women, and the poor, disabled persons.

It is well-known that in second half of the 20th century international system of protection of civil rights was created, including activity of international bodies, legal procedures, etc. During the last years there have arisen serious obstacles not allowing citizens of some countries to use the indicated opportunities. Some governments intimidate, use repressions to those who aspires to cooperate with the United Nations, other international organizations working in the field of human rights.

§ 2. Civil Human Rights in Modern Russia

The situation with realization of civil human rights in modern Russia is extremely inconsistent and the objective analysis allows coming to the conclusion that negative tendencies prevail. However, in the beginning we should mention positive changes in this sphere.

As it is known, the Constitution of the Russian Federation, 1993 has harmonized the contents of the civil rights and freedoms recorded in it with international standards; it has expanded their legal guarantees. The Constitution has recognized the conventional principles and standards of international law, international treaties of the Russian Federation as a component of Russian legal system (Article 15). It has proclaimed that the rights and freedoms of a person and a citizen are recognized and guaranteed according to the indicated principles and propositions and according to the Constitution. constitutionally-legal bases of the of the state remedial system (the President of the Russian Federation, courts, Human Rights Commissioner, Office of Public Prosecutor) are also fixed there. According to the Constitution civil human rights should determine the meaning and contents of laws, activity of governmental bodies and local self-management. However, it is necessary to remark that the current legislation, law enforcement practice quite often contradict the constitutional propositions.

Being a member of the United Nations, OSCE and the Council of Europe, Russia has taken up obligations to guarantee to its citizens rights and freedoms of a person stipulated by standards of international law. The important international-legal guarantee of civil human rights is the European Convention for the Protection of Human Rights and Basic Freedoms ratified by Russia in 1998. The serious step in development of legal guarantees of civil rights (first of all the rights to impartial and fair trial) was a started judicial reform (increase in number of judges, introduction of institution of Justice of the Peace, a jury aspiration of the legislator to ensure the provision of independence of judges, etc.). Acceptance in 2001 of a new Code of Criminal Procedure of the Russian Federation should be considered as an attempt of the fundamental solution of the problem of perfection of criminally-remedial guarantees of personal immunity, the rights of the imprisoned and accused persons, other civil rights. The Code of Criminal Procedure (2001) has fixed the principles of equality of the parties, competitiveness in the proceeding. The rights of lawyers have been expanded.

Decisions of the Constitutional Court of the Russian Federation in 1992-2003 played a serious role in definition of the contents of civil (personal constitutional) rights.[11] Thus, considering the complaint of a citizen of V.V. Scheluhin in 1996, the Constitutional Court of the Russian Federation came to the conclusion that "part 5 of Article 97 of the Code of Criminal Procedure RSFSR gave to limitation of the right on freedom at imprisonment arbitrary character" and consequently recognized its unconstitutional.[12]

In some cases Russian justice has executed its role in civil human rights enforcement characterized by the Constitution. Thus, on case of Poegly (1994) the regional court of Moscow defended the constitutional principle of equal protection of the law of citizens and court, having forced the important official to give a testimony. In criminal case of ecologist A. Nikitin accused of espionage, the city court of St.-Petersburg passed the verdict "not guilty" and the Supreme Court of the Russian Federation upheld it (1999). In criminal case on T. Rohlina's charge in murder of the husband the Supreme Court of the Russian Federation found no necessary proofs for her return guilty (2003). In these litigations the judicial authority provided realization of a principle of presumption of innocence. In 2003 the court of Rostov-on-Don as a result of long-term proceeding returned guilty the colonel J. Budanov in murder of the Chechen girl, having protected the constitutional rights of a victim of a crime.

The role of international-legal guarantees of civil rights is increasing. In this connection it would be desirable to mention the decision of Human Rights Committee of the complaint of Mr. Gridin returned guilty in murders. This decision accepted on the basis of the procedure, approved by the Optional protocol to international Covenant on Civil and Political Rights, has established the facts of the roughest infringements of presumption of innocence, the right of an accused of defence, admitted by Russian courts.

The decision of the European Court on Human Rights to Kalashnikov's case against Russia (2002) recognized that conditions of the imprisonment of the condemned contradict international standards of human rights, is also very important. Besides, their right to fair proceeding during reasonable term has been outraged.

The facts connected with case of Nikishina against Russia testify the role of this court in Russian judiciary practice. Russian courts have deprived this woman with from the right to bring up her child and passed them to their father basing the given decision on the mother's creed. After submission of Nikishina's complaint in the European Court on Human Rights, the Supreme Court of the Russian Federation, having considered case by way of supervision, has cancelled all decisions and has complied the request of mother. Thus, one appeal of a citizen in the European Court on Human Rights has served as stimulus for more attentive attitude of judges to the complaint and the fair sanction of case according to the constitutional principle of freedom of conscience.

Finally, a new phenomenon in the human rights mechanism of our country has become the activity of Human Rights Commissioner in the Russian Federation. In 1998-2003 officers of the Commissioner Apparatus have considered and assisted to satisfy significant number of complaints of citizens connected with protection of civil rights. In the annual and special reports the Commissioner stated an objective estimation of realization of these rights. In 2000 O.O. Mironov has subjected to the sharp criticism the infringement of the human rights, made by federal armies in the Chechen Republic. In the Commissioner's Report the terrible facts of infringement of the right to personal immunity and the right to freedom from tortures, cruel and inhuman treatment made in bodies of the Ministry of internal Affairs have been named. However, ignoring of references of Russian ombudsman concerning human rights becomes practice of many state departments.

And it not the unique negative phenomenon connected with realization of civil human rights in Russia. The most serious and mass infringements of these rights are made in the Chechen Republic. Among them are murders hostage taking, disappearance of people, trade in people, tortures, destruction of property. In 2003-2004 there were some positive changes; nevertheless, the Chechen problem has not been solved till now that is confirmed by the murder of the president of the Chechen Republic Kadyrov on May, 9th, 2004.

Serious threat to the right to life in Russia is increase of acts of terrorism which victims are peaceful citizens. At that the actions of the organizations aimed at preventing these criminal acts appear to be insufficiently effective. As "International Amnesty" has informed, none of the officials responsible for safety of citizens in Moscow, has retired in connection with hostage taking at the theatre in October, 2002.[13] "The law accepted in 1998 on struggle against terrorism, it is noted in the report of "International Amnesty", makes practically impossible for a person injured due to counterterrorist operation, to receive indemnification".[14] It seems that this law really requires specification. In particular, it would be necessary to ensure the provision of procedure of parliamentary investigation of the events connected with inability to organize officials, called to prevent acts of terrorism and to carry out acts of antiterrorism. It is expedient to expand legal guarantees of the rights of victims of acts of terrorism.

Enforcement of the right to life in the Russian Federation is connected with the problem of death penalty. Russia has not yet ratified the Protocol 6 to the European Convention for the Protection of Human Rights and Basic Freedoms and has not excluded death penalty from types of punishment in the Criminal Code. It is well-known that the public opinion in our country mostly favours reservation of this criminal sentence. Some politicians and scientists support the preservation of death penalty which has not been used in Russia till 1996. Meanwhile Russia, having entered the Council of Europe, has taken up the obligations connected with observance of the European Convention for the Protection of Human Rights and Basic Freedoms. Therefore from the legal point of view there is an alternative here: to abolish the death penalty or to leave the Council of Europe. It is necessary to add that during the last decades the tendency to refuse from the death penalty is obviously traced in many states all over world. Unabolition of the death penalty and judicial errors of which the imperfect and corrupted Russian justice is not relieved, make impossible the use of this feudal sentence in the 21st century. It is necessary to add that the Protocol 6 concerning abolition of the death penalty, 1983 assigns this obligation to the state only in peacetime. Clause 2 of the European Convention supposes lawful deprivation of life of a person at necessary defense, at realization of lawful imprisonment, at prevention of breach of prison and at suppression of mutiny.

In our opinion, the exaggerated significance is quite often given to the problem of death penalty. Supporters of this sentence consider it as a certain absolute means with the help of which it is possible to prevail criminality. For example, professor D. Koretsky considers that the actual abolition of the death penalty at increase of number of murders in Russia during the last years "contradicts not only the idea of adequacy (i.e. proper response of the state to increase of dangerous crimes. - *F.R.)* but also to common sense!"[15]

In our opinion, today the main problem consists not in how to punish criminals but how to find them out and prosecute. Not cruelty of punishment but inevitability of the legal responsibility should provide the reality of the right to life. Professor D. Koretsky cites data from which it appears that in 2001 only 31.9% of criminals were solved and made answerable among all the registered crimes.[16] According to investigatory Committee at the Ministry of internal Affairs of the Russian Federation, in the first half-year of 2003 a level of crime detection in comparison with 1993 decreased on 21.6%.[17]

It is necessary to say that to threats of human life in Russia not only growth of murders and other crimes against a person belong but also other factors. In particular, increase in road accidents. According to official data, in 1997-2002 from 27,000 up to 33,000 people died annually in car accidents. During the last 10 years 315,100 people have died in that way.[18]

The number of murders increased in Russia from 15,600 in 1990 up to 31,100 in 1999.[19] In 1993 the number of murders decreased up to 28,980.[20] However, the gangs of professional criminals represent serious danger: killers, dealers in women, children, and human organs. Besides, 60,000 suicides annually happen in Russia.[21] Therefore the problem of the right to life enforcement is quite serious.

The started judicial reform is called to ensure the provision of right of a person to fair independent impartial trial. However, in practice these undertakings are not provided with sufficient financial and personnel resources. Judges have not released from the pressure of executive authority and commercial structures. Many lawyers have appeared unable to work in new conditions. The accusatory bias, callousness, the scornful attitude to citizens, to lawyers continues to remain the integral part of psychological line of many judicial, public prosecutor's and militia officers. The low salary of law-enforcement system officers, incompetent management of its many parts have led to outflow of the qualified professionals from the Ministry of internal Affairs, Office of Public Prosecutor. The lack of professionalism can be found in their activity. The part of law enforcement bodies is corrupted and bureaucratized. Criminalization of a society leads to increase of number of the crimes made by officers of these organizations. In criminology a special direction has appeared called criminality in the sphere of struggle against criminality.[22] There is a merging the underworld to the corrupted officials of law enforcement bodies. There has appeared a so-called "shadow justice" by means of which citizens search for ways of protection of the rights. All the indicated phenomena testify to crisis of the state institutions, inefficiency of legal guarantees of civil rights. As Human Rights Commissioner in the Russian Federation O.O. Mironov has fairly noted, the state loses the war with criminality.

And it has led to serious threats for the realization of civil human rights. The negative factor is lacks and contradictions in the legislation. As it was noted in the special literature, a new Code of Criminal Procedure of the Russian Federation has led to deepening of inequality in the rights between accused and victims. Unlike suspected and accused, whose rights are in details registered in the Code of Criminal Procedure of the Russian Federation 2001, the mechanism of realization of the rights of victims has not been developed yet.[23]

The Federal law "On Lawyer's Activity and Legal Profession of the Russian Federation", 2002 has established the tight state control over this organization which as it is fairly said in Article 3 of the given instrument, is the institution of a civil society. As participants of the workshop "Civil Society and Judicial-Legal System" of the All-Russia Conference of civil organizations (2003), declared, the modern legal profession turned into the governmentalized corporation monopolized the enforcement of the right of defence on criminal cases within the limits of which many lawyers have been turned into 'driving belts' of corruption. Certainly, there are a lot of fair professionals among lawyers (as well as among judges, law enforcement bodies officers), nevertheless, the breach of confidence of clients, unreasonable and overestimated fees have become a certain tendency.[24] In opinion of participants of the conference, office of Public Prosecutor has practically ceased to realize human rights functions.[25] It is necessary to add to it inefficiency of activity of Human Rights Commissioners in the Russian Federation and subjects of Federation as ay are not authorized by powers which would allow them to become valid defenders of human rights.

There is the problem of realization of human rights to freedom from any intervention in the private and family life. Cases of high rank officials V.A. Kovalev and J.I. Skuratov, accompanied by public television demonstration of circumstances of their private life, have shown, that even for such statesmen this right cannot be guaranteed.

The serious threat to the right to move and the right to residence represent the archaic institution of residence permit revived in the way of registration. According to the conclusion of "International Amnesty" to 2003 approximately in 10 subjects of the Federation, including Moscow, St.-Petersburg, Stavropol and Krasnodar Territories, there were illegal limitations of the indicated human rights. Thus it is necessary to note that infringements of the right to move in the country quite often are accompanied with the encroachments on the constitutional principle of equality of the rights and freedoms irrespective of race, nationality, fixed in Article 19 of the Constitution of the Russian Federation.

Finally, there are serious problems in the sphere of realization of freedom of conscience and creeds. Namely, clericalization of authorities, a world outlook inequality, infringements of the rights of the atheists, believers, religious minorities. There is no appropriate level of sense of justice among the population in the country. Activity of the mass-media spreading a cult of sex, violence, interferes with formation of cultural guarantees of civil rights. All the above-stated circumstances allow drawing a conclusion about serious deformations of civil human rights in Russia, weakening and undermining of their guarantees. The situation is so serious that absence of the measures aimed at its overcoming, can lead to actual elimination of civil rights. The reasons of this status of a society root in inefficiency of economic reforms, falling of a standard of life of significant number of the population, deepening of a social inequality, bureaucratization of authorities. The culture of human rights has not become property of a society and representatives of authority.

Overcoming of the indicated negative phenomena will allow to fill civil human rights with the real contents and to guarantee real individual freedom.

We have dwelled on the most general problems of civil human rights. In the subsequent Chapters of the given work certain aspects of this subject will be opened.

Notes

1. See: UN Economic and Social Council. Main session 1995. June 29 − 28 July. Paragraph 5d of the preliminary minutes. Crime Prevention and Criminal Sentence in the World. Death Penalty and Realization of Measures for Protection of Rights of those Facing the Death Penalty. Secretary General Report. Geneva, 1995. P. 47-51. / См.: Организация Объединенных Наций. Экономический и Социальный Совет. Основная сессия 1995 г. 26 июня−28 июля. Пункт 5 д предварительной повестки дня. Предупреждение преступности и уголовное правосудие. Смертная казнь и осуществление мер, гарантирующих защиту прав тех, кому грозит смертная казнь. Доклад Генерального секретаря. Женева, 1995. С. 47−51.

2. See: UN Economic and Social Council. Human Rights Commission. 59th session. Paragraph 17 a of the preliminary minutes. State of international Covenants on Human Rights. Death Penalty. Secretary General Report, presented according to the Commission resolution 2002/77 January, 27, 2003. P. 14-22. / См.: Организация Объединенных Наций. Экономический и Социальный Совет. Комиссия по правам человека. 59-я сессия. Пункт 17 а предварительной повестки дня. Состояние международных

пактов о правах человека. Вопрос о смертной казни. Доклад Генерального секретаря, представляемый в соответствии с резолюцией 2002/ 77 Комиссии 27 января 2003 г. С. 14–22.

3. Human Rights Commission. Report of 59th session (March, 17 – April, 24, 2003). P.1. Geneva, 2003. P. 286. / Комиссия по правам человека. Доклад 59-й сессии (17 марта – 24 апреля 2003 г.) Ч. 1. Женева, 2003. С. 286.

4. See: Ibidem.

5. USA. Fatal Mistakes: innocence and Death Penalty. international Amnesty. 1998. P. 2. / Соединенные Штаты Америки. Смертельные ошибки: невиновность и смертная казнь. Международная амнистия. 1998. С. 2.

6. See: Ibidem. P. 3.

7. See: UN Economical and Social Council. Human Right Commission. 54th session. Paragraph 10 of preliminary minutes. Violation of human rights and basic freedoms in any part of the world, especially in colonies and other dependent countries and territories. Extrajudicial executions, executions without appropriate trial or arbitrary executions. Mr. B.V. Ndyay report presented in accordance with Commission resolution 1997/61. Addition. USA Mission. January, 22, 1998. p. 18. / См.: Организация Объединенных Наций. Экономический и Социальный Совет. Комиссия по правам человека. 54-я сессия. Пункт 10 предварительной повестки дня. Вопрос о нарушении прав человека и основных свобод в любой части мира, особенно в колониальных и других зависимых странах и территориях. Внесудебные казни, казни без надлежащего судебного разбирательства или произвольные казни. Доклад г-на Б. В. Ндиайе, представленный в соответствии с резолюцией 1997/61 Комиссии. Добавление. Миссия в США. 22 января 1998 г. С. 18.

8. See: UN Economical and Social Council. Human Right Commission. Subcommision on Human Rights Enforcement, 55th session. Paragraph 6 of preliminary minutes. Specific Questions Concerning Human Rights. Human rights and weapons of mass destruction or nonselective action or weapons able to cause excessive damage or unnecessary sufferings. Working paper presented by E.K.E. Yeng Sic Yun. / См.: Организация Объединенных Наций. Экономический и Социальный Совет. Комиссия по правам человека. Подкомиссия по поощрению и защите прав человека. 55-я сессия. Пункт 6 предварительной повестки дня. Конкретные вопросы в области прав человека. Права человека и оружие массового уничтожения или неизбирательного действия или оружие, способное причинить чрезмерные повреждения или ненужные страдания. Рабочий документ, представленный Е.К.Е. Енг Сик Юном. Женева, 2003. С. 16.

9. See: Human Rights Commission. Report on 59th session. March, 17 – April, 24, 2003. P.1. Geneva, 2003. p. 164. / См.: Комиссия по правам человека. Доклад о работе 59-й сессии, 17 марта – 24 апреля 2003 г. Ч. 1. Женева, 2003. С. 164.

10. See: Human Rights Commission. Report on 59th session. March, 17 – April, 24, 2003. P.1. Geneva, 2003. p. 186. / См.: Комиссия по правам человека. Доклад о работе 59-й сессии, 17 марта – 24 апреля 2003 г. Ч. 1. Женева, 2003. С.186

11. See: Commentary to Legal Resolutions of Russian Constitutional Court: in 2 vol. Vol. 2: Protection of Human Rights and Freedoms / Resp. Editor B.S. Ebzeev. Moscow, 2000. P. 43-132. / См.: Комментарий к постановлениям Конституционного Суда РФ: В 2 т. Т. 2: Защита прав и свобод граждан / Отв. ред. Б. С. Эбзеев. М., 2000. С. 43 132.

12. See: Ibidem. P. 43-50.

13. See: Searching For Justice: Law and Human Rights in the Russian Federation. Moscow. 2003. P. 57. / См.: В поисках справедливости: закон и права человека в Российской Федерации. М., 2003. С. 57.

14. Ibidem. P. 56.

15. Koretsky D. Are Measures of Combating Criminality Adequate to Its State? // Legality. 1993. #2. P. 27. / Корецкий Д. Адекватны ли меры борьбы с преступностью ее состоянию? // Законность. 1993. № 2. С. 27.

16.. See: Gavrilov B. Novels of Criminal Procedure on the Background of Criminal Statistics // Russian Justice. 2003. #10. P. 5. / См.: Гаврилов Б. Новеллы уголовного процесса на фоне криминальной статистики // Российская юстиция. 2003. № 10. С. 5.

18. See: State Report "On Road Safety in RF" // Rossiiskaya gazeta. 2003. Sept. 11. / См.: Государственный доклад "О состоянии безопасности дорожного движения в РФ // Российская газета. 2003. 11 сент.

19. See: Russian Statistical YB. Statistical collection. Moscow, 2000. P. 243. / См.: Российский статистический ежегодник: Статистический сборник. М., 2000. С. 243.

20. See: Scrobot A. The Ministry of internal Affairs of Russia Sums Up the Last Year // Nezavisimaya Gazeta. 2004. January, 14. / См.: Скробот А. МВД России подводит итоги минувшего года // Независимая газета. 2004. 14 янв.

21. See: Data of the State Scientific Centre of Social and Judicial Psychiatry Named after Serbsky // Nezavisimaya Gazeta. 2003. August, 11. / См.: Данные Государственного научного центра социальной и судебной психиатрии им. Сербского // Независимая газета. 2003. 11 авг.

22. See: Golik Y.V. Globalization of Criminality and Russian Reality. Russia in Focus of Criminal Globalization. Vladivostok, 2002. P. 31. / См.: Голик Ю. В. Глобализация преступности и российские реалии. Россия в фокусе криминальной глобализации. Владивосток, 2002. С. 31.

23. See: Shestakova T. Impaired Rights of the Sufferred // Legality. 2003.8. P. 21-22. / См.: Шестакова Т. Ущемленные права потерпевших // Законность. 2003. № 8. С. 21–22.

24. See: All-Russia Conference of Civil Organizations on October, 27-28th, 2003. Materials and reports // Legal Expert. 2003.4. P. 56-59. / См.: Всероссийская конференция гражданских организаций 27–28 октября 2003 г. Материалы и выступления // Правозащитник. 2003. № 4. С. 56–59.

25. See: Ibidem. P. 65.

PART II

SYSTEM OF CIVIL HUMAN RIGHTS

Chapter 3. THE HUMAN RIGHT TO LIFE

Human life is the greatest value of a democratic society. The right to life, heading the system of civil human rights, is fixed in international statutory acts (the Universal Declaration of Human Rights, international Covenant on Civil and Political Rights, the European Convention for the Protection of Human Rights and Basic Freedoms, etc.) and also in the majority of Constitutions of the countries of world.

The right to life is a natural opportunity of protection of inviolability of life integral with a person and freedom to handle it, guaranteed by the propositions of the internal legislation and international-legal regulations.

The natural character of the given right is understood as a "mother of the absolute law is human nature".[1] Theory of natural human rights formed in 16th-17th century, considered the right to life as an integral property of life: "a person is born having the right to full freedom and limitlessness of using all rights and privileges of the natural law... and by nature he has authority to protect their property that is the life, freedom and property".[2]

International community, recognizing the right to life as a born right, establishes the basic criteria on which each state declaring its respect of the rights and freedoms of a person, should determine the position concerning life of each individual.

In the Russian Federation the right to life is fixed in Russian Declaration of Civil Human Rights and Freedoms, 1991 and also in Article 20 of Russian Constitution, 1993.

Object of protection of legal provisions of Article 20 of Russian Constitution is the life of any person, irrespective of presence or absence of Russian citizenship.

Let's remark that in some cases the object of a legal protection is life itself as a value provided by the right to inviolability, i.e. the right to live without any encroachment, able to entail death of a person (it is so-called aspect of "inviolability of life").

In other cases the right protects not life as value but the real opportunity of a person to use it freely, having put in dangerous position (such act is encouraged with the state at presence of socially useful purposes).

In modern jurisprudence criterion of "life" at an estimation of a status of a human body is presence of a brain as a basic instrument of self-identification of a person and "the coordinating center" all physiological activity of an organism. The fact of presence of a live brain is established according to existing medical criteria (one of them is the ability to submit signals registered by the special device called electroencephalograph).

Thus, "life" as object of a legal protection in narrow meaning is understood as a form of biological existence of the born human body adjustable and coordinated by the present brain activity.

In a broad meaning "life" includes also the social relations providing ability to live of the subject, their socialization.

Holders of the right to inviolability of life and the right to freedom dispose of life are not identical.

The major element of the right to life is the right to inviolability of life.

The subject whose inviolability of life is certainly protected by the law, any is live-born human being with present brain activity. All other factors as: anomalies of physical and mental health, features of psycho-logical qualities and also citizenship, age, national, racial or any other belonging do not matter.

Let's remark that the history of mankind has not always showed a celebration of the humanistic approach to life. Thus, for example, in the Middle Ages a woman given birth to a child with strong anomalies of physical development (freak/lusus naturae), was accused of intimate connection with a devil and executed. According to Prussian land law, 1794 killing of "a being having no human image" was considered not a murder but ordinary police offence. As to Russia the first interdiction of murder of such persons occurred in Peter's the Great epoch, exclusively with the purpose of their use as cabinets of curiosities aids. In 1718 Peter I even published the decree "On Observance in Russia of any Human and Bestial Ugly Creature".

The position of the French legislator of the 19th century which have proclaimed is most approached to the modern concept of the holder of the right to inviolability of life that "any creation as though strange and ugly it was if it was born by a person, should use protection of the law".[3]

However, not only individuals can be recognized as subjects of the right to inviolability of life but also their communities (people, nationalities, and the whole mankind). Such approach to concept of the subject is expedient at the analysis of international aspect of the given right considered as a right to peace.

Among the most debatable and complicated questions in the sphere of the right to life is the question of life beginning. Its uniform understanding is necessary, first of all, for correct use of legal provisions about the responsibility for crimes against life.

Now in Russian criminal law there is an approach which presupposes the beginning of life as a moment since which it is possible to harm life of the child, not causing any harm to life and to health of mother. Thus taking into consideration the existing medical criteria of a newborn child.[4]

However, the discussion about admissibility of artificial interruption of pregnancy does not lose its acuteness.

According to Russian legislation of 18th century a murder of a child in a womb of mother was considered as "infanticide". All other kinds of murder of children by parents were called "childicide".[5]

From the point of view of religious canons abortion is a heavy sin. According to the words of one of religious thinker, a human foetus "is not her (i.e. mother's- N.K.) body; it is body and life of another human being entrusted to their mother's care for feeding".[6]

From the point of view of modern biology (genetics and embryology) life of a person as biological individual begins from the moment of merge of man's and female's gametonucleuses and formation of a uniform nucleus included unique genetic material.[7]

The fact of presence of a live brain as it has noted been above, is the criterion of "life" acting as object of legal protection. In the end of the 20th century the scientists could register electro-physiological activity of the brainstem at a six-week foetus. It is logical to assume that the given circumstance should be put in a basis of the edge separating "life" from the previous stage of its development.

For today the domestic legislator considers a not born foetus as a component of a parent organism connected with it physiologically and psychologically that, in essence, is not medical and, more likely, socially-pragmatical criterion of the decision of a question of the legal protection of life beginning and in particular criminal protection.

According to operating "Bases of the Legislation of the Russian Federation on Health Protection of Citizens" a woman can interrupt pregnancy at her desire till 12 weeks.

Besides, in the legislation of the Russian Federation there are a lot of so-called "social indications" stipulated, entitling a woman to interrupt pregnancy on a late term of its development (till 22 weeks).[8]

It is thought that the moral estimation of the given act (if we accept not medical but exclusively social indications) can be only negative.

Only formal legal criterion - the physiological connection with an organism of mother does not allow considering "a product of conception" as a holder of the right to inviolability of life.

It seems that at the moment the problem of legitimacy of abortions in our country is solved by a principle of preference of a "smaller harm". The full failure in the sphere of realization of social and economic human rights serves the moral justification of prevention of birth of not desired children, whom the state (in parents' refusal from them) is not capable to guarantee a necessary minimum of social values.

Naturally that the life traditionally relates to the most significant cultural wealth of any society. However, the right to life is not absolute (i.e. it is not a subject to lawful limitation in any situation); operating Russian legislation stipulates some bases of lawful deprivation of life which executors act as private persons (some situations of necessary defense, emergency) or as representatives of the state.

The legal fact stopping legal relationships connected with the right to inviolability of life is biological death.

The reason of biological death can be natural and unnatural. Modern scientific data allow claiming that the border between life and death is determined by viability of the brain. The establishment of precise medical criteria of the fact of death is necessary for delimiting it from boundary statuses of a person, reminding death, for example from coma or clinical death. The modern medicine replaces the usual concept of death as one-stage act with a certain graded process. Cerebral cortex providing realization of maximum personal qualities as thinking and will perishes first. After it brainstem perishes, there is a status of "total brain death". Heart and many internal bodies, owing to use of complex medical techniques, can continue the activity but a person at that is no longer capable to perceive the surrounding world. He exists, not coming to consciousness. And, finally, the final stage is the death of internal. At the lost brain it puts the end under complete existence of a person.

In 1993 in Russia the Ministry of Health of the Russian Federation instruction providing the whole complex of clinical attributes at the presence of which the diagnosis of brain death is established has been developed and accepted.

Certainly, the detailed regulation of diagnostics of biological death of a person is rather essential guarantee of the right to life; however, it is impossible to disagree with the opinion that such an important medical criteria should be given the shape of the Federal law, rather than departmental statutory acts.

In general the medical practice faces with three possible variants of brain pathology:

—Destruction of all brain, including its brainstem, with irreversible unconsciousness, the termination of independent breath and disappearance of all brainstem reflexes;

—Destruction of a brainstem (attributes of viability of cerebral hemispheres, in particular their electric activity can be saved);

—Destruction of parts of brain responsible for consciousness, thinking, i.e. for safety of a person as an individual.

Now our medicine has recognized the first of the indicated variants as criterion of biological death. As to the state of a person in the second and third variants we should note that the given problem is connected not only with a question of legitimacy of the termination of reanimation actions but also an opportunity to use these persons as donors for transplantation of bodies.

The second of the mentioned variants of ascertaining of death is accepted, in particular, in England and characterized as a rule, by inevitable and fast enough cardiac arrest.

The third variant causes the greatest amount of ethical disputes. The patient with the diagnosis "a chronic vegetative status" can stay in this status from several days to many months and even years.

The position existing in a science which essence was expressed by the academician of V.A. Negovsky: "Ascertaining of death of a brain (the third variant - N.K.) gives a legal and moral opportunity to stop methods of maintenance of meaningless vegetative existence".[9] But, for the sake of justice, it is necessary to remark that there have been such cases when people left this vegetative status and were normally socialized. In opinion of the academician P. Behtereva, the supervisor of studies of a centre "Brain" of science-practical institution of Human Brain, "it is a miracle of concealed reserves of brain which it keeps for such extreme cases. There are practically no reliable criteria of death of brain".[10]

Differently, now nobody can give 100% guarantee of that the brain of a person with the diagnosis "chronic vegetative status" can never return to a normal "working" status.

Thus, the medical and legal problem of expediency of maintenance of persons with such diagnosis remains acute.

Unlike natural death, the unnatural death is caused by influence of any external factors on a human organism, making changes incompatible with live functions. The unnatural death can be both a result of lawful deprivation of life and a result of illegal act.

According to part 2 of Article 2 of the European Convention for the Protection of Human Rights and Basic Freedoms, 1950, deprivation of life is not considered as infringement of that clause if it is the result of use of force, no more than absolutely necessary:

—for protection of any person against illegal violence;

—for realization of lawful imprisonment or prevention of runaway of a person detained on the lawful bases;

—for lawful suppression of revolt or mutiny.

Besides, operating Russian legislation stipulates some more bases, entitling lawful causing of death under certain conditions. In particular:

—deprivation of life if it is accomplished by a person in a state of emergency (at conditions indicated in Article 39 of the Criminal Code of the Russian Federation);

—deprivation of life at realization of the activity regulated by the Charter of garrison and guard services of Armed Forces of the Russian Federation;

—deprivation of life during participation in confrontations of international and not international character.[11]

However, legitimacy of the actions directed on destruction of the opponent, is determined, among other conditions, by the character of means and methods used at it.

The first basis of lawful deprivation of life noted by the European Convention in our legislation is reflected in institution of necessary defense. Anyone can be recognized as a subject of legally used force - a victim of illegal violence as well as any private person or an official acting with the purpose of suppression of illegal encroachment.

The equal right to necessary defense has all persons irrespective of their professional or other special training and service position.

An opportunity of causing damage to the encroaching person irrespective of their opportunity to escape or to address other people or corresponding bodies for help mentioned in Article 37 of the Criminal Code of the Russian Federation is important.

The question of objects, encroachments on who generates the right to necessary defense integrated to deprivation of life of the encroaching person is traditionally debatable.

According to one of the modern Paragraphs of view the use of any force including entailing death of an encroaching person is lawful for defense:

—from an encroachment menacing by death;

—from an encroachment menacing by causing heavy harm to health;

—from rape or violent actions of sexual character;

—from an encroachment on the property, integrated to violence or threat of its use;

—from penetration into premises by breaking or violence and also from penetration made by group of persons.[12]

I believe that the given position is not indisputable. But we should notice that criminal theory supposes that the harm caused on an encroaching person by a person in a status of necessary defense, can be more significant in comparison with that harm which could have been prevented by necessary defense. It is important that this harm was not obviously disproportionate in comparison with prevented harm.

For the "special subjects" of defense belong officers of law-enforcement bodies in situations when an attack represents threat of life and to health of other person (persons), actions on suppression of an illegal encroachment are a professional *duty but* not a right.

General leitmotif of all international documents considering questions of use of firearms by officials on maintenance of the law and order to whom belong also militia officers, the regulations about scope are that "in any case deliberate use of force with a fatal outcome can take place only when it absolutely inevitable for protection from death".[13]

Besides, one of supervising principles of regulations about use of firearms by the above-stated persons is the interdiction of use of such firearms and ammunition rendering extremely heavy wounds or being a source of unjustified risk.[14]

Condition of realization of the second form of lawful limitation of the right to life, stipulated by the European Convention, is the realization of lawful imprisonment or prevention of runaway of a person detained on the lawful bases.

In Russian criminal law the first of the indicated bases is invested with the legal provision fixing legitimacy of causing damage at detention of a person committed a crime.

If detention is integrated with causing death on imprudence it is not beyond lawful behaviour (at conditions of legitimate causing damage at detention stipulated by the criminal law).

The question of admissibility of deliberate deprivation of life at detention is debatable. Some scientists believe that such act is illegal, except for cases when actions of the detained person create threat of committing of a new criminal encroachment.

At the same time in the literature there is the point of view according to which at detention causing death is admissible in unusual cases.[15]

At detention it is possible to relate the following to the basic conditions of legitimacy of limitation of the right to life:

—confidence that the crime is committed by that very person;

—at these conditions it is impossible to detain a person committed by other means;

—at grounds to believe that, having escaped, the given person will continue the criminal activity;

—the detained has committed the crime representing increased public danger (grave or especially grave).

Concerning the latter of the conditions we should notice that it should be considered not only a category of crime but also a character of object of an encroachment; as a rule, such acts as murder in aggravating circumstances, gangsterism, terrorism, etc. At the same time it is hardly justified at detention, for example, of a briber trying to escape.[16]

The European Convention and Russian legislation stipulates also such basis of lawful deprivation of life as suppression of breach of prison. Particularly, it means a suppression of breach of prison of a person detained on suspicion in committing a crime; detained persons; persons condemned to imprisonment and also for suppression of attempts of violent discharge of these persons.[17]

Law enforcement body's officers using firearms as a rule detain the given category of persons. It is thought that undoubtedly, the statement that "using of arms at breach of prison doesn't depend on the kind of crime the prisoner has committed" is correct.[18]

Besides, the legislator regulating a question of use of firearms in such situations does not make stress on the status of a person: suspected accused or condemned.

The actions made in a state of emergency can be recognized as grounds of lawful deprivation of life.

The modern Russian criminal law provides two groups of the conditions excluding illegality of such acts.

The first characterizes direct danger at which presence the actions harmed the interests protected by the criminal law are made. The impossibility of elimination of harm by other means and absence of excess of limits of emergency relate to the second group of conditions.

When it is a question of an opportunity of ascertaining of the state of emergency, the described deprivation of life of a person (persons) as one of criteria of legitimacy objective circumstances, i.e. the caused harm (the number of killed persons) should be smaller than the prevented harm (the number of the rescued lives). It is possible to say that emergency is based on the principle of outweighing value of smaller harm. Such objective criterion of estimation of the compared values importance (on the one hand, the values are protected, on the other they are subjected to lawful encroachment) starts with a concept of equivalence of life of various subjects. For the law in situations of emergency the lives of law abiding persons and criminal, juvenile and old persons, being either healthy or hopelessly sick have equal value.

In the recent past many scientists did not consider the opportunity to refer to a state of emergency at causing death even if by life of one person the lives of many people were rescued. Some of them considered an opportunity of such situations with the clause that the rescue was not made by cannibalism.[19]

In the operating the Criminal Code of the Russian Federation the excess of limits of emergency is causing not only greater but also equal harm in comparison with the harm prevented. Thus, the controversial problem is how to qualify rescue by a person of their life due to life of other person (if danger threatened one and the other died rather than them) has received the legal sanction. According to The Criminal Code of the Russian Federation in this case the excess of limits of emergency is present.

Specificity of the situations arising at realization by subjects of activity, caused by execution of the army regulations, consists in non-recognition of the rights to protect of the interests due to causing damage to interests of the state.

Thus, according to the Charter of garrison and guard services of Armed forces of the Russian Federation hour has no right to leave the post until it will be replaced or removed when due hereunder even if its life is threatened with danger (Article 187 of the Charter). If a sentry under the threat of life autocratically leaves a post, he cannot refer to a state of emergency.

The bases of using firearms by a sentry are also interesting enough. Thus, for example, the proposition of Article 190 of the above-mentioned Charter *obliges* the sentry to use firearms without warning in case of obvious attack on them or on another object protected by them.

If any person (persons), except for listed in Article 191 of the Charter, comes nearer to a post or to prohibited area the sentry after a corresponding precautionary hail at continuation of attempt should come nearer to make a precautionary shot upwards. At default by the infringer to fulfill this requirement and its attempt to get on a post (to cross the prohibited area) or at the attempt to flee the sentry can use the firearms.

It is necessary to note that for a legal estimation of actions the sentry it does not matter what is the purpose of protection of object for which the given post has been established: a warehouse with ammunition which plunder as obvious is fraught with threat to life of many persons, or Fighting Banner plunder of which means only material and moral damage. Use of firearms during guarding in some cases can formally excess the limits of necessary defense but thus completely meeting the requirements of the Charter. Actions of the sentry in such cases will be recognized as lawful.

Last of the bases of lawful deprivation of life analyzed in given work is caused by the fact of realization of military operations during participation in international and interstate confrontations.

There is the whole branch of international law called the humanitarian law within the limits of which there is system of the legal instructions known as "law of war".

Their purpose is to limit arbitrariness concerning human life during a confrontation, in particular by limitation of means and methods of conducting military actions.

The appeals to forbid war as a way of conflicts resolution without making efforts to its humanization are quite often. But, firstly, it is impossible to solve the problem of confrontations by interdictions; and secondly, some lawyers believe that use of armed forces can be morally justified if there is a struggle for liberation of enslaved people or for overthrow of totalitarian regime.

For the first time general principles of "the law of war" was formulated in the St.-Petersburg Declaration of 1868 which limited the "needs" of war by requirements of philanthropy. The declaration forbids the use of those kinds of firearms which wounding the enemy increase sufferings of people or make their death inevitable.[20]

According to Geneva Convention (1949) and Additional Protocols, the victims of war[21] should have under all circumstances the protection and human treatment. The Convention forbids any encroachment for their life and physical inviolability.

Provisions of the first Additional Protocol establish the list of the forbidden methods and means of conducting war. Among them there are:

use of poisons and the poisoned firearms; perfidy; murder or drawing of wounds to the opponent who, having combined the firearms, surrenders in a captivity; statements that nobody will be given mercy; use of firearms, shells, materials which are capable to cause excessive sufferings; illegal using a flag of the truce envoy, national colours or military signs of distinction and uniform of the enemy.

The Hague Convention (1907) fixed the provision for protection of civilians from disasters of war; meaning is in an interdiction of use of firearms operating nonselective, i.e. both against militaries and against civil persons.

In the legislation of some states the death penalty as one of forms of lawful limitation of the right to life to this day is saved.

The problem of use of the death penalty in the form of death penalty is reflected in a number of international documents: in the Universal Declaration of Human Rights, international Covenant on the civil and political rights and the Second optional protocol to them.

The named report accepted by General Assembly of the United Nations in December, 1989, obliges the states signed them and ratified to refuse use of death penalty in a peace time. The Euro Parliament in October, 1994 has supported abolition of death penalty in all European countries.

We believe that all possible arguments of opponents and supporters of the death penalty have already sounded in numerous discussions. Therefore, it is necessary to ascertain only observance by Russia of the moratorium concerning execution of capital sentence. We should note only that in Russian legislation the death penalty is stipulated in the form of the sanction for especially grave crimes integrated to deliberate deprivation of life of one or more persons. Such position corresponds to provision of Article 20 of the Constitution of the Russian Federation limiting a circle of acts, punishable by death penalty, "especially grave crimes against life".

The analysis of the foreign legislation allows noting some general features inherent in the countries which keep death penalty. Practically all the states, irrespective of features of their culture and customs, use it as a sanction for murder (allocating such structures as "infanticide", "patricide"), various kinds of high treasons ("mutiny", "attempt to conduct war against their Majesty Sultan"), etc.

However, in a number of the countries of world (Islamic, in particular) there are the specific structures of crimes punished by death penalty (in some cases as an uncontested sanction): "adultery", "non-observance of laws of Islamic religion and renunciation of it", etc.

Another element of the right to life is the right *to free disposition of life*. The given right is considered as an opportunity of voluntary acceptance by a person of the decision about putting their life in dangerous situation caused by the free, realized expression of the will directed on achievement of a certain positive purpose in interests of a person, other persons and the whole society. The duty of the state in the sphere of maintenance of a favorable mode of realization of the given right consists in creation of conditions to minimize the degree of risk.

Among the basic forms of lawful putting a person's life in dangerous situation there are:

1) involvement in some kinds of professional work (a military man, a militia officer, a test-pilot, etc.), initially assuming existence of certain degree of risk for life of a person even under condition of observance of the necessary measures determined by safety precautions regulations;

2) Refusal of medical aid of any sort (surgical intervention, blood transfusion, etc.) at presence of the medical parameters testifying to real threat to life;

3) The consent to an ex-plantation of organ or tissue for the subsequent transplantation to another person aiming at rescuing their life or health care;

4) By realization of medical and biologic tests with participation of a person as an examinee;

5) Actions to rescue human life not included into a circle of professional duties of this person.

The professional risk can be characterized as an opportunity of undesirable accident of a great or small probability. "There are two types of professional risk threatening life and health of a person", M. Tkachevsky considers, "the first of them is characterized by the fact that a person who takes it exposes themselves to the risk of losing life or health (for example, at fire extinguishing by the fireman). The second is a person taking a professional risk carries out the actions directed on rescue of life and health of another person. In this case the justified risk can be combined with emergency".[22] As a subject of a professional risk absolutely capable person who has reached civil majority can act.

The analysis of the second of the mentioned forms of lawful putting one's live in dangerous situation allows to answer the following question, whether a person has a right, being guided by certain reasons (religious, ethical, etc.) to refuse from the help of medical character, including surgical intervention?

We believe, that yes, but provided that their physical and mental status does not represent potential danger to a society.[23] Certainly, thus he should be informed on possible negative consequences for life and health in default.

It is remarkable that the right of the decision of such question concerning children (persons under 15-years age) and incapable persons our legislator has assigned to their trustees and lawful representatives. The logic of the legislator recognizing the given right behind them even in a situation when refusal of the help of medical character means real threat to life of the child or the incapable person is not absolutely clear.[24]

It seems that given by the legislator to hospitals the right to address the court with the appeal of such refusal cannot serve as an effective guarantee of the right to life as in such situations the questions of life and death sometimes are solved in hours and even minutes.

To more expedient legislative fastening the commission order of acceptance by medical workers of the decision on rendering urgent medical aid is represented to the indicated categories of persons. At the same time it is necessary to recognize that complexity of the put problem causes necessity of the careful analysis of all aspects of it: ethical, medical and legal.

Certain share of risk concerning the life of a donor as well as a recipient is represented with operation on transplantation of an organ (tissue) from the live donor.

Therefore the subject of an ex-plantation (withdrawal) can be only a person capable to the reasonable order by the health and, simultaneously, realizing degree of risk for life.

Russian law on transplantation of organs and (or) tissues of a person limits a circle of alive donors, excluding persons under 18 years and incapable.[25]

According to the given normative-legal instrument the live donor should necessarily be with the recipient in genetic connection, except for cases of change of marrow and blood transfusion. We believe that the ethical contents of the given provision is rather ambiguous as are many arguments in favour of giving to transplants, withdrawn from an alive organism, the state of objects of a material world and, hence, legalizations of transactions on their term and in particular sale and purchase.

It, firstly, would allow the representatives of socially made destitute layers to dispose on a legal basis lifetime or posthumous onerous of alienation of organs with the purpose of material maintenance of maintenance of health of the relatives (for example if there is a need for an expensive surgical operation for a sick child); secondly, it would considerably lower profitableness for a long time of the existing and prospering underground market of donor organs.

Withdrawal of organs and tissues is not permitted if is established that they relate to a person, suffering from an illness dangerous to life and health of the recipient (for example, AIDS) and also if it is established that forthcoming operation on an ex-plantation represents real threat to life of the donor or is capable to cause irreversible frustration of their health.

Change of organs and tissues is carried out under the written approval of the recipient (at blood transfusion the oral consent is enough), however, the consent is not required, when delay in realizing of corresponding operation threatens life of the recipient and to receive such consent it is impossible (for example, he is in a unconsciousness). Practically, such situations can become the reason of the conflict as some people do not accept transplantation on religious and other grounds.

As to the questions connected with withdrawal of bodies and (or) tissues at the donor-corpse the principle is put in a basis of Russian normative base of "a presumption of the consent", meaning an opportunity to use a corpse as a donor if during lifetime of a person did not declare the disagreement on a posthumous ex-plantation.

We believe, that is it an example of the utilitarian approach to an estimation of a human being which dignity should be respected and protected even after death.

It is thought that in a basis of the law regulating the relations in the sphere of transplantology, the principle of "a presumption of disagreement" should be settled.

Firstly, it will allow solving the problem of moral character noted above.

Secondly, the given principle can play a role of the deterrent during increase of the illegal case connected with sale of bodies abroad and simultaneously to become certain guarantee of the prevention of criminal abusing in the given sphere of medical activity, down to actual self-elimination of medical workers from actions on rescuing life of the dying person considered by them as a potential donor.

Last from the analyzed aspects of the right to dispose of one's life is connected with the practice of attraction of persons for participation in medical and biologic researches as examinees. Such researches are spent with the purpose of approbation of new medical products, new methods of relations.

It is necessary to distinguish two categories of the volunteers who are participating in such researches: in the first case the researcher acts as a volunteer; in the second there is a person not involved in the research.

Now in the majority of the states medical and biologic researches are carried out under aegis of the main principles proclaimed by the Helsinki Declaration of world Medical Association, accepted in 1964 on 18-th World Assembly. This standard which has received the name "Qualitative Clinical Practice" is characterized by strict legal regulation of tests that provides it with international acceptability.

Its main principle is the priority of interests of the examinee: interests of a person should be considered always in a greater degree, than interests of a science and a society. It is also necessary to note the following rules:

—With participation of a person the careful analysis of probable risk in comparison with prospective benefits to the examinee and other persons should precede each project of research;

—The potential subject of research should be informed on its purposes, methods and possible negative consequences.

Voluntariness presupposes that a person can realize the essence, value and possible consequences of test and also to express in this connection the will. However, sometimes there is a necessity of carrying out an experiment on a child's organism or an organism of the insane (incapable) person.

The Helsinki Declaration in the principles proclaimed by it supposes such researches on the basis of the consent of trustees, lawful representatives of the indicated categories of persons. It is not excluded that final transition of medicine to a contract basis (many decades in our country participation in medical and biologic researches was carried out gratuitously) will cause "trade" in children from parents is representatives of socially made destitute layers.

We believe that involvement in experiments of such persons should be carried out only on the basis of the conclusion of a competent medical board on ethics, with participation not interested in an outcome of certain experiment of doctors and lawyers, after careful studying the purpose of research, competence of the researcher, a person of the examinee and conformity of a degree of risk of value of expected result.

Creating of Russian normative base of realizing of medical and biologic researches with participation of a person on the basis of an available positive experience, embodied in propositions of "Qualitative Clinical Practice" is thought to allow creating an effective system of legal guarantees of the right to life and also the rights to the highest achievable level of physical and mental health.

It is necessary to remark that not all forms of realization of the right to free disposition of life are subject to legal regulation. In some cases it is objectively impossible (for example, at suicide).

The given act is an extreme degree of an actual opportunity of a person to dispose of life. However, the expression "the right to suicide" is legally insignificant as suicide does not give the shape of the legal right imposing a duty on the state or the third parties to assist its realization. Certainly, "the existing normative concept of the right should extend only on the actions made in a society and concerning mutual relations of people among themselves but not relations of a person with the destiny if he has wanted to select it".[26] At the same time Russian legislator in propositions of criminal law-executive fixes an interdiction of certain category of persons to encroach for own life.[27]

Recently hot discussions have been conducted on the problem of euthanasia. (Euthanasia is the easy, painless death relieving a person from intolerable sufferings, caused by illness that can't be cured in terminal or preterminal stage).

As a rule, it is a question of a situation when a person not capable for physiological reasons to commit suicide to free themselves from sufferings, is compelled to address the associates with such request (doctors or relatives).

In medical deontology there are two forms of euthanasia: passive (acceleration of death by the termination of active therapeutic reanimation actions) and active (use of means and the actions directly leading to the death of the patient).

All religious doctrines are extremely unanimous in the denying euthanasia. "Do not kill", is proclaimed in Old and New Testament. "As a owner of a fig knows time of its maturing, the God knows when to withdraw the righteous from this world", the Talmud says.

The basic argument of secular opponents of the indicated way of deprivation of life is the statement that the concept of legitimacy of euthanasia will lead to destruction of the public morals, to rough infringement by physicians of the Ascepiades' Oath.

Modern the Criminal Code of the Russian Federation considers euthanasia as a form of deliberate deprivation of life; however, it can be a motive of compassion as a circumstance commuting punishment (Article "D" Article 61 of the Criminal Code of the Russian Federation).

The interdiction of euthanasia (both active and passive) contains in Article 45 of Bases of the legislation of the Russian Federation on health protection of citizens. However, Article 33 of the named legal instrument provides the right of the patient to refusal of rendering to them medical aid (artificial measures enter into concept of medical aid on maintenance of life also) that in itself there is not that other as passive euthanasia.

In the foreign medical literature the position is stated following which the doctor can make a decision on refusal of the reanimation undertaken for prevention of death of the patient from cardiac imprisonment or breath. "The basic justification of such order is the proved opinion of the doctor that the patient is in far come and not on reversible stage of fatal disease and should die during a short time interval".[28]

If the patient is in consciousness this information is provided to them, in case the patient asks for reanimation, the doctor *is obliged* (here and below our italics.-*N.K.*) to make an attempt to save their life.

In case of unconsciousness of the patient, the doctor makes this decision himself and records it in the case record. "Except for cases when the patient is under legal guardianship of relatives, the consent of the last to refusal of reanimation *is not obligatory*".[29]

Passive euthanasia it is already legalized in twelve states of USA. A person, who is being sensible mind, makes the document fixing that "if I am ill with incurable illness for which, in opinion of two doctors, there are no reasonable bases to expect recover, I want to be allowed to die, rather than being supported by artificial means or by heroic efforts".[30]

Council on ethics and actions of proceeding of the American Medical Association has introduced the concept "supported suicide". It differs from active euthanasia that the doctor does not make the actions directed on deprivation of life and only provides the patient with medical products necessary for it or the information (for example, about a lethal doze of prescribed somnolent).[31]

We believe that statements about humanity of process of maintenance of life of hopelessly patient, the suffering person is rather doubtful. Denying euthanasia as an instrument opposite to ethical principles of a society, the state, hiding the prosecution in clothes of humanism that illustrates Berdyaev thesis that "any ethics of the law should recognize that the abstract goods above certain, individual person, even the abstract goods was understood as a principle of a person or a principle of happiness".[32]

"A person appears on light not at the will and them, even for the sake of justice, freedom to decide should be given, whether he wishes to continue the life or not".[33]

The criminal law forms of violent intervention in another's rights should restrain only at obvious desire of their separate person to save. Certainly that theoretically the subject euthanasia the capable person, i.e. can be active only. A person capable to adequate estimation of a situation and acceptance of the realized, strong-willed decision.

We consider possible to express solidarity with the authors, offering to legalize instruments of voluntary euthanasia with the consent of hopelessly sick, under condition of fixing the given consent in the form established by the law.

Is worthy and the offer stated in the literature on inclusion in general part of the Criminal Code of the Russian Federation the provision providing the consent of the victim as circumstance, act excluding criminality, including the act integrated to deliberate deprivation of life.[34]

The right to life is the first human right. In our opinion, the further theoretical research of its realization should be aimed at searches of new effective guarantees of the given right.

Notes

1. Grotsy G. About the Right of War and Peace., 1957. P. 45. / Гроций Г. О праве войны и мира. М., 1957. С. 45.

2. Locke J. Two Treatise About Government // Works: in 3 Vol., 1988. Vol. 3. P. 310. / Локк Д. Два трактата о правлении // Соч.: В 3 т. М., 1988. Т. 3. С. 310.

3. Tagantsev N.S. About Crimes against Life by Russian Law. S.-Petersburg, 1870. P. 47–48. / Таганцев Н. С. О преступлениях против жизни по русскому праву. СПб., 1870. С. 47–48.

4. The specified criteria are reflected in the order of Ministry of Health of the Russian Federation of December, 4th, 1992 318 "About transition on recommended by the World Health Organization criteria of viviparity and stillbirth" / Указанные критерии отражены в приказе Минздрава РФ от 4 декабря 1992 г. № 318 «О переходе на рекомендованные Всемирной организацией здравоохранения критерии живорождения и мертворождения»

5. See: Antsiferov K.D. Compilation of clauses and notes on criminal law and legal proceedings. S.-Petersburg, 1898. P. 53. / См.: Анциферов К. Д. Сборник статей и заметок по уголовному праву и судопроизводству. СПб., 1898. С. 53.

6. Harakas S. Orthodoxy and Bioethics // Person. 1994.2. P. 93. / Харакас С. Православие и биоэтика // Человек. 1994. № 2. С. 93.

7. See: Siluyanova I.V. Bioethics in Russia: Values and Laws, 1997. P. 90. / .: Силуянова И. В. Биоэтика в России: ценности и законы. М., 1997. С. 90.

8. Since 1996 in Russia the expanded list of social indications for abortions operates including: a recognition of the woman to be jobless or having the jobless husband, absence of constant habitation (residing in a private apartment or in a hostel), possession of many children, etc. See: Siluyanova I.V. Specified works. P. 86. / С 1996 г. в России действует расширенный перечень социальных показаний для абортов, в который вошли такие основания, как: признание женщины безработной или имеющей безработного мужа, отсутствие у женщины постоянного жилья (проживание на частной квартире или в общежитии), многодетность и т. п. См.: Силуянова И. В. Указ. соч. С. 86.

9. Negovsky V.A. Death, Dying, Revival: Ethical Aspects // Doctor. 1992.8. P. 24. / Неговский В. А. Смерть, умирание, оживление: этические аспекты // Врач. 1992. № 8. С. 24.

10. Brainstorming // Komsomolskaya pravda. June, 23. 1998. / Атака на мозги // Комсомольская правда. 1998. 23 июня.

11. Second Additional Protocol to Geneva Conventions (1949) defines confrontations of not international character as conflicts between armed forces of the state and antigovernmental armed groups or other organized armed groups. / Второй Дополнительный протокол к Женевским конвенциям 1949 г. определяет вооруженные конфликты немеждународного характера как конфликты между вооруженными силами государства и антиправительственными вооруженными группами или другими организованными вооруженными группами.

12. See: Yusupov R.M. Necessary Defense in Legislation and Judiciary Law: Thesis of dissertation ... Candidate of Jurisprudence, 1999. P. 22-23. / См.: Юсупов Р. М. Необходимая оборона в законодательстве и судебной практике: Автореф. дис. ... канд. юрид. наук. М., 1999. С. 22–23.

13. Article 9 "Main Principles of Use of Force and Fire-arms by Officials in Law and Order Enforcement" / Статья 9 «Основных принципов применения силы и огнестрельного оружия должностными лицами по поддержанию правопорядка».

14. See: Ibidem. Paragraph 11.

15. : Pobegajlo E.F., Revin V.P. Necessary Defense and Detention of a Criminal in Activity of Law-Enforcement Bodies., 1987. P. 43; Ivanov A.B. institution of Causing Harm at Detention of a Person Who Have Committed a Crime: Thesis of dissertation ... Candidate of Jurisprudence, 1999. P. 18. / См.: Побегайло Э. Ф., Ревин В. П. Необходимая оборона и задержание преступника в деятельности органов внутренних дел. М., 1987. С. 43; Иванов А. Б. Институт причинения вреда при задержании лица, совершившего преступление: Автореф. дис. ... канд. юрид. наук. М., 1999. С. 18.

16. The qualified structures of bribery are referred to the category of grave crimes. / Квалифицированные составы взяточничества отнесены к категории тяжких преступлений.

17. See: About Militia: The Law of the Russian Federation. Paragraph 6. Part 1. Article 15. / См.: О милиции: Закон РФ. П. 6. Ч. 1. Ст. 15.

18. Minges A.V. Special Measures of Administrative Suppression: Use of Fire-arms, Physical Strength and Special Means by the Representatives of Executive State Authorities. Volgograd, 1999. P. 105. / Мингес А. В. Специальные меры административного пресечения: применение огнестрельного оружия, физической силы и специальных средств представителями исполнительной власти государства. Волгоград, 1999. С. 105.

19. See: Ovezov N.A. To the Question on the Circumstances Eliminating Public Danger and Illegality of Act in the Soviet Criminal Law. Ashkhabad, 1972. P. 96. / См.: Овезов Н. А. К вопросу об обстоятельствах, устраняющих общественную опасность и противоправность деяния в советском уголовном праве. Ашхабад, 1972. С. 96.

20. See: Materials of the international Symposium Devoted to the "Right of War" // State and Law. 1994.4. P. 147. / См.: Материалы международного симпозиума, посвященного «праву войны» // Государство и право. 1994. № 4. С. 147.

21. Persons who are not directly involved or stopped participating since certain moment in military actions are referred to "victims of war": wounded people and patients in field armies, prisoners of war, civilians (including the population of occupied territories). / К «жертвам войны» относятся лица, которые не принимают непосредственного участия в военных действиях или прекратили участие в них с определенного момента: это раненые и больные в действующих армиях,

военнопленные, гражданское население (в том числе население оккупированных территорий).

22. Tkachevsky Y.M. Justified Professional and industrial Risk as the Circumstance Reducing Criminal Liability // Bulletin of Moscow University. #3 1991. P. 19. / Ткачевский Ю. М. Оправданный профессиональный и производственный риск как обстоятельство, смягчающее уголовную ответственность // Вестник Моск. ун-та. 1991. № 3. С. 19.

23. See: Article 33 of Bases of Legislation of the Russian Federation about Citizens' Health Care // Rossiiskaya gazeta. 1993.August, 18. / См.: Статья 33 Основ законодательства РФ об охране здоровья граждан // Российская газета. 1993. 18 авг.

24. See: Ibidem.

25. See: Rossiiskaya gazeta. 1993. January, 9.

26. Ковалев M.I. Right to Life and Right to Death // State and Law. 1992.7. P. 71. / Ковалев М. И. Право на жизнь и право на смерть // Государство и право. 1992. № 7. С. 71.

27. See: On Imprisonment of the Suspected and Accused of Crimes: Law of the Russian Federation. Paragraph 9. Paragraph 36. / См.: О содержании под стражей подозреваемых и обвиняемых в совершении преступлений: Закон РФ. П. 9. Ст. 36.

28. Don H. Decision-Making in intensive Therapy, 1995. P. 204. / Дон Х. Принятие решения в интенсивной терапии. М., 1995. С. 204.

29. Ibidem.

30. Walker A. Death of Brain., 1988. P. 207. / Уолкер А. Смерть мозга. М., 1988. С. 207.

31. See: Siluyanova I.V. Specified work. P. 165. / См.: Силуянова И. В. Указ. соч. С. 165.

32. Berdyaev N.A. About Purpose of a Person, 1993. P. 93. / Бердяев Н. А. О назначении человека. М., 1993. С. 93.

33. Krasikov A.N. Crimes Against Human Right to Life. Saratov, 1999. P. 203. / Красиков А. Н. Преступления против права человека на жизнь. Саратов, 1999. С. 203.

34. See: Ibidem P. 207.

Chapter 4. THE HUMAN RIGHT TO DIGNITY

Scientific Categories "Honour" and "Dignity", Their Historical Development

Dignity and honour are concepts of moral consciousness, ethical categories. These are multiple-valued, polysemantic concepts. In ethics theoretical bases of these categories their correlation is comprehensively developed. Dignity is identified with value of a person (a person in general or certain person) or with comprehension of this value by them or with the behaviour of a person expressed in a worthy way of life.

The major aspect of the contents of dignity is in consciousness of absence of compulsion, i.e. consciousness of freedom.

In the philosophical and legal literature 70 is 80th and also in modern researches (works of V.A. Bljumkina, V.P. Tugarinova, N.A. Pjatak, N.A. Pridvorova, etc.) in the concept of dignity as a rule, there is the objective moment (a concept of value of a person) and the subjective moment, i.e. feeling and comprehension of the moral value. In the objective moment of this concept it is possible to emphasize the following aspects:

1) Human dignity, value of a person in general, irrespective of its certain qualities and features;

2) Personal dignity, i.e. value of certain individual, set of their positive cultural and physical qualities;

3) The dignity connected with belonging to a certain social community, group, etc. (for example, dignity of the worker, scientific, national dignity, and dignity of a woman).

The subjective moment of dignity is comprehension by an individual of the value as person in general as certain person as representative of certain social group (a class, the nation, etc.).

Other aspects of general concept "dignity" are also possible. Sometimes it is identified with moral behaviour, a worthy way of life. But the main thing in its contents is a concept of dignity of a person.

The idea of dignity in all its aspects has deep social meaning.

Humanistic ethics recognize that idea of human dignity means a concept of a person of the maximum, with what incomparable value. The concept follows from a concept of the maximum value of the subject of freedom, equality, having them the rights and duties of a person and a citizen.

The category "honour" is also considered in ethics as multiple-valued concept, i.e. as a public estimation of a person, their positive moral reputation, either the moral attitude, or comprehension and feeling abuse, or set of the best sincere qualities.

In jurisprudence "honour" as a rule, is identified with an estimation of a person by a society. There are also objective (external estimation) and internal (consciousness, experience of this estimation) aspects.

Correlation of abuse and dignity is determined by the following position: there is no dignity without honour and honour without dignity. These categories are considered as interconnected, interpenetrating but not identical concepts. The correlation between concepts "dignity" and "honour" corresponds to a correlation between categories "value", "estimation". Obviously, it is impossible to draw an absolute side between these concepts. An idea stated by Voltaire seems interesting: "Honour is a status of faultless moral dignity".[1] The correlation between concepts of honour and dignity in ethics is usually expressed in the following. The common thing is that they are determined on the basis of the same social criteria; open the attitude of a person both to them from a society; play such role in regulation of moral relations. Distinction consists that in dignity notion about value of any person (is reflected. It starts with a principle of equality of all people in the moral attitude) and in a category "honour" moral values of a person contact merits of people, their differentiated estimation from a society.

The category of "dignity" is also connected with other ethical categories, in particular with conscience, i.e. feeling of the moral responsibility for the acts to the surrounding people, internal consciousness, a self-estimation of own behaviour. Conscience is especially closely connected with subjective aspect of dignity. Comprehension of conformity of the behaviour to moral principles (as is usually said, "clear conscience") strengthens self-respect and is shown externally in a worthy way of life.

Dignity is connected with the category of a duty as social human nature it is necessary demands from them the ability, skill to coordinate the acts with interests of a society. In particular it relates to dignity of a citizen. It is inseparable from fair execution of the civic duty.

And if democracy is inconceivable without respect of the state to the citizens, the functioning of democratic institutions of authority cannot be normal if citizens honesty do not carry out the duties before the state.

Dignity, spotless honour is an indispensable condition of happy human life. A person who has lost self-respect, do not enjoy confidence and respect of associates, loses correct orientation in life, sense of happiness.

Concepts of honour and dignity of a person have started to be formed already at the first stages of development of a human society. During those far times people did not divide themselves from a tribe, a clan. As K. Marx indicated, "a person stands apart as an individual only by force of historical process. Originally he acts as a public being, a breeding essence, a gregarious animal".[2]

In this connection the insult of a person belonging to any clan was perceived as an insult of the whole clan. The custom of blood feud has arisen on this basis.

At the same time in conditions of a primitive-communal system the elementary-moral concepts of honour and dignity of a person have been formed.

In a slaveholding society there are concepts of social value of representatives of ruling classes. The doleful cult that existed in Ancient Egypt testifies the fact that by means of special rituals of burial rich people expected to save the exclusive position and in the other world. However, in these conditions in moral consciousness of people the ideas of moral value, honour and dignity of a person have arisen and developed. Thus, in Egyptiac collection "Doctrine of Life and Values" (XI century A.D.) national saying goes: "it is better to be the fair person, than a rich predator".[3] In the doctrine of the early Buddhism the protest against exclusive constraint and privileges has been made. "A person becomes a Brahman not ... because of the family tree or a birth", is said in "Dhammapada" (the collection of Buddhist sayings of IV-III century A.D.).[4]

Ideas of value of a person, their freedom for the first time find all-round development in philosophical, moral and politically legal doctrines of the Ancient Greece and Rome. In public live various aspects of concepts "dignity" and "honour": dignity of a citizen, self-respect of a person, etc have been recognized there and have become the object of theoretical analysis.

"A lot of great is on light as an ancient Greek playwright Sofokl said but nothing is greater than a person".[5]

One of the highest tops of ancient Greek humanism was Protagor's doctrine that proclaimed the well-known thesis: "a person is a measure of all things".

Protecting the idea of human equality, he considered that such dignity as wisdom, virtue, an opportunity to participate in the state life, were accessible to all people.

Glorifying a person, recognizing their absolute value, Protagor greatly outstripped their time. In certain respect he anticipated the ideas of humanists of Renaissance and other thinkers of the next century.

Certainly, social value of a person, their freedom in a classical antiquity had a burden of class limitation. Slaves were completely excluded from the sphere of freedom and according to dominating slaveholding morals could not be bearers of such moral qualities as honour and dignity.

Roman law has reflected the notion which generated in the classical antiquity about a free person as a participant of legal relationships, at the same time it considered the slave as speaking instrument (instrumentum vocale). Human qualities of slaves were recognized by stoics (Zenon, Seneca) for whom only internal, cultural freedom which was not connected with any sociopolitical status of a person did matter.

The feudalism which came in the stead slaveholding I build became a new stage in development of a human being.

However, the class partitions connected with feudal hierarchy, fixed a social inequality, held down its creative opportunities. Put forward in early Christian the doctrine of the principle of equality of people to the god was a form of the statement of a human being. The well-known statement of the Christ: "It is not a person for Saturday but Saturday for a person" has been filled by humanistic meaning.

The ancient idea of similarity of a person apprehended by Christianity good luck ("on an image and similarity divine") ennobled a person though basically the myth about Adam and Eve's creation called to prove abjection of a person before a person of the almighty creator.

"A person is a greater miracle, than any miracle accomplished by a person" as Augustine wrote (IV-V).[6]

But, in our opinion, the doctrine of the Fall is incompatible with the concept of human dignity, as a basis of the sermon of Christian self-killing of flesh that is ascetism, nunhood, solitary life, self-destruction of a person.

Finally, practice of Catholic and other Christian churches (activity of inquisition, prosecution of heretics, etc.) over centuries interfered with the statement of human dignity.

In Renaissance this humanistic idea receives a new, secular substantiation. This time puts forward an ideal of enlightened formed person (homo eruditus), a person-citizen, and the participant of political life.

The originality of culture of Renaissance was expressed and thus paved the way for blossoming of individualism, developed the rationalistic approach to the validity.

The 16th-17th century is an epoch of Reformation and early bourgeois revolutions became a new stage in development of idea of dignity of a person. The bourgeoisie going to authority were interested in elimination of class partitions, in the statement of new bourgeois concepts of freedom and equality. Reformation undermined cultural domination of Catholic Church.

The most outstanding thinkers of 16th-17th century saw social value of a person in their creative activity, in their aspiration to increase the authority above the nature (D. Bruno, F. Bacon). The advanced philosophers of new time were impressed by the belief of virtue of human mind. Also it is a prominent aspect of becoming of human dignity.

"I think, hence, I exist", as R. Descartes proclaimed. This thesis about power of a human idea became a sign of new time.

It is necessary to note that during new time there was deepening of the contents of concept of human dignity. And it is connected with formation of concepts of a person as a subject of personal freedom and the bearer of inalienable human rights.

Originality of ethical, political and legal doctrines of the 15th-18th century is that social value of a person was considered by them from views of school of the absolute law.

Development of the problem of dignity of a citizen as a subject of personal freedom takes the central place in J. Locke's political doctrine. "Freedom of a person in a society, as he wrote, is that he does not submit to any other legislature, except for that which is established under the consent in the state ... Where there are no laws, there is no freedom".[7]

Here the bases of western concept of equal protection of the law of citizens are formulated. Both in theory and in a political practice (originally in Holland, England) that time formed the concepts of civil human rights.

One of the first found the legal embodiment in British Habeas Corpus (1679) there was a right to personal immunity. Rudiments of this right have been recorded in Magna Carta (1215).

One of the first rights affirmed during new time was freedom of conscience.

During new time various aspects of the problem of honour and dignity of a person were developed in detail. Thus, T. Hobbes in the "Leviathan" in detail analyzed a correlation between such moral categories as power, value, dignity, respect of a person.

He equated cost, or value of a person to cost of things and considered it as a price which "makes so much, as much as possible to give for using their force".[8] Hobbes called dignity the public value of a person, i.e. the price which gives them the state. Hence, public dignity of a person merges with civil. Obviously, bourgeois approach to dignity of a person in aspect of the economic theory of cost where it was equated to a thing, to goods is also rather characteristic. In this case Hobbes theoretically expressed a public practice of an arising new society.

Bourgeoisie, wrote K. Marx and F. Engels, "has transformed personal dignity of a person into an exchange value and has put on a place uncountable welcome and acquired freedom one unscrupulous freedom of commerce".[9]

At the same time already in 16th-18th century there was expressed an idea of dignity of a person-worker released from social oppression (T. More, T. Campanella). The American scientist and the politician of the 18th century B. Franklin recognized work as a greatest moral value.

The advanced thinkers of the epoch of Enlightenment saw social value of a person as a subject of freedom. "A person is born free, Rousseau claimed in the "Public Contract". To refuse from freedom means to renounce the human dignity, from the right of human nature, even from their duties".[10]

During this epoch the substantiation idea of political freedom and its essential elements as equal protection of the law of citizens, personal immunity, and freedom of conscience. "The fair person, is wrote Voltaire, is possible to subject to prosecution but to not disgrace".[11]

As Mably noted, "the feeling of equality is not that the feeling of our dignity".

An outstanding philosopher and lawyer of the 18th century Ch. Montesquieu, the founder of theory of division of authorities, deeply realized idea of universal dignity. "First of all, I am a person and then the Frenchman", he wrote.[12]

The German classical philosophy made significant contribution to development of idea of dignity of a person. Here again first of all it is necessary to emphasize the role of I. Kant. "In everything created anything can be used only as means for everything; only a person, with each sentient being is the purpose in themselves".[13]

These views of the German philosopher are dictated by sincere humanism. Virtually Kant's ethics is that he connected the category of dignity with the concept of "duty". The duty at the Kant is "loftily a great word".

All representatives of German classical philosophy defended the idea of human dignity but everyone gave it the special meaning.

Kant believed that the social value of a person was identified with execution of a duty, i.e. categorical imperative, Hegel considered an individual an element of general, moral totality, and Feuerbach perceived dignity as greatness of a person, their highest value. "Homo hominy deos est", he claimed.[14]

But all the mentioned philosophers considered a person the subject of freedom. In the end of the 18th - the beginning of the 19th century honour and dignity became objects of the constitutional protection. In the USA Declaration of independence (1776), in the French Declaration of Civil Human Rights ((1791)) the democratic principles of freedom and equality of people, were proclaimed, i.e. the essential elements of concept of value of a human being.

Bourgeois revolutions and the statement of a capitalist society were the important factors of development of a person and their rights. The first generation of human rights received legal recognition. In the 19th century such representatives of western liberalism as B. Constant, A. Tocqueville, D.S. Mill, Spencer, represented themselves as supporters of dignity of a person and their rights.

During this period the Danish philosopher, the forerunner of existentialism S. Kierkegaard opposed the concepts of a person as a public being. The main thing in a person is their individuality, rather than sociality. A person is primary and a society is a secondary thing. Kierkegaard's subjective-idealistic theory led to their conclusion that "a person is a spirit". The principal value in human life is not public work but "frontage inside", "in a chasm of a private world".[15] Kierkegaard wrote about dignity of a person but he put their greatness in dependence on their attitude to the god.

In opinion of the Danish philosopher, a person is great not by the public merits but during that moment when he "plunges into the depth of consciousness of their sinfulness".[16]

The 19th century was a century of a wide circulation of socialist and communistic doctrines which aspired to prove and protect dignity of a labour person. Development of trade-union movement, appearing of social-democratic parties, appearing of international I promoted formation of concepts of the second generation of human rights. S. Fourier for the first time distinguished the right to work as a first of human rights. In the future communistic society, K. Marx and F. Engels wrote, free development of everyone would become a condition of free development of everybody.

In the 20th century the problem of dignity of a person became extremely aggravated. During this century two inconsistent tendencies were showed. Two World Wars killed tens of millions of human lives. Oswiencim and Hiroshima, these ominous symbols of imperialism are challenges to the very idea of dignity of a person. Arising of globalism led to strengthening of inequality between the countries and continents, to violation of the basic human rights, deepened and expanded such social ulcers as unemployment, racism, militarism, omnipotence of bureaucracy, alienation of a person from a society.

On the other hand, the development of science and technical equipment, democratic movements, progressive development of a society, crash of colonial system, despotic modes, finding of independence by many countries led to the statement of idea of value of a human being.

In the Charter of the United Nations the aspiration to approve the belief in basic rights of a person, in dignity and value of a human being has been proclaimed. The Universal Declaration of Human Rights begins with the statement: recognition of the inherent dignity and of equal and inalienable rights of all members of the human family is the foundation of freedom, justice and peace in world. The Declaration has proclaimed equality of people in their dignity and rights.

In UN Declaration on Race and Racial Prejudice (1978) the nature of universal dignity is revealed: "All human beings relate to a single species and are descended from a common stock. All peoples of world possess equal faculties for attaining the highest level in intellectual, technical, social, Economic, cultural and political development" (Article 1).

Thus, dignity of a person is based as is said in this Declaration, on organic unity of mankind and, hence, on equality of all people and people, "finding expression in the most raised concepts of philosophy, morals and religion".

In this Declaration not only dignity of separate persons but also dignity of peoples was recognized.

In Declaration on Social Progress and Development of the United Nations (1969) it is proclaimed that "social progress and development are based on respect of dignity and value of a human being".

It is necessary to say that the category "human dignity" in the 20th century has become a fundamental basis of all international-legal regulations of the United Nations, other international organizations and the integral part of the majority of modern Constitutions.

In international-legal documents of the 20th century not only the right to human dignity of all people but the right to dignity of separate social groups (women, children, workers, mentally retarded persons, etc.) is fixed.

In political, ethical and legal doctrines of our time various aspects of the category "dignity" develop. The deep humanistic meaning contains in A. Schweitzer's concept "awe of life".

The problem of dignity of a person is a component both theological and secular philosophical concepts. Thus, for existentialist philosophies the identification of value of a person with absolute freedom is characteristic. People "are thrown among freedom", "are sentenced to freedom". J.-P. Sartre came to the conclusion that a person (even the prisoner and the slave) was always free.

In the Neo-Thomist concept a person acts in two aspects: as an individual, i.e. as a component of a society and as a person. Dignity of a person, their greatness arises from the order of things, "having on itself the mark of the father of life" (Maritain) and consists in that "completely to give themselves to service to the god" (Gilson).

In political science doctrines it is possible to emphasize three basic interpretations of the category "dignity": liberal, socialist, including Marxist and national-democratic.

The liberal concept is based on individualistic interpretation of value of a person which interests are put above all. Freedom and human rights, intolerance to any forms of the state arbitrariness, the sermon of equality are the major postulates of the liberal theory. And in this theory the basic accent is on universal understanding of dignity of a person, maintenance of civil and political rights. Philosophical sources of substantiation of liberal understanding of freedom can be the diversified concepts (from Hegel both Hegelian up to existentialistic and positivistic).

Dignity in Marxist understanding is considered neither as an embodiment of divine forces, nor as a moment of development of Hegel's absolute idea or Kant's categorical imperative, nor as reflection of existential existence of an individual, "thrown in freedom" and as result of social development. "We should know, K. Marx wrote, what human nature is in general and how it is modified during each historical epoch".[17] It means that explanation of essence of a person of certain historical period presupposes definition of their social value.

Criticizing the liberal theory for it denying or belittling the importance of the economic and social rights, Marxism pays special attention to protection of dignity of workers, their liberation from operation and oppression.

The Constitution of RSFSR (1918) recognizing work as a duty of all citizens reproduced an evangelical principle: "Who doesn't work – doesn't eat". In Marxist understanding dignity of a person is shown not only in their rights and freedoms but also in their duties before a society.

During different historical epochs the contents of concept "dignity of a person" was changing. In the religious medieval interpretation dignity is a person, obedient to the will of church; during the epoch of Renaissance it is a homo sapiens; in the 17th - 19th centuries a person is the subject of political freedom, in the 20th century in conditions of western mass consumer society there is a person-consumer. The Marxism put forward the understanding of human dignity which was successfully formulated by Nikolay Ostrovsky: meaning of life is in struggle for liberation from mankind.

Chernyshevsky wrote about national-democratic understanding of dignity in the 19th century: "Historical value of each Russian great person is measured by their merits to the Native land, their human dignity by the force of their patriotism".[18] In the 20th century the struggle of oppressed people for liberation filled the contents of dignity of a person with ideas of aversion of racism, xenophobia and statement of national equality.

In the African Charter of Human Rights and People (1981) it is said about dignity of historical traditions and values of the African civilization which should find reflection in the contents of the concept of human rights and people.

Contents of the Right to Honour and Dignity

There are two aspects of the category "dignity" in the law and in jurisprudence.

The first is human dignity as one of basic principles of the law. The second aspect is honour and dignity as a legal right belonging to the separate person.

The respect for a person, concept of their maximum value underlies modern democratic jural relationship. In the domestic legal literature the idea of dignity as principle of the right comprehensively was proved by N.A. Pridvorov.

It is necessary to say that a number of modern Constitutions have highlighted the principle of respect of human dignity. Thus, in Article 1 of the Constitution of Germany it is said, "Dignity of a person is inviolable. Any government should respect and protect them". In the Modern Greek Constitution this principle is recorded in Article 2. Other Constitutions fix a principle of respect of dignity of a person in clause opening the Chapter about the rights and freedoms of a person (Article

7 of the Swiss Constitution, Article 10 of the Italian Constitution). In Article 30 of the Constitution of Poland the contents of this principle and its value for all institution of the rights and duties of a person is rather successfully opened: "Natural and integral dignity of a person forms a source of freedom and civil human rights. It is inviolable and its respect and protection are a duty of public authorities".

In the Constitution of Belgium other approach to dignity of a person is recorded. Here it represents itself as one of constitutional rights of person: "Everyone has a right to conduct life corresponding to human dignity" (Article 23). In this case the right to dignity contacts the right to adequate standard of living.

The Portuguese Constitution gives modern interpretation of the indicated right, guaranteeing the right of citizens to personal dignity and genetic individuality of a person and also on good reputation (Article 26) and equality in public dignity (Article 13).

As to the Constitution of the Russian Federation 1993, it, on the one hand, has followed the Greek sample, having fixed in Article 2 the idea of human dignity as general law: "a person, their rights and freedoms are the maximum value. A concept of, observance and protection of the rights and freedoms of a person and a citizen is a duty of the state". On the other hand, Russian Constitution has recorded in Chapter II the right to dignity as one of civil human rights: "Dignity of a person is protected by the state. Nothing can be the basis for its belittling" (part 1 Article 21). The analysis of the Constitution of the Russian Federation shows that here in different constitutionally-legal institutions dignity of a person as representative of separate social groups is also recognized: racial, national, sexual, religious, ideological, etc. As a Constitution fixes equality of the rights and freedoms of a person irrespective of their belonging to different social groups so far as equality in dignity of these people (Article 19) is legally guaranteed. Proclaiming maintenance of the state support of motherhood, paternity, the childhood, invalids, older persons, the Constitution recognizes social value of these citizens (Article 7). Fixing system of civil human rights (first of all such as freedom and personal immunity, personal privacy, personal and family secret, protection of honour and reputation), the Constitution guarantees also the right to dignity of a person as an individual (Article 23).

It is necessary to recognize that in the country where tens millions people are below poverty where trade in children and women, and other heavy encroachments on the human rights exist, it is difficult to recognize the indicated constitutional guarantees as real. But legal recognition of the maximum value of a human being, firstly, has serious humanistic meaning; secondly assigns to the state the obligations connected with protection of a person and their rights.

Addressing to theoretical analysis of human rights to honour and dignity, it is necessary to remark that it can be considered in two aspects: 1) as a complex legal institution including propositions of constitutional, international, civil, criminal and other branches of law; 2) as a legal right.

Honour and dignity of people find the external display in moral relations and certain part of these relations requires legal fixing and protection. Certainly, the court cannot oblige a society to have any opinion on a person but he can oblige it not to express unfair and offensive opinion for a person. Besides, the decision of court has not only a validity but also moral authority and consequently it can influence public opinion.

The right to honour and dignity presupposes, firstly, the right of a citizen to demand that moral, politically legal, professional and other social estimation of their person was formed on the basis of correct perception of their acts.

Here it is said about the differentiated estimation of acts of a citizen, their reputation, i.e. about the right to honour. Secondly, it is necessary to say about the right of a citizen to their respect as person in general and as a certain person. Thirdly, the given right fixes and guarantees conditions of formation of subjective aspect of honour and dignity, i.e. self-respect, a correct estimation a person of public opinion about them.

The self-estimation by a person of their public importance cannot directly be regulated by legal provisions but this self-estimation can become a reality only under certain social conditions. Even V. Belinsky indignantly wrote about imperial Russia, "where people themselves were called by nicknames: Vanjka, Vasjka, Steshka, Palashka" where there were no "guarantees for a person and honour".[19]

Originality of dignity as objects of the constitutional protection is that these valuable personal values are protected not only by means of a subjective fundamental right on honour and dignity but also by the system of all constitutional rights, freedoms and duties. Thus, infringement of any of the rights (for example, illegal imprisonment, a search, an illegal dismissal from work, discrimination on political, national, religious grounds) as a rule is considered as an encroachment on honour and dignity of a citizen.

Hegel noted, "The self-respect of a person and respect for them of others are proportional to the size of the community to which this person relates to".[20]

The high importance of the given right and that honour and dignity, being the important element of social orientation of a person, promote education at citizens of feeling of civilization, the responsibility, act as motive and stimulus to performance of a public duty.

It is possible to emphasize two basic elements of this right:

1) The right of a citizen to respect from all state bodies, officials, public organizations, individuals;

2) The right to the deserved reputation, i.e. on the fair differentiated estimation of its acts, a way of life.

The legal regulations fixing the right to honour and dignity are rather numerous. They enter into all branches of the law. Among them the central place is occupied by international-legal and constitutionally-legal provisions.

Among international-legal provisions it is necessary to mark out; first of all, the Charter of the United Nations in which Preamble it is said that one of the purposes of this international organization is the aspiration to approve belief in dignity and value of a human being. In many clauses of the Charter the principle of respect for human rights and basic freedoms (Article 1, 8, 13, 55, 62) is fixed. The Universal Declaration of Human Rights begins with the concept of "dignity". Here two basic ideas connected with this concept are fixed: 1) dignity is inherent in all members of human family, i.e. to all people of world; 2) the concept of dignity, equal inalienable laws is a basis of freedom, validity and universal peace, i.e. the normal existence of mankind.

Clause 1 of the Universal Declaration of Human Rights fixes the following principle: equality of people in the dignity and the rights. From this point of view among Russian constitutional propositions what are fixed in Article 2 and 21 Constitutions of the Russian Federation have major importance. In first of them the following principle is recorded: "a person, their rights and freedoms are the maximum value". Here the term "dignity" is not used but it is the question of this category. In this case its maintenance is considered as one of general principles of the right, bases constitutional system and objects of the state protection. Besides, the rights and freedoms of a person are considered as an embodiment of idea of the maximum value of a person.

In Article 21 and part 1 Article 23 of the Constitution dignity and honour are fixed as human rights.

In Part 1 of Article 21 two provisions are fixed: "Dignity of a person is protected by the state. Nothing can be the basis for its belittling". In first of the indicated positions the constitutional principle is formulated as binding provision. Here it is emphasized that the state is the guarantor of the given right. In the second provision it is a question of inherence of the given right. And this part of Article 21 can be understood in a combination with part 3 of Article 56 of the Constitution where the right to dignity is listed among those constitutional rights which are not subject to limitation.

Part 1 of Article 23 of the Constitution where the human rights to protection of honour and a reputation are guaranteed, deserves the special analysis.

It seems that in above-stated clauses of the Constitution the uniform human rights to honour and dignity are recorded. Here already it is a question not of dignity of a person as general law a principle but as about the legal right.

Finally, the special role relates to part 2 of Article 21 of the Constitution of the Russian Federation.

There is the separate human right - the right to freedom from torture and other cruel, inhuman treatment or punishment to which one of the subsequent Chapters of this book is devoted. But in this constitutional provision there is the provision of the right to dignity: incompatibility of all kinds of violence, cruel treatment or degrading human dignity.

Finally, in the same part 2 of Article 21 it is written down: "Nobody can be subjected to medical, scientific or other experiences without the voluntary consent".

This principle opens new, arisen in the end the 20th - the beginning of the 21st century aspects of human dignity. In the modern world the grandiose international project "Human Genome" is carried out. Such programs are realized in the USA, Russia and in other countries. The Council of Europe, UNESCO, international organizations of scientists-physicians have accepted the special documents, devoted to these questions. New discoveries in the sphere of genetics open huge opportunities in treatment and prophylaxis of diseases. On the other hand, there are the dangers connected with use of the genetic information for discrimination of people. In the Declaration of Bilbao accepted at the meeting of international working group on legal aspects of the project "Human Genome" (1993), it was emphasized that in this sphere a new legal approach was necessary but it was not always realized. Progress of biotechnology, which speed gradually increases, makes their necessity still more urgent.[21]

UNESCO General Conference accepted on November, 11th, 1997 the Universal Declaration on the Human Genome and Human Rights.

The first section is called "human dignity and human rights". As it is emphasized in Article 1, "the human genome underlies the fundamental unity of all members of the human family, as well as recognition of their inherent dignity and diversity. The human genome is the heritage of humanity".[22]

The Declaration proclaims the right of each person to respect for their dignity and for their rights irrespective of their genetic characteristics. People cannot be reduced to their genetic characteristics (Article 2). This question is similarly solved in the Convention accepted by the Council of Europe on protection of rights and dignity of a person in connection with use of achievements of medicine: Convention on Human Rights and Biomedicine (1996) there it is indicated: "any form of discrimination on the basis of the genetic status of certain person is forbidden".[23]

Thus, it is possible to come to the following conclusion: in international law a new genetic understanding of universal dignity and equality of people in the dignity, irrespective of their genetic features is being formed.

Proving this thesis, authors of the Declaration of Bilbao wrote that in history there were a lot of the ingenious people who had those or other infringements but manage to achieved significant attainments (Milton, Goya, Beethoven).[24]

Besides, one more principle providing genetic safety of a person is formulated: intervention in a human genome, directed on its updating, can be carried out only in the preventive, therapeutic or diagnostic purposes and only provided that such intervention is not directed on change of genome of the descendants of the given person (Article 13 of the above-stated Convention of the Council of Europe).[25]

It seems that these new international-legal principles bring a new contents in the legal provisions fixed in Article 21 of the Constitution of the Russian Federation.

The analysis of the Constitution of the Russian Federation allows coming to the conclusion that in it there is legally recorded not only the right of a person to human dignity but also human right to dignity as a member of certain social group. Thus, Article 19 of the Constitution fixes equality of the rights and freedoms of a person and a citizen irrespective of sex, race, nationality, attitude to religion, believes and other circumstances. Here the term "dignity" but meaning of this constitutional provision is not used in providing equality of people, representatives of different social groups (men and women, representatives different racial, national, religious, etc.) in their dignity.

Finally, fixing such rights as a right to life, freedom and security of person, the right of defence of private life, the Constitution provides personal dignity. However, the degree of real maintenance of various aspects of the right to honour and dignity of a person in modern Russia is low.[26] Here we pass to a question of efficiency of guarantees of this right.

Problem of Guarantees of the Right to Honour and Dignity

Human rights to honour and dignity should be provided by system of guarantees: material, political, ideological.

We should dwell on legal guarantees in more detail. The domestic branch legislation provides the following legal guarantees of this right: criminal; criminal-remedial; civil; civil-remedial; the guarantees stipulated by propositions family, labour, of criminal law-executive and also administratively-legal guarantees. We should consider each kind of guarantees separately.

Criminal guarantees are the guarantees included in the propositions of the Criminal Code of the Russian Federation. First of all, the criminal legislation is based on the principle of humanism: punishment and other measures of criminal character used to a person, committed a crime, and cannot have the purpose of causing of physical sufferings or humiliation of human dignity.

Dignity can be considered, on the one hand as a universal value inherent in it from birth and on the other hand as dignity of separate social groups, nations, nationalities, a person, it is lawful to emphasize two kinds of criminal guarantees.

Firstly, the responsibility for all personal crimes can be referred to guarantees of the human right to dignity. Thus, the Criminal Code of the Russian Federation establishes the responsibility for the following crimes against life: murder, finishing before suicide, criminal causing damage to health, etc.

Secondly, Chapter 17 of the Criminal Code of the Russian Federation is directly devoted to crimes against freedom, honour and dignity and provides the corresponding responsibility for slander and insult.

The part of 2 of Clause 129 of the Criminal Code of the Russian Federation contains qualifying attributes among which there are: slander in the public performance {statement}, publicly shown product or mass media. In mass media it is necessary to understand the products discrediting honour and dignity of a citizen as slander, carried out in the typographical way, sounded on radio or TV.

The most dangerous kind of slander is the slander connected to charge in fulfillment heavy or especially of grave crime (part 3 Article 129 the Criminal Code of the Russian Federation).

The part of 2 clauses 130 Criminal Code provides The Russian Federation as qualifying attributes of the insult: deliberate humiliation honour and dignity in public performance, in publicly shown product or in mass media.

It is especially necessary to pay attention to clause 282 of the Criminal Code which has appeared in a new wording The Russian Federation "Excitation of hatred or enmity and the humiliation of human dignity" in which the responsibility including humiliation of dignity of a person or group of persons on the grounds of sex, race, a nationality, language, origin, attitude to religion, belonging to certain social group which is accomplished publicly or with use of mass media is established.

Criminally-remedial means of protection of human rights for dignity are stipulated by propositions of the Code of Criminal Procedure of the Russian Federation. One of principles of criminal legal proceedings is the respect to honour and dignity of a person (Article 9 of the Code of Criminal Procedure of the Russian Federation). Actions humiliating honour and dignity of a person and decisions integrated to violence, threats, offensive statements and also depriving a person from opportunities to defend and protect the rights and legitimate interests as an equal in rights of a subject should be admitted. As it was noted in the Decision of May, 3rd, 1995 4-P the Constitutional Court of the Russian Federation,[27] maintenance of dignity of a person presupposes that a person in their mutual relations with the state acts not as object of the state activity but as a subject equal in rights who can protect the rights in all ways not forbidden by the law and to argue with the state on behalf of any bodies. The given provision is directed on protection of a person, their honour and dignity first of all from abusing from those officials who are distinguished during the imperious powers allowing them to apply measures of compulsion concerning other participants of the process and to make other actions connected with limitation of the rights and freedoms of citizens. At the same time the above-stated principle presupposes a duty of bodies and the officials who are carrying out criminal legal proceedings, to take measures to protection of the rights and legitimate interests of participants of the process against encroachments of others.

As it is known, publicity as one of the major principles of legal procedure is proclaimed in part 1 of Article 123 of the Constitution of the Russian Federation, Article 241 of the Code of Criminal Procedure of the Russian Federation. Trial of affairs in all courts is open and hearing of affairs in a closed meeting is supposed in the cases stipulated by the Federal law.

Thus, at disposal of legal proceeding about crimes in the sphere of sexual relations and also about the crimes mentioning honour and dignity of a person, the court has to discuss in each case the question of carrying out of closed meeting, proceeding first of all from interests of the victim to which the open hearing of case can cause excessive moral sufferings.

Code of Criminal Procedure of the Russian Federation especially emphasizes that at reception of samples for comparative research methods which are dangerous to life and health of a person or humiliating their honour and dignity should not be used.

Civil--legal and civil-remedial guarantees are stipulated by propositions of the Civil Code of the Russian Federation and the Civil Remedial Code of the Russian Federation. In civil law the right to honour and dignity relates to the number of a personal non-right of property. The Civil Code of the Russian Federation attributes dignity of a person to the non-material values (Article 150 of the Civil Code) as, firstly, this concept is deprived from the property contents, it is impossible to estimate it in the Russian Federation in money terms and secondly, it is inseparably linked with a person of its bearer that means impossibility of its alienation.

Their civil protection is possible in two cases. Firstly, when the essence of the infringed non-right of property and character of consequences of this infringement supposes an opportunity to use general ways civil protection and, secondly, when for protection of these rights in the Civil Code of the Russian Federation or other laws are stipulated by special ways. Such special ways are established for protection of honour, dignity and business reputation of citizens in the form of a refutation of the widespread damning information. This way can be used if there is a set of the following conditions: 1) if data is widespread or should be widespread; 2) they should not correspond to the validity. Thus data is considered mismatching the reality until distributed they will be not proved by the return; 3) should be discrediting.

A citizen has a right to demand on court of a refutation discrediting their honour, dignity or business reputation of data if distributed such data will not prove that they correspond to the validity.

Plenum of the Supreme Court of the Russian Federation[28] pays attention to a number of problems which arise at courts by consideration of the given category of affairs. Thus, in cases of the given category citizens considering that about them damning information mismatching the reality are widespread have the right to bring an action (Article 152 of the Civil Code of the Russian Federation). The Supreme Court of the Russian Federation especially emphasizes that at distribution of damning information concerning lawful representatives minor or incapacitated for protection of their honour and dignity can bring an action. On demand of interested persons protection is supposed honour and dignity of a citizen and after their death.

At presentation of such claims it is not stipulated by the law the obligatory preliminary appealing with such requirement to the respondent, including the case when the claim is shown to the mass media, spreading the information indicated above. A citizen, concerning whom mass media published data striking their right or interest protected by the law, has a right to publication of the answer in the same mass media (Article 3, 7 Article 152 of the first part of the Civil Code of the Russian Federation).

The respondents under claims for a refutation of data discrediting honour and dignity or business reputation are persons spreading such information. If the claim contains the requirement about a refutation of data widespread in mass media the author and edition of corresponding mass media are involved as respondents. In case the editors of mass media are not legal persons, the founder of the given mass media should be involved in participation in case as a respondent.

In case actions of a person spreading information discrediting another person, contain attributes of the crime stipulated by Article 129 and 130 of the Criminal Code of the Russian Federation, the victim has a right to address in court with the statement for bringing the guilty to account and also to bring an action about protection of honour and dignity or business reputation by way of civil legal proceedings.

Thus, criminal guarantees of the given right are combined with civil ones.

The Civil Code of the Russian Federation specially marks outs the order of a refutation of damning information which have been widespread in mass media (Paragraph 2 of Article 152 of the Civil Code of the Russian Federation).

Presence of circumstances which by virtue of Article 57 of the law of the Russian Federation "On mass media"[29] can form the basis for condonation of the editors, the editor-in-chief, the journalist for distribution of data mismatching the reality both discrediting honour and dignity of citizens, does not exclude an opportunity of consideration by court of the claim of a citizen about a refutation of such data.

It is especially necessary to note that limitation of actions do not extend on the requirement about protection of honour, dignity, the business reputation, declared by paragraphs 1-3, 5-7 of Article 152 of the first part of the Civil Code of the Russian Federation.

According to paragraph 5, 7 of Article 152 of the first part of the Civil Code of the Russian Federation a citizen concerning whom spread information, discrediting honour, dignity or business reputation has a right to demand alongside with a refutation of such data the indemnification of the moral damage, caused by their distribution. Indemnification of moral damage the guilty official or a citizen or mass media is determined by court at making a decision in money terms. If damning information mismatching the reality has been widespread in mass media, court, determining the size of indemnification of moral damage, has a right to consider also the character and the contents of the publication, a degree of distribution of doubtful data and other worthy circumstances.

At default of the decision on case about protection of honour and dignity and also business reputation in the term established by court he has a right to impose the penalty claimed to the income of the state on the infringer.

The property and non-property damage which was caused by infringement of honour, dignity and business reputation is subject to compensation on the propositions included in Ch. 59 of the Civil Code of the Russian Federation (obligations owing to causing damage). According to these propositions the compensation of property damage (losses) is probable only at guilty distribution of data (Article 1064 of the Civil Code) and indemnification of moral damage is irrespective of fault (Article 1100 of the Civil Code). in addition to mentioned can be used and any other general ways of protection, in particular suppression of the actions breaking the right or creating threat of its infringement (withdrawal of circulation of a newspaper, magazine, book, prohibition of the publication of the second edition , etc.).

It is necessary to remark that civil protection of honour and dignity is widely used by citizens. Some cases of this kind were rather popular. Thus, during the election campaign of 1999 Mayor of Moscow Luzhkov sued on protection of honour and dignity the television leader Dorenko and has to gain a suit at law.

Specificity of the given right consists that its subjects are not only alive but also the dead people. Memory of a person cannot be discredited; their honour and dignity continue to remain object of legal protection. Several years ago the group of citizens addressed in court with the claim to a television channel of NTV with the claim in protection of Lenin's honour and dignity, to whose life and activity the television leader Kiselyov had devoted a special film. The court accepted the statement of claim, having recognized as that legitimacy of such claims. However, claimants could not result a sufficient legal substantiation of the claim requirements and the court has given up in the claim.

Special kinds of guarantees given to those rights which are stipulated *by propositions of the family law*. The Family Code of the Russian Federation refers to the number of the basics of this branch of the right the necessity to strengthen the family, building of family relations on feelings of mutual love and respect, maintenance of unobstructed realization with members of family of the rights (Article 1). The family law forbids any forms of discrimination of people at the introduction into marriage and in family relations, guarantees equality of spouses in family, equality of the rights and duties of parents (Article 1, 31, 61).

The Convention on the Rights of the Child (1989) is penetrated by idea of respect of human dignity of children, concept of their right to preservation of individuality. Chapter II of the Family Code of the Russian Federation implements in the domestic legislation the major legal rights of the child, recognizing their value as persons.

There are guarantees of the given right, stipulated *by propositions of the labour right*. Thus, the Labour Code of the Russian Federation fixes as main principle of legal regulation of labour relations enforcement of the right of workers on protection of the dignity during labour activity (Article 2).

The propositions of the labour right providing dignity of the worker also relate to this group of guarantees: freedom of work and an interdiction of forced labour and discrimination in the sphere of work, equality of the rights and opportunities of workers, protection of their personal data. As it is indicated in Article 86 of the Labour Code of the Russian Federation, "workers should not refuse the rights to preservation and protection of secret". The employer does not have the right to receive the information on political and other belief of the worker, their private life, a state of their health (if it does not concern the fulfillment of work).

Protection from unemployment and enforcement of the right on duly and full size payment of the fair salary providing worthy personal existence, is one of the most essential aspects of the right to dignity following from Article 11 of international Covenant on Economic, Social and Cultural Rights, Article 7, 37 of the Constitution of the Russian Federation, Article 2, 133, 142 of the Labour Code of the Russian Federation. Such phenomena as poverty of a significant part of a society, extinction of the population of Russia, grow out infringements of the indicated propositions, the roughest encroachment on dignity of a person.

There are guarantees of the labour rights of women and the workers who are under 18-years (Ch. 41 of the Labour Code of the Russian Federation) where the protection of their dignity is shown.

The guarantees established by the criminally-executive legislation are extremely important.

The criminally-executive legislation of the Russian Federation and practice of its use should be based on strict observance of guarantees of protection from torture, violence and cruel or degrading treatment of condemned (Article 3 of the Correctional Code of the Russian Federation). However, regular infringements of these propositions in places of imprisonment till now have not been overcome.

The Correctional Code of the Russian Federation establishes that condemned have the right to the polite treatment from a personnel of the establishment executing punishments. Measures of compulsion to condemned can be used precisely on the basis of the law. Condemned irrespective of their consent cannot be subjected to medical and other experiments threatening their life and health.

In the basis *of administratively-legal guarantees there is* a principle: administrative punishment cannot have for an object humiliation of human dignity of the physical person who has made an administrative offence, or causing to them of physical sufferings (Article 3.1).

There are different kinds of the indicated guarantees. Thus, Administrative Code of the Russian Federation establishes the responsibility for a unaccordance of an opportunity to promulgate a refutation or other explanation in protection of honour, dignity or business reputation (Article 5.13 of the Administrative Code). On the other hand, appearing of a person in public places in the state of intoxication offending human dignity and public morals, leads to the administrative responsibility (Article 20.21 of the Administrative Code).

The system of legal guarantees of the right to honour and dignity requires perfection. For these purposes in 1999 in the State Duma of Federal Assembly of the Russian Federation the bill of the Federal law was proposed "On constitutional law of citizens of the Russian Federation on protection of honour and dignity and on enforcement of this right by the state and a society"[30] by the State deputy I.D. Kobzon.

Necessity and the purpose of the given law were based on requirements of the state protection from all encroachments of honour and dignity of citizens in the widest value of the named values. Such protection has been dictated by the constitutional concept of priority of the rights and freedoms of a person and a citizen of the Russian Federation.

In essence, any encroachment on the rights and freedoms of a person and a citizen is infringement of human and civil dignity.

Necessity of acceptance of such law has been caused, first of all, by orientation to creating of a social lawful state which presupposes a complex of legislative and other measures under the statement in a real life of human values. in an explanatory note to the bill the need for the given law it was said that the current legislation didn't protect honour and dignity in full; it only fragmentary regulated separate displays of encroachments on these values and actually did not contain the propositions specially directed on creation of a mode of general respect for honour and dignity of a citizen of the Russian Federation, education of civilization. Experts in international-legal protection of the rights and personal freedoms and remedial features in consideration of a corresponding category of legal affairs.

Let's especially note that the given bill in many respects had innovative character, in a world practice there have not been such analogues.

If we address to the legal characteristic of the given bill it is possible to emphasize the following: it would be the Federal law as regulation of the rights and freedoms, according to Article 71 of the Constitution of the Russian Federation, concerning the conducting The Russian Federation; frame as in conformity from Article 72 of the Constitution of the Russian Federation protection of the rights and freedoms of a person and a citizen, maintenance of legality jointly conducting The Russian Federation and subjects of the Russian Federation. The law gives to subjects of the Russian Federation and representative bodies of local self-management an opportunity to develop establishments included in them in aspect of their fullest carrying out during life.

This law would have consolidating character as in them attempt to reduce many propositions included in various statutory acts is done in one instrument.

The structure and the contents of the given bill during its preparation varied. The disorder of opinions concerning the bill was rather significant: from complete support up to resolute aversion. The majority of experts were the Chapter of administrations and legislative assemblies of subjects of the Russian Federation which in the majority have approvingly met ideas of the bill. Thus, in opinion of governors Sverdlovsk, Novosibirsk, Ulyanovsk and some other areas, heads of some republics in structure of the Russian Federation, a legislature of subjects of the Russian Federation, the bill was important and duly. "Entirely I support suggested in the State Duma of Federal Assembly of the Russian Federation the given project of the Federal law as I consider that declared by the Constitution of the Russian Federation the right of citizens to protection of honour and dignity requires acceptance of the Federal law concretizing it" (D.F.Ayatskov). "(E.S.Savchenko) and completely agree with the text of the above-mentioned bill directed on protection of honour and dignity of citizens of Russia".

However, it is necessary to note that as a whole sharing ideas of the bill, many responses contained serious remarks and the offers which were sent to completion and processing of the bill.

Doubts in necessity of such law, accompanied criticism of its substantive provisions, have been stated to basics of the state-legal management of Administration of the President of the Russian Federation, Committee of Council of Federation under the constitutional legislation and judicial-legal questions, governmental body of the Russian Federation, a number of legislative assemblies of subjects of Federation.

Many remarks have been considered and the given bill has been accepted in the first reading in the following kind. The project consisted of a preamble, five Chapters and 22 clauses.

In the Chapter "General Provisions" the basics of a state policy in the field of the statement and protection of honour, dignity, reputation and a reputation of a citizen (Article 1 of the project) have been formulated. Attempt is made to determine much more precisely and more particularly, on the one hand, the duties of the state on creation of a mode of general respect for honour and dignity of each citizen and on the other hand, the duties of a citizen in relation to the state.

By means of the category of honour and dignity the civil meaning of service to Fatherland (Article 2) is revealed. in this Chapter guarantees and the bases of occurrence of the right of defence of honour and dignity of a citizen (Article 4,5) ; principles of protection of honour and dignity of a citizen (Article 6); the responsibility for encroachments on honour and dignity of a citizen (Article 7) are also formulated.

Special contents of Chapter II "On maintenance of constitutional law of citizens on protection of honour and dignity" in which propositions are placed, binding corresponding institutions of a civil society, the state bodies, mass media to the activity forming necessary personal qualities of a citizen.

Protection especially regulated honour and dignity of a citizen outside Russia (Chapter III). In Chapter IV the attempt to formulate a guarantee of execution of the given law is made. In final provisions of the law (Chapter V) the propositions connected with its coming into force and action are contained.

Those social expectations attract attention which the authors of the project wished to see from acceptance of the given law. Developers of the bill considered that acceptance of the law and its carrying out during life will promote increase of civil consciousness, understanding a citizen of the Russian Federation of the place and a role in life of Russia; to real warranting of the rights and freedoms of a person and a citizen, in particular appropriate state protection of dignity of citizens.

It is possible to agree with many ideas and views of the authors of the given project. However, the bill was criticized in some respect and, unfortunately, was not accepted in the second reading by the State Duma. Therefore now in Russia there is no special law fixing mechanisms of protection and guarantees of human rights to protection of honour and dignity. We wish that such law were accepted. As it will allow creating more favorable conditions for protection of human dignity in our country.

Notes

1. Quoted on: Einstein I. Dignity in Legal Philosophy. S.-Petersburg, 1895. P. 79. / Цит. по: Эйнштейн И. Честь в философии права. СПб., 1895. С. 79.

2. Marx K. Forms Preceding Capitalist Production, 1940. P. 30. / Маркс К. Формы, предшествующие капиталистическому производству. М., 1940. С. 30.

3. Sketch of History of Ethics / Edited by B.A. Chagin, M.I. Shahnovich, Z.N. Meleshchenko, Moscow, 1969. P. 21. / Очерк истории этики / Под ред. Б. А. Чагина, М. И. Шахновича, З. Н. Мелещенко. М., 1969. С. 21.

4. Dhammapada. 1960. P. 125.

5. Bowl of wisdom. Aphorisms, sayings of domestic and foreign authors, 1978. P. 41. / Чаша мудрости. Афоризмы, высказывания отечественных и зарубежных авторов. М., 1978. С. 41.

6. See: Dushenko K.V. Thoughts and sayings of the ancient with the indication of a source, 2003. P. 553. / См.: Душенко К. В. Мысли и изречения древних с указанием источника. М., 2003. С. 553.

7. Locke J. The Selected Philosophical Works. Vol. 2. P. 16, 34. / Локк Д. Избранные философские произведения. Т. 2. С. 16, 34.

8. Hobbes T. The Selected Works: in 2 vol., 1964. Vol. 2. P. 118. / Гоббс Т. Избранные произведения: В 2 т. М., 1964. Т. 2. С. 118.

9. Marx K., Engels F. Compilation of works. 2nd edition. Vol. 4. P. 426. / Маркс К., Энгельс Ф. Сочинения. 2-е изд. Т. 4. С. 426.

10. Rousseau J.-J. Treatises, 1969. P. 152, 471.

11. Voltaire F. M. Ideas. S.-Petersburg, 1904. P. 28.

12. Masters of aphorisms, Moscow, 2001. P. 129. / Мастера афоризмов. М., 2001. С. 129.

13. Kant I. Compilation of works: in 6 vol., 1965. Vol. 4. Part 1. P. 415. / Кант И. Сочинения: В 6 т. М., 1965. Т. 4. Ч. 1. С. 415.

14. Feuerbach L. Selected Philosophical Works, 1955. Vol. 2. P. 308. / Фейербах Л. Избранные философские произведения. М., 1955. Т. 2. С. 308.

15. Quoted on: Bykhovsky B.E. Kierkegaard, Moscow, 1972. P. 94-97. / Цит. по: Быховский Б. Э. Кьеркегор. М., 1972. С. 94–97.

16. Ibidem. P. 199.

17. Marx K., Engels F. Compilation of works. 2nd edition. Vol. 23. P. 623.

18. Chernyshevsky N.G. Full Compilation of works. Vol. 3. P. 137. / Чернышевский Н. Г. Полн. собр. соч. Т. 3. С. 137.

19. Belinsky V.G. Selected works, Moscow, Leningrad. 1949. P. 890. / Белинский В. Г. Избранные сочинения. М.; Л., 1949. С. 890.

20. Hegel G.V. Political works, 1978. P. 89. / Гегель Г. В. Политические произведения. М., 1978. С. 89.

21. See: Ethical and Legal Aspects of the Project "Human Genome" (international documents and analytical materials), Moscow, 1998. P. 45. / См.: Этико-правовые аспекты проекта «Геном человека» (международные документы и аналитические материалы). М., 1998. С. 45.

22. Ibidem. P. 102.

23. Ibidem. P. 88.

24. See: Ibidem. P. 43.

25. See: Ibidem. P. 89.

26. See: Report on Activity of the Commissioner for Human Rights in the Russian Federation in 1999, 2000. / См.: Доклад о деятельности Уполномоченного по правам человека в РФ в 1999 г. М., 2000.

27. See: Decision of the Constitutional Court of the Russian Federation of5/3/1995 4-P "On the case of check of constitutionality of the clauses 220.1 and 220.2 of the Criminally-Remedial Code of RSFSR in connection with the complaint of the citizen V.A. Avetjan" // Bulletin of the Constitutional Court of the Russian Federation. 2-3.1995. / См.: Постановление Конституционного Суда РФ от 03.05.1995 № 4-П «По делу о проверке конституционности статей 220.1 и 220.2 Уголовно-процессуального кодекса РСФСР в связи с жалобой гражданина В. А. Аветяна» // Вестник Конституционного Суда РФ. № 2–3. 1995.

28. Concerning some questions arisen by Court consideration of cases of protection of honour and dignity as well as business reputation of citizens and legal persons: Decision of Plenum of the Supreme Court of the Russian Federation of 8/18/1992 11 (Edit. of 4/25/1995) // Bulletin of the Supreme Court of the Russian Federation. 1992. #11. / О некоторых вопросах, возникших при рассмотрении судами дел о защите чести и достоинства граждан, а также деловой репутации граждан и юридических лиц: Постановление Пленума Верховного Суда РФ от 18.08.1992 г. № 11 (ред. от 25.04.1995 г.) // Бюллетень Верховного Суда РФ. 1992. № 11.

29. On mass media: Law of the Russian Federation of 12/27/1991 2124-1 (Edit. of 12/8/2003) // Sheets of SND and SC of the Russian Federation. 1992. # 7. Article 300. / О средствах массовой информации: Закон РФ от 27.12.1991 г. № 2124-1 (ред. от 08.12.2003 г.) // Ведомости СНД и ВС РФ. 1992. № 7. Ст. 300.

30. See: On the bill "On the constitutional law of citizens of the Russian Federation on protection of honour and dignity and about maintenance of this right with the state and a society": Decision of the State Duma of Federal Assembly of the Russian Federation

of 3/10/1999 3728-II GD // Sheets of the Federal Assembly of the Russian Federation. 1999. # 9. Article 612. / См.: О проекте Федерального закона «О конституционном праве граждан РФ на защиту чести и достоинства и об обеспечении этого права государством и обществом: Постановление Государственной Думы Федерального Собрания РФ от 10.03.1999 г. № 3728-II ГД // Ведомости Федерального Собрания РФ. 1999. № 9. Ст. 612.

Chapter 5.   THE RIGHT TO PERSONAL IMMUNITY

§ 1.   Concept of the Right to Personal Immunity

The right to personal immunity is one of the most ancient ones. The indication on the right of the accused to be released under a condition of the guarantee was included into the treatise of Glanville about laws and customs of England (12th century). Rudiments of this right are recorded in Magna Carta (1215).

During then epoch of bourgeois revolutions of 17th -18th centuries it found the legal embodiment in British Habeas Corpus Act (1679), in the French Declaration of Civil Human Rights (1789) (Article 2, 7), in the American Bill of Rights (Amendments IV, V) (1791). Despite some distinctions in principles on which these historical documents are constructed, the right to personal immunity was considered by them as set of guarantees from illegal imprisonment and judicial arbitrariness as one of "freedom-limitations".

The Universal Declaration of Human Rights (Article 3, 9), International Covenant on Civil and Political Rights (Article 9, 10, 11), regional international documents record this right today.

French political scientist Burdeau G. saw the content of personal safety (surete) in the fact, "that any person cannot be detained in another way than is stipulated by the law"[1]. He connected freedom of a person with personal safety to exist without risk, freedom of movement, personal physical freedom, a guarantee against imprisonment, detention, criminal sentences.[2]

In the Great Britain, the USA and some other western countries the problem of personal immunity, as a rule, is connected with the procedure of Habeas Corpus.[3]

The majority of modern constitutions proclaim personal immunity (for example, Article 22 of the Constitution of the Russian Federation, Article 2 of the Organic Law of Germany, Article 33 of the Constitution of Japan, etc.) but this right is regularly broken in many countries of world.

The question of the right to personal immunity in domestic legal, and mainly, in state - legal literature has its history. E.A. Elistratov in 1922 defined the given right as "the complex of the legal regulations determining the limit for intrusion of the government into the area of physical inviolability of a person … by means of which the known divide of the state compulsion is reached".[4] The right to personal immunity acts here as a guarantee from illegal actions of the state bodies and officials. In essence, E.A. Elistratov was within the limits of traditional understanding of this question which existed in Russian pre-revolutionary literature and in the literature of the period of revolution. B.A. Kistyakovsky considered personal immunity as lawful limit for powers of authorities to suppress infringement of law in a lawful state.[5] B.P. Vysheslavtsev in 1917 wrote that it is "the right to demand that the government did not concern a person of citizens unless they do something illegal".[6]

But there was also another, wider understanding of the problem. In 1917 of P.I. Lublinsky determined personal immunity as "the right basing on understanding the opportunity to act and work in conformity with the belief within the limits set by the law, not being afraid of violent counteraction from authority or private persons".[7]

Thus, the attention was drawn not only to the question of protection from illegal state-imperious compulsion but also from compulsion in relations between separate citizens. However, "the right to work in conformity with the belief" about which P.I. Lublinsky wrote in his article, characterizes not personal rights to which the right to personal immunity refers, but freedom of speech, freedom of press and other political rights. In this case limits of the concept of personal immunity are excessively expanded.

In the Encyclopedia of the State and the Law published in 1926 the author of the clause concerning personal immunity A.S. Gluzman determined it as follows, "Personal immunity in the broad meaning aims at ensuring of individual freedom and legal protection of everyone from arbitrariness of others. In the narrow sense personal immunity aims at ensuring the ensuring of an individual from any imprisonment and detention, or as said in Article 5 of the Code of Criminal Procedure, "nobody can be imprisoned and detained otherwise than in the cases indicated in the law and by the law".[8]

In our opinion, it is right to emphasize that personal immunity cannot be considered only in criminally-remedial aspect as freedom from any imprisonment and detention. The concept of personal immunity in the wide sense, about which A.S. Gluzman wrote, contains a number of rational items. In particular, the right indicated in general plan is connected with individual freedom and represents legal protection not only from arbitrariness of the state bodies but also from other subjects. As a whole, A.S. Gluzman was, certainly, closer to truth than P.I. Lublinsky. But at the same time in some respects the definition of A.S. Gluzman is vulnerable. Apart from personal immunity, inviolability of dwelling and privacy of correspondence are also connected with individual freedom. In interpretation of A.S. Gluzman the right to personal immunity does not have specific features, and it is not separated from other rights of person, almost merging with them.

In courses and textbooks on the state (constitutional) law, published in 1930-60s, as a rule, the right to personal immunity was considered as freedom of a citizen from any arbitrary imprisonment[9] or as their right to defence by the state from illegal imprisonment.[10]

Remaining within the limits of traditional understanding of personal immunity, authors of the textbooks published in 1938 and 1948, saw in the content of this right not only freedom from illegal imprisonment but also guarantees from illegal searches, seizure, surveys of personal correspondence and other measures limiting personal freedom of a citizen.[11] Personal immunity was almost identified by them with wide patrimonial concept of personal constitutional rights.

In the legal literature of 1970-90-s there also attempts to define the right to personal immunity. "As personal immunity, as V.A. Ivanov wrote, it is necessary to understand free, not dependent on someone's will the state of a citizen at which he can realize at own discretion the rights belonging to them and assigned to them. It is quite obvious that the main attribute of a considered status is the freedom of movement, visiting those places with which the satisfaction of these or another needs of a person is connected. Deprivation of the right to personal immunity means also deprivation an individual of freedom".[12]

The relations of the right to personal immunity do not raise the doubts in this formulation as "status of a citizen". Any legal right is a kind and a measure of possible behaviour. A status is possible to call not the right but its constant realization. Thus, V.A. Ivanov, obviously, says not about the legal right but about its realization. It is also incorrect to see the meaning of the indicated right that a citizen can realize at own discretion as the right to act. As N.I. Matuzov remarks, the right serves as an official criterion of operating freedom, its provision, and the index of borders of due and possible.[13]

Existence of any legal right in general presupposes that a person knows opportunities of a choice.

One of stages of realization of any freedom is freedom of will connected with all set of the legal rights and legal duties of citizens, including with the right to personal immunity.

It is impossible to agree with the statement of V.A. Ivanov that freedom of movement is the main attribute of the right to personal immunity as freedom of movement is the independent legal institution recording the specific personal right.

Obviously, the connection between personal immunity and freedom of movement exists, as a rule, limitation of the first right (for example, custody) automatically entails limitation of the second. But, on the other hand, not always limitation of freedom of movement means also limitation of the right to personal immunity (for example, a recognizance not to leave). Anyway, to include freedom of movement in the content of the right to personal immunity means to admit displacement different by the legal nature and sociopolitical purpose of rights of person.

Somewhat the given lack was inherent and I.P. Gorshenev which saw meaning of the right to personal immunity in ensuring to each citizen of individual freedom and safety, relative independence in questions of free choice of a place of stay, occupation, etc.[14] In our opinion, freedom of choice of occupation is an element of the right to freedom of work.

In the master's thesis I.P. Gorshenev has even more moved beyond the frameworks of the right to personal immunity, in fact, including in its content parliamentary immunity but calling it "a special personal immunity".[15] A.A. Bezuglov also connected personal immunity with parliamentary immunity.[16] Apparently, the reason of such rapprochement or identification of the concepts roots in the term "inviolability". But more close examination of this question leads to other conclusions.

Historically deputy immunity appeared considerably earlier than personal immunity. According to the expert on the British parliamentary procedure T.E. May, "the privilege of freedom from imprisonment and detention" was known in England in the end of the 6th century, during Ethelbert.[17]

But the main distinction is in social purpose of these institutions. In fact, the term "inviolability" concerns here different subjects of social relations. In one case it is a question of inviolability of an individual, in other is a member of national notion. The right to personal immunity provides personal safety of individuals. The right of parliamentary immunity is intended for other purposes. Its purpose, as M.A. Ameller wrote, is "to guarantee trouble-free work and full independence of parliament. Immunity is established in interests of parliament, rather than in personal interests of its members".[18]

In all constitutions the provisions providing personal immunity and the provisions describing deputy immunity are recorded in different clauses and represent different institutions. As an individual a person elected as a deputy of the parliament, certainly, uses the right to personal immunity. As to guarantees of parliamentary immunity they are given by the special law to a deputy and create conditions for normal activity of the parliament. Hence, there are no bases to consider parliamentary immunity as "a special personal immunity".

However, let us come back to the definition of I.P. Gorshenev. There are, certainly, some positive aspects in it, and first of all that he included in the content of personal immunity personal safety (to tell the truth, he puts it out of the limits of individual freedom, while personal safety, in our opinion, is one of its major aspects). The idea supported by him on the necessity to emphasize physical (corporal) and mental (moral) inviolability is rather fruitful. The definition given by L.D. Voevodin seems also interesting in this respect. He considered the right to personal immunity as a right of each citizen to the state protection and protection from criminal encroachment of anybody for the life, health, freedom, honour and dignity.[19] The right to personal immunity is connected by L.D. Voevodin with a right protection from the state (the idea, formulated by A.S. Gluzman in 1926). However, in this regard personal safety is not considered as a social value, which, in our opinion, should be on the first place in the list of objects of protection.

Personal safety is included in the definition suggested by V.A. Patulin. Personal immunity (legal institution) was determined by him as a set of legal provisions providing criminal, criminally-remedial, administratively-legal, civil and other means of ensuring by the state of an opportunity of a person to freely to dispose of oneself, protection and protection of the life, health, individual freedom and safety, honour and dignity against illegal encroachment of anybody.[20]

Basically, it is possible to agree with the given definition though it also has some discrepancies. Thus, in listing of means of protection of the given right (criminal, criminally-remedial, etc.) the state-legal is not called. Besides, individual freedom is put in one line with life, health, personal safety, etc. while all of them are aspects of individual freedom.

And it is possible to find different approaches in the modern scientific literature to definition of the right to personal immunity. First is the wide approach when in its content protection of life, health, honour, dignity (M. V. Baglay) or freedom of movement (E.I. Kozlova) are included. Second is the narrow one, which is reduced to understanding of this right as inadmissibility of illegal limitation of freedom.[21]

The basic approaches to understanding of the right to personal immunity, the 20th century developed in the domestic literature are the following.

In modern conditions this concept cannot be formulated without taking into account internationally-legal regulations concerning human rights. In Article 9 of International Covenant on Civil and Political Rights, Article 5 of the European Convention on Protection of Rights and Basic Freedoms is a question of the right to freedom and security of person. In such edition this right is formulated in Article 22 of the Constitution of the Russian Federation (1993). Analyzing practice of the European Court on Human Rights, D. Gomien, D. Harris and L. Zvaak wrote: "Frequently terms "liberty" or "freedom" are given in connection with the concept which is much wider in comparison with what covers the given provisions of the Convention. In Article 5 which is the most important among these provisions, it is a question of deprivation of physical freedom. Clause 5 guarantees mainly freedom from any imprisonment and detention".[22] Thus, the indicated authors refer to the decision of the European Commission of Human Rights (1978) on the case Arrowsmith vs. the United Kingdom on which this commission balanced the right to freedom and inviolability.

Thus, it is possible to emphasize the following versions of the concept "freedom":

1) in the narrow sense, i.e. physical freedom which can be limited by detention and imprisonment (in the spirit of Article 5 of the European Convention); 2) in a more wide sense, i.e. as individual freedom (not political, social, etc.) in which the whole system of civil rights is expressed; 3) in the widest sense, i.e. as freedom which is embodied in the whole system of human rights. In such meaning the term "freedom" is used in the first paragraph of the Preamble of the Universal Declaration of Human Rights.

It seems that in part 1 of Article 22 of the Constitution of the Russian Federation there is a question of two rights: the right to individual freedom and the right to personal immunity. Such conclusion can be mad, after analyzing of the new Code of Criminal Procedure of the Russian Federation (2002) which used the term "personal immunity" (Article 10) in understanding of this right traditionally for our country, i.e. as freedom from false imprisonment and custodial placement. Obviously, the legislator interprets Article 22 of the Constitution in this way.

In our opinion, the right to personal immunity is the legal right of each person recorded in the Constitution to the state protection and protection from illegal encroachment of anybody on the freedom and personal safety.

Regarding personal safety it is possible to emphasize three kinds of inviolability: physical (life, health, corporal integrity), moral (honour, dignity) and cultural (the opportunity on the basis of freedom of will to have the acts not to be subjected to illegal compulsion). The indicated social values are essential aspects of individual freedom of a citizen.

The given provisions were put forward by the author of this chapter in 1976[23] and recognized in the modern literature by a number of authors (A.P. Morozov, K. Eckstein, etc.).

The detailed substantiation of this definition can be given only by consideration of the content of the right to personal immunity.

§ 2. Content of the Right to Personal Immunity

The content of the right to personal immunity is described in internationally-legal regulations and the Constitution of the Russian Federation.

In Articles 3, 9 of the Universal Declaration of Human Rights the principle of personal immunity and its essential element is recorded as follows: freedom from any imprisonment, detention or exile.

These provisions are developed in Article 9 of the International Covenant on Civil and Political Rights in more detail.

It is necessary to add to it Article 11 where guarantees of freedom from debt servitude are formulated, emphasizing inadmissibility of imprisonment on grounds of default by the debtor of the contracture obligation.

Thus, the International Covenant on Civil and Political Rights marks out the following elements of personal immunity: 1) The right to freedom from arbitrary, i.e. groundless, unmotivated imprisonment and detention; 2) The right to freedom from illegal imprisonment; 3) The right to freedom from debt servitude.

The originality of the European Convention for the Protection of Human Rights and Basic Freedoms means that it not only reproduces the basic elements of the content of the right to personal immunity but records its guarantees in more detail. In particular, in part 1 of Article 5 of the Convention thee kinds of lawful imprisonment and detention of persons and also the right to complain (guaranteed in part 4 of Article 5) are listed.

The Constitution of the Russian Federation (1993) briefly reproduces logic structure of the content of the given right recorded in internationally-legal documents. In part 1 of Article 22 of the Constitution a principle of personal immunity is proclaimed. In part 2 it is said, "Imprisonment, custody and holding in custody are supposed only under a court decision. Prior to a court decision a person cannot be subjected to detention for the term of more than 48 hours". Here it is a question of guarantees of freedom from illegal imprisonment or detention.

Obviously, all kinds of administrative and criminally-remedial limitations of such type are meant under the terms "imprisonment" and "detention". The term "custody" has only criminally-remedial meaning. As to the constitutional term "holding in custody" it, in our opinion, covers all kinds of imprisonment (holding in custody of the accused, imprisonment of the condemned).

Theoretical consideration of a question of the content of the right to personal immunity in the domestic literature was connected with certain difficulties. At the analysis of the Soviet Constitutions among theorists there was no common opinion on this question. Thus, I.P. Gorshenev in the above-mentioned works totaled three elements in the right to personal immunity: the right to individual freedom, the right to defence of life and health, the right to necessary defense. I.E. Farber has increased the number of these elements up to five: the right of a citizen to legal protection from bodies of the state and bodies of public organizations; the right to personal freedom and safety, guarantees from any imprisonment; the right of defence in court; the right to necessary defense; the right to inviolability of dwelling.[24]

It is difficult to agree with such opinions that the right of defence in court and the right to inviolability of dwelling are independent constitutional rights, rather than elements of personal immunity. As to the right of necessary defense it is criminal institution and the right to personal immunity is state-legal. The right to necessary defense is used not only for protection of interests of one person but also of other persons, and the state. Therefore, it is not absorbed by the content of the right to personal immunity and can be considered only as one of criminal guarantees of rights of person (the right to personal immunity and inviolability of dwelling).

The right to legal protection is connected not only with personal immunity but also with the whole system of the legal rights of citizens and consequently it is considered as an independent fundamental law. Thus, the legal rights, which I.E. Farber and I.P. Gorshenev considered as elements of personal immunity, have quite independent value and do not refer to the given constitutional law.

Subsequently the right to legal protection was included in the Constitution of the Russian Federation (1993) as a separate right (Article 46, 48).

Similarly to any legal right the right to personal immunity consists of the right-requirement, the right to positive actions which are expressed in using certain social values and the rights-claims. The right-requirement in this case means that the opportunity to demand from the state bodies is given to a citizen, officials, public organizations, individuals of observance of a legal duty not to break their personal safety, an opportunity to have honour and dignity.

In the content of the indicated competence it is necessary to emphasize two aspects:

Freedom from illegal and unreasonable imprisonment, detention, personal searches, witnessing and other precautionary measures used by the state bodies and officials;

Freedom from criminal encroachment of individuals' life, health, and corporal inviolability of a person.

Division goes on subjects who can act as infringers of the right: or agents of the government (the state bodies, officials), or private persons.

In abusing by separate state bodies and officials there is no necessity in see a unique threat to the right to personal immunity, limiting its content by measures of judicial control over imprisonment in the spirit of the Anglo-Saxon concept of Habeas Corpus.

It is impossible to see in personal immunity only legal means forms of protection of the rights of the imprisoned who the offender, as a rule, is.

Subjects of this right are all persons (citizens, foreign citizens, and stateless persons). Freedom from encroachment of any offenders for life, health and personal safety of an individual is the major part of this right. Inevitability of the legal responsibility for crimes and other offences against a person is provided by the activity of law enforcement bodies directed on struggle against dangerous crimes: murders, physical injuries, rapes, etc. that carries out the provisions recorded in Article 22 of the Constitution of the Russian Federation.

It would be simplification of the question to believe that in any case when the court determines sentence in the form of imprisonment, it negatively affects realization of the right to personal immunity and if criminal sentence is not connected with imprisonment it is positive. Superficial liberation from the sentence of the dangerous criminal encroaching on safety of citizens stipulated by the law, threatens the opportunity of normal realization of their right to personal immunity. And, on the contrary, deprivation of this criminal of freedom on the basis of the law promotes strengthening of a regime of legality, the law and order, protection of personal safety of citizens.

The second competence of each legal right is the right to positive actions and it is the main thing in the legal right. It is necessary to note also that the right to positive actions merges here with the right to use certain social values.

Feature of the right to personal immunity consists in the fact that it is directed mainly on ensuring and protection of personal safety of a citizen. Personal safety is an acute status of an individual at which they are guaranteed against any illegal encroachment on their corporal, moral and cultural inviolability. Personal safety is the important social value assuming absence of illegal violence or threat of personal violence and giving confidence, calmness, opportunities of participation in all spheres of social life.

The idea of protection of personal safety was put forward in 17th century by V. Blackstone and Ch. Montesquieu. But even earlier, in 17th century, J. Locke saw problems of the state in ensuring, preservation and achievement of own civil interests, to which they referred life, freedom, health and absence of corporal sufferings and also the property.[25] At V. Blackstone's the doctrine about personal safety gets the finished legal form. Distinguishing the right of personal safety (the right of personal security) and the right of personal freedom (the right of personal liberty), he wrote, "the right of personal safety consists in lawful and continuous having life, members of the body, the health and the reputation by a person".[26] As for the right of personal freedom, it consisted "in traficability, change of a situation or movement of any person in any place at own will without imprisonment or limitation which are admissible only after appropriate lawful procedure".[27]

Virtually, the right to personal safety at V. Blackstone's is rather close to the modern wide concept of the right to personal immunity. Here it is possible to see also rudiments of the right to life, health, honour and dignity. Criminally-remedial aspect of personal immunity and freedom of movement is seen in the right to personal freedom.

Ch. Montesquieu in the well-known work "Spirit of Laws" raised personal safety up to the level of political freedom, identifying these concepts. "Political freedom, as he wrote, consists in our safety or, at least, in our confidence that we are in safety".[28] Ch. Montesquieu gave special attention to criminal and criminally-remedial guarantees, in particular to high quality of criminal laws, the best rules of legal proceedings. "If innocence of citizens is not protected, the freedom is not protected either".[29]

The problem of safety excited also some other philosophers and lawyers. For example, V. Humboldt considered safety as "confidence of natural freedom".[30] Significant value of safety was seen by K. Marx, recognizing as its maximum social concept of a civil society.[31]

It is necessary to remark that the right to personal safety is legally recorded in the European Convention on Protection of Rights and Basic Freedoms (Article 5) and it is considered in these documents as a synonym of personal immunity.

The right to personal immunity is not unique legal means of ensuring personal safety of citizens. And other human rights, and constitutional rights (for example, the right to life, the rights of the accused) and also the rights established by the current legislation (the right of necessary defense, etc.), guarantee personal safety.

On the other hand, the right to personal immunity is in a meaning directed on protection of some other social values, for example to honour and dignity of citizens. Thus, illegal imprisonment represents not only encroachment on personal safety but also on personal dignity of a citizen. Interests of personal safety nevertheless are solving at definition of sociopolitical purpose of the indicated right. It is more distinctly shown at comparison of the rights of personal immunity and inviolability of dwelling (Article 25 of the Constitution of the Russian Federation).

Guaranteeing from unreasonable searches and other illegal intrusions into a house of a citizen, the right of inviolability of dwelling protects also personal safety but in the foreground there are other social values: opportunity of an individual, private life and privacy of a person.

Let's consider three aspects of personal safety: physical, moral and cultural personal immunity.

Physical and moral personal immunity were distinguished by I. P. Gorshenev (in the above-mentioned dissertation). However, they did not connect this question of personal safety and did not found this classification in detail.

As to protection of life and health, i.e. physical inviolability as the component of personal safety we see in it, first of all, the protection from violent actions from offenders. This aspect of personal safety is provided, first of all, by means of the right to life. As to the right to personal immunity it, being freedom from any illegal compulsion to a person, creates conditions for ensuring of inviolability of the life and health.

Moral inviolability is an acute status at which there are absent illegal compulsion or threats of such compulsion encroaching on honour and dignity of a person.

Moral inviolability presupposes protection of honour and dignity of a person. Dignity and honour are ethical categories, the major social values, being object of legal protection, in particular, in the civil and criminal legislation, on what we wrote in the previous chapter.[32]

The modern Russian Constitution records the rights to dignity, honour, reputation (Article 21, 23). These are the special rights having the wide content, various forms of realization and protection. As to moral inviolability as the component of personal safety it expresses only one aspect: inadmissibility of violent encroachment on honour and dignity of a person.

Cultural but, nevertheless, different concepts are closely connected with moral inviolability. If, for example, a person, wishing to offend another one, will give him a slap in the face (the assault) the attempt at a moral personal immunity will take place.

If someone forces the witness or of the accused to give false testimonies, then the cultural inviolability will act as an object of encroachment.

Cultural inviolability is the acute status excluding an opportunity to use illegal compulsory methods of influence by means of which opinions of a citizen, their ideas; court decision can be presented in the deformed, forged kind or are suppressed.

M. A.Cheltsov-Bebutov saw one of guarantees of the rights of the accused in criminal trial in freedom of mentality of the accused, their opportunities to self-determination, to determine the remedial behaviour within the limits of position of the accused.[33] Virtually, here is a talk about cultural inviolability with reference to the accused but the same it is possible to speak about of the suspected, the victim, the witness. Freedom of mentality, an opportunity of self-determination, to determine the position within the law are generally guaranteed to a citizen in all spheres of social life. The legal principle is well-known: the violence over receiving of indications cannot be used to anybody. In our opinion, this important legal establishment characterizes one of the essential aspects of the right to personal immunity.

The value of criminally-remedial and criminalist aspects of the problem of cultural inviolability is especially great. During preliminary investigation the inspector renders certain mental influence on the interrogated, of the accused, the victim, the witness but this influence, certainly, cannot act in the form of mental violence.

Criminalist science and investigatory practice have developed various tactical methods of lawful psychological influence with the purpose to receive from the interrogated truthful indications: a method of exposure, a method of belief, a method of an example, etc. However, it is impossible to use breach of confidence, falsifications, threats and other methods of an illegal encroachment on cultural inviolability interrogated.

Cultural inviolability is connected with using the major social values as an opportunity of a citizen to dispose of oneself. This opportunity is considered in this case only in sphere individual but not political or social freedom.

The opportunity to dispose of one consists in aspect of the right to personal immunity that a person free but within the law determines the behaviour in sphere moral-household and private life.

The important element of any legal right is assertion of right, i.e. the guaranteed opportunity of its protection. Assertion of right it is realized in the right of a citizen to address in the state bodies and organizations with complaints, statements and requests for protection from illegal encroachment. The given competence is indicated in international, constitutional law, in criminally-remedial, administrative legislation guaranteeing the rights of victims of crimes (victims), detained, detained, imprisoned. First of all, it is provided by means of constitutional rights on the state, judicial protection and the qualified legal aid (Article 45, 46, 48 Constitutions of the Russian Federation).

Special value of criminally-remedial provisions making institution of excitation of criminal case (has the section VII of the Code of Criminal Procedure of the Russian Federation 2002). These provisions regulate the procedure of consideration of corresponding treatment of citizens. On the other hand, the institution of the right of the complaint provides the rights of all persons, including the imprisoned persons, detained, and arrested (Ch. 16 of the Code of Criminal Procedure of the Russian Federation, Ch. 30 Administrative Code of the Russian Federation).

Thus, we see the following basic competences (elements) in the content of constitutional law of personal immunity: 1) Human right to physical inviolability (life, health, corporal integrity); 2) Human right to moral inviolability (honour, dignity, inadmissibility of illegal compulsory intervention in the moral-ethical sphere of life); 3) Human right to cultural inviolability (an opportunity to dispose of oneself in the sphere of individual freedom); 4) Human right to demand observance of legal duty not to encroach for the above-stated social values; 5) Human right to address with complaints and statements into the state bodies and international organizations with the request to protect the given legal right.

§ 3. Legal Nature of the Right to Personal Immunity

The right to personal immunity is a human right (a constitutional personal right) which assumes the presence at the state and international community of a duty to ensure the provision of personal safety of a citizen, i.e. life, health, corporal integrity, honour and dignity.

A.A. Piontkovsky considered this right "absolute".[34] However, for its realization only passive abstention of associates from its infringement that is characteristic for absolute civil rights is not enough. For realization of the right to personal immunity the vigorous activity of the state, especially bodies of the Ministry of Internal Affairs, on struggle against the criminals encroaching on personal safety of citizens is required.

There are a significant number of legal provisions recording of the right to personal immunity. Internationally-legal, constitutionally-legal, criminally-remedial, criminal, administratively-legal, administrative-remedial and also civil provisions.

Their core is in the provisions recorded in Article 22 of the Constitution of the Russian Federation. Therefore, the analysis of their internal structure has the greatest value. It seems that five constitutionally-legal provisions are recorded in this clause.

In the first part of the clause ("Everyone has a right to freedom and personal immunity") two provisions are recorded: the right to freedom and the right to personal immunity. In the scientific literature it was said that in this case it is a question of the uniform right.[35] Moreover, the court decision that the indicated uniform right includes other constitutional rights (inviolability of dwelling, freedom of movement, etc.) has become widespread.[36] And it is characteristic for some foreign researchers. Thus, F. Lusher refers to personal immunity the right to justice, endowment of persons, and legal protection of a person.[37]

However, the majority of experts on constitutional law estimate personal immunity as an independent constitutional law connected with the right to freedom but not identical with it.[38] And it is correct. At the whole internal affinity of freedom and inviolability they are different sides of life of an individual. In one case it is a question of an opportunity to choose various variants of behaviour and inadmissibility of illegal limitation of such opportunity, in another it concerns protection of personal safety and inadmissibility of illegal compulsion. Thus, these are two various, though rather close by the nature, human rights, incorporated by the authors of the Constitution of the Russian Federation (1993) in one formula. It is necessary to remind also that Article 3 of the Universal Declaration of

Human Rights says: "Everyone has the right to life, liberty and security of person". Here three rights are incorporated in one clause. However, no one will claim that the indicated rights represent the uniform right.

It is thought that the authors including in the content of Article 22 of the Constitution of the Russian Federation other civil rights (on inviolability of dwelling, on guarantees of privacy, etc.), without the sufficient bases identify the right to freedom and the right to personal immunity with the whole system of civil rights. Such identification may lead only to mess in the concepts. The Constitution precisely determines the system of constitutional rights, differentiating one right from another. The meaning of scientific research consists in perceiving the essence of each of them, to reveal their specific attributes, ways of their realization. Including one right in the content of another one, we stay away from fulfilling of this task.

Both provisions which have been included in Article 22 of the Constitution of the Russian Federation have entitling and regulative character. Allocating a person the legal right to personal immunity, the Constitution Thus, assigns a duty to the state to ensure the provision of them. These are provisions-principles which were developed in the branch legal provisions. The second part of Article 22 of the Constitution records three provisions which concretize the above-mentioned principles. At the same time these are provisions-guarantees of the right to personal immunity. The formula "Imprisonment, custody and holding in custody can be realized only under a court decision" contains two rules. One of them basically forbids the state bodies to encroach on security of citizens. The word "only" emphasizes the exclusiveness of imprisonment, and custodial placement. Virtually, this interdiction opens the content of the first part of Article 22 of the Constitution. Other rule (legal proceedings of imprisonment, the conclusions) is called to guarantee a reality of personal immunity. Finally, the third provision provides the maximum 48-hour term of detention of a person before adjudication about custodial placement.

The part of the second Article 22 of the Constitution, is, certainly, connected with the content of a part of the first clause as guarantees of personal immunity are recorded there. At the same time the provisions recorded in the part 2 of Article 22 have independent value as they are detailed and developed in criminally-remedial legislation. On the other hand, Article 22 of the Constitution of the Russian Federation indicated parts 1-3 of Article 8 of the Declaration of Rights and Freedoms of a Person and a Citizen of RSFSR (1991) All the above-mentioned provisions have reproduced substantive provisions of Article 3, 9 of the Universal Declaration of Human Rights, and Clause 1 of Article 9 of International Covenant on Civil and Political Rights.

The legal nature of the right to personal immunity is characterized by the fact that its realization, as a rule, does not require any actions from subjects of this right; they become necessary only in the case of infringement of this right.

The originality of constitutional law of personal immunity means that it in fact, represents itself as one of inter-branch principles of the right. These principles of the right can be subdivided into types depending on the area of legal regulations on which they extend. It is well-known that there are four kinds of principles: general, inter-branch, branch, and separate legal institutions. All personal constitutional rights in the sphere of individual freedom are recorded and indicated in other branches of the law. But unlike them the right to personal immunity plays the role of one of the supervising principles expressing the content of certain groups of branches of the law.

In terms of it is possible to speak about a principle of personal immunity. Value and the role of this principle till now in the scientific literature have not been sufficiently cleared up.

In some sections of jurisprudence, in particular in the science of criminal trial, the role of the right to personal immunity is quite often narrowed up to a branch principle, in others (for example, in the science of criminal law) it is underestimated even more.

Meanwhile, the ensuring of this right is connected with such different questions as, for example, deprivation of criminals of freedom and isolation of mental patients, detention of the suspected and administrative imprisonment.

On the other hand, it would be wrong to overestimate the value of the right to personal immunity, characterizing it as the general principle of the right. There are such branches (for example, labour, financial, ground, family law) where the constitutional principle of personal immunity is not evenly expressed.

In our opinion, the right to personal immunity, being recorded in provisions of constitutional law, is developed and indicated in criminally-remedial, criminal, administrative, administrative-remedial and criminal law-executive. The inter-branch principle of personal immunity in the ratio with the general principles of the right can be considered as specific display of general law principles of humanism and legality in some branches of the law.

Personal immunity is realized in relations of citizens with the state bodies, and among themselves.

Three kinds of relations with the state bodies are possible:

1. All citizens vs. bodies of the Public Prosecutor and the Ministry of Internal Affairs protecting their personal safety.

2. Separate citizens vs. judges, militia officers and Office of Public Prosecutor. Relations arise at detention, custody, imprisonment, administrative imprisonment and cover the procedure and the kind of limitation of personal freedom.

3. The imprisoned persons, detained, of the condemned (citizens, whose security of person on the basis of the decision of court is limited) vs. bodies of the Ministry of Justice, the Ministry of Internal Affairs and the Office of Public Prosecutor providing personal safety of these persons in places of imprisonment.

If we speak about subjects of the right to personal immunity the following position of the Constitutional Court of the Russian Federation has the main value: "With reference to ensuring of constitutional rights of citizens the concepts "imprisoned", " of the accused", "accuse" should be interpreted in the constitutionally-legal, rather than in narrower meaning applied to them by the Code of Criminal Procedure of the Russian Federation".[39]

Citizens in relations among themselves should not encroach on personal safety of each other. The problem of personal immunity has special value for the question of the right of citizens on necessary defense, on suppression of criminal encroachment and also on detention of criminals for their delivery in militia.

§ 4.   System of Guarantees of the Right to Personal Immunity

The system of guarantees of the right to personal immunity includes material, political, cultural and legal guarantees. Protection of the right to personal immunity demands well-known financial expenses (charges on the maintenance of law-enforcement bodies, Offices of Public Prosecutor, etc.) but these expenses are necessary for protection of other constitutional rights and consequently cannot be considered as special guarantees of this right.

However, there are also some special material guarantees. It is well-known that for a long time in the Great Britain, the USA and other countries the procedure of Habeas Corpus was connected with the payment of the monetary mortgage, and the lawyer's fee. F. Engels wrote in the 19th century: "This so praised right is the privilege of rich. Poor cannot present the guarantee and should be sent therefore, to prison".[40]

It seems that the correct court decision has not lost its value in the 21st century. Cheapness or, at least, financial availability to the usual person of lawyer's services at choosing of the preventive punishment to the imprisoned person, or of the accused is necessary to consider as a special material guarantee of the right to personal immunity. After introduction of the Code of Criminal Procedure of the Russian Federation 2002 (Article 108) this problem became acute for Russia. Not every of the accused is similar to the billionaire Khodorkovsky who has an opportunity to invite the most fashionable Russian foreign lawyers to participate in a judicial sitting on the basis of Article 108 of the Code of Criminal Procedure of the Russian Federation. Therefore, there is a necessity to set guarantees of financial availability of lawyer's services for deprived of the accused and victims. And it corresponds to principles of the legal and social state (Article 1, 7 of the Constitution of the Russian Federation).

A political guarantee of the right to personal immunity is first of all a democratic political regime in the state, excluding illegal detention and imprisonment of citizens, stability of their rights and freedoms. Political guarantees consist in consecutive realization in practice of the constitutional principle of division of the authorities that assumes the independence of judicial authority in ensuring of human and civil rights. Finally, political guarantees of the right to personal immunity in the democratic state assume also wide participation of citizens in activity of justice at the decision of the questions connected with limitation of the rights of imprisoned and of the accused persons. It seems that it also corresponds to Clause 5 of Article 32 of the Constitution of the Russian Federation. From this point of view the new Code of Criminal Procedure of the Russian Federation 2002, which has established rules, at which the overwhelming majority of criminal cases and the questions connected with them (in particular, concerning choosing of the preventive punishment in the form of custody) are solved only by professional judges without participation of jurymen, is a step back in ensuring of political guarantees of the right to personal immunity.

Cultural guarantees of this right should be provided with educational institutions, the cultural, educational and other organizations which are preparing judges, law enforcement bodies officers respect for the rights of the imprisoned, detained, of the accused and of the condemned, intolerance to infringement of the right to personal immunity. It is a component of formation of professional sense of justice and culture of human rights. It is necessary to note that an accusatory bias, the scornful attitude to human rights of the accused, imprisoned persons is rather characteristic for many professional lawyers.

According to the sociological researches carried out in 1999-2000 in 14 subjects of the Russian Federation, 67% of inspectors and investigators and 68.4% of judges, 69% of workers of the Office of Public Prosecutor consider that custody as the preventive punishment is a penalty. In fact, they consider imprisonment before adjudgement as evidence of fault of an imprisoned person. The overwhelming number of these workers (from 89 up to 93%) has supported the opinion on an opportunity to use imprisonment before accusing.[41] Therefore, it is necessary to develop the measures aimed at overcoming of these phenomena. As it is known, the Code of Criminal Procedure of the Russian Federation (2002) allows the use of the preventive punishment to the suspect before accuse only in exceptional cases. In practice such opportunity is considered as usage. It is impossible to disagree with V.I. Rudnev that "in the Code of Criminal Procedure of the Russian Federation the use of custody only after accuses" should be stipulated.[42]

The major role in enforcement of the right to personal immunity is played by special legal guarantees.

P.I. Lublinsky referred to the guarantees of personal immunity the following: the exact indication in the law of the cases when a citizen can be subjected to compulsion; determining by a court the presence of the conditions supposing using of such individual measure; granting to a citizen an opportunity to give the reasons against use of compulsion.[43] In A.I. Denisov's opinion, the following aspects are referred to the indicated guarantees: granting of the right to deprive of personal freedom only to court and Office of Public Prosecutor; establishment of the disciplinary, administrative and judicial responsibility of everyone (irrespective of their rank), illegally infringed the right to personal freedom: definition of cases in which deprivation of a citizen of personal freedom can take place; observance of the forms of limitation of personal freedom recorded in the law.[44]

Hungarian political scientists J. Beer, I. Kovach, L. Samel, listing guarantees of the right to personal immunity, mentioned many of them mentioned by the above-stated authors and, besides, referred to them the following: the verdict about imprisonment can be made on the basis of adversary proceedings, only by court, with observance of rules of judicial protection; in the case of the proved imprisonment before trail case should be considered in certain term, with the expiration of the term established by the law a person is subject to clearing even if on this case he/she has not been sentenced yet by trial court.

The analysis of views of all these authors allows coming to the conclusion that many of theoretical regulations concerning a guarantee of the right to personal immunity formulated by them are correct and are the result of studying the legislation and practice of its use. However, the exhaustive list of guarantees and their classification has not been provided yet.

Among guarantees of the given right we shall mark out the following: constitutionally-legal, internationally-legal, criminally-remedial, criminal, administratively-legal, administrative-remedial and civil. The specificity of constitutionally-legal guarantees consists in the fact that they are top-priority for all other legal guarantees of the given constitutional law. These guarantees of the right to personal immunity are shown, firstly, in the constitutional recording of this right; secondly, in establishment of legal institutions which are central for all legal guarantees of protection of the given right; thirdly, in ensuring of the judicial control over activity of the state bodies, called to protect the right to personal immunity.

Value of the guarantees recorded in part 2 of Article 22 of the Constitution of the Russian Federation is based on the fact that they: basically establish inadmissibility of imprisonment; regulate the imprisonment procedure, being exception of general principle; determine special legal procedure of imprisonment; cause the control over imprisonment from court. Certainly, the Constitution records only the major guarantees of the right to personal immunity.

During 1996-1998 the Constitutional Court of the Russian Federation made three decisions devoted to the problems of realization of the right on personal immunity. The meaning of these instruments is that the current legislation of the Russian Federation and its subjects cannot contradict constitutional and internationally-legal guarantees of the indicated right. In particular, considering the complaint of a citizen of V.V. Scheluchin, the Court has recognized unconstitutional part 5 of Article 97 of the Code of Criminal Procedure of RSFSR and has also indicated inadmissibility of superfluous or unlimited imprisonment of a citizen.[45] In J.D. Gafur's complaint the Court denied the present point of view that Article 22 of the Constitution of the Russian Federation refers only to Russian citizens, not to foreigners.[46]

The system of internationally-legal guarantees involves the system included into the instruments of international law and also legal procedures, called to ensure the provision of personal immunity. In particular, Article 5 of the European Convention provides six kinds of procedures of detention and imprisonment which should be stipulated by the law of each country. Practice of the European Commission and the European Court on Human Rights has special value.

We refer the system of criminally-remedial conditions and means of protection of the mentioned right to criminally-remedial guarantees. Conditions of realization of the right to personal immunity, in our opinion, are as follows:

1) Strict regulation of conditions of legality and validity of detention, custodial placement and other measures of remedial compulsion by the legislator;

2) Necessary observance of the terms of person's security limitation stipulated by the law;

3) Inadmissibility of secret detention, custodial placement and other secret limitations of security of person;

4) Observance of presumption of innocence and inadmissibility of putting of burden of witnessing on of the accused.

The question of guarantees of the suspected in committing of a crime deserves special attention. The Code of Criminal Procedure of the Russian Federation (2002) has introduced a lot of novelties. Firstly, a new basis for detention of the suspected was established: judicial recourse of the inspector and the investigator by permission of the public prosecutor with the petition to choose preventive punishment in the form of custody (part 2 Article 91 of the Code of Criminal Procedure). Secondly, the maximal term of detention can be prolonged by court for five days (part 7 of Article 108 of the Code of Criminal Procedure 2002) rather than for three according to the Code of Criminal Procedure of RSFSR (1960). Thirdly, the new Code of Criminal Procedure has given the right of detention of the suspected to inquiry agencies. Already the number of the detained by investigators has increased in the first half-year of 2003 in 2,3 times in comparison with 2002, though, as a whole, the number of detention decreased.[47] At the same time it is necessary to note that the new Code of Criminal Procedure has indistinctly determined the concept of criminally-remedial detention. Chapter 12 of this Code is made so that there are difficulties with understanding of the moment of the term of detention beginning: from the moment of the suspect's capture on the place of committing of a crime, from the moment of delivery into militia or from the moment of signing the report of detention. After acceptance of the Code of Criminal Procedure the discussion about these disputable moments has begun in the literature.[48] Such "white spots" in the legislation will hardly lead to strengthening of guarantees of the right to personal immunity.

Existence of institution of custody is caused by reasons of emergency which now are expressed in the bases listed in Chapter 13 of the Code of Criminal Procedure, in particular in Article 108.

In unusual cases and under certain conditions this preventive punishment can be used to the suspected (Article100 of the Code of Criminal Procedure).

The right to personal immunity is guaranteed in the case of:

Strict observance of legal proceedings of custody (Article 10, 108, 109 of the Code of Criminal Procedure).

Enforcement of the rights of detained persons, including the right to appeal the decision of the judge about choosing the preventive punishment (Article 11, part 11 Article 108 of the Code of Criminal Procedure);

Inadmissibility to use regarding indicated persons the measures that cause physical suffering or are degrading (Article 9 of the Code of Criminal Procedure).

The following to rules about clearing the indicated persons from arrested in the case of a cancelling, changes of the preventive punishment or expiry of the term of holding in custody (part 2 Article 10, part 4 Article 109 of the Code of Criminal Procedure).

Supervision by public prosecutors of observance of legality in jails (Federal law "Office of Public Prosecutor in the Russian Federation", Article 22 of the Criminal Code of the Russian Federation).

In the problem of criminally-remedial guarantees the validity of custodial placement is very important. Clause 97 of the Code of Criminal Procedure says about using of the preventive punishment as "the sufficient bases". The unreasonable charge put forward against a citizen can lead to undesirable consequences but the unreasonable custody in the most pernicious image affects not only on of the accused but also members of their family, has a negative public resonance.[49] Any mistake connected with custody is incompatible with principles of legality as well as the law and order.

Studying of investigatory practice allows emphasizing some typical mistakes connected with infringement of personal immunity. The illegal custody can be the result of a mistake a law-enforcement person at a legal estimation of actions of the accused. Thus, sometimes the provision about necessary defense is not taken into consideration; the subjective party of structure of a crime is not researched.

Investigatory mistakes quite often says about wrong estimation of proofs (imprisonment on the basis of one confession of the accused or indications of the victim without appropriate check and confirmation by objective proofs, change of indications of witnesses, wrong carrying out of identification, etc.). Untimely carrying out of urgent investigatory actions, haste at choosing the preventive punishment and other circumstances testifying to low quality of consequence, can also be the reasons of the mistakes leading to infringement of constitutional law of personal immunity.

Significant danger seems by abusing of officers of law enforcement bodies. It is impossible to disagree with conclusions of the international remedial organization "Human Rights Watch" which carried out the research Russia in 1995-1999: scales of use to imprisoned persons of illegal methods at detention and during the period directly following it have got a scandalous character in today's Russia.[50] In 1999-2002 they prepared a special report "reports of the Representative testifying to infringement of the rights of citizens by employees of the Ministry of Internal Affairs of the Russian Federation and also Criminal Executive System the Ministry of Justice of the Russian Federation" where it is noted that 22% of all complaints of victims are devoted to the unlawful methods and remedial infringement at carrying out of inquiry and preliminary investigation. Inspectors of the Council of Europe recognize investigatory cells of Russia as a place equal to torture.[51]

According to Minister of Justice, through investigatory cells annually pass up to 2 million prisoners that almost twice exceeds the amount of persons subject to imprisonment and inhuman conditions of stay in pretrial detention centre contradict international standards of human rights. Studying materials of the Representative concerning human rights, independent human rights organizations allow to draw some conclusions about detention of the suspected and custodial placement in 1999-2002:

In practice of law enforcement bodies detention and custody are considered as means of receiving of accusatory proofs. "For the sake of receiving of a confession or evidence against other persons at first hours after detention people in militia quite often are beaten and subjected to cruel treatment and torture. besides, they practice placement of the preliminary imprisonment to force them to cooperate with militia ... Courts, as a rule, do not call in question the concept of received Thus, which become a basis of the charge".[52] Amazing is the fact that from professional sense of justice of lawyers, from investigatory and judiciary practice in the end the 20th - the beginning of the 21st century feudal concepts of a concept of the accused as to "tsarina of proofs" have not been eradicated! Therefore, inspectors as a rule aspired to select of the suspected or of the accused the preventive punishment in the form of custody. As a result thousands of fine offenders are arrested. There are the following questions: whether these ideas form component of judicial politics of the state? And whether it is valid or may become legal? Obviously, archaic institution which has not casually saved in the Anglo-Saxon right of the transaction of the accused with justice is included in the new Code of Criminal Procedure of the Russian Federation (Ch. 40). In the country where corruption is prospering and where it is officially recognized that torture are widely used by inquiry agencies and inquest, introduction of such criminally-remedial provisions seems unreasonable.

Typical infringement of the right to personal immunity in Russia is the discrimination treatment by law enforcement bodies national minorities – natives of Central Asia, Caucasus, gypsies. It is shown in illegal and unreasonable detention. Mass detention and imprisonment of such kind took place in the Chechen Republic. After events on Dubrovka cases of falsification of criminal cases, charges in illegal storage of firearms and imprisonment of Chechens have extended.[53]

Operations with use of automatic weapons, camouflage, handcuffs, and masks with a view of detention of the suspected are practiced.[54] Violent methods of suppression of a person in isolation ward of temporary custody and a pre-trial detention centre are widely used. In places of imprisonment they use putting criminals into cells in penal institutions.

Rather disturbing tendency of increase of a crime rate in the environment of law enforcement bodies officers is observed. Finally, it is necessary to note superficial character of public prosecutor's supervision and absence of public control over places of imprisonment.

The new Code of Criminal Procedure establishing the judicial control stipulated by the Constitution over imprisonment and custodial placement and also the necessity of the consent of the public prosecutor on excitation of criminal case, it is necessary to estimate introduction as strengthening of criminally-remedial guarantees of personal immunity. As a result according to the Ministry of Internal Affairs the number of the detained, suspected and accused in the first half of 2003 in comparison with the same period of 2000 decreased in 2.2 times.[55] As Minister of Justice of the Russian Federation J. Chaika has informed in 2002-2003, the number of persons included in pre-trial detention centre, reduced on 70, 000 people. For the first time in history of Russia the amount of all prisoners became less 1 million (i.e. less than 900,000 persons). It allowed finishing filling of the pre-trial detention centre on the average to the established European standards.[56] "The qualitative characteristic of criminally-executive politics of the state is a withdrawal from an excessive retaliatory orientation to increase of the importance of observance of the rights of certain person" as the minister writes. It seems that this conclusion is excessively optimistic. Firstly, the new Code of Criminal Procedure has introduced the principles of equality of the sides and competitiveness only at the stage of proceeding, having saved mixed inquisitional-competing process at the stage of preliminary investigation. Secondly, the Code of Criminal Procedure has saved the institution of custody of charge of the suspected up to presentation (Article 100 of the Code of Criminal Procedure of the Russian Federation). Thirdly, judges, the staff of law enforcement bodies, including investigators, inspectors, and employees of pre-trial detention centers are growing old. The culture of human rights yet has not become a dominating element of their professional consciousness. And, finally, pressure upon court, Office of Public Prosecutor, and trial from executive authority, commercial structures continues to remain the serious problem interfering realization of personal immunity.

Criminally-remedial provisions provide compulsion of immediate liberation from everyone illegally imprisoned or holding in custody over the term stipulated by the law or the adjudication (part 2 Article 10 of the Code of Criminal Procedure of the Russian Federation). Terms of detention and custody are set by the legislator and have exclusive value for ensuring of the given constitutional law. Every day and hour of detention essentially infringe on interests of the imprisoned person, members of their family. Therefore, the question of conditions of limitation of the right to personal immunity is very important.

In part 12 of Article 108 of the Code of Criminal Procedure of the Russian Federation it is emphasized that a person against whom there is a criminal case, is immediately obliged to inform relatives about holding in custody of the suspected or of the accused about a place or about the change of this place.

The important guarantee of personal immunity is presumption of innocence and inadmissibility of putting on of burden substantiation on the accused. As it is known, the presumption of innocence means that any citizen is considered innocent while their guilt is not proved in the order established by the law. The guilty person is that one whose charge is recognized by the proved adjudication which has introduced validity admits only. This principle is recognized by criminally-remedial legislation of many states of world, in particular in Article 49 of the Constitution of the Russian Federation, Article 10 of the Code of Criminal Procedure of the Russian Federation.

In criminally-remedial literature it is common to connect a principle of presumption of innocence with the right of the accused on protection. But it would be inexact to deduce presumption of innocence only from the content of Article 47 of the Constitution of the Russian Federation. In our opinion, it follows also from the meaning of Article 22. If basically a person is inviolable, he/she can become "implicated" only if their guilt in committing an offence that according to the law entails imprisonment is proved. The content of the guarantees recorded in Article 22 of the Constitution of the Russian Federation, in that also means that citizens basically are considered innocent and, hence, inviolable. If in advance to consider all of them guilty the judicial control over imprisonment loses any sense. It is necessary to note also that the right of defence is under certain conditions carried out when the presumption of innocence is not used. Action of the indicated presumption comes to an end during the moment of a return of a person guilty by the order established by the law, for example during the moment of the introduction of a verdict of guilty by virtue of. "After the introduction of a verdict into validity the presumption of innocence gives the place of a presumption of the verity of a verdict".[57]

However, the right of defence of the condemned realizes in these conditions as well (in supervising instance, etc.) Therefore, this right cannot be connected under all circumstances with presumption of innocence.

The new Code of Criminal Procedure (Articles 92, 108, 109) provides a number of the important guarantees of legality and validity of detention (in particular, drawing up of the report of detention, the right of the imprisoned person to appointment of the defender, the information to the public prosecutor about detention), custodial placement (the petition, judicial sitting, participation of the accused, the defender, etc.). Special value has a right to rehabilitation of persons illegally involved in the criminal liability (Ch. 18 of the Code of Criminal Procedure of the Russian Federation).

Criminal guarantees have great value. In the scientific literature on criminal law there is a question of protection or guarantees of the right to personal immunity and imprisonment, etc. In our opinion reducing to the analysis of the responsibility for obviously illegal imprisonment, detention, not only the provisions provide punishment for illegal imprisonment, detention and imprisonment but also the provisions establishing some major provisions and principles of criminal law as branch of the right, play an essential role in ensuring of constitutional law of personal immunity.

Criminal guarantees represent the system of criminal conditions and means of protection of constitutional law of personal immunity. To guarantees-conditions are referred the following:

— Recording in the criminal law conditions of inadmissibility to limit security of innocent persons. Structure of a crime is the unique basis of the criminal liability;

— A strict regulation in criminal law of the bases of imprisonment as measures of punishment;

— Conformity of a kind and term of imprisonment as measures of criminal sentence, weight of a crime;

— Inadmissibility of return force of the criminal law establishing punishability of act or strengthening punishment.

The indicated principles are recorded in Articles 6, 8, 10, 53-57 of the Criminal Code of the Russian Federation. Infringement of any of them can lead to illegal imprisonment.

— to means of protection of the right to personal immunity we refer the legal provisions establishing the criminal liability for crimes against life, health, freedom, honour and dignity of a person to criminal guarantees (Ch. 16, 17 of the Criminal Code of the Russian Federation), crimes against justice (Article 299, 301, 303, 305 of the Criminal Code of the Russian Federation), etc. All criminally-legal provisions directed on protection of personal safety of a citizen, life, health, freedom, guarantee the right to personal immunity.

In our opinion, the criminal liability for encroachment on the right to personal immunity should come not from the moment of false imprisonment but from the moment of illegal delivery of a citizen and it is necessary to recognize as subjects of the responsibility not only civil servants but also private persons.

Administratively-legal and administrative-remedial guarantees, similarly to other legal guarantees are subdivided into conditions of realization and means of protection of the right to personal immunity. To conditions of realization the following things are referred:

— Regulation in provisions of administrative and administrative-procedural law of the conditions of legality and validity of measures of administrative compulsion;

— Performance of the terms stipulated by the law for detention, imprisonment and other measures of administrative compulsion;

— Observance of rules about presumptions of innocence and objectivity in an estimation of proofs, in particular explanatory of an accused person of committing of administrative offence by consideration of case.

The authorities have certain means of protection of the right to personal immunity. Among them first of all it is necessary to emphasize law-enforcement: law-enforcement bodies, state security, and justice.

There are many cases when lawful administrative methods of protection, including direct physical influence and even use of firearms (if they are used within the law) are unique and the most effective ways of protection of personal immunity (for example, suppression by the worker of militia of an attack of the criminal on a citizen; operation on clearing the hostages grasped by armed terrorists).

The following things are also referred to administratively-legal guarantees as to means of protection: the interdepartmental control over law-enforcement bodies, state security, justice, Office of Public Prosecutor behind legality of imprisonment, detention, etc. a disciplinary responsibility of the officials guilty of infringement of the right to personal immunity; the administrative responsibility of persons encroaching on personal safety of citizens.

A new Code of the Russian Federation about administrative offences provides two basic kinds of lawful limitation of personal immunity: 1) measures of ensuring of cases about administrative infringement (administrative delivery, detention, personal inspection and a drive); 2) administrative punishment (administrative imprisonment, administrative exclusion for limits of the Russian Federation of the foreigner or a person without citizenship). The given Code provides the administrative-remedial form of consideration of such type of affairs, guarantees of the rights of a person.

It is necessary to note that the measures of administrative compulsion limiting the right to personal immunity are used in Russia rather widely. Thus, according to official data in 2002 to administrative imprisonment were subjected to by regional courts 387,900 persons (43.1% of all subjected to official criminalities).[58]

It seems that legislative grounds of such coercive actions as administrative delivery and administrative detention are formulated in the legislation not clearly enough. And this circumstance creates conditions for militia arbitrariness.

The law records the civil guarantees of the given right. In the case when as a result of infringement of the right to personal immunity there was a property damage which suffered on the basis of Ch. 18 of the Code of Criminal Procedure of the Russian Federation, Ch. 59 of the Civil Code of the Russian Federation have the right to address with the requirement about compensation of property damage in the body which decided a verdict or has taken out definition about the termination of criminal case.

Protection of property interests and those citizens to which the damage by crimes against a person is caused is provided. They are distinguished with the rights of the civil claimant in criminal trial (Article 44 of the Code of Criminal Procedure of the Russian Federation).

This party of a question has crucial importance as concerns fair citizens, whose personal safety became object of criminal encroachment. In terms of it the great value has Definition of the Constitutional Court of the Russian Federation under T.N. Alikina complaint of December, 4th, 2003, which means that Clause 1 of Article 1070 of the Civil Code constitutionally-legal interpretation should be understood as follows: harm, caused to a citizen as a result of illegal limitation of freedom, including false imprisonment, is subject to the full indemnification at the expense of the treasury.[59] In this clause of the Code "false imprisonment" is not mentioned. The Constitutional Court, proceeding from the content of Article 52 of the Constitution of the Russian Federation, has given legally proved interpretation of the legal provision, having expanded, thus, civil guarantees of personal immunity.

Notes

1. Burdeau G. Les libertes publiques. Paris, 1961. P.89.

2. See: Ibidem. P. 103.

3. About the Concept of This Institute and Its History See: Deruzhinsky V.M. Habeas Corpus Act and its Suspension by the English Law. Yuriev, 1895. P. 113 /О понятии этого института, его истории см.: Дерюжинский В. М. Habeas Corpus Act и его приостановка по английскому праву. Юрьев, 1895. С. 113.

4. Elistratov E.A. Essays of Administrative Law. Moscow, 1922. P. 118. / Елистратов Е. А. Очерки административного права. М., 1922. С. 118.

5. See: Kistyakovsky B.A. Social Sciences and the Law. Moscow, 1916. P. 561./ См.: Кистяковский Б. А. Социальные науки и право. М., 1916. С. 561.

6. Vysheslavtsev B.P. Guarantees of the Rights of Citizens. Moscow, 1917. P. 7./ Вышеславцев Б. П. Гарантии прав гражданина. М., 1917. С. 7.

7. Lublinsky P.I. Inviolability of a Person, 1917. P. 6-7. / Люблинский П. И. Неприкосновенность личности. 1917. С. 6–7.

8. The Encyclopedia of the State and the Law. Vol. 2. Moscow, 1925-1926. P. 1371. / Энциклопедия государства и права. Т. 2. М., 1925–1926. С. 1371.

9. See: Denisov A.I. Soviet State Law. Moscow, 1947. P. 345; Lepeshkin A.I. Course of the Soviet State Law. Vol. 1. Moscow, 1961. P. 519;, etc. / См.: Денисов А. И. Советское государственное право. М., 1947. С. 345; Лепешкин А. И. Курс советского государственного права. Т. 1. М., 1961. С. 519; и др.

10. See: Soviet State Law / Under edit. of S.S. Kravchuk. Moscow, 1958. P. 270. / См.: Советское государственное право / Под ред. С. С. Кравчука. М., 1958.   С. 270.

11. See: Soviet State Law. Moscow, 1938. P. 566; Soviet State Law. Moscow, 1948. P. 166-167. / См.: Советское государственное право. М., 1938. С. 566; Советское государственное право. М., 1948. С. 166–167.

12. Ivanov V. A Guarantees of the Rights of a Person in the Sphere of Administrative Compulsion // Soviet State and the Right. 1972.8. P. 55-56. / Иванов В. А. Гарантии прав личности в сфере административного принуждения // Советское государство и право. 1972. № 8. С. 55–56.

13. See: Matuzov N.I. Acute Problems of the Theory of the Law. Saratov, 2003. P. 41. / См.: Матузов Н. И. Актуальные проблемы теории права. Саратов, 2003. С. 41.

14. See: Gorshenev A.P. Theoretical Questions of Personal Constitutional Rights of the Soviet Citizens. Saratov, 1972. P. 39. / См.: Горшенев А. П. Теоретические вопросы личных конституционных прав советских граждан. Саратов, 1972. С. 39.

15. See: Gorshenev A.P. Personal Constitutional Rights of the Soviet Citizens: Cand. Dissertation Saratov, 1972. P. 88. / См.: Горшенев А. П. Личные конституционные права советских граждан: Канд. дис. Саратов, 1972. С. 88.

16. See: Bezuglov A.A. Soviet Deputy. State-Legal Status. Moscow, 1971. P. 174-175. / См.: Безуглов А. А. Советский депутат. Государственно-правовой статус. М., 1971. С. 174–175.

17. See: May T. A Treatise on the Law, Privileges, Proceedings and Usage of Parliament. L. Moscow, 1863. P. 117.

18. Ammeler M. Parliaments. Moscow, 1967. P. 114. / Амеллер М. Парламенты. М., 1967. С. 114.

19. See: State Law of the USSR. Moscow, 1967. P. 225. / См.: Государственное право СССР. М., 1967. С. 225.

20. See: Patulin V.A. Inviolability of a Person as a Legal Institution // Soviet State and the Law. 1973.11. P. 18. / См.: Патюлин В. А. Неприкосновенность личности как правовой институт // Советское государство и право. 1973. № 11. С. 18.

21. See: Baglai M.V. Constitutional Law of the Russian Federation, 1999. P. 179; Kozlova E. I., Kutafin O.E . Constitutional Law of Russia, 2002. P. 261; Kutafin O.E . Inviolability in Constitutional Law of the Russian Federation. Moscow, 2004. P. 121. / См.: Баглай М. В. Конституционное право Российской Федерации, М., 1999. С. 179; Козлова Е. И., Кутафин О. Е. Конституционное право России, М., 2002. С. 261; Кутафин О. Е. Неприкосновенность в конституционном праве Российской Федерации. М., 2004. С. 121.

22. Gomien D., Harris D., Zvaak L. European Convention on Human Rights and European Social Charter: Law and Practice. Moscow, 1998. C.160. / Гомьен Д., Харрис Д., Зваак Л. Европейская конвенция о правах человека и Европейская социальная хартия: право и практика. М., 1998. C.160.

23. See: Rudinsky F. M. Person and Socialist Legality. Volgograd, 1976. P. 79, 80. / См.: Рудинский Ф. М. Личность и социалистическая законность. Волгоград, 1976. С. 79, 80.

24. See: Farber I. . A Constitutional Right to Personal Immunity of the Soviet Citizens // Jurisprudence. 1973.3. P. 16. / См.: Фарбер И. Е. Конституционное право на неприкосновенность личности советских граждан // Правоведение. 1973. № 3. С. 16.

25. See: Locke J. Selected Philosophical Works: In 2 vol. Vol. 2. Moscow, 1960. P. 50, 51, 145. / См.: Локк Д. Избранные философские произведения: В 2 т. Т. 2. М., 1960. С. 50, 51, 145.

26. Blackstone W. Commentaries on the Laws of England in Four Books. Philadelphia, 1859. P. 129.

27. Ibidem. P. 134.

28. Montesquieu Ch. Selected Works. Moscow, 1955. P. 317. / Монтескье Ш. Избранные произведения. М., 1955. С. 317.

29. Ibidem. P. 318.

30. Humboldt W.F. Experience of Establishment of the State Activity Limits. St. Petersburg, 1908. P. 89. / Гумбольдт В. Ф. Опыты установления пределов государственной деятельности. СПб., 1908. С. 89.

31. See: Marx K. Engels F. Works. Vol. 1. P. 401. / См.: Маркс К., Энгельс Ф. Сочинения. Т. 1. С. 401.

32. See: Belyavsky A.V., Pridvorov N.A. Protection of Honour and Dignity of a Person in the USSR. Moscow, 1971. P. 6-21; Vilnjanskij S. N. Protection of Honour and Dignity of a Person in the Soviet Law // Jurisprudence. 1965.3. P. 139; Rafieva L.K. Honour and Dignity as Legal Categories // Jurisprudence. 1966.2. P. 57. / См.: Белявский А. В., Придворов Н. А. Охрана чести и достоинства личности в СССР. М., 1971. С. 6–21; Вильнянский С. Н. Защита чести и достоинства человека в советском праве // Правоведение. 1965. № 3. С. 139; Рафиева Л. К. Честь и достоинство как правовые категории // Правоведение. 1966. № 2. С. 57.

33. See: Chelstsov-Bebutov V.A. The Accused and His Evidence in the Soviet Criminal Trial. Moscow, 1947. P. 13. / См.: Чельцов-Бебутов М. А. Обвиняемый и его показания в советском уголовном процессе. М., 1947. С. 13.

34. See: Piontkovsky A.A. Illegal Arrest and Resistance to a Militia Officer or to a National Combatant // Soviet State and the Law. 1966.4. P. 130. / См.: Пионтковский А. А. Незаконное задержание и сопротивление работнику милиции или народному дружиннику // Советское государство и право. 1966. № 4. С. 130.

35. See, for example: Bezuglov A.A., Soldatov S.A. Constitutional Law of Russia: In 3 vol. Vol. 1. Moscow, 2001. P. 448; Krasavchikova L.O. Concept and System of Personal Rights not Connected with the Property Rights (of Physical Persons) in the Civil Law of the Russian Federation: Abstract of Dissertation of Doctor of Jurisprudence. Ekaterinburg, 1994. P. 30. / См., например: Безуглов А. А., Солдатов С. А. Конституционное право России: В 3 т. Т. 1. М., 2001. С. 448; Красавчикова Л. О. Понятие и система личных, не связанных с имущественными прав граждан (физических лиц) в гражданском праве РФ: Автореф. дис. ... д-ра юрид. наук. Екатеринбург, 1994. С. 30.

36. See: Stetsovsky J.I. Right to Freedom and Inviolability of a Person. Norms and the Reality. Moscow, 2000. P. 101, 272, etc.; Tolkachyov K.B. Theoretical and Methodological Basis of Realization of Personal Constitutional Laws of a Person and a Citizen: Abstract of Dissertation of Dr. of Jurisprudence. St. Petersburg 1998. P. 21; Morozov A.P. Constitutional Right of a Person and a Citizen to Freedom and Inviolability of a Person in the Russian Federation: Abstract of Dissertation of Cand. of Jurisprudence. Saratov, 2002. P. 22. / См.: Стецовский Ю. И. Право на свободу и личную неприкосновенность. Нормы и действительность. М., 2000. С. 101, 272 и др.; Толкачев К. Б. Теоретико-методологические основания реализации личных конституционных прав человека и гражданина: Автореф. дис. ... д-ра юрид. наук. СПб., 1998. С. 21; Морозов А. П. Конституционное право человека и гражданина на свободу и личную неприкосновенность в РФ: Автореф. дис. ... канд. юрид. наук. Саратов, 2002. С. 22.

37. See: Lusher F. Constitutional Protection of Rights and Freedoms. Moscow, 1993. P. 286-337. / См.: Люшер Ф. Конституционная защита прав и свобод. М., 1993. С. 286–337.

38. See: Kozlova E. I., Kutafin O. E. Constitutional Law of Russia: Textbook. Moscow, 1995. P. 199; Constitutional Law: Textbook / Edited by V. V. Lazareva. Moscow, 1998. P. 93; Baglai M. V. Constitutional Law of the Russian Federation: Textbook. Moscow, 2000. P. 179. / См.: Козлова Е. И., Кутафин О. Е. Конституционное право России: Учебник. М., 1995. С. 199; Конституционное право: Учебник / Под ред. В. В. Лазарева. М., 1998. С. 93; Баглай М. В. Конституционное право Российской Федерации: Учебник. М., 2000. С. 179.

39. Definition of the Constitutional Court of the Russian Federation under the complaint of a citizen of T.N. Alikina to infringement of her constitutional laws, Clause 1 of Article 1070 of the Civil Code of the Russian Federation of December, 4th, 2003 // Rosiiskaya Gazeta. 2004.17, Feb. / Определение Конституционного Суда РФ по жалобе гражданки Т. Н. Аликиной на нарушение ее конституционных прав п. 1 ст. 1070 ГК РФ от 4 декабря 2003 г. // Российская газета. 2004. 17 февр.

40. Marx K., Engels F. Works. Vol. 1. P. 635. / Маркс К., Энгельс Ф. Сочинения. Т. 1. С. 635.

41. See: Rudnev V. I. Imprisonment and the Problem of Reduction of Number of People Put into Cells. Results of the Sociological Research. Moscow, 2002. P. 6, 8. / См.: Руднев В. И. Заключение под стражу и проблема уменьшения количества лиц, находящихся в следственных изоляторах. Результаты социологического исследования. М., 2002. С. 6, 8.

42. Ibidem.

43. See: Lublinsky P.I. Inviolability of a Person. Moscow, 1917. P. 7. / См.: Люблинский П. И. Неприкосновенность личности. 1917. С. 7.

44. See: Denisov A.I. Soviet State Law. Moscow, 1947. P. 345-346. / См.: Денисов А. И. Советское государственное право. М., 1947. С. 345–346.

45. See: Comment to Decisions of the Constitutional Court of the Russian Federation. Vol. 2. / Edited by B.S. Ebzeev. Moscow, 2000. P. 43-56. / См.: Комментарий к постановлениям Конституционного Суда Российской Федерации. Т. 2. / Отв. ред. Б. С. Эбзеев. М., 2000. С. 43–56.

46. See: Ibidem. P. 65-69.

47. See: Gavrilov B. Novels of Criminal Trial on the Background of Criminal Statistics // Russian Justice. 2003.10. P. 6. / См.: Гаврилов Б. Новеллы уголовного процесса на фоне криминальной статистики // Российская юстиция. 2003. № 10. С. 6.

48. See: Abdurahmanov R. Problems of Criminally-Remedial Detention // Legality. 2003.3. P. 21-22; Nazarov S. Detention is "another" remedial action // Russian Justice. 2003.7. P. 48-49. / См.: Абдурахманов Р. Проблемы уголовно-процессуального задержания // Законность. 2003. № 3. С. 21–22; Назаров С. Задержание – «иное» процессуальное действие // Российская юстиция. 2003. № 7. С. 48–49.

49. Voltaire F.M. Selected Works on Criminal Law and Trial. Moscow, 1956. P. 267./ Вольтер Ф. М. Избранные произведения по уголовному праву и процессу. М., 1956. С. 267.

50. See: Special Reports of Human Rights Commissioner in the Russian Federation O.O. Mironov. Moscow, 2003. P. 135-136. / См.: Специальные доклады Уполномоченного по правам человека в Российской Федерации О. О. Миронова. М., 2003. С. 135–136.

51. See: Ibidem. P. 128-129.

52. Report on Human Rights Commissioner's Work in the Russian Federation in 1999. Moscow, 2000. P. 54. / Доклад о деятельности Уполномоченного по правам человека в Российской Федерации в 1999 году. М., 2000. С. 54.

53. See: Report on Human Rights Commissioner's Work in the Russian Federation O.O. Mironov in 2002. Moscow, 2003. P. 104. / См.: Доклад о деятельности Уполномоченного по правам человека в Российской Федерации О. О. Миронова в 2002 году. М., 2003. С. 104.

54. See: Ibidem. P. 21.

55. See: Gavrilov B. Specified Works P. 6. / См.: Гаврилов Б. Указ. соч. С. 6.

56. See: Chaikal Y. The Third Century of the Ministry of Justice // Russian Justice. 2003.4. P. 4. / См.: Чайка Ю. Третье столетие Министерства юстиции // Российская юстиция. 2003. № 4. С. 4.

57. The Theory of Proofs in the Soviet Criminal Trial. General Part. Moscow, 1966. P. 455. / Теория доказательств в советском уголовном процессе. Общая часть. М., 1966. С. 455.

58. See: Statistics. Work of Courts of the Russian Federation in 2002 // Russian Justice. 2003.8. P. 77. / См.: Статистика. Работа судов РФ в 2002 г. // Российская юстиция. 2003. № 8. С. 77.

59. See: Definition of the Constitutional Court of the Russian Federation under the Complaint of a Citizen T.N. Alikina to Infringement of her Constitutional Rights. Clause 1 of Article 1070 of the Civil Code of the Russian Federation of December, 4th, 2003 // Rossiiskaya Gazeta. 2004.Feb.,17. / См.: Определение Конституционного Суда РФ по жалобе гражданки Т. Н. Аликиной на нарушение ее конституционных прав п. 1 ст. 1070 ГК РФ от 4 декабря 2003 г. // Российская газета. 2004. 17 февр.

Chapter 6. THE RIGHT TO FREEDOM FROM TORTURE AND
OTHER KINDS OF INHUMAN TREATMENT AND
PUNISHMENT

The question of freedom from torture and other cruel, inhuman or degrading treatment or punishment[1] is one of the most important for international and interstate legal regulation. A plenty of them testify to internationally-legal regulations and legal regulations of the Russian Federation, foreign countries. The part of 2 clauses 21 of the Constitution of the Russian Federation (1993) sounds as follows: "Nobody should be subjected to torture, violence, another cruel or degrading treatment or punishment. Nobody can be subjected to without the voluntary consent to medical, scientific or other experiments". Historical predecessors of indicated clause were Article 19 of the Declaration of Rights and Freedoms of a Person and a Citizen of the Russian Federation, Article 5 of the Universal Declaration of Human Rights, Article 7 of International Covenant on Civil and Political Rights and also Article 3 of the European Convention.

At the same time it is necessary to remind that in history of development of a human civilization and statehood the attitude to the problem of non-use (use) of torture or other kinds of inhuman treatment or punishment was not unequivocal. Therefore, it is obviously necessary to carry out the historical analysis of separate aspects of legal regulation of the given problem.

If we address to the history of the Ancient Greece it is possible to be convinced that during litigation torture, having such form with ordain, was considered as one of the major kinds of proofs. Thinkers of the Ancient Greece extolled torture as the best of proofs.[2]

In litigation of Ancient Rome, since Octavian Augustus (31 B.C. - A.D. 14), a new form of court - inquisitive one appeared that assumed a wide use of torture. Special interest in terms of it seems in Digest of Justinian, with mentioning questions of use torture to witnesses (1.10 Digests, 48.4; 1.7 Digests, 48.4; 1.15 Digests, 48.18).[3]

Since the 12th century the search process in which torture is distinguished for special legal purpose starts to develop. Thus, the first mention about inquisitional process in France can be found in Ordinance (1254) and Ordinance, 1498 and 1539 with the full description of the developed inquisitive system and contained the remedial provisions regulating use of torture. "Big Criminal Ordinance" (1670) considers torture as one of the proofs in search process and the core one in cases of shortage of the collected accusatory proofs. This rule has existed in France up to the end of 17th century and was cancelled only before revolution by Edict (1788) who forbade using torture.

In turn since the 14th century in many cities of Germany torture became the widespread means of substantiation. And in the end the 15th - the beginning of the 16th century torture finds the legal recording in codes of some the federal grounds: in the Tyrolean Charter 1499, in Criminal Charter of Bamberg episcopacy 1507 which issued introduction of ex-ordinary process with obligatory torture; in the Brandenburg charter 1516 almost literally repeating provisions of the Bamberg Charter.

The special place in this list occupies the code having the official name "Code of Emperor Charles V of Sacred Roman Empire" (1532), more known under a short name "Carolina".

German codes of the 17th - 19th centuries (Prussian 1756, Austrian (1776), Bavarian 1806) updated the system of search process, giving a number of the rights of the accused to protection and cancelling torture as means of receiving of proofs. However, a number of codes kept the measures of compulsion directed on receiving of evidence from the accused.

English legal proceedings traditionally differ from the exclusively competing. However, England, as well as other countries, has not avoided the period of inquisitional process but by virtue of the historical reasons this form of justice has not received such development as on the European continent. It was promoted also by acceptance of Magna Carta (1215), the recorded basis of civil freedom and determined character and a direction of the further development of judicial system to Engle.

At the same time the history of England knows examples of use various cruel and inhuman treatment in legal proceedings. It is possible to recollect inquisitional process with use torture in activity of Star Chamber and the High Commission of the Secret Council, distinguished by competences on realization of justice.

By guarantee of personal freedom and guarantee of protection from use of cruel and inhuman treatment at realization of justice the "Bill of Rights" (1689), approved that it, "can be considered "that the requirement of excessive judicial mortgages, imposing of excessive criminalities or cruel and unusual punishment is inadmissible".[4]

In Russian laws the first mention of torture as judicial action was in laws of Grand Duke John (Code of Laws, 1497).[5] The institution of torture received the further legal regulation in the Lip letters establishing new local bodies for struggle against robbers where it was recommended to these bodies to use torture with a view of receiving of a confession that was recorded in the subsequent laws of Russia (Code of laws 1550, etc.)[6]

Fuller regulation to use torture can be found in Peter's I Decree 1697, cancelling the process in legal proceedings and in the Brief image of processes and judicial trials,[7] 1715, recorded detailed rules of carrying out of search process with use inquiry with predilection and torture.[8]

The legal interdiction of use torture in Russia was established by Decree of Alexander I in 1801. As a whole, numerous examples of use torture as way (means) of substantiation with a view of the decision of problems of legal proceedings are known.

In the middle of the 20th century, "considering that the neglect and contempt for human rights have led to barbarous instruments which revolt conscience of mankind", General Assembly of the United Nations on December, 10th, 1948 proclaimed the Universal Declaration of Human Rights[9] which recorded as natural and basic human rights to freedom from torture and other kinds of inhuman treatment or punishment in the following form: "No one shall be subjected to torture or to cruel, inhuman or degrading treatment or punishment" (Article 5).

During the same period the major-legal provisions of the humanitarian law which are directly connected with warranting freedom against torture and other kinds of inhuman treatment or punishment and which allow to open the legal content of the researched right are accepted is international. The Geneva Convention on improvement speed up wounded men and patients in field armies (1949)[10] has referred to gross infringement of international obligations such actions as: torture and inhuman treatment, including biological *experiments*, deliberate causing of heavy sufferings or serious mutilation (Article 50). This position is reproduced in Article 51 of the Geneva Convention on improvement speed up wounded men, patients and persons who have suffered ship-wrecks, from structure of armed forces on the sea (1949).[11]

From torture and other kinds of inhuman treatment and punishment it is necessary to recognize as an essential contribution to development of the concept of freedom the acceptance of such major legal document for international community as International Covenant on Civil and Political Rights (1966).[12] Having validity and being obligatory for all participants, this legal instrument has recorded: "No one shall be subjected to torture or to cruel, inhuman or degrading treatment or punishment. In particular, no one shall be subjected to without his free consent to medical or scientific experimentation" (Article 7).

In this connection it is necessary to recollect regional international instruments which, certainly, have brought the contribution to establishment of legal bases of freedom from torture and other kinds of inhuman treatment and punishment, supplementing universal international ways of its warranting.

The European Convention on Protection of Human Rights and Basic Freedoms (1950)[13] not in recommendatory but in the obligatory form recorded: "Nobody should be subjected to torture or inhuman or degrading treatment or punishment" (Article 3). However, unlike the Universal Declaration of Human Rights it excluded cruel treatment and punishment from the content of the mentioned right.

The researched right received the registration in other regional international instruments as well: in Article 5 of the inter American Convention on Human Rights (1969)[14] and also in Article 5 of the African Charter of Human Rights and Rights of People (1981).[15] Besides, this right is recorded in Article 3 of the Convention of the CIS about the rights and basic freedoms of a person (1995).[16]

Development of the concept of freedom from torture and other kinds of inhuman treatment and punishment happened in several directions that presupposes specificity in the field of legal regulation of the given right depending on the sphere of its realization; the subjects, called to ensure the provision of its protection and subjects of realization.

Thus, human rights with reference to imprisoned persons, including the right to freedom from torture and other kinds of inhuman treatment or punishment, became a subject of "the minimal standard rules of treatment of prisoners"[17] which were developed on the basis of standards of treatment of prisoners and were accepted on June, 31st, 1957

The main applicability of the Arch of principles of protection of all persons, subjected to detention or the conclusion in any form (1989),[18] the establishment of internationally-legal standards for an estimation of treatment of a person subjected to detention in any form, including interdiction of torture and other kinds of inhuman treatment or punishment.

According to Main Principles for the Treatment of Prisoners (1990)[19] the rights of prisoners correspond to the human rights stated in the Universal Declaration of Human Rights, International Covenant on

Civil and Political rights and other Covenants of the United Nations (5 principle).

The minimal standard rules of the United Nations concerning the measures which were not connected with imprisonment (the Tokyo Rules)[20], accepted in 1990, provide: "the measures not connected with imprisonment exclude carrying out of medical or psychological experiments with the offender or unjustified risk of causing to them physical or cultural wounds" (a rule 3.8).

Thus, the result of activity of bodies of international community for this historical period became the creation of the system of internationally-legal regulations providing realization of the mentioned right of a special category of persons, i.e. persons, subjected to detention or imprisonment of any form or to the measures which were not connected with imprisonment.

At the same time the correct functioning of law enforcement bodies is considered by a condition of effective protection of basic rights and freedoms of a person, including the given right. The first document in there was the Code of Conduct for Law Enforcement Officials (1979)[21] which presupposes transformation in the national legislation of Article 5 of the Universal Declaration of basic rights of a person and Article 7 of International Covenant on Civil and Political Rights recording of the right to freedom from torture and other kinds of inhuman treatment or punishment (Article 5 of the Code).

It seems necessary to recollect the European Declaration on Police (1979) according to which "punishment without court and investigation, torture and other forms of inhumane or degrading treatment or punishment remain under interdiction under any circumstances" (Article 3).

The importance of the given international instruments in guarantying of the rights to freedom from torture and other kinds of inhuman treatment or punishment means that character of functions on ensuring of the law and order and ways of their realization render direct influence on realization of the given right.

Process of preparation, acceptance and use the whole system of internationally-legal regulations, has both obligatory and the recommendatory character, directed on formation of the concept and the content of the considered right and also its realizations regulating separate aspects and protection, led to an opportunity and necessity of development of the special fundamental legal regulations directly expressing the concept of freedom of a person from torture and other kinds of inhuman treatment and punishment. To such international instruments accepted by international community it is necessary to refer the Declaration on the Protection of All Persons from Being Subjected to Torture and Other Cruel, Inhuman or Degrading Treatment or Punishment (1975) and the Convention against Torture and other Cruel, Inhuman or Degrading Treatment or Punishment (1984).

The analysis of the content of the legal regulations, concerning legal regulation of freedom from torture and other cruel, inhuman or degrading treatment and punishment, enables to emphasize the concepts, allowing to open the content of the researched right. It is necessary to refer to them: "torture", "cruel treatment (or punishment)", "inhuman treatment (or punishment)", "degrading treatment (or punishment)", "medical or scientific experiments", "violence".

Thus, it is necessary to make the clause. The European Commission and Court on Human Rights at interpretation of Article 3 of the European Convention on protection of human rights and basic freedoms, recording the researched right, distinguish three concepts: "torture", "inhuman treatment or punishment", "degrading treatment or punishment".

From the analysis of the above-stated instruments it is obvious that the term "cruel, inhuman or degrading treatment and punishment" is a generalizing and basic determinant of the acts, forbidden by internationally-legal regulations, the Constitution of the Russian Federation and other legal regulations.

Internationally-legal regulations and Russian legislation normative do not determine the concept of "cruel, inhuman or degrading treatment or punishment". Alongside with it normative definition of torture takes place.

For the first time the concept "torture" received the normative definition and recording in the Declaration. It would be desirable to remind that one of the first scientific definitions of torture is the definition given by Caesarea Bekkaria in the well-known work "Crimes and Punishment" (1764).[22]

Developing sights at concept of torture, the Declaration in Article 1 determines torture as "any act by which severe pain or suffering, whether physical or mental, is intentionally inflicted by or at the instigation of a public official on a person for such purposes as obtaining from him or a third person information or confession, punishing him for an act he has committed or is suspected of having committed, Or intimidating him or other persons".

The convention in Article 1 gives fuller definition of torture, opening the content of this concept as "any action to which to any person the severe pain or suffering is deliberately caused, physical or moral to receive from them or from the third party of data or a concept of, to punish them for action which it or has made the third party or of which carrying out it is of the suspected and also to intimidate or force its or the third party, or for any reason based on discrimination of any character when such pain or suffering is inflicted by the state official, acting in official capacity, or on their instigation, or from them is conducted or a tacit consent".

The definition of torture recorded by the Declaration and the Convention is constructed by means of a legal design of legal behaviour. The legal model of illegal behaviour as well as any model of jurisprudence has an interpreting and explaining function.[23] Therefore, such model (a legal design) as a structure of an offence, can serve as means to interpretation of the act expressed in the form of torture.

According to a common view about structure of an offence torture determines the special structure having in the structure the following elements: the subject, object, the subjective party, the objective party.[24]

The subject of torture, proceeding from the content of Article 1 of the indicated Declaration, is the official. The convention specifies that as a subject of a considered offence the state officials acting in official quality are assumed. Both the Declaration and the Convention recognize commitment of the given offence in the form of partnership if it is carried out on instigation or with is conducted or a tacit consent of officials.

In spite of the fact that internationally-legal regulations do not contain definition of general concept of the official person, it is possible to find interpretation of the concepts of separate kinds of officials in international law. In particular, Code of Conduct for Law Enforcement Officials has a comment according to which "the official on ensuring of the law and order" includes the term of all prescribed or elected officials connected with use the right who have police powers, especially powers on detention of fenders.

General Assembly of the United Nations connects allocation of the given group officials with character of functions carried out by them and an opportunity of abusing at realization of their powers and, first of all, an opportunity of use by them torture and other inhuman kinds of treatment or punishment (Article 5 of the present Code).

As it has been noted above, officials make actions in the form of torture if these actions are carried out can and not: on instigation, i.e. as a result of declination of the subject by the official to participation in carrying out of torture; with it is conducted by officials, i.e. when the official has all necessary information on use torture; from a tacit consent of the official, i.e. when the official does not interfere or even eliminates obstacles in carrying out of torture. The subject, who has made given actions, not being the official, is considered by the accomplice of such official offence as torture.

It is an object of the offence accomplished in the form of torture, personal safety of the victim or the third parties (physical, moral and cultural). Thus, a personal safety for the first time recorded by the Declaration of Civil Human Rights (1789) as a principle of a civil society is the important social value regarding a person.

In the legal literature there is no common opinion concerning definition of personal safety. According to the "Dictionary of Russian" it is necessary to understand position at which danger does not threaten the safety of anybody or anything. Thus, danger is understood as an opportunity of threat by something dangerous, capable to cause any harm or misfortune.[25]

In legal understanding personal safety presupposes a status of security of the vital properties of a person from internal and external threats. A.A. Ter-Akopov considers that safety of a person represents the complex status including physical, mental, genetic, reproductive and cultural health and provides corresponding system of ensuring.[26]

In opinion of F.M. Rudinsky, it is necessary to consider personal safety in three aspects: 1) physical lives assuming protection, health and a body; 2) moral assuming protection of honour, dignity and reputation; 3) cultural assuming protection of consciousness, ideas and opinions of an individual.[27]

The following position of the mentioned Convention allows determining object of torture: causing as a result of torture of a severe pain or suffering physical (i.e. infringement of physical safety); causing of moral suffering (i.e. infringement of moral safety); intimidation (i.e. infringement of cultural safety). However, here they do not join pain and sufferings which arise only as a result of lawful sanctions and are inseparable from them or are caused by them.

It is required to specify that personal safety is expressed in an acute status of an individual at which there is no illegal, compulsory infringement of their physical, moral or cultural integrity.[28]

The objective party, in conformity with Article 1 of the Declaration, includes such elements as actions and consequences in the form of causing a severe pain or suffering, physical or intellectual (see: "or moral" is established by Article 1 of the Convention).

The court decision of attributes of the objective party of torture allows determining structure of the given offence as material, i.e. when the fact of committing an offence is connected with approach of certain consequences. Therefore, explainable normative recording of definition of torture as any actions, i.e. without attributes qualifying them.

During use torture various ways and methods can be used. The most widespread methods, according to messages of legal experts, are rapes, suffocations by polyethylene packages or any chemicals, use of electric bludgeons and electric shockers, deprivation of sleep and meal, torture by cold and heat, beating, thrashing.[29] Methods and instruments of torture became a subject of various researches.[30]

Consequences of the actions determined as torture have only the special legal importance. In objective to the form of a consequence of torture are determined as causing of a severe pain and suffering, physical or moral, essential physical and moral damage.

It seems that "severe pain" specifies the concept of a significant degree of painful senses, their danger to ability to live and infringement of normal functioning of an organism[31]. Severe pain can result from physical injuries among which it is possible to mark out: mutilation and wounds, beating and torture, damages and frustration of health. Thus, physical injuries can render not only physical but also mental influence.

Concerning the concept of "suffering" it is noted in the literature that actions of a harm-doer should necessarily reflect in consciousness of the victim and cause certain mental reaction. Thus, nocuous changes reflect in consciousness in the form of senses (physical sufferings) and notions (moral sufferings).[32] Physical sufferings are connected with certain external influence on physical and mental well-being.

Thus, Russian judiciary practice recognizes that moral sufferings can arise "in connection with loss of relatives, impossibility to continue an active social life, loss of work, disclosing of family, medical secrecy, distribution of data mismatching the reality discrediting honour, dignity or business reputation of a citizen, time limitation or deprivation of any rights..."[33]

Thus, in the case of consideration Ireland against the Great Britain (1978) the European Court on Human Rights has paid attention that for ascertaining infringement of regulations about interdiction of torture in practice of achievement of a minimum level of cruelty should be revealed, considering some factors, such as sex, age and a state of health of a victim and also duration of such treatment, the physical and moral sufferings.[34] Thus, the estimation of this minimum has relative character.

The subjective party of the given kind of an offence is characterized by direct intention. The declaration in clause 1 of Article 1 determines the form of fault through concept "the carrying out of actions". Simultaneously in Article 2 deliberate character of its carrying out is emphasized. The convention also normative records the deliberate form of carrying out of the given offence. Thus, the direct intention is necessary and at partnership in the indicated kind of an offence.

As an obligatory qualifying element of the subjective party the purpose of carrying out of torture should be considered. In conformity with Article 1 of the Declaration the purpose is: 1) receiving of the information or a confession; 2) punishment for action which has made a person subjected to torture (note: "or the third party" is established by the Convention) or of which carrying out of the suspected; 3) its intimidation or the third party. The convention, except for noted above things concerning the purposes of carrying out of torture, records compulsion and limitation or deprivation of the rights of certain categories of citizens based on discrimination character (segregation, genocide, etc.).

By results of the questioning carried out among chiefs of local police precincts of the Astrakhan, Volgograd, Ulyanovsk areas and Republic Kalmykia and also inspectors of the Volgograd area, 65% of interrogated inspectors and 24% of interrogated chiefs of local police precincts consider that there are the purposes justifying the use of illegal physical and moral compulsion during inquiry or investigation. For example: with a view of disclosing of any kinds of crimes is accordingly 8.5 and 55%; with a view of disclosing of crimes against the state is 58 and 18%; with a view of disclosing of grave crimes is 25 and 35%; with a view of protection of a person is 8.5 and 8.5% of respondents.

The facts of use torture in activity of office of Public Prosecutor and the Ministry of Internal Affairs with a view of receiving of a confession of or other information having demonstrative value became object of separate journalistic investigations.[35]

Despite of available divergences in international, regional and interstate practice of qualification of the torture, the given act should be estimated as an aggravated and going kind of cruel, inhuman or degrading treatment or punishment.

It is necessary to emphasize that the concept of "cruel, inhuman or degrading treatment or punishment" represents itself as estimated. In the legal literature under estimated concept general attributes recording most generalized remedial phenomena and interpreted by estimation during law enforcement concepts are considered.[36] Thus, they, as a rule, relate to the group of current concepts at which basis the ethical standards act.[37]

During interpretation of estimated concepts the role doctrinal interpretation and also judiciary practice is great. Proceeding from it, great value in interpretation of the concept "cruel, inhuman or degrading treatment or punishment" refers to law enforcement to practice of international and regional bodies and also judiciary practice of the separate states.

It would be desirable to emphasize that internationally-legal regulations differentiate between inhuman treatment and inhuman punishment. General for them is that they act as not a legal form of the state compulsion. Thus, if the first carries precautionary or secured character, from the point of view of a person making these actions the second, in their opinion, carries out functions of the state sanctions.

It is required to recollect that statements for interdiction of cruel and unusual punishment (Article 10 of the English Bill of Rights 1689) have been included in many early Constitutions of American states, together with in the Constitution of the USA (1791) as an Eighth Amendment. The Canadian Bill of Rights 1960 established the interdiction of the cruel and unusual treatment and punishment. The identical formulation was included in the Canadian Constitutional Charter of Rights and Freedoms (1982) and is included in Constitutions of other countries.

It is necessary to note that in the modern world still there are the countries legislatively establishing cruel kinds of punishment. For example, Article 119 of the Islamic Criminal Code of Iran contains a regulation of punishment in the form of throwing stones. The punishment prescribed by court (thrashing and amputation of hands) are still used in Iran, Saudi Arabia and the United Arab Emirates.[38]

The American judiciary practice does not regard corporal punishment as a form of inhuman punishment and only in the case of excessive and unreasonable use of force considers it as a kind of inhuman treatment. At the same time the Human Rights Committee of the United Nations considers that prohibition of inhuman treatment and punishment should extend on corporal punishment, including those which are used as educational or a disciplinary means.[39]

The problem of the death penalty as inhuman punishment is also interesting. Speech in this case goes about the death sentences which have been taken out any way and also without observance of corresponding remedial measures.

Special kinds of inhuman treatment (punishment) by international and regional community and also by the separate states are considered as institutionalization of certain practice.

Firstly, there is discrimination. In the case of East-Africans when the United Kingdom refused to recognize as immigrants approximately 30 people, the European Commission, having found out that the legislation of the United Kingdom discriminated these people on the basis of their color of skin and race, decided that such legalized racism was degrading according to international standards concerning interdiction of inhuman treatment.[40]

Secondly, there is extradition and exile. According to Article 3 of the Convention, "No State Party shall expel, return (*"refouler"*) or extradite a person to another State where there are substantial grounds for believing that he would be in danger of being subjected to torture", considering existence of practice of rough, scandalous and mass infringement of human rights in the given state.

According to "Amnesty International", Russian authorities in 1996 Elgudga Hutaevich Meshia, a member of the governmental opposition, have been forcibly repatriated to Georgia where he could be subjected to torture and cruel treatment and Rathem Kasiev, former Minister of Defence of Azerbaijan, possible passing a death sentence was forcibly returned to the country where he was threatened with cruel treatment.[41]

Thirdly, there is "expectation of death". Thus, the European Commission, considering case of Kirkwood against the Great Britain (1984), noted that it was impossible to suppose that this long period of uncertainty ("expectation of death penalty") dropped out of the concept of inhuman or degrading treatment or punishment.[42]

Fourthly, there is violence. In 1993 in the Constitution of the Russian Federation the violence was recognized as an independent kind of inhuman treatment (punishment).[43] It is necessary to note that the subjects of the given act are not only officials but also any persons encroaching on personal safety. Thus, Russian legislation, unlike internationally-legal regulations, not only marks out a special kind of inhuman treatment and punishment but also changes the scope of the content of the concept of the latter.

Fifthly, there are experiments. Recording interdiction of inhuman treatment and punishment, internationally-legal regulations and Russian legislation use such concept as carrying out of medical, or scientific and other experiments without the free consent of a person subjected to them (Article 7 of International Covenant on Civil and Political Rights, Clause

2 of Article 21 of the Constitution of the Russian Federation, etc.) but do not contain normative definition of the given offence.

It seems that compulsory experiments concerning people can be seen as a special kind of inhuman treatment or punishment and at the same time as a version of torture or other kinds of inhuman treatment and punishment. Thus, according to the Uruguayan Medical Association about 600 doctors were involved in carrying out of torture in Uruguay during existence of a dictatorial regime.[44]

Thus, depending on features of the subject having personal safety, international and Russian legal practice marks out as a special kind of inhuman treatment conditions of keeping of imprisoned persons and prisoners and military men mismatching international standards; any displays of inhuman treatment and punishment concerning children and women; having discrimination, offensive or humiliating character of treatment of invalids, persons of a various national identity; any displays of intolerance from the state and its officials concerning a person professing other religion or having other belief; the facts of inhuman treatment or punishment concerning prisoners of war and civilians during military actions, etc.

It is possible to assume that features of the state of the subject, whose personal safety acts as an object of inhuman treatment and punishment are or limited individual freedom, or incapacity (the limited capacity), or available social distinctions.

It is necessary to emphasize that a lot of infringement of interdiction of inhuman treatment and punishment is found out, thus, it is possible to speak about using of torture and other kinds of cruel, inhuman or degrading treatment and punishment. Two elements are necessary to determine the existence of the given practice: repeatability of actions and official tolerance.[45]

The significant number of cases of torture or other kinds of inhuman treatment or punishment which reflect general situation are considered as "repeatability of actions". "The official tolerance" means that though instruments of torture or other kinds of inhuman treatment or punishment are accomplished illegally, with them are reconciled in the meaning that chiefs who bear the direct responsibility, know about such instruments but nevertheless do not undertake any actions to punish guilty or not to admit their recurrence; or that the higher body, having numerous statements, shows indifference, refusing to carry out appropriate investigation with a view of definition of reliability or unauthenticated, or that at proceeding impartial hearing such complaints is not observed.

Despite of available facts of inhuman treatment or punishment in the Russian Federation, in 1995 the experts of the Council of Europe concerning conformity of a legal order of Russia to the main European principles have noted that they have not been find "traces of serious and regular infringement of human rights, especially regular practice of torture".[46] At the same time in the Special Report on Human Rights Commissioner in the Russian Federation about infringement of the rights of citizens by employees of the Ministry of Internal Affairs of the Russian Federation and criminally-executive system of the Ministry of Justice of the Russian Federation in 2000 the essential growth of number of complaints to illegal actions of law enforcement bodies' officers was emphasized. Thus, in spite of "the recommendation of international organizations, data of independent mass media, and numerous complaints and statements of persons who have really suffered from torture, officials of Russian state do not wish to recognize the problem of torture in our country really existing".[47]

In the literature the opinion is expressed that "prohibition to subject to torture, to inhuman or degrading treatment or punishment is an extremely serious right by nature".[48] Thus, Donna Gomien, David Harris, Leo Zvaak think, "The right to be free from torture and the right to be free from inhuman or humiliating treatment is one of the most important human rights …".[49]

Being an international law and normatively recorded by the Universal Declaration of Human Rights and International Covenant on Civil and Political Rights, the right to freedom from torture and other kinds of inhuman treatment or punishment can have the constitutional form and should be considered as a basic guaranteed civil human right. The analysis of the constitutional development of the Russian Federation and the foreign states shows the obviously expressed tendency to recording in Organic laws of the above-mentioned right, despite of certain divergences in forms of expression of its content in Constitutions of these countries.

The Constitution of Japan (1947) approves that "the use by public officials of torture and cruel punishment (Article 36) is strongly forbidden." The Organic law records also special guarantees, "the confession made on compulsion, under torture or under threat of or after unfairly long imprisonment or holding in custody cannot be considered as a proof" (part 2 Article 38).[50]

According to the constitutional provisions of Sweden, "each citizen should be protected from corporal punishment. Similarly they should be protected from torture and from medical influence with a view of compulsion or contrary to their desire" (Ch. 2 5 Forms of Board).[51]

According to Article 2.54 of the Constitution of the Hungarian Republic, 1949 (in edition of 1990): "Nobody can be subjected to torture, cruel, inhumane, degrading treatment or punishment; carrying out on a person without his consent of medical or research experiments" is strongly forbidden.

Such formulations of attributes and guarantees of the right to freedom from torture and other kinds of inhuman treatment or punishment are used in the constitutional instruments of other states. It is necessary to note that, from the point of view of legislators of some the countries, the given right not always is issued as an independent constitutional law and can be considered as one of the competences included in the content of personal freedom and inviolability, or as a guarantee of the latter (or other freedom).

At the same time it is necessary to remark that the constitutional reforms happening during the modern period, give to the researched right character of an independent fundamental law, alongside with the rights to life, to respect of dignity, to freedom and personal immunity, etc. It says the increased value of international law during regulation of personal freedom within the limits of legal system of the state, a concept of the countries of human rights and a principle of a primate of international law above internal.

The Constitution of the Russian Federation (1978) in the first edition did not provide as a core right to freedom from torture and other kinds of inhuman treatment and punishment. The mentioned right received the constitutional concept as a result of political reforms in the country, expressed in acceptance on November, 22nd, 1991 by the Supreme Soviet of the Russian Federation of the Declaration of Rights and Freedoms of a Person and a Citizen who provisions were included then into the text of the Constitution of Russia.

According to Clause 4 of Article 8 of the present Declaration it is recorded: "Nobody can be subjected to torture, violence, other cruel or degrading treatment or punishment. Nobody can be subjected to medical, scientific or other experiments without his voluntary consent".[52]

The given formulation of the right was completely reproduced in part 3 Article 59 in the last edition of the Constitution of the Russian Federation, 1978.[53]. It was also saved in the Constitution of the Russian Federation.[54]

The right to freedom from torture and other kinds of inhuman treatment or punishment is natural, inalienable, termless, directly operating, not subjected to any limitations, obtained international and constitutional concept and recording in the civil human rights, expressed in having personal safety, excepting use torture and other inhuman treatment or punishment, which realization and protection is guaranteed by international and state-compulsory influence.

The important role in the system of international warranting of the given right refers to control and supervising of international bodies. The special control and supervision over the sphere of enforcement of the right to freedom from torture and other kinds of inhuman treatment or punishment is carried out by Committee against Torture which activity provides the system of granting reports and special lecturers concerning torture of the Commission of the United Nations on Human Rights.

Besides, it is necessary not toe, that the question of torture was also considered by Human Rights Committee; Special lecturer concerning executions without appropriate proceeding or any executions and also working group on detention of the Commission of the United Nations on Human Rights.

In the system of warranting of the given right preventive measures among which it is necessary to mention the activity of the European Committee on the Prevention of torture and inhuman or degrading treatment or punishment have special value. Development of international preventive measures within the limits of preparation of the Optional Protocol for the Convention against Torture proceeds. Besides, the African Commission of Human Rights and People decided to realize the preventive measures.

The element of international system of warranting is the established measures of protection of the infringed right. Messages on infringement of the mentioned right can be considered by Human Rights Committee and also by the Committee against Torture. However, the activity of these organizations, providing restoration of the infringed right, does not provide compensation of damage and neutralization of consequences.

The European system has a more effective mechanism of protection of human rights and basic freedoms, including the considered rights according to which the state-offender is obliged to make changes in legislative and law-enforcement personal practice, paying to a victim an indemnification for an offence.

The guarantees providing the effective use of internationally-legal provisions recording the given right are the measures of international responsibility. So, the creation of international tribunals (for example, international tribunals for the former Yugoslavia and Rwanda) is stipulated.

Thus, international community pays special attention to the problem of establishment of international criminal court and acceptance of the Code of crimes against world and safety of mankind among which torture and other inhuman kinds of treatment or punishment are mentioned.

Among interstate guarantees of the right to freedom from torture and other kinds of inhuman treatment or punishment the main place refers to the constitutional guarantees. A special guarantee of the given right is its constitutional recording (Clause 2 of Article 21).

Alongside with it, constitutionally-legal ensuring is based on the mechanism of general constitutional warranting of basic rights and freedoms of a person and a citizen in the Russian Federation.

Criminal guarantees of protection of the considered right are presented in the form of the criminal liability for committing actions that contradict to the internationally-legal standards.

Up to 2003 of the Criminal Code of the Russian Federation did not contain a normative definition of torture. In 2003 addition was made to Article 117 of Criminal Code in the form of the note where torture was characterized as follows: "causing of physical or moral sufferings with a view of compulsion to evidence or other actions contradicting will of a person and also with a view of punishment, or in other purposes".

This short story can be considered as a step forward in development of the given kind of guarantees that characterized more widely what is formulated in Article 1 of the Convention against Torture.

In the system of warranting of the right to freedom from torture and other kinds of cruel, inhuman or degrading treatment or punishment it is necessary to consider criminally-remedial guarantees as well. In Clause 2 of Article 9 of the Code of Criminal Procedure of the Russian Federation it is established: "Anybody from participants of criminal legal proceedings cannot be subjected to violence, torture, other cruel or degrading treatment". Simultaneously with it Clause 1 of Article 75 of the Code of Criminal Procedure records a rule: "the proofs received with infringement of requirements of the present Code are inadmissible. Inadmissible proofs have no validity and cannot be put in a basis of a charge ...." Thus, "the confession of the accused in committing of a crime can be necessary in a basis of charge only at confirmation of his guilt by set of proofs available on criminal case" (Clause 2 of Article 77 of the Code of Criminal Procedure of the Russian Federation).

The criminal statistics annually registers the facts of compulsion to evidence by use of threats or other illegal actions from a person making inquiry or preliminary investigation.[55]

In the Report on activity of Human Rights Commissioner in the Russian Federation in 2003 the typical ways of torture used in places of imprisonment are listed: beatings of the suspected and of the accused, depriving them of food and water, blocking of access of air, and threats.[56]

The special group of guarantees of the right to freedom from torture and other kinds of inhuman treatment or punishment is made by the guarantees which provide conditions of holding in custody under corresponding international standards of the suspected and of the accused. In this connection the great value has the federal law[57] accepted on June, 21st, 1995, devoted to these questions which provide significant expansion of the rights and freedoms of the suspected and of the accused, holding in custody, and their guarantees.

Criminally-executive guarantees also have great value in the system of guarantees of the right to freedom from torture and other kinds of cruel, inhuman or degrading treatment or punishment.

It is necessary to recognize as a special guarantee of the mentioned right the provision according to which the practice of use the criminally-executive legislation is based on "strict observance of guarantees of protection from torture, violence and other cruel or degrading treatment of the condemned" (Clause 3 of Article 3 of the Correctional Code of the Russian Federation).

Besides, according to Clause 2 of Article 12 of the Correctional Code of the Russian Federation, "The condemned have the right to the polite treatment from personnel of the prison. They should not be subjected to cruel or degrading treatment. Measures of compulsion to the condemned can be used precisely on the basis of the law" (Clause 2 of Article 12 of the Correctional Code of the Russian Federation). Simultaneously, "the condemned irrespective of their consent cannot be subjected to medical and other experiments threatening their life and health" (Clause 3 of Article 12 of the Correctional Code of the Russian Federation).

Certainly, positive moment in criminally-executive reforming is recording in the criminally-executive legislation of basic rights of the condemned, including a concept of the right to personal safety (Article 13 of the Correctional Code of the Russian Federation).

Alongside with it, other criminally-executive guarantees of the indicated right are also stipulated.

Realization and protection of the right to freedom from torture and other kinds of cruel, inhuman or degrading treatment or punishment demands the presence of administratively-legal guarantees.

It is obviously necessary to consider the problem of presence of special structures of administrative offences, which attributes come within the concept of cruel, inhuman or degrading treatment.

Within the limits of administratively-legal guarantees of the right to freedom from torture and other kinds of inhuman treatment or punishment it is also required to solve the problem of admissibility to use measures of direct compulsion (special measures of administrative suppression). In conditions of sharp increase in number of law enforcement bodies and officials which are distinguished by the right of use measures of direct compulsion (administrative suppression), the special importance is given to the perfection of laws and statutory acts regulating these questions. Thus, codification of laws on measures of direct compulsion (measures of special administrative suppression) seems necessary.[58]

Speaking about civil and civil-remedial guarantees of the given right, it is necessary to emphasize that the Civil Code of the Russian Federation considers life and health, dignity of a person, security of person, honour and reputation, inviolability of private, personal and family life (Clause 1 of Article 150) as an object of civil protection, and also establishes measures of protection of the infringed right (Article 12, 15, 16 of the Civil Code of the Russian Federation).

However, the institution of compensation of the damage caused by illegal actions of law enforcement bodies, established by the Decree of Presidium of the Supreme Soviet of the USSR on May, 18th, 1981, does not include torture and other kinds of cruel, inhuman or degrading treatment or punishment as an acute basis for a duty of the state to compensate the damage as it is stipulated by the constitutional provisions (Article 53), and a number of functions on protection of the infringed right by the state bodies, and human rights organizations do not incur.

It is possible to recognize as conditions of ensuring of the researched right cultural guarantees that consist in formation at representatives of Russian and world community of knowledge of the given right and feelings of intolerance to torture and to those who use them. Thus, the basic purpose in this the sphere of are achievement of general understanding of interdiction of torture and other kinds of inhuman treatment or punishment, awareness and knowledge of the public concerning realization and protection of the given right and also aspiration to work according to these international standards. Therefore, education of all population of Russia and other states in the spirit of respect of the right to freedom from torture and other kinds of cruel, inhuman or degrading treatment or punishment should become one of the major directions in guarantying of this right.

Notes

1. Hereinafter the replacement onto «freedom from the inhumane treatment or punishment» is possible.

2. In detail see: Vallon. History of Slavery in the Ancient World. Moscow, 1941. P. 13. / Подробнее см.: Валлон. История рабства в античном мире. М., 1941. С. 13.

3. See: Pokrovsky I.A. The History of the Roman Law. 1917. P. 17. / См.: Покровский И. А. История римского права. 1917. С. 17.

4. The Collection of Documents on General History of the State and the Law. Moscow, 1977. P. 53. / Сборник документов по всеобщей истории государства и права. Л., 1977. С. 53.

5. See: The Reader on History of the State and the Law. The pre-October period. Moscow, 1990. P. 44-55. / См.: Хрестоматия по истории государства и права. Дооктябрьский период. М., 1990. С. 44-55.

6. Ibidem. P. 58.

7. See: Ibidem. P. 104.

8. See: Ibidem. P. 116.

9. See: United Nations Organization. Official reports of the first part of the third session of General Assembly. A/810. P. 39-42. / См.: Организация Объединенных Наций. Официальные отчеты первой части третьей сессии Генеральной Ассамблеи. А/810. С. 39–42.

10. See: Geneva Conventions of August, 12th, 1949, and Additional Protocols to them. Moscow, 1994. P. 25. / См.: Женевские конвенции от 12 августа 1949 года и Дополнительные протоколы к ним. М., 1994. С. 25.

11. See: Ibidem. P. 52.

12. See: USSR and International Cooperation in the Sphere of Human Rights: Documents and materials. Moscow, 1989. P. 302. It was signed by the USSR on March, 18th, 1968, and ratified on September, 18th, 1973, came into force on March, 23rd, 1976 / См.: СССР и международное сотрудничество в области прав человека: Документы и материалы. М., 1989. С. 302. Подписан СССР 18 марта 1968 г., ратифицирован 18 сентября 1973 г., вступил в силу 23 марта 1976 г.

13. See: Ibidem. P. 160.

14. See: International Acts on Human Rights: Comp. of Documents. Moscow, 1999. P. 720. / См.: Международные акты о правах человека: Сб. документов. М., 1999. С. 720.

15. See: Ibidem. P. 737.

16. See: Ibidem. P. 712.

17. See: Collection of Standards and Norms of the United Nations in the Sphere of the Criminality Prevention and Criminal Justice. The United Nations. New York, 1992. P. 102. / См.: Сборник стандартов и норм ООН в области предупреждения преступности и уголовного правосудия. ООН. Нью-Йорк, 1992. С. 102.

18. See: Ibidem. P. 319.

19. See: Ibidem. P. 129.

20. Ibidem. P. 132.

21. See: United Nations Organization. General Assembly. Official Reports. 34-th session. Add. 46 (A/34/46). P. 238-240. / См.: Организация Объединенных Наций.

Генеральная Ассамблея. Официальные отчеты. 34-я сессия. Доп. № 46 (А/34/46). С. 238–240.

22. See: Beccaria C. About Crimes and Punishments. St. Petersburg, 1803. P. 96-97. / См.: Беккария Ч. О преступлениях и наказаниях. СПб., 1803. С. 96–97.

23. About the Role of the Legal System see: Cherdantsev R.F . Logical and Language Phenomena in the Law, Jurisprudence and Practice. Ekaterinburg, 1993. P. 126-127. / О роли юридической конструкции см.: Черданцев Р. Ф. Логико-языковые феномены в праве, юридической науке и практике. Екатеринбург, 1993. С. 126–127.

24. See: The Course of the Soviet Criminal Law, 1970. P. 17-18, 52; The Course of the Soviet Criminal Law. Moscow, 1981. P. 97, 173. / См.: Курс советского уголовного права М., 1970. С. 17–18, 52; Курс советского уголовного права. Л., 1981. С. 97, 173.

25. See: Ozhegov S.I. Dictionary of Russian. Moscow, 1987. P. 33, 388. / См.: Ожегов С. И. Словарь русского языка. М., 1987. С. 33, 388.

26. See: Ter-Akopov A.A. About Legal Aspects of Mental Activity and Psychological Safety of a Person // The State and the Law. 1993.4. P. 88. / См.: Тер-Акопов А. А. О правовых аспектах психической активности и психологической безопасности человека // Государство и право. 1993. № 4. С. 88.

27. See: Rudinsky F. M. Person and Socialist Legality. Volgograd, 1976. P. 76-78; In the legal literature the regulations about psychological aspect of personal safety are stated. See: Constitution. The Comment / Under gen. edition of V.A. Topornin. Moscow, 1994. P. 144. / См.: Рудинский Ф. М. Личность и социалистическая законность. Волгоград, 1976. С. 76–78; В юридической литературе высказано положение о психологическом аспекте личной безопасности. См.: Конституция. Комментарий / Под общ. ред. Б. А. Топорнина. М., 1994. С. 144.

28. So, the American Convention fixing in Clause 5 the researched right, in the same article specifies physical, spiritual and moral integrity of a person. See: International Acts on Human Rights: Comp. of Documents. P. 721. / Так, Американская конвенция, закрепляющая в ст. 5 исследуемое право, в той же статье указывает на физическую, духовную и моральную целостность личности. См.: Международные акты о правах человека: Сб. документов. С. 721.

29. See: The Annual Report of the Organization «Amnesty International about Infringement of Human Rights» for 1993 // Express chronicle. 7-14th July, 1994.28.; 21-28th July, 1994.30.. / См.: Годовой отчет организации «Международная амнистия о нарушении прав человека» за 1993 г. // Экспресс-хроника. 1994. № 28. 7–14 июля; 1994. № 30. 21–28 июля.

30. See, for example: Bryan L. Torture and Punishments. Smolensk, 1997. / См., например: Брайен Л. Пытки и наказания. Смоленск, 1997.

31. See: Textbook of Russian Criminal Law / Edited by L.S. Belogrits - Kotlyarevsky. Kiev, 1903. P. 370-337. / См.: Учебник русского уголовного права / Под ред. Л. С. Белогриц-Котляревского. Киев, 1903. С. 370–337.

32. See, for example: Erdelevsky A.M. Moral Harm and Indemnification for Sufferings: Scientific and practical textbook. Moscow, 1998. P. 1. / См., например: Эрделевский А. М. Моральный вред и компенсация за страдания: Науч.-практ пособие. М., 1998. С. 1.

33. The decision of Plenum of the Supreme Court of the Russian Federation // Rossiiskaya Gazeta. 1995.Feb., 8 / Постановление Пленума Верховного Суда РФ // Российская газета. 1995. 8 февр.

34. See: The Judgement on the Case of Ireland versus the United Kingdom of January, 18th, 1978 Series A. 26. P. 65, par. 162. / См.: Судебное решение по делу Ирландия против Соединенного Королевства от 18 января 1978 г. Series A. № 26. P. 65, par. 162.

35. See: The Report on Human Rights Commissioner's Work in the Russian Federation in 2000. Moscow, 2001. / См.: Доклад о деятельности Уполномоченного по правам человека в Российской Федерации в 2000 году. М., 2001.

36. See: Vlasenko N.A. Problems of Accuracy the Form of the Law Expression (the linguistics-logical analysis): Abstract of Dissertation of Dr. of Jurisprudence Ekaterinburg, 1997. P. 57; Kashanina T V. Estimated Concepts of the Soviet Law: Abstract of Dissertation of Cand. of Jurisprudence. Sverdlovsk, 1974. P. 6-8. / См.: Власенко Н. А. Проблемы точности выражения формы права (лингво-логический анализ): Автореф. дис. ... д-ра юрид. наук. Екатеринбург, 1997. С. 57; Кашанина Т. В. Оценочные понятия в советском праве: Автореф. дис. ... канд. юрид. наук. Свердловск, 1974. С. 6–8.

37. According to the explanatory dictionary "severe" - the extremely severe, ruthless, brutal; "brutal" - very severe; "to humiliate" - to offend someone's pride or dignity. See: Ozhegov S.I.The Dictionary of Russian. P. 42, 72, 166. / Согласно положению толкового словаря «жестокий» – крайне суровый, безжалостный, беспощадный, бесчеловечный; «бесчеловечный» – очень жестокий; «унизить» – оскорбить чье-нибудь самолюбие или достоинство. См.: Ожегов С. И. Словарь русского языка. С. 42, 72, 166.

38. See: The Annual Report of the Organization «Amnesty International on Infringement of Human Rights» for 1993 / См.: Годовой отчет организации «Международная амнистия о нарушении прав человека» за 1993 г.

39. See: Human rights and Imprisonment Before Trail // Comp. of International Standards, concerning imprisonment before trail. The United Nations. New York; Geneva, 1994. P. 75. / См.: Права человека и предварительное заключение // Сб. междунар. стандартов, касающихся предварительного заключения. ООН. Нью-Йорк; Женева, 1994. С. 75.

40. See: Ibidem. P. 141.

41. See: Index MA: EUR 46/46/96R.

42. See: Gomien D., Harris D., Zvaak L. European Convention on Human Rights and European Social Charter: Law and Practice. Moscow, 1998. P. 124. / См.: Гомьен Д., Харрис Д., Зваак Л. Европейская конвенция о правах человека и Европейская социальная хартия: право и практика. М., 1998. С. 124.

43. In detail see: Violent Criminality / Edited by V. N. Kudryavtsev, A. V. Naumov. Moscow, 1997. / Подробнее см.: Насильственная преступность / Под ред. В. Н. Кудрявцева, А. В. Наумова. М., 1997.

44. See: The Report of Committee Against Torture. General Assembly. Official reports. 47-th session. Add. 44 (A/47/44). The United Nations. New York, 1992. P. 34. / См.: Доклад Комитета против пыток. Генеральная Ассамблея. Официальные отчеты. 47-я сессия. Доп. № 44 (A/47/44). ООН. Нью-Йорк, 1992. С. 34.

45. See, for example: Greece against the United Kingdom. Comm. Report 5.11.69, par. 28-29; Yearbook 12. P. 195-196. From: Gomien D., Harris D., Zvaak L. European Convention on Human Rights and European Social Charter: Law and Practice. P. 134, 135. / См., например: Греция против Соединенного Королевства. Comm. Report 5.11.69, par. 28–29; Yearbook 12. P. 195–196. Приводится по: Гомьен Д., Харрис Д., Зваак Л. Европейская конвенция о правах человека и Европейская социальная хартия: право и практика. С. 134, 135.

46. Human Rights in Russia - International Estimation. Moscow, 1995. P. 125. / Права человека в России – международное измерение. М., 1995. С. 125.

47. The Special Report of the Human Rights Commissioner in the Russian Federation. Moscow, 2000. P. 216. / Специальный доклад Уполномоченного по правам человека в Российской Федерации. М., 2000. С. 216.

48. Gomien D. Guidebook on the European Convention on Protection of Human Rights. The Council of Europe, 1994. P. 14. / Гомьен Д. Путеводитель по Европейской конвенции о защите прав человека. Совет Европы, 1994. С. 14.

49. Gomien D., Harris D., Zvaak L. European Convention on Human Rights and European Social Charter: Law and Practice.P. 133. / Гомьен Д., Харрис Д., Зваак Л. Европейская конвенция о правах человека и Европейская социальная хартия: право и практика. С. 133.

50. See: Ibidem. P. 446, 447.

51. See: Constitutions of the States of the European Union. Moscow, 1997. P. 703, 706. / См.: Конституции государств Европейского Союза. М., 1997. С. 703, 706.

52. Quoted on: The Constitutional (State) Law of the Foreign States: In 4 vol. Vol. 1. Moscow, 1995. P. 93. / Цит. по: Конституционное (государственное) право зарубежных государств: В 4 т. Т. 1. М., 1995. С. 93.

53. See, for example: Ebzeev B.S. Constitution. Democracy. Human rights. Moscow, 1992. P. 159. / См., например: Эбзеев Б. С. Конституция. Демократия. Права человека. М., 1992. С. 159.

54. See: The Declaration of Rights and Freedoms of a Person and a Citizen // Sheets of the Council of People's Deputies and the Supreme Soviet of the Russian Federation. 1991.52. Clause 1865. / См.: Декларация прав и свобод человека и гражданина // Ведомости Совета народных депутатов и Верховного Совета РФ. 1991. № 52. Ст. 1865.

55. See: The Criminal Situation in Russia and its Changes. Moscow, 1996. P. 41-42. / См.: Криминальная ситуация в России и ее изменения. М., 1996. С. 41–42.

56. See: The Report on Human Rights Commissioner's Work in the Russian Federation in 2003. P. 10. / См.: Доклад о деятельности Уполномоченного по правам человека в Российской Федерации в 2003 году. С. 10.

57. See: About Detention of the Suspected and Accused: Federal Law of the Russian Federation // Assembly of the Legislation of the Russian Federation. 1995.29. / См.: О содержании под стражей подозреваемых и обвиняемых в совершении преступлений: Федеральный закон Российской Федерации // Собрание законодательства Российской Федерации. 1995. № 29.

58. See: Oparin V. N. Legal Regulation of Using of Measures of Direct Compulsion by Officials of Law Enforcement Bodies of the Russian Federation: Abstract of dissertation of Cand. Of Jurisprudence. Omsk, 1998. P. 5. / См.: Опарин В. Н. Правовое регулирование применения мер непосредственного принуждения должностными лицами правоохранительных органов Российской Федерации: Автореф. дис. ... канд юрид. наук. Омск, 1998. С. 5.

Chapter 7.   THE FREEDOM OF MOVEMENT AND RESIDENCE

One of historical features of Russia that has not been provided nor in pre-revolutionary, nor during the Soviet period was the freedom of movement in the country and freedom of residence.

This freedom has received a legislative concept and practical embodiment within the borders of the Russian Federation followed a way of wide democratic reforms. The beginning was necessary with acceptance on November, 22nd, 1991 by the Supreme Soviet of RSFSR of the Declaration of Rights and Freedoms of a Person and a Citizen. Recording of the given right in the operating Constitution (part 1 Article 27) has made its organic component of bases of a legal status of a person in the Russian Federation.

The right to freedom of movement and freedom of residence, according to the character of the values mediated by them, has been always concerned and related to the basic civil (personal) rights and freedoms of a person. In turn in the system it has been related to specific group of rights and freedoms, described by an opportunity of self-determination in space and also of the protection from illegal intervention in the sphere of an individual life, and encroachment on it. The right to freedom, the right of free departure beyond the borders of the state and unobstructed returning are also related to this group.[1]

The freedom of movement and freedom of residence is natural and inalienable, belonging to everyone from birth. It entirely keeps within general estimation of inalienable laws and freedoms of a person which are called to approve dignity and freedom of a person, their high cultural and moral principles irrespective of a status of a society and in this respect first of all to protect them as spiritual essence from arbitrariness of the most powerful force in a society as authorities, and their aspirations to dominate over a person.[2] As those, i.e. universal and standing in a number of the cores, it is recognized by international community and recorded in all basic internationally-legal regulations about human rights.

Internationally-legal regulation is worth mentioning. By virtue of natural character of the indicated opportunity it is carried out practically in all leading international documents on human rights, both on universal and regional level. For example, the Universal Declaration of Human Rights says that "everyone has the right to freedom of movement and residence within the borders of each State" (part 1 Article 13). In International Covenant on Civil and Political Rights it is said that "to everyone who lawfully is in territory of any state, refers to, within the limits of this territory, the right to free movement and freedom of residence" (Clause 1 of Article 12). In fact, such formulation included in the Covenant and in Report 4 to the European Convention for the Protection of Human Rights and Basic Freedoms is used. But with only one difference that "freedom of residence" is designated in the Convention in the form of "the rights to freedom of residence" (Article 2 of Report 4)[3]. In the Parisian Charter for a new Europe (Final document of OSCE on November, 21st, 1990)[4] in section "Human Rights, Democracy and Leadership of the Law" it is said that "each person has a right to ... freedom of movement".

As "the rights to freedom" competence of a person to move and choice of residence, being the stipulated condition of "observance of the law", 1981 (in the African Charter of Human Rights and People. Part 1 of Article 12)[5]. Such legal formulation with reference to freedom of residence is contained in the Convention of the Commonwealth of Independent States on the rights and basic freedoms of a person 1995[6] (part 1 Article 22) but with reference to movement it is said about the right to its free realization.

By the way, the term "the right to freedom "seems not absolutely successful from terminological point of view. Speech as it seems, should be either about individual freedom, or about human rights as they are standard basic elements of a legal status of a person with known specificity of their content.

Absence of accuracy in distinction of considered concepts "freedom" and "right" of a person sometimes leads to that in one clause competence to move and choice of residence moves simultaneously as a right and as freedom. For example, Article 22 of the American Convention on human rights 1969[7] is called "the freedom of movement and settlements" and in part 1 of the mentioned clause it is said already about corresponding human rights: "Everyone, lawfully being in the territory of the state-participant, has a right to move on it, to choose a residence with observance of provisions of the law". Certainly, it can be regarded as a certificate of identity of understanding of subjective "right" and subjective "freedom" but in such submission the meaning of their parallel use as independent elements of a legal status of a person is basically lost. Here at their all similarity there nevertheless should be a conceptual clearness and definiteness, i.e. the legal opportunity of a person acts in the form of the right, or in the form of freedom.

In the considered plan it is expedient to analyze a regulation of competence of a person to move and to choose residence in the constitutional normative-legal regulations of the foreign democratic countries in which it is proclaimed alongside with other fundamental rights and personal freedoms. Mainly there are two already described ways of its terminological legal recording. In a number of the countries it is considered directly as individual freedom, interdiction of use of administrative measures limiting it. Thus, in the Organic law of Federal Republic of Germany (1949) it is said, "All Germans use freedom of movement in all territory of Federation" (part 1 Article 11)[8]. In Austria the Organic law of the state (1867) says, "general laws of citizens of kingdoms and the grounds presented in imperial light": "The freedom of movement of a person and property within the borders of the state are not subject to any limitation" (part 1 Article 4).[9] The Constitution of the Italian Republic (1947) says: "Each citizen can freely move and live in any part of national territory, with the limitations which established by the law in the interests of health protection and safety. No limitations can be established on political grounds" (Article 16)[10]. In the Constitution of Greece it is said about prohibition "to apply individual administrative measures limiting freedom of movement or residing in the country" (part 4 Article 5)[11]. In the Constitution of Sweden it is said that each citizen should be provided with "the freedom of movement within the borders of the state" (§8)[12].

Frequently in constitutions there is a regulation of considered subjective freedom through the corresponding legal right, i.e. "the right to freedom". For example, according to the Constitution of Spain (1978) "Spaniards have the right to choose freely a residence and to move on territory of the country" (Article 19)[13], according to the Constitution of the Portuguese Republic 1976 "all citizens have the right to move freely on the national territory and to live in any part of it" (part 1 Article 44).[14]

Let's notice that in the modern constitutional legislation of some democratic states neither freedom, nor the right to freedom of movement and freedom of residence is mentioned. It logically follows from the democratic, legal device of the state, from general concept of the state of personal freedom and its basic inalienable laws and freedom. As an evident illustration the Great Britain where in general is not present separate codified the constitutional instrument about a legal status of citizens can serve but their freedom of movement among other basic rights and freedoms is guaranteed. It is mentioned in Magna Carta (1215) where it is said that all merchants should have the right to go safely to England and to leave England, to stay and go across England as overland and on water ... (Article 41)[15]. In the Great Britain the rights and freedoms of a person and a citizen, not being recorded in the constitutional document are recorded as it is noted in the literature, the constitutional customs which have developed in the country which are on occasion supported by laws and judiciary practice.[16]

In the Constitution of Ireland the whole section is devoted to the basic rights of person but among them there is no considered subjective freedom. Meanwhile it follows from regulations about scope that "the state guarantees respect to the laws and as far as they are feasible laws, protection and restoration of rights of person of citizens" (subparagraph 3.1). In favour of its concept it can testify that constitutional limitations of much more strict by way of realization (with the purpose of safety of the state) freedom is freedom of travel between the state and other country are not supposed (subparagraph 4)[17].

As the analysis of the constitutional legislation of the different countries shows, the legal opportunity of a person to move and choose residence is extremely seldom designated without a mention of freedom, i.e. only in the form of the legal right as it, in particular, takes place in the Constitution of Finland (1919). There it is emphasized that "a citizen of Finland has a right to stay in the country, to choose there a residence and move from one district in another if the law does not establish otherwise" (§ 7)[18].

Thus, the aforesaid concerning a legal opportunity of a person to move and choose residence, including its characteristic internationally-legal and interstate constitutional regulation, allows to make a number of conclusions. Firstly, this competence in strict understanding is referred in a greater measure to a category not the basic rights, but basic freedoms of a person, apparently, a community of the content and absence of rigid differences between them in structure of a legal status of a person. But it also is impossible not to see differences. In fact, not casually the legal opportunity to work under the operating Constitution of Russia is not recorded in the form of the right and replaced with freedom of work (part 1 Article 37).

Proclaimed in the Constitution of the Russian Federation the right of everyone to move freely chooses a place of stay and residence forms legal base for its certain definition in the current legislation. It, in particular, concerns general definition of the concept of a residence in Article 20 of the Civil Code of the Russian Federation as places where a citizen constantly or mainly lives; normative-legal recording of scope and features of realization of the given right for foreign citizens and stateless persons in the Federal law "a legal status of foreign citizens in the Russian Federation" (Article 11).

With reference to Russian citizens it is necessary to mention especially the law of the Russian Federation concretizing a corresponding constitutional law (1993) "the right of citizens of the Russian Federation to freedom of movement, a choice of a place of stay and residence within the borders of the Russian Federation"[19]. The law has determined the basic concepts concerning a subject of its regulation, detailed the provisions, concerning corrected registration of citizens in a place of stay and a residence and also has established the bases of possible limitation of the given right.

On a large scale the freedom of movement and freedom of residence can *be determined as naturally arising, integral, legislatively recorded and guaranteed opportunity of a person to use the values in the form of unobstructed moving on territory of the country where he lawfully is and also its unobstructed time or constant residing at personally them a determined place.*

Analyzing freedom of movement and freedom of residence in the system of other rights and freedoms of a person and a citizen, it is necessary to remark that it does not relate to the absolute from the point of view of realization of character, i.e. the main thing is not in scope of realization of a constant and not subjected to any limitations as, say, human rights to freedom from torture and inhuman treatment and punishment. The freedom of movement and freedom of residence refers to the rights and personal freedoms which do not exclude lawful, compatible to other inalienable laws and freedom of limitations for reasons of protection of the rights and freedoms of other persons, protection of state security, a public order, health and morals of the population. Such it is possible with reference to a border land, zones of ecological disaster, territories where it is introduced by extreme or the martial law. Limitations in movement and freedom of residence of certain persons can be caused by circumstances of disclosing and investigation of the crimes integrated by virtue of necessity with detention of the suspected, by use of such preventive punishment as imprisonment and a capture of a recognizance not to leave.

As to the form of realization the freedom of movement and freedom of residence as a matter of fact refers to individual rights and freedoms, i.e. such which each person can have and use separately that, however, does not exclude the collective realization (separate family, group of immigrants, etc.). In comparison: there are rights and freedoms, the possessing and using of which is supposed in the collective form, as, for example, the right to be going to peacefully, without the firearms, to carry out assemblies, meetings, processions and picketing (Article 31 of the Constitution of the Russian Federation).

Rather important definition of the place and the importance of freedom of movement and freedom of residence among the rights and personal freedoms are at their classification on social purpose and the content.

Acute free movement of an individual on territory is equal definition to them at sole discretion where to stay and where to live, eat is not only the value in itself. It is simultaneously a condition of using many other values underlying the constitutional and branch rights and personal freedoms and sometimes the means of ensuring and protection of somebody from them. The freedom of movement and freedom of residence relate to the category of civil rights and freedoms. Being closely connected with other human rights, it provides their realization.

In itself movement of a person and change of a place of stay and a residence by them in case of military actions, ecocatastrophes, interethnic conflicts and in some other extreme situations often acts hardly probable not as a main means of rescue of life, health, property, rescue from violence and etc. can serve as vivid examples of moving of people from places, suffered from radioactive infection because of Chernobyl accident; from the Chechen Republic where military actions are conducted and also there are open threats of terrorism, kidnapping by gangster formations, etc.

Choosing of the preventive punishment can depend on presence or absence of a constant residence concerning a person at investigation of crimes. Thus, one of the bases of detention of a crime of the suspected of carrying out on Article 122 of the Code of Criminal Procedure of RSFSR[20] is absence of a constant residence. Absence of this does not allow applying if necessary to the accused a recognizance not to leave and frequently attracts as a compelled measure is his custody.

Certainly, the freedom of movement and freedom of residence plays a big role not only in the mentioned extreme situations and not only in criminally-remedial sphere. It is very important that in movement and a choice of residence may seriously influence the character and the content of rights and freedoms of a person. In particular, it can concern political rights. Thus, because of moving from one city into another, entering into other constituency, the access to public service automatically varies for a citizen, candidates for whom they have a right to vote at their election in bodies of the government and institutions of local government do vary.

Use of the rights and personal freedoms directly depends on realization of constitutional law on freedom of movement and a choice of a place of stay and a residence in many situations in the sphere of an economic, social and cultural life. For example, realization by citizens of the right to introduce price and other economic activities is not forbidden by the law and often is connected with movement or a choice of a place of stay or a residence; the rights freely to dispose of the abilities to work, to choose a sort of activity and a trade; rights to rest; rights to health protection and medical aid, the rights to a favorable environment; the rights to education; the rights to participation in cultural life, etc.

By the way, there is a category of citizens, whose working conditions are directly connected with constant movement (workers of geological, search and prospecting expeditions, the linear creating, mobile mechanized columns, persons of floating structure of fleet, etc.). Privileges can depend on a residence of citizens and a privilege in realization of the social and economic rights by them, for example at receipt in high schools of inhabitants of the Far North, the extra charge to their salary and increase of holiday time.

On occasion the legislation directly connects with a residence of a person of its opportunity to use the rights in the field of protection. In particular, it concerns treatment of a person in certain court of general jurisdiction according to the law of the Russian Federation "the appeal in court of actions and the decisions breaking the rights and freedoms of citizens"[21]; to the Federal law "protection of the rights of consumers"[22].

Rather essential is that the right to housing directly depends on officially registered residence of a person, i.e. an opportunity of stable using premises available in houses of the state and municipal available housings on treaty provisions of hiring, inviolability of such dwelling and also a legal opportunity of improvement of living conditions by receiving by requiring persons from the state of other habitation. If the dwelling is not privatized, only through registration on a residence it is possible to legally realize a right to housing.

Thus, the freedom of movement and freedom of residence on the socially-legal value and the content of the mediated values in the form of an opportunity of people free to move, be and live in various places represents itself not only subjective freedom (the legal right). It simultaneously acts as a legal guarantor of ensuring of many other things ass right to freedom of a person which realization presupposes moving a person on territory or is connected directly with the given place of its residing.

The freedom of movement and freedom of residence evenly refers to the sphere of private life of a person where other civil rights and freedoms also matter.

The mechanism of realization of freedom of movement and choice of a residence does not exclude certain limitations of realization. It corresponds to also to international standards. Thus, Report 4 (Article 2)[23] to the European Convention for the Protection of Human Rights and Basic Freedoms marks out some cases which basically are covered by the part 3 Article 55 of the Constitution of the Russian Federation.

It is, first of all, said about the standard limitations of the rights and freedoms of a person and a citizen of the law in that measure in what it is necessary with a view of protection of bases constitutional system, morals, health, the rights and legitimate interests of other persons, ensuring of defense of the country and safety of the state. As to direct an object of research according to the law "the right of citizens of the Russian Federation to freedom of movement, a choice of a place of stay and a residence within the borders of the Russian Federation" (Article 8) the given right can be limited in territories with certain mode: in a border zone, in the closed military stations; in the closed administrative-territorial educations; in zones of ecological disaster; in separate territories and in settlements where in the case of danger of distribution infectious both mass noninfectious and poisonings of people special conditions and modes of residing of the population and economic activities are introduced; in territories where it is introduced extreme or the martial law. In the Federal constitutional law of the Russian Federation from May, 30th, 2001[24] "state of emergency" it is directly said that the establishment of limitations on freedom of movement on territory on which state of emergency is introduced and also introduction of a special regime of entrance on the indicated territory and departure it, including establishment of limitations on entrance on the indicated territory and stay on her of foreign citizens and stateless persons" is possible ".

As a leading guarantor of realization of the rights and freedoms of a person and a citizen the state as it is known, acts. It is called to create necessary conditions for their favorable realization during life. Specificity of the majority of civil rights and freedoms, including freedom of movement and freedom of residence, presupposes their ensuring and by means of legal support and by means of non-interference of authority, i.e. observance.

Given freedom first of all is provided by the President within the limits of its measures on consolidation of legality in the country, on reduction the federal legislation of the legislation of subjects of the Russian Federation.

From the point of view of realization by bodies of general competence of providing functions concerning freedom of movement and first of all a choice of a place of stay and a residence it is possible to emphasize activity of the Government of the Russian Federation. In this case special value has a Governmental order from July, 17th, 1995 713 by which Rules of registration and removal of citizens of the Russian Federation from the registration account in a place of stay and on a residence within the borders of the Russian Federation are approved[25]. The government was authorized on their acceptance by the legislator in part 4 Article 3 of the law "the right of citizens of the Russian Federation to freedom of movement, a choice of a place of stay and a residence within the borders of the Russian Federation".

As to activity of bodies of the registration account till now there are many negative sides of their work. Among them the facts of bureaucratism, the unreasonable administrative discretion is distinguished at registration law enforcement. Registration should have strictly notifying character but in any way allowing. On a large scale the problem of acceptance by officials of unusable decisions concerning a person the President of the Russian Federation in the message to Federal Assembly in 2001. As they said has not casually paid attention, "we practically are standing at a dangerous boundary when the judge or other a law-enforcement person can choose at sole discretion provision which seems to them to the most comprehensible ... Obviously that such use the right creates also a huge field of opportunities for abusing in the sphere of enforcement of the rights and freedoms of citizens".[26]

Meanwhile the question of observance in Russia of freedom of movement and freedom of residence causes trouble not to special cases, but to wide prevalence of infringement. As consequence, Human Rights Commissioner in the Russian Federation presents the Special report "Constitutional Law on Freedom of Movement, a Free Choice of a Place of Stay and a Residence in the Russian Federation"[27]. Feature of this document is that it allows to see laws and tendencies of infringement of the indicated right. Concerning fences in this the sphere of it is said and in the Report of Human Rights Commissioner of the Russian Federation in 2003 (P. 34-35).

Today as hardly probable appears not most widespread kind of infringement of the mentioned personal freedom as limitation in the legislation of subjects of the Russian Federation. In a number of subjects the normative-legal regulations regulating registration of citizens in a place of stay and a residence are accepted in such a manner that it essentially deforms their lawful legal opportunities in the considered sphere. The conclusion about characteristic ways of such limitations to which it is paid attention of Human Rights Commissioner logically follows.

Firstly, there is a direct interdiction of registration in a place of stay or on a residence of citizens who are arriving on territory of the subject of the Russian Federation from territory of other countries or other subjects of the Russian Federation and not having close connections with given region (the Kabardino-Balkarian Republic). Secondly, there are relapses in establishment of the allowing order of realization of the right freely to move and choose a place of residing (Republic Adygea, Krasnodar territory). Thirdly, the normative-legal establishment of dignity in registration on a residence for separate categories of persons (Krasnodar territory) is used. Fourthly, introduction of special conditions of registration of citizens in a place of stay and a residence (Nizhniy Novgorod, Yaroslavl, Kurgan areas) takes place. Fifthly, various deadlines of registration in a place of stay and a residence of citizens (Moscow, St.-Petersburg, the Volgograd, Smolensk areas, etc.) are established. Sixthly, additional obstacles for realization of freedom of citizens are established to choose a place of stay and a residence (Tatarstan, Republic Mary Al, the Chuvash Republic, the Kaliningrad area, etc.) Seventhly, additional (in comparison with the Administrative Code of RSFSR) measures of the responsibility for infringement of rules of registration in a place of stay and a residence, such as administrative imprisonment and exclusion for limits of the subject of the Russian Federation (Moscow, St.-Petersburg, Stavropol Territory, etc.) are introduced.

The special place in protection of the rights and personal freedoms occupies the Constitutional Court of the Russian Federation which, protecting constitutional rights and freedoms, simultaneously carries out function of protection of the Organic law.

The analysis of practice of the Constitutional Court of the Russian Federation shows its exclusively important role in counteraction to "rule-making" encroachment directly on freedom of movement and freedom of residence. Confirmation to that is a lot of decisions. It is possible to mention, for example, the decision of the Constitutional Court of April, 4th, 1996 9-E "Check of Constitutionality of some statutory acts of city of Moscow and the Moscow area, Stavropol Territory, the Voronezh area and city of Voronezh, regulating the order of registration of citizens arriving on a constant residence in mentioned regions"[28]; the decision from July, 2nd, 1997 10-E "Check of Constitutionality of parts of the firstly, second and third clause 2 and a part of sixth clause 4 of the law of the Moscow area from July, 5th, 1996 "gathering on indemnification of expenses of the budget of the Moscow area on development of an infrastructure of cities and other settlements and ensuring with social conditions of citizens arriving to the Moscow area on a constant residence in connection with complaints of citizens I.V. Shestopalko, O.E. Sachkova and M.I. Krjuchkova".[29]

The law of the Russian Federation "Right of Citizens of the Russian Federation to Freedom of Movement, a Choice of a Place of Stay and a Residence Within the Borders of the Russian Federation", besides, judicial protection, provides the appeal of encroachment on the given right in administratively-legal forms.

Effective guarantee in the given aspect is activity of the Office of Public Prosecutor. The sphere of public prosecutor's supervision is directly connected with protection of the rights of citizens has great value settled in clauses 1, 26, 27, 28 and other clauses of the Federal law "Office of Public Prosecutor of the Russian Federation"[30]. In the law it is indicated that the Office of Public Prosecutor "supervises the observance of the rights and freedoms of a person and a citizen by the federal ministries and departments, representatives (legislative) and agencies of subjects of the Russian Federation, institutions of local government, bodies of the control, their officials and also by directors and heads of the commercial and noncommercial organizations". In the law (Article 22) there are certain powers of the public prosecutor in the given area, including an opportunity to protest on the instrument violating the rights and freedoms. With reference to an object of research it is possible to give a certain example, when the public prosecutor of Moscow on July, 9th, 1997 under Article 33 "Conditions of Stay in Moscow for the Foreign Citizens Who Have the Right of Visa-Free Entrance to Russia" addressed in court with the claim for a concept of mismatching the federal legislation of separate provisions of the Law. In these provisions the term of a finding of a citizen in certain place of time stay that should be determined by a citizen was illegally limited to the subject of the Russian Federation. The Moscow City Court satisfied the claim of the public prosecutor and the judicial board on civil cases of the Supreme Court left the decision without changes.[31]

As a whole, administratively-legal forms of protection of freedom of movement and freedom of residence can be the most various. The majority of them are uniform for basic rights and personal freedoms[32].

They include already mentioned functions of the President of the Russian Federation, activity of Human Rights Commissioner, etc. With reference to an object of research it is possible to emphasize the opportunities of the departmental appeal of illegal actions of employees of passport and visa service of law-enforcement bodies in the sphere of realization of freedom of movement and freedom of residence according to operating departmental instruments.

As an independent question it is possible to speak about protection of freedom of movement and freedom of residence human rights public organizations, through mass media, etc. In connection with connection of the Russian Federation to the European Convention for the Protection of Human Rights and Basic Freedoms the opportunities for international protection of freedom of movement and freedom of residence have appeared. Though It is necessary to remark, that practice of the European Court by the rights concerning given freedom, in comparison with other basic rights and freedoms of a person, is limited[33]. It appears as one of certificates of achievements of the democratic states by members of the European community in a concept of and observance of freedom of movement and freedom of residence. Russia should also aspire to high achievements as a democratic state.

Notes

1. In a science there is a judgement that the corresponding basic personal rights and freedoms are the component of the independent right of inviolability of a person. (see, for example: Lukasheva E.A. Socialist Law and a Person. Moscow, 1987. P. 130). / (См., например: Лукашева Е. А. Социалистическое право и личность. М., 1987. С. 130).

2. See: Alexeev S.S. Law: Alphabet - Theory - Philosophy: Experience of the Complex Research. Moscow, 1999. P. 621. / См.: Алексеев С. С. Право: азбука – теория – философия: Опыт комплексного исследования. М., 1999. С. 621.

3. See: Ibidem. P. 553-555.

4. See: Ibidem. P. 664-666.

5. See: Ibidem. P. 737-747.

6. See: Ibidem. P. 711-719.

7. See: Ibidem. P. 720-736.

8. Constitutions of the States of the European Union. Moscow, 1997. P. 183. / Конституции государств Европейского Союза. М., 1997. С. 183.

9. Ibidem. P. 93.

10. Ibidem. P. 425.

11. Ibidem. P. 246.

12. Ibidem. P. 703.

13. Ibidem. P. 375.

14. Ibidem. P. 246.

15. See: The Collection of Documents on General History of State and Law. Moscow, 1977. P. 32. / См.: Сборник документов по всеобщей истории государства и права. Л., 1977. С. 32.

16. See: Krylov B.S. Introduction // Constitutions of the States of the Europe: In 3 Vol. T. 1. Moscow, 2001. P. 501. / См.: Крылов Б. С. Вводная статья // Конституции государств Европы: В 3 т. Т. 1. М., 2001. С. 501.

17. See: Constitutions of the States of the European Union. P. 350, 351. / См.: Конституции государств Европейского Союза. С. 350, 351.

18. Ibidem. P. 614.

19. See: Sheets of Congress of People's Deputies of the Russian Federation and the Supreme Soviet of the Russian Federation. 1993.32. Clause 1227. / См.: Ведомости Съезда народных депутатов Российской Федерации и Верховного Совета Российской Федерации. 1993. № 32. Ст. 1227.

20. See: Sheets of the Supreme Soviet of RSFSR. 1960.40. Clause 592 (with the subsequent changes and additions). / См.: Ведомости Верховного Совета РСФСР. 1960. № 40. Ст. 592 (с последующими изменениями и дополнениями).

21. See: Sheets of Congress of People's Deputies of the Russian Federation and the Supreme Soviet of the Russian Federation. 1993.19. Clause 685. / См.: Ведомости Съезда народных депутатов Российской Федерации и Верховного Совета Российской Федерации. 1993. № 19. Ст. 685.

22. See: Assembly of the Legislation of the Russian Federation. 1996.3. Clause 140. / См.: Собрание законодательства Российской Федерации. 1996. № 3. Ст. 140.

23. It is ratified by the Federal law «Ratification of the Convention on Protection of Human Rights and Basic Freedoms and Protocols to it » // Assembly of the Legislation of the Russian Federation. 1998.14. Clause 1514. / Собрание законодательства Российской Федерации. 1998. № 14. Ст. 1514.

24. See: Assembly of the Legislation of the Russian Federation. 2001.23. Clause 2277. / См.: Собрание законодательства Российской Федерации. 2001. № 23. Ст. 2277.

25. See: Assembly of the Legislation of the Russian Federation. 1995.30. Clause 2939. / См.: Собрание законодательства Российской Федерации. 1995. № 30. Ст. 2939.

26. Rossiiskaya Gazeta. 2001. Apr., 4.

27. See: The Report on Human Rights Commissioner's Work in the Russian Federation in 2000. Moscow, 2001. P. 174-207. / См.: Доклад о деятельности Уполномоченного по правам человека в Российской Федерации в 2000 году. М., 2001. С. 174–207.

28. See: Bulletin of the Constitutional Court of the Russian Federation. 1996.2. / См.: Вестник Конституционного Суда Российской Федерации. 1996. № 2.

29. See: Ibidem. 1997.5.

30. See: Assembly of the Legislation of the Russian Federation. 1995.47. Clause 4472; 1999.7. Clause 878. / См.: Собрание законодательства Российской Федерации. 1995. № 47. Ст. 4472; 1999. № 7. Ст. 878.

31. See: Bulletin of the Supreme Court of the Russian Federation. 2001.8. P. 1-2. / См.: Бюллетень Верховного Суда Российской Федерации. 2001. № 8. С. 1–2.

32. About it in more detail see: Administratively-Legal Forms of Protection of Rights and Freedoms of a Person and a Citizen // Human rights: Textbook for high schools. Moscow, 1999. P. 378-410. / Об этом подробнее см.: Административно-правовые формы защиты прав и свобод человека и гражданина // Права человека: Учебник для вузов. М., 1999. С. 378–410.

33. See: Gomien D., Harris D., Zvaak L. European Convention on Human Rights and the European Social Charter: Law and Practice. Moscow, 1998. P. 467-470. / См.: Гомьен Д., Харрис Д., Зваак Л. Европейская конвенция о правах человека и Европейская социальная хартия: право и практика. М., 1998. С. 467–470.

Chapter 8. THE RIGHT TO PRIVACY

In the beginning of the 20th century the majority of the constitutional legal regulations did not provide normative recording for the right to personal privacy. The preference was given only to the right to privacy of correspondence, cable, telephone messages. Only after the end of the Second World War at reforming of the state systems of the European countries in new Constitutions private life of a citizen was mentioned.

Normative recording of the right to personal privacy was found in the Universal Declaration of Human Rights (1948): "No one shall be subjected to arbitrary interference with his privacy, family, home or correspondence" (Article 12). It, most likely, is not right, concerning to the subject and a corresponding duty assigned on associates. The European Convention for the Protection of Human Rights and Basic Freedoms (1950) provides that everyone has a right to respect of personal and family life. Mentioning the European Convention for the Protection of Human Rights and Basic Freedoms, it is necessary to speak about discrepancy of translating of the Clause 8. The English text sounds like "Everyone has a right for his private and family life ...". "Private" will correspond to Russian "private" that is the European Convention says just about respect of private life. Translating into Russian of international Covenant is also inexact. The English primary source uses the term "privacy". The attention has been already paid to the given circumstance in Russian legal press.

The Constitution of the USSR (1977) proclaimed the right of defence of private life (Article 56)[1] that reflected in Constitutions of the Union republics. The Soviet doctrine researched the right of defence of private life as display of the right to personal immunity is "personal immunity can be understood in wide and narrow sense. In the wide sense it is possible to include all complex of the cultural values and the rights describing a person in this concept. In a narrow sense personal immunity means protection of various displays of personal, family, intimate human life and inviolability of his personal freedom".[2]

Development of the Constitution in Russia regarding regulation of the given right was inconsistent: from full denying before recording of the right to privacy of correspondence and eventually up to a concept of the right of defence of private life. But at absence of direct action of provisions of the Organic law it was emasculated at realization in the branch legislation. It is necessary to note that in history of Russian jurisprudence the right of defence of private life much earlier was recognized by a science, than has found the normative recording. Thus, I.A. Pokrovsky, analyzing the basic problems of civil law, results in the "special" rights: "secrecy of letters, of own image, etc., or more generally is about the rights on protection of intimate sphere ("Das Recht auf die eigene Geheimspehre") or on the statement of individuality ("Das Recht auf Behauptung der Individualitat")"[3].

During action of the Constitution of the USSR (1977) the right of defence of private life was understood as "a personal non-right of property of a citizen to freedom of definition of the behaviour in individual ability to live at own discretion, excluding any intervention in their private life from other persons, except for the cases directly stipulated by the law"[4].

And "private life" was considered as an object of protection; hence, it should be coordinated to the concept "person". However, neither the law, nor the scientific doctrine gave a precise definition of a person; therefore, the right of defence of private life was treated otherwise. There were many questions, in particular: whether is a person the child of the condemned, incapacitated. There was also an opinion that private life is the sphere of "an individual way of satisfaction of material and cultural needs of a person in social life".[5] At such approach it has lost its own value and "was dissolved" in social life.

Personal privacy is a wide enough and capacious concept. It is possible to include in it, first of all, a complex of the social relations describing a person and a citizen as a subject, having the full freedom determined even by the French thinkers as "natural".

To reveal a certain place of the right to personal privacy (as a legal right recorded in Article 23 of the Constitution of the Russian Federation) in the hierarchy of values, protected by the law, it is necessary to determine its internal elements: the content of the given right, its essence and structure.

N.I. Matuzov determines that the content of the legal right "is formed by those certain legal opportunities, competences which are given and guaranteed to the subject (authorized)"[6]. As a whole, agreeing with the given definition, it would be necessary to note the following: Hegel considered that the content was deduced from the concept, found out its originality. With reference to the legal right its content can be revealed through will, following this philosophy, the content is defined as "the nature and the external validity".[7]

The structure, according to N.I. Matuzov, "acts as interrelation of these opportunities (elements), their relative positioning and subordination as a form of the organization of the content of the legal right, its internal unity and a structure".[8]

By general definition given above, the content can be expressed from interpretation of the concept, to be exact, through consideration of its elements "inviolability" and "private life".

"Inviolability" in lexical meaning is understood, first of all, as non-interference. If we treat inviolability only as non-interference it will be right, recorded by Article 23 of the Constitution of the Russian Federation, to have only negative semantic meaning. Thus, recognizing narrowness of the rights to protection of the private life, shown that it includes only guarding activity of competent bodies, at the aforesaid conclusion we give also to the right to personal privacy not a full meaning, not including in it law enforcement. As a branch of the constitutional legislation concerns the theory of the law to public branches, therefore, imperious influence on regulation of social relations is one of its basic methods.

The theory of the law marks out, besides protection, one more positive element that "in most general meaning ... there is a counteraction to illegal infringement and limitations of the rights, freedom and interests of a person, the prevention of infringement and limitations and also compensation of the caused harm in case to warn or reflect infringement and limitation was not possible"[9]. Therefore, analyzing Article 23 of the Constitution of the Russian Federation, it is possible to come to the conclusion that inviolability includes three sides of protection; as protection is, in fact, non-interference.

Protection in the theory of the law is understood as measures carried out by the state bodies and other subjects of the right, directed on the prevention of infringement of the rights and freedoms of a person and a citizen, on elimination of the reasons, generating them, removal of obstacles and realization of the rights promoting freedom established by the law[10].

Protection is understood as set of the measures directed on non-admission of infringement of the rights and freedoms of a person and a citizen and also "a compulsory way of realization of the right, used when due hereunder competent bodies or an authorized person"[11]. It is necessary to say that as an object of protection act not only the rights and freedoms but also object or the subject of these or other legal relationships.

Both of them are directed on non-admission of infringement of the given right of a citizen and make, as a rule, problems and functions of corresponding bodies and as an object of influence the third party is the potential or acute offender acts. At visibility of concurrence of the concepts of protection and protection all the same at close interdependence and interrelation they have also own attributes which allow distinguishing them. Though the given border is transparent enough, that gives the basis to many jurists to apply these terms as synonyms. "Protection is the moment of the protection, and one of its forms"[12] is the most widespread point of view.

Protection as it seems, is the activity directed on the future, its primary goal is not to admit an offence, to eliminate barrier to realization of competence, precautionary activity. Protection is the activity arising in the case of presence of a certain offence or elimination of such status which will really lead to approach of negative consequences and also directed on restoration of the infringed right. as a rule, there is already certain offender and a person, whose right is limited by guilty actions. In fact, non-interference is a duty of the state to ensure the provision of positive regulation of the given right and also recording of a status of certain autonomy of a person from the state, societies, such and can be regulated by the state doubly:

1) Through establishment of interdictions;

2) Through recording of certain legal status of the subject or through recording of certain regime of social activity of a person.

Apart from general recording of the right to personal privacy in Russian Constitution, in Article 23, the rights to personal and family secrecy and protection of honour and reputation are also stipulated. The part 2 in addition says about the right to privacy of correspondence, telephone conversations, post cable and other messages. Also in part 2 there are general bases of limitation of the right to secrecy of a mail service. Thus, the general plan of Article 23 consists of five elements:

— The right to personal privacy;

— The right to personal and family secrecy;

— The right of defence of honour and reputation[13];

— The right to secrecy of a mail service;

— The bases of limitation of the right to secrecy of a mail service.

Apparently, Russian Constitution marks out the right to personal secret and the right to family secrecy as independent elements. Sociologist George Merdok determined family as "the social group, defined by joint residing, general housekeeping and reproduction. It includes adult of both sexes and, at least, two from them maintain socially approved sexual relations and one or more own or adopted children"[14]. One of the bases of family life is joint residing. Similarly, the concept of family cannot be reduced only to joint residing of persons of different sexes as a husband and a wife. The concept of family will cover also joint residing of mother (father) and the full age child, etc. Therefore, it is necessary to agree with S.I. Golod's point of view and to consider family "as set of an individuals consisting of, at least, in one of three kinds of relations: consanguinity, generation, property"[15].

In relations inside of family it is sometimes difficult enough to determine a personal belonging to for this reason[16]. The Constitution of the Russian Federation marks out two these independent rights. It is possible to ask a question: if family secrecy is general property whether it is necessary to use these values? Whether it means that in questions of disclosing of family secrets it is necessary to be guided by opinion of each member of the family? M.N. Maleina considers that "if it is impossible to isolate, "to pull out" the data concerning only of one member of the family the consent to disclosure of all other members which have the right of secret of family life, should be asked". Besides, M.N. Maleina specifies: "Thus, the question cannot be solved by the number of voices. Even presence of one contra should lead to refusal of disclosing secret of family life. Thus, members of the family have the right to family secrecy and simultaneously each of them is obliged to save family secrecy". For example, spouses have lived together for some time, trusting each other various secrets. In the subsequent life cannot develop, a result is divorce. One of spouses starts to spread information on features of a joint life. Very serious harm to other spouse can be caused then.[17] Naturally, there is a question how to protect the rights of the affected party? Whether a citizen the claim for indemnification can submit in this case, or address in court with the request to withdraw circulation of the published materials, or to put interdiction on the publication of memoirs? More than there are enough examples of such situations. It seems that by the coordination of disclosure of data making general family secrecy should not solve the given question. It is, apparently, a moral choice of each member of the family. Recording of the recorded model of behaviour in the law will not result in what as to putting in a Procrustean bed such different situations which cannot be comprehensively estimated by means of the hand-written law.

Personal secrets have independent recording in the branch legislation, including in relation to citizens who are married. A citizen, having personal secret, has a right to dispose of it: to clue it to members of the family or not to clue it. The example is the Bases of the Legislation of the Russian Federation about health protection of citizens.[18] Clause 61 of Bases on health protection of citizens records that "the information on the fact of treatment to medical aid, a state of health of a citizen, the diagnosis of its disease and other data received at its inspection and relations, make medical secrecy". And the guarantee of confidentiality of data passed by him should be confirmed to a citizen. The same clause provides that the information that is a medical secret can be passed to other persons only by permission of the patient. Without the consent of a citizen it is possible to distribute such data only in cases directly stipulated by the law. Thus, granting of the medical information to parents of the patient is possible only in the case of rendering assistance to the minor in the age under 15 years. If a medical worker gives the data to close relatives without the consent of the patient who has reached 15 years it will be considered as illegal disclosure of medical secrecy. The confirmation of recording of personal secret is Article 15 of the Family Code of the Russian Federation[19], establishing the opportunity of medical examination of marrying persons. Medical examination is possible only by permission of persons who are marrying and results of inspection of a marrying person "can be given to a person, whom he/she is going to marry, only by permission of a person who was last of inspection". Otherwise, the medical secrecy is personal secret and can be disclosed to other members of the family only by permission of a person who received some medical aid. The doctor broken the given interdiction, can become the subject of bringing to court under Article 137 of the Criminal Code of the Russian Federation "Infringement of Personal Privacy".

As it has been noted, the Constitution of the Russian Federation, simultaneously having designated the patrimonial characteristic of the right to personal privacy, also marks out in Article 23 the independent right to privacy of correspondence, telephone conversations, post, cable and other messages (some scientists use for brevity the term is the right to secrecy of a mail service what, apparently, is possible to use in the present research). It is necessary to note that the given right has older history than the right to personal privacy.

The right to secrecy of a mail service has been traditionally considered in the context of an opportunity of law enforcement bodies to carry out criminal investigation actions. According to the Federal law "Criminal Investigation Activity"[20] the bodies carrying out criminal investigation actions can apply various methods of gathering of the information, i.e.

the detective methods limiting private life of citizens: the control of mail, cable and other messages, listening of telephone conversations, removal of the information from technical liaison channels.

Clause 8 of the mentioned Federal law records that the basis of limitation of secrecy of a mail service is the court decision. Criminal investigation actions can be carried out at presence of the information concerning:

1. Attributes of the prepared, committed or absolutely illegal act on where preliminary investigation is obligatory.

2. Persons preparing, committing or having committed illegal acts where preliminary investigation is obligatory.

3. Events or actions threatening the state, or military, economic and ecological safety of the Russian Federation.

In urgent cases, it is enough to have a motivated decision of one of heads of the body which is carrying out criminal investigation actions, with the obligatory notice within 24 hours of judicial bodies which within 48 hours can start authorized actions.

Tapping of telephone conversations under a personal statement or by the written approval of the owner of the device is possible under the decision approved by the head of body that is carrying out criminal in- vestigation actions, with the obligatory notice of court within 48 hours. There is nothing said in the law about legal consequences of refusal in authorization of such actions. The Constitution of the Russian Federation especially determines that the secrecy of a mail service can be limited only on the basis of a court decision. The word "only" in formulations of the Federal law is absent that essentially changes meaning of the constitutional rule.

Apparently, the given circumstances also have generated the complaint in the Constitutional Court of the Russian Federation concerning the given Federal law. On July, 14th, 1997 the Definition of the Constitutional Court of the Russian Federation 86-D "Case of Check of Constitutionality of Separate Provisions of the Federal Law" concerning criminal investiga- tion activity "under the complaint of a citizen I. Chernov was accepted". The Constitutional Court of the Russian Federation made a decision to refuse in consideration of the complaint though without the established procedure a question of conformity of the given law of the Constitution of the Russian Federation was practically solved. This definition caused an ambiguous estimation at human rights organizations as proceeding from provisions of the Federal law "Criminal Investigation Activity" and the conclusions stated in the Definition of the Constitutional Court of the Russian Federation on case of the citizen I. Chernov, there will be formally lawful carrying out of the criminal investigation actions limiting the right to secrecy of a mail service, on any crimes irrespective of their degree of weight.

An indirect confirmation of validity of the complaint of the citizen Chernov is in the fact that in 2001 changes were made to the law of "Criminal Investigation Activity" according to which tapping of telephone and other talks was possible only concerning suspected or accused persons in committing grave or especially grave crimes and also persons who can have data on the indicated crimes.

In many countries there are certain limitations on privacy of correspondence, telephone conversations, post, cable and other messages. The legislator of the developed countries tries to find the compromise between realization of the given right and the state interests and also to protect the state bodies from disclosure of the state and military secret. For control of activity of special services the special judicial body which could carry out the control over activity of security service, the guarantor of protection, to be right and freedom of citizens and at the same time to ensure the provision of privacy, protection of the state interests is created.

Thus, in the Great Britain there is a law on security service (1989) which provides supervision of activity of prospecting body of Great Britain MI5. It authorized (commissioner) on affairs of security service and carries out the tribunal on consideration of illegal actions of service.

According to the Appendix 1 to the given law which regulates the order of activity of the tribunal, "any British believing that in his house the bugging equipment is installed, his telephone conversations are tapped and correspondence is opened, or considering that he is being shadowed, say, thinking is conducted that he or his property has became an object of illegal actions of Security service, has a right to direct the complaint to the tribunal and to demand official explanations".[21]

If the complaint is thorough, the tribunal checks legality of actions MI5, at absence of those, MI 5 stops work and destroys all data on this person and also monetary indemnification is paid to him.

In the USA a major landmark in history of regulation of the right to secrecy of a mail service is case of Katz against the USA (Katz vs. United States, 1967), considered by the Supreme Court. Till this moment law enforcement practice started with the mechanical approach to the protection of the right to personal privacy. Otherwise, a citizen and his rights were not subject to protection, there has not been yet a material infringement of his house. The Fourth amendment was not used to the procedure of tapping of telephone conversations. Proceeding from the decision of the Supreme Court of the USA on case of Olmstead vs. US (1928) under protection of the Fourth Amendment[22] the actions of police which would not lead to damage of dwelling were not included: so the bugging device which was built in without the judicial sanction by means of a nail, hammered into a wall, is the infringement of the Constitution pasted by an adhesive tape is not considered as an infringement. In 1967 in the case of Silverman vs. United States the Court rejected "the proofs received by means of the bugging device, introduced into a wall of the house the suspected".[23] Precisely the same attitude existed to telephone lines. If they are outside of a residence of citizens, it means that there is no search and judicial authorization is necessary. Still at that time on case Olmstead in special opinion they defended a position of the concept of the right to secrecy of telephone conversations: "Installation of interception of telephone conversations breaks the right to private life of both talking persons; besides, conversations, that do not have any forbidden content and also confidential and secret conversations are all overheard. Moreover, installation of interception on a telephone set of one person designates interception of all other persons to whom this person will call or to whom they will call"[24].

Almost in forty years the Supreme Court of the USA has determined, "The Fourth Amendment protects people, rather than places. That the given person exposes on a public review, even it happened in his own house, or in a place of work, not subject to protection. However, the fact that he aspires to leave it as a private affair, even in a place accessible to all, can be protected by the Constitution" (in opinion of the majority of the authorship of Judge Stuart)[25].

In view of expansion of opportunities of electronic listening in 1986 the Congress of the USA introduced supervision over wandering object (roving surveillance), for a person without dependence from what communication facility they would use. "In the Memorandum of the Ministry of Justice of the USA, accompanied with the project of a new law, it was said that "the law does not contain the exact indication of a subject of listening and, thus, allows to receive the warrant on listening of conversations of certain person, rather than a telephone set or a premise"[26].

In affairs concerning the threat of national safety the judge of the special court formed by chairman of the Supreme Court of the USA from seven judicial districts of USA stands out the warrant on electronic listening[27].

Analyzing international experience of regulation of the criminal investigation actions mentioning the right to personal privacy, it is possible
to emphasize some general tendencies of development of the legislation.
Firstly, the order of preliminary authorization concerning foreigners and
citizens of the state is different. In the first case, as a rule, there is no
preliminary judicial control. Moreover, the official laws establishing the
official order of carrying out of private actions concerning foreigners
cannot be used. Secondly, precise recording of the bases of carrying out
of such actions and first of all certain list of crimes on which criminal
investigation activity is possible is worth mentioning. The legislation
emphasizes that the indicated activity always has the exclusive character as concerns the basic (constitutional) rights. Thirdly, the legislation
outlines a circle of data having evidentiary value which character should
be always indicated in the judicial warrant. Thus, obligatory destruction
of the materials which do not have the relations to investigated criminal
cases is recorded.

As the given examples show, the content of the legal right is a multi-
pronged concept and it would be impossible to open it not paying attention to its structure. The theory of the law considers an opportunity as a
key element of structure of the legal right. "This attribute is patrimonial,
general for all types of the legal right"[28]. Therefore, the following structure
of the legal right was built:
— An opportunity of action;
— An opportunity of the requirement;
— An opportunity of protection;
— An opportunity to use the social values (the given competence is
distinguished with some authors as additional).

Such classification is not absolutely comprehensible to the analysis of
structure of the right to personal privacy as naturally there is a question:
whether all citizens in such context have the right to personal privacy?
Really, Constitution of the Russian Federation proclaims (Article 23):
"Everyone has a right..." But as a basic key element of the legal right
that is covered by a verb "can" (competence). Otherwise, the right is the
right when the owner can use it, by means of which to determine certain
actions, whether to create duties for other persons, etc. For example, is
such opportunity incapacitated? Can they similarly estimate the indicated
non-material values? The feature of the right to personal privacy means
that a citizen "experiences" the given right. They realize that these or
other sides of its world should not be made public. They carefully hide
them, expecting from others the behaviour which does not break the own

borders of private life. Many mentally unhealthy people lose that valuable component of the right as internal comprehension. Their activity in most cases has no latent character; such persons do not give the report that any actions are necessary for hiding not to undergo public condemnation or for any other reasons. They simply do not realize that they are surrounded by other people, which are not regulated completely too present private world on a general review. The same it is possible to say about juvenile while they still "are not infected" by social rules of behaviour.

As an example of essential denying of separate elements of the right to personal privacy for persons condemned for violent crimes, it is possible to result distribution of the information by a number of newspapers to the Great Britain and Italy about citizens to whom charges in depravity juvenile were shown. On the one hand, the lawful purpose is pursued to protect the rights and freedoms of citizens, on the other these are the rights of a citizen who has already served time for the illegal act. That expiates the fault before a society and whether in this case there is a necessity for further informing about the fact of committing of a crime[29]. In this case about a person, his incomplete characteristic is intentionally disclosed. It is necessary to consider also a degree of perception of this information by citizens, whether they can adequately react to it, state a fair estimation to all vital way of a citizen. Even in courts of the United States of America at investigation of criminal case the information, concerning the previous wrong actions or condemnation of the accused, "is saved as fiduciary from the judge and the jurymen participating in certain case"[30] that in advance there was no accusatory bias.

There is no necessity in considering the given circumstances as the basis of denying of the right to personal privacy for such category of citizens, having agreed with M.N. Maleina, "that the uniform model of a personal non-right of property (structure of its competences) cannot consider features of all non-right of property and consequently does not require designing"[31]. In this case the right to personal privacy is recorded not only as a right, giving socially active effect from conscious actions of citizens but also as a guarantee of an autonomy of internal space of a person from the state and societies.

It would be desirable to pay attention to the fact that the right to personal privacy is the right, rather than a duty. Any person can protect the "vital space" but they can and make its open for all. And such displays can be as socially caused as well as to depend only on personal will. The attitude to virginity of the bride, characteristic for many people can be an example of it in the first case. Thus, in the Vladimir area "if the bride was a virgin she was shown in her shirt to the guests. The groom bowed to her parents, thanked them for "good power". Guest started to beat crockery. If the bride was not honest, her parents were given a "bad" glass of wine, a "bad" pot and sometimes put on a collar. In that case the feast stopped and parents of the bride soon leaved"[32]. The series of experiments carried out with participation of mass media can serve as a characteristic example in the second case. The group of people of different sexes is located for some time in the limited space "stuffed" by video cameras. Thus, tracking devices are installed so that it is impossible to be hidden somewhere. Thus, all internal life, bar none, of the small "commune" is broadcast on TV and on the Internet[33].

Simultaneously, basing on works of researchers of this subject, it is possible to emphasize the following elements of the given right:
— The right to solitude;
— The right to communication.

The right to privacy was considered during the Soviet period through a prism of the concept "secret"[34]. The American doctrine also sees a basic element in "privacy" as the right to be left alone. The modern psychology remarks need for privacy as natural property of any developed person[35]. Accordingly the recording of the given right is caused by features of mentality of a person.

The right to privacy can be determined as a negative element of the right to personal privacy. A citizen himself determines the sides of life (or all ability to live) which would be undesirable to publicity. Creation of own "small world", as a rule, happens not by means of the state and is independent. In this key the greatest value refers to self-defense. Display of self-defense can be very simple. The majority of families with the beginning of darkness use lightproof curtains to protect themselves from possible peeping from passers by or by people living in opposite houses. While living in the house the tenants give a lot of attention to sound insulation of apartments. Till now the significant sales scope of phones with an automatic determinant of number is saved. The purpose of such purchase is to protect from an "uninvited" visit.

Simultaneously the solitude can designate the various phenomena. And in a greater measure psychologists attached the analysis of its semantic meaning significance. (Thus, the term "interpersonal distance" is used. It is specially created by a person with the purpose of delimitation the internal space from other persons by means of the unwritten rules depending on culture, religion, education. It is known that inhabitants of Western Europe are individualists by nature and inhabitants of the

African continent are inclined to collectivist type of residing)[36]. In these cases there will be also various legal understanding.

Firstly, it is "an objective status of the compelled physical or social isolation, participation in communications with people in general or with any socially and personal significant categories of people"[37]. The given status will be compulsory solitude. Imprisonment as a measure of the criminal liability can serve as a widespread example.

Secondly, it is possible to speak about a voluntary solitude: "isolation, limitation "external" connections and contacts for the sake of the profound autocommunications, reflection, contemplation of art, merge to the nature, etc."[38] The history of Lykov's family, who lived in the Siberian taiga, far from a society, serves as a confirmation of when a person independently makes a decision on limitation of interpersonal contacts. Since 1998 Vera and Erofey who refused from world vanity and joined Agafia Lykova, a unique survived from the family[39].

Thirdly, the solitude can become compelled neither by virtue of command of the state, nor on own grade. Psychological features of a person can serve as a reason: absence of sociability, presence of complexes, external isolation. A person, on the contrary, ceases to appreciate privacy as a value which is a subject to protection by means of the right. In this case they need a communication with other people. The state does not carry out any ordered actions; it cannot forcibly organize such a communication. Influence is shown indirectly through creation (or financing, or encouragement) of networks of psychological services, telephone hotlines, by formation of the requirements shown to preschool education and different training with the purpose of inculcation of skills of interpersonal communication.

Apparently, the solitude is a passive element of the right; therefore, it is necessary to emphasize an active element as the right to communication acts. A communication in this context is understood in the wide sense, not being limited to establishment of language contacts. If we consider the French doctrine it is possible to determine this element as freedom to have oneself[40]. The subject party of freedom to have one is also certain widely enough that some authors entail its allocation not from the right to personal privacy but from personal freedom. "A person can live at the choice; hence, they cannot impose certain way of life or to forbid any vital ritual in the name of in advance stipulated moral concept which besides, is shared by everybody"[41].

Apparently, the first element, the right to solitude, it is necessary to determine as an autonomy of a person from the world, the right to interrupt connections with any subject of relations at own discretion and the right to non-interference.

The second (the right to a communication) is understood as independence in creating of connections with the state bodies, enterprises, organizations, organizations associations, citizens under own discretion.

It is worth mentioning that Article 23 of the Constitution of the Russian Federation specifies that the social relations arising in case of personal privacy act as a protected object, i.e. the Constitution precisely determines that the private life is inviolable.

The relativity of private life of a person was simultaneously absolutized. The Lenin phrase "to live in a society and to be free from a society is impossible" proved that private life if not a version of public life, at least, is caused by it. It is necessary to recognize that the ideas of Russian socialism refracted in history of development of the Soviet state are completely not original and should not be considered as bugaboo of totalitarianism. Still Plato in "State" explained that all should be regulated and ordered that it will create new type of a person. Thomas More in "Utopia" admired at the device which was thought up by them, at which "... stay on a kind at all creates necessity to be engaged in habitual work or decently to have a rest"[42]. The given thesis is very convenient for a manipulation a society; therefore, it was used (and still is used) by the state irrespective of the formative accessories or dominating ideology. They can be carefully latent but not be subject to full denying.

Basic approaches (two of them) to understanding of private life are added up to the following. The first starts with detailed elaboration of elements of private life by means of which an attempt to outline all the sides of the concept of the whole is made. As a rule the developed concept acts as a result[43].

The second approach concerns creating of a negative element. In the beginning general principle is built: everything that does not relate to public activity is private life, and then exceptions are deduced from them. "From my point of view, the secret of private (personal) life is made with data on certain person, not connected with his professional or public work and assessing his character, shape, health, the material status, the marital status, a way of life, the separate facts of the biography and also his relations with relatives, friends, and etc."[44], M.N. Maleina considers, having outlined private life as data... except for concerning to professional or public work.

Both from them are noteworthy though they have some drawbacks. Scope of all sides of private life will represent a bulky design in which the concept can "sink". Simultaneously definition only through a negative element suffers absence positive, in fact, the content of the legal right is based not only on questions of protection but covers also positive actions both from the state and a citizen.

It seems that, closely studying all aspects of private life: sociological, culture-logic, philosophical, etc. the jurisprudence should draw more precise conclusions, clear to any citizen and especially for law enforcement.

The culture-logic approach to understanding of private life is wider than legal. The private life is the sphere of the direct communication of people[45]. Really, a person who is being a full solitude does not require private life as in the institution requiring protection. There are no other people who could disturb his rest. It does not mean that a person does not have private world, it remains with him. The concept of private life which emphasizes isolation of an individual from such has been lost. Its inviolability is caused only by human intrusion, by virtue of his mental originality, in personal space. Intrusion of the person into a world cannot be considered as infringement of personal privacy. Otherwise, the right stipulated by Article 23 of the Constitution of the Russian Federation, is the right from a person. Accordingly the communication of a person, their functioning in a society, also adds value to his private life, is which it is recorded and guaranteed in the subsequent by means of the right.

A person cannot survive alone. The problem to survive absorbs in itself some values; it concerns also some aspects of freedom. Proceeding from it, likely, it is impossible to say that during ancient times people were not civilized as they did not know many modern values which are declared sacred, inalienable, born. It concerns understanding of private life. Ancient times laid down such conditions in which before everyone there was a choice is or to survive but to obey to collective, or to die. And the destiny of collective education quite often depend on an act of certain person is families, sorts, communities. In the latter case any discussions about inalienable laws would be useless. We from height of our time can easily condemn the whole generations as easily we condemn some people, having mentioned their primitive. But whether mankind could survive, having built that culture which we use in the 21st century if the system of human rights of the third millennium were imparted 1000 years ago? The destiny of small radical people of the North who were destined to jump from the 15th century into the 20th century can serve as confirmation. The result was their full destruction as ethnos. As it was correctly noted by Norbert Rouland, "... It is much easier to describe the world, than to explain. Depending on an epoch our manner to ask questions also changes"[46]. The history does not stand a subjunctive mood. Apparently, the attitude to private life during the various periods has somewhat an objective substantiation.

At the early stage of development of social relations the private world was not individual but collective. It was also built by community as a whole, and was protected also by it. Therefore, cruel ethnic wars were possible. In its opposition of a private world of one ethnos in relation to another was expressed. At this time national traditions were developed that as a matter of fact and expressed the collective private life.

At formation of the uniform nation (which, as a rule, was accompanied by creation of the mononational state) the private world was differentiated. Its "creating" happened within the limits of less extensive communities: there are friendly associations, professional castes, estates, etc.

Later a family becomes the basis of private life. Literary criticism serves as a perfect parameter. Since the middle of the 19th century, the majority of books have been devoted to a recreating of history of families (and there is not an epic narration, namely the description of interfamily relations).

A celebration of individuality has already marked the 20th century. A person is put onto the first place in the hierarchy of public values. And if earlier the conflict "between fathers and children" was solved always in favour of parents, giving questions of education of children at the discretion of family justice now legal regulations emphasize the protection of a certain person. If parents do not cope with education they can be deprived from the parental rights.

That should not be said about boundaries of private life but about a boundary between a private and a collective world which is built proceeding from the corresponding reasons during the various historical periods. For this reason the legislator gradually asks questions of regulation of intimate relations (in meaning internal is private) making significant only the external party of behaviour. The law did not try to change a private world; it imposed an external stereotype of behaviour. The more rigidly it was imposed; the distinction of a private world and external actions was more brightly shown. From the point of view of psychology it is possible to state that consecutive introduction of external canons of behaviour also created the subjective attitude to the acts. Through any time the subsequent generation did not reflect any more on necessity of certain model of behaviour: It is necessary to do so because all ancestors did so. Strict ritualizedness, guaranteed by cruel methods of compulsion is unequivocally created ground for conflicts inside of a society. It is impossible to say that the right did not provide performance of these specifications. The initial right provided the system of punishment down to an excommunication from church and burning in fire. Excommunication was the derelict of a society. The degree of an excommunication from church could reach that the person was put beyond the framework of the civil law. He could be killed, beheaded, sold unpunished in slavery. Such system was supported by legal recording of the system of family legal proceedings.

Simultaneously propagation of cleanliness of customs without their legal (formal-normative) recording obliges each individual to carry out shadowing "for the neighbour". Only-imperious command state would provide just supervision from police bodies that, in turn, could encounter aversion from a society. Other model is provided with a society as a whole, in this case the ruling elite requires, first of all, the skill to operate (and to correct in the necessary manner) the collective processes.

Given reasons show the ambiguity of the approach to definition of the content of private life that accordingly attracts washing out of criteria of possible limitations of the right to personal privacy and division of private and social life. The various states build the system of principles of mutual relations between a person and the state. In this context it is possible to mention general approach developed by the Supreme Court of the USA on case Katz versus the USA (Katz vs. United States, 1967), to an estimation of legitimacy of intervention of authorities during the private life, received the name "the proved expectation on personal privacy " ("reasonable expectation of privacy"). Its essence consists in how the author - Judge Harlan expressed that he based on two preconditions: "Firstly, the given person should show the valid (subjective) expectation of observance of the right to private life; secondly, this expectation should be such that the society could recognize it "proved" ("reasonable")"[47]. Making a start from such characteristic of the legal right, it is possible to develop criteria of definition of private life, proceeding from "the proved expectation". In this case such sphere which similarly a citizen disappears from extraneous persons will relate to private life. Thus, a citizen realizes the value of the behaviour on concealment of certain information, these or other actions. His internal belief is under creating that he soundly expects inadmissibility of any intervention. As a private life as a category is a watershed between, in fact, private and public in definition of its content is inadmissible to be based only on subjective criterion of the owner of the values. Therefore, the additional condition is also a concept by a society of the proved reference of these or other sides of activity of a person by their private life. The American judiciary practice at the legal proceeding, the sides of private life connected with disclosing, now bases on the given rules: the publication of a certain fact of private life is considered as encroachment on the sphere of private life if it was proved, "that the publication of this fact was reprehensible from the point of view of the homo sapiens distinguished by usual sensitivity"[48].

From the point of view of positive jurisprudence it is impossible to forget that any textual recording of the competence and the protected values entails also the right to claim protection and accordingly and the right of defence by means of the state. Therefore, in this case the **private life** should be determined **as a non-material value belonging to each citizen from birth, consisting of such sides of his internal life and spheres of communication which similarly are saved by them as fiduciary from other subjects and are subject to unconditional protection in the democratic state as in the cases directly stipulated in the law and in other cases in those limits which follow from an essence of the given values and a degree correlation of its realization with the rights and freedoms of other citizens**.

While considering the various sides of private life depending on a way of protection they can be divided on two big groups:

— What persons themselves in a status to protect from extraneous intervention according to Article 45 of the Constitution of the Russian Federation: "Everyone has a right to protect the rights and freedoms in all ways which have been not forbidden by the law";

— What the state takes under the special protection; these are the most valuable sides of private life, intervention in which would render essential harm to a person and authority of the state.

The second group includes such sides of private life which undertake under special protection in the branch legislation. These sides as a rule are determined by means of the term "secret". Their difference means that they are determined precisely enough. The method of the legislator seems as follows: to outline legal relationships, having the greatest value, to isolate and protect. Thus, in the branch legislation it was reflected in notarial secrecy, bank, lawyer, medical and other secrets. By development of the mechanism of regulation of a certain kind of secret the following requirements should be considered:

The subject of the secret obliged it to keep any person who is on a duty of service or by virtue of specificity of the work gets access to such data should act;

The law should determine the exhaustive list of the subjects having access to data that makes certain secret and also the bases and the procedure of presentation of such requirement;

There should be a legislative recording of an opportunity of a citizen to appeal in the judicial order on the actions directed on acquaintance with data; making secret protected by the law if a citizen considers that they are unreasonable or illegal. And a citizen should be informed of use the information which is subject to him unless otherwise stipulated by the Federal law;

The scope of secret protected by the law should cover not only the data, which a citizen independently gives into an organization (the credit organization, notary's office, legal consultation, etc.) but also any information, received from communication with a citizen and also the fact of treatment in such organizations or absence of such fact.

Realization of constitutional law on protection and on personal privacy is connected with serious problems. In particular, in the Report of Human Rights Commissioner in the Russian Federation in 2003 the following infringement of this right are indicated: illegal intrusions of militia officers into dwellings of citizens; illegal use of the information bases including data of the private life of citizens (a surname, names, home addresses and phones) in political and other purposes; offenders are not legally responsible for it; editions of telephone directories where data about citizens without taking into account their opinions is published[49].

Realization of the legal right by an individual can concern the rights and legitimate interests of other persons. Philosophers considered that there were times when freedom of everyone faced with freedom of others that led to war of everybody against everybody. It also has forced people to create the state to bridle customs of a person that already freedom of everyone was compatible to freedom of other persons. The need for such regulation has generated limitations of some civil human rights. By means of limitations the good purpose of social cohabitation that is joint residing of people in one territory for achievement of general uniform problems, first of all, such as achievement of the highest level of individual development is reached. The state in this case acts as the most convenient way (but not the only thing) in achieving of such purpose.

The Constitution of the Russian Federation supposes establishment of limitations of the right to personal privacy but it should respond the following conditions:

— The opportunity of penetration into the sphere of private life should be indicated only in the law and respond to the purposes of Article 55 (part 3) Constitutions of the Russian Federation;

— In the law the circle of persons should be indicated, having the right to interfere in private life;

— Penetration into the sphere of private life should be not any, with observance of corresponding procedure.

All the indicated conditions make the most rigid demands to a remedial basis of realization of limitations. Unfortunately, the Soviet jurisprudence least attention gave a remedial basis of activity of public bodies.

The right to personal privacy directly is connected with a legal regime of the information. Data on private life of a person can be collected in various information databases. Transfer of this data also happens in the form of transfer of the information. Therefore, the Constitution of the Russian Federation provides the special clause devoted to this problem. Clause 24 of the Constitution of the Russian Federation proclaims: "Gathering, storage, use and distribution of the information on private life of a person without his consent is not supposed".

The Federal law "the information, and protection of the information" determines the information as follows is "data on persons, subjects, the facts, events, the phenomena and processes irrespective of the form of their notion" (Article 2)[50]. The given definition says that the unessential information should be documented that its use and distribution is according to the Constitutional interdiction. Therefore, the information can be given as in oral and in writing. The most acute problem of use the information nowadays is its finding in electronic databanks.

At presence of uniform information space the legal aspect of gathering and use of the information on private life of a person qualitatively becomes complicated as any treatment of citizens is recorded in an electronic database. Necessity of it is dictated not by a duty before the state or heads of organizations but convenience and economic feasibility. The reviewer is the worker of shop or the insurance company writing the information into the computer does not think at all that there is an interest in that someone had a full picture about life of a citizen. And a citizen least reflects that on them there is any special file where the part of their private life is reflected. In this case the right cannot determine a legal regime only by means of permissions any more and interdictions. Moreover, in the beginning banks of electronic data began to be formed and already there was a need to put them under the special control of the society and the state. The given problem has global value especially for the developed countries basing on the mobile information resources and precision technologies. In Soviet Union there were no such problems because of backwardness of PC, concerning western countries it moved as a special way of suppression of a person a capitalist society.

Ordering of personal data is facilitated at introduction of uniform identification number of a citizen. It means that within the limits of any relations to a citizen is given personal individual number which is necessary to specify at appealing into any organization. In this case accumulation of all personal data is made by processing all file of the information through personal number. That in all electronic system is "a thread", having pulled which (the main task is to know personal number), it is possible to receive full scope of the processed information. The given problem is called the problem of "Big Brother"[51].

Clause 83 of the Tax Code of the Russian Federation[52] provides that "with a view of carrying out of the tax control taxpayers are subject to statement on the account in tax bodies..." Clause 84 supplements that "to each taxpayer the taxpayer identification number" is given uniform by all kinds of taxes and tax collections, including a subject payment in connection with moving of the goods through customs border of the Russian Federation and in all territory of the Russian Federation. Otherwise, the operating Russian legislation provides assignment of uniform personal number (TIN), including to citizens. The Tax Code establishes that each taxpayer specifies identification number in submitted in tax body of the declaration, the report, the statement or other document and also in other cases stipulated by the legislation.

Simultaneously the data on identification number of the taxpayer does not relate to tax secret. Practice testifies that at payment of any compensation to physical persons the accounts department of enterprises, organizations, demands the indication of TIN. The foreign practice testifies that the direct interdiction on compulsion of the indication of a uniform code of the physical person is quite often introduced at carrying out of transactions or rendering of services.

In the Russian Federation the Federal law "Information and protection of the information" was accepted in 1995. In spite of the fact that the law itself has a frame character and contains a lot of provisions to yet not accepted legal regulations, the basic provisions directed on guarantees of privacy of citizens, in them are. Thus, Article 14 records: "Citizens have the right of the organization to access to the documentary information on them, on specification of this information with a view of ensuring of its completeness and reliability, have the right to know, who and in what purposes uses or used this information. Limitation of access of citizens and organizations to the information on them is possible only on the bases stipulated by Federal laws". The documentary information on citizens should be given free of charge on demand of those persons whom it concerns. Limitations are possible only in the cases stipulated by the legislation of the Russian Federation. Refusal of the owner of information resources to the subject in access to the information on them can be appealed against in the judicial order.

The indicated Federal law for the first time introduces into Russian practice concept "personal data": "Information on citizens (personal data) is data on the facts, events and circumstances of life of a citizen, allowing identifying his personality" (Article 2). The decree of the President of the Russian Federation of March, 6th, 1997, # 188 approves the List of data of confidential nature[53] in which there are the facts, events and circumstances of private life of a citizen are also included", allowing to identify his personality (personal data), except for data which are subject to distribution in mass media in cases established by Federal law". Apparently, the Decree "corrects" provisions of the law, having a little limited the concept of "personal data", having included in it only circumstances of private life of a person and having excluded the data which is subject to distribution in mass-media.

Simultaneously indicated interdiction does not have an absolute character. Moreover, the legislation provides activity of organizations, engaging it on a professional basis. Those are, for example, law enforcement bodies.

Law enforcement bodies, as it was said, accept active participation in gathering the information. It is necessary not to that gathering of the information is not always connected with reaction to any offence. Law enforcement bodies are interested in creation of card files which would render the essential help in prophylaxis and disclosing of crimes: dactyloscopic maps, photographic albums, etc. It is connected by that some attributes inherent in a person are especially individual. Presence of prints of fingers can speak that the given citizen was in the given place. Therefore, presence of dactyloscopic data will help to identify, for example, a personality of the offender. Also the design of DNA which formula can be deduced from the smallest particle left on a place of an offence is individual. In many states it is offered to carry out full "inventory" of citizens to some attributes. The most widespread method is a formation of bank of dactyloscopic data.

In the Russian Federation in 1998 was passed the Federal law "The State Dactyloscopic Registration in the Russian Federation"[54]. At acceptance of the law by some politicians it was offered to introduce obligatory dactyloscopic registration for all citizens.

The purpose of the state dactyloscopic registration is recorded in Article 2 of the law is identification of a person of a person.

The law, recording voluntary and obligatory dactyloscopic registration, started with its purpose. Thus, representatives of law enforcement and other bodies and organizations are subject to obligatory registration, whose professional work is connected with risk for life (FSB, the Ministry of Internal Affairs, FIS - SVR (Foreign Intelligence Service), etc.).

Any citizen of the Russian Federation has a right to the voluntary state dactyloscopic registration carried out by law enforcement bodies. For this purpose a personal will in written form is enough.

Simultaneously it is necessary to dwell on one aspect of definition of the right to personal privacy is guarantying of it. As George Ellinek noted, "an essential attribute of the concept of the right is... not compulsion but a guarantee, serves one of which kinds compulsion"[55].

Accordingly, the following generalizing definition of guarantees of the right to personal privacy is a legally significant mechanism of ensuring of the considered right, strictly set on the basis of the constitutional recording both on legislative and on a law enforcement level.

Special guarantees are the legal ways and means providing certain conditions and the order of realization of the legal provision, therefore, in theory of the right and guarantees of its realization[56]. There are a lot of special guarantees, but all of them are incorporated by one purpose – the creation of the legal mechanism of realization of the right to personal privacy. As it seems, the legislation of the Russian Federation should contain in this sphere: establishment of the responsibility for infringement of the right to personal privacy, judicial control of activity of the state bodies, including the right to the judicial appeal of actions and decisions breaking the given right and the right to the constitutional appeal as a guarantee from a legislative arbitrariness and also observance of secrecy of the private life which has become at interaction with public bodies, organizations, enterprises in case of realization of the rights belonging to them.

In the Russian Federation the criminal liability for infringement of privacy of correspondence, telephone conversations and cable messages is provided. Infringement can be in the form of acquaintance with the mail, the content of telephone conversations or cable messages without the consent to that of addressees and also in the form of disclosure of the message irrespective of, in the oral or written form it was made. The given provision is characteristic for the criminal legislation of the majority of the countries.

A new Criminal Code of the Russian Federation provides new Chapter 19 "Crimes Against Constitutional Rights and Freedoms of a Person and a Citizen" in which it is possible to find clause 137 recording the criminal liability for general delict as infringement of personal privacy: "Illegal collecting or distribution of data on private life of persons making his personality or family secrecy without his consent or distribution of this data to the public, publicly shown product or mass media if these acts are accomplished from mercenary or other personal interest and have harmed the rights and legitimate interests of citizens".

In the Criminal Code of France the responsibility of any person having the confidential information which was entrusted in connection with performance of professional functions and divulged is stipulated[57]. Russian legislation provides also remedial guarantees of preservation of personal privacy at realization by a citizen of the rights in public bodies. Establishing such principle as publicity of proceeding, in the Code of Criminal Procedure of the Russian Federation and the Remedial Code of the Russian Federation provide the necessity of closed hearings. Such session happens under motivated decision of the court to prevent the disclosure of corresponding data to the participants of a process.

In any case the final decision on a civil case is made publicly. The given rule, in fact, crosses out guarantees of observance of secrecy of private life. In some decisions there is practically no opportunity to hide (not to announce) circumstance because of which the session was declared closed even if it is disclosed only partly resolute. Rules of civil legal proceedings in the USA predetermine that in some category of affairs "the rights of the parties to privacy are protected by means of designations by their fictitious names, such as "Richard Rowe" and "Mary Rowe"[58].

Summing up, we should pay attention to some most essential moments: a person as an individual is characterized not only by a multivariate inclusiveness in social bonds but also by the unique individuality, allowing bringing in social life the moment of subjective creativity. On the other hand, the society, protecting individuality of a person, recognizes a certain level of freedom. The private life is an element of freedom of an individual, simultaneously reflecting his public and individual nature. From this point of view personal privacy acts as social value in which protection both a person and a society are evenly interested. From here there is also the problem of a right protection of personal privacy.

The content which is put in the concept of private life has historical character and its relations depend on many factors: customs, foundations, characteristic for the majority of the population, a level of culture of a society, national and religious features of its development. It is possible that in internationally-legal documents quite often feature of regulation of these or another relations in the states for which communal way is characteristic are reflected. And it should not be confused with a communal system as a kind of socioeconomic structures. Community is considered as a form of joint residing when the private life of everyone is included in the life of social structure (the expanded family, a kin, etc.); it is protected jointly and is regulated also jointly.

It seems that the right to personal privacy refers to a person irrespective of the fact whether the given institution is recorded by the legislation of that or another state. But, recording the given right in an official source, the state thus points to its legal significance. The right to personal privacy becomes a legal category and accordingly, gets the content, structure, and elements.

Use of classical system of the content of the legal right and the analysis of the right to personal privacy allows revealing features of its legal nature. The given right is difficult to determine as a measure of legal behaviour (an opportunity of action, requirement, using the social values). It, first of all, is a barrier from any intervention into a private world of a person, from imposing certain behaviour, possible limitation of daily freedom of choice and is not on a law enforcement person's level, rather than on the level of lawmaking. Necessity of presence of the private world of a person is predetermined by special properties of human mentality.

The Constitution of the Russian Federation has proclaimed the right to personal privacy to assume that unique declaration will provide that inviolability. At the same time the attitude to the Constitution as to the document for "external using" has led to the fact that the constitutional aspect of any legal right in its branch refraction is seldom deduced. Absence of the Constitution "in blood" at many practicing lawyers leads to increasing mistrust to the essence of basic rights of a person. It obliges to pay special attention of jurisprudence to problems of the content of basic rights and freedoms of a person and a citizen.

On the basis of it is possible to emphasize the general concept of the right to personal privacy. It is necessary to understand an inalienable right of a person to independent definition of the way of life as it is, free from any regulations, intervention and encroachment as from the state, a society or a person and also protected by the law from any stereotype imposing.

Notes

1. It is necessary to note that the Constitution of the USSR does not fix the subjective right, fixing: «Private life of citizens, secret of correspondence, telephone conversations and cable messages are protected by the law».

2. Малеин N.S. Protection of rights of a person by the Soviet Legislation. Moscow, 1985. P. 49. / Малеин Н. С. Охрана прав личности советским законодательством. М., 1985. С. 49.

3. Pokrovsky I.A. Basic of the Problem of Civil Law. Moscow, 1998. P. 125. / Покровский И. А. Основные проблемы гражданского права. М., 1998. С. 125.

4. Krasavchikova L.O. Personal Life under Protection of the Law. Moscow, 1983. P. 39. / Красавчикова Л. О. Личная жизнь под охраной закона. М., 1983. С. 39.

5. The Constitutional Status of a Person in the USSR. Moscow, 1980. P. 184. / Конституционный статус личности в СССР. М., 1980. С. 184.

6. Matuzov N.I. Person. Rights. Democracy. Theoretical problems of the subjective right. Moscow, 1972. P. 93. / Матузов Н. И. Личность. Права. Демократия. Теоретические проблемы субъективного права. М., 1972. С. 93.

7. Hegel G.V. F. Philosophy of the Law. Moscow, 1990. P. 79. / Гегель Г. В. Ф. Философия права. М., 1990. С. 79.

8. Matuzov N.I. Specified work. P. 93.

9. The General Theory of Human Rights. Moscow, 1996. P. 169. / Общая теория прав человека. М., 1996. С. 169.

10. See: The Constitutional Status of a Person in the USSR. Moscow, 1980. P. 202. / См.: Конституционный статус личности в СССР. М., 1980. С. 202.

11. Ibidem. P. 203.

12. Vedyahin V.M., Shubina T.B. Protection of the Right as a Legal Category // Jurisprudence. 1998.1./ Ведяхин В. М., Шубина Т. Б. Защита права как правовая категория // Правоведение. 1998. № 1.

13. It is necessary to note that the given competence has the indirect reference to the "base" right as honour and a reputation require protection, first of all, when they are discredited (Clause 152 of the Civil Code of the Russian Federation). Protection of a private life happens at distribution of truthful information in which publicity the citizen is not interested.

14. Quoted on: Thompson D.L., Priestley D. Sociology: Introductory Course. Moscow, 1998. P. 162. The traditional understanding of family is challenged by modern sociology. Remarkable is the sanction in some countries to homosexual marriages, and also to having children in them by artificial way. / Цит. по: Томпсон Д. Л., Пристли Д. Социология: Вводный курс. М., 1998. С. 162. Традиционное понимание семьи современной социологией оспаривается. Примечательным выглядит разрешение в некоторых странах на гомосексуальные браки, а также на появление в них детей искусственным путем.

15. Golod S.I. Family and Marriage: Historically-Sociological Analysis. St. Petersburg, 1998. P. 91. / Голод С. И. Семья и брак: историко-социологический анализ. СПб., 1998. С. 91.

16. Note: Are features of a joint intimate life of spouses a personal secret of each of them or they form the family secret?

17. Maleina M.N. Personal Non-property Rights of Citizens: Concept, Realization, Protection. Moscow, 2001. P. 175. / Малеина М. Н. Личные неимущественные права граждан: понятие, осуществление, защита. М., 2001. С. 175.

18. See: Sheets of Congress of People's Deputies of the Russian Federation and the Supreme Soviet of the Russian Federation. 1993.33. Clause 1318. / См.: Ведомости Съезда народных депутатов РФ и Верховного Совета РФ. 1993. № 33. Ст. 1318.

19. See: Assembly of the Legislation of the Russian Federation. 1996.1. Clause 16. / См.: Собрание законодательства РФ. 1996. № 1. Ст. 16.

20. See: Assembly of the Legislation of the Russian Federation. 1995.33. Clause 3349. / См.: Собрание законодательства РФ. 1995. № 33. Ст. 3349.

21. Domrin A. Law of Security Service of the Great Britain // Socialist Legality. 1991.12. P. 59. / Домрин А. Закон о службе безопасности Великобритании // Социалистическая законность. 1991. № 12. С. 59.

22. It is necessary to bear in mind that the right to inviolability of private life in many respects in judiciary practice of the USA is deduced from the contents of the Fourth amendment to the Constitution. Similarly the procedure of receiving a sanction to restrictions of the right on secret of a mail service is considered by analogy to procedure of delivery of the warrant on a search.

23. Peshkov M. Bugging and Electronic Supervision in Criminal Trial of the USA // Russian Justice. 1997.4. P. 55. / Пешков М. Прослушивание и электронное наблюдение в уголовном процессе США // Российская юстиция. 1997. № 4. С. 55.

24. Frankovsky S., Goldman R., Lentovska E. Supreme Court of the USA about Civil Rights and Freedoms. Warsaw, 1997. P. 190-191. / Франковски С., Гольдман Р., Лентовска Э. Верховный суд США о гражданских правах и свободах. Варшава, 1997. С. 190–191.

25. Ibidem. P. 189. The essence of Katz case was the following. The accused organized illegal gambling by phone. The judge admitted as the proof the record of the telephone conversation made from a pay phone. The overhearing device has been established by agents of FBI outside.

26. Peshkov M. Bugging and Electronic Supervision in Criminal Trial of the USA // Russian Justice. 1997.4. P. 56. / Пешков М. Прослушивание и электронное наблюдение в уголовном процессе США // Российская юстиция. 1997. № 4. С. 56.

27. See: Nikolaichik V.M. Criminal Justice in the USA. Moscow, 1995. P. 94. / См.: Николайчик В. М. Уголовное правосудие в США. М., 1995. С. 94.

28. Матузов N.I. Person. Rights. Democracy. Saratov, 1972. P. 97. / Матузов Н. И. Личность. Права. Демократия. Саратов, 1972. С. 97.

29. In the middle of 90th in the United States America the law was passed ordering «to the condemned persons for sexual crimes, within 10 years after clearing from prison to register in police of a state, and for some of them with extreme aggression to registrate constantly - without limitation in time. Communities are notified that the given criminal lives in their territory or goes to them » (Nikiforov A.S. The USA: The Law on the Control over Violent Criminality // The State and The Law. 1996.3. P. 127). / (Никифоров А. С. США: закон о контроле над насильственной преступностью // Государство и право. 1996. № 3. С. 127).

30. William G. Young. The USA: Courts and Mass Media // Russian Justice. 1996.1. P. 58. / Уильям Дж. Янг. США: суды и средства массовой информации // Российская юстиция. 1996. № 1. С. 58.

31. Maleina M.N. Content and Realization of Personal Non-property Rights of Citizens: Problems of the Theory and the Legislation // The State and The Law. 2000.2. P. 17. / Малеина М. Н. Содержание и осуществление личных неимущественных прав граждан: проблемы теории и законодательства // Государство и право. 2000. № 2. С. 17.

32. Leschenko V. J. Family and Russian Orthodoxy (XI - XIX centuries). St. Petersburg, 1999. P. 125. / Лещенко В. Ю. Семья и русское православие (XI – XIX вв.). СПб., 1999. С. 125.

33. The example is the project «Behind Glass» (like "Big Brother"), created by a telechannel TV-6.

34. See: Guliev V.E., Rudinsky F.M. Socialist Democracy and Personal Rights. Moscow, 1984. / См.: Гулиев В. Е., Рудинский Ф. М. Социалистическая демократия и личные права. М., 1984.

35. See in more detail: Kon I.S. Friendship: Ethical - Psychological Sketch. Moscow, 1987. P. 308. / См. более подробно: Кон И. С. Дружба: Этико-психологический очерк. М., 1987. С. 308.

36. See: Godfruat J. What is Psychology: In 2 vol. Vol. 2. Moscow, 1992. P. 73. / См.: Годфруа Ж. Что такое психология: В 2-х т. Т. 2. М., 1992. С. 73.

37. Kon I.S. Friendship: Ethical - Psychological Sketch. Moscow, 1987. P. 308. / См. более подробно: Кон И. С. Дружба: Этико-психологический очерк. М., 1987. С. 308.

38. Ibidem.

39. See: Peskov V. Taiga Deadlock // Komsomolskaya Pravda. 2000. Oct., 27. / См.: Песков В. Таежный тупик // Комсомольская правда. 2000. 27 окт.

40. See: Lusher F. Constitutional Protection of Personal Rights and Freedoms. Moscow, 1993. P. 91. / См.: Люшер Ф. Конституционная защита прав и свобод личности. М., 1993. С. 91.

41. Ibidem.

42. More T. Utopia // Utopian Socialism: Reader. Moscow, 1982. P. 68. / Мор Т. Утопия // Утопический социализм: Хрестоматия. М., 1982. С. 68.

43. So, the detailed characteristic is given by L.O. Krasavchikova, considering 10 sides of a private life display. (See: Private Life under Protection of the Law. Moscow, 1983. P. 16). / (См.: Личная жизнь под охраной закона. М., 1983. С. 16).

44. Maleina M.N. Personal Non-property Rights of Citizens: Concept, Realization, Protection. Moscow, 2001. P. 153. / Малеина М. Н. Личные неимущественные права граждан: понятие, осуществление, защита. М., 2001. С. 153.

45. See: Person in a Family: Sketches on History of Private Life in the Europe Prior to the Beginning of New Time. Moscow, 1996. P. 13. / См.: Человек в кругу семьи: Очерки по истории частной жизни в Европе до начала нового времени. М., 1996. С. 13.

46. Rouland N. Legal Anthropology. Moscow, 1999. P. 49. / Рулан Н. Юридическая антропология. М., 1999. С. 49.

47. Frankovsky S., Goldman R., Lentovska E. Supreme Court of the USA about Civil Rights and Freedoms. Warsaw, 1997. P. 192. / Франковски С., Гольдман Р., Лентовска Э. Верховный Суд США о гражданских правах и свободах. Варшава, 1997. С. 192.

48. Ivansky V.P. Legal Protection of the Information on Private Life of Citizens. Moscow, 1999. P. 8. / Иванский В. П. Правовая защита информации о частной жизни граждан. М., 1999. С. 8.

49. See: The Report on Human Rights Commissioner's Work in the Russian Federation. Moscow, 2004. P. 24-29. / См.: Доклад о деятельности Уполномоченного по правам человека в Российской Федерации. М., 2004. С. 24–29.

50. Assembly of the Legislation of the Russian Federation. 1995.8. Clause 609. / Собрание законодательства РФ. 1995. № 8. Ст. 609.

51. In honour of Georges Oruell's novel «1984».

52. See: Assembly of the Legislation of the Russian Federation. 1998.31. Clause 3824. / См.: Собрание законодательства РФ. 1998. № 31. Ст. 3824.

53. See: Assembly of the Legislation of the Russian Federation. 1997.10. Clause 1127. / См.: Собрание законодательства РФ. 1997. № 10. Ст. 1127.

54. See: Assembly of the Legislation of the Russian Federation. 1998.31. Clause 3806./ См.: Собрание законодательства РФ. 1998. № 31. Ст. 3806.

55. Ellinek G. General Doctrine of the State. St. Petersburg, 1908. P. 246. / Еллинек Г. Общее учение о государстве. СПб., 1908. С. 246.

56. Patulin V.A. The State and The Person in the USSR. Moscow, 1974. P. 233. / Патюлин В. А. Государство и личность в СССР. М., 1974. С. 233.

57. See: Yefimov L. Bank Secrecy: Comparative Aspect // Business and Banks. 1991.46. P. 2. / См.: Ефимова Л. Банковская тайна: сравнительный аспект // Бизнес и банки. 1991. № 46. С. 2.

58. Young William G. The USA: Courts and Mass Media // Russian Justice. 1996.1. P. 58. / Янг Уильям Дж. США: суды и средства массовой информации // Российская юстиция. 1996. № 1. С. 58.

Chapter 9. THE FREEDOM OF CONSCIENCE
IN THE RUSSIAN FEDERATION

Legal grounds of freedom of conscience can be found in a number of international legal documents among which it is necessary to emphasize the Universal Declaration of Human Rights (1948), International Covenant on Civil and Political Rights (1966), the European Convention for the Protection of Human Rights and Basic Freedoms (1950), the Declaration on the Elimination of All Forms of Intolerance and of Discrimination Based on Religion or Belief (1981).

The Declaration (1948) served as model at definition of standards of human rights for a newest Constitutions accepted in many countries of the world, including Russia. Having headed for creating of a lawful state in the end of 1980s, the Russian Federation has undertaken to bring the national legislation into accord with provisions of internationally-legal documents. Confirming conformity to the conventional principles and standards of international law, the Constitution of the Russian Federation has recorded as a legal basis such civilized provisions as freedom of conscience (Article 28) and secularity of the state (Article 14).

According to Article 28 "Everyone is guaranteed the freedom of conscience, including the right to profess individually or together with others any religion or not to profess any, freely to choose, have and distribute religious and other believes and to work according to them". Clause 14 declares: "1. The Russian Federation is a secular state. No religion can be established as state or obligatory. 2. Religious associations are separated from the state and are equal before the law". The part 2 of Article 19 seamlessness supplements Article 14 and 28. It says, "The State guarantees equality of the rights and freedoms of a citizen irrespective of ... attitude to religion, belief, belonging to public associations and other circumstances".

Historically in the basic international legal documents and in Constitution of the Russian Federation following their example, the standards of freedom of conscience are considered exclusively in connection with their religious aspects, i.e. religious-confessional. Accordingly, the legal concept of freedom of conscience (freedom of choice of a world outlook) has got narrower meaning as the right of an individual to solve the problem independently, whether to be guided in an estimation of the acts and ideas by lectures of religion or to refuse them.

Gloria M. Moran says in this occasion, "The Universal Declaration (1948) and a newest Constitutions are following its example, speaking about "freedom of thought, conscience and religion". In this connection scientists cannot come to the consent opinion whether there is only one - global freedom considered in three different aspects, or it is necessary to distinguish three independent kinds of freedom? Since the fiftieth and up to the end of the seventieth years the majority of the European scientists preferred the last variant, considering a specific goal of religious freedom but recently tend to the opinion that this term is inseparably linked with freedom of conscience"[1].

It is impossible to challenge a main role which the Universal Declaration played in development of legal and political philosophy of the second half the 20th century but as a result of such inconsistency the wide, scopetric concept concerning literally everyone individual "freedom of conscience" was shown exclusively to freedom of creeds (i.e. to freedom concerning only individuals, considering believers) and even the activity of religious associations (i.e. to the collective form of realization of the right to freedom of creeds). In fact, the right of individuals considering with non-believers appears outside the legal scope.

In connection with that criteria and limits of freedom of conscience in international legal documents and in the Constitution of the Russian Federation are certain in general view, without taking into account the essence, nature and value of this right, its realization is exposed to "special" limitations according to the state religious politics which is carried out by means of state-confessional relations.

Among consequences of religious politics there is limitation of a political competition, infringement of human rights, stimulation of nationalism, phobias, violence over intolerance, terrorism.

Thus, legal regulation in the field of freedom of conscience "historically" is based on incorrect principles from the legal point of view, not having precise legal criteria and the corresponding conceptual device partially borrowed from theology that is why it is obviously unusable.

The freedom of conscience is substituted for freedom of creeds, human rights - for the rights of associations, religion for ideology, in summary the priority of the right is substituted for a priority of politics, interests of "elites".

In opinion of the author, **freedom of conscience** is the backbone right in the system of the human rights, the basic inalienable law of each person to the free world outlook choice which is not entailing "special" limitations in other civil rights and freedoms or their loss.

Accordingly, **freedom of creeds (religion)** is one of elements of freedom of conscience. It includes a number of elements: 1) the right to profess any religion; 2) the right of carrying out of religious practices; 3) the right to change religion; 4) the right of propagation of religion; 5) the right to charities; 6) the right to religious education; 7) cultural-educational religious activity; 8) equal protection of the law of all citizens, irrespective of their attitude to religion, etc.

Freedom of Conscience in the Context of Problems of Creating of the Legal Democratic State Formation of a Civil Society

Declaration of freedom of conscience not casually ranks as major gains of mankind. The freedom of conscience as means of protection of a person, a society from ideological domination of any doctrines and structures acts as a basis of each legal democratic state, set as a purpose of creating of the open civil society.

Suppressing freedom of conscience the totalitarian regimes achieve transformation of a person into an instrument for achievement of purposes. They wish to remain with authority as longer as possible if not forever. Therefore, today as before, imperious groups are interested in the control and limitation of freedom of a world outlook choice that, having played "a religious map", without problems to use public, group and individual consciousness of "simple" people during next elections, by its involving in the sphere of religious authorization.

As a result the society receives only mythological imitation of freedom of conscience, human rights and democracy for the wide use, the imperious groups formally recognizing the higher authority of people and using political strategists - legend-makers on a regular basis dominate over successful overcoming of democratic procedures.

The right of each person to freedom of conscience is, as a matter of fact, one of the backbones in the system of human rights. Without realization of this right other human rights lose the most part of the real content and turn into the empty declaration.

Realizing the right to freedom of conscience, a person realizes himself, in fact, a person, finds the meaning and determines the place in life. The freedom of conscience, thus, includes all variety of forms of the systems of orientation (including mentioned religious), sold individually and (or) collectively on principles of equality. And real equality can and should be based on the principle of limitation of a regulation of culturally-moral sphere from the state. Granting to the state the special powers on regulation of the given sphere inevitably leads to an interpretation of it (according to personal interests and group confessional preferences of government officials) and as consequence, to an inevitable abusing.

The choice of the form of the system of orientation of each person in accuracy corresponds to the system of orientation of ancestors or that is the most probable in modern realities, considerably differs. It is possible to assume that development of above-mentioned forms is inseparably linked with evolution of mankind, as a whole. Hence there is a necessity of equality of new forms in relation to existing. As "primordial" and "traditional" forms were in due time new and accordingly "nonconventional".

Becoming of a civil society appreciably depends on a status of freedom of conscience and in particular its normative-legal base. Prosperity of a society and the state depends on realization of the right to freedom of conscience in many respects and as a whole, of mankind. With a view of protection of world outlook pluralism as a major component of a civil society, alongside with ideological variety, it is necessary to protect religious sphere from political interests and claims of the state. In the given context creating of the legal democratic state formation of a civil society are incompatible with clericalization of the state institutions from any religious faith, legislative recording of the rigid control and in equality in relation to other faiths.

Difficulties of realization of the constitutional principles of freedom of conscience and secularity of the state in Russia are caused, alongside with other factors, in many respects by scientific unavailability and absence of the wide concept of freedom of conscience.

Legal regulation of freedom of conscience in the modern democratic lawful state which has determined as a purpose creating of an open civil society, demands radical audit and reform of principles on which this regulation is based. Otherwise the domestic science still will long go "a vicious circle" and lawmaking is "successfully" to carry out political orders of imperious groups, contrary to interests of a society.

The Problem of a Correlation between Freedom of Conscience and Freedom of Creeds

The understanding of necessity of religious tolerance, free-thinking, legal protection of the people, adhering various outlook was affirmed in public consciousness in the process of historical development. Today the freedom of conscience, ideas and religions is the integral component of universal values, the basic democratic rights and freedoms of a person. However, it is necessary to remark that the principle of freedom of conscience was theoretically comprehended and evolutionized more likely as a historical and philosophically-ethical, rather than a legal category.

It is possible to say that all over world the concept in a greater measure was won with an ideal of religious freedom, therefore, its principles have found the normative importance. The freedom of conscience is only declared, along with freedom of religion, in standards of international law and Constitutions of many states. Thus, the right of everyone to freedom of conscience is mentioned everywhere only as a declaration, in fact, being outside of the legal scope.

One part of the problem means that the principle of religious freedom has, in fact, been based on the division of a society into the "believers and non-believers", and appreciably caused by provisions of knowledge and belief of separate people, sciences and religions in a society. The other part of the problem is caused by the fact that in jurisprudence as well as in lawmaking the freedom of conscience is, as a rule, a synonym of religious freedom (i.e. the wide concept is substituted narrow, reflecting absence of notion about freedom of conscience as a universal phenomenon).

Thus, the legislation which, logically, should be directed on realization of freedom of a world outlook choice, is substituted by "special religious" for regulation of activity of religious associations.

This "special" legislation interferes with realization of the constitutional rights by each person and allows the state to interfere with activity of religious associations. And the state, as a rule, interferes with the religious associations, which having integrative opportunities traditionally are an object of political interests and the "special" control over authority, both in Russia and in many countries of the world.

As a result of law enforcement of the above-mentioned "special" legislation not only the rights of religious minority are broken, a lot of the democratic principles making a basis constitutional system is diffused, freedom of a world outlook choice but, possibly suppresses, the chance by the separate states and world community fully is missed to use progressive opportunities of globalization and to find the worth mentioning answer to its calls.

It is obvious that for formation of an effective legal mechanism of realization of the right to freedom of conscience a wide legal concept of religion that is free from especially confessional is necessary and equal also atheistic limitations; otherwise it is necessary to refuse from this term in general use in the system of the right. Absence of a wide legal concept of religion aggravates that fact that definition and the intrinsic content of freedom of conscience as a legal category, is, in fact, deformed and determined through other uncertain enough concept "freedom of religion". According to the expert in the field of Cole Duram's religious freedom, "the most obvious is value of the term "religion" for definition of legitimacy of statements for the right to freedom of religion. A number of other terms often meeting by consideration of questions of freedom of religion is close connected with these problems, for example "church", "a religious community", a "sect", etc. Complexity means that formulations almost inevitably lead to the threat of discrimination of the religious groups appearing on the border of the definition".[2]

In jurisprudence the use the incorrect terms which do not have precise legal criteria, provokes occurrence of obviously false situations creating initially absolute obstacles in the way of realization of declared principles. Therefore, it is necessary to differentiate of legal terms and other terms. Abundantly clear that, for example, sociological or even theological definition of religion and the legal content of religion is not always the same.

Fundamental value, in the case of practical realization of the proclaimed principles of freedom of conscience, has comprehension of above-mentioned principles as legal category. Result of such court decision could become a uniform legal (as wide as possible) understanding of a phenomenon of freedom of conscience at formation of the correct conceptual device connected with this understanding based on the use of precise legal criteria that corresponds to orientation to creating of the open democratic society and a lawful state. In reality the main aspect of freedom of conscience is comprehension of variety of relations and respect for a correlation between knowledge and belief at different people in a society. Accordingly, freedom of creeds is a special case of freedom of conscience.

At the same time in the system of the right, both on international and on national levels, is an incorrect mixture and substitution of legal concepts for the essence of the right to freedom of conscience is certain take place is inexact and in practice is reduced to its religious part, putting its realization in dependence from real state-confessional relations, creating, thus, the space for restrictive lawmaking.

Freedom of Conscience and Relations of the State with Religious Associations

Historically the realization of human rights in the sphere of freedom of conscience in general formation of corresponding legislative base in particular has very much depended on relations of the state with religious associations. These relations are determined as a "set of historically developing and changing forms of interrelations between institutions of the state and institutional religious educations (religious associations, religious parties, religious movements, international confessional centers), as one of components of the internal foreign policy of the state. In their basis is the concept of the place of religion and Church in life of a society and the state at a certain stage of development.[3] In 2001 there were the real bases; allowing assuming that in Russia the concept of relations of the state with religious associations will be created.[4] Forces on which the authority will base at formation of the given concept, is MT Russian Orthodox Church, the orthodox public are also certain. Review of above-mentioned forces was carried out on July, 6th, 2001 in the form of parliamentary hearings "The Problem of Legislative Ensuring of State - Church Relations in a View of the Social Concept of Russian Orthodox Church", organized by Committee on Affairs of Public Associations and Religious Organizations of the State Duma.

The abovementioned concept of relations of the state with religious associations is called to make a basis of a scientific substantiation of real politics of the state in the given sphere and to generate a base for transformation of the legislation on freedom of conscience in the form of inclusion of elements of selective partnership of the state with "traditional" religious associations in structure of the Federal law "Freedom of Conscience and Religious Associations". Elements of confessional preferences, recorded in a preamble in normative meaning of the Federal law, the interested circles try to fill with the real content and to issue in the form of the "special" concept of relations of the state and religious associations.

Finally such model will promote domination in relations with the state of one faith to "most traditional". As history shows, not all faiths appear to be equally useful to authority, even among "traditional" ones. From here inevitability of the further selection already among the "traditional" religious organizations, in the form of even big privileges for one and persecutions for others arises. But the most important is that legal criteria of "traditional character" do not basically exist.

The statement correctness of the problem of the concept state-confessional relations formation concerning problems of realization of the constitutional principles in the sphere of freedom of conscience is very doubtful.

In the Constitution of the Russian Federation and in provisions of international law, being priority for legal system of Russia, nothing is said about state-confessional relations and the state religious politics as self-sufficient phenomena.

State-confessional relations and the state religious politics existed historically. But from the moment of acceptance of the Universal Declaration of the Rights and Freedoms of a Person in 1948 for Russia, at least, from the moment of acceptance in 1993 of the Constitution of the Russian Federation, state-confessional relations and the state religious politics should also be considered as derivative from the above-mentioned constitutional principles and they should correspond to them.

Relations of the democratic lawful state which was laid down as an aims formation of an open civil society should be under creating with religious associations on uniform legal grounds with other public non-commercial associations. The secular state, especially multinational and polyconfessional should not have any "special" relations with the religious organizations at all and consequently the concepts of these relations. In means that all relations should be carried out on generally basis with other associations of citizens. Otherwise, the principle of secularity of the state is diffused (and together with them other democratic principles) and "special" state-confessional relations of the state and the selected faiths get self-sufficing character, acquiring "special religious" privileges.

Freedom of Conscience and Secularity of the State

Today it is difficult to present principles of freedom of conscience and secularity of the state separately from the mutual connection and dependence. "The branch of church from the state means that the state does not interfere with an internal, religious life of church and does not charge it to carry out any state functions and the church does not interfere with the affairs of the state. It is the most important guarantee of freedom of conscience as liberation from conscience of compulsory state trusteeship gives to them independently to solve the problem on the belief. The religious organizations turn to private societies which cannot use authority against "otherwise-minded" or non-believers".[5] The majority of domestic authors (M. Kirichenko, V.V. Scraps, S.A. Mozgovoi, M.M. Persic, A.J. Rosenbaum, F.M. Rudinsky, etc.) in the works on the given problems relate a principle of branch of church from the state to one of the major guarantees of freedom of conscience.

The modern Russian history, more evidently, than any other, shows that a principle of secularity of the state, underlying equality of people without dependence from the attitude to religion and equality of religious associations, itself requires guarantees. Such guarantee shows that there should be a limitation of a "special" regulation of the sphere of freedom of conscience from the state.

Today in Russia a principle of secularity and other constitutional principles interdependent with them (they make sense and work only in mutual connection) have fallen a victim on an altar of sacralization to authority (including the form of clericalization of authorities and the government).

Clericalization of "especially dear" faiths (basically it concerns the Moscow patriarchy of Russian Orthodox Church, in a number of subjects of the Federation these are the Muslim organizations) authorities, school, culture, army has a mass character[6].

Practice of teaching of the religious and church-focused disciplines by orthodox clerics is introduced in many state educational institutions that contradicts the Constitution of the Russian Federation and the Federal law "Education", providing secular character of educational process in the state educational structures. In the state high schools of some regions (for example in Altai territory, Omsk, Tver, Ivanovo areas) faculties and faculties of divinity on the basis of local dioceses Russian Orthodox Church work for many years. In August, 1999 the contract about cooperation between the Ministry of Education and Russian Orthodox Church, bringing a certain legal base under clericalization the state education was concluded.

Clericalization of the army was promoted appreciably by signing in 1994 of the contract about cooperation between the Ministry of Defence and Russian Orthodox Church. In conditions of military discipline religious ceremonies in military units (consecration of banners, rockets, submarines, etc.) are carried out that contradicts the Constitution of the Russian Federation and also the Federal law "The status of military men", forbidding the organized religious activity in military units. "Now in parts of the Ministry of Defence already work or are under creating up to hundred orthodox temples and chapels...

Agreements about cooperation with Russian Orthodox Church the Ministry of Internal Affairs, the Federal Frontier service, Federal agency of the governmental connection and in formation (Federal agency for government communication and in formation), Ministry of Health, and the Ministry of culture have also signed it.

Imperious groups are always interested in the sacralization, i.e. use integrative opportunities of faiths for deduction of authority and corporate interests of faiths, as a rule, reach for limits of religious freedom (absence of discrimination, equality of faiths), namely in the sphere of the state preferences.

Thus, the basis of unity of a society and stability of the state is initially undermined. The division of religions into "dominating" and "tolerant", "top-quality" and "second-grade" in the conditions of Russia will mean the division of their followers and even all people onto categories as in public consciousness there is an identification of a national and religious belonging"[7].

Sacralization of authorities with the purpose of privatization is one of the main reasons of approach to the rights and freedoms of a person in Russia. The corresponding state policy, by creation of legislative base in the form of "special" restrictive lawmaking is formed.

This legislative base is based on use of incorrect principles at jurisprudence and not legal terms, including those borrowed from theology. Hence, any interpretation of the legislation in the sphere of freedom of conscience, according to personal interests and corporate ideological preferences of government officials, in many respects predetermines numerous infringement of the rights and freedoms of a person.

With coming into force of the Federal law "Freedom of Conscience and Religious Associations" anticonstitutional processes in the sphere of its regulation are in fact, legalized and have accepted the character of a state policy.

The Federal law "Freedom of Conscience and Religious Associations" and Its Subordinate Base

In 1997 the campaign initiated by "traditional" religions against "nonconventional" religions and actively supported by interested political groups, came to an end with introducing of a new bill about freedom of conscience of essential restrictive provisions. The Federal law "Freedom of Conscience and Religious Associations" was accepted by the State Duma on September, the 19th, 1997 and came into force on October, 1st.

The Federal law "Freedom of Conscience and Religious Associations" got support from Russian Orthodox Church which is indignant by inflow to Russia that it calls "foreign" religions. Evangelic Christians, Mormons, Roman Catholics, etc. are referred to them. Patriarch Alex II has compared in trusion of foreign religious groups into Russia to expansion of NATO into the East Europe.

A new Federal law unlike earlier law in force of RSFSR "Freedom of Creeds" (1990) has recorded confessional preferences of the states (preamble), has significantly toughened the order of creation of the religious organizations (Article 9-12), has limited activity of "nonconventional" and especially foreign religious organizations (Article 13). The bases for acceptance of a court decision on elimination of religious association (Article 14) are considerably expanded. A repressive innovation of the law is introduction of institution of prohibition of activity of the religious organization (Article 14). Unlike elimination, the institution of civil-legal prohibition concerns both registered and not registered associations.

Transfer in a preamble of the Federal law "Freedom of Conscience and Religious Associations" to some religious faiths is perceived on places as a basis to consider all others, except for mentioned in a preamble, confessional educations by "sects" with negative legal consequences following from here. Cases when government officials refer to statements of eparchial managements of Russian Orthodox Church and directory of Russian Orthodox Church "destructive and occult character of new religious organizations of Russia" are frequent.

In our opinion, the most important contradictions and repressive potential of the Federal law "Freedom of Conscience and Religious Associations" are covered in Clause 1 of Article 6 defining the attributes of a religious association and Article 12 about the created organization determining non-recognition of religious as a basis for refusal in the state registration. According to Clause 1 of Article 6 of the indicated law, "religious association in the Russian Federation are voluntary association of citizens of the Russian Federation living in territory of the Russian Federation, formed on the lawful bases with a view of joint confession and distribution of belief and having attributes corresponding to these purpose: creed; carrying out of divine services, other religious practices and ceremonies; training of religion and religious education of the followers". It is not clear, why these attributes are set as legal. It is obvious that not everything from the existing and studied religions can fully correspond to the set forth attributes, let alone new and able to arise in the future.

For definition of religious character of associations the Advisory Council for carrying out state theological examinations was created at the Ministry of Justice of the Russian Federation which Regulations concerning activity were approved by the order of the Ministry of Justice dd. October, 8th, 1998, # 140. Advisory councils at enforcement authorities in subjects of the Federation are formed according to the instruction of the Government of the Russian Federation dd. June, 3rd, 1998.

Till now uniform legal and even theological definitions of religion have not existed (all in all they are more than 200) Thus, experts, in fact, determine external displays of "religiousness" of associations for conformity to own concepts of religion. Besides, as shows the analysis of functioning of advisory councils at enforcement authorities in subjects of the Federation, last influence on the end result of their work is far not render a principle of formation and personal structure. For example, "formation of expert bodies in the Kostroma, Voronezh, Oryol and Lipetsk areas were carried out to "an ideological attribute". In two of four advisory councils studied by us in Voronezh and Kostroma among members of advisory councils there were regular employees of dioceses of Russian Orthodox Church and orthodox active workers from among laymen and in Voronezh a member of advisory council is the eparchial expert-specialist in sects"[8].

Some of religious associations try to register the charters and to receive the state of the legal person as public organizations around of the legislation. For example, after the administration of Primorye Territory has carried out thirteen sessions of the expert-advisory council on which charters and activity of fifteen religious organizations have been considered, ten have not been recommended for registration of charters in regional Justice Department, some of them have tried to be registered as public. By them it was given up, "theological examination with the purpose of definition of public or religious character of the given organizations is planned".[9]

Granting to judicial authorities of rather wide control rights allows supervising activity of religious associations around of the operating criminal and civil legislation.

In February, 1998, during that time when President B.N. Yeltsin met Pope John-Paul II, in Moscow the decision "Order of Registration, Opening and closing in the Russian Federation of notions of the foreign religious organizations" was signed and published[10]. This decision in execution of part "Freedom of Conscience and Religious Associations" the same position according to which the foreign religious organizations having divisions in Russia, should be registered in six-monthly term according to part 3 of Article 13 of the Federal law.

If earlier the notion could be open at any Russian organization registered when due hereunder now such right is only centralized. In conformity with Article 5 of Provision on notions of the state of the religious organization does not extend, they "cannot be engaged in cult and other religious activity". In fact, the decision "Order of Registration, Opening and Closing to the Russian Federation of notions of the foreign religious organizations" is directed on strengthening of the "special" control and limitation of activity of the corresponding religious organizations.

On August, 2nd, 1995 the order of the President of the Russian Federation 357-rp, with the changes brought by the order of the President of the Russian Federation dd. March, 17th, 2001 133-rp, approved the Regulations of Council on Interaction with Religious Associations at the President of the Russian Federation. The Council is an advisory body. According to the Provision, the basic functions of Council are the following: "ensuring of interaction of the President of the Russian Federation with religious associations; assistance to strengthening of the public consent, achievement of mutual understanding, tolerance and mutual respect in questions of freedom of conscience and freedom of conscience"[11].

The structure of Council approved by the order of the President of the Russian Federation dd. March, 17th, 2001 133-rp. attracts attention by the fact that out of 24 person of structure of Council there are 5 representatives from Russian Orthodox Church, 10 are from other religious organizations (Old Believers, Buddhists, Moslems, Catholics, Baptists, Jews, Pentecost's, Lutherans, Adventists of the Seventh Day), 5 are representatives of the official science, and 4 are state officials. Chairman of Council was a head of Administration of the President of the Russian Federation A.S. Voloshin.

It is obvious that representatives of Russian Orthodox Church have acute dignity in this Council.

In April, 1999 Human Rights Commissioner in the Russian Federation O.O. Mironov published the conclusion on the Federal law "Freedom of Conscience and Religious Associations" in a view of internationally-legal obligations of the Russian Federation. The conclusion admitted that a number of provisions of the law of the Constitution of the Russian Federation contradicted international contracts of Russia. In particular, it is emphasized be recording by the law of exclusive position of separate religions (Article 4-5 of a Preamble); on differentiation between religious associations and religious groups (Article 6-7), depriving the last from rights of the legal person (Clause 1 of Article 7); on differentiation of "traditional" faiths and the religious organizations which do not have the document, confirming their existence in corresponding territory for not fewer than 15 years (Clause 1 of Article 9) that leads to deprivation of last many rights (Clause 3 of Article 27); on deprivations of the state of religious associations of notions of the foreign religious organizations

(Clause 2 of Article 13); on the contradiction to international provisions of limitations of freedom of religion for reasons of "national safety" (Clause 2 of Article 3).[12]

The Federal law "Freedom of Conscience and Religious Associations" has essentially undermined guarantees of freedom of conscience. Its characteristic features are the following: illegal character of principles and ambiguity of many formulations in turn creating conditions for subjective and corporate interpretation, predetermining, thus, skews to law enforcement, abusing, infringement of the rights, and use religion in political aims.

The Regional Legislation in the Sphere of Freedom of Conscience

In more than thirty subjects of the Federation laws and by-law instruments breaking a principle of equality of religious associations before the law are passed in excess of the powers established by the Constitution. Division of religious associations on the one hand onto traditional, and on the other onto foreign missionaries, missionary societies, foreign religious organizations, sects. In some regions such acts directly set exclusive faiths (for example, in Republic Tyva it is shamanism, Buddhism and Orthodoxy).

As occasion to acceptance of regional laws and decisions about missionary and other religious activity acted usually "imperfection" (from the point of view of regional authorities) the law "Freedom of Creeds" (1990) However, even with acceptance of the Federal law (1997) proceeds the regional lawmaking contradicting this new law. It leads to arbitrariness of officials on places, who are free to use certain law at own discretion. Thus, on November, 24th, 1994 in the Tula area "the law was passed concerning missionary (religious) activity in territory of the Tula area". It subjected to essential limitations the activity of the religious organizations, ordered the collection of gathering for delivery of sanctions to religious activity, demanded from missionaries in advance to coordinate the program of predicant activity with local authorities. After Tula such statutory acts have been accepted in Tver, Tyumen, Kostroma, Kaluga, Tatarstan and other regions.

On December, 23rd, 1997 in Republic Buryatiya "the law was passed concerning religious activity in territory of Republic Buryatiya" according to which the religious organizations were obliged to receive the special sanction to realization of predicant and charities for which delivery gathering is raised from religious communities at the rate of 110 minimum monthly wages.

Above-mentioned regional laws are discrimination and (or) illegally limit and regulate religious activity. These laws contradict the Constitution of the Russian Federation and the federal legislation in the field of freedom of conscience.

Simultaneously, bodies of the government of many subjects of the Federation, ignoring the constitutional principles of equality of religious associations before the law and their branches from the state, accept numerous decisions and orders giving privileges and dignity to separate "traditional" faiths and even to certain church structures and also illegally connect them to financing due to tax-payers.

Problems of Law Enforcement, Abusing, Xenophobia, Infringement of the Rights in the Sphere of Freedom of Conscience

Separate provisions of the Federal law "Freedom of Conscience and Religious Associations" have been already twice appealed against in the Constitutional Court of the Russian Federation.[13] The Constitutional Court of the Russian Federation has avoided a concept of unconstitutional provisions appearing in complaints, however, having replaced literal perusal of the law revealed "Constitutionally-legal meaning", slightly softening the law and satisfying certain applicants.

Decisions of the Constitutional Court of the Russian Federation, positively apprehended by the public, in our opinion, finally bring to noting democratic gains in the sphere of the freedom of conscience connected with its legal regulation. In particular, the Decision of the Constitutional Court of the Russian Federation dd. November, 23rd, 1999, in fact, introduces into Russian legal space a number of not legal concepts: "sect", "missionary activity", "proselytism", "and recruitment".

Besides, courts of general jurisdiction consider dozens of civil cases connected with the use of separate provisions of the law "Freedom of Conscience and Religious Associations" which on classification of the lawyer of V.V. Ryahovsky can be subdivided in to two basic categories:

1. Case, started under the initiative of the religious organizations and citizens.

2. Case, started under the initiative of judicial authorities, offices of Public Prosecutor and institutions of local government[14].

"Absence of a plenty of such affairs does not testify to absence of infringement of the rights of believers. As the analysis of actions of proceeding about elimination of the religious organizations arising under the initiative of judicial authorities or Office of Public Prosecutor shows, their general lack is impreparation and full groundlessness of the declared requirements"[15].

As an example evidently describing law-enforcement to practice, it is possible to recall the proceedings against Moscow religious community "Witnesses of Jehovah", preceded two a year. On February, 23rd, 2001 the court gave up in satisfaction of the claim of the Office of Public Prosecutor of Northern district of the capital about elimination of the community. All charges of the Office of Public Prosecutor (in kindling of interreligious break, destruction of family, etc.) were completely rejected. However, the Office of Public Prosecutor didn't reconcile to defeat and on May, 30th, 2001 the Moscow city court made a decision about returning the case in Golovinsky court for consideration in a new structure of judges. This time the Office of Public Prosecutor rejected the case. In opinion of experts, decisions of Russian courts on this case are not supported by critics.

According to the lawyer A. Krylova having wide experience of judicial protection of the rights of religious associations, "the use of the Federal law "Freedom of Conscience and Religious Associations" roughly breaks constitutional rights and freedoms of citizens and contradicts the Constitution of the Russian Federation"[16]. In her opinion, "the state protectionism is used as a clincher in public doctrinal disputes"[17].

Infringement of the rights of the religious organizations has become usual in Russia. Not only new religious movements and marginal groups are restrained in the rights. Catholics and Protestants also almost everywhere are discriminated. At the same time the Moscow Patriarchy receives enormous latifundium and the real estate.

Cases when the religious organizations are cancelled are frequent or are not prolonged agreements rent of premises, belonging to them made decisions on granting the ground areas under creating of cult buildings are cancelled earlier.

In a number of regions the facts of hindrances to carrying out of divine services, uses of threats and violence over believers both from militia officers and from informal national patriotic groupings take place.

Local authorities provoke propaganda of "antisectarian" campaigns. There were tendencies to return of retaliatory psychiatry, the use of medicine for struggle with different believes has also become a reality.

In 2002 the Federal law about alternative civil service was passed. Before its acceptance litigations against denied persons from the military service, demanding realization of constitutional law took place. Last years the tendency to acceptance by courts of decisions not in their dignity was outlined. Cases of a premise in prison for refusal from military service on belief of conscience have been recorded. For example, on November, 10th, 1997 Kurchatovsky city court of Kursk area sentenced to one and a half years of imprisonment on part 1 of Article 328 of the Criminal Code ("Evasion from obligatory military service") a 22-years assembler Vitaly Guschin, a member of a community of Witnesses of Jehovah. Guschin was released on June, 10th, 1998 only after intervention of the deputy of the State Duma and the organization "Amnesty International" but the Office of Public Prosecutor refused to take the charge off him.

Most likely, the realization of constitutional law on replacement of military service by alternative civil one in many respects depends on realization of the right to freedom of conscience as from the derivative.

Practically everywhere in Russia unreasonable refusals in re-registrations, illegal requirements of a re-registration, oppression of foreign missionaries took place, starting with visa limitations and finishing by exile.

Russian legislators and civil servants were not able to distinguish cultural life from cult, undertaking incessant attempts of creation of acceptable committees and strengthening pressure with support of the mass information. Attempts of introduction of censorship of mass media by creation of new socially-state structures with participation of representatives of the Moscow patriarchy and other "traditional" religious organizations are noted.

In a number of statements church and public figures threats to address of journalists and employees of mass media contain.

Russia, Freedom of Conscience, Globalization

In view of realities of the 21st century and the more so sight in the future, the mutual relations arising in the sphere of freedom of conscience, being reflection of mutual relations between a science and religion, have global universal character. In this connection an effective legal mechanism of realization of the right to freedom of conscience is the necessary factor of overcoming of the dividing principles, being a basis of existence of traditional political structures, a condition of formation of a political management of the national states, capable to carry out integration into world community. Finally efficiency of this legal mechanism will influence adequacy of answers of people to calls of globalization and will the determine ability of a society to protect religion from use in political aims and to avoid kindling of ethno-confessional conflicts as means in struggle for repartition of world.

Thus, the value of elimination of incorrect dividing principles from legal bases of existence of a society is beyond the decision of narrow legal problems and realization of ideals of religious freedom. "That is really necessary, so this notion about religious freedom which could prove that is based on the values shared both by the religious as well as secular traditions"[18].

Realization of these ideals today is possible only in the expanded frameworks of freedom of conscience for everyone, based on principles of a concept of variety of forms and respect for a correlation between knowledge and belief at different people in a society. For full realization of ideals of religious freedom (for believers) it should be derivative of freedom of conscience (for everyone).

Today, in the 21st century interdependence and interaction of the states is blocked by globalization is increasing interaction, increase of a role and change of a correlation in favour of structures and the phenomena which are being outside of jurisdiction of the national states.

Intensively global systems in technological, financial, information, cultural-language spheres develop.

Integration with the purpose of steady development and overcoming of global problems is resisted with breaks between inevitable global tendencies and activity of the traditional political structures which are based on national consciousness and have inherited deeply taken roots of the problems of opposition of the majority against minority, "the contra another's", the main things among which there is ethno-confessional.

Interethnic relations are knitted with inter-confessional and turn into ethno-confessional. The incorrect dividing principle on "believers and non-believers" underlies the division between faiths, their followers and also the people who do not belong to any faith. The same division underlies the division of people and the nations, in connection with yet not got rid identification of religious-confessional and also national identification. "Concurrence of national and confessional self-identifications, religious and national consciousness shows that not only believers but also non-believers relate themselves to certain religious tradition: Russian to Orthodoxy, Tatars to Islam, Buryats and Kalmyks to the Buddhism, etc."[19]

In view of the inevitable tendencies of globalization which were making demands to integration, the modern political system on the basis of the national states is not always capable to respond to the calls of new time. However, the national states serve as a starting point for formation of the uniform world system called to solve global problems facing the mankind at a new level.

In the widest meaning it is necessary to realize the necessity of perfection of normative-legal base for realization of human rights in the sphere of freedom of consciencc as a global universal problem.

Formation of the legal mechanism of overcoming the dividing ethno-confessional factors and breaks in the form of realization of freedom of a world outlook choice is determined by necessity:

Overcoming of a combination of national consciousness by global;

Prevention of use of religion in political aims and kindling of ethno-confessional conflicts to the purpose of repartition of world;

Prevention of opposition between a science and religion in a society, knowledge and belief of each person, on the basis of reflection of change of a correlation between them in the system of the right, also makes demands:

— Conformity of the tendency to growth of degrees of freedom of an individual in the form of necessity of limitation of a "special" regulation of world outlook sphere from the state;

— Differentiations religious and legal provisions, with the purpose of their reduction conformity with standards of international law;

— Unifications state-confessional relations, their submission to principles of secularity of the state, human rights, other democratic principles, down to refusal from "special" relations with faiths as at the level of international legal provisions and national Constitutions;

— Development of declared democratic constitutional principles in their interrelation, with the purpose of realization.

Real ensuring of freedom of conscience and other human rights will determine both the level of international integration and principles on which it will be based, and equality and partnership or the domination of "great" powers based on force and hegemony.

Planetary mutual understanding and cooperation of civilizations, cultures and faiths, coexistence of various ways of life, traditions and valuable preferences is impossible without realization of principles of freedom of conscience in as much as possible wide legal understanding.

In this connection the necessity of perfection of normative-legal base of realization of the right to freedom of conscience as a legal mechanism of easing of intensity has global universal character.

Unfortunately, the state policy of Russia in the sphere of freedom of conscience, in our opinion, does not respond to humanistic problems.

Directions of Perfection of the Normative-Legal Base in the Sphere of Freedom of Conscience

The legal mechanism of realization of freedom of conscience in a modern democratic lawful state demands radical audit and reform of basic principles and the conceptual device. In particular, there was a necessity of creation of the wide legal concept of freedom of conscience; elimination from the system of the right incorrect from the legal point of view of a dividing principle "believers and non-believers"; overcoming of substitution of the concepts "freedom of conscience" and "freedom of religions", "religion" and "faith". Differentiation of legal and other terms, elimination of theological terms from the system of the right seems expedient; use in jurisprudence of as much as possible wide definition of the "religion" concerning each separate person, or in general refusal from its use in the system of the right. Modern legal definition of religion should be free from specially confessional and atheistic limitations. It is necessary to refuse from the "special" religious legislation and from granting powers on identification of religion to any persons, bodies, structures in view of basic impossibility of definition of their precise legal criteria. The refusal to use religious studies in the decision of questions of legal character in the sphere of freedom of conscience as right obviously not responding to the principles is quite reasonable.

Criminally-legal protection of a society from possible abusing in the sphere of freedom of conscience should exclude "special" religious prophylaxis, owing to the absence of precise legal criteria of this the sphere.

Limitations of the rights should consider the essence of the right to freedom of conscience in a wide legal meaning, not putting its realization in dependence on the factors which do not have precise legal criteria, such as state-confessional relations and the state religious politics.

Legal regulation of the activity of the religious associations, corresponding effective legal mechanism of realization of freedom of conscience, in our opinion, is expedient to carry out in view of the following **principles:**

— The rights of associations should be considered as derivatives from the rights and freedoms of a person, in order to prevent their substitution;

— Registration of religious associations as well as others public and noncommercial ones should have an appealing character;

— Refusal from "special" regulation of activity of religious associations means that it should be carried out in accordance with the general practice with other associations;

— Refusal from "special" privileges for religious associations means that privileges can be given generally to other public noncommercial associations;

— Refusal from "special" religious administratively-legal limitations with the purpose of prophylaxis of illegal activity in the sphere of freedom of conscience from religious associations;

— Administratively-legal regulation of activity of the religious organizations (as well as other public noncommercial associations) should be carried out only within the limits of and the scope, connected with their activity as legal persons for conformity to the noncommercial status.

Freedom of conscience in full as freedom of a world outlook the choice for everyone and not just for believers as a result of its data to freedom of creeds (now) or only for atheists (during the Soviet period) in Russia and its principles as legal category have not been realized completely. Except for weak scientific readiness on a status of freedom of conscience significant influence is rendered with special interests of authority and confessional to bureaucracy. These factors today determine a status of freedom of conscience which is formed at the levels of science, lawmaking and law enforcement.

Owing to weak scientific readiness the given problems and backwardness of the constitutional principles of freedom of conscience as to a legal category Russian lawmaking in this sphere is devoted exclusively to freedom of creeds. Thus, the legislation which on logic should be directed on realization of freedom of a world outlook choice is substituted with "special religious" for regulation of activity of religious associations. As a result of law enforcement of the given "special" legislation not only the rights of believing and religious minority are broken but also a lot of the democratic constitutional principles making a basis constitutional system are diffused.

That regarding provisions in the sphere of freedom of creeds during the last years remains disturbing and it is characterized by strengthening of restrictive-prohibitive tendencies.

The control, limitation of world outlook sphere and infringement by authority of human rights over the sphere of freedom of conscience, the use of religion in political aims and sacralization of authorities, a withdrawal from the constitutional principles of secularity of the state and clericalization of institutions of the state, confessional preferences of the state and a religious inequality have become habitual and daily. These phenomena underlie ethnic-confessional intensity, stimulate separatism, integrity of federal system threaten.

The analysis of a state policy in the sphere of freedom of conscience allows drawing a conclusion that Russia has no time to reflect on the global changes generated by new tendencies, essential problems sufficing it. However, ignoring them and also discrepancy to requirements of one of the main tendencies of historical process to growth of degrees of personal freedom[20] can turn back the disintegration of the Federation which settled the old imperial bases of unity and have not found a new, universal integrated to violence.

Notes

1. Moran G.M. What is the Religious Freedom? What Should the Law Guarantee? // Religion and Law. 1997.1. P.14. / Моран Г. М., Что такое религиозная свобода? Что должен гарантировать закон? // Религия и право. 1997. № 1. С. 14.

2. Duram U.K. Freedom of Religion or Belief: the Laws Influencing Structuring of Religious Communities. Reference document БДИПЧ 1999/4. P.22. / Дурам У. К. Свобода религии или убеждений: законы, влияющие на структуризацию религиозных общин. Справочный документ БДИПЧ 1999/4. С. 22.

3. State and Church Relations in Russia (experience of the past and the modern state). Moscow, 1996. P.4. / Государственно-церковные отношения в России (опыт прошлого и современное состояние). М., 1996. С. 4.

4. In the summer of 2001 in the newspaper "NG - Religion" an abridged version of the project «Conceptual Bases of State and Church Relations in the Russian Federation», developed by public organization «Institute of State-Confessional Relations and the Law» and Senior management of the Ministry of Justice of the Russian Federation on a to Moscow on behalf of the deputy chief of Senior management Zhbankov V.N. were published (complete variants of projects of concepts may be found in the Internet: www.state-religion.ru).

5. Rudinsky F. M. Law, Religion, Offences. Volgograd, 1971. P.36. / Рудинский Ф. М. Закон, религия, правонарушения. Волгоград, 1971. С. 36.

6. The information on infringements of human rights in the sphere of the right of conscience, used by the author, is in «White book , published in 1997 by the Public Committee of Protection of a right of conscience; in the Report «Infringement of human rights in the sphere of the right of conscience in the Russian Federation», prepared by Regional public organization of assistance to the right of conscience together with the Moscow Helsinki Group and Christian social movement in the end of 1998; in periodicals and the Internet.

7. Mozgovoi S.A. Armed Forces of Russia and Religious Associations: State and Prospects of Interaction // Religious Organizations and the State: Prospects of Interaction. Moscow, 1999. / Мозговой С. А. Вооруженные силы России и религиозные объединения: состояние и перспективы взаимодействия // Религиозные организации и государство: перспективы взаимодействия. М., 1999.

8. Zherebyatiev M.A. Practical Religious Studies. State Theological Examination in the Subjects of the Russian Federation // Religion and Law. 2001.3. P.5. / Жеребятьев М. А. Практическое религиоведение. Государственная религиоведческая экспертиза в субъектах РФ // Религия и право. 2001. № 3. С. 5.

9. Fadeev P.G. Realization of the Federal Act « The Right of Conscience and Religious Associations» in Primorye Territory // Russian Legislation about the Right of Conscience in 1980-90s of the 20th century: Theoretical Disputes, Reforming of Legal Bases, Practi-

cal Realization of Legislative Acts. Moscow, 1999. P.143. / Фадеев П. Г. О реализации Федерального закона «О свободе совести и о религиозных объединениях» в Приморском крае // Российское законодательство о свободе совести в 80–90-х гг. XX в.: теоретические споры, реформирование правовых основ, практическая реализация законодательных актов. М., 1999. С.143.

10. Rossiiskaya Gaseta, 1998, Feb. 12 / Российская газета. 1998. 12 февр.

11. Regulations about Council on Interaction with Religious Associations at the President of the Russian Federation // Religion and Law. 2001.2. P.35. / Положение о Совете по взаимодействию с религиозными объединениями при Президенте РФ // Религия и право. 2001. № 2. С. 35.

12. See: Religion and Lawe. 1999. #2. P.6. / См.: Религия и право. 1999. № 2. С. 6.

13. See: Judiciary Law on the Cases Connected with Realization of the Right of Conscience and Activity of the Religious Organizations. Moscow, 2000. / См.: Судебная практика по делам, связанным с реализацией права на свободу совести и деятельностью религиозных организаций. М., 2000.

14. See: Ryahovsky V.V. Federal Act «Right of Conscience and Religious Associations». Law Enforcement Practice // Legislation about the Right of Conscience and Law Enforcement Practice in the Sphere of its Action. Moscow, 2001. P.175. / См.: Ряховский В. В. Федеральный закон «О свободе совести и о религиозных объединениях». Правоприменительная практика // Законодательство о свободе совести и правоприменительная практика в сфере его действия. М., 2001. С. 175.

15. Ryahovsky V.V. Specified work. P.177-178. / Ряховский В. В. Указ. соч. С. 177–178.

16. Krylova G.A. Freedom of Conscience on the Weights of Justice. Moscow, 1998. P.227. / Крылова Г. А. Свобода совести на весах правосудия. М., 1998. С. 227.

17. Ibidem. P. 16.

18. Durem U.K. Prospects of Religious Freedom: Comparative Analysis. Moscow. 1999. P.14. / Дурэм У. К. Перспективы религиозной свободы: сравнительный анализ. М.,. 1999. С. 14.

19. Mozgovoi S.A. Ethno-Religious Relations and Problems of the Civil World in Russia // Religion and Nationalism. Moscow, 2000. P.157. / Мозговой С. А. Этнорелигиозные отношения и проблемы гражданского мира в России // Религия и национализм. М., 2000. С. 157.

20. In the program article published on December, 30, 1999 in «Nezavisimaya Gazeta», V. Putin said that we couldn't live without collectivism and without the strong government, and connected it with historical and cultural tradition.

Chapter 10. THE RIGHTS OF THE SUSPECTED AND ACCUSED

§ 1. Concept and Content of the Rights of the Suspected and Accused

The Universal Declaration of Human Rights[1] records the system of civil human rights.

Many human rights included in the mentioned Declaration influencing formation of international status of the accused and suspected are indicated in the provisions of International Covenant on Civil and Political Rights and the European Convention for the Protection of Human Rights and Basic Freedoms dd. November, 4th, 1950.[2]

The given Convention provides the developed enough guarantees of the rights of the accused and suspected, down to creation for these purposes of special institutions in the form of the European Commission of Human Rights and the European Court on Human Rights. The list of conditions at which deprivation of a person of freedom can be considered lawful (Article 5) is developed. Moreover, in part 3 of Article 6 of the Convention the minimal list of the legal rights of person of the accused of committing of a crime, having especially criminally-remedial character and opening the content of the right of the accused on protection is determined :

To be immediately and in detail notified on clear language about the character and the basis of the charge shown to them;

To have sufficient time and opportunities for preparation of the protection;

To protect themselves personally or via the defender chosen by them or if they do not have sufficient money for payment of services of the defender, to have the defender prescribed to them free of charge when it is demanded by the interests of justice;

To interrogate witnesses giving evidences against them or to have the right to that these witnesses have been interrogated and to have the right to call and interrogation of the witnesses, on the same conditions as a witnesses giving evidence against them;

To use free help of the translator if they do not understand the language used in court, or do not speak it.

As Russia recognizes and joins the mentioned conventions and other international statutory acts on human rights, its Constitution and criminally-remedial legislation basically are given and partially are subject to fast reduction conformity with them. Thus, the priority is legislatively established internationally-legal provisions (part 4 of Article 15 of the Constitution of Russia, part 3 of Article 1 of the Code of Criminal Procedure of the Russian Federation).

In view of the said, practically international standards in the field of enforcement of the rights of the suspected and accused are reproduced directly in the Constitution of Russia. In particular, by the Organic law there are established: equality of everybody before the law and court (Article 19); granting of the accused committed especially grave crime of the right to consider his case by court with participation of jurymen (Article 20); interdiction of torture, violence, and other cruel treatment and punishment (Article 21); the right to freedom and security of a person, shown in particular that imprisonment, custody and holding in custody are supposed only under a court decision. Prior a court decision a person cannot be subjected to detention for the term of more than 48 hours (Article 22); personal privacy, personal and family secrecy, the right of defence of honour and reputation, the right to privacy of correspondence, telephone conversations, post, cable and other messages, which limitation is supposed only on the basis of a court decision (Article 23); the inviolability of dwelling limited only in cases, established by the Federal law, or on the basis of a court decision (Article 25); the right of protection of the rights and freedoms in all ways which have been not forbidden by the law (Article 45); guarantees of judicial protection of the rights and freedoms, including by the judicial appeal of decisions and actions of the state bodies and officials down to treatment in interstate bodies on protection of the rights and freedoms of a person if available interstate means of legal protection (Article 46) are settled; inadmissibility of deprivation of the right to consideration of case of the accused of that court and that judge which jurisdiction it is referred by the law (Article 47); the right to receive the qualified legal aid rendered free of charge in cases, stipulated by the law, the including of the right for the suspected and accused to use the help of the lawyer (defender) from the moment of detention, custody or accuse (Article 48); presumption of innocence (Article 49); inadmissibility of use the evidence received with infringement of the Federal law (Article 50); the right not to testify against oneself, the spouse and close relatives (Article 51); the right to compensation by the state of the harm caused by illegal actions (or inactivity) bodies of the government or their officials (Article 53); limits of limitation of the rights and freedoms (Article 55).

The majority of the rights and freedoms of the given extensive list are not subject to limitation even in conditions of the state of emergency (Article 56).

The given constitutional provisions make bases of the legal status of the accused and suspected. Criminally-remedial legislation of Russia completely perceives these provisions, specifies, details them and creates the mechanism and guarantees of their certain practical realization. Constitutional remedial spirit penetrates all creating of the system of criminal trial. The provisions-principles of criminal legal proceedings concentrated in Ch. 2 of the Code of Criminal Procedure of the Russian Federation, alongside with the legal rights of the accused and suspected and their guarantees in the form of the rights and duties of other participants of legal proceedings, in aggregate form the unique legal phenomenon known as a *right of the accused on protection* which in many respects determines the purpose of criminal legal proceedings[3].

The enhanced attention to problems of the legal status of researches of position of a person of the suspected and accused of the block in the criminal legal proceedings, carried out within the limits of the domestic theory of criminal trial is traditional, quite natural and justified. It is possible in future that the suspected and accused will be the same persons but already in the state of the defendant of the condemned or justified personify is the central figure in criminal legal proceedings. It is connected by that criminal case is started directly concerning these persons as "committers" in the opinion of representatives of the party of charge or criminal action. For this reason in the further the same persons become the basic participants of the most significant legal relationships, arising at conducting of a criminal case.

In view of the mentioned circumstance, namely that the same person in process of development of criminal legal proceedings can consistently stay in a role of the suspected, accused, the defendant of the condemned or justified, in the legal literature enough for a long time the term "the accused" has been used as a collective concept simultaneously meaning (if it specially does not stipulate) all listed participants of legal proceedings[4]. It is necessary to recognize this approach justified, as, besides, the bearer of all mentioned statuses as a matter of fact, is the same person, the legislator determines the list and the content of the legal rights and the duties of general character forming a basis of corresponding statuses. The given similarity is especially obvious in the ratio of the list of the rights of the accused, the defendant of the condemned and justified that does not demand the special analysis as in part 2 of Article 47 of the Code of Criminal Procedure of the Russian Federation directly is emphasized: "the accused on whom criminal case proceeding is conducted, is called a defendant. The accused concerning whom the verdict "guilty" is passed is called the condemned. The accused concerning whom the verdict of "not guilty" is passed is called "justified". Further part 4 of Article 47 of the Code of Criminal Procedure of the Russian Federation is contained with the list of the rights of the accused which by virtue of the above-stated provision we should fully apply to all other "updating" of the concept of the accused.

The said, certainly, does not mean full identity of remedial position of preliminary investigation of the accused of a stage and in the subsequent judicial stages of criminal legal proceedings. In this connection in the literature the practical importance of necessity of differentiation of the legal rights of the accused on two categories, is fairly noted, i.e. the rights of general and special character. Thus, to general usually relate the rights which the accused uses during the whole period of being in criminal trial; to special - the rights which the accused gets in connection with participation in certain remedial action[5].

However, proceeding from practical interests, it is obviously important to expand and to specify a little this classification. A distinctive attribute according to which procedural rights can be referred to a category in general, it is necessary to consider not only the fact that these rights the accused uses during all period of stay in this status but also relation of a certain right to all without exception to the mentioned versions of the accused, irrespective of his special status.

According to it, general laws of the accused, with reference to part 4 of Article 47 of the Code of Criminal Procedure of the Russian Federation, it is necessary to consider the following: the nobility of what it is of the accused (Article 1); to represent evidence (Article 4); to declare petitions and removals (Article 5); to use the help of the defender (Article 8); to complain to actions (inactivity) and decisions of the investigator, the inspector and court and to participate in their consideration by court (Article 14); to be protected by other means and the ways which have been not forbidden by the Code of Criminal Procedure (Article 21).

The special rights, in turn, can be subdivided on two basic categories:

1. The Rights following from features of special statuses of the accused, among which there is rather an independent group of rights caused by specificity of a remedial stage in which legal proceedings proceeds and also the character of the preventive punishment used concerning the accused. For example, the right to get acquainted upon termination of preliminary investigation with all materials of the criminal case and to write out from criminal case any data and in any scope (Article 12, part 4 of Article 47 of the Code of Criminal Procedure of the Russian Federation); to appeal against a verdict, definition, the decision of court and to receive copies appealed decisions (Article 18 part 4 of Article 47 of the Code of Criminal Procedure of the Russian Federation); to participate in consideration by court of a question of election concerning the preventive punishment (Article 16, part 4 of Article 47 of the Code of Criminal Procedure of the Russian Federation); to have appointments to the defender alone and confidentially, including before the first interrogation of the accused, without limitation of their number and duration (Article 9, part 4 of Article 47 of the Code of Criminal Procedure of the Russian Federation).

Other subgroup of the special rights of this category form the rights displaying other features of a person of the accused (represent a person who didn't know the language of legal proceedings; the minor, etc.). It, in particular, is the right to testify and speak the native language or language which they speak; to use the help of the translator free of charge (Articles 6, 7, part 4 of Article 47 of the Code of Criminal Procedure of the Russian Federation); the right of the accused military man at his custody to demand the notice of command of military unit on a place of his detain or about change of a place of holding in custody (part 12 of Article 108 of the Code of Criminal Procedure of the Russian Federation).

2. The Rights which the accused gets in connection with participation in certain investigatory (remedial) action form the second in dependent category of the special rights of the accused. For example, to give a petition to the inspector for use during his interrogation of photographing, audio-and (or) video recordings, filming (part 4 of Article 189 of the Code of Criminal Procedure of the Russian Federation); by making a confrontation from the sanction of the inspector to ask questions to the second interrogated person (part 2 of Article 192 of the Code of Criminal Procedure of the Russian Federation), etc. Definition of the exhaustive list of the special rights of the accused are represented are real but enough inconvenient problems of many procedural rights, not being directly recorded in the law, follow from character of duties of

a person who are carrying out proceedings on case by virtue of them. Thus, from part 12 of Article 47 of the Code of Criminal Procedure of the Russian Federation, demanding on behalf of which there is a criminal case, immediately to notify someone from close relatives of the accused, at their absence - other relatives about the place of holding in custody or about the change of the place of holding in custody, his right to demand such notice. It is necessary to also consider that many legal rights of the accused by virtue of their specific orientation can follow from provisions of others, besides, the Code of Criminal Procedure of the Russian Federation, Federal laws (Custody of the accused and suspected arrested; Office of Public Prosecutor; Legal profession and lawyer activity, etc.) and by-law legal regulations. Thus, Ch. 2 of the Federal law dd. July, 15th, 1995, 103-Federal law "Holding in custody of the suspected and accused of committing of crimes", called "The Rights of the suspected and accused and their ensuring", unite in themselves the corresponding numerous provisions determining specificity of the status of the suspected and accused at their holding in custody. Moreover, the content of Article 6 of the same law called "The Legal status of the suspected and accused" is characterized by provisions-principles.

Corresponding remedial orientation fills also many provisions of "Regulations of cells of the time of the custody of the suspected and accused by law-enforcement bodies", the Ministries of Internal Affairs of Russia approved the Order dd. January, 26th, 1996, # 41.

Besides, presence of one right quite often generates occurrence of another. For example, the right of the accused to resort to services of the defender presupposes also the right to have with them of appointment alone and confidentially.

The given classification of the legal rights of the accused fully (with separate nuances) is applicable to the characteristic of the legal status of the suspected[6] as this participant of criminal legal proceedings comes within collective concept "of the accused" and being of a person, subjected to criminal prosecution in the status of the suspected, as a rule, precedes his introduction into the status of the accused and in his subsequent special statuses.

In the remedial literature and in the legislation the term "right" of the accused (of the suspected) is frequently used in aggregate with the term "legitimate interests". Therefore, it seems worth mentioning a question of a correlation between these concepts.

The content of the rights are certain interests because investment with the right means an opportunity of satisfaction of the interests, provided by the state[7]. However, concurrence in some cases of an interest with the legal right yet does not allow an occasion to consider these concepts identical. Interest makes a basis of any legal right established by provision of the law. Interest is lawful not only because it is recognized by the law, and recorded in it, that is why that it is those in essence, i.e. not contradicting the law[8]. Far not all interests of the suspected and accused, being in essence lawful are recorded in the law. Therefore, it is incorrect to unite, in our opinion, the legal rights and legitimate interests of the uniform concept "the rights of the subject"[9].

As legal rights the most important are made out only, essential, from the point of view of the legislator, socially and personal significant interests. The impossibility of recording of all legitimate interests in the form of legislatively guaranteed legal rights is determined by their practically immense variety and in equality in the attitude to each other. It is important that some interests of the suspected, being, certainly, lawful, cannot be guaranteed by virtue of economic, organizational and other reasons of not legal character.

For example, interests of the suspected, the imprisoned person by way of Article 91 and 92 of the Code of Criminal Procedure of the Russian Federation in participation as his defender of certain lawyer can be realized not in all cases. According to part 4 of Article 50 of the Code of Criminal Procedure of the Russian Federation if mentioned of the suspected the lawyer cannot introduce the case as a defender within 24 hours after detention the inspector is obliged to ensure the provision of participation of other lawyer in the same term. Thus, in this case at of the suspected there is a right to demand participation of certain defender but is not right on its unconditional participation. However, by virtue of legality and the big remedial importance of such interest the inspector is obliged to use all opportunities available them for ensuring of participation as a defender of the demanded person. Moreover, in case the materials proving impossibility of participation of the demanded lawyer (the information or the telephone message of lawyer office on case trip of the corresponding lawyer and should contain it).

In the given example the legitimate interest of the suspected about participation in his case of certain lawyer as a defender, undoubtedly, is more significant, than his some legal rights firmly guaranteed by the law. For example, the right to make plans, drawings, figures, diagrams by the accused during the interrogation for familiarizing with the report of interrogation (part 5 of Article 190 of the Code of Criminal Procedure of the Russian Federation). Nevertheless this significant interest can be unrealized and little significant for the majority of cases the right to make on a course of interrogation of the plan and etc. is provided in the unconditional order. It is also the basic criterion allowing delimiting a legitimate interest from the legal right.

Thus, concepts of a "right" and "legitimate interests" are one-serial and quite often coincide in the content. They should be considered as independent in the attitude to each other in cases when legitimate interests are not mediated by the corresponding legal rights, i.e. are not issued normative as those.

In the literature the questions on the scope of the list of procedural rights of the suspected and accused, about their content and the problems connected with their realization on a practice have been researched full enough and enough for a long time[10]. However, the modern updated criminally-remedial legislation represented the basic set of provisions of the Code of Criminal Procedure of the Russian Federation, accepted on December, 18th, 2001 (174, Federal law) and has been operating since July, 1, 2002, appreciably indicated, has indicated and even has partially changed statuses of the suspected and accused (as well as other participants of criminal legal proceedings), with serious image has expanded guarantees of their rights and legitimate interests. Thus, powerful development was received by institution of the judicial appeal, having distributed the action on pre-judicial proceedings. Mechanisms of the judicial control over remedial activity of bodies of the preliminary investigation, connected with an opportunity of limitation of the basic constitutional rights of person are finally created. There have arisen new, earlier unknown remedial institutions, for example, the special order of acceptance of a final court decision at the consent of the accused with the charge shown to it, etc. All this should regard the content of remedial statuses of the accused and suspected, including such its important element as legal rights.

By virtue of the insignificant period of time of action of new criminally-remedial legislation and as the consequence, insufficiency of its practical court decision, the publications of a monographic level displaying a modern status of remedial position of the suspected and accused are not extremely numerous. The absence of stability of the legislative base, connected with the tendency of introducing into operation of the Code of Criminal Procedure of the Russian Federation numerous changes and additions, does not create a stimulus to systematic basic research of corresponding problems.

First of all, the problem of a correlation between statuses of the suspected and accused from the point of view of realization in a stage of preliminary investigation of function of the party of protection is worth mentioning. The matter is that before coming into force of the operating Code of Criminal Procedure of Russia this question hasn't arisen seriously. As for the suspected there was a preliminary investigation during rather a short time interval for no more than 10 days. It was determined by specificity of ways of occurrence of the suspected in criminal case: 1) by way of detention on suspicion in committing of a crime for the term of 72 hours; 2) by way of use to a person before accuse of one of the preventive punishment that assumed in the further compulsion of accuse before the expiration of 10-days term since the indicated moment. Thus, the figure of the suspected of criminal trial was the time and corresponding status provided conditions for collecting evidence of guilt of the suspected person and distinguished this person with lawful opportunities to resist to criminal prosecution, using the rights recorded by the law given for it of the suspected. The situation was resolved either by clearing from the imprisoned and cancelling of the used preventive punishment in the indicated terms, or by accusing a person with all consequences following from it.

During present time the suspected can act in the role of the constant participant of a stage of preliminary investigation for longer period and even, than it is peculiar - the accused. It is connected with the expansion of the bases of occurrence in case of the suspected and acute elimination of the accused of the preliminary investigation which is carried out in the form of inquiry. Thus, besides two mentioned ways of occurrence in case of the suspected, there has appeared an additional instituting of criminal case concerning a certain person (Article 1, Part 1 of Article 46 of the Code of Criminal Procedure of the Russian Federation). Thus, the legislator does not establish any limitations on terms of possible stay of such person in the status of the suspected if the given way of occurrence of the suspected is not integrated to simultaneous use to them of detention or the preventive punishment. Thus, in fact, a person now can be in the status of the suspected during all preliminary investigation in view of an opportunity of numerous prolongations of terms of investigation down to the moment of deciding about its bringing as of the accused. Procedure of bringing of a person as of the accused, including the instrument official accuse, on quite lawful bases can be carried out in day of making a decision by the inspector in the end of preliminary investigation.

Whether the right of the accused on protection is violated, thus, depriving from his duly opportunity to resort to realization of the legal rights inherent in him? The answer to this question as it seems, is possible on the basis of results of the comparative analysis of the legal status of the suspected and accused and, first of all, on the basis of comparison of the list and certain content of the legal rights belonging to them and finding-out the presence or absence of any essential dignity or limitations for someone from them.

Such analysis allows approving that, firstly, the list and scope of rights of special character of all mentioned subspecies at of the suspected and accused on preliminary investigation are practically identical. The leveled approach in the decision of this problem by the modern legislator (unlike approaches of the former the Code of Criminal Procedure of RSFSR, represented some dignity for of the accused) is precisely shown. For example if before the inspector has not been obliged to acquaint of the suspected with the decision about purpose of examination with the conclusion of the expert, now according to part 3 of Article 195 and part 1 of Article 198 of the Code of Criminal Procedure of the Russian Federation, the suspected is distinguished with the right of such acquaintance alongside with the accused.

Secondly, such picture is observed by comparison of the list and the content of the rights of the suspected and accused. The given circumstance represents special value as an essence and value of one of the major for criminal trial of the legal phenomenon called by the right of defence of the suspected and accused, in basic is determined by set of the legal rights of the mentioned persons and their real guarantying of reached degree.

The list of general and the most significant from provisions of enforcement of the right to defence the legal rights of the suspected and accused is concentrated accordingly in part 4 of Article 46 and in part 4 of Article 47 of the Code of Criminal Procedure of the Russian Federation. Thus, the list of the rights of the suspected is settled by 11 Article and the same list for of the accused is presented already by 21 Paragraph. It, however, does not mean that the accused at the stage of preliminary investigation is distinguished with great scope of rights in comparison with the suspected. Expansion of the list is connected basically with inclusion in it of some special rights with which the rights of the defendant of the condemned are distinguished and justified, and also the rights of the accused which they use after the announcement to them about the end of investigation. Besides, inclusion of the separate rights of the accused of the corresponding list seems excessive and testifies, in our opinion, to imperfection of the used legal technical equipment at a formulation and editing of Article of the list. For example, Article 11, part 4 of Article 47 of the Code of Criminal Procedure of the Russian Federation gives of the accused the right to get acquainted with the decision about purpose of judicial examination, to put questions to the expert and to get acquainted with the conclusion of the expert. This provision as a matter of fact, duplicates already mentioned provisions part 3 of Article 195 and part 1 of Article 198 of the Code of Criminal Procedure of the Russian Federation which directly concern and to the suspected.

Really, rights of the suspected, not listed in part 4 of Article 46 of the Code of Criminal Procedure of the Russian Federation, will as follows be coordinated with the corresponding rights of the accused, mentioned in part 4 of Article 47 of the Code of Criminal Procedure of the Russian Federation. We should consider this question in more detail:

1. The right to know what are the suspected and to receive a copy of the decision about starting instituting against them legal proceedings or a copy of the decision about use to them of the preventive punishment.

In Article 1 and 2 part 4 of Article 47 of the Code of Criminal Procedure of the Russian Federation, i.e. with reference to the accused, there is the right to know what is the accused; to receive a copy of the decision about him being as the accused, a copy of the decision about use to him of the preventive punishment, a copy of the bill of particulars or the indictment.

Undoubtedly, the formulation of charge included in the decision about bringing as the accused, differs by greater completeness, clearness of the form of recording, and contains a necessary legal substantiation down to of the Criminal Code qualifying attributes of the absolute crime. All this far is not always inherent in the formulations of suspicion following from the content of decisions about instituting of a case, about use of the preventive punishment and the prologue of the report of interrogation of the suspected. However, action of provision of Article 1 part 2 of Article 75 of the Code of Criminal Procedure of the Russian Federation, recognizing as the inadmissible proof the prejudicial evidence of the suspected, of the accused, data during pre-judicial conducting of a criminal case for the lack of the defender, including cases of refusal from the defender and not confirmed of the suspected and accused of court, have in fact, predetermined compulsion of participation of the defender on any criminal case. Even in cases of un- conscientiousness or incompetence of the inspector the defender, by virtue of his duty to render legal aid of the suspected, in a status to give the essence and possible consequences of existing suspicion. Besides, in practice cases of presentation to a person so-called "flying", are widespread. Time of the charge displaying only separate episodes of criminal activity of the accused but all spectrums of "claims" of body of criminal prosecution to the accused. This practice is connected with necessity to legalize the fact of the content of a person arrested or with reasons of, obviously, tactical character more often.

Thus, both comments formulations of the corresponding right, in our opinion, will be coordinated between themselves.

2. The right to give an explanation and the prejudicial evidence in case of available concerning its suspicion or to refuse giving of explanations and prejudicial evidences.

In Clause 3 of Article 47 of the Code of Criminal Procedure of the Russian Federation there is the right to object charges, to testify on the charge shown to them or to refuse evidence. That is practically full coordination is noted. The basic part of prejudicial evidences of the suspected also can have character of objections against the declared suspicion. Presence at the suspected of the right to give an explanation is connected with a corresponding requisite in the formalized form of the report of detention of the suspected[11]. However, the right to give in certain measure puts explanations of the suspected in more exclusive position in comparison with the accused, i.e. having refused evidence, they at the same time have an opportunity to state the attitude to the fact of their detention by giving explanations.

3. The right to use the help of the defender since the moment stipulated by the law and to have with him appointments alone and confidential before the first interrogation of the suspected.

In Article 8 and 9, part 4 of Article 47 of the Code of Criminal Procedure of the Russian Federation the meaning and the content of this provision as a matter of fact, is generating. Further it is possible to mention eight more rights of the suspected: the right to present the proof; to declare petitions and removals; to testify and explain on the native language; to use the help of the translator free of charge; to get acquainted with reports of the investigatory actions made with its participation and to submit on them remarks; to participate from the sanction of the inspector or the investigator in the investigatory actions made under his petition, the petition of his defender or the lawful representative; to complain to actions (inactivity) and decisions of court, the public prosecutor, the inspector and the investigator; to be protected by other means and the ways which have been not forbidden by the Code of Criminal Procedure.

The corresponding rights of the accused of Article 4-7, 10, 14, 21 part 4 of Article 47 of the Code of Criminal Procedure of the Russian Federation are formulated practically similarly.

Stated as it seems, allows to approve the maximal degree of similarity of legislative ensuring of the suspected and accused opportunities for realization of their right for defence and about absence any violation of remedial position of the suspected in comparison with position of the accused. Hence, in modern criminally-remedial legislation the difference between the suspected and accused is not completely certain.

A unique way of occurrence of the accused on preliminary investigation is the decision about bringing of a person as of the accused which should be made only at presence of the sufficient evidence, giving the bases for charge of a person in committing of a crime (part 1 of Article 171 of the Code of Criminal Procedure of the Russian Federation) but it does not always mean big dignity of charge unlike suspicion. At least, the given circumstance almost does not render influence on a degree of security of a person concerning which criminal prosecution is carried out.

Probably, the legislator, duplicating a role and a place of the suspected and accused on preliminary investigation, in essence, has created pre conditions for statement of a question of necessity of elimination of such duality. It is thought that the problem could be resolved due to the further strengthening of the role of the suspected by his final transformation into the constant and basic participant of preliminary investigation as the main bearer of criminally-remedial function of protection down to the final stage of investigation. Only by the results of all-round and full investigation of circumstances of case it is possible to speak seriously about the presence of the necessary evidence, allowing to formulate proved and lawful and the most important is the final charge to a person who has committed a crime. In this connection the moment of deciding about bringing of a person (i.e. of the suspected) as of the accused it would be necessary to connect, in our opinion, with the moment of decision-making of the inspector about the end of investigation. That the same moment would communicate with the advent in case of the accused as a legal fact meaning finality of accusatory conclusions of the inspector.

Such idea, probably, seems disputable. However, the problem of a duality of statuses of the accused and suspected, undoubtedly, demands the sanction and deserves a special research.

It is necessary to note that the legislator, as a matter of fact, already uses the offered approach in the definition of the moment of occurrence in the case of preliminary investigation of the accused in the form of inquiry. Here the indictment is analogue to the bill of particulars as not only the final remedial instrument of preliminary investigation but also simultaneously the instrument of bringing of a person as of the accused (part 1 of Article 47 of the Code of Criminal Procedure of the Russian Federation). Only in cases of choosing of election the preventive punishment in the form of custody concerning of the suspected and impossibility, thus, to draw up the indictment in 10-days term, the suspected is charged by the way, stipulated for preliminary investigation (Part 2 and 3 Article 224 of the Code of Criminal Procedure of the Russian Federation).

It is interesting that by the given provision the legislator, most likely unconsciously, has already taken steps in diffusion of distinctions between statuses of the accused and suspected and transformation of the last into a constant remedial figure of the stage of preliminary investigation. According to made comments, it appears that at inquiry there is unessential for the accuse of the suspected after 10-days term from the moment of use to him any other preventive punishment, apart from custody, including such as house arrest. In this case the collision between made comments and the provision of general character included in Article 100 of the Code of Criminal Procedure of the Russian Federation, any preventive punishment unequivocally not supposing the use without accusing for the term of more than 10 day is created. The arisen collision, in our opinion, should be resolved in favour of instructions of general provision.

Clear and already obviously to transform the realized aspiration of the legislator of preliminary investigation of the suspected by the constant participant is shown now in the form of discussion in the State Duma of the bill of introducing in of the Code of Criminal Procedure of the Russian Federation of changes and the additions providing an opportunity of detention of persons, of the suspected in participation in terrorist activity, within 30 days without accuse. It is necessary to note obvious anticonstitutionality of the given project.

§ 2. Humanization of the Modern Criminal Trial: The Rights of the Suspected and Accused

Many scientists-proceduralists addressed to the analysis of position of a person in criminal trial in general and a legal status of separate participants of criminal legal proceedings that in many respects promoted development of legislative regulation of protection of human rights in this branch of Russian legislation. The most significant contribution to the given direction such scientists as scientifically-used researches have brought M.S. Strogovich, L.D. Kokorev, I.M. Larin, and I.L. Petruhin. M. Kudin, V.M. Kornukov, V.S. Shadrin, etc[12].

Unfortunately, it is necessary to ascertain that the majority of researchers of position of a person in criminal legal proceedings, showing heightened interest to enforcement of the rights of the suspected, of the accused and other representatives of the party of protection, practically, with rare exception, left outside the sphere of the attention the problem of the legal status of victims of criminal encroachment and furthermore the position of other subjects of criminally-remedial relations, corresponding to the operating Code of Criminal Procedure to the category of "other participants of criminal legal proceedings" (Ch. 8 of the Code of Criminal Procedure). Such obvious skew of a scientific orientation of corresponding researches the provisions of the Code of Criminal Procedure of RSFSR (1960) to small degree stimulated the state of participants of criminal trial. For example, the witness is the most widespread subject of criminally-remedial relations, on earlier operating Code of Criminal Procedure basically was distinguished with duties (to testify, be on calls of the official who is carrying out legal proceedings, etc.). Some legal rights, given to them, had special character, i.e. reflected possible specificity of a person (minors), or followed from its participation in certain investigatory action (the right with own hand to write down the prejudicial evidences in the report of interrogation, the right to get acquainted with the report, etc.). Obviously, these rights do not have remedial essence.

Such skew in balance of the rights and duties of participants of criminal legal proceedings is somewhat overcome the operating Code of Criminal Procedure of the Russian Federation.

Acceptance by the Federal law dd. December, 18th, 2001 174-Federal law of the new Code of Criminal Procedure of the Russian Federation is a logic stage in the system of measures on realization of provisions of the judicial-legal reform which are carried out in our country. The given event in itself should not be considered as "revolution" in Russian criminal legal proceedings. Many provisions and institutions of the new Code of Criminal Procedure have been prepared by changes and additions, introduced in the Code of Criminal Procedure of RSFSR during all post Soviet period of its action, provisions of the Constitution of Russia, practice of activity of the Constitutional Court and supervising explanations of the Supreme Court of the Russian Federation. Besides, there were known to the legal public of some groups of the authors on preparation of projects the new Code of Criminal Procedure, carried out during the last years. As a result Russian criminal legal proceedings have found features of adversary proceedings of the guarding type excluding any limitation of constitutional rights of citizens.

It is possible to consider as doubtless positive innovations of the Code of Criminal Procedure legislative definition of the concept of participants of criminal legal proceedings, their classification, proceeding from carried out remedial function; expansion of guarantees of the rights and legitimate interests of participants of criminal trial, a certain definition and specification of their status; expansion of remedial opportunities of the chief of an investigatory department under the control over activity of inspectors; precise definition of the moment from which current term of detention starts; giving to inquiry the features of independent obvious simplification of its procedure in comparison with preliminary investigation; expansion of the bases for stay of the case in view of modern needs of law enforcement experts; introduction of certain mechanisms of safety for the participants of a process; occurrence of worth mentioning alternative to custody as house arrest; "Legalization" checks and specifications of prejudicial evidences on a place; introduction of the special order of acceptance of a final court decision at the consent of the accused with the charge shown to them; scope by criminally-remedial regulation of proceedings concerning separate categories of persons, rehabilitations and international cooperation on criminal cases. It is not a full list of positive innovations in of the Code of Criminal Procedure.

At the same time some provisions of operating criminally-remedial legislation are speculative, untold, inconsistent and mutually exclusive. Blanket (reference) character of many provisions creates serious inconveniences at work with the text of the law enforcement persons and trained.

Causes of bewilderment evasion of the legislator from a precise formulation of the purpose and problems of criminal legal proceedings. The content of Article 6 of the Code of Criminal Procedure hardly can be considered in such quality. Ensuring of balance of interests of charge and protection really is one of the major, basic provisions adversary proceedings. However, it only creates conditions for appropriate realization of criminally-remedial activity but at all does not focus on its desirable result.

Unequivocally rectilinear reference of the investigator, the inspector and the public prosecutor to the party of charge seems tactless, stimulating displays of an accusatory bias. They really carry out criminal prosecution but they should carry out and other criminally-remedial functions.

Absence in a new law of an opportunity of returning to additional investigation has put court; impossibility of prolongation of terms of inquiry will undoubtedly create in practice an absolute obstacle to the proved and fair consideration of criminal cases.

The provision of Article 1 is incorrect. Part 2 of Article 75 of the Code of Criminal Procedure, in fact, carries out compulsion of participation of the defender on preliminary investigation on any criminal case (refusal from the accused from the prejudicial evidences given from his consent without participation of the defender, makes these prejudicial evidences inadmissible). There is no explanation of the concept of the civil suit in criminal trial and its content. Leveling distinctions by way of legal procedures of general jurisdiction, in juries and at Justice of the Peace is obviously looked through.

Numerous innuendoes and contradictions of new criminally-remedial law are caused as it seems, by unduly hasty and non-critical perception by the legislator of a scopetric package of "presidential" amendments in already accepted by the State Duma of the Russian Federation in the third reading the completed project of the Code of Criminal Procedure. In the subsequent additional work of corresponding structures of a legislature of the country, result in acceptance of a new Federal law on modification and additions in text of the Code of Criminal Procedure[13] that is unprecedented in relation to already accepted was required but not to come into force Federal law. During the first period of action of the Code of Criminal Procedure there was a need to accept all series of additional federal acts for introducing into them of changes and additions[14].

Unfortunately, even after these legislative measures many innuendoes of the law still remain.

Nevertheless, it is necessary to note that provisions of the new Code of Criminal Procedure correspond to the Constitution and in a sufficient measure will be coordinated with the bases of general theory of human rights. First of all, it is necessary to pay attention to the fact that Ch. 2 of the Code of Criminal Procedure "Principles of criminal legal proceedings" as first such principle purpose of criminal legal proceedings determines (Article 6). The concept of "purpose of criminal legal proceedings" is new to criminally-remedial legislation. It is possible to say that somewhat this term has replaced the used in the Code of Criminal Procedure of RSFSR term "problems of criminal legal proceedings". But the legal applicability of use in the Code of Criminal Procedure a new term seems to a little bit others.

From the etymological point of view, the given terms correlated as one of interpretation of a word "purpose" - "problem" and both of them have general concept of "purpose"[15].

At the same time "problem" designates more certain, practical purpose, that someone is necessary for carrying out. Such approach was used in of the Code of Criminal Procedure of RSFSR to the characteristic of problems of the criminal trial consistent fast and full disclosing of crimes, exposure guilty, correct use the law for their fair punishment. Therefore, in the previous paragraph at definition of problems of Russian criminal legal proceedings their direct connection with certain stages and the content of remedial activity was emphasized (functions) of its separate participants.

Another meaning is put in the content of the purpose at use the term "purpose" for which it is a prospective role, by expediency of use by something, mission, i.e. has a big degree of generalization in comparison with the purposes arising at the solution of problems. Thereof the legislator erects the purpose of criminal legal proceedings in a rank of basic position.

Such change of sights at the role of criminal justice was a natural result of transformation of legal priorities concerning the state to the right of person, interests of a society and problems of criminality. Accordingly, legal recognition of that fact that the purpose of criminal legal proceedings is not struggle against criminality as a social phenomenon and demanding for this adequate complex of measures but protection of a society against crimes by realization of the criminal law, protection of the rights and legitimate interests of citizens who have got in the sphere of criminally-legal relationships. Only functioning of law enforcement bodies of the state is not capable to lead to reducing of the criminality but can provide the legal decision of a question of guilt of the separate person in certain act and about purpose to them measures of punishment. As realization of the criminal law in that case it is understood not only bringing to account and purpose of punishment but also refusal from criminal prosecution of the innocent. All the indicated purposes should be reached in the special remedial order.

The stated fact was recorded in Article 6 of the Code of Criminal Procedure, determined the main purpose of criminal legal proceedings **as protection of the rights and legitimate interests of persons and organizations which have suffered from crimes and also protection of a person against illegal and unreasonable charge, condemnation, limitation of their rights and freedoms.**

Thus, it is emphasized that criminal prosecution and purpose guilty fair punishment are not an end in itself, a priority of criminal legal proceedings, they in the same degree respond to the purpose of criminal legal proceedings as refusal from criminal prosecution of the innocent, their impunity, and rehabilitation of everyone who has unreasonably undergone to criminal prosecution.

Thus, the original purposes of criminal justice responding to its nature and opportunities are recognized, as liquidated it narrowness in the form of an accusatory bias and also the former purposes on struggle against criminality and its eradication which generated aspiration of law enforcement bodies officers to achieve it by any means are eliminated and to that led to quite often unreasonable and illegal limitations or even infringement of the rights and personal freedoms.

It seems, that it allows to ascertain that the legislator at designing provisions the operating Code of Criminal Procedure initially starts with basic regulations concerning necessity of ensuring of balance of the rights and legitimate interests of the sides and whenever possible all other participants of criminal legal proceedings. In particular, for the first time concerning the problem of legal protection earlier as it was already noted as a matter of fact the deprived of civil rights participant of process was the witness. Thus, according to part 4 of Article 56 of the Code of Criminal Procedure the witness has the right: to make a petition and to complain about actions (inactivity) and decisions of the investigator, the inspector, the public prosecutor and court; to be on interrogation with the lawyer; to make petitions for the use of measures concerning his security. The witness, as a rule, cannot be forcibly subjected to judicial examination or survey (part 5 of Article 56 of the Code of Criminal Procedure)...

The opportunity of use security measures in relation to participants of process for the first time is recorded at a legislative level. Thus, if necessary to ensure the provision of safety of the victim, his representative, close relatives and close persons the inspector has a right in the report of investigatory action in which the victim participates, not to cite the data about this person. In this case the inspector by approbation of the public prosecutor makes the decision in which the reasons of decision-making on preservation as fiduciary this data is stated, the pseudonym of the participant of investigatory action is emphasized and the sample of his signature which they will use in reports of the investigatory actions made with its participation is given. The decision is put into an envelope which after that is sealed up and put into the criminal case (part 9 of Article 166 of the Code of Criminal Procedure). At presence of threat of violence, extortion and other criminal acts concerning the victim, the witness or their close relatives, relatives or close persons control and record of telephone and other negotiations are supposed under the written statement of the indicated persons and at absence of such statement is on the basis of a court decision (part 2 of Article 186 of the Code of Criminal Procedure). With a view of safety of a person identifying presentation for an identification under the decision of the inspector can be carried out in the conditions excluding visual supervision identifying him (part 8 Article 193 the Code of Criminal Procedure). On the basis of definition or the decision of court the closed proceeding in cases when it is demanded by the interests of safety of participants of proceeding, their close relatives, or close persons is supposed. (Article 4, part 2 of Article 241 of the Code of Criminal Procedure). In the same purposes the court without announcement of original data about a person of the witness has a right to carry out its interrogation in the conditions excluding visual supervision of the witness by other participants of proceeding about what the court makes definition or the decision (part 5 of Article 278 of the Code of Criminal Procedure). To the category of the legislative measures directed on safety of participants of criminal legal proceedings, it is necessary to refer to the provision of part 3 of Article 170 of the Code of Criminal Procedure, allowing proceedings of investigatory actions without participation understood in the cases integrated to possible danger to life and health of people by their proceedings.

As a whole, the system of principles of Russian criminal trial is penetrated by spirit of ensuring of human rights that is seen even from the name of the majority of the provisions-principles included in Ch. 2 of the Code of Criminal Procedure: legality by conducting of a criminal case (Article 7); realization of justice only court (Article 8); respect to honour and dignity of a person (Article 9); personal immunity (Article 10); protection of the rights and freedoms of a person and a citizen in criminal legal proceedings (Article 11), etc.

As the consequence of it, interests of protection of human rights penetrate also the system of rules and conditions of process substantiation, representing a rod basis of criminally-remedial activity in general.

However, the current legislation and law enforcement practice not in all cases are not always consecutive in formation of balance of the rights and legitimate interests of participants of criminal legal proceedings. Quite often, probably secretly, the priorities in enforcement of the rights and legitimate interests of representatives of the party of protection to the detriment of interests of other persons nevertheless are looked over.

Such approach contradicts the constitutional instruction about inadmissibility of realization of the rights and freedoms of a citizen in cases when it leads to infringement and infringement of the rights of other persons (part 3 of Article 17 of the Constitution).

Unfortunately, it is necessary to ascertain that many of the accused frequently abuse the right of defence presented to them by the Constitution and criminally-remedial law. The concept is already introduced in to theory of criminalistics "counteraction to investigation" which is understood as any illegal activity of the accused, of the suspected and persons assisting them with the purpose of evasion from the criminal liability or its unreasonable mitigation[16].

There is a question: whether it is an abusing of the right of defence by obviously false statement of the accused about participation in a crime of the innocent person? Judiciary practice goes on a way of denying of infringement of the law to noted actions of the accused that is connected with boundless understanding of the right of defence. There is a definition of Judicial board of the Supreme Court of RSFSR where it was noted that "a person does not have the responsibility for giving of false testimonies about criminal acts of the given person if they were means of own protection from charge in concealment of a crime"[17].

Is such approach correct? The Constitution in part 2 of Article 45 about the right of everyone to protect unequivocally determines the rights and freedoms in all ways which have been not forbidden by the law. It is known that realization of the right of defence should not break the rights of other persons. And here, first of all, dignity of a person is touched (Part 1 of Article 21 of the Constitution), the right to security of a person (Article 22 of the Constitution)[18]. Besides, the Convention on Protection of Human Rights and Basic Freedoms in part 2 of Article 10 are limited with the right of free expression of opinion with the purpose of protection of reputation or the rights of other persons[19].

The European Court on Human Rights also adheres to such position. Thus, on case "Brandesteter against Austria" (1991) Court has decided that Clause 3 of Article 6 of the aforesaid Convention does not provide the unlimited right to use any means of protection and has recognized slander as an inadmissible argument of protection[20].

A lot of authors specify the necessity to protect the interests of all participants of criminal legal proceedings, irrespective of their remedial position.

The significant role in enforcement of the rights of legitimate interests of participants of preliminary investigation is played by the inspector as he is the first defender of the rights and legitimate interests of a person[21]. Really, whether so the inspector in activity on criminal case and so he is protected from possible pressure from participants of preliminary investigation or their relatives and friends is remedially independent? The question is rather acute. The remedial opportunity of the inspector to limit considerably constitutional rights and freedoms of a person and a citizen, being the participants of the preliminary investigation, entitles to rank them as officials having special powers. The inspector determines a direction of preliminary investigation, he estimates the evidence collected on case and makes the decisions determining the development of the case both concerning the rights and interests of certain people. Therefore, the participants of preliminary investigation are not indifferent to the question that solves the destiny of criminal case as remedially independent or dependent on the public prosecutor, the chief of an investigatory department or criminal elements. We should notice that than it is more given guarantees of safety to the inspector and his relatives, it is especially active to protect legitimate interests of other participants of preliminary investigation. In fact, he is dependent on various officials, he is not free from pressure upon them of other citizens, and they have no real remedial independence. As N.I. Kulagin remarks, "not overloaded by affairs and having legal immunity and powers the inspector will qualitatively carry out the functions assigned to him that will help to protect effectively the rights and legitimate interests of victims of crimes and also those persons who have committed them"[22]. It is impossible to disagree with it. In this connection some authors consider necessary to bring in Article 10 of Article 448 of the Code of Criminal Procedure the change according to which the right of the decision of a question of instituting of criminal case, bringing as a of the accused inspector the public prosecutor of the subject of Russia (his assistant), rather than the supervising public prosecutor as it is stipulated in the mentioned provision would have[23]. Such addition is really necessary, because, as a rule, the public prosecutor of area (city) carries out supervision of activity of the inspector. The inspector can appeal against its instructions to the higher public prosecutor in this connection there can be intense relations between the public prosecutor and the inspector.

At possible occurrence of disputed situations objectivity of the public prosecutor in the decision of a question of instituting of criminal case or accuse concerning the inspector, is put under doubt. It is impossible to exclude an opportunity of instituting of case or accuse (or threat of proceedings of the given actions) concerning the inspector with the purpose of rendering on them pressure.

The mechanism of protection of the inspector from pressure from criminal elements is created by the state. According to part 2 of Article 2 of the Federal law "The State Protection of Judges, Officials of Law-Enforcement and Supervising Bodies"[24], the inspector is referred to a category of persons who are a subject to the state protection at encroachment on their safety and also creation of appropriate conditions for departure of justice and struggle against crimes. A guarantee of safety of the inspector is also the responsibility of persons for disclosure of data on the security measures used concerning the judge and other participants of criminal trial (Article 311 Criminal Code), the increased responsibility of persons for carrying out (or threat of carrying out) them of a criminal encroachment for life and health of the inspector in connection with realization of the official duties by them (Article 295, 296 Criminal Code).

Certainly, the question of granting big powers to the inspector is necessary to solve extremely cautiously. Excessive freedom and in dependence of the inspector can lead to negative consequences. But one is obvious is remedial independence of the inspector and its security from criminal encroachment in connection with performance official duties by them is one of mechanisms of enforcement of the rights and legitimate interests of participants of criminal legal proceedings.

In this connection it is necessary to hope that the reform of law enforcement bodies assumed in particular and creation uniform extradepartamental of the investigatory device carried out now in Federal service of investigation, will promote, including much greater in comparison with a modern level, degrees of security of protection of human rights in criminal legal proceedings.

Notes

1. See: Rossiiskaya Gazeta,1995, April, 5.

2. See: Assembly of the Legislation of the Russian Federation. 1998. #4. Clause 1514; Rossiiskaya Gazeta. 1995.April, 5. / См.: Собрание законодательства Российской Федерации. 1998. № 4. Ст. 1514; Российская газета. 1995. 5 апр.

3. See: Strogovich MS. The Right of the Accused to Defense and Presumption of Innocence. Moscow, 1984. / См.: Строгович М. С. Право обвиняемого на защиту и презумпция невиновности. М., 1984.

4. See, for example: The Right of the Accused to Defense in the Socialist Criminal Procedure / Edited by V.M. Savitsky. Moscow, 1983. P.12. / См., например: Право обвиняемого на защиту в социалистическом уголовном процессе / Под ред. В. М. Савицкого. М., 1983. С. 12.

5. See: Gutkin I. M. Pressing Questions of Criminally-Remedial Detention. Moscow, 1980. P.75. / См.: Гуткин И. М. Актуальные вопросы уголовно-процессуального задержания. М., 1980. С. 75.

6. In more detail see: Kolosovich S.A., Parii A,V. The Legal Status of the Suspected and Problems of its Improving. Volgograd, 1997. P.28-31. / Подробнее об этом см.: Колосович С. А., Парий А. В. Правовой статус подозреваемого и проблемы его совершенствования. Волгоград, 1997. С. 28–31.

7. See:Malein N.S. The Interest Protected by the Law // Soviet State and the Law. 1982.4. P.8-9. / См.: Малеин Н. С. Охраняемый законом интерес // Советское государство и право. 1982. № 4. С. 8–9.

8. See: Public and Personal Interests in the Criminal Trial / Edited by L.D.Kokoreva. Voronezh, 1984. P.21. / См.: Общественные и личные интересы в уголовном судопроизводстве / Под ред. Л. Д. Кокорева. Воронеж, 1984. С. 21.

9. See:Malein N.S. An Offence: Concept, Reasons, Responsibility. Moscow, 1985. P.64. / См.: Малеин Н. С. Правонарушение: понятие, причины, ответственность. М., 1985. С. 64.

10. See, for example: Akincha N.A. Suspected and Accused in Preliminary Investigation. Saratov, 1964; Bekeshko S.P., Matvienko. E.A. Suspected in the Soviet Criminal Procedure. Minsk, 1969; Denezhkin B.A. Suspected in the Soviet Criminal Procedure. Saratov, 1982; Korotkii N.N. procedural Guarantees of the Inviolability of a Person of the Suspected and Accused in Preliminary Investigation. Moscow, 1981; Strogovich M.S. The Right of the Accused to Defense and Presumption of Innocence. Moscow, 1984; Stetsovskij J.I., Larin A.M. The Constitutional Principle of guaranteeing of the Right to Defense to the Accused. Moscow, 1988, etc. / См., например: Акинча Н. А. Подозреваемый и обвиняемый на предварительном следствии. Саратов, 1964; Бекешко С. П., Матвиенко Е. А. Подозреваемый в советском уголовном процессе. Минск, 1969; Денежкин Б. А. Подозреваемый в советском уголовном процессе. Саратов, 1982; Короткий Н. Н. Процессуальные гарантии неприкосновенности личности подозреваемого и обвиняемого в стадии предварительного расследования. М., 1981; Строгович М. С. Право обвиняемого на защиту и презумпция невиновности. М., 1984; Стецовский Ю. И., Ларин А. М. Конституционный принцип обеспечения обвиняемому права на защиту. М., 1988 и др.

11. See: Appendix 28 to Clause 476 of the Code of Criminal Procedure of the Russian Federation. / См.: Приложение 28 к ст. 476 УПК РФ.

12. See, for example: Strogovich M.S. The Right of the Accused to Defense and Presumption of Innocence. Moscow, 1984; Public and Personal Interests in the Criminal Trial / Edited by L.D. Kokoreva. Voronezh, 1984; Kornukov V.M. The Constitutional Bases of the Status of the Person in the Criminal Trial. Saratov, 1987; Stetsovskij J.I., Larin A.M. The Constitutional Principle of Guaranteeing of the Right to Defense to the Accused. Moscow, 1988; KudinF. M. Compulsion in the Criminal Trial. Krasnoyarsk, 1985; Petruhin I.L. Personal Privacy of a Person at Investigation of Crimes. Volgograd, 1997; VolodinaL.M. The Mechanism of Protection of the Personal Rights in the Criminal Procedure. Tyumen, 1999; Lebedev V.M. Judicial Protection of Freedom and Security of Citizens. Moscow, 2001. / См., например: Строгович М. С. Право обвиняемого на защиту и презумпция невиновности. М., 1984; Общественные и личные интересы в уголовном судопроизводстве / Под ред. Л. Д. Кокорева. Воронеж, 1984; Корнуков В. М. Конституционные основы положения личности в уголовном судопроизводстве. Саратов, 1987; Стецовский Ю. И., Ларин А. М. Конституционный принцип обеспечения обвиняемому права на защиту. М., 1988; Кудин Ф. М. Принуждение в уголовном судопроизводстве. Красноярск, 1985; Петрухин И. Л. Личная жизнь личности при расследовании преступлений. Волгоград, 1997; Володина Л. М. Механизм защиты прав личности в уголовном процессе. Тюмень, 1999; Лебедев В. М. Судебная защита свободы и личной неприкосновенности граждан. М., 2001.

13. See:5/29/2002 58-Federal Law.

14. See:7/24/2002 98-Federal Law, 7/24/2002 103-Federal Law, 7/25/2002 114-Federal Law, 7/4/2003 94-Federal Law, 7.17.2003 111-Federal Law, 12/8/2003 161-Federal Law.

15. See: Explanatory Dictionary of Russian / Edited by D.N. Ushakov. Moscow, 1935. Vol. 1. P.923;, 1938. Vol. 2. P.356. / См.: Толковый словарь русского языка / Под ред. Д. Н. Ушакова. М., 1935. Т. 1. С. 923; М., 1938. Т. 2. С. 356.

16. See: Stulov O. How to Interfere with Counteraction of Investigation // Legality. 2000.1. P.26-27; Polyakov M.P. Protection of the Accused and «Protection from the Accused» // State and Law. 1998.4. P.94-98. / См.: Стулов О. Как препятствовать противодействию расследования // Законность. 2000. № 1. С. 26–27; Поляков М. П. О защите обвиняемого и «защите от обвиняемого» // Государство и право. 1998. № 4. С. 94–98.

17. The Criminal Code of the Russian Federation with Decrees and Comments / Ed. S.V. Borodin, S.V. Zamyatin; Edited by V.M. Lebedev. Moscow, 1998. P.828. / Уголовный кодекс РФ с постановлениями и комментариями / Сост. С. В. Бородин, С. В. Замятина; Под ред. В. М. Лебедева. М., 1998. С. 828.

18. See: Nafilov S., Vasin A. The Right to Defense is not Boundless // Legality. 1999.4. P.6. / См.: Нафилов С., Васин А. Право на защиту – не беспредельно // Законность. 1999. № 4. С. 6.

19. See: The Convention on Protection of Human Rights and Fundamental fFeedoms and Protocols to it. Official Translation to Russian in edition of 2001 // Newsletter of the Council of Europe in Uralsk region. Ekaterinburg, 2001. P.10. / См.: Конвенция о защите прав человека и основных свобод и Протоколы к ней. Официальный перевод на русский язык в ред. 2001 года // Информационный бюллетень Совета Европы в Уральском регионе. Екатеринбург, 2001. С. 10.

20. See: Gomien D., Harris D., Zvaak L. European Convention on Protection of Human Rights and the European Social Charter: Law and Practice. Moscow, 1998. P.251. / См.: Гомьен Д., Харрис Д., Зваак Л. Европейская конвенция о защите прав человека и Европейская социальная хартия: право и практика. М., 1998. С. 251.

21. See: Shmatov V.M. Development of the Private Criminalistic Theory of Studying of a Person and Enforcement of its Rights: Abstract of thesis of a Cand. of Jurisprudence. Volgograd, 2000. P.20; Kulagin N.I. In Protection of the Rights and Legitimate Interests of the Inspector // Human Rights and Law-Enforcement Activity. Volgograd, 1995. P.102-106. / См.: Шматов В. М. Развитие частной криминалистической теории изучения личности и обеспечение ее прав: Автореф. дис. ... канд. юрид. наук. Волгоград, 2000. С. 20; Кулагин Н. И. В защиту прав и законных интересов следователя // Права человека и правоохранительная деятельность. Волгоград, 1995. С. 102–106.

22. Kulagin N.I. Specified work. P.106.

23. See: Egorova M.S. The Institution of Suspension of Proceeding on Criminal Case and Enforcement of the Rights and Legitimate Interests of Participants of the Criminal Procedure at Realization of its Norms: Thesis of a Cand. of Jurisprudence. Volgograd, 2004. P.148-150. / См.: Егорова М. С. Институт приостановления производства по уголовному делу и обеспечение прав и законных интересов участников уголовного процесса при реализации его норм: Дис. ... канд. юрид. наук. Волгоград, 2004. С. 148–150.

24. See: 20.04 1995 48-Federal Law.

Chapter 11.   THE RIGHTS OF VICTIMS OF CRIMES
AND ABUSE OF POWER

The Constitution of the Russian Federation (1993), focusing on international standards of human rights, raised many questions which decision demands special scientific researches. Among them in the context of updating of Russian legislation the great value has the legal status of victims of crimes and abuse of power.

Separate aspects of the rights of victims of crimes were developed in jurisprudence. The problem of protection of victims of crimes always caused interest and drew attention of scientists in the field of criminal law, criminal trial and criminology. Accordingly various used aspects of the problems of victims of crimes were from this point of view considered.

In connection with the constitutional recording of the rights of victims as rights of a citizen (Article 52 of the Constitution) there arisen the necessity to consider their content through a prism of human rights and the rights of a citizen and to find out a correlation between the rights of victims as human rights from provisions of modern international and constitutional law.

The theoretical aspect of distinctions between the content of the rights of victims as human rights and the rights of a citizen and distinctions between guarantees of human rights and the rights of a citizen seems extremely important in the research of problems of system of guarantees.

In this respect it is difficult to overestimate the big contribution which was made into the development of the problem of rights of victims of crimes by scientific researches and publications of V.P. Bozhiev, A.D. Voikov, P.S. Dagel, V.A. Dubrivnoi, L.D. Kokorev, A.M. Larin, J.O. Motovilovker, V.J. Ponarin, I.I. Poteruzh, R.D. Rahunov, and V.M. Savitsky. L.V. Frank, V.S. Shadrin, P.S. Janie, etc.

There is also an acute problem of protection of the rights of persons subjected no to the breaking the criminal legislation acts but there is an infringement of ratified internationally-legal contracts and the criminal legislation at the moment of it has not been brought into accord with them.

The concept of the rights of victims of crimes and abuse of power as human rights has been formed in international law within several decades. The significant contribution to comprehension by the states of the world the necessity to cooperate in the sphere of struggle against criminality and abuse of power and creation of means of legal aid to victims refers to the United Nations and the Council of Europe.

It is necessary to note that necessity of theoretical development of the rights of victims as human rights and its reflection in international documents have been realized by lawyers and representatives of world community only during last decades. However, international community pays attention to the problems of rights of victims of infringement of basic rights and freedoms of a person from the end of 1940s. Meanwhile the increase of criminality in 1980s became a serious problem of national and international scale interfering political, economic, social and cultural development. It led to a series of measures at the national and international level, directed on struggle against criminality and abuse of power. Process of development of international documents where there were the attempts to formulate the content of the indicated right, begun in 1940-60s, became especially active in 1980s. This activity is carried out by the Commission of the United Nations on the Prevention of Criminality and Criminal Justice (up to 1992 the Committee of the United Nations on the Prevention and Struggle against Criminality), the Congresses of the United Nations on the Prevention of Criminality and Treatment of Offenders.

The result of activity of the indicated bodies became the creation of the system of international documents both of recommendatory and binding character, concerning, on the one hand. The assistance to enforcement of the rights of victims in the sphere of justice and in other organizations and bodies of criminal justice.

Turning point in the development of the concept is also the content of internationally-legal mechanism of realization of the rights of victims of crimes and abuse of power accepted on 96th plenary session of General Assembly of the United Nations on November, 29th, 1985. The Declaration of main principles of justice for victims of crimes and abuse of power which text was developed on VII Congress of the United Nations was accepted. From the analysis of the Declaration it follows that in its provisions a number of the generated elements of the considered right contain: the right to access to mechanisms of justice and the right on restitution (compensation) from a harm-doer or from the third parties bearing the responsibility for the behaviour and also in provisions of the

Declaration there were new kinds of the rights of victims, in particular, the right to financial indemnification of the caused damage due to the state if the victim cannot receive compensation from other sources.

For the subsequent registration of the concept of the rights of victims influence of documents of the United Nations on rule-making in the Council of Europe was not less significant. Since 1970 the Council of Europe, in particular the European Committee on Problems of Criminality (European Commission for the Prevention of Torture (ECPT), carried out a number of researches, concerning victims of crimes and accepted the documents included principles of criminal politics on this question[1]. European Commission for the Prevention of Torture (ECPT) prepared the Convention "Indemnification of Victim of Grave Crimes" that came into force on February, 1st, 1988.

For Russia the constitutional recording of the rights of victims appeared due to the experience of the interstate legislation of the USSR and the Russian Federation and implementation of provisions about the rights of victims recorded in international legal regulations, it was originally in the Declaration of Rights and Freedoms of a Person and a Citizen (1991) (Article 33), later the given right was recorded in Article 52 of the Constitution of the Russian Federation (1993).

The term "victim" is used not only in the standard meaning but also in international[2] and in interstate legislation[3].

Constitutional rights of people suffered from crimes and abuse of power are considered through a prism of the rights of victims as human rights in such branches as international humanitarian right; the term "victim" is used. The victim, having special social and legal status, demands to him compassion and respect of his dignity and pursues as interest exposure guilty, his bringing to the responsibility and restoration of the infringed rights though in criminal trial the victim is considered as one of bearers of evidence. Thus, J.I. Stetsovsky directly approves, "The purpose of giving victims the rights is receiving additional help in disclosing crimes from them"[4].

More correctly as it seems, was to use in Article 52 of the Constitution of the Russian Federation the uniform concept: a victim of a crime and abuse of power.

As I. Lukashuk remarks, "At interpretation of provisions of the Constitution on human rights we should take into consideration corresponding standards of international law. If the last represent wider interpretation of human rights they are used alongside with the constitutional provision"[5]. Completely agreeing with the given position, at definition of attributes of the concept of subjects of the given constitutional law we are guided by legislative and scientific definition of a victim in Russian legal language and on definition of a victim in provisions of internationally-legal regulations. Before turning to the concept of the rights of victims, it is necessary to formulate the concept of subjects of the given rights. The theory of the legal status of a person became the basis of methodology of research of the concept of the subject of the rights of victims. The legal status of victims should be referred to the special (patrimonial) status which, being based generally on the constitutional status of a person, nevertheless, reflects feature of a position of the given category of citizens.

In our opinion, the following relate to attributes of the subject of the rights of victims:

— The victim can be both a physical and a legal person;

— The victim can be both individual and collective;

— A victim can be a citizen of the Russian Federation, the foreign citizen and a person without citizenship;

— The victim is a person to whom physical, property or moral damage is caused and a person concerning whom a threat of causing of such harm is made;

— In case of a death of a direct victim close relatives of a victim and his dependent can act as the subject of the rights of victims.

In of the Code of Criminal Procedure of RSFSR only natural person (Article 53) were referred to victims, however, still M.S. Strogovich did not have doubts that victim under the current legislation "can be both a natural person and a legal person as an organization, an enterprise, or a establishment".[6] In Article 42 of the Code of Criminal Procedure of the Russian Federation (2001) it is recorded, "Victim is a natural person to whom the crime causes physical, property, or moral damage and also a legal person in the case of causing harm to his property and business reputation".

The listed attributes should be referred to general but at the same time an attribute which distinguishes a victim as a subject from other subjects of the right, the basis for its concept of those. Besides, in our opinion, categories "a victim of a crime" and "a victim of abuse of power" do not coincide at all and criterion, delimiting one concept from another, is the basis for a concept of victims of a crime or abuse of power.

Speaking about the rights of victims as about constitutional rights, some authors do not make a distinction between concepts "the victim of a crime "and "the victim of abuse of power" and consider that in Russian terminology a word-combination "the victim of a crime and abusing" represents a designation of overlapping concepts partially conterminous on the scope. "Some abuse of power" forms certain kind of crimes and alongside with it the abusing which is not criminal but disciplinary or administrative offences is possible. At the same time set of crimes there are outside the concept of "abuse of power". Then it possible to conclude that the clause (Article 52 of the Constitution) proclaims and provides protection of the rights of victims both from criminal and from other abuse of power"[7].

As it is a question of the rights of victims as constitutional rights, for them a lot of attributes of the given system of the rights is characteristic[8]. In particular, the rights of victims are the cores as mediate the most essential relations between the state and its citizens in connection with their place in the major areas of life and activity. By virtue of it, it is impossible to recognize the relations arising from abusing as not a criminal but a disciplinary or administrative offence, basic, essential, radical relations between the state, a society and a person and the rights of victims of such abusing of Constitutional.

To have an opportunity to open the content of the rights of victims, to identify certain kind of victims with victims of a crime or with victims of abuse of power, it is necessary to find out the content of those bases which entail a concept of a person as a victim of a crime or a victim of abuse of power.

At definition of the bases for a concept of persons as victims we recognize that in a basis of Article 52 of the conventional provisions of the Declaration of main principles of justice for victims of crimes and abusing the authority accepted by General Assembly of the United Nations in 1985 in which as a basis for a concept of a person causing damage as a result of the act breaking national criminal laws is called as a victim of a crime, "including the laws forbidding criminal abusing by authority" and a victim of abuse of power is causing damage as a result of act, " not yet representing infringement of national criminal laws lay but infringing international recognized provisions, concerning human rights". Literal interpretation of the text of the Declaration allows recognizing that criminal abuse of power is completely covered by the concept "crime".

If a crime is a bases for occurrence of the rights of victims of crimes which is specially stipulated in a hypothesis of the Especial part of the criminal legislation of the country such behaviour of a person is understood by virtue of it the crime has an attribute illegality such acts as an abuse of power at the moment of its carrying out that does not only break the criminal legislation of the state, but at the same time breaks the conventional provisions and principles of international law, concerning the rights and freedoms of a person.

There is a question: at what conditions an abuse of power generates legal consequences for the corresponding subject in national legal system if this act breaks standards of international law?

Before answering this question, we should note that we understand two kinds of the act as abuse of power, differing under the content.

The first kind of abuse of power is abusing of power to publish normative-legal regulations which contain the provisions interfering realization by a person of a certain right, recorded in an internationally-legal document.

The second kind of abuse of power is infringement of criminal interdictions included in provisions of international contracts of the USSR (the Russian Federation) which are ratified but in conformity with which Criminal Code has not been given at the moment of carrying out of the act. A condition of occurrence of legal consequences at abuse of power is the concept of the Russian Federation in part 4 of Article 15 of the Constitution of the Russian Federation of the conventional standards of international law on human rights as a source of the national right.

Let's consider a certain example of the first kind of abuse of power. It is known that yet in 1968 the USSR signed and in 1973 ratified international Covenant on Civil and Political Rights. According to this document each person has a right to leave the country, including his own. It is necessary to note that in the Covenant it was stipulated, that this right cannot object of any limitations, except for what are stipulated by the law and are necessary for protection of state security, a public order, and health and moral of the population or the rights and freedoms of other persons. However, in Criminal Code of RSFSR there existed such a provision restricting to fly abroad or refusing to come back from abroad as a version (one of ways) of treason to the Native land (Article 64).

Thus, realization of the indicated human rights (freedom of departure from the country, freedom of residence) formed by the basis for bringing someone to account for especially grave treason and that led to infringement of internationally recognized provisions concerning human rights.

We agree with I.V. Naumov who writes: "The concept of Russian conventional standards of international law (in the Declaration of Rights and Freedoms of a Person and a Citizen and in the Organic law) means that flight abroad or refusal to come back home not only legally (at the constitutional level) decriminalized but also the direct use these standards of international law means also simultaneous distribution on these cases of a principle of return force of the criminal law, i.e. the changes of the condemned earlier for the indicated form to the Native land on Article 64 of the Criminal Code of the Russian Federation (if their actions do not comprise to the structure of treason of the Native land to other attributes or structure of other crime for example stipulated by same Article 83 Criminal Code) rehabilitations with all consequences of the legal and moral respect following from here[9].

Only after declaration of the conventional principles as Russia and standards of international law a component of its legal system in the Declaration (1991) the criminal liability for infringement of laws on branch of church from the state and schools from church (Article 142 Criminal Code), for infringement of the rules of passport system (Article 198 Criminal Code), for begging or conducting other parasitic way of life (Article 209 of the Criminal Code), for private business and commercial intermediary (Article 153 Criminal Code) and for some other activities was cancelled[10].

Hence, actions of the officials who instituted criminal proceedings of citizens on the basis of criminal interdictions, roughly breaking the rights and freedoms of a person, did not have legal basis according to the interstate legislation. However, if such charges were forged using illegal methods of investigation the officials guilty of crimes against justice are subject to the criminal liability.

Confirming to the given thesis we should refer to Article 5 of the law "Rehabilitation of Victims of Political Reprisals"[11] from which it follows that not the fact of condemnation of persons under indicated clauses of the Criminal Code is illegal but the activity of the legislator on institution of the given acts in the rank of the crimes, caused reprisals, for example, inclusion into the Criminal Code (1926) of the section "Counterrevolutionary Crimes".

As researchers mark, "within a totalitarian regime there was a practice of acceptance without publication in press of laws, by-law instruments and departmental instructions on establishment of various kinds of the legal responsibility. Thus, according to the Decree of Presidium of the Supreme Soviet of the USSR dd. October, 9th, 1951, the Minister of State Security in the order 00776 on October, 24th, 1951 demanded to declare on receipt to Germans, Chechens, Kalmyks, Ingush, Balkarians, Karachai people, to Greeks and the Crimean Tatars that they are left on special settlements forever"[12].

Abuse of power was also an activity of the legislator on inclusion in the criminal legislation of Russia of counterrevolutionary crimes (1918-1958) and after acceptance of the criminal legislation (1958) some crimes accomplished on anti-Soviet, antisocialist grounds and the purposes and statutory acts about use of criminal sentences administratively.

Thus, one of the kinds of abuse of power is an act which yet does not break the criminal legislation of the state but breaks internationally recognized provisions proclaiming the rights and freedoms of a person irrespective of the fact, whether the state joined to internationally-legal instrument proclaiming human rights, or not.

However, in the internationally recognized provisions, concerning human rights, the rights and freedoms of a person can not only be proclaimed but they can contain criminal interdictions. But even at recording in the Constitution of regulations of inclusion of internationally-legal provisions into the national legal system, **these provisions** cannot work outside of the mechanism determining their action in the internal right[13].

With reference to conventional criminally-legal provisions about the responsibility for international crimes it is impossible to realize a principle of a priority of standards of international law above provisions of the national right as the given provisions do not contain criminal sanctions. In this connection if provisions of internationally-legal convention have not been introduced in to Russian criminal legislation, a law-enforcement person it is not capable to apply the corresponding convention directly. And in this case the priority of interstate provisions in relation to standards of international law is, in fact, saved. That is nobody can be involved in the criminal liability for the act which was not stipulated by the internal criminal legislation.

The Russian Federation in 1991 (in the subsequent Constitution of the Russian Federation) provisions of international contracts a component of its legal system means a concept that a victim of a socially dangerous act recorded in criminal provision of international contract of the USSR and also international contract of the Russian Federation, in conformity with which at the moment of carrying out of the act the criminal legislation of Russia has not been given, though doesn't have has the right to count on bringing harm-doer to the criminal liability within the limits of interstate procedures, however, he has a right to restoration of the infringed legal status due to means of the state budget. Thus, a duty of the state to establish measures of protection for victims arises as result of not ensuring of the responsibility of a natural person within the limits of interstate criminal law.

Hence, the rights of victims of abuse of power arise on the basis of general condition (a concept of Russia the conventional standards of international law about human rights a source of the national right), however, as a basis (the legal fact), in one case, can act abusing power to accept normative-legal regulations which contain the provisions interfering a person to realize certain right, recorded in internationally-legal instrument, on the other it is infringement of criminal interdictions included in provisions of international contracts of the USSR (the Russian Federation) which are ratified but in conformity with which of the Criminal Code has not been given at the moment of carrying out of the act. The condition and the bases predetermining the character of actions of the obliged subjects. Thus, in the case of committing of a crime a person recognized by a verdict of court guilty in committing of a crime, has a duty to be responsible for the act (to incur legal (criminal) responsibility) and in the case of abuse of power the state has a duty to carry out measures of protection (regenerative).

Measures of protection are united with measures of the responsibility by that they also are a kind of the state compulsion, i.e. they are established by the state in legal provisions which realization in all cases is provided with compulsory force of the state. However, as it was shown above, measures of protection distinguish the bases of use from the legal responsibility.

Besides, measures of protection are directed on elimination of consequences of infringement of the human rights recorded in provisions of international instruments, on restoration of the infringed rights. Accordingly, they are turned not so much to the infringer of legal provisions, but to the authorized, to the victim and, unlike measures of the responsibility, do not attract adverse consequences for the offender (direct harm-doer).

On the basis of the abusing victims by authority persons to whom physical, property and moral damage is caused are equal to persons whose interests are threatened causing such harm by the act which is yet not breaking the criminal legislation but breaking internationally recognized provisions proclaiming the rights and freedoms of a person, or the act breaking criminal interdictions, included in provisions of international contracts, ratified by the USSR (the Russian Federation), in conformity with which the criminal legislation at the moment of their carrying out has not been given.

If the Constitution implemented the provision about the rights of victims from the Declaration of the United Nations, the approach will be preferable, allowing to identify the concept "victims of crimes", recorded in the Constitution not with criminally-remedial concept of the victim which, in our opinion, is too narrow but with "the victim of a crime", formulated in the Declaration concerns only one party suffered from crimes.

It is possible to define victims of a crime as follows, "Victims of a crime are physical and legal persons to whom physical, property and moral damage was caused and they are equal to persons whose interests are threatened by causing such harm by the act forbidden by the Criminal Code of the Russian Federation under threat of punishment and also their close relatives and dependents, in the case of death of a direct victim".

The analysis of internationally-legal documents allows to draw a conclusion that the rights of victims as human rights represent the system of the legal rights providing an opportunity of restoration of the legal status of a person, infringed by illegal behaviour. The mentioned system attributively includes guarantees of all other rights and freedoms.

The subject analysis of the rights of victims allows to emphasize their following substantial components: the right to the fair treatment; the right to access to mechanisms of justice; the right to compensation of damage from a harm-doer or from the third parties responsible for his behaviour (hereinafter referred to as third parties); the right to financial indemnification of the caused damage due to the state; the right to receive social aid.

Let's consider the constitutional provisions recording of the rights of victims, proceeding from their legal nature.

Provisions of Article 52 of the Constitution are based on the complex legal institution of victims of crimes and abuse of power. The first provision, from the point of view of a degree of definiteness, is provision-principle as it formulates only general provisions, determining the character and orientation of legal regulation of the given kind of social relations. The second provision refers to representative-binding, regulating attitude together with other provisions. The prejudicial evidence on the subject of the given constitutional rights refers to the conditions at which presence the provision can or should be realized. The provisions recording circumstances (the legal facts) at which presence the subject admits to victims from a crime or abuse of power and legal consequences in the case of infringement of a disposition of Article 52 contain in sources of other branches of the law. The disposition of rules of behaviour is of binding character. The state incurs the obligation on ensuring, warranting of the rights of victims, namely: the rights to access to justice and the rights to receive indemnification of the caused damage from a harm-doer (third parties).

At comparison of provisions of Article 52 of the Constitution with internationally-legal provisions recording the considered right, it is necessary to note that its provisions on the whole do not contradict the position expressed both in documents of the United Nations and in regional internationally-legal regulations. However, in provisions of Russian Constitution the content of the rights of victims as civil rights is recorded not completely as only two kinds of the rights are presented.

The rights of victims as civil rights are the system of the legal rights providing an opportunity of restoration of the legal status of a person, incurred harm as a result of the act forbidden by the Criminal Code of the Russian Federation under threat of punishment (or breaking criminal provisions of international contracts ratified by the USSR (the Russian Federation), in conformity with which it is not given the criminal legislation of Russia at the moment of their carrying out), by means of the system of interstate bodies on protection of civil human rights.

In theoretical meaning rights of victims civil rights consist of the same elements as human rights.

In connection with recording of the given international standard in the Constitution of Russia, the right of victims has got a new quality: they began to be the center of the legal status of victims that is why the rights of victims included in the branch Russian legislation, in aggregate concretize the content of constitutional rights of victims.

The analysis of the current legislation allows to draw a conclusion that, as a whole, victims of crimes have four kinds of the rights: the right to access to justice; the right to indemnification from a harm-doer (or from the third parties); the right to financial indemnification of the caused harm due to the state and the right to receive the social aid. Last two rights in Russian legislation are recorded to victims of acts of terrorism, besides; the right to receive the social aid is for those victims of crimes who suffered from harm to life and to health.

At victims of abusing the authority in fact, records three kinds of the rights: the right to access to justice; the right to indemnification from a harm-doer (or from the third parties); the right to receive the social aid.

In the scientific literature there were approaches to define the rights of person through competences (the right of use, the right of the requirement, the right of action, the right of claim) and through using the values. We apply the last approach, including that the formulation of the legal rights through "behavioural aspects" is hardly applicable to all elements of the system of the rights of victims, the majority of the rights concerning a category mediating social values, having and using which depends not on purposeful actions of a person but on the acts of corresponding subjects.

From these provisions the right of victims of crimes to access to justice represents an opportunity to use such complex social values that are: competence of a victim personally and actively to accuse a person caused harm as a result of act, forbidden by the Criminal Code under threat of punishment and actively to defend the legitimate interests and actions of investigation bodies and their officials on duly bringing the guilty to account.

The right of victims of crimes to access to justice includes some elements of legal rights: the right to demand suppression of criminal actions preparing or made against a victim; the right to demand bringing the guilty to account; the right to participate in criminal prosecution; the right to defend the legitimate interests at charge of a victim in illegal or immoral behaviour.

The rights of victims of crimes arise from the fact of causing damage as a result of the act forbidden by the criminal legislation. By virtue of that they have material character. There are various points of view concerning a concept of non-recognition of the victim as the subject of criminal legal relationships[14].

We completely share the arguments in favour of the concept of people suffered from a crime as subject s of criminal legal relationships and recording of their rights in the criminal legislation. The state, having imperious powers for restoration of the infringed rights for putting on criminal liability on guilty, is obliged to consider interests of a victim. Criminal legal relationships are necessary for regulation of disputed relations both between the state and the criminal and between the criminal and a victim. The new Code of Criminal Procedure of the Russian Federation for the first time recognized that criminal legal proceedings have a **purpose of** "protection of the rights and legitimate interests of persons and organizations which suffered from crimes" (Article 1, part 1 of Article 6). The given position, developing the constitutional provision of Article 52: "The rights of victims and abuse of power are protected from crimes by the state", underlies a complex of criminally-remedial provisions recording a legal status of victims of crimes.

The important element of the right to access to justice is the competence to demand bringing the guilty to account which received due settlement in the new Code of Criminal Procedure. Thus, the victim has a right to start criminal prosecution and to formulate charge on the affairs of private charge listed in part 2 of Article 20 and also on affairs of private-public charge (part 3 of Article 20) which, however, are not subject to the termination in connection with reconciliation, except for the cases stipulated by Article 25 of the Code of Criminal Procedure. One of the elements of the right of victims on access to justice is the competence to participate in criminal prosecution (charge) of a person who has committed a crime. For a long time in jurisprudence a notion about exclusively public character of criminal prosecution and the circle of its subjects joined only the inspector (body of inquiry) and the public prosecutor existed.

In works of last years the victim is recognized as a subject of criminal prosecution within the limits of the procedural rights given to him[15]. Within the limits of criminally-remedial relations and according to the Code of Criminal Procedure of RSFSR, the victim had the right to present evidence; to declare petitions; to get acquainted with all materials of case from the moment of the end of preliminary investigation; to participate in proceeding, to declare removals, to complain to a verdict. The rights and duties of the inspector were the following: to ask questions to a person with whom the confrontation (Article 163) is carried out; to make remarks which are a subject to introducing in the report of investigatory action in which the victim takes part (Article 141). During proceeding they have a right to interrogate the defendant (Article 280), witnesses (Article 283), to represent in written form questions to the expert for drawing up of the conclusion by the latter (Article 288), to interrogate the expert (Article 289), to examine the material evidences (Article 291) and an area or a premise, in case the court recognizes the given investigatory action necessary (Article 293).

In the new Code of Criminal Procedure of the Russian Federation for the first time in section "Substantive Provisions" the base competence of victims is recorded as the right to participate in criminal prosecution of the accused (Article 22) and a complex of the rights of victims on participation in criminal prosecution considerably is expanded, it causes also its reference to participants of criminal legal proceedings from charge (Ch. 6). Thus, in conformity with Article 42 of the new Code of Criminal Procedure of the Russian Federation, the victim has a right to know about the charge of the accused, to participate in the investigatory actions made under his petition or the petition of his Commissioner under the sanction of the investigator, to support charge. If in the operating Code of Criminal Procedure the victim has a right to get acquainted with all materials of case from the moment of the end of preliminary investigation, according to Article 42, they have a right to get acquainted with reports of the investigatory actions made with their participation and to make remarks and also with the decision about purpose of judicial examination and the conclusion of the expert, has a right to receive copies of decisions about instituting of criminal case. The victim leveled with other participants of process is distinguished by the right to collect and represent written evidence and subjects for familiarizing with the criminal case as evidence (Article 86).

The Code of Criminal Procedure of the Russian Federation (2001) records a number of the important guarantees of the rights of victims on access to justice among which it is necessary to emphasize the right of suffered to use free of charge the help of a translator, the right to use security measures concerning victims and also their close relatives, relatives or close persons, at presence of sufficient data about threats of murder, use of violence or damage of property.

The increase in the rights of the victim as a side of charge has soundly entailed the recorded measures of responsibility which can be assigned to them in the case of abusing these rights. Thus, according to Article 75, the prejudicial evidence of the victim based on a guess, assumption is considered in admissible evidence. In the cases stipulated in the Code of Criminal Procedure, the investigator, the inspector, the public prosecutor or the court has a right to apply to the victim a measure of remedial compulsion in the form of the obligation about appearance, a drive and monetary collecting (Article 111).

Last years after accepting of the new Code of Criminal Procedure of the Russian Federation science officers and lawyers-experts stated the proved court decisions that the rights of victims in comparison with the rights of the accused are restrained in them. The mechanism of realization of the rights of victims in the Code of Criminal Procedure of the Russian Federation (2001) in detail is not registered. We support assumptions of their equation with the rights of the accused, in particular, about the right to use services of a free lawyer[16]. And it is necessary, for the number of crimes against a person in Russia increases.

Material consequences of a crime can be considered in two aspects: harm and damage as different sides of the same phenomena. Firstly, the crime to a person causes "harm". Harm in civil law is understood as adverse changes in the values protected by the law which can be both property and non-property, it "is compensated". Secondly, material consequences can be considered in terms of money – it is damage. The legislation knows three kinds of harm: property, physical and moral (Article 53 the Code of Criminal Procedure). Physical harm in jurisprudence is understood as set of evenly happened changes in a status of a person as physical essence or creation of threat of such changes.

I.M. Erdelevsky considers that physical harm from the point of view of causing is simultaneously material as negative changes happening in an organism, lead to negative changes in the property sphere of a person and non-property as the changes lead to negative changes in a status of mental well-being of the victim[17]. Changes in the property sphere are expressed in loss of earnings by victim or means of subsistence persons who are being on its expense but had the right on reception from them means for existence and also the charges suffered on recovery of health and in the case of death of a victim is charges on its burial. Hence, physical harm is compensated by indemnification of moral damage, the reimbursement suffered as a result victimization (the charges carried out for relations, the strengthened food, sanatorium relations and (or) burial), compensation of the missed benefit, granting of services (recovery of health of a victim by forces harm-doer).

Moral damage is determined in the legal literature otherwise. One authors understand the harm as am, caused abuse, to dignity[18], others is infringement of a mental status of a person[19]. The concept of moral damage of the legislation, of the most general form, opens part1 Article 151 the Civil Code of the Russian Federation.

The developed definition gives Plenum of the Supreme Court of the Russian Federation: "Moral damage are the moral or physical sufferings caused by actions (inactivity), encroaching on belonging to a citizen from birth or by virtue of the law the non-material values (life, health, dignity of a person, business reputation, personal privacy, personal and family secrecy, etc.) or breaking his personal non-right of property (the right to using the name, a copyright and other non-right of property according to laws on protection of the rights to results of intellectual activity) or breaking right of property of a citizen.

Moral damage, in particular, can consist in moral experiences in connection with loss of relatives, impossibility to continue an active social life, loss of work, disclosing of family, medical secrecy, distribution of data mismatching the reality discrediting honour, dignity or business reputation of a citizen, time limitation or deprivation of any rights, the physical pain connected with the caused mutilation, other damage of health or in connection with the disease born as a result of moral sufferings, etc."[20] According to Article 1101 of the Civil Code of the Russian Federation moral damage is subject to compensation in the monetary form irrespective of property damage subject compensation.

In connection with that that both physical and moral damage are compensated in the monetary form, in the decision of a question of unity or differentiation of the given legal institutions in a domestic science various court decisions are stated. In opinion of I.M. Erdelevsky, "mediated through compensation of property damage compensation of organic harm is directed on elimination or easing of dysfunctions of an organism or their external displays while indemnification of moral damage is directed on elimination or smoothing of experiences and the sufferings connected with causing damage to an organism of a person"[21]. As at realization of the right to indemnification of moral damage the victim pursues the independent interest, the given right we emphasize as one of competences in constitutional law of victims for indemnification.

In the content of the right to indemnification from the offender or persons bearing the responsibility for its behaviour, it is possible to mark out: the right to return of the property; the right to compensate the cost of the lost property; the right to reimbursement, suffered as a result of victimization; the right to receive the missed benefit; the right to indemnification of moral damage; the right to granting of services (restoration of a property status or health of a victim); the right to restoration in the rights.

The given right mediates the complex social values of property; the sums of money making: cost of the lost property, the charges made for restoration of the infringed right (for example, the sums of charges carried out for relations, on restoration of the damaged property, etc.), not received in comes (for example, the sum of the lost earnings, etc.), additional losses (for example, the sums of charges on the food, sanatorium, etc.); compensatory payments for the suffered moral and physical sufferings; actions on granting services and restoration in the rights.

In the Soviet jurisprudence disagreements were observed at the decision of a question of indemnification of moral damage. Thus, S.A. Aleksandrov considered practically impossible, proceeding from features of criminal case, a degree and character of moral sufferings, a property status of the victim and doer, to determine the size of monetary compensation for the caused mental cruelty, moreover, the idea of indemnification of moral damage on the essence admitted to him bourgeois, alien to the Soviet society[22].

O.S. Ioffe who supposed compensation of moral damage even by way of criminal legal proceedings referred to the number of supporters of the opposite point of view[23]. Under the fair remark I. M. Belyakova, collecting of material means in favour of the victim in compensation of moral damage it is directed on smoothing the inconveniences which have arisen at them, to enable suffered to satisfy usual vital needs which they have lost because of the received mutilation, losses of the close person or the suffered property losses[24].

Institution of indemnification of moral damage in Russian legislation is rather new. Before acceptance of the Civil Code of the Russian Federation the provision about compensation of moral damage contained in Article 131 of Bases of the civil legislation 1991 unlike Article 131 of Bases which provided an opportunity of the victim to receive indemnification of moral damage in all cases of its infringement both property and non-property right, Article 151 and after it Article 1099 of the Civil Code of the Russian Federation establish an opportunity of indemnification of moral damage when it is caused by the actions breaking a personal non-right of property (values) and indemnification of the moral damage caused by infringement of right of property of citizens, it is supposed only in the cases specially stipulated by the law. It is understood as a law according to Clause 2 of Article 3 of the Civil Code of the Russian Federation and the Federal law accepted according to them. Such law is the law of the Russian Federation "Protection of Consumer Rights".

Concerning victims of a crime it is explained in the indicated decision of Plenum of the Supreme Court of the Russian Federation: "With reference to clause 29 of the Code of Criminal Procedure of RSFSR the victim that is a person, to whom the crime causes moral, physical or property damage (clause 53 of the Code of Criminal Procedure of RSFSR), has a right to start a civil suit about indemnification of moral damage by conducting of a criminal case"[25]. In part 3 of Article 42 of the Code of Criminal Procedure (2001) the right of the victim to compensation of moral damage in the monetary form are directly recorded for the first time: "Under the claim of the victim for compensation of the moral damage in money terms caused to him the size of compensation is determined by court by consideration of criminal case or by way of civil legal proceedings". From provisions of the Civil Code it follows that victims of crimes have the right to indemnification of moral damage if socially dangerous act are infringed or threatened by infringement rights of a person. Thus, if concerning a person one of socially dangerous acts, stipulated by Article 158 (theft), Article 159 (swindle), Article 160 (assignment or waste), Article 161 (robbery), except for Article part 2 of Article 161, Article 164 (plunder of the subjects having special value), Article 165 (causing of property damage by a deceit or breach of confidence), Article 166 (illegal taking of a car or another vehicle without the purpose of plunder), Article 167 (deliberate destruction or damage of property) and a number of other acts stipulated by the Criminal Code, which object are only rights of property of the victim, they does not have the right to indemnification of moral damage.

The right to indemnification to victims of crimes is provided as follows: establishment of a rule according to which the state is directly obliged to compensate the harm caused by officials of the state bodies and institutions of local government; establishment of the responsibility of the employer for the harm caused by its worker; indemnification to persons to whom the damage at attempt to assist is caused to a direct victim of a crime. Besides, victims enduring harm to life or to health at execution of duties under a labour contract, acquired the right to compensation of this harm by granting in full all kinds of ensuring on insurance, including the payment of expenses for medical, social and professional rehabilitation according to the Federal law of the Russian Federation dd. July, 24, 1998 # 125 "Obligatory Social Insurance from Accidents and Occupational Diseases".

Article 1069 of the Civil Code of the Russian Federation stipulated extra-contractee responsibility of the Russian Federation, its subjects and municipal institutions for harm, caused to a citizen or a legal person by illegal actions (inactivity) of the state bodies, institutions of local government and also their officials. I.N. Polyakov names special conditions of the responsibility of the state: actions of the mentioned bodies and officials should be given the shape the instrument of authority which can be both normative and not normative; the instrument of authority should be published by the guilty official or group of the officials forming joint body; officials, publishing imperious instruments are obliged to execute the service powers[26]. Illegality of instruments can be expressed in limitation or deprivation of citizens or organizations of any rights (for example, infringement of equality of citizens is part 2 of Article 136 of the Criminal Code, infringement of personal privacy - part 2 of Article 137 of the Criminal Code, infringement of inviolability of dwelling is part 3 of Article 139 of the Criminal Code; hindrance of lawful enterprise activity is Article 169 of the Criminal Code, etc.).

The bases of compensation of the harm caused by illegal actions of inquiry agencies, preliminary investigation, Office of Public Prosecutor and court are established in Article 1070 of the Civil Code of the Russian Federation. The victim from illegal actions of officials of law-enforcement and judicial bodies has a provisional list of property losses, the right to which compensation, in particular, victims of crimes stipulated by Article 299, 301, 305 of the Criminal Code of the Russian Federation, is given in "Regulation of the procedure of compensation of the damage, caused to a citizen by illegal actions of inquiry agencies, preliminary investigation, Office of Public Prosecutor and court", approved by the Decree of Presidium of the Supreme Soviet of the USSR dd. May, 18th, 1981[27].

The victim, first of all, has a right to demand compensation of earnings and other labour incomes. Plenum of the Supreme Court of the USSR, explaining the order of compensation of material harm, indicated, "The Damage caused by loss of earnings and other labour incomes in connection with illegal bringing to the criminal or administrative responsibility or illegal condemnation, is subject to compensation during holding in custody as the preventive punishment, serving sentence in the form of imprisonment or corrective works, during discharge from a post under the decision of the inspector or the public prosecutor, a finding on stationary examination and in time during which a citizen was absent from work in connection with his call in bodies of investigation or in court as of the suspected, of the accused, the defendant.

The damage is subject to compensation also in time from the date of declaration of the verdict of "not guilty" and up to its introduction into dignity and in time, during which (within the limits of established by Article 5 of three-month term) a citizen took measures to restoration of his infringed labour rights, before acceptance by administration of the enterprise of the decision on this question in the established monthly term"[28].

In due time L.V. Boitsova noted that the tendency of narrow interpretation of the concept "causal relationship" reflected in the decision of Plenum between illegal actions of law enforcement bodies and deprivation of a citizen of earnings and other incomes as loss of work can be consequence not only discharges from work under the initiative of bodies of investigation but also the fact of bringing to account. The given drawback is eliminated in provisions of the new Code of Criminal Procedure of the Russian Federation, recording of the rights of the rehabilitated. Thus, according to Article 1, part 1 of Article 135 compensation of property damage to the rehabilitated includes compensation of wages, pension, grants, and other funds which they have lost as a result of the criminal prosecution. Thus, the concept of "criminal prosecution" is wider in comparison with the concept of "bringing to account" as it represents the remedial activity which is carried out by the party of charge with a view of exposure of the suspected crime of the accused.

Are subject to return of the number of the criminalities claimed on the basis of a verdict of court on criminal case or the decision and also: claimed under the civil suit; brought by them by way of voluntary indemnification or on demand of administration in a place of work; payment of a fare in connection with calls to judicial-investigatory bodies; hiring of premises; payment of legal aid[29]. The victim should be returned: confiscated movable and real estate; the subjects filed as material evidences; things on which imprisonment in ensuring of the civil suit was imposed and also the withdrawn money, currency, securities and contributions together with the prizes which dropped out on them and the added interests. Movable and the real estate, material evidences should be returned to a nature and in the case of their damage, losses or destructions their cost on the market prices should be paid.

In the new Code of Criminal Procedure of the Russian Federation for the first time at a legislative level the complex of the provisions regulating the right of property on compensation property and moral damage and also on restoration of labour, pension, housing and other rights is recorded.

The right to receive social aid is also not a uniform legal right as its material content is made by the following competences: the right to the information on presence of the social aid; the right to receive material aid; the right to receive medical aid; the right to receive psychological help; the right to receive legal aid (the information on the rights and the help during legal proceedings); the right to receive the information for prevention of victimization.

The right to receive financial indemnification of the caused harm due to the state consists of two elements: the right to financial indemnification of the charges suffered as a result victimization and the right to financial indemnification of cost of lost property.

In connection with the situation which has developed in the country caused by confrontations in territory of Republics Dagestan, the Chechen Republic, barbarous acts of terrorism in the cities of Budyonnovsk, Buinaksk, Moscow, Volgodonsk, Volgograd, the provisions assigning to the state a duty to compensate harm to victims, caused as a result of act of terrorism have appeared in Russian legislation.

Comparison of provisions of instruments of the Government of the Russian Federation and the Federal law of the Russian Federation

"Struggle against Terrorism"[30] shows that the state incurs the obligation of indemnification of the caused damage only in case when the victim cannot receive indemnification from a harm-doer that unites the given documents with internationally-legal regulations in the given sphere (the Declaration, the European Convention "Indemnification for Victims of Grave Crimes") in attempt to decide the acute problem of indemnification in the case of indetermination of a person who has committed a crime. Thus, it is a question not of clearing guilty from the responsibility but about the replacement of a subject, authorized to receive the compensation: rather than the victim it becomes or the Russian Federation, or the subject of the Russian Federation.

Legal regulations are uniform and that in the case of death of a direct victim or essential undermining of his physical or mental health as a result of a grave crime the state is obliged to compensate damage to the family of a victim, in particular to his dependents. In the Governmental order of the Russian Federation dd. January, 23rd, 1996, # 58[31] lump-sum compensatory payments is determined in conformity with a degree of weight of a physical injury, proceeding from the established minimal monthly payment.

According to orders of the Government of the Russian Federation dd. September, 22nd, 1999 1499 and dd. September, 23rd, 1999 #1503, compensatory payments for the lost members of the family and the damage, rendered to health of citizens injured with act of terrorism in Volgodonsk on September, 16th, 1999 and acts of terrorism in Botlihsky and Tsumadinsky areas of Republic Dagestan in August, 1999, should be made by way of and on the conditions stipulated by the governmental order of the Russian Federation dd. January, 23rd, 1996 #58.

The procedure of realization of the right to receive the social aid for victims of terrorism is certain in the governmental order of the Russian Federation dd. February, 6th, 2001 #90 according to the law of the Russian Federation "Struggle against Terrorism"[32].

Theoretically, victims of abuse of power have all complex of the rights of victims of crimes. However, in the content of the separate competences making in aggregate the rights of victims of crimes and abusing by authority, there are certain features. If the victim of a crime at realization of the right to access to justice mediates the moral-psychological interest consisting of establishment of dignity which in this case is understood as condemnation, punishment of a person guilty of causing damage and clearing from the criminal liability of the innocent, a victim of abuse of power, addressing in bodies of justice, pursues the purpose to rehabilitate;

to establish the fact of causing damage as a result of the act which yet has been not criminalized in the national criminal legislation but breaks internationally recognized provisions.

Let's emphasize two kinds of victims of abusing by authority: victims of political reprisals and victims of use the forbidden means and methods of conducting war during settlement of the crisis in the Chechen Republic.

To persons referring to the first group, harm is caused as a result of condemnation on the basis of the normative-legal instrument in a rank of a crime realization of human rights, or use reprisals on the basis of the statutory act on political grounds, than roughly broken internationally recognized provisions proclaiming human rights.

To persons referring to the second group, harm is caused as a result of the act breaking criminal interdictions, included in provisions of international contracts ratified by the USSR, in conformity with which the criminal legislation at the moment of their carrying out has not been given.

According to provisions of international humanitarian law, the armed conflict in the Chechen Republic (1994-1996) can be determined as a confrontation of not international character as it completely corresponds to the attributes stated in Report II to the Geneva Convention dd. August, 12th, 1949. Thus, on the Chechen conflict the provisions stated in the Additional report, concerning protection of victims of confrontations of not international character in which criminal interdictions of use the forbidden means and methods of conducting war are recorded extend. The given international legal instrument was ratified by the Supreme Soviet of the USSR on August, 4th, 1989; however, the indicated requirements of the Geneva Conventions (1949) are realized in Russian criminal legislation only in 1997, with introduction in action new of the Criminal Code of the Russian Federation, providing in Article 356 the corresponding structure of a crime.

The content of the right of victims on access to justice is made by the following competences: the right to demand rehabilitation (a concept of suffered from political reprisals); the right to demand establishment of the fact of causing property damage as a result of the Chechen conflict; the right to participate during rehabilitation; the right to participate in confirmation of the fact of causing of property harm.

Legal rehabilitation of the collective subject of the right of victims (people, nations, etc.) is carried out not by officials of the state bodies as rehabilitation of citizens on political grounds but by the legislator and its legal bases have been incorporated by the law of RSFSR "Rehabilitation of People Subjected to Repression" dd. April, 24th, 1991, in edition of the law dd. July, 1st, 1993. Legal rehabilitation happens in two stages. The content of the first is the legislative cancelling of all illegal regulations accepted concerning subjected to repression people. Thus, Article 12 of the law says: "All instruments of allied, republican and local bodies and the officials, accepted concerning subjected to repression people, except for the instruments restoring their rights, admit unconstitutional and become invalid". The content of the second is legal rehabilitation of all people separately. Clause 1 of the law contains a legislative imperative about rehabilitation of all subjected to repression people and is a basis for the edition of normative-legal regulations about personal legal rehabilitation of all people.

The material content of the right to indemnification of individual subjects of the rights of victims of political reprisals is made by the following competences: the right to return the property; the right to compensation of the cost of the lost property; the right to monetary indemnification of property harm; the right to restoration in the rights.

The material content of the right to indemnification of collective subjects of the rights of victims of political reprisals is made by the following competences: the right to restoration in the rights (political, cultural, etc.) and the right to compensation of property harm.

The special role in ensuring and protection of the rights of victims of abusing by authority is played by administratively-legal and remedial guarantees. In the system of the rehabilitation legislation first of all we should emphasize Laws of RSFSR "Rehabilitation of Victims of Political Reprisals" and "Rehabilitation of People Subjected to Repression" and also by-law instruments of the Government of the Russian Federation: "Regulations of the Procedure of Return to Citizens of Illegally Confiscated, Withdrawn or Otherwise Left Property in Connection with Political Reprisals, Compensation of its Cost or Payment of Monetary Indemnification", approved by the decision dd. August, 12th 1994; "Regulations of the Procedure of Granting of Privileges to the Rehabilitated Persons and Persons Recognized as Suffered from Political Reprisals", approved by the decision dd. May, 3rd, 1994. In the given normative-legal regulations (and many other things, making the rehabilitation legislation) the rights of victims of the given category are indicated, a group of obliged persons and their powers are detailed, the order of realization of the rights is remedially determined.

The procedure of realization of the rights of the suffered during the crisis in the Chechen Republic is established in by-law instruments, in particular "Procedure of Payment of Indemnification for the Lost Habitation and (or) Property to the Citizens Suffered during the Crisis in the Chechen Republic", approved by the governmental order of the Russian Federation dd. April, 30th, 1997.

In jurisprudence the question of referring the rights on protection of other rights and freedoms to a certain group of writes has not been solved yet. In our opinion, it is necessary to agree with the point of view of the scientists (L.D. Voevodin, S.F. Kechekjan, etc.), defending notion of five-steps classification of the rights on spheres of realization the rights on protection of other rights and freedoms are not introduced: the right to the complaint, the right to the judicial claim, the rights of the accused and, in particular, the rights of victims. The given group of rights should be made for frameworks of the standard classification on the civil, political, social and economic and cultural rights, uniting them into the group of the rights-guarantees on the relation to the whole complex of civil human rights.

Notes

1. See: Recommendation R (85 11 by the state of victims within the limits of criminal law and process (1985); Recommendation R (87 21 Help to Victims and Prevention of Victimization (1987) // Russian Justice. 1997.7. / См.: Рекомендация R (85)11 по положению потерпевших в рамках уголовного права и процесса (1985 г.); Рекомендация R (87)21 о помощи потерпевшим и предотвращении виктимизации (1987 г.) // Российская юстиция. 1997. № 7.

2. The Declaration of Main Principles of Justice for Victims of Crimes and Abuses of Power; the Additional Protocol to the Geneva Convention dd. August, 12, 1949, concerning the protection of victims of international confrontations; the Additional Protocol to the Geneva Conventions dd. August, 12, 1949, concerning the protection of victims of internal confrontations. / Декларация основных принципов правосудия для жертв преступлений и злоупотреблений властью; Дополнительный протокол к Женевским конвенциям от 12 августа 1949 г., касающийся защиты жертв международных вооруженных конфликтов; Дополнительный протокол к Женевским конвенциям от 12 августа 1949 г., касающийся защиты жертв вооруженных конфликтов немеждународного характера.

3. The Declaration of Rights and Freedom of a Person and a Citizen of Russia; Rehabilitation of Victims of Political Reprisals: the Law of RSFSR; Assistance to the Persons Becoming the Victims of the Terrorist Act in Budennovsk of Stavropol Territory: the Decree of the President of the Russian Federation dd. June, 19, 1995. / Декларация прав и свобод человека и гражданина России; О реабилитации жертв политических репрессий: Закон РСФСР; Об оказании помощи лицам, ставшим жертвами террористического акта в г. Буденовске Ставропольского края: Указ Президента РФ от 19 июня 1995 г.

4. Stetsovsky J.I. The Soviet Legal Profession. Moscow, 1989. P.276. / Стецовский Ю. И. Советская адвокатура. М., 1989. С. 276.

5. International norms on human rights and their application by courts of the Russian Federation: Practical booklet. Moscow. 1996. P.12. / Международные нормы о правах человека и применение их судами Российской Федерации: Практ. пособие. М. 1996. С. 12.

6. Strogovich M.S. The Course of the Soviet Criminal Procedure. Moscow, 1968. P.253. / Строгович М. С. Курс советского уголовного процесса. М., 1968. С. 253.

7. The Constitution of the Russian Federation. The Comment / Editors: V.A. Topornin. M. Baturin. R.G. Orehov. Moscow, 1994. P.277. / Конституция РФ. Комментарий / Ред. Б. А. Топорнин, Ю. М. Батурин, Р. Г. Орехов. М., 1994. С. 277.

8. See: Voevodin L. D. The Legal Status of a Person in Russia: Studies. Moscow, 1997. P.147. / См.: Воеводин Л. Д. Юридический статус личности в России: Учеб. пособие. М., 1997. С. 147.

9. Naumov A.V. Crimes Against Peace and Safety of a Person and International Crimes // State and Law. 1995.#6. P.55. /Наумов А. В. Преступления против мира и безопасности человека и преступления международного характера // Государство и право. 1995. № 6. С. 55.

10. See: Ibidem.

11. Article 5 states: «The listed acts are recognized as not having social danger and persons condemned for them shall be rehabilitated irrespective of actual validity of charge: Anti-soviet propaganda and propagation; Distribution of false fabrications discrediting the Soviet State or social order ... »

12. Lunev V.V. Political Criminality // State and Law. 1994.# 7. P.111 / Лунев В. В. Политическая преступность // Государство и право. 1994. № 7. С. 111.

13. So, Article 5 of the Law of the Russian Federation «International Treaties of the Russian Federation» dd. June, 16, 1995 establishes that provisions of officially published international treaties which are not requiring issuing of interstate acts for application, act in the Russian Federation directly, and for realization of other provisions of international treaties corresponding legal acts shall be passed.

14. See: Bozhiev V.P. Criminally-Remedial Legal Relations. Moscow, 1975. P.117. / См.: Божьев В. П. Уголовно-процессуальные правоотношения. М., 1975. С. 117.

15. See: Sheifer S. A., Petrova N.E. Problems of Procedure Reforming in the Cases of Request of the Aggrieved Party in the Spirit of Expansion of Private Basis in the Criminal Procedure of the Russian Federation // State and Law. 1999. # 6. P.51-56. / См.: Шейфер С. А., Петрова Н. Е. Проблемы реформирования производства по делам частного обвинения в духе расширения частных начал в уголовном процессе РФ // Государство и право. 1999. № 6. С. 51–56.

16. See: Shestakova T. The Violated Rights of the Victims // Legality. 2003. # 8. P.21, 22; Koretsky D. Are Measures of Crime Control Adequate to its Condition // Legality. 2003. # 2. P.27-29. / См.: Шестакова Т. Ущемленные права потерпевших // Законность. 2003. № 8. С. 21, 22; Корецкий Д. Адекватны ли меры борьбы с преступностью ее состоянию // Законность. 2003. № 2. С. 27–29.

17. See: Erdelevsky A.M. Indemnification of Moral Harm: Analysis and Comment of the Legislation and the Judiciary Law. Moscow, 1999. P.3. / См.: Эрделевский А. М. Компенсация морального вреда: анализ и комментарий законодательства и судебной практики. М., 1999. С. 3.

18. See: Kuznetsova N.F. Crime and Criminality. Moscow, 1969. P.52. / См.: Кузнецова Н. Ф. Преступление и преступность. М., 1969. С. 52.

19. See: Dubrivny V.A. A Victim on Preliminary Investigation. Saratov, 1966. P.10. / См.: Дубривный В. А. Потерпевший на предварительном следствии. Саратов, 1966. С. 10.

20. Some questions of application of legislation on indemnification of moral harm: Decree of Plenum of the Supreme Court of the Russian Federation dd. December, 20, 1994 # 10 // Report of the Supreme Court of the Russian Federation. 1995. # 3.

21. Erdelevsky A.M. Specified work. P.5. / Эрделевский А. М. Указ. соч. С. 5.

22. See: Alexandrov S.A. Legal Warranties of Reimbursement of Damage in the Criminal Procedure. Gorki, 1976. P.22. / См.: Александров С. А. Правовые гарантии возмещения ущерба в уголовном процессе. Горький, 1976. С. 22.

23. See: Ioffe O.S. Protection of Honour and Dignity of Citizens // Soviet State and Law. 1962. # 7. / См.: Иоффе О. С. Охрана чести и достоинства граждан // Советское государство и право. 1962. № 7.

24. See: Belyakova A.M. Property Responsibility for Damnified. Moscow, 1979. P.10. / См.: Белякова А. М. Имущественная ответственность за причиненный вред. М., 1979. С. 10.

25. The Report of the Supreme Court of the Russian Federation. 1995.3. / Бюллетень Верховного Суда РФ. 1995. № 3.

26. See: Polyakov I.N. Responsibility under Obligations as a Result of Injury. Moscow, 1998. P.53-54. / См.: Поляков И. Н. Ответственность по обязательствам вследствие причинения вреда. М., 1998. С. 53–54.

27. Sheets of the Supreme Soviet of the USSR. 1981. # 21. Clause 741. / Ведомости Верховного Совета СССР. 1981. № 21. Ст. 741.

28. The Report of the Supreme Court of the USSR. 1989. # 1. P.10. / Бюллетень Верховного Суда СССР. 1989. № 1. С. 10.

29. See: The Report of the Supreme Court of the USSR. 1989. # 1. P.10-14. / См.: Бюллетень Верховного Суда СССР. 1989. № 1. С. 10–14.

30. Struggle against Terrorism: the Federal act of the Russian Federation dd. July, 25, 1998 130-Federal Law // Assembly of the legislation of the Russian Federation. 1998.31. Item 3808. / О борьбе с терроризмом: Федеральный закон РФ от 25 июля 1998 г. № 130-ФЗ // Собрание законодательства Российской Федерации. 1998. № 31. Ст. 3808.

31. Assistance to persons who have become victims of the terrorist act in January, 1996 in Republic Dagestan: the Governmental order of the Russian Federation dd. January, 23rd, 1996 # 58 // Assembly of the legislation of the Russian Federation. 1996.5. Article 483. / Об оказании помощи лицам, ставшим жертвами террористического акта в январе 1996 г. в Республике Дагестан: Постановление Правительства РФ от 23 января 1996 г. № 58 // Собрание законодательства РФ. 1996. № 5. Ст. 483.

32. Procedure of social rehabilitation of persons injured as a result of an act of terrorism: the Governmental order of the Russian Federation dd. February, 6th, 2001 # 90 // Rossiiskaya Gazeta. 2001. Feb.,10. / О порядке осуществления социальной реабилитации лиц, пострадавших в результате террористической акции: Постановление Правительства РФ от 6 февраля 2001 г. № 90 // Российская газета. 2001. 10 февр.

Chapter 12. ENFORCEMENT OF CIVIL RIGHTS
OF THE CONDEMNED

The problem of the rights of the condemned to imprisonment became a point of issue in a society and then and a theoretical and scientific research in the end 80-90-s of the last century, when domestic corrective-labour (today it is criminally-executive) system under pressure of the world and Russian public became more open, "transparent", has appeared an opportunity of receive the information, let not always quite authentic and objective, about activity of organizations and the bodies executing punishment which testified to existence of serious problems in places of imprisonment. Major of them represented the problem of ensuring of the legal status of the condemned is human rights and their other legal rights, legitimate interests and legal duties which make a legal status of this category of citizens of Russia.

According to theory of criminal law-executive the *legal status of the condemned* is "based on generally status of citizens of Russia and position determined by means of legal provisions of the condemned during criminal sentence"[1].

Any person has three versions of the legal status: a general legal status of a person and a citizen, a special legal status as Commissioner of certain category, group of persons and also an individual legal status.

The legal status of the condemned is also considered similarly. Being a person and a citizen of the state, they use general civil rights, simultaneously being the subject of the special rights connected with conditions of the punishment and individual rights caused by socially-demographic features of a person (sex, age, a state of health, etc.) and behaviour during punishment.

Within the limits of the declared subject we should consider the problem of ensuring only one element of the legal status of the condemned, i.e. their *legal rights* under which, by definition of the professor V.I. Seliverstov, it is necessary to understand "granting of the condemned real opportunities of certain behaviour and using the social values. Which is provided by legal duties of administration of the bodies executing punishment and other subjects of legal relationships"[2]?

According to the theory of human rights and constitutional law the civil, political, social, economic and cultural rights are distinguished. We should stick to the analysis of process of enforcement of civil rights of the condemned (the right to life and respect of dignity of a person, inadmissibility of torture, violence, cruel or degrading treatment or punishment, freedom of conscience, etc.), i.e. civil human rights, stipulated by Articles 20-29 of the Constitution of the Russian Federation.

The indicated rights form a legal basis of the status of any person and a citizen, they are not subject to limitation (except for the cases specially stipulated in the legislation as it concerns the condemned to imprisonment); the majority of them have an absolute character, a high degree of protection and ensuring[3].

Preservation for the condemned of citizenship, warranting of its civil rights theoretically has a deep social meaning. The state, punishing the criminal, pursues the purpose not to punish him (though the term "penalty" has disappeared from Russian legal terms), but to raise educational potential of punishment, to generate civil qualities of the condemned, to impart feeling of responsibility and respect for the law and people to them.

Process of enforcement of civil rights of the condemned can be divided in to three stages:

1) Declaring or warranting of the rights and freedoms of a person and a citizen at international and national levels;

2) Legislative recording - development of the mechanism of enforcement of the rights and freedoms in laws and by-law normative legal regulations;

3) Practical realization is enforcement of civil rights of the condemned during serving sentence.

Only at presence of these three components and under condition of their effective realization it is possible to speak about original enforcement of civil rights of the condemned.

The first stage is *declaring* that is a formulation of the basic civil rights in internationally-legal regulations, being a component of Russian legal system and also in the Constitution of the Russian Federation.

Internationally-legal documents on human rights, struggle against criminality and treatment of offenders were developed during long-term international cooperation and have incorporated the huge experience which was saved by a human civilization and the various bases of classification are accepted by internationally-legal regulations: on specialization (general, or universal and specialized), on scales of action (universal and regional), on compulsion (included provisions-principles and pro-visions-recommendations), etc[4]. We should address to consideration of documents, dividing them on two basic groups: general, or universal and specialized and should analyze them only in that respect in which they concern the civil rights of imprisoned persons making the significant scope of legal provisions in rather various forms.

In the first group it is especially necessary to emphasize the Universal Declaration of Human Rights (1948) which proclaimed such vital rights as a right to life (Article 3), the right not to be subjected to torture, cruel treatment, inhuman or degrading or punishment (Article 5), freedom of thought, conscience and religion (Article 18). We deliberately do not quote the clauses of the Universal Declaration formulating the right of a person to freedom of movement, to non-interference in private or family life and a number of other civil rights as according to Russian legislation which will be analyzed below, these rights of the condemned are limited by a verdict of court to punishment in the form of imprisonment.

In the context of our research the major is the International Covenant on Civil and Political Rights (1966) which value consists of "… not only that … it at a higher level, with a greater degree of detailed elaboration and a detail, than in the Universal Declaration … has determined international standards in the considered area but also that … it is an international contract included legally obligatory provisions for its participants and establishing certain procedures of its realization"[5]. At the analysis of certain provisions of the given covenant attracts attention first of all to Article 6, included the important provisions concerning the status of persons, whose rights are limited by criminal justice. In particular, it is guaranteed in the right to life.

Clause 7 of the Covenant says about inadmissibility of torture, cruel, inhuman treatment or punishment, medical or scientific experiments without free consent of a person.

In clause 10 the right of imprisoned persons to humane treatment and respect of the dignity inherent in a human being is recorded. In this clause it is specially emphasized that the penal system should provide such regime of the content of the condemned, "which essential purpose is their correction and social re-education".

Thus, International Covenant on Civil and Political Rights has not only recorded the basic civil human rights (of the condemned, in particular) but also has planned ways and means of their ensuring during serving sentence by means of creation of certain regime requirements which should be analyzed with reference to the Russian criminally-executive system.

Among universal international instruments it is also necessary to emphasize the Declaration on Protection of All Persons from Being Subjected to Torture and Other Cruel, Inhuman or Degrading Treatment or Punishment (1975) and also the Convention against Torture (1984) which start with the Universal Declaration and international Covenant on Civil and Political Rights. Doubtless dignity of the Declaration is that fact that in it (Article 1) the concept "torture" is characterized.

Unlike the Declaration, the Convention against Torture contains legally obligatory for the states - members of the United Nations position and also determines the mechanism of international reaction to actions of the separate states breaking the given Convention.

In the Code of Conduct for Law Enforcement Officials (1979), developed on the basis of Article 10 of the Universal Declaration of Human Rights and Article 14 of International Covenant on Civil and Political Rights the basic requirements to moral and professional qualities of officials of bodies and organizations executing punishment are formulated: they should observe provisions of moral and ethics, to have necessary vocational training, to have skills of dialogue and cooperation with the public, etc.

First of all, the Code determines that at performance of law enforcement duties the officials "shall respect and protect human dignity and uphold the human rights of all persons" (Article 2). In the comment to given clause the link to the major documents of the United Nations which were analyzed by us above is made and also the requirement to the states about necessity to specify in national comments the regional or national provisions establishing and protecting these rights contains. In the Code inadmissibility of use force without the objective and lawful bases (Article 3), as well as torture, cruel or degrading treatment and punishment (Article 5) is also emphasized. The requirement to ensure the provision of health protection and to render medical aid to all persons is obligatory.

Among specialized internationally-legal documents it is necessary to mark out, first of all, the Minimal standard rules of treatment of prisoners (1955) that is not an international agreement and has only recommendatory character. As it was noted in resolution ECOSOC 663 "C" (the 21V) on July, 31st, 1957, the United Nations "... pay attention of the governments to these Rules and recommends ... to concern benevolently to their acceptance and use in penal and corrective institutions".

However, a number of provisions of the Minimal standard rules have basic character and should be considered as legally obligatory as follow from spirit and the letter considered above documents. In particular, Article 6 "Main Principle" demands from the states to apply Rules with impartiality, not to suppose "discrimination on the basis of race, color of skin, sex, language, religious, political or other belief, national or a social origin, a property status, a family origin or a social status. On the other hand, it is necessary to respect religious beliefs and moral of the prisoners belonging to these or other groups of the population".

Regarding I "Generally applicable rules" it contains also recommendations on health protection of the condemned (Articles 22-26), especially pregnant women, lying-in women and feeding mothers, ensuring of their right to freedom of conscience and creeds (Articles 41, 42).

Important is the section "Personnel of Institutions" (Articles 46-54) in which long before acceptance of the Code of Conduct of Law Enforcement Officials the basic requirements to employees of penal organizations , their duties on ensuring of basic rights of the condemned have been formulated.

The part II "Rules used to special categories" determines supervising principles of management penal institutions, major of which, in opinion of developers that "the prison system should not aggravate suffering" (Article 57) "in circulation with prisoners it is necessary to emphasize not their exception of a society and that circumstance that they continue to remain its members" (Article 61).

It is necessary to add that such documents are accepted on regional and the European level: the European Convention for the Protection of Human Rights and Basic Freedoms (1950), the European Convention of the Prevention of Torture and Inhuman or Degrading Treatment or Punishment (1987), the European Prison Rules (1987).

Continuing the analysis of a stage of declaring, we should address to consideration of the Constitution of the Russian Federation.

In an estimation of the nature of the state as legal attitude at the constitutional level to persons who have violated the law, returned guilty and the condemned it is especially indicative. Besides, it serves as an indicator of humanity of the state and a society, testifies to a level of moral which reigns in a society or, at least, should be inherent in a society aspiring a high degree of a maturity and development. Therefore, not casually Article 2 of the Constitution of the Russian Federation, recognizing a person, his rights and freedoms as the maximum value, does not at all stipulate the special or individual status of a person.

At the same time, proclaiming that "the rights and freedoms of a person are inalienable and relate to everyone from birth", the Constitution in part

3 of Article 17 warns that realization of these rights and freedoms "should not break the rights and freedoms of other persons". In this position it is possible to see some clause concerning imprisoned persons as limitation of their personal freedom, for example the constitutional civil law on freedom of movement (Article 27), will be coordinated with the nature of institution of the imprisonment called, in particular, to ensure the provision of the right of other persons, societies and the states as a whole.

As to the civil rights of the condemned on personal privacy, personal and family secrecy (Article 23), distribution of the information on private life of a person without his consent (Article 24), inviolability of dwellings (Article 25), these constitutional rights according to Russian legislation are limited on the basis of part 3 of Article 55 of the Constitution of the Russian Federation and of the Criminal Code of the Russian Federation.

Summing up the consideration of a stage of declaring of civil rights of the condemned on international and national levels, it is possible to approve that this part of process of enforcement of rights of imprisoned persons, it is realized fully, in view of the wide experience which was saved in the century of a human civilization, on the basis of theoretical provisions of constitutional law and theory of human rights and simple common meaning which should be present always when an object of research become a person and also the phenomena and the processes making an essence of the life.

Legislative recording of the legal status of the condemned is contained in of the Criminal Code-executive of the Russian Federation which has taken effect since July, 1st, 1997, it provides the system of guarantees of enforcement of the rights and freedoms of the condemned, establishes control measures and supervision of their realization that favourably distinguishes them from other branches of the legislation.

Developers of the project of the Code have paid big attention to regulation of the legal status of the condemned and consider it "as an important gain and purchase as basic rights and duties of the condemned now are registered in the law. No other normative legal regulations and first of all federal enforcement authorities, can change, narrow or add them. It is the major guarantee of the rights, freedom and legitimate interests of the criminal sentences of the condemned at execution"[6].

Unlike operated earlier correctional labor colony in RSFSR, contained three clauses with the general definition of the legal status of the condemned, a new Code has given this question the whole Chapter consisting of six clauses.

It is difficult to agree with the aforesaid of the professor C. V. Borodin that the domestic corrective-labour legislation of 80th "is fuller, more purposefully and more effectively" regulated system of execution of punishment, in comparison with that as it was recommended the Minimal standard rules of treatment of prisoners.[7] If we speak about legal regulation of the organization of a mode, work the indicated authors were right. However, regarding enforcement of civil rights of the condemned, correctional labor colony of RSFSR has fully reflected underestimation and even full ignoring of human rights.

Article 10 of the Correctional Code of the Russian Federation has confirmed aspiration of the state to respect and protect the rights, freedom and legitimate interests of the condemned, to ensure the provision of legality of use means of their correction, their legal protection and personal safety. At execution of punishment of the condemned the rights and freedoms of citizens of the Russian Federation with withdrawals and the limitations established by criminal, criminally-executive and other legislation of the Russian Federation are guaranteed.

Last position has essentially a great value as no other infringement of the rights of the condemned are supposed, except for regulated by the law. In earlier operated legislation limitations of the legal status of the condemned, not only stipulated by the legislation but also vessels following from a verdict and a regime of serving of a certain kind of punishment were established. It created ground for rather free and extended interpretation of various sorts of rights limitations, many of which were formulated in departmental normative legal regulations is orders, instructions, orders which are started with necessity of ensuring of a regime of the content, rather than observance of the rights of the condemned.

Clause 12 of the Correctional Code of the Russian Federation formulates basic rights of the condemned, irrespective of a kind of punishment or a kind of establishment where it is left. First of all, the right to receive the information about rights (part 1). Simultaneously the duty is imposed on administration to give the indicated in formation. In it feature of legal regulation in criminal law-executive is brightly shown: by granting certain right to one of subjects of criminally-executive legal relationships other subject is distinguished with a duty on ensuring.

According to given clause all the condemned have the right to the polite treatment from personnel of the establishment executing punishment, i.e. here Article 21 of the Constitution of the Russian Federation is reflected, which says: "Dignity of a person is protected by the state".

Anything, even the fact of condemnation and serving sentence, cannot be the basis for infringement of human dignity.

The clause also confirms provisions of internationally-legal documents and the constitutional provision about inadmissibility of cruel or degrading treatment of the condemned, irrespective of their consent, cannot be subjected to medical or other experiences threatening their health and life.

In development of Article 26 of the Constitution of the Russian Federation in part 5 of Article 12 of the Correctional Code of the Russian Federation it is stipulated that of the condemned can use the native language or any language which they can speak and in necessary cases to use services of the translator. In part 6 of the analyzed clauses prove to be true "the right of the condemned on health protection, including receive primary medico-sanitary and specialized medical aid".

The final part of the clause (part 11 Article 12) contains the important provisions concerning the procedure of the condemned the rights, in particular, it is emphasized that at realization of the rights of the condemned "should not be broken the order and conditions of serving sentence and also to violate the rights and legitimate interests of other persons".

The right of the condemned for life, proclaimed in Article 20 of the Constitution of the Russian Federation, is indicated in Article 13 of the Correctional Code of the Russian Federation "The Right of the Condemned to Personal Safety" which provides the mechanism of its realization: at occurrence of threat to personal safety from others, a condemned person has a right to address to administration of the corrective institution requesting to transfer him into a safe place or accepting other measures eliminating this threat, down to transfer in other institution. The chief of establishment under the statement of the condemned and in some cases and under own initiative, is obliged to take appropriate measures for non-admission of fatal consequences both for the most of the condemned for safety of other persons or establishment, as a whole, as of the condemned. If on the one hand, he cannot independently provide the safety by virtue of specific conditions of serving of imprisonment, then on the other, he can resort to illegal methods of the resolution of conflict that will cause large excesses, mass disorders, crimes, including murders and runaways.

On the basis of Article 28 of the Constitution of the Russian Federation in the Correctional Code of the Russian Federation made a new edition of the clause concerning ensuring of freedom of conscience and freedom of conscience of the condemned. "They have the right to profess any religion or not to profess any religion, freely to choose, have and share religious beliefs and to work according to them" (part 1).

Obligatory conditions of realization of this right are voluntariness and non-admission infringement of regulations and also infringement of the rights of other persons (part 2).

According to part 4 of the given clause under the request of the condemned priests can be invited to the imprisoned. The condemned can practice religion, use subjects of a cult and religious literature. The administration is obliged to give them some premises for this purpose.

The law for the first time has provided an opportunity of visiting of the condemned in the cells by clerics, (penal isolation wards), single chambers of colonies of a special mode, in disciplinary cells (disciplinary isolation ward) educational colonies for minors and also in premises of chamber type (cells), under condition of absence of threat to personal safety of attendants of a cult (part 5 of Article 14). The condemned that are seriously ill under their request have an opportunity to make all necessary religious practices with the invitation of the cleric (part 6).

Additional guarantees of realization of the rights of the condemned are recorded in Article 15 of the Correctional Code of the Russian Federation "Treatment of the condemned and the order of their consideration" on which meaning of the condemned can direct offers, statements and complaints, connected with infringement of their rights, both in oral and in written forms. They should be considered by administration of the establishment.

The statement and the complaint of the condemned to the imprisonment, addressed in the bodies which are carrying out the control and supervision of activity of organizations and bodies, executing punishment are not subject to censorship. These treatment should be directed to belonging to not later than one day (except for days off and holidays) and bodies and officials to whom offers are directed, statements and complaints of the condemned, should consider them to the Russia established by the legislation terms and to bring made decisions to the notice of the condemned (part 4 and 6 of Article 15 of the Correctional Code of the Russian Federation).

The dignity of the Code is also in that fact that control of bodies of the government and local self-management (Article 19), the judicial control (Article 20), the departmental control (Article 21) and public prosecutor's supervision (Article 22), the control of public associations (Article 23) are regulated.

The Criminal-Executive Code of the Russian Federation accepted in December, 1996 didn't determine the place and the role of Human Rights Commissioner in the Russian Federation in the mechanism of the control of the activity of criminally-executive system on enforcement of the rights of the condemned as a corresponding federal constitutional law accepted a little bit later. Nevertheless, it is possible to consider with good reason that, in particular, Chapter I "General Provisions" and Chapter III "Competence of the Representative" of the given law have the most direct attitude to legislative recording enforcement of civil rights of the condemned.

Human Rights Commissioner in the Russian Federation in November, 1999 sent a letter to the Committee of the State Duma about introducing of the addition into Article 24 of the Correctional Code of the Russian Federation "Visiting of organizations and the bodies executing punishment", suggesting to give to the Commissioner the right at execution of official duties to attend organizations and the bodies executing punishment, without the special sanction to that. "It will allow Human Rights Commissioner in the Russian Federation in due time and freely to carry out checks in case of the information about mass or rough infringement of human rights or in cases having special public value or connected with necessity of protection of interests of persons, not capable independently to use legal means of protection and at carrying out of checks under certain complaints ..."[8].

Questions of realization of the legal status of the condemned and, in particular, their rights of person were specified and defined in Regulations of Corrective Organizations, in by-law normative legal instrument approved by the order of the Ministry of Justice of the Russian Federation and coordinated with the State Office of Public Prosecutor of the Russian Federation. As it is indicated in 1 "General Provisions", Rules on the basis of the Correctional Code "regulate the Russian Federation and concretize corresponding questions of activity of corrective colonies, medical corrective organizations, relations-and-prophylactic organizations and prisons with a view of creation of optimum opportunities for ... protection of the rights, legitimate interests of the condemned and carrying out of duties by them".

In particular, in the document basic rights of the condemned (3) are listed; the order of dialogue between employees of correctional organizations and of the condemned is established: "Workers of organizations address to the condemned as "you" and "citizen", "a citizen" and on a surname" (4) name them "the condemned", procedure of submission of statements and complaints of the condemned (13) is stated in detail; the organization and of the relations-and-prophylactic and sanatorium-preventive granting help to the condemned (19) are explained; the order of transfer of the condemned in a safe place (25) is stated in more detail.

Thus, the analysis of legal regulation of enforcement of civil rights of the condemned allows to draw the following conclusions: firstly, the Correctional Code of the Russian Federation accepted in 1996 is basically based on provisions-principles and provisions-recommendations of human rights, included in internationally-legal documents which form a part of legal system of Russia; secondly, in the Code the constitutional provisions on basic rights of a person are recorded, the mechanism of their ensuring is developed; thirdly, the Correctional Code represents a legal basis for practical realization of the rights of the condemned in activity of criminally-executive system; and finally, the control over ensuring of the legal status of the condemned is legislatively recorded in realization of their rights and freedoms.

Consideration of the question *of realization* of civil rights of the condemned as shows studying the special literature, the analysis of experience of activity of criminally-executive system, acquaintance with the information of human rights organizations and other sources, even at presence of legal guarantees of protection of the rights of the condemned, infringement by virtue of objective and subjective circumstances seems to the most complex.

The matter is that enforcement f the rights of the condemned is connected with the whole complex of the problems standing not only before criminally-executive system but also before the state and a society.

Now it is accepted, analyzing difficulties in activity of the criminally executive system, on the first place to put forward the problem of financing. Not a belittling importance of its decision for increase of efficiency of execution of punishment, we, nevertheless, would like to note first of all the absence in modern Russia of original respect for a person, his rights and freedoms, deformation of sense of justice, a low level of moral. In this situation even legislative citizens cannot feel protected, confident in ability of authority to defend their interests.

The criminally-executive system with hundreds and thousands people working there, hundreds of thousands of the condemned, is just a product of our society, having its negative features.

Culture of human rights, education of a society in the spirit of moral, inculcation of respect for the law, people, is the criterion of success in the case of original ensuring of human rights.

Fortunately, it is understood in the Central Administration of Penal Executions of the Ministry of Justice of Russia where "essential upgrade of the system of personnel ensuring is provided, education of employees of a new formation …"[9]

In ensuring of human rights the deep moral meaning is incorporated. The constitutional principle "realization of the rights and freedoms of a person and a citizen should not break rights and freedoms of other persons" is based on ideals of goods and dignity, eternal human values which our society is obviously lacking.

Therefore, one of the major problems, in our opinion, is the problem of personnel ensuring of criminally-executive system, its acquisition not only professionally prepared but the main thing is highly moral people, with positive valuable orientations.

However, realization of new personnel selection is directly connected with the decision of problems of financing of the Criminal Executive System as a whole, and endowment of its employees in particular. According to Central Administration of Penal Executions Ministry of Justice Russia, "for some years the Criminal Executive System was provided with budgetary funds in the size not exceeding 60% of needs of organizations …"[10] Simultaneously the average salary of employees makes 1000-1200 roubles a month. Such figures are given in the letter of Human Rights Commissioner in the Russian Federation in the State Duma dd. October, 2, 2000 "Financing of the Organizations of the Criminally-Executive System"[11].

Substantially, the financial position of employees affects then estimation of their status, on prestige of service in Criminal Executive System and as a result is on their attitude to work, on quality of work.

During the research carried out in Khabarovsk territory, it was found out that 49.5% of employees consider that people surrounding them disapprove of workers of the execution of punishment system. Such negative opinion of a society is one of the factors of falling prestige of service in Criminal Executive System and substantially "demoralizing influences on employees, reduces their self-estimation, promotes falling prestige of service with problems following from here in selection of qualified personnel"[12].

Consequence of underfinancing of the Criminal Executive System is also lack of money on the maintenance of the condemned (food, ware, medical and household ensuring) that is directly connected with ensuring of their rights to life and health protection. As it was indicated in the same letter of Human Rights Commissioner in the Russian Federation,

"… rather than 18 rubles put on established provisions day on food of one person is really distinguished from the federal budget only nearby 9 rubles"[13]. It is the reason of the increased disease and death rate of the condemned. In circulation of the Human Rights Commissioner addressed to Minister of Justice J. Chaika (on October, 31, 2000) it is emphasized that only during three years in corrective organizations more than 20 thousand people have died from various illnesses. In some regions of Russia numerous cases of death of the condemned from a dystrophy are registered. In a number of organizations owing to infringement of sanitary-and-hygienic provisions, the uses of substandard food took place mass poisonings, group infectious, parasitic and gastroenteric diseases[14].

The problem of disease tuberculosis in organizations UIS continues to remain acute. The parameter of distribution of this disease among of the condemned 23 times exceeds the average indices in the country, as the main phthisiatrician of medical management Central Administration of Penal Executions Ministry of Justice of Russia admits[15]. In comparison with 1998 in 1999 the death rate from tuberculosis in corrective organizations increased on 8.2% and amounted at 238 cases on 100 thousand of the condemned that 12 times exceeds the average registered level among the population of the country[16].

According to special census of the condemned in 1999, for that period 84% of the condemned did not suffer from this disease, 4% had it but managed to be cured, the other 12% have tuberculosis and 3% of them have it in the open form[17].

If in 1990 there were 38,517 people who had tuberculosis in organizations UIS, by the end of 2001 this figure increased up to 92 201 people. The predicted growth of amount of the condemned, who have active tuberculosis, in 2002 will make not less than 10.4% to the level 2000 and in absolute figures (together with people in pre-trial detention centre) will amount at 101,478 people[18].

"In conditions when the state cannot provide normal conditions of the maintenance … of the condemned, still existing practice of infringement of human rights is especially intolerant, humiliations of dignity of a person and simple mockeries from employees of criminally-executive system", it is said in the Special report of Human Rights Commissioner in the Russian Federation[19].

The certificate of it is collective and individual complaints of the condemned brought to the Commissioner.

Thus, under the complained of the condemned from Murmansk area that "in a diet there is not a tenth part of that is necessary, just water, only 150g of bread a day during 10 days, no sugar was given within three months. In a colony the scurvy rages, the dystrophy is widespread, some of the condemned fall in hungry faints. The medical personnel refuse to treat the condemned ..."[20] During the check the facts, stated in the complaint of the condemned, proved to be true.

20 people of the condemned sick of a tuberculosis, from the Amur area complained to Human Rights Commissioner informing that "as soon as are leaves any commission, the medical corrective establishment at once turns to a colony of a strict regime though for a long time has a state of medical establishment. For the slightest fault the guilty are put into a criminal cell where in the winter the temperature falls below zero, thus, they deprive the condemned of all warm things ... the condemned are beaten by legs and rubber sticks"[21].

As we see, infringement not only of the rights of the condemned to life and health but also humiliation of their human dignity and use of torture took place.

The same case was revealed during the check of one of organizations of the Kirov area where the major showed roughness concerning the condemned, for what he was brought to a disciplinary responsibility[22].

However, in our opinion, in both cases actions took place, for which guilty "Abusing Official Powers" should be brought to the criminal liability according to the Article 285 of the Criminal Code of the Russian Federation.

In the Report of Human Rights Commissioner in the Russian Federation in 2003 the facts of infringement of the rights of the condemned in republic Komi, the Orenburg area and other regions (illegal use of physical strength and special means against the condemned, their illegal putting in criminal cells, etc.) are mentioned.

Despite of democratization of procedure of custody on the new Code of Criminal Procedure of the Russian Federation, judiciary practice continues to be guided by use the most rigid kinds of criminal sentence: for insignificant crimes the cruel penalty follows.

Such practice contradicts Covenants on human rights and promotes infringement of the rights of the condemned as well as inhuman treatment of them.

The analysis of such cases shows the obvious necessity of modification and additions in Ch. 19 of the Criminal Code of the Russian Federation "Crimes Against Constitutional Rights and Freedoms of a Person and a Citizen" in which such structures of crimes as humiliation of human dignity, use of torture, kinds of cruel, inhuman or degrading treatment from officials of organizations executing punishment are not reflected.

Chapter 17 of the Criminal Code of the Russian Federation providing the responsibility for crimes against honour and dignity does not consider specificity of law-enforcement activity during which realization the indicated crimes can be committed. The legal estimation of actions of officials existing today creates ground for abusing, an atmosphere of the tolerant attitude to persons breaking the civil rights of the condemned. To some extent it is possible to understand but not to justify the decisions accepted by heads of territorial bodies of UIS, which are compelled to shut eyes to such facts if we mean personnel deficiency in corrective organizations.

According to Human Rights Commissioner, in 65% of cases of infringement of the rights of the condemned the facts did not prove to be true and their check was carried out by managements on execution of punishment Ministry of Justice of Russia[23].

In our opinion, it is possible to explain this circumstance in two ways. Firstly, heads of territorial bodies, protecting "official authority", could hide and really do hide the facts of infringement of the rights of the condemned. Secondly, the condemned, the majority from which arc well informed on the rights, knowing that the correspondence aimed at authorities and managements and also in human rights organizations, is not opened, could direct false data, wishing to get even with the administration showing to them legal requirements. Unfortunately, there is a set of such examples and the skilled employees of the Criminal Executive System well knowing psychology of the condemned, can successfully understand such situations. The third variant is also possible: rendering of psychological and other pressure on the condemned from administration with the purpose to intimidate them to force to refuse the complaint.

It seems that civil (and others) rights of independent subjects of the control but over bringing of advisers from other regions knowing specificity of activity of corrective institutions and feature of a person and behaviour of the condemned should carry out check of statements of their infringement.

In our opinion, the civil law of the condemned on ensuring of freedom of conscience and freedom of conscience (Article 14 of the Correctional Code of the Russian Federation) is most successfully realized. However, here again there are certain problems.

In second half of 1980s, before introducing in Correctional Labour Colony of Article 8 "Ensuring of Freedom of Conscience of the Condemned", have started to develop contacts of corrective-labour system to representatives of the religious organizations which incidentally attended organizations. The decision of a question of the admission of attendants of a cult in pre-trial detention centre and colonies depend on a higher management and sometimes and from persistence of the condemned. Position significantly changed, when the order of the Ministry of Internal Affairs of Russia dd. October, 10, 1989 # 250 had approved recommendations on mutual relations of correctional labour institution with the religious organizations and attendants of a cult. Relations between of the condemned, religious organizations and administration of organizations accept more and more steady character. In pre-trial detention centre and then and in colonies prayful rooms are created, chapels and temples hands of the condemned are under creating. The first temple was incorporated in the autumn 1991 in CI-32 of Irkutsk area. To 1993 in organizations UIS 17 churches and 310 prayful rooms, in 1996 is accordingly 113 and 455 were already totaled[24].

One more serious step was a joint statement of Minister of Internal Affairs of the Russian Federation and the Patriarch of Moscow and All Russia Alex II of September, 6, 1994 in which readiness for cooperation in the case of struggle against criminality and immorality was expressed, in the field of educational and educational work among of the condemned, wishing to follow a way of correction. We should notice that, thus, the freedom of conscience and freedom of conscience of the condemned as integral civil rights were not mentioned.

In 1996 the Cooperation agreement in the case of culturally-moral education of the condemned between Russian Orthodox Church and the Ministry of Internal Affairs of Russia in charge of which at that time there was a criminally-executive system was concluded.

It is necessary to note that representatives of Russian Orthodox Church actively cooperate with criminal executive system, however, on materials of last census of the condemned, the majority of them (63.2%) refer themselves to non-believers (in 1994 of those there were 76.7%). Among believers over 82.9% consider themselves orthodox (30.5% from all the condemned), 9%- Moslems (3.3% from all the condemned). Among serving time there are Christians of other faiths (Catholics, Protestants, Baptists, etc.) and also professing other religions[25].

The analysis of the given figures and also vigorous activity Russian Orthodox Church in organizations UIS testifies not so much to aspiration to ensure the provision of freedom of conscience and freedom of conscience of the condemned, but to expand influence of Orthodox

Church due to involving in belief a numerous and very specific category of citizens of Russia.

It is possible to understand aspiration of administration of organizations any lawful means to achieve the purposes of punishment is corrections of the condemned as a law as one of the basic means of correction provides public influence (Article 9 of the Correctional Code of the Russian Federation). In this case the religious organizations can be considered as those. It is possible to understand also the possibly of sincere desire of some of the condemned to change the life by means of religion. It is possible to accept, eventually, the position of the majority of the condemned which see orthodox ceremonies as an opportunity to diversify a sad life in establishment, to communicate to other, clever educated people. In our opinion, such practice has no attitude to ensuring of freedom of conscience and freedom of conscience and contradicts Article 14 of the Constitution of the Russian Federation. In particular it refers to faithless representatives of Muslim, Catholic, and Jew religions. Their rights are restrained during mass religious actions.

It is characteristic that complaints to Human Rights Commissioner complaints from the condemned on infringement of their right to freedom of conscience and creeds do not act. It is thought what to explain it is possible not so much the fact of absence of such displays, how much, in our opinion, absence of need for upholding this right, absence of true religiousness at the majority of the condemned.

Thus, having analyzed all stages of enforcement of civil rights of the condemned, it is possible to draw the following conclusions. Firstly, internationally-legal regulations and the Constitution of the Russian Federation guarantee full scope of the indicated rights but with the limitations stipulated by the legislation; secondly, the declared rights, the mechanism of their realization are recorded in the legislation which is based on internationally recognized provisions and corresponds to the Constitution of the Russian Federation; thirdly, in Russia preconditions for effective realization of civil rights of the condemned are not created yet. The decision of the problems indicated above depends on a state policy which should be based on respect of dignity of citizens, both legislative and violated the law.

Notes

1. Criminally-Executive Law: Textbook / A.S. Mihlin, P.G. Ponomarev, etc.; Edited by Pr. I.V. Shmarov. Moscow, 1998. P.65. / Уголовно-исполнительное право: Учебник / А. С. Михлин, П. Г. Пономарев и др.; Под ред. проф. И. В. Шмарова. М., 1998. С. 65.

2. Seliverstov I.V. Theoretical Problem of a Legal Status of Imprisoned Persons. Moscow, 1992. P.68-69. / Селиверстов В. И. Теоретические проблемы правового положения лиц, отбывающих наказания. М., 1992. С. 68–69.

3. See: Voevodin L.D. The Legal Status of a Person in Russia. Moscow, 1997. P.172-204; Kozlova E. I., Kutafin O.E. The Constitutional Law of Russia. Moscow, 1996. P.198-203; Constitutional Law / Edited by V.V. Lazarev. Moscow, 1999. P.13-150, etc. / См.: Воеводин Л. Д. Юридический статус личности в России. М., 1997. С. 172–204; Козлова Е. И., Кутафин О. Е. Конституционное право России. М., 1996. С. 198–203; Конституционное право / Под ред. В. В. Лазарева. М., 1999. С. 13–150 и др.

4. See: Bekuzarov G.O., Seliverstov V.I. Criminally-Executive Law of Russia. General and special parts: Schemes and tables / Edited by V.I. Seliverstov. Moscow, 1998. P.207. / См.: Бекузаров Г. О., Селиверстов В. И. Уголовно-исполнительное право России. Общая и Особенная части: Схемы и таблицы / Под ред. В. И. Селиверстова. М., 1998. С. 207.

5. Borodin S.V. Lyahov E.G. International Cooperation in Struggle against Criminality. Moscow, 1983. P.148. / Бородин С. В., Ляхов Е. Г. Международное сотрудничество в борьбе с уголовной преступностью. М., 1983. С. 148.

6. The Comment to the Criminally-Executive Code of the Russian Federation / Edited by A.I. Zubkov. Moscow, 1997. XI. / Комментарий к Уголовно-исполнительному кодексу Российской Федерации / Под ред. А. И. Зубкова. М., 1997. С. XI.

7. See: Borodin S.V. Lyahov E.G. Specified work. P.156. / См.: Бородин С. В., Ляхов Е. Г. Указ. соч. С. 156.

8. Protection of human rights. The collection of documents (1998-2000). Moscow, 2001. P.687-688. / Защита прав человека. Сборник документов (1998–2000 гг.). М., 2001. С. 687–688.

9. Shamsunov S. X. Conceptual Aspects of Reforming Criminally-Executive System// Sheets of criminally-executive system. 2000. # 4. P.2. / Шамсунов С. Х. Концептуальные аспекты реформирования УИС // Ведомости уголовно-исполнительной системы. 2000. № 4. С. 2.

10. Ibidem.P.2-3.

11. See: Protection of human rights … P.720-722. / См.: Защита прав человека… С. 720–722.

12. Stepanov E. Factors Influencing Fluctuation of the Personnel // Sheets of criminally-executive system. 2001. # 4. P.38. / Степанов Е. Факторы, влияющие на текучесть кадров // Ведомости уголовно-исполнительной системы. 2001. № 4. С. 38.

13. Protection of human rights … P.721.

14. See: Ibidem.P.643.

15. See: Sidorov S. Tuberculosis in the Places of Confinement and Measures of Struggle against it // Sheets of criminally-executive system. 2001. # 3. P.9. / См.: Сидорова С. Туберкулез в местах лишения свободы и меры борьбы с ним // Ведомости уголовно-исполнительной системы. 2001. № 3. С. 9.

16. See: Ibidem.

17. See: Characteristic of the Condemned. Materials of Partial Census 1999 / Edited by Dr. of Jurisprudence, Pr. A.S. Mihlin. Moscow, 2001. P.20, 22. / См.: Характеристика осужденных к лишению свободы. По материалам специальной переписи 1999 г. / Под ред. д-ра юрид. наук, проф. А. С. Михлина. М., 2001. С. 20, 22.

18. See:Konotets A. Consolidation of Efforts in Struggle against Socially Significant Diseases // Sheets of criminally-executive system. 2002. # 1. P.2-3. / См.: Кононец А. Консолидировать усилия в борьбе с социально значимыми заболеваниями // Ведомости уголовно-исполнительной системы. 2002. № 1. С. 2–3.

19. The special report of the Human Rights Commissioner in the Russian Federation «Infringements of the rights of citizens by employees of the Ministry of Internal Affairs of

the Russian Federation and Criminally-executive system of the Ministry of Justice of the Russian Federation » dd. 2000, 2000. P.26. / Специальный доклад Уполномоченного по правам человека в Российской Федерации «О нарушениях прав граждан сотрудниками Министерства внутренних дел Российской Федерации и Уголовно-исполнительной системы Министерства юстиции Российской Федерации» за 2000 г. М., 2000. С. 26.

20. Ibidem. P.27.

21. The special report of the Human Rights Commissioner in the Russian Federation …, 2000. P.27-28. / Специальный доклад Уполномоченного по правам человека в Российской Федерации… М., 2000. С. 27–28.

22. Ibidem. P.31.

23. See: The Special report of the Human Rights Commissioner in the Russian Federation …, 2000. P.29. / См.: Специальный доклад Уполномоченного по правам человека в Российской Федерации… М., 2000. С. 29.

24. See: Davydenko V. With Belief in one's Heart (by anniversary of signing of the Working agreement of the Ministry of Justice of the Russian Federation and the Moscow patriarchy of Russian Orthodox Church) // Sheets of criminally-executive system. 2001. # 1. P.29-30. / См.: Давыденко В. С верой в душе (к годовщине подписания Соглашения о сотрудничестве Министерства юстиции Российской Федерации и Московской патриархии Русской Православной Церкви) // Ведомости уголовно-исполнительной системы. 2001. № 1. С. 29–30.

25. See: The Characteristic of the Condemned … P.27-28. / См.: Характеристика осужденных к лишению свободы… С. 27–28.

PART III

PROBLEMS OF CIVIL HUMAN
RIGHTS GUARANTEES

Chapter 13. SOCIAL AND LEGAL MECHANISM OF REALIZATION
OF CIVIL RIGHTS AND FREEDOMS OF A PERSON

The value of all without exception rights and freedoms of a person consists in an opportunity of their high-grade realization. The regulations about the scope are axiomatical that democratism of the state and a degree of freedom of its citizens are determined not so much by formal adherence to high international standards of rights and freedoms of a person, but rather by perfection and efficiency of the mechanism of their realization. The said entirely refers to civil rights and freedoms of a person. The realization mechanism of the majority of them has its specificity reflecting the known features of the content of the given kind of rights and freedoms. The given specificity can be seen with the help of the overall characteristic of the socially-legal realization mechanism of human rights and freedoms in its basic features and constitutive elements which are, in fact, universal for all kinds of rights and freedoms.

Realization of any legal right (freedom) is its materialization, i.e. the direct use by a person of certain value which makes the content of a certain right (freedom). With reference to civil rights and freedoms of a person the speech is accordingly about the values of the sphere of personal freedom, the sphere of private life (dignity, physical inviolability, family secrecy, etc.).

Thus, the realization of a certain legal right (freedom) can be considered both as the process of achieving the result in its stages and as a final analysis which is in fact the acquisition by a citizen of a certain value, its use and command.

Thus, the question of realization of human rights and freedoms, in this case civil rights and freedoms, cannot be considered especially in the formal-legal aspect. The special attention is given here to the factors of political, economic, moral, organizational-technical, socially-psychological and some other procedures which cause the process of realization of rights and freedoms and in many respects determine its efficiency and result. A lot of the indicated factors, as far as their nature and content allow, are considered in the legislation and regulated by it. However, it is impossible to issue legally all the variety of phenomena of social life influencing efficiency of realization of legal rights and freedoms, its required result. The realization is determined by the development of economy, political stability, well-being of the population, an overall performance of law-enforcement structures, a level of legal culture of corresponding officials and other phenomena and factors various on character and importance that in a complex allow to present the process of realization of human rights and freedoms in the form of the original mechanism.

The mechanism of realization of the legal right (freedom) is understood in the wide sense as socially caused and legislatively stipulated opportunity of person's behaviour in the first place as a legal owner in a combination to guaranteeing actions of obliged and other subjects to the purpose of reception by the interested person of certain values mediated by the right (freedom). In other words, it is in itself realization plus phenomena favorably influencing it.

Through a category "mechanism" the structure, a consecutive arrangement, interrelation and interaction of stages and factors of realization of the legal rights and freedoms are revealed; efficiency of its ensurance and protection by various subjects, the role of an environment comes to light; value of qualities of a person for realization of rights and freedoms is estimated. As a phenomenon of socially-legal order the mechanism of realization of human rights and freedoms allows not only to consider in a complex all aspects of realization but also to emphasize from them both legal and sociological and psychological ones.

The characteristic of the content of the mechanism of realization of civil rights and freedoms of a person, no less than all others, naturally presupposes research of the social environment influencing them. It is in the wide sense understood as the public conditions rendering on a person direct or indirect influence, in this case determining behaviour of a person who is carrying out the rights and freedoms and also other subjects involved in realization.

In jurisprudence the question of the role of the social environment in the realization of human rights and freedoms has received the developed coverage mainly through a prism of their warranting, i.e. factors positively influencing the realization. There are two principal causes here, though they are different. Firstly, all the legal rights, in particular civil human rights are inseparably linked with guarantees, and without them lose the quintessence of the content as a provided opportunity of reception by an individual of certain values. It is simply impossible to neglect this basic statement. Secondly, any social environment for human rights should be considered in aggregate both positive and evenly existing undesirable phenomena. Thus, the positive phenomena remain constant in the scientific estimation as guarantees of rights and freedoms of a person.

With some variations but affirmed strongly enough, certain classifications of the indicated guarantees have become axiomatic. The majority of provisions of scientists are incorporated by understanding the fact that the system of warranting develops of general social conditions and also legal and other special means which give to the human rights and freedoms the character really embodied in practice, provide their lawful and high-grade use and protection in cases of encroachment and infringement.

Certainly, behind frameworks of guarantees of rights and freedoms there are separate negative factors in certain sphere of social relations. However, their analysis and the account are extremely important for their elimination, for the decision of questions of perfection of the mechanism, in this case, realizations of civil human rights and freedoms. Unfortunately, while the negative phenomena are not eliminated, they keep the nocuous influence on the rights and freedoms in the mechanism of realization.

For a short period of time Russia has made some important steps on a way of democratic development. The rights and freedoms of a person have received the constitutional recording in the form of the maximum value. It is necessary to speak about some success in the realization of civil rights and freedoms of a person.

In turn, complex processes of public transformations have caused not only successful but also opposite results, have exposed old ones and have revealed new illnesses of a reformed Russian society.

The conclusion here is unequivocal: action of the legal mechanism of realization of human rights and freedoms as it was already noted is not only inseparable from the social one but also due to disruptiveness of the latter can come to naught. The history shows that infringement of social justice, a low standard of citizens' well-being, a long absence of attributes of its growth on a background of inculturality, a magnificent life of the few, political instability, powerlessness of the government before criminality, its decision-making which nobody seems to take into account, may lead to social shocks, mass protests, disorders, growth of criminality, etc. And attempts to resist that by means of only legal methods and authorities are unproductive from the point of view of problem solution of human rights and freedoms enforcement.

Theory and practice of bases formation of a legal status of a person on principles of democracy and legal statehood as a whole, have affirmed in some standards of the content of general social guarantees without which a legal status, civil rights and freedoms remain only beautiful legislative formulations. The mentioned guarantees are usually classified onto economic, political, and cultural (ideological), i.e. according to the basic spheres of social life. General guarantees do not work directly. They represent the basic preconditions of the reality, effectiveness of civil and equally all other kinds of human rights and freedoms.

Economic guarantees of realization of human rights and freedoms are material wealth and values of a society, national property, development of the economy in all its manifestations, the level of income of citizens, etc. Among patterns of ownership great value is given to the development of constitutionally proclaimed in today's Russia the private property as a guarantee of material independence of a person and from here its individual freedom with the rights mediating it and freedom.

Certainly, the value of material-economic guarantees is most brightly shown with respect to the same rights of citizens. For example, the realization of a right to housing directly depends on rates of housing creating and its fund, a right to health protection depends on financing and development of the system of public health services. Therefore, an exclusively important role in enforcement of rights and freedoms of a person and a citizen is played by the directly social and economic politics and economic functions of the state. Russian state is not casually designated in the Constitution as social (Article 7). It predetermines service to a person and their rights as its final and main purpose.

Though economic guarantees to a greater extent provide the social and economic rights of person, they are sometimes essentially important both for the realization of the separate civil rights and freedoms of a person. As an example it is possible to emphasize freedom of movement and freedom of residence. Its violation during the Soviet period was in many respects a consequence of an over-organized economic policy of the state with the use of forced labour in the country that demanded recording citizens on a residence. On the other hand, in conditions of democracy the level of a material well-being of citizens directly influences the realization of freedom of movement by them and freedom of residence. Thus, the absence at a citizen of necessary money resources does not allow getting vehicles in the property, to get tickets on railway, air and other types of transport. The lawful aspiration to change a residence is often complicated because of the problems of employment in another region, the cost of dwelling offered for purchase non-comparable to wages.

Political guarantees have the major value for civil rights and freedoms. Here the regime of democracy, development of its institutions forms, first of all, concerns. In terms of it, the recording in the Constitution of the democratic legal device of Russia, the republican form of board (Article 1), a person and his rights as a maximum value (Article 2) is especially significant. High-grade realization of rights and freedoms of a person in the system of free elections, political variety, division of authorities on legislative, executive, judicial are called to ensure the provision of, other systems of "checks" and "counterbalances".

The state acts as a guarantor of a reality of human rights and freedoms the effective recognizing in mutual relations with a person, his priority on the basis of leadership of the right, maintaining political stability in a society, capable if necessary to effectively protect the democracy, the proclaimed rights and freedoms. In the final bill the question of dependence of civil rights and freedoms of a person on democratic character of the organization and activity of political authority has not less fundamental underside: the state does not exist as legal in general outside of an embodiment of the civil and political rights and freedoms. The most vivid is the example of everybody's right to judicial protection of rights and freedoms which is an integral component of a democratic regime.

It is possible to refer to the becoming of principles of social solidarity, tolerance and friendship of people to the number of social guarantees favorable for civil human rights and freedoms. It is necessary to remark that these factors appeared today are subjected to unreasonable oblivion.

An independent kind of guarantees of human rights and freedoms is cultural, including ideological. They render significant influence on favorable realization of civil rights and freedoms. It is the level of culture of a society, its scientific and creative potential, erudition, moral views of its members which finally determine a level of culture of human rights. As a special guarantor, the Constitution marks out a concept of ideological variety in Russia and at the same time unequivocally forbids to kindle social, racial, ethnic and religious discord. (Part 1, 2, 5 Article 13).

The public and individual sense of justice, politically legal culture of the society, separate citizens, including officials, called to ensure the protection of rights and freedoms serve as a component of ideological guarantees. There is a problem of overcoming of stereotypes of the last long-term vision of a person in whom a passive acceptance of a mode, a blind submission of authority, a timid attitude to an individual initiative are inherent. Traditional for Russia belittling of the role of a person, neglect of his dignity, individuality, the rights and freedoms as it is fairly noted in science, first of all, determine immorality of a modern Russian society[1]. It is necessary to use all means, including ideological ones to overcome it.

The integral condition of a reality of civil rights and freedoms of a person is people's knowing them, understanding of their high value, skill to use and effectively protect, respect of such rights of associates. The role of formation of a high level of citizens' sense of justice is great among ideological factors of ensuring of civil rights and freedoms: the concept of rights and freedoms of a person the maximum value, respect of honour and dignity of each individual, observance of legality and the law and order as the bases of rights and freedoms realization.

Economic, political and cultural guarantees form a complex of basic conditions which, once again we should emphasize it, predetermines as a whole the reality of civil as well as all other rights and freedoms of a person and a citizen, is the deciding precondition of formation at an individual of an interest in their realization. However, general social factors in themselves cannot always provide high-grade use of rights and freedoms, especially protect from encroachment and infringement. Any competences demand special legal support. For this purpose there are some legal guarantees including current principles, legal provisions, other legal phenomena and more particularly speaking, legislatively recorded ways (means, measures) which are called to ensure directly the provision of realization and also protection of legal rights and freedoms and, as a result, using by an individual of the values laying in their basis.

The mentioned guarantees at a known community uniting them in an independent kind of attributes, properties, qualities have two big divisions: guarantees of use (realization) of rights and freedoms, i.e. legal means which provide their high-grade realization and guarantees of protection of rights and freedoms, i.e. the legal means protecting them. In essence such gradation is accepted in science, reflected in the legislation and shown in practice.

In the considered context it is necessary to note one detail. The legislator frequently uses such concept as "observance" of rights and freedoms of a person and a citizen (for example, Article 2 of the Constitution of Russia). It is quite sound. Basically the indicated concept can be considered as a version of enforcement of rights and freedoms but with the specificity. From the point of view of "observance" there is non-interference (usually through realization of legal interdictions) mainly by the subjects distinguished by authority in civil human rights and freedoms. Being figuratively expressed, it is "passive ensuring" of the given kind of rights and freedoms.

Special guarantees of ensuring lawful realization by a person of rights and freedoms are aimed at creation of the optimum socially-legal environment of their realization and, unlike the guarantees of their protection are not connected with offences. Here, the whole legal system and, first of all, the democratic legislation regulating the rights and freedoms, mainly, refers: their importance, reality, content, scope, limits of use, remedial procedures of realization, including legal facts, with which it communicates, etc.

The way to legal enforcement of human rights and freedoms on a large scale opens from legislative registration of essence of the state, a social order, adherence to democratic political-legal principles, such as legal statehood, leadership of the right, division of authorities, a priority of a person in mutual relations with the state, etc.[2] Direct enforcement of civil rights and freedoms originates from their concept of the state and corresponding normative-legal regulation. The character of regulation, including the level of implementation of international instruments on human rights and also social and legal meaning officially given to the rights and freedoms is determined. Russia as it is known, has joined the Covenant on Civil and Political rights of person, to other major internationally-legal documents on human rights, and has recognized their priority. Besides, basic rights and freedoms of a person and a citizen are recorded at the constitutional level as directly current ones that give to them the maximum reality concerning rule-making, law-enforcement activity of all state bodies and officials.

As guarantees of rights and freedoms of a person it is possible to emphasize principles of harmony of their limitation and preservation of their intrinsic democratic content. General meaning of it consists in inadmissibility of weakening, excessive limitation by authority of rights and freedoms, even due to the arisen danger for the constitutional system, the rights and legitimate interests of other persons, the law and order, etc. It is rather significant for civil rights and freedoms the realization of which at known infringing circumstances does not exclude lawful use by the state of force and compulsion (limitation of freedom of movement, detention and imprisonment of a person, etc.). It is forbidden to regard the essence of the content of basic rights and freedoms. There is no direct formulation about it in the Constitution of the Russian Federation as, say, in the Organic Law of Germany (Clause 2 of Article 19), however, there is a number of provisions in it, which can be interpreted similarly (Article 18, Part 2 of Article 55).

The important role in realization of human rights and freedoms is played by their certain definition, in particular limits of their use by an individual and also the content of rights and freedoms, the circle of their owners, a circle of the obliged persons and power belonging to them, etc. Certain definition of rights and freedoms, including civil, is carried out, as a rule, normatively: by means of detailed elaboration of rights and freedoms provisions of the law regulating them, by means of the current legislation and on occasion by official interpretation of rights.[3] One of the initial provisions of a certain definition is served with the establishment of subjects who are the bearers of the right. Russian Constitution (Part 2 of Article 6) says that each citizen of the Russian Federation has in the territory all rights and freedoms and performs the equal duties stipulated by the Constitution. The subject of almost every proclaimed in Ch. 2 Organic laws of civil rights and freedoms is each person. It at the same time does not exclude the detailed elaboration of subjects in the legislation, with the consequences following from here. For example, in the Constitution it is emphasized that everyone can freely leave the borders of the Russian Federation. But only its citizens have the right of unobstructed returning to the Russian Federation (Part 2 of Article 27).

The great value has the normative-legal definition of reasonable limits of realization of human rights and freedoms in a democratic society irrelevant of the bearers. The general provision of the Constitution of the Russian Federation is the following: realization of rights and freedoms of a person and a citizen should not break the right and freedom of other persons (Part 3 Article 17). Their use, according to the recognized international standards, for a violent change of the constitutional system, kindling of racial, national, class, religious hatred, for propagation of violence and war are forbidden (this position was still recorded in Part 2 of Article 4 of Russian Declaration of Rights and Freedoms of a Person and a Citizen in 1991). There are direct instructions in the branch Russian legislation on inadmissibility of use of rights and freedoms with a view contradicting their purpose. There is an especially devoted Article 10 "Limits of Realization of Civil Rights" in the Civil Code of the Russian Federation in particular. It is said there about the interdiction of actions of citizens carried out exclusively with an intention to harm another person and also abusing the right in other forms; about inadmissibility of use of civil rights with a view of the limitation of a competition; about reasonableness and conscientiousness of realization of rights.

Ways of realization of human rights and freedoms can be indicated through a certain set of concretizing competences, their interrelation. For an illustration we should name Article 28 of the Constitution, recording freedom of conscience and freedom of religion that, in turn, includes the right to profess individually or together with others any religion or not to profess any, to choose freely, have and distribute religious and other beliefs and to work according to them. It is remarkable that the given clause supposes the opposite legal behaviour of a person within the limits of the designated subjective freedom, i.e. one person can be an active believer and another can be an active atheist.

For realization of human rights and freedoms the specifying regulation of their content, first of all, the objects including the various values, legitimate claims inducing a person to realize rights and freedoms is important. Concerning some of them on a number of the objective reasons it is quite logical or even necessary. Thus, the Constitution, proclaiming the right of a private property in whole (Article 35), especially marks out as an object of the mentioned right the ground (Part 1 Article 36). As far as civil rights and freedoms are concerned, the majority of them do not demand the developed detailed elaboration of an object: the right to life, to a concept of legal personality, on citizenship, the right to determine and specify the national identity, on use of the native language, etc.

Legal ensuring of realization of rights and freedoms of a person and a citizen is not at all limited by the above-mentioned legal ways. In the interests of lawful realization in statutory acts the special indication on the legal facts with which the opportunity of use is soundly connected by an individual of the right (freedom) often is made, the indication on the order of its use and measures of ensuring is made. Definition in the law of the list of certain persons which should guarantee realization of rights and freedoms by means of execution of the functional duties is exclusively significant. The normative regulation of duties is also important, i.e. their list, appropriate execution.

As it is known, each right or personal freedom has its order and character of realization. Realization of the majority of civil rights and freedoms by virtue of specificity of their content is organized by a person, under their initiative, outside of direct dependence on anybody. Thus, some competences making the content of freedom of conscience and freedom of religion, the right to determine and specify the national identity are realized, etc.

Alongside with the above-stated initiative form of use of rights and freedoms of a person there exists a remedially-procedural one when the law to some definiteness provides the rules of their use. The remedially-procedural order is in fact, a legal design of realization of rights (less often than subjective freedom by virtue of the specificity of their content expressed in greater independence of their realization from the state). It usually presupposes a coordination of active actions of the legal owner and the obliged subjects, a precise normative regulation of these actions under the form, methods, means, time, to a place of realization, etc. The Coordination is set first of all through the system of the legal facts, legal (acute) structures which cause the indicated actions and are also generated by them. Thus, Ch. 2 of Federal Law of the Russian Federation "Conscience and Religious Associations" directly regulates the basic forms of realization of the right to freedom of creeds that, in particular, includes an opportunity to create the corresponding associations. Corresponding procedures of realization of the right to entrance to the country and departure from the country are provided with the Federal law "The Order of Departure from the Russian Federation and Entrance to the Russian Federation".

In the given context special value has a remedially-procedural procedure of realization of rights of a person which includes rendering by these or other competent bodies law enforcement instruments: allowing, registration regulating, certifying, ascertaining and others[4]. They are necessary with respect to the rights the realization of which cannot evenly have any optional character, to be legally uncontrolled. First of all, these are some economic rights.

Law enforcement instruments are elements of the mechanism of realization and some civil rights and freedoms. Realization of the indicated rights and freedoms demands a law-enforcement control when there is an obvious necessity of ensuring individual and state security, the increased ensuring of the law and order, protection of rights and freedoms of other citizens. For an illustration it is possible to mention two above-mentioned laws again. The first of them provides registration of the charter of a religious association. The second establishes the delivery of corresponding visas. It is also characteristic here the registration procedure of realization of the right to freedom of residence by citizens that is standard in Russia. In the law "The Right of Citizens of the Russian Federation to Freedom of Movement, a Choice of Residence within the Borders of the Russian Federation"[5] it is said that registration aims at ensuring of necessary conditions for realization by citizens of rights and freedoms and also executions of duties by them before other citizens, the state and the society (Part 1 of Article 3).

The main task is to make such instruments evenly necessary and clear to the legal owner in the legal and social applicability, i.e. provided appropriate realization of rights and freedoms, rather than created artificial complexities and obstacles in it. The practice of introduction in the USSR the allowing order of freedom of residence (a registration and an extract), trip abroad, creation of religious associations etc. is sadly memorable.

Speaking about realization of civil rights and freedoms of a person, it is necessary to say and that its mechanism referring to a number of rights and freedoms is quite original. It is expressed in the fact that a person sometimes uses values of the sphere of private life and individual freedom not due to the active actions on realization of the corresponding rights and freedoms but due to the observance of interdictions by other persons.

The given aspect is emphasized already in the formulation of some basic civil rights and freedoms. Thus, according to the Constitution of the Russian Federation honour and dignity are subject to observance (Part 1 of Article 21); the right not to be subjected to torture, violence, other cruel or degrading treatment or punishment (Part 2 of Article 21); freedom and security of a person (Article 22); the right to personal privacy, personal and family secrecy (Part 1 of Article 23); the right to privacy of correspondence, telephone conversations, post, cable and other messages (Part 2 of Article 23); inviolability of dwelling (Article 25); presumption of innocence (Article 49), etc.

The need for in fact, protection of human rights and freedoms, including civil ones, arises in cases of their infringement (or real threat), whether it is rendering of unlawful legal regulations interfering with their realization, an unreasonable refusal in a concept for a person of the right, default of a legal duty by someone as a correlate of rights and others, including an open encroachment for life, honour and dignity of a person, etc.

Protection of rights and freedoms begins with a basic rule-making definition of punishable encroachment on them and also main principles and opportunities of legal protection of a person in the state, including nation-wide obligations, its main ways, and admissible limits. The major role here refers to the Constitution which has recorded adherence of Russia to corresponding international standards according to which human rights are necessary for protecting "authority of the law with a view of ensuring that a person has not been compelled to resort means to revolt against tyranny and oppression" (The Preamble of the Universal Declaration of Human Rights).

The Constitution of the Russian Federation approves equality of all people before the law and court (Part 1 of Article 19); records the observance and protection of rights and freedoms of a person and a citizen as a duty of the state (Article 2); does not presuppose the use of normative-legal regulations connected with the rights and freedoms if they are not published officially for general data (Part 3 of Article 15); proclaims the state protection of security of rights and freedoms and an opportunity for everyone to protect the rights in all possible ways which have been not forbidden by the law (Part 1, 2 of Article 45), etc. In the branch legislation many provisions are developed, indicated, supplemented. Thus, the aiming at the safety of a person as a whole is characteristic, as well as in a significant part, at the protection of human rights and freedoms, provisions of the new Criminal Code of the Russian Federation determining a number of encroachment on them as criminal with the consequences following from here. Simultaneously the Code regulates legitimacy of self-defense through the concepts of necessary defense (Article 37), emergency (Article 39), regulates legitimacy of causing damage to a person detained for committing a crime (Article 38), including that against a person and their rights, etc.

It is possible to determine already a guarantee of protection of human rights and freedoms on a large scale through the development of democratic institution of the responsibility of the state before citizens for the infringement of their rights and freedoms[6]. The current Constitution has confirmed adherence of the Russian Federation to this axiom of legal statehood, having established not only the protection by the law of the victims' rights from abuse of power (Article 52) but also in general the right of everyone to compensation of the harm caused by illegal actions (or inactivity) of the government bodies or their officials (Article 53). The mentioned institution includes the whole complex of necessary guaranteeing measures of especially guarding character (are considered further) and some, providing frequently in aggregate: property indemnifications, instruments of moral rehabilitation, punishment guilty, establishment of preferential modes for victims, etc. As it is known, today the question consists in due realization of the state responsibility institution that becomes complicated because of the problems of its material-financial ensuring, etc.

The list of the basic guarantees of protection of rights and freedoms of a person and a citizen includes: revealing of the facts of infringement of rights and freedoms; means of their restoration; measures of the legal responsibility; the preventive punishment of the actions breaking the rights and freedoms or creating that threat; remedial forms (procedures) of rights and freedoms protection. Sometimes narrowly graded ways of protection of rights are distinguished, in particular (Article 12) stipulated by the Civil Code: by the concept of some transactions void, the terminations or changes of legal relationships, etc.

In most cases some ways of protection are used in various combinations. It is remarkable that as an infringement or other encroachment on the right or freedom basically can take place in any stage of their realization the necessity for their protection can arise at any moment and then the realization regularly proceeds.

The check-supervising functions of many authorities and managements and, certainly, court are directed at the revealing of the facts of civil human rights and freedoms infringement. The activity of the Public Prosecutor Office, the Human Rights Commissioner in the Russian Federation, and human rights commissioners in its subjects are directly subordinated to it. Separate control problems are carried out by the presidential structures: the Commission of Human Rights, the Central administrative board concerning the constitutional guarantees of rights of citizens and distinguished in the Administration of the President of the Russian Federation. In particular, operatively-search, investigatory activity of law-enforcement bodies and of some judicial authorities is directed in many respects to the achievement of the indicated purpose. Registration with the purpose of the control over conformity to the law of the departmental statutory acts regulating the rights and legitimate interests of citizens.

Restoration of the infringed civil human rights and freedoms is carried out, as a rule, by means of: understanding by a person of the right (freedom) that was illegally rejected; rejections or concept of illegal and normative and individual legal regulations of imperous subjects; putting on a duty to compensate the caused damage and also to eliminate the obstacles that prevented the legal right realization; adjustment or other imperous instruction to execution of an unfulfilled duty; return of property to the proprietor; refutations of data discrediting honour and dignity, etc. In the case of restoration of rights and freedoms the role of court is exclusively significant, whose decisions allow not only to satisfy legitimate interests of the claimant but also to approve the legal principles of statehood, reality, a regime of democratic legality and the law and order.

Measures of the legal responsibility for infringement of human rights and freedoms are certain kinds of sanctions, in this case, punishment (sometimes in aggregate with compensatory measures), the rights stipulated by various branches (criminal, civil, administrative, etc.) in compliance with seriousness and a kind of the deed. Special value is given to the constitutional responsibility of the maximum officials for default of the functions on ensuring, protection and also for non-observance of rights and freedoms of a person and a citizen, including the responsibility for rule-making, beyond provisions about basic rights and freedoms.

Among the guarantees of protection of human rights and freedoms the specific place is occupied by special stopping measures. Separate from them, including the preventive punishment, there is the criminally-remedial sphere: detention, imprisonment, personal recognizance not to leave the country, mortgage, search, imposing of imprisonment on property, etc. There are also administratively-legal, disciplinary-legal, and civil-legal: a passenger removal from a vehicle for a stowaway fare, discharge from work for the infringement of certain rules, distrain, etc. On occasion when the encroachment for life, health, physical inviolability is available, coercive actions with the use of firearms, force of special means are included.

In the basis all measures on protection of rights and personal freedoms, especially stipulated by sanctions of legal provisions are used in the order established by law. A precise legal regulation of such order, their strict abidance is a reliable guarantee of legality and efficiency of rights and freedoms protection[7]. It is not casual that the Constitution of the Russian Federation itself establishes a number of civil rights of remedial meaning. As a matter of fact they are the fundamental rights-principles, the rights-guarantees on which legal procedures are based and which are extremely significant for protection of a person in guarding legal relationships: legal proceeding according to the law by way of jurisdiction with the participation of jurymen (Article 47); security of legal aid to everyone, including the lawyer from the moment of detention, custody or charge (Article 48); the presumption of innocence, absence of a duty to prove the innocence, interpretation of ineradicable doubts about guilt of a person in favour of the accused (Article 49), etc.

Clearly, in the case of infringement of civil as well as other rights and freedoms, each person is allowed to protect it with the help of the various, not forbidden by law ways, including self-defense. However, more often people have to address officially the law enforcement bodies. From here, in the wide sense, the classical legal procedure of protection of rights and freedoms invariably includes the will of the victim (the initiative of the most competent subject, court, the Office of the Public Prosecutor, etc. is possible), rendering decision to the instrument of law enforcement and if necessary it's further practical execution. Sometimes the requirements and submission by a citizen of the statement for a certain fact, of infringement of their rights (payment of a State Tax, observance of hierarchy of instance, correct official registration of papers, etc.) can be normatively established. For example, how to address the Constitutional Court with an individual complaint is in details defined in the Federal constitutional law "The Constitutional Court of the Russian Federation" (Ch. 5)[8].

The main thing nevertheless is that the procedure of the most law-enforcing activity of the state bodies, their officials is almost always legislatively settled. Thus, if a person has addressed in court for protection of the civil law or freedom on the basis of the law of the Russian Federation "the appeal in court of actions and decisions breaking the rights and freedoms of citizens"[9], all further activity of the court will be carried out under the established remedially-legal rules opened for acquaintance by any interested persons. It is, by the way, one of the confirmations that justice is the most effective and democratic form of protection of civil and all other rights and freedoms of a person and a citizen. It is not casual in modern Russia that it receives the increasing development and is put by the citizens in the first place in the system of guarantees of their rights and freedoms[10].

There are guarantees of human rights and freedoms the specificity of which does not allow considering them in one line with the general conditions and legal means of warranting. First of all, it refers to organizational guarantees which should be understood as the special organizational, technical, informational and suchlike activity of competent subjects directed at the assistance to the process of realization of rights and freedoms, to effective functioning of general social and special guarantees. Perfection of work of the whole state apparatus is an effective utilization of economic potential, institutions of democracy, social forecasting and so forth by the authority. Organizational sort of activity as a whole is based on the law though, it is not, as a rule, connected with a rigid, detailed normative regulation, is not directly carried out through rule-making, law enforcement but "penetrates" them. It appears quite often as understood in a civilized society. It is obvious, for example, that each state body (establishment, organization), is officially called to execute their functions honestly, to correspond to the status in everything. The style of work of competent persons on whom the realization and protection of rights depend is also important here. It is first of all, respect of a person, his rights and freedoms, honour and dignity. It is professionalism, responsibility, honesty, efficiency, keenness in a counterbalance of illiteracy, bureaucratism, graft, inefficiencies, callousness which can bring very good legal and material guarantees of a person's legal status to naught.

Summing up the above-stated concerning the mechanism of realization of civil and other human rights and freedoms, including their guarantees, we should note that the problem can be considered wider, in other planes, with other emphasis. It concerns the sphere of international guarantees. Here the activity of the United Nations and its structures, particularly specialized, prosecuting with subjects of human rights observance (the Supreme Commissioner on Human Rights, the Commission on Human Rights, the Human Rights Committee, etc.) is distinguished. The cooperation of Russia with other European states in the field of human rights, including participation in the work of the European Court on Human Rights deserves the increasing scientific attention[11]. The cooperation of the states within the limits of OSCE on humanitarian problems is theoretically and practically acute. The interaction of the states within the limits of the Interpol, the Europol in the context of guarantees of human rights is important. The work on protection of human rights by nongovernmental formations of the type widely known as "Amnesty International", "Human Rights Watch", International Committee of the Red Cross, etc. is productive.

It is necessary to note that the problems of realization of civil rights in Russia are, as a rule, connected with inefficiency of the guarantees, called to ensure the provision of their real implementation. For example, the tragic events in the Chechen Republic, which caused mass infringement of civil and other rights of citizens, in many respects were predetermined by the inability of the government to settle the conflict through political means in the initial stage of its occurrence and at later stages. In this case it is a question of absence of political guarantees or their inefficiency. But the most visible place in the system of guarantees of civil human rights is occupied by the legal guarantees. Among their disadvantages it is necessary to mention discrepancy, deficiencies of law and instability of the legislation, poor-quality work of legislature. Thus, the hasty acceptance of the new Code of Criminal Procedure of the Russian Federation (2002) and the following numerous amendments did not promote a successful struggle against criminality, protection of rights of a person. The bureaucratic principles, corruption in the activity of court, law enforcement bodies have not been overcome till now. Our legal system calls to combat criminality and this circumstance affects the sphere of civil human rights realization. And finally, a low level of ideological guarantees of these rights (backwardness of culture of human rights, legal nihilism in consciousness of many citizens, officials, etc.) is a serious obstacle in the realization of the indicated rights.

Overcoming of these negative phenomena will allow to fill civil rights of Russian citizens with the real content.

Notes

1. See: Lukasheva E.A. Rights of a Person as a Criterion of Politics and State Power Moral Measure // Rights of a Person and Political Reformation. Moscow, 1997. P. 36. / Лукашева Е. А. Права человека как критерий нравственного измерения политики и государственной власти // Права человека и политическое реформирование. М., 1997. С. 36.

2. See: Rights of a Person. History, Theory and Practice. Moscow, 1995. P. 141-144. / Права человека. История, теория и практика. М., 1995. С. 141-144.

3. Thus, concretization of basic rights and freedoms of a person is acceptable through their interpretation by the Constitutional Court of the Russian Federation within its exceptional prerogative to interpret constitutional propositions (Part 5 Article 125 of the Constitution).

4. Find more about the kinds of law enforcement acts in the mechanism of realization of the rights of a person: Rostovschikov I. V. Rights of a Person in Russia: Ensuring and Protection by the Bodies of Internal Affaires. Volgograd, 1997. P. 131-146. / Ростовщиков И. В. Права личности в России: их обеспечение и защита органами внутренних дел. Волгоград, 1997. С. 131–146.

5. See: Journal of the Convention of People's Deputies of the Russian Federation and Supreme Soviet of the Russian Federation. 1993. № 32. Article 1227. / Ведомости Съезда народных депутатов Российской Федерации и Верховного Совета Российской Федерации. 1993. № 32. Ст. 1227.

6. See more, for example, in: Boitsova L. A. A Citizen against the State? // Social Sciences and Modern Age. 1994. № 4. P. 42-50; General Theory of Human rights. Moscow, 1996. P. 297-301. / Бойцова Л. Гражданин против государства? // Общественные науки и современность. 1994. № 4. С. 42–50; Общая теория прав человека. М., 1996. С. 297–301.

7. In a number of countries the statement 'protection of the rights of a person through the procedures' is an inseparable condition of the constitutionality of the state authority corresponding decisions. See more, for example, in: Ledyah I. A., Vorobyov O. V., Kolesova N. S. Mechanism of Rights and Freedoms Protection of the Citizens // Human Rights: Problems and Perspectives. Moscow, 1990. P. 144-147. / Ледях И. А., Воробьев О. В., Колесова Н. С. Механизмы защиты прав и свобод граждан // Права человека: проблемы и перспективы. М., 1990. С. 144–147.

8. See: The Corpus of Legislation of the Russian Federation. 1994. № 13. Article 1447. / Собрание законодательства Российской Федерации. 1994. № 13. Ст. 1447.

9. See: Journal of the Convention of People's Deputies of the Russian Federation and Supreme Soviet of the Russian Federation. 1993. № 19. Article 685. / Ведомости Съезда народных депутатов Российской Федерации и Верховного Совета Российской Федерации. 1993. № 19. Ст. 685.

10. See: Kashelov V. P. The Institute of Judicial Protection of Rights and Freedoms of Citizens and Means of their Realization // State and Law. 1998. № 2. P. 66-71. / Кашепов В. П. Институт судебной защиты прав и свобод граждан и средства ее реализации // Государство и право. 1998. № 2. С. 66–71.

11. See: Rolv Risdal. The problem of human rights protection in the united Europe // Human Rights Protection in the Modern World. M., 1993. P. 122-133; Glotov S. A. Constitutionally legal problems of the cooperation of Russia and the European Commission in the field of human rights. Saratov, 1999. / См.: Ролв Рисдал. Проблема защиты прав человека в объединенной Европе // Защита прав человека в современном мире. М., 1993. С. 122–133; Глотов С. А. Конституционно-правовые проблемы сотрудничества России и Совета Европы в области прав человека. Саратов, 1999.

Chapter 14. THE RIGHT TO LEGAL PROTECTION
          AND REMEDIAL LEGAL RELATIONSHIPS

The embodiment of civil rights and freedoms of a person during life, their statement as the greatest universal value always appears connected with a qualitative level of their scientific-theoretical comprehension. In the Russian Federation the course on creating of a lawful state is proclaimed, rights and freedoms of a person are constitutionally recognized and taken under protection by the state. It has given an impulse to the development and formation of the domestic concept of civil rights and freedoms of a person. During a rather short period of time the problems connected with civil human rights and their protection have turned from narrow profiled to one of the development mainstreams of Russian jurisprudence. However, our society should apply many efforts to transform these rights into a real value for everyone and for all on both the scientific and practical level.

It is necessary to note that modern domestic scientific researches of the rights and freedoms of a person incorporate the achievements of a universal philosophical and legal idea and the corresponding development of the domestic scientists of the 19th - the 20th centuries. It is one of the reasons why Russian researches of civil rights and freedoms of a person get a more and more mature and fundamental character.

The expansion of the theory and practice of human rights, active formation of scientific views on this problem in the 20th century, a real embodiment of problems of protection of the rights and freedoms of a person during life have reflected in the processes of the states association in various international communities (League of Nations, the United Nations, the Council of Europe, OSCE, etc.). Such cooperation leads to the increase of the role of international law, the statement and a general recognition of the universal concept of human rights.

The most important and paramount question both for theory and practice of civil human rights is the question about what such phenomenon as "civil rights and freedoms of a person". Scientific searches for the answer to this question have led to the understanding of the fact that

human rights including civil rights and freedoms of a person are a continuation of socially-natural and intellectual-cultural properties of a person. Proceeding from such understanding of human rights there is, in our opinion, the search for the most capacious and substantial approaches to studying civil rights and freedoms of a person.

The analysis of the specially-scientific literature shows that by the present time several somewhat isolated directions in the research of civil human rights have already been formed in the Russian jurisprudence.

Within the limits of the first direction the basic accent is made on ontological problems of civil human rights. With respect to this, it is possible to mention **the philosophical-legal approach.** Here the questions of the origin of civil human rights and the logic of acquisition by them of the legal nature are exposed to theoretical analysis. Under this angle, I.E. Farber, E.A. Lukasheva. N.V. Vitruk, B.L. Nazarov, N.I. Matuzov. F.M. Rudinsky L.I. Gluhareva and others carried out their researches of human rights. Such major properties of this phenomenon as the essence of civil human rights, their absoluteness and inalienability and also a regular property in their correlation with subjective and objective right are revealed and considered by them in detail. Generalizing scientifically-practical utility of such researches, it is possible to draw a conclusion that the basic value of the philosophical-legal approach consists in its ability to open socially-natural and legal sources of civil human rights as a uniform and complete formation. And in this quality, in many respects "unfamiliar" for both objective and legal right, the philosophical-legal approach offers the scientific community as well as the legislature to perceive civil human rights.

The understanding of civil human rights as a special way of legal regulation of social relations that has been actively developing during recent five-six years is not less significant both for theory and practice. This is **a regulative approach to the problems of civil human rights,** if it is possible to say so, it is based on a concept of the fact that the civil human rights recognized by the international community and the state, introduce corresponding regimes, procedures and algorithms of the legal realization both in internationally-legal and in national-legal systems. This regulative effect of civil human rights has found its theoretical substantiation in the works of V.I. Kartashev, M.F. Orzih, N.I. Matuzov, A.V. Malko and others who have convincingly shown that the implementation of human rights in legal systems with relentless logic leads to radical restructurings in the mechanisms of legal regulation. The past of many states and the experience of new, democratic Russia confirm this law.

Owing to such fundamental conclusion it becomes obvious that the attention to civil human rights is a general thing that unites legal systems of the states which have acquired the quality of being legal. It means that not any democratic society has a special (dropping out of this logic) way to an evolutionary development of its legal system. Regulative properties of civil human rights unify the practice of legal dialogue of a person and the state, a person and other subjects of legal system. As a result of this, legal systems get similar and even common features. However, it does not lead to sanitization of legal ways of life in the democratic states. Alongside with the said, it is necessary to note such regulative meaning which, being incorporated in civil human rights is to legal systems of societies as a precisely designated limit of legal regulation of a person's activity. An attempt to state the generalized estimation of civil human rights researches in a regulative approach leads to the conclusion that this is a scientifically proved and dictated by practice needs point of view on civil human rights aspiring to answer the question of how to build the system of legal regulation of social relations in a lawful state.

In one line with the above-mentioned directions of research of civil human rights there is **a human rights direction**. The essence of this approach consists in the understanding of the fact that civil human rights turn to real value only when they are reliably guaranteed and protected. The most consecutive and full research of this aspect of human rights has been found in the works of A.J. Azarov, L.B. Alekseeva A.S. Mordovets, I.V. Stremouhov and others. These authors consistently carry out an idea on the obligatory inclusion in the definition of the general concept of "rights and freedoms of a person" instructions on the necessity of their protection. The fact that the protection of human rights is based on such human right as its right to legal protection acts as a basic reason in favour of such understanding of civil human rights. This right, in the opinion of the above-mentioned scientists, has no other purpose, except for elimination of drawbacks in the way of realization of all other human rights, restoration of already infringed rights and under threat of the use of compulsion measures making their infringement unprofitable. In our opinion, the basic scientific and theoretical value of such approach in the understanding of civil human rights means that it focuses on the search of more effective means and mechanisms of uninterrupted embodiment of civil human rights during life.

The consideration of the basic directions of research of civil human rights in the domestic jurisprudence helps to make a conclusion about their reality, urgency and importance both from the methodological and practical point of view. However, if we consider the originality of the historical period experienced by the Russian Federation, some features of the place and role of the state in the affairs of the society, social groups and a separate person, it is impossible to disagree that from the practical point of view it is the legal aspect of studying civil human rights that is characterized by the greatest sociopolitical and legal pressure that this tension is known to the corresponding scientific researches as well, in which the alarm for the status of civil human rights security in Russia is traced. The special reports by O.O. Mironov, the Human Rights Commissioner in Russia, are the most convincing confirmation of it. It unequivocally follows from them that infringement of human rights in general and civil human rights in particular, from the bodies of the state has become really mass that the mechanisms calculated on non-admission of the human rights infringement, in some cases are not formed and do not work for this reason, and in other cases they are openly trampled by officials. Unfortunately, this is a reality which cannot be ignored. Therefore, in our opinion, these are the problems of human rights that should draw today's attention to the increasing number of lawyers and, thus, turn to a strategically important direction of the development of the theory of human rights.

Speaking about a remedial direction in the theory of human rights, it is necessary to remark that the thesis used here about a methodologically-constructive role of the human right to legal protection should not interfere with the statement of the question, namely, from the point of view of its analysis in interrelation with corresponding legal duties. It is true that studying of human rights to legal protection separately from those duties that make this right by the legal phenomenon proper, reduces its both scientific and practical value while if they are taken in unity, it is possible to express and realize the idea of legal protection of human rights in a wider sense. It is thought that **a complex research of civil human rights protection (the right of a person to legal protection with legal duties providing this right) can overcome the existing separation of civil human rights in general and the right of a person to legal protection in particular, from those real mechanisms which the subjective and objective right has.** We mean the following: as S.S. Alekseev notices, from the legal point of view, the specificity of a human right to legal protection means that it is designed by the principle "the right for the right". It initially presupposes the existence of legally obliged party and through legal duties of this party the civil right of a person to legal protection interferes "in the legal matter, in the complex of legal mechanisms expressed in legal regulations, laws, and objective properties of the right"[1]. In other words, through legal duties the right to legal protection has an opportunity to involve almost the whole mechanism of legal regulation of human rights protection. The absence of any theoretical researches of a human right to protection in the noted unity and interrelation with legal duties interferes with knowledge of its essence.

The structure of the right of a person to legal protection is formed by the following competences: 1) an opportunity of a person to use such value as legal protection of the natural and inalienable rights (right-use). The given competence was recorded in the Preamble of the Universal Declaration of Human Rights where the following is written, "It is essential, if man is not to be compelled to have recourse, as a last resort, to rebellion against tyranny and oppression, that human rights should be protected by the rule of law". It is further indicated in Article 1 of the Convention on Protection of Human Rights and Basic Freedoms in which the duty on the states which have signed the Convention is assigned to ensure the provision of security of human rights. "The High Agreeing Parties, it is said in this clause, provide each person who is being under their jurisdiction with the rights and freedoms stated in Section I of the present Convention". At a national level this competence, as a rule, is recorded in the Constitution and other federal laws. The right to legal protection in the Russian Federation is recorded in part 1 of Article 17 where it is said that "in the Russian Federation the rights and freedoms of a person and a citizen are admitted and guaranteed according to the conventional principles and standards of the international law and according to the present Constitution"; 2) an opportunity for a person to demand from legally obliged persons diligent and absolute fulfillment of the requirements by them following from their right to legal protection (right-requirement). It is possible to illustrate this competence by the indication to Article 1 of the International Act on the Main Principles, concerning the role of lawyers the United Nations accepted by the Eighth Congress on the Prevention of Criminality and Treatment of Offenders, Havana, dd. August, 27 - September, 7, 1990) in which it is written that "each person has a right to address to any lawyer for protection and upholding of their rights and their protection at all stages of criminal proceedings"; 3) an opportunity of a person by means of the actions to carry out protection of the rights belonging to him (right-behaviour). Various forms of self-defense are meant in this case.[2] In the Constitution of the Russian Federation this competence is recorded in Part 2 of Article

45. It is written there, "Everyone has a right to defend the rights and freedoms in all ways possible which have been not forbidden by law"; 4) an opportunity of a person to involve human rights organizations, states, international community and the public in the realization of the right to legal protection. The given remedial competence is recorded in Part 1 of Article 45 of the Constitution of the Russian Federation, in Article 34 of the Convention on Protection of Human Rights and Basic Freedoms.

The right to legal protection is realized in special legal relationships which have received the name remedial in the scientific literature. Thus, for example, A.V. Stremouhov, characterizing the category "legal activity on protection of human rights", comes to the conclusion that it is realized only in remedial relations, "in which one entitled party has a right to demand non-admission of encroachment on the rights, freedoms and legitimate interests, i.e. their protection and, in the case of such, their restoration (protection) and another one (obligatory) should not admit any infringement of the right or restore it if it is infringed by it".[3]

It is well-known that the terms "legal aid", "legal expert" in our country have been historically linked to the activity of nongovernmental public organizations. Now they are used in the scientific literature in a wider sense. It is the activity of all structures, state and public, aimed at human rights protection.

It is necessary to note that the traditional classification of legal relationships happens according to a branch attribute (constitutionally-legal, administratively-legal, civil legal relationships, etc.).

Allocating remedial relations, we bring to a focus another criterion of their classification: a way of realization and a kind of the used guarantees of human rights. If human rights are realized freely by a person, without any obstacles guarantees-conditions of realization are carried out.

In this case human rights materialize within the limits of legal relationships, embodying possession and use of these rights by a person. When a citizen uses freely rights to life, dignity, personal immunity, it means that with the help of guarantees-conditions of realizations appropriate conditions for the realization of these rights are created. If human rights are broken, a person uses the right to legal protection the realization of which leads to the occurrence of remedial relations.

Thus, these legal relationships become the form of use of legal guarantees which are the means of human rights protection. As legal guarantees play the main role in the realization of civil human rights, remedial relations get a special value.

Remedial relations are a new phenomenon in our legal system that is why they, in fact, have not been researched by experts yet.

Their specific features consist in the following:

1. Remedial relations arise on the basis of such legal phenomenon as a human right to protection. This right generates remedial attitude irrespective of its presence or absence in the national legislation. In any case an individual has a right to carry out the protection of his rights independently or by means of other subjects, using within the limits of these relations of both interstate and international remedial bodies and organizations.[4] 2. Human rights relations are characterized by a legal connection between the parties, in which the entitled party (the holder of the right to legal protection) assigns a corresponding legal duty to another. 3. The realization of a human right to legal protection and the execution of the legal duty connected with it are provided by an opportunity of the state compulsion but can be realized without any intervention by remedial bodies and organizations.

The indicated features allow emphasizing remedial relations from the whole number of legal relationships, being formed in very various areas of the vertical and horizontal cut of the whole system of legal relationships. First of all, it is necessary to refer to the following ones: the relations between the state (its bodies) and each person, social groups and the society as a whole; the relations inside the state, between its bodies in the case of normative-legal and organizational-legal human rights ensuring; strong-willed relations between the people involved in the process of realizing human rights to legal protection; relations between the state and the international community, on behalf of its remedial organizations; relations between the states in the case of and in connection with human rights ensuring.

The originality of remedial relations is expressed to the fullest in its element structure which is the object, the subject and the content. The specificity of the properties of these elements directly results in a conclusion that remedial attitude is that form in which the human right to legal protection is joined to a legal duty and further develops in the whole system of remedial regulations. And it is just the confirmation of the fact that the remedial attitude can and should act as the starting point from the position of which there appears an opportunity to reveal and eliminate the blanks in the legislation and to put up reliable barriers to stop officials being nihilistic towards human rights.

The object of legal relationships is understood as those phenomena (subjects) of the world surrounding us and also socially efficient duties and their results to which the legal rights and legal duties are directed.[5]

The object legal relationships should not be mixed with the object of legal regulation. If the object of legal relationships is always that value in case of which the legal relationship itself arises and develops, the object of legal regulation is understood as a public attitude to which the regulative influence of the right is directed.

During the analysis of the object of remedial relations a great importance is acquired by the interrelation of the object of the legal relationships and the legal right noted by practically all experts[6]. The main thing in this interrelation is concluded in the fact that the circle of objects of legal relationships is set by the legal right which, in turn, directly expresses the interests the entitled parties. Owing to that, the object as a legal phenomenon is revealed from the utility, i.e. abilities to satisfy a person's need.

In view of the noted object (subject) of remedial relations it is necessary to recognize those properties of a person and also the material and non-material values, socially significant actions and their results, possession and use of which are connected with a status of worthy existence of a person and which are put under protection of its right.

Remedial relations develop in connection with certain values which, in one case, have a person as a source (freedom of a person, human life) and in another one they have external phenomena in relation to them (things from the material and inner world, ecology, socially efficient duties and their results: habitation, clothes, information, education, medical and legal aid, etc.) which have the vital value for their worthy existence.

Every remedial attitude has its object. In a generalized and ordered presentation all objects of remedial relations can be subdivided into the following kinds: 1) personal (life, health, freedom, honour and dignity of a person, etc.); 2) social and economic (food, clothes, habitation, medical care and necessary social service, etc.); 3) political and civil (participation in politics and management, freedom of speech and information, opportunity of citizens to carry out meetings, demonstrations, processions and picketing, etc.). Remedial relations arising in the sphere of civil rights, come into use through the first group of objects.

While characterizing the list of objects of remedial relations it should be noted that it (the list) basically coincides with the structure of the basic rights and freedoms of a person, recorded in the fundamental international documents under human rights. However, such statement requires some specification. The thing is that in addition to the values following from the human nature and a level of socio-economic and political development of a society and being an object of remedial relations, it is difficult to refer so-called procedural human rights which arise within the limits of remedial relations. Hence, the values, standing up for these rights, cannot unequivocally be considered as objects of remedial relations (but they certainly are a subject of legal regulation). For example, it is written in Part 1of Article 6 of the European Convention for the Protection of Human Rights and Basic Freedoms: "Each person when defending his civil rights and duties or while considering any criminal charge brought against him has a right to a fair and public trial of the case in a reasonable term by an independent and impartial court created on the basis of law". Is it possible to consider a public trial, its reasonable term, an impartiality of court, etc. as an object of remedial relations? In our opinion, it is impossible as here it is a question of legal duties execution of one of the participants within the limits of the existing uniform remedial relations.

As an additional argument of such statement it is possible to refer to the conclusion of V.P. Bozhiev of that "the object of criminally-remedial legal relationships is a criminally-legal relationship in its objective (i.e. trustworthy) status".[7]

Subjects of remedial relations are those physical and legal persons who have a legal connection with a subject (object) of remedial relations. This legal connection means that subjects of remedial relations have legal personality (competence) which allows them to act as participants of remedial relations. Subjects of remedial relations are all participants of the given relations interconnected through the reciprocally corresponding rights and duties. Thus, it is necessary to draw distinction between the concepts "the holder of the right to legal protection" and "the subject of remedial relations". The circle of subjects of remedial relations is much wider than subjects of the right of human rights defence.

The analysis of the normative documents on human rights allows referring to two categories of participants among the number of subjects of remedial relations. The first category are subjects of human rights to legal protection and the second category are those participants of remedial relations who are involved in them on the basis of an available legal duty not to break human rights and to carry out their protection by virtue of the legal duties assigned to them.

Subjects (bearers) of all generations of human rights relate to the first category, namely, a separate person (a natural person), a social community (people, nation, and group) and all mankind.[8]

The second category of subjects of remedial relations are organizations (international, state, private, public), officials and just citizens who have to respect and protect human rights. A separate individual (an official, citizen), thus, acts in two legal strata, namely, as an authorized person (a right to legal protection belongs to him from birth, it is universally and inalienable) and as a person, legally obliged to respect, observe and realize the protection of human rights.

The presence of two strongly pronounced categories of subjects of remedial relations enables to establish a correlation between them and to emphasize the primary and secondary among them. From our point of view, it is necessary to refer exclusively the bearers of human rights to legal protection to the number of basic subjects. The second group of subjects of remedial relations are those persons (natural and legal) who are legally obliged not to break human rights and to execute the requirements incorporated in human rights to legal protection.

The place and role of each subject in a remedial relation are determined by his legal status (competence).

A feature of a legal status of physical subjects of remedial relations is inseparability of the categories of legal competence and capacity. The unity of legal competence and capacity reflects a principle of the unity of rights and duties in a legal status of a person. On this occasion it is written in the Universal Declaration of Human Rights that "each person has duties before a society in which free and full development of their personality is only possible "that the realization of the rights and freedoms by a citizen demands "a due concept and respect of the rights and freedoms of others, satisfactions of fair moral requirements, general order and well-being in a democratic society".

The unshared state of legal competence and capacity explains also the interdiction to abuse human rights by one party to the detriment of interests of another.

At a more detailed approach to the problem of legal properties of physical subjects of remedial relations it is possible to reveal material and formal conditions of their legal personality. The material condition of a legal personality is an ability of the given person to have the right to legal protection, in other words, the property inherent in a person from birth. A formal condition of a legal personality is a concept of external legal authority (the state, international community) the indicated ability in the given person. It is expressed in the concept of human rights in general. Only the unity of these two conditions can characterize more exhaustively a natural person as a subject of remedial relations.

A legal person as a subject of remedial relations is lodged with remedial competence. The competence is a concept designating a legal expression of the set of powers and functions of the given subject. Remedial competence is a set of remedial powers realized in basic directions of the activity of a legal person. A feature of such competence means that a remedial body (organization) does not have its own right to legal protection as it is not the subject of human rights. The meaning of the presence of remedial competence at a certain body of the state, international community, public organization completely follows from the purpose of human rights and their protection. In this connection it will not be superfluous to remind that according to Article 18 of the Constitution of the Russian Federation "the rights and freedoms of a person and a citizen are directly current. They determine the meaning, the content and use of laws, the activity of legislative and executive authority, local self-management and are provided by justice". "It means, N.I. Matuzov writes, that Russian citizens as bearers of these rights act in relation to the state as the authorized and the state in relation to them is a law authorized party".[9] Therefore, it is necessary to recognize as an axiom that the legal person as a subject of remedial relations has a right on behalf of and in favour of a certain bearer of human rights, and hence human rights to legal protection to make legally relevant actions. Forms, structure, functions and limits of this activity are determined by the content of those functions which are assigned to them by the subject who created them.

"The bearer of the sovereignty and a unique source of authority in the Russian Federation are its multinational people", which is written in Article 3 in the Constitution of the Russian Federation. These are people who assigned a duty on protection of human rights to the state. From here the remedial competence of all bodies of the state follows.

Similarly, the formation of remedial international bodies (organizations) and their competence, with the only difference that the role of a source of international authority is carried out by the states that signed and ratified the documents on recognition and protection of human rights. Thus, for example, the states that signed the European Convention on the Protection of Human Rights and Basic Freedoms formed such body as the European Court on Human Rights.

The legal personality and competence of subjects of remedial relations, being recorded in the corresponding legal sources, is expressed in the same way in a general legal status of subjects of remedial relations. The specificity of the formation and content of the initial legal status of subjects of remedial relations, firstly, testifies to the existence of a special (intended only for the regulation of remedial relations) way of the remedial relations regulation and, secondly, essentially influences its features and orientation of influence.

There are certain features that are inherent in the content of remedial relations. We agree with a number of the authors who consider the content of legal relationships as its internal structure consisting of acute (real behaviour of participants of legal relationships, expressed in their action or inaction) and legal (legal rights and legal duties of the legal relationships parties).[10] Thus, we recognize that the material content inseparably connects a legal relationship with real social relations and a legal one serves as legal means of ensuring and, in some cases, formation of the material content of legal relationships. The legal element of remedial relations represents a connection of a human right to legal protection, on the one hand, and a corresponding legal duty, on the other. Besides, this connection is the most obvious proof of the fact that we witness a legal relationship. "The connection between the right and duty, to be exact, between their bearers, is also a legal relationship," N.I. Matuzov remarks.[11]

It is necessary to note that the legal content of remedial relations is a form of a detailed definition and record of those basic legal instructions (interdictions, permissions and obligations) which represent a human right to legal protection in an extremely generalized way. These general legal instructions, owing to the ability to be recorded in the legal rights and legal duties, acquire a quality of behaviour regulators of subjects of remedial relations. Outside of their expression in the form of the legal right they cannot execute the role of ways and means of legal regulation.

As a legal category, a subjective human right to legal protection is revealed through a set of corresponding remedial powers that form its internal structure.

The above basic remedial powers set forth correspond to the legal duties of the other party of remedial relations. This correspondence is characterized by law. "In real life, S. S. Alekseev emphasizes, there is no legal right (as a legal phenomenon) if it not "the right" in relation to someone, i.e. if it is not anyhow connected with duties. There is also no duty (as a legal phenomenon) if the right of the requirement does not correspond to it. The right which is not provided by duties and the duties which have been not been supported by the right of the requirement, turn to "a [12]legal zero"".

The purpose of legal duties in a remedial attitude is to satisfy, execute remedial competences. Therefore, **the structure of legal duties corresponds to the structure of human rights to legal protection.** "The structure of a legal duty, N. I. Matuzov writes, corresponds to the structure of the legal right (as if being its underside) and also includes four components: 1) the necessity to perform certain actions or to refrain from them; 2) the necessity for a law authorized person to react to the legal requirements turned to him by the authorized; 3) the necessity to bear the responsibility for any default of these requirements; 4) the necessity not to interfere with the counterpart to use that value to which they have a right".[13]

Alongside with the legal content in the remedial attitude, there is also an acute element that is legal behaviour. This element of remedial relations is presented by legally significant actions of its parties which are subjects of remedial relations.

It is known that the term "legally significant behaviour" covers two variants of behaviour of subjects: lawful behaviour and unlawful behaviour.

The unlawful illegal behaviour with reference to remedial relations acts as one of its bases and proves itself in the form of the legal fact which is behaviour (action or inaction), that breaks human rights. Therefore, the unlawful behaviour lies outside current remedial relations. However, it does not mean that it does not have any legal properties. All the attributes of the illegal behaviour are recorded in the legislation and form structures of human rights infringement. The realization of such behaviour is forbidden by this legislation under the threat of the use of corresponding sanctions.

The main specific feature of the illegal behaviour is that the subject has not executed the duty assigned to him which is called to satisfy a certain remedial competence. Such duty can be formulated quite particularly in the form of the corresponding obligation, or indirectly, in the form of the permission or interdiction.

The lawful behaviour of subjects of remedial relations is a set of actions or inactions the realization of which, firstly, corresponds to the requirements of the provisions about human rights and secondly, means the realization of these instructions. "...The realization of the rights and freedoms in a general view, I.V. Rostovschikov writes, is the practical use of the social opportunities stipulated by legal provisions and as a result, a person receives various material and other values to satisfy individual and, to a certain extent, public interests and needs".[14] The legal behaviour as an element of remedial relations can be only lawful.

The lawful behaviour represents a transformation of the inwardness of a person into an action under the influence of the right.[15] It reflects a direct contact of the subject to the legal reality during which strong-willed efforts are revealed and the objectivization of the legal content of legal relationships is carried out.

In the remedial attitude the lawful behaviour is presented by actions or inactions of its participants. In this behaviour the legal content of remedial relations is materialized. However, this general provision demands explanations.

Legal rights and legal duties influence directly the behaviour of remedial relations participants. The essence of this influence is expressed in the fact that rights and duties act as legal programs of the behaviour itself. Their orientation is caused by the character of remedial competences and a corresponding legal duty. They bring order to the actions of the parties of a legal relationship.

The lawful behaviour of the entitled party of a remedial relation should be distinguished from the lawful behaviour of a legally obliged one. If the behaviour of the entitled party is the form of the legal rights use, the behaviour of the counterpart is the execution of legal duties (interdictions). Depending on where the active legal center in a certain remedial relation is situated, in a plane of competences or duties, all human rights relations are subdivided into active and passive.[16] Remedial relations of the active type are characterized by the fact that a legally obliged subject should make certain active actions with a view of satisfaction of remedial powers of the other party. In passive human rights relations this subject is obliged to abstain from actions which can lead to failure, infringement of the realization process of the rights of the entitled party.

Passive human rights relations are always a general legal relationship. Active ones, on the contrary, can take place only as certain remedial relations.

At present the problem of general legal relationships still remains debatable. We share the point of view according to which general legal relationships exist and play an important role in the mechanism of legal regulation, i.e. act both as a means and a form of the realization of the right. Therefore, we support N. I. Matuzov, who writes, "...General legal relationships, unlike specific ones, express legal connections of a higher level between the state and citizens and also the latter between themselves in case of warranting and realization of the basic rights and personal freedoms (the right to life, honour, dignity, safety, inviolability of dwelling, freedom of speech, and others) and equally the duties (to observe laws, the law and order). They arise mainly on the basis of provisions of the Constitution, other basic instruments and are basic, initial for the branch legal relationships".[17] N. I. Matuzov's words can entirely and completely be applied to the characteristic of general remedial relations. They arise from the fact of a concept of human rights and act as a form of their realization.

In general remedial relations of a legally obliged subject correspond to certain remedial competences, abstains from the realization of the forbidden behaviour patterns.

General remedial relation is a way of realization of both human rights to legal protection and all other rights.

The regulatory instructions recording human rights to legal protection have a representatively-binding character. Hence, the interrelation between a duty to abstain from illegal actions and a human right to demand execution of this duty is ideally simulated in them. **This interrelation is an "interdiction-right" in the process of legal regulation and is indicated in general remedial relations. The legal content of the given relation is concluded in the fact that on the basis of such interrelation a person has a right to demand strict observance of the law instructions (interdictions) and the duty not to make such actions lays on the state and other subjects. These rights and duties (interdictions) are, in fact, carried out by the behaviour of the obliged subjects that are active actions of the entitled party towards the realization of human rights and abstention from the forbidden patterns.**

It is possible to refer to the institution of personal immunity as an example of the real confirmation of the above mentioned reasoning. It is known that the right of a person to inviolability stands against the duty of all other persons not to encroach on this right. Such connection is a general legal relationship. It is realized without any infringement of the rights of the entitled person. But as soon as a right of a person is infringed, the duty of the infringer in relation to it precisely comes to light and the general legal relationship itself turns in the form into a specific one. In this case the legal connection between the participants of remedial relations is specified and a legally obliged party performs active actions directed at the fulfillment of the requirements that follow from remedial powers of the entitled party.

Thus, the division of remedial relations into active and passive inevitably leads to a concept of their division into general and specific remedial relations.

Notes

1. Alekseev S.S. Law: Alphabet – Theory – Philosophy: the Results of a Certain Research. Moscow, 1999. P. 631. / Алексеев С. С. Право: азбука – теория – философия: Опыт конкретного исследования. М., 1999. С. 631.

2. Outside the problems, to which this topic is devoted, there are such forms of self-defence, permitted by law and morally approved, as a necessary defence, namely, an action, though being by the characteristics a crime on the objective part, but carried out "during the defence ... of human rights or the rights of the defendant or another person against a socially dangerous endeavour by doing harm to the offender" (Article 13 of the Penal Code of RSFSR). The same should be said about such a form of self-defence as an extreme necessity - an action, though being by the characteristics a crime, but carried out to eliminate the danger for the person's interests or rights of this person or other citizens, if this danger in this circumstances could not be eliminated by other means and if the caused harm is less significant than the averted harm.

3. Stremouhov A.V. Legal Protection of a Person: Theoretical aspect: A Synopsis of the Thesis ... of the Doctor of Jurisprudence. S.-Petersburg, P. 12. / Стремоухов А. В. Правовая защита человека: Теоретический аспект: Автореф. дис. ... д-ра юрид. наук. СПб., 1996. С. 12.

4. See: Rostovschikov I.V. The Human Rights Realization and the Activity of the Internal Affaires Authorities. Volgograd, 1996. P. 7-8. / См.: Ростовщиков И.В. Реализация прав личности и деятельность органов внутренних дел. Волгоград, 1996. С. 7-8.

5. See: Alekseev S.S. The Basic Theory of Law: in 2 volumes. Volume 2. Moscow, 1982. P. 154; Problems of the Basic Theory of Law and the State / ed. by V.S. Nersesyants. Moscow, 1999. P. 382. / См.: Алексеев С. С. Общая теория права: В 2 т. Т. 2. М., 1982. С. 154; Проблемы общей теории права и государства / Под ред. В. С. Нерсесянца. М., 1999. С. 382.

6. See more in: Tolstoy Yu.K. To the Theory of Legal Relations. Leningrad, 1959. P. 42; Grevtsov Yu.I. Problems of the Theory of a Legal Relation. Leningrad, 1981. P. 81; Osnovin V.S. Soviet State-Legal Relations. Moscow, 1965. P. 62. / Подробнее см.: Толстой Ю. К. К теории правоотношения. Л., 1959. С. 42; Гревцов Ю. И. Проблемы теории правового отношения. Л., 1981. С. 81; Основин В. С. Советские государственно-правовые отношения. М., 1965. С. 62.

7. Bozhiev V.P. Criminal Procedure Relations. Moscow, 1975. P. 139. / Божьев В.П. Уголовно-процессуальные правоотношения. М., 1975. С. 139.

8. Thus, an American professor L. Son writes: "An international law admits not only inseparable laws of the individuals, but also some certain group rights, which are realized together by the individuals, organized into large groups of people, including peoples and nations. These rights are the rights of a person; the effective realization of group rights is a condition of the realization of other rights, both political and economic ones." Cit.: The Basic Theory of Human Rights / Ed. by E. A. Lukasheva. M., 1999. P. 489-490. This conclusion is shared by the absolute majority of the domestic legal scholars. / Цит. по: Общая теория прав человека / Под ред. Е. А. Лукашевой. М., 1999. С. 489-490.

9. Matuzov N.I. Human Rights and General Regulative Legal Relations // Legal Science.1996. № 3. P. 27-39. / Матузов Н. И. Права человека и общерегулятивные правоотношения // Правоведение. 1996. № 3. С. 27-39.

10. See: Yavich L.S. Law and Public Relations. Moscow, 1971. P. 117; Alekseev S. S. Problems of the Theory of Law. Vol. 1. Sverdlovsk, 1972. P. 256-301; Halphina R. O. The Basic Study of a Legal Relation. Moscow, 1998. P. 257 and others. / См.: Явич Л.С. Право и общественные отношения. Moscow, 1971. С. 117; Алексеев С. С. Проблемы теории права. Т. 1. Свердловск, 1972. С. 256-301; Халфина Р.О. Общее учение о правоотношении. М., 1998. С. 257 и др.

11. Matuzov N.I. Basic Legal Relations and Their Specificity // Legal Science.1976. № 3. P. 23. / Матузов Н. И. Общие правоотношения и их специфика // Правоведение. 1976. № 3. С. 23.

12. Alekseev S.S. The Basic Theory of Law: in 2 Volumes. Vol. 2. Moscow, 1982. P. 86. / Алексеев С.С. Общая теория права: В 2 т. Т. 2. М., 1982. С. 86.

13. The Theory of the State and Law: A Series of Lectures / Ed. by N.I. Matuzov, A.V. Malko. Moscow, 1997. P. 492. / Теория государства и права: Курс лекций / Под ред. Н.И. Матузова, А.В. Малько. М., 1997. С. 492.

14. Rostovschikov I.V. Human Rights Realization and the Activity of the Internal Affaires Authorities Volgograd, 1996. P. 63. / Ростовщиков И. В. Реализация прав личности и деятельность органов внутренних дел. Волгоград, 1996. С. 63.

15. See more in: Lazarev V. V. The Influence of the Regular Patterns of Lawful Behaviour // The Soviet State and Law. 1983. № 11. P. 20. / Подробнее см.: Лазарев В. В. Влияние закономерностей правомерного поведения // Советское государство и право. 1983. № 11. С. 20.

16. On the Division of Legal Relations into Active and Passive see: Alekseev S. S. The Basic Theory of Law: in 2 volumes. Vol. 2. Moscow, 1982. P. 108-109. / О делении правоотношений на активные и пассивные см.: Алексеев С. С. Общая теория права: В 2 т. Т. 2. М., 1982. С. 108-109.

17. The Theory of the State and Law: A Series of Lectures / Ed. by N. I. Matuzov, A. V. Malko. Moscow, 1997. P. 478. / Теория государства и права: Курс лекций / Под ред. Н. И. Матузова, А. В. Малько. М., 1997. С. 478.

Chapter 15. THE RIGHT TO FAIR, IMPARTIAL
AND LAWFUL TRIAL

One of basic rights and freedoms of a person recorded in the world standards is the human right to fair, impartial and lawful proceeding. For the first time it was formulated in the British Magna Carta (1215) and then in the American Bill of Rights (1791) and in the French Declaration of Civil Human Rights (1789) Thus, in Article 20 of the British Magna Carta it was proclaimed that each free person would be fined for a little offence only in compliance with a sort of an act for everyone large precisely in proportion to importance of this act. The rule recorded in Article 39 of Magna Carta was also important, providing that any free person couldn't be imprisoned, deprived, outlawed, expelled, or by otherwise made destitute as on a lawful verdict equal to them and according to the law of the country.

In the American Bill of Rights the elements of human rights to fair, impartial and lawful proceeding are included in the Sixth Amendment providing the right of the accused to urgent and public trial of a case by an impartial jury of that state or district in which the crime was committed. Thus, the accused has a right to be informed about the essence and the bases of a charge, to the legal aid of the lawyer for the protection. In the French Declaration of Civil Human Rights elements of this right are included in Article 7 according to which nobody can be subjected to charge, detention or imprisonment otherwise than in the cases stipulated by the law and in the forms ordered by them.

Human rights to fair, impartial and lawful proceeding have considerably developed and enriched as a result of long historical formation. During the modern period they have been already recorded in the Universal Declaration of Human Rights accepted by the General Assembly of the United Nations on December, 10th, 1948 and have become a basis of international standards for understanding of rights and freedoms of a person as a whole, and the given right in particular.

In Article 7-11 and other clauses of the Universal Declaration equality is stipulated: all people are equal before the law without any distinction;

the right of each person to restoration in the rights in competent national courts; prohibition of any imprisonment, detention or exile; the right of each person for definition of their rights and duties and organization of reality of the criminal charge brought to him, on the basis of full equality on that its case was considered publicly with observance of all requirements of reality by independent and impartial court. It is proclaimed that everyone of the accused of committing a crime has a right to be considered in innocent while his fault is not proved legislatively by public proceeding at which all opportunities for protection are provided to them.

But most fully and in details this right is formulated in Article 14 of International Covenant on Civil and Political Rights, accepted by the United Nations on December, 16, 1966 and Article 6 of the European Convention for the Protection of Human Rights and Basic Freedoms dd. November, 4, 1950. According to the mentioned legal provisions all persons are equal before trials and tribunals. Everyone has a right to consideration of any criminal charge, brought to him, or at definition of rights and duties in any civil process on fair and public trial of a case in reasonable term, by the competent, independent and impartial court created on the basis of the law.

Neither in pre-revolutionary Russia, nor during the Soviet period of history of our country in theory and in law enforcement practice the concept of "human right to fair, impartial and lawful proceeding" was used and is used. This circumstance has also caused the occurrence of some problems in the given area during the modern period. As legislative base for the solution of these problems and also the Declaration of Rights and Freedoms of a Person and a Citizen, accepted on November, 22, 1991 serve the Constitution of the Russian Federation (1993).

The indicated right, certainly, refers to the number of human rights and consequently it has natural and in alienable character. Features, characteristic for human rights are inherent in them. Nevertheless, neither the Constitution of the Russian Federation, nor the Declaration of Rights and Freedoms of a Person and a Citizen has directly recorded the concept of civil human rights on fair, impartial and lawful proceeding.

By consideration of one of the cases in February, 2004 the Constitutional Court of the Russian Federation indicated that in conformity with Article 6 of the Convention on Protection of Human Rights and Basic Freedoms and Article 14 of International Covenant on Civil and Political Rights "everyone at definition of his civil rights and duties or by consideration of any criminal charge to him, has a right to fair public trial of a case in reasonable term by the competent, independent and impartial court created on the basis of the law". The indicated provisions as concerning the conventional principles and standards of international law, according to part 4 Article 15 of the Constitution of the Russian Federation, are a component of legal system of the Russian Federation.

Besides, the Constitution and the Declaration contain all major elements of this right. First of all, Article 46 of the Constitution has proclaimed that everyone is guaranteed judicial protection of his rights and freedoms. In detail the indicated elements are recorded in the current legislation. Therefore, it is possible to admit that human rights to fair, impartial and lawful proceeding are recorded in the modern Russian law and are a constitutional law of a person and a citizen of the Russian Federation.

The question is to what kind of human rights it can be referred: to civil, political or to another. At first sight, it refers to the number of civil human rights as it provides to them personal safety and protection of various interests. By the character and nature it is close to such rights as a right to personal immunity, the right to inviolability of dwelling, etc. But at the same time by means of the right to fair, impartial and lawful proceeding it is possible to refer protection of not only personal safety and personal (individual) freedom but also such values as property, free work, etc. Therefore, it seems that the given right refers to the number of a special kind of rights: rights-guarantees which use is directed to protection of the whole system of rights and freedoms of a person.

On the structure the right to fair, impartial and lawful proceeding has a complex character. Let's consider the content of this right. Its basic elements from our point of view are the following:

1) the right to fair proceeding;
2) the right to consideration of a case by impartial court;
3) the right to the public (open) proceeding;
4) the right to consideration of a case by competent court;
5) the right to lawful proceeding;
6) the right to consideration of a case by independent court;
7) the right to consideration has put the court created on the basis of the law;
8) the right to consideration of a case in reasonable terms.

Each of the listed elements represents the separate legal right following from the Constitution of the Russian Federation, the Declaration of Rights and Freedoms of a Person and a Citizen, the Federal constitutional law "Judicial System of the Russian Federation" and the law of the Russian Federation "State of Judges of the Russian Federation". Any of these rights from the point of view of internal structure can be researched by revealing their content of the right-behaviour, the right-requirement, the right-claim and the right to use social values.

For example, the right to consideration of a case by independent court includes, firstly, the right-behaviour, i.e. the right of a citizen to address in court which is created on the basis of Article 120 of the Constitution of the Russian Federation within the limits of judicial system established by the law and the Federal constitutional law "Judicial System of the Russian Federation"; secondly, it has also the right-requirement, i.e. can appeal during the litigation, the independence of court directed on ensuring (for example, the right to declare removal the court or somebody from judges); thirdly, the right-claim means that a citizen can appeal against actions of court if there are doubts in its independence. And finally, the right of using social values which means that all the above-mentioned powers allow a citizen to protect the rights. High-grade and all-round protection of civil human rights also makes in this case the major social value.

The right to fair proceeding, in opinion of western authors analyzing the European Convention on the rights and basic freedoms of a person, contains both objective and subjective elements. To objective elements one can refer the constitutional principle of division of authorities when, for example, a case was considered not by a judicial but by an administrative body or in structure of court there were employees of government agencies[1]. The subjective moments, from our point of view, assume the creation of such conditions at which the court has an opportunity and aspires to establish original true in a case in conditions of equality and competitiveness of the parties. According to the decision of the Constitutional Court dd. November, 28th, 1996 19-P, fair justice, in particular, it means "bringing to trial only problems to make a decision in case of criminal charge already brought to a person, rather than to formulate them independently".[2]

The right to fair proceeding recorded in Article 6 of the European Convention on Protection of Rights and Basic Freedoms, follows from of some clauses of the Constitution of the Russian Federation (Article 47, 123, etc.) and also from Article 8 of the Federal constitutional law "Judicial System of the Russian Federation" which provide participation of jurymen in legal proceedings, competitiveness and equality of the parties.

In our opinion, the right to fair proceeding includes also such legal guarantees as a right to protect personally or via a chosen defender, the right to participate in interrogation of witnesses, to use the help of the translator free-of-charge and other rights recorded in Clause 3 of Article 6 of the European Convention. Guarantees of reality should be provided by all possible legal means of protection of rights of person.

The right to consideration of a case by impartial court presupposes equality of the parties during absence of preferences, subjective aspiration of court to reveal true, and an estimation court of the obtained evidence on the basis of unemotional and unbiased attitude to all participants of the process. The European Court on Human Rights has determined impartiality as an "absence of bias". The objective factor of this concept is the aspiration to establish personal belief of the judge on the given case and subjective is definition of, whether they have given sufficient guarantees to exclude any lawful doubt in this respect[3].

The principle of impartiality of court is expressed in Clause 1 of Article 47, Clause 3 of Article 118 and also Article 121-123 of the Constitution. The right to consideration of a case by an impartial court in the most detailed way is formulated in Clause 2 of Article 7 of the Federal constitutional law "Judicial System of the Russian Federation".

The right to the public (open) proceeding follows from Article 123 of the Constitution of the Russian Federation and Article 9 of the Federal constitutional law "Judicial System of the Russian Federation", records a principle of publicity in activity of courts.

The right to consideration of a case by competent court follows from Article 119 of the Constitution and Ch. 2 of the same Federal constitutional law, Article 4-6 in which the list of necessary requirements is given to candidates on a post of a judge. The meaning of the indicated legal regulations consists in that functions of justice were carried out by legally competent, serious professionals having sufficient professional and life work experience.

The right to lawful proceeding is recorded in Article 47-52, 118 of the Constitution of the Russian Federation and Article 3 and 11 of the Federal constitutional law "Judicial System of the Russian Federation". The indicated right presupposes that protection of human rights is carried out by means of the Russian Federation established by the Constitution by the form of legal proceedings and any distortions of legal procedures are inadmissible by consideration of certain case.

The right to consideration of a case by independent court is recorded in a number of the clauses of the Constitution of the Russian Federation. Thus, in Article 10 of the Constitution the principle of independence of judicial authority is proclaimed. In Article 120 independence of judges is stipulated. The constitutional guarantees of this independence are recorded also in Article 121, 122 and 124 of the Constitution where it is emphasized that judges are permanent and in violable and financing of courts can be made only from the federal budget. These provisions are indicated in the above-mentioned Federal constitutional law "Judicial System of the Russian Federation" (Clause 2 of Article 1, Article 5, Clause 3 of Article 11, Articles 14-16). In particular, in Article 5 of the indicated law the content of the concept of independence and in dependence of judges is revealed. It means that courts have judicial authority irrespective of someone's will, being subject only to the law. Some clauses of the law of the Russian Federation "State of Judges of the Russian Federation" are devoted to this element of human rights also considered by us.

The right to consideration of a case by a court was created on the basis of the law directly following from provisions of Clause 3 of Article 118 by the Constitution of the Russian Federation and the Federal constitutional law according to which the judicial system of Russia is established. Creation of extreme courts is not supposed. Such requirements are contained in Article 4 of the Federal constitutional law "Judicial System of the Russian Federation".

Human rights to consideration of a case in reasonable terms are recorded in Article 14 of the International Covenant on Civil and Political Rights and Article 6 of the European Convention. The concept of "reasonable term" is revealed neither in the Constitution of the Russian Federation, nor in the current legislation. In the Code of Criminal Procedure of RSFSR and the Code of Civil Procedure of RSFSR there are established terms of legal proceeding in courts and also terms of preliminary investigation which in many cases have appeared as unreal. It is one of the most complicated questions requiring a special research. Tendencies to direct use of provisions of the European Convention were outlined in judiciary practice of Moscow concerning the terms of legal proceeding.

New criminally-remedial and civil-remedial legislation has expanded guarantees of human rights to consideration of a case in reasonable terms. In particular, new the Code of Civil Procedure of the Russian Federation provided a two-month's term of consideration of civil cases in court. And it basically corresponds to real opportunities of bodies of justice. The new Code of Criminal Procedure of the Russian Federation establishes terms of carrying out of preliminary investigation, detention of the suspected, holding in custody, etc. In particular, the suspected is subject to clearing after 48 hours from the moment of detention if the preventive punishment in the form of custody has not been elected or the court has not prolonged the term of detention in the order established by the law (Clause 2 of Article 94 of the Code of Criminal Procedure of the Russian Federation). In conformity with Article 109 of the Code of Criminal Procedure the term of holding in custody on preliminary investigation, as a rule, cannot exceed two months and under exclusive circumstances is prolonged for 18 months. "The further prolongation of the term is not supposed", is the Russian Federation is emphasized in Clause 4 of Article 109 of the Code of Criminal Procedure.

In the Decision of the Supreme Court of the Russian Federation dd. March, 5, 2004 "Use of Provisions of the Code of Criminal Procedure of the Russian Federation by Courts" judiciary practice connected with the realization of the Code of Criminal Procedure of the Russian Federation (2001) and, in particular, gave judicial interpretation of some problems concerning the correct understanding of the concept "reasonable terms".

The right to fair, impartial and lawful proceeding is provided with the guarantees recorded in the legislation. Legal guarantees relate to their number (for example, procedure of investment by powers of judges in the Russian Federation, presence of bodies of judicial community, etc.), economic guarantees (such as financing of courts from the federal budget), political guarantees (first of all, it is democratic regime in the state), organizational guarantees (for example, procedure of work of the qualified board of judges), moral guarantees (for the first time introduced by the law of the Russian Federation "State of Judges of the Russian Federation" the oath of the judge).

It is difficult to overestimate the importance of the right to fair, impartial and lawful proceeding in the system of civil human rights. Without exaggeration it is possible to say that this right is a gain of people that emphasizes democracy of Russian judicial system. It can be considered as an effective way of protection of rights and freedoms of a person and a citizen and as means of struggle against offences, means for strengthening legality as well as law and order. At the same time it is necessary to note the existing problems connected with the indicated right.

In the Report on activity of Human Rights Commissioner in the Russian Federation in 2003 such typical infringement of this right as encroachment of the right of citizens to consideration of their case in bodies of preliminary investigation and in court in reasonable term which appear in judicial red tape, unjustified postponement of litigation is noted; hindrance to the right to access to justice (refusal in acceptance of applications of victims, infringement of terms and order of consideration of these applications, not their consideration in criminally-remedial order, etc.)[4].

At the session of the Council that took place in May, 2004 at the President of the Russian Federation concerning perfection of justice the Chairman of the Constitutional Court of the Russian Federation of V.D. Zorkin noted that financial support of courts improved, legal and organizational bases of functioning of judicial authority were created. However, at the majority of the population the negative attitude to judicial authority didn't change. "Courts appeared to be rather vulnerable for corruption attack than they have declared. Bribery in courts appeared to be as one of the most powerful corruption markets in Russia, built in the various corruption networks acting on the different levels of authority, including technologies on disorder of criminal cases and interception of another's case"[5].

It is necessary to remark that activity of judges excludes reality, impartiality and legality of proceeding. The second problem mentioned on V.D. Zorkin, is instability of the legislation. Up to 80% of all bills in the State Duma are amendments to laws in force of the Criminal Code of the Russian Federation and of the Code of Criminal Procedure of the Russian Federation; they are hardly accepted even being half changed. To ensure the provision of legality of proceeding in such conditions begins rather inconveniently. And finally, the third problem about which the Chairman of the Constitutional Court of the Russian Federation spoke is the lack of qualified legal staff. It seems that they spoke not only about drawbacks of juridical education. The low wage of inspectors and other workers of law enforcement bodies, a low level of organization of their work have led to mass lay-offs of qualified personnel from law enforcement bodies, especially investigatory, experiencing an urgent need and lack of qualified employees and not capable to ensure the provision of a sufficient level of preliminary investigation. Thus it undermines legality of proceeding. Lack of personnel is felt during formation of the system of Justice of the Peace. Thus, it is necessary to note the problem of special preparation and retraining of judges. In the country there are basically only educational institutions in which lawyers of general jurisdiction are prepared. From this point of view the occurrence of numerous higher educational institutions specially intended for preparation of judges is worth mentioning. It would be necessary to pay special attention to the question of retraining of judges which owing to the huge loading practically have no an opportunity in due time to watch changes in the current legislation and judiciary practice. For example, practice of the Moscow city court on carrying out of periodic employment with judges is, certainly, insufficient. It would be expedient even once in 1-3 years to release judges from work that they could devote this time to occupation concerning legislation.

Recently, particularly in Moscow, plans of equipment of courts with modern technology have started to be realized. Creation of information network covering federal and world courts would allow to ensure the provision of judges with the legal information in due time.

Until recently in many cases problems with jurymen prevented effective justice. The difficulties connected with their attraction to judicial activity, frequently led to a tightening, red tape by consideration criminal and civil cases. Introduction of a jury has revived this problem. Courts experience significant difficulties with attraction of jurymen.

The principle of equality of participants of process recorded in the legislation quite often contradicts inequality of these participants. Not each of the parties has an opportunity to pay court costs or to use the qualified legal aid. It would be desirable to emphasize that this inequality is especially shown in conditions of competitiveness of process by consideration of civil and other cases.

Till now a problem in criminal cases is the presence of an accusatory bias not only at inspectors and public prosecutors but also at judges. As expertise shows, despite short stories in criminally-remedial legislation, the number of verdicts of "not guilty" does not increase.

In some cases poor-quality investigation gets especially negative attitude. There has appeared a new tendency: the judge makes a verdict of guilty on the basis of materials of poor-quality investigation, using the special order of acceptance of the comprehension, stipulated by Ch. 40 of the new Code of Criminal Procedure of the Russian Federation. The accused shall show "consent with the charge to him" and the verdict is made without proceeding. In this case it is not necessary to speak about the right to fair, impartial and lawful proceeding.

Indifferent and bureaucratic attitude from judges and other employees of court to participants of a process is also a very serious problem. The question of ensuring of judges impartiality in the legislation is not absolutely settled. But for the sake of justice it is necessary to note that judges still have the burden repeatedly exceeding established there is no time the specifications so far from a real life as well as those who established them. This circumstance evenly does not allow judges to properly execute their official responsibilities, for example, to consider a case in the terms established by the law. Important factors in the decision of the given problem are again the revived system of Justice of the Peace, the overwhelming number of cases considered by them individually included in jurisdiction and also provisions of the new Code of Criminal Procedure which provide procedure of consideration of many criminal cases by individually judges. It is supposed that it will allow creating normal conditions for judges' activity.

Judges experience certain difficulties, working in conditions which deprive them from the opportunity to consider a case independently and evenly. As a rule, judges still feel the dependence on local authorities (for example, in questions of improvement of living conditions) and also from chairmen of courts and qualified boards of judges. Pressure upon judges from the Office of Public Prosecutor also happens. But pressure upon judges from mass media when frequently ignorant of legal questions journalists using the rank to carry out direct pressure upon court try to make certain decisions is especially unbearable. Thus, the widely known practice of the publication of custom-made clauses has recently extended.

Judicial reform that happens today should provide wider and all-round guarantees of human rights to fair, impartial and lawful proceeding. However, as the Chairman of Council has noted at the President of the Russian Federation on judicial reform V. A. Tumanov at the session in May, 2004, "Legal reform is at a deadlock"[6]. Therefore, studying and analysis of the problems connected with real realization of considered human rights have the most serious scientific and practical value. On the foreground there are, certainly, practical results according to which it is possible to judge a real status of these problems. However, the importance's got also by the scientific party allowing theoretically developing ways, and estimations of realization of these human rights which in the further will be used in practice.

Notes

1. See: Gomien D., Harris D., Zvaak L. European Convention on Human Rights and the European Social Charter. Law and Practice. Moscow, 1998. P. 217-219. / См.: Гомьен Д., Харрис Д., Зваак Л. Европейская конвенция о правах человека и Европейская социальная хартия. Право и практика. М., 1998. С. 217–219.

2. The comment to decisions of the Constitutional Court of the Russian Federation: In 2 vol. Vol. 2. Moscow, 2000. P. 819. / Комментарий к постановлениям Конституционного Суда Российской Федерации: В 2 т. Т. 2. М., 2000. С. 819.

3. See: Gomien D., Harris D., Zvaak L. Specified work. P. 219. / См.: Гомьен Д., Харрис Д., Зваак Л. Указ. соч. С. 219.

4. See: The Report on Human Rights Commissioner Activity in the Russian Federation. Moscow, 2004. P. 42-47. / См.: Доклад о деятельности Уполномоченного по правам человека в Российской Федерации. М., 2004. С. 42–47.

5. Verdict at a Price-List // Rossiiskaya Gaseta. May, 19, 2004. / Приговор по прейскуранту // Российская газета. 2004. 19 мая.

6. Verdict at a Price-List // Rossiiskaya Gaseta. May, 19, 2004. / Приговор по прейскуранту // Российская газета. 2004. 19 мая.

Chapter 16. THE RIGHT TO LEGAL AID AND THE ROLE
OF THE LEGAL PROFESSION IN THE
PROTECTION OF CIVIL RIGHTS

§ 1. The Concept and Content of the Right to Legal Aid

The opportunity to receive legal aid by each person is an important value in any civilized society. Radical economic and sociopolitical transformations in modern Russia have led to occurrence of new social relations, democratization of forms and methods of their regulation. Against this background the need of participants of civil, criminal, administrative and other legal relationships to receive qualified legal aid has increased. It is not by chance that in the Constitution of the Russian Federation (1993) the right to reception of legal aid is especially distinguished.

Traditionally the need for legal aid is connected with corresponding participation of persons in criminal and procedural criminal relations. It is also necessary to point out that in the last decade there has been a considerable expansion of the circle of the bases of legal aid granting in the indicated sphere. Thus, the right to reception of qualified legal aid rendered by an expert is now really provided to the participants of criminal legal proceedings at not only during the of the proceeding but also at the stage of inquiry and preliminary investigation.

With development of civil and other legal relationships the situations, when it is hard (and sometimes practically impossible) to solve a certain problem without the consultation of a qualified expert, are becoming more frequent. The necessity for reception of legal services in cases which were irrelevant 10-20 years ago (e.g. private property relations, ecological legal relationships, indemnification of moral damage, etc.) has increased dramatically.

Legal aid as a social value in fact can be necessary for any society. Formation of its content has developed progressively for many centuries: certain elements of legal aid developed more or less dynamically at different stages of civilization. As a whole, the institution of legal aid has got more precise contours during occurrence of the constitutional system.

Occurrence of legal aid is inseparably linked with occurrence of the right and formation of the state. As an example the Athenian state should be marked out where in the 6th-7th centuries B.C. everyone had the right to seek legal aid from three "expounders of the sacred right". In the heyday of the Athenian democracy there developed a particular specialization of persons rendering legal services. It is notable, that in the Athenian the social attitude to logographs, receiving a payment for their services, was distinctly negative while those rendering help free of charge "out of friendship" were much respected[1].

An even more detailed division of labour on rendering legal aid took place in Ancient Rome. It was divided into three types: cavere (to make new claims and transactions), agere (to run a case in court), respondere (to give answers)[2]. Occurrence of the term "lawyer" is usually connected with legal proceedings in Ancient Rome. The term comes from the Latin word *advocatus* which in republican Rome meant friends and relatives of the litigant who accompanied them in court and gave advice during the session.

The institution of the right to legal aid gets its second wind during the period of formation of the bourgeois state legal relationships in the Middle Ages. One of the first states where the constitutional system appeared was England. It was not by chance that in the 17th century the need for legal services promoted occurrence of the profession of a legal counselor in the country.

Whereas there was no written constitution in England, the first written constitutions in a number of western countries contained the rights and freedoms providing guarantee of privacy of citizens, limiting the state from excessive intervention into it. Among the abovementioned rights and freedoms was one of the elements of the right to legal aid – the right to defense while being brought to account. Thus, the sixth amendment to the Constitution of the United States of America has established the right of the accused to demand a compulsory call of the witnesses and to use the help of the lawyer for defense[3].

In Russia the creation of the legal profession jury under the Judicial Charter of 1864 can be considered the beginning of professional rendering of legal aid[4]. While solving the problem concerning the persons rendering legal aid, Russia followed the German-Austrian example, according to which the defender (lawyer) executed two functions: those of defense and judicial notion. Organization of legal profession was adopted from the French system of organization of legal aid.

Certain development of the right to legal aid took place during the period between 1905 and October of 1917, when first autocracy and then the Provisional government carried out some liberal-democratic reforms. Development of legal aid in Russia after the revolution of 1917 was connected with appearance of Decree 1 "On Court" of 22 November 1917, according to which the defender was allowed to participate in preliminary investigation of all criminal cases. The Constitution of RSFSR of 1918 did not fix the Right to Legal Aid. However, it still contained its elements. The right to legal aid appeared in it as the right to know the text of the Constitution and also as the right to its explanation and interpretation. Thus, according to the Preamble of the Constitution, the National Commissariat of Education was entrusted to introduce the study of the main provisions of the Constitution as well as their explanation and interpretation in all schools and educational institutions without exception[5].

The right to legal aid was fixed in Article 111 of the Constitution (Organic Law) of the USSR of 1936[6]. It was recorded in the Constitution (Organic Law) of the USSR of 1977 (Article 158)[7]. The special law regulating the mechanism of legal aid rendering on a professional basis was the Law of the USSR of 1979 "Legal Profession"[8].

The right to legal aid is recorded practically in all modern constitutions (for example, in Article 37 of the Constitution of Japan). Most fully and precisely the right to legal aid is registered in the constitutions adopted during the last decades. Thus, practically all organic laws of the post Soviet states contain an article, and in some cases a whole chapter, devoted to legal aid. For example, Article 40 of the Constitution of the Armenian Republic, Article 62 of the Constitution of Byelorussia, Article 42 of the Constitution of Republic Georgia, Article 26 of the Constitution of Republic Moldova, Article 29 of the Constitution of Ukraine, Article 31 of the Constitution of Lithuania, etc.

Legal aid is also recorded in the norms of international law. The first international document which has recorded the Right to Reception of Legal Aid is the Universal Declaration (the right of a person to defense during the proceedings - Article 11).

The International Covenant on Civil and Political Rights of 1966 recorded the right of every person during consideration of any criminal charge to protect themselves personally or via the defender prescribed to them (part 3 Article 14)[9]. Here it is also possible to mention the minimal standard rules of treatment of prisoners. This document gives the person on trial the right to address free legal consultation where possible and also while imprisoned to meet the legal adviser who has taken up their defense (Article 93)[10]. The main principles concerning the role of lawyers fully enough regulate the questions of realization of the right to legal aid on the international level[11].

The considered right was reflected in international normative-legal regulations of regional character. For example, the European Convention for the Protection of Human Rights and Basic Freedoms of 1950 recorded the right of every person to defense personally or via a defender chosen by them or if they do not have sufficient means to pay for the services of a defender, to have a defender prescribed to them free of charge when it is necessary in the interests of justice[12].

The content of Article 48 of the Constitution of the Russian Federation (1993) about the right to legal aid was borrowed from the Declaration of Rights and Freedoms of a Person and a Citizen of RSFSR of 1991 practically without changes.

The whole history of formation and development of the right to legal aid indicates both the many-sided nature of the given legal phenomenon and its increasing importance in the world community, including modern Russia.

The right to legal aid is the right recorded in the Constitution in ac- cordance with the international standards which entitles every person to receive legal services to ensure economic, cultural, political interests and favourable vital activity of a person in different social spheres.

In law there are several terms which are either close in meaning or are identified with the term "legal aid". It is necessary to distinguish between the concepts of "legal aid" and "legal redress" according to the international agreements of the Russian Federation legal aid on civil, family and criminal cases is carried out between the sides which have signed the international agreement. Thus, in conformity with Article 5 of the decision of the Supreme Soviet of the Russian Federation of October 9, 1992 "Ratification of the Agreement on the Order of the Resolution of Disputes, Connected with Realization of Economic Activities" competent courts and other bodies of the states - participants of the Commonwealth of Independent States undertake to render mutual legal redress. The meaning of the term "legal redress", unlike that of the term "legal aid", has narrowed lately: this word combination is used at interaction of the states within the limits of international legal relationships. The term "legal aid" includes delivery and transfer of documents, performance of remedial actions, in particular examination, hearing of the sides, wit- nesses, experts and other persons.

Legal aid can be carried out in the form of representation. Many works of civilians are dedicated to the institution of representation, though some of the authors refer to the given institution as an inter-branch[13]. There is representation in material and a procedural right: "If in civil law representation is connected with taking legal actions on behalf of the represented, generating obligatory legal consequences for them, in criminal and civil process persons who render legal aid to the represented are also called representatives"[14]. The line between representation and legal aid is determined according to the following principle: a representative acts on behalf of the represented taking legal actions causing certain remedial or material consequences for the represented. While rendering legal aid the representative is working on their own behalf.

In the works of civilians legal aid is identified with so-called remedial representation. The latter seems to us not absolutely correct: legal aid is also carried out in the course of material representation because material representation is "settlement of transactions and other legal actions by one person - the representative - within the limits of power on behalf of another person – the represented"[15]. It is impossible to render legal actions without legal aid.

There are also inter-branch attributes of representation[16]. Let us view the attributes of considered institutions, i.e. institution of representation and legal aid, which are in common or different.

The common attributes are:

1) the institution of representation as a form of legal aid regulates relations, within the limits of which one person (the representative or the person rendering legal aid) renders legal assistance to another one (the represented or the person receiving legal aid);

2) legal assistance is carried out in interests of the represented or the person receiving legal aid;

3) there are no legal consequences in relation to the third parties resulting from realization of power or legal aid of the representative and the person rendering legal aid,

It is considered that in connection with similarity of some attributes of legal aid and representation they are quite often identified, which is wrong. There are differences between these institutions:

1. Representation regulates relations between the representative and represented in purchase of the legal rights and duties of the latter, in their relations with the third parties. Relations between the person rendering legal aid and the person receiving it can be closed and not concern the third parties. For example, reception of the legal information.

2. The limits of interaction of the representative and the represented are determined by competence - the legal right of the representative. The

person rendering legal aid cannot have such legal right as competence. For example, the lawyer who has made a statement of claim does not get any competence.

Legal aid should be divided into activity of rendering legal services which require settlement by legal provisions and those which do not require them. For example, when parents explain to the child to what signal of a traffic light they should cross the street, it is also considered legal aid rendered beyond legal relationships.

The notion of legal aid as the corresponding opportunities of a person put to trial as well as in the case of their participation in criminal, civil, administrative, jurisdictional processes is still dominant in law nowadays. Such approach narrows the subject of legal aid. The subject of legal aid is any legal relationships, arising in the course of reception by a person of practically any services of legal character. Such services can actually be, for example, legal education while ensuring and realizing the rights and personal freedoms.

It is necessary to specify the content of legal aid through such of its attributes as being qualified. Nowadays there are different points of view on the problem of being qualified (i.e. the degree and level of professional efficiency)[17]. Thus, on the one hand, it seems unproductive to create conditions in which a certain body (in this case) acquires exclusive rights to render qualified legal aid (monopoly will badly influence the quality of the rendered legal services). On the other hand, the uncontrolled power of certain persons to provide legal services can also influence their quality in a negative way.

The requirement of efficiency of legal aid presupposes introduction of a special term - "the minimal standards of qualified legal aid" which should include:

— juridical education of a person rendering legal aid;

— special requirements which should be met by the person rendering certain kinds of legal aid (a promotion examination, the experience, etc.);

— activity of rendering of legal aid.

These are the minimal standards of qualified legal aid. To certain kinds of legal aid (for example, when a person is put to trial) additional increased requirements can be made.

There are two groups of the subjects participating legal relationships concerning the right to legal aid: they are persons who receive legal aid and persons who render legal aid.

If we consider the right to legal aid from the point of view of basic rights and freedoms the subject of this right will certainly be an individual exclusively. However, in the widest meaning the right to legal aid includes its granting not only to an individual but also to other subjects of the law.

For example, states, their bodies, public organizations and other associations can be holders of the right to legal aid. Any persons requiring legal aid and having the lawful bases to receive it can be the subjects receiving qualified legal aid,

The human right to legal aid has all the attributes of legal right. The basic attribute is that it allows everyone to receive the corresponding values – that is, legal services.

The human right to receive legal aid is not only subjective but also has all the attributes of the constitutional legal right, i.e. the fundamental right. There are four main attributes of subjective constitutional rights.

The attribute of special importance of the right to legal aid means that without realization of the given right in the modern world favorable vital activity of a person is difficult. Accordingly the right to legal aid will relate to the basic inalienable law even without being recorded in the Constitution. It is not by chance that it is recorded in international documents.

The constitutional right of every person to receive legal aid records the most essential, basic connections and relations between the society, the state and the citizen. The right to legal aid guarantees realization and protection of all other rights and freedoms of a person and a citizen. The right to legal aid is reflected in the overwhelming majority of social relations. We realize the right to legal aid even when using public transport as a form of reception of information on what penalty can be imposed for fraudulent travel.

The right to reception of legal aid as a constitutional right has a maximum reality. It means that all the branch rights and duties must not contradict it. Even punishment in the form of imprisonment cannot belittle the right of a person to legal aid reception.

The right to legal aid in its objective meaning is a legal institution representing a set of international, constitutional and branch legal provisions, establishing the right to legal aid and its guarantees.

Besides the Constitution the right to legal aid is recorded and developed in other normative-legal regulations. The number of the normative-legal regulations including provisions, regulating the right to reception of legal aid is great enough. Among them it is possible to emphasize the Code of Criminal Procedure of the Russian Federation, the Code of Civil Procedure of the Russian Federation, the Code of the Russian Federation on administrative offences, the Federal law "On Legal Profession And Lawyer Activity in the Russian Federation", etc.

It is necessary to point out that the provisions establishing the right to reception of legal aid are disseminated under various normative-legal regulations. Meanwhile their analysis allows to draw a conclusion that recording of the right to legal aid in the Constitution of the Russian Federation, in the branch federal legislation, the legislation of subjects of the Russian Federation says about gradual formation of a new legal institution in the basis of which lies reception of qualified legal aid.

The question of reference of the right to legal aid to a certain group of civil human rights is interesting.

Reference of the right of the accused to defense in court (an element of the right to legal aid) to any of the groups immediately caused certain difficulties. There existed and still exist various scientific provisions.

According to one of them, the right to legal aid relates to the group of civil rights. Thus, this group is subdivided in two subgroups: the first one, more general, includes such rights as the right to life, the right to personal freedom, the right to physical integrity; the second subgroup includes the rights concretizing those belonging to the first subgroup – they are the right to freedom of thought and conscience, freedom of private life and communications, criminal and remedial guarantees of personal rights and freedoms[18]. The right to legal aid relates to remedial guarantees of civil rights and freedoms.

The given classification, in our opinion, is disputable. When in the Constitution of the USSR only one element of the right to legal aid – that is, the right of the accused to defense in the course of a criminal trial - was recorded, some authors indicated that the given right was personal[19]. Indeed, in this form the right to legal aid reflects only one aspect – protection of the personal safety in the form of freedom from a groundless charge and accusation. In the current Constitution of the Russian Federation the right to legal aid is recorded in full and provides not only personal safety but other rights as well. Legal aid should be rendered both when a person is put on trial and when they are being employed, when a civil dispute has occurred, or a will is being drawn, etc.

Some authors used to refer the right of the accused to defense in court to the group of political rights[20].

Meanwhile the questions concerning legal aid arise not only in the field of politics but also in the spheres of economy, education, culture, etc.

The third stream in science marks out a separate, sixth group of constitutional rights. The majority of the authors name this group the constitutional guarantees of the rights and freedoms. In the given group the constitutional guarantees of the rights and freedoms are singled out as two subgroups: general guarantees of the rights and freedoms of a person and a citizen and legal guarantees. The right to reception of qualified legal aid refers to the last group.

Development of the institution of guarantees of the rights of a person has served as a basis for the sixth group.

Authors soundly motivate existence of the institution of constitutional guarantees with the fact that without corresponding guarantees the rights and freedoms proclaimed in the Constitution will only be of declarative character. In jurisprudence guarantees act as a part of a more general institution of application of legal provisions. It seems to us that the problem of guarantees is also close to the problem of division of legal provisions into material and remedial. Remedial provisions serve realization of provisions of the substantive law and in this formulation are closer to the concept of guarantees.

What is the ground for viewing the constitutional guarantees of the rights and freedoms as a separate group? Views on this problem differ.

The conventional doctrine recognizes that the rights, duties, guarantees are elements of the legal status of a person. "The greatest necessity for guarantees of the right and freedom is felt because they make a mobile, dynamical element of the bases of the legal status of a person"[21].

Viewing the institution of guarantees as an element of a legal status of a person allows to see the essence of the given phenomenon better. However, this must not influence the classification of the rights and freedoms of a person and a citizen.

The Constitution contains special clauses (Articles 45-54) establishing guarantees of realization of the rights and freedoms of citizens, as M.V. Baglay and B.N. Gabrichidze write[22]. Reasoning from such logic of thought, in Ch. 2 of the Constitution of the Russian Federation there exist two kinds of provisions which contain either rights or guarantees. This concept gives rise to obvious objections.

Firstly, the title of Ch. 2 of the Constitution of the Russian Federation mentions the rights but nothing is said about the guarantees.

Secondly, separation of the guarantees from the constitutional rights has put the latter into the position of remedial ones serving other constitutional rights and freedoms. Is the separation of the abovementioned rights on this basis well-grounded? We do not think so as the given rights do not only have remedial value.

In works of the authors which we are studying the given group of rights is refers to the constitutional guarantees of justice (Article 46-54 of the Constitution of the Russian Federation). Indeed, most of the indicated rights start to work only in the course of realization of justice in court. However, it does not always happen so. For example, Article 54 of the Constitution of the Russian Federation establishes interdiction of return force of the law. The indicated right works not only when the case is being heard in court but also in other cases: when a person is called to account for an administrative, disciplinary offence by officials and other persons, the right not to testify against oneself and one's spouse and close (Article 51 of the Constitution of the Russian Federation), presumption of innocence (Article 49 of the Constitution of the Russian Federation) also represent realization of justice. The right to legal aid studied by us all the more does not exclusively refer exclusively to justice but also to the group of civil human rights.

Being a part of the constitutional-legal status of a person, the right to legal aid does not exist independently. It closely cooperates with other rights and freedoms.

The right to legal aid comprises three elements: legal aid with formation of the sense of justice (legal culture), legal aid with enforcement of the rights and personal freedoms, legal aid with protection of the rights and personal freedoms.

In their turn, each kind of legal aid includes some subgroups. Within the limits of formation of the sense of justice (legal culture) the following rights are distinguished: the right to reception of legal information, the right to explanation of the content of legal provisions, the right to reception of juridical education.

The base element of the right to legal aid is the right to reception of legal information. It can be realized in the form of official or informal rendering of the content of legal provisions. Receiving legal information of normative character, apart from formation of the sense of justice, the person concerned also have an opportunity to realize their rights more fully and to protect their interests using the given kind of legal aid.

It is necessary to mark out the principles of reception of legal information. They are availability; reliability; responsibility for refusal in granting of the information, for granting of doubtful or incomplete legal information.

As a subspecies of the right to reception of legal aid the right to explanation of the content of legal provisions acts. It can be classified as official, informal and normative (interpretation in mass media, doctrinal comments) and casual (judicial, administrative, legal examination) interpretation.

The right to reception of juridical education is, in our opinion, an important subspecies of the right to receive legal aid. The term "education" is used by us in the widest meaning and with reference to the right to legal aid includes a total amount of legal knowledge received by a person to increase their legal culture and to get a possibility to realize and protect their rights and freedoms.

The right to receive juridical education can come in two forms: propagation of legal knowledge and general juridical education (secondary and higher juridical education).

It is necessary to point out that creation of the jural state in Russia without realization of the given kind of legal aid is extremely difficult. The concept of a "jural state" implies that the citizens of the state must have a highly developed sense of justice the formation of which is impossible without considerable legal aid.

It is also important to point out such kind of right to legal aid as help to citizens to ensure their rights and freedoms. In any legal right there are two elements, two functional cuts of this right. On the one hand, a personal right determines a measure of their freedom, i.e. guarantees certain values (life, education, health, legal aid, etc.). On the other hand, any personal right, in its turn, is to some extent a guarantee of realization of other rights and freedoms.

The correlation of the given functions in various rights and freedoms of a person and a citizen is unequal: in some the first is dominating, in others it is the second. The dominating function of the right to legal aid is that of ensuring and protection of other rights and freedoms. However, in the three abovementioned subspecies of the right to legal aid the role and correlation of the two functions of legal rights is unequal. Thus, the informational legal aid equally realizes both the first and the second functions.

While studying the essential attributes of the right to legal aid to ensure other rights and freedoms, it is necessary to specially view the competences arising from interaction of the person receiving legal aid and persons rendering it. Within the limits of the fundamental human right to legal aid there is a certain group of competences, namely:

1. The right to free choice of the person rendering legal aid means unobstructed choice of such person. Here access to trustworthy information concerning powers and the competence of the person rendering legal aid is important.

2. The right to free dialogue with the person rendering legal aid means the possibility to use the lawyer at any moment and under any circumstances. A person can be limited in these or other rights but cannot be limited in reception of legal aid. For example, in a criminal trial it means the right to access the defender, in a civil procedure it is the right to case management through the representative.

3. The right to confidential dialogue with the person rendering legal aid means that the information which is exchanged during the dialogue between the person assisting and the person receiving aid, cannot be divulged to the third parties without consent. In particular, the given right is recorded by Article 202 of the Code of Criminal Procedure of RSFSR according to which the defender of the accused can have conversations alone with the accused or has the right stipulated by international provisions to be outside of so-called limits of audibility during the conversations with the defender within the precincts of the investigatory cell.

The competence to give the person rendering legal aid special rights refers to the competences arising from interaction of the person receiving and the person rendering legal aid. The right of the person rendering legal aid to address the state bodies and other ones for the information necessary for realization of their functions also refers to such competences.

There are following subspecies of the personal right to legal aid to ensure other rights and freedoms: the right to legal consultation, the right to draw up documents of legal character, the right to representation, the right to reception of free legal aid.

Legal consultation judging by its content is a kind of competence to inform persons about the content of legal provisions or a kind of casual interpretation. It can be both written and oral. The main person rendering this kind of help is a lawyer. Alongside with legal profession legal aid in the form of legal consultations is rendered by other subjects including the state bodies and institutions of the local government.

One of subspecies of the right to legal aid to ensure personal rights and freedoms is the right to draw up documents of legal character. The distinctive feature of the given competence is its casual character. The document for each certain case is made individually. There are two basic variants of realization of the given right: documents of legal character can be drawn fully and partially.

According to the first variant the person rendering legal aid studies the matter of the case, selects the legal provision which will be used to settle the arisen legal relationships or the relationships which the person receiving legal aid aspires to create, and draws a legal document which is supposed to become a legal fact with a view of ensuring of defense of some right. The given document can be drawn in the form of a complaint, a petition, a statement of claim, a statement of acceptance of legacy, etc. Documents of legal character can be drawn up by a notary, which is a variety of realization of the right. For instance, the notary must explain to the parties the meaning and value of the presented project of the transaction.

The meaning of partial drawing up is in the fact that the person is granted a form of the legal document which they must fill in with the personal data. An example of such legal aid is the use of forms of various contracts of sale and purchase, donation, hiring of premises. Especially popular have recently become special forms of letters of attorney for driving a vehicle. Ready forms of these letters of attorney are on free sale. A doubtless advantage of the given kind of legal aid is its availability, its disadvantage is uniformity and therefore the possibility opportunity of a legal mistakes.

The right to representation in the course of civil and administrative legal relationships is realized first of all by means of legal aid of a lawyer. The lawyer's help comes in the form of representation in courts and also while asserting their interests in other organizations. Development of the principle of competitiveness has led to the fact that a significant part of duties of the court connected with rendering legal aid should pass to a representative qualified and skilled in questions of civil legal proceedings. Representation of a lawyer in the sphere of administrative legal relationships, unfortunately, is not so widely spread nowadays and is limited to rendering legal aid when drawing up complaints, statements, petitions, etc.

Legal aid in the form of representation is also rendered by the state bodies. Thus, a big role in the case of rendering of legal aid in civil legal proceedings belongs to the Office of Public Prosecutor.

The importance of legal aid as a social value means that a person feels a particular need for it in the cases of infringement of their rights and freedoms. Therefore, an important element of the content of the right to legal aid is its rendering while giving legal assistance.

When a person is brought to account the danger of infringement of their rights and freedoms increases sharply. It is not by chance that in such cases the corresponding branch legislation practically always provides the person on trial with the right to receive legal aid. For example, within the limits of the criminal, administrative responsibility the right to services of a lawyer (Article 49 of the Code of Criminal Procedure of the Russian Federation, Article 25.5 Administrative Code of the Russian Federation) is stipulated.

It is necessary to pay special attention to the problem of protection of the considered legal right itself. Its protection is carried out in two ways: protection of the right to legal aid from illegal behaviour of persons rendering legal aid and protection of the given right from illegal behaviour of the third parties.

The problem of protection of the right to legal aid from illegal behaviour of persons rendering legal aid has remained serious up to this day. It is obviously necessary to improve the Russian market of legal services having directed its development in the civilized course. Recently the problem of lawful realization of the state control over the activity of persons rendering legal aid has become especially urgent. First of all it is necessary for the persons in question to observe the conditions and requirements of the legislation on granting legal aid.

Protection of the right to legal aid is also carried out by establishment and use of the legal responsibility for infringement of the given constitutional law. It would be expedient to draw a provision in the Criminal Code of the Russian Federation ensuring criminal liability for infringement of the right to legal aid, for persecution of the lawyer.

In conformity with Article 48 of the Constitution of the Russian Federation everyone has a right to qualified legal aid, and the lawyer cannot refuse to defend the suspected or the accused after taking up this duty. If the lawyer refuses to render legal aid or does not adequately execute their professional duties their status of a lawyer can be eliminated.

We should point out that it is necessary to distinguish between the measures to protect the given right from legal responsibility for infringement of the right to legal aid. In particular, cancellation of an illegal act breaking the right to legal aid is a measure of protection.

§ 2. The Activity of the Legal Profession as a Form of Realization of the Human Right to Legal Aid

Functioning of legal profession as an independent institution of a civil society is a way of realization of the human right to legal aid.

Thus, in Part 1 of Article 48 of the Constitution of the Russian Federation it is said about the right of "each person on the territory of the Russian Federation to receive qualified legal aid". It is also pointed out that in the cases stipulated by the law legal aid is granted free of charge. Nothing is said directly about paid qualified legal aid. However, it is obvious that in some cases legal aid can be rendered free of charge. The meaning of this provision is that, as a rule, qualified legal aid is paid – which is normally a rule.

In Part 2 of Article 48 of the Constitution of the Russian Federation it is emphasized: "Each imprisoned person accused of a crime has a right to use the help of a lawyer (defender), from the moment of detention, custody or arraignment".

To this it is necessary to add a number of the constitutional provisions important for definition of the legal status of the lawyer. In this case we are talking about Ch. 7 of the Constitution of the Russian Federation devoted to judicial authority. In Part 3 of Article 123 of the Constitution of the Russian Federation it is emphasized that "legal proceedings are carried out on the basis of competitiveness and equality of the sides". In this clause the term "lawyer" is also absent but it is absolutely clear that the principle of competitiveness means, first of all, the possibility of the lawyer's participation. The principle of competitiveness is spoken about in the Federal Constitutional Lights "On the Constitutional Court of the Russian Federation" (Article 35) and "On the Arbitration Courts in the Russian Federation" (Article 6). It is well-known that these principles are recorded in the Criminally-Remedial, Civil Remedial and other Codes. The Constitution of the Russian Federation also gives an opportunity of participation of the lawyer in protection of the rights of citizens by means of definition of some legal guarantees of the major civil human rights.

Those rights are the right to freedom and securities of person: "Imprisonment, custody and holding in custody are only possible by the court order"; personal privacy: "The right to privacy of correspondence, telephone conversations, post, cable and other messages the limitation of which is possible only on the basis of the comprehension". This also concerns limitation of the right to inviolability of dwelling (Article 22, 23, 25 of the Constitution of the Russian Federation).

It seems, this is only a question of judicial protection of the indicated civil rights and freedoms of a person but since the lawyer has the right to participate in judicial consideration of such affairs, the Constitution gives ample opportunities for the lawyer's activity.

For the bases of the constitutional system of our state a great role is played by Article 15 of the Constitution of the Russian Federation, in Part 4 of which it is noted that "the conventional principles and standards of the international law and the international agreements of Russia are a component of its legal system".

This clause in the Constitution of the Russian Federation means that the major standards of the international law concerning activity of the lawyer are in force on all the territories of our country. First of all, it refers to Clause 3 "D" of Article 14 of the International Covenant on Civil and Political Rights. In the indicated clause it is recorded:

1) the right of each citizen to choose a defender;

2) the right to be notified that they have this right;

3) the right to have a defender prescribed to them if they have not used the right to choose one;

4) the right to gratuitous defense in the cases when they do not have sufficient means to pay for it. We believe that is it the most fundamental international-legal ground for the activity of the lawyer. The given legal provision is adjoins Clause 3 of Article 6 of the European Convention for Protection of Human Rights and Basic Freedoms in which, though briefly, the provisions of Article 14 of the International Covenant on Civil and Political Rights is reproduced.

Constitutional-legal status of the lawyer is also determined by the Substantive Provisions about the role of the lawyers accepted during the Eighth Congress of the United Nations on crime prevention in August, 1990. This document defines essential legal guarantees of the lawyers' activity and their duties in relation to clients.

In Article 93 "The Minimal Standards of Rules of Treatment of Prisoners" approved by the Economic and Social Council of the United Nations it is emphasized that prisoners on trial should have the right to use the services of a lawyer. With this purpose it is necessary to provide them with writing materials, and their appointments with the lawyer should occur in the presence of police officers or jail superintendents but beyond the hearing distance.

Finally, the principle formulated in the document of the Copenhagen Meeting-Conference on Human Measurement OSCE in 1990 where it is written down that the states should provide independence of the lawyer, in particular as far as it concerns the conditions of their employment and practice (Clause 5.12) is rather important

In Clause 5.17 of the same document it is noted that the right to be defended by the lawyer chosen by the accused must be provided immediately.

Thus, the indicated constitutional and international legal provisions generally characterize the constitutional-legal status of the lawyer. This is closely connected with the Federal law "On Advocacy and Legal Profession in the Russian Federation" of May, 31st, 2002, Federal Law №63.

The new law on legal profession is controversial. On the one hand, it contains progressive provisions which are stated in Article 3: "The legal profession is a professional community of lawyers and as an institution of a civil society does not belong to the system of the governmental bodies and institutions of local government".

According to this clause, legal profession acts on he basis of principles of legality, independence, self-management, corporation and as well as the principle of equality of lawyers.

To ensure availability of legal aid to the population and assistance to advocacy the governmental bodies guarantee independence of legal profession, ensure financing activity of the lawyers rendering legal aid to citizens of the Russian Federation free of charge in the cases reflected in the legislation of the Russian Federations and if necessary give advocatory groups office accommodations and communication facilities. Social security is guaranteed to each lawyer.

A rather democratic provision expanding the competence of the lawyer, is Part 3 of Article 6 of the Law which affirms that "the lawyer has the right to collect data necessary for rendering of legal aid, to request information, characteristics, to interrogate persons by their consent, to collect proofs, etc.".

An essential provision of the given Law is Article 8 that tells about advocatory secrecy. We can consider the provisions of Article 18 of the Law where guarantees of independence of the lawyer are recorded extremely important for the lawyer's activity.

At the same time in this law there are a lot of provisions that put legal profession under control of the state and give a chance to bureaucracy to interfere with advocacy. In our opinion, the law breaks three basic principles of advocacy:

— independence of legal profession as lawyer community;

— independence of the lawyer at legal proceedings;

— provision of the constituent's right to choose the lawyer.

Thus, the structure of legal profession is determined by government officials and officials of legal profession. It is them who decide who will be included into the corresponding Register of lawyers (Article 14,15).

As a result, modern advocacy, in fact, ceases to be a homing organization, as it is becoming completely dependent on the government.

And directing bodies of legal profession – Councils of Chambers and especially qualifying commissions which include justice officials turn to the instrument of bureaucratic pressure upon ordinary lawyers realizing their powers, imposing disciplinary punishment, partially and totally terminating the lawyers' status (Articles 16, 17, 33 of the Law).

Speaking about the correlation between competences of the Ministry of Justice and chambers of lawyers, we can see that the Ministry of Justice tries to limit independence of advocacy by intervention in its internal affairs. This is testified by the materials of the interdepartmental meeting "On the Results of Realization of the Federal Law" in the Far East federal district and prospects of interaction **of the lawyer case** with judicial authorities, the government of subjects of the Russian Federation, the law-enforcement and judicial bodies, that took place in Khabarovsk on October 16, 2003. In the theses of his report deputy minister of justice M. K. Kislitsin expressed regret about the fact that the new Law has significantly changed the role and the place of legal profession in the Russian society, has arranged the interrelations of the lawyer community and judicial authorities in a new way. This Law has deprived the Ministry of Justice and its territorial bodies of any significant levers to influence the advocacy, having left only formal powers to them. Elimination of legal grounds that would enable the judicial authorities to influence the lawyer community, in their opinion, cannot be recognized as a positive factor in strengthening of the system of legal aid rendering. In M. K. Kislitsin's opinion, further changes can only be connected with strengthening of the role of the Ministry of Justice and its territorial bodies in the field of legal profession[23].

However, there is another opinion on the state of affairs in modern Russian legal profession. It was formulated by the participants of the section "The Civil Society and Judicial-Legal System" at the All-Russian Remedial Conference of Civil Organizations in 2003

In the resolution of that section it is said: "Russian legal profession experiences deep crisis. Transformation of legal profession into one of the sources of a large-scale infringement of human rights, first of all, in criminal trial is a consequence of this crisis".

Certainly, many lawyers selflessly protect the rights of their principals. But the presence of greatly respected lawyers in the corporation does not remove the question concerning legal profession as a whole, concerning the tendencies which are dangerous for the society, concerning the serious, nowadays typical phenomena distorting the essence of legal profession.

The Federal Law "Advocacy and Legal Profession in the Russian Federation" determines legal profession as and institution of the civil society.

Despite this declaration, advocacy in modern Russia has intrinsic characteristics which allow to estimate it as **a governmentalized corporation which has monopolized the right of defense in criminal cases.**

Governmentalization of legal profession is a consequence of its compulsory verticalization into a uniform Federal Chamber (that creates conditions for controllability of lawyers and deprives them of independence). Governmentalization of legal profession is a consequence of being controlled by judicial authorities having the right to collect materials compromising lawyers and to initiate deprivation of their status.

Advocacy's monopolization of the right to defense in criminal cases is provided by the Code of Criminal Procedure of the Russian Federation which, in fact, expelled the lawyers who are not lawyers, and public defenders from criminal procedure "[24].

Legal experts have noted such negative qualities of modern advocacy as low professional level of many of its many, transformation of lawyers into driving belt of corruption, breach of the clients' confidence, concealment of the clients' procedural rights, collusion with the prosecution party and "deals" with judges, unreasonable and overestimated fees[25].

At the same time it is necessary to point out that in the advocatory environment the distribution of affairs can be unfair, which mostly comes from heads of advocatory constitutions, their presidiums therefore, as a result of which many talented, fair lawyers remain jobless and unpaid.

Generally, the situation with the state of affairs in legal profession signifies serious problems in realization of the Human Right to Legal Defense.

On the other hand, the illegal practice of infringement of the rights of lawyers by the bodies of Public Prosecution and preliminary investigation is widely spread. Some of their illegal actions are typical infringement of the kind. For example, there are obstacles preventing the lawyer from meeting the client at the initial stage of inquiry or preliminary investigation when the presence of the defender under the agreement is undesirable for prosecution. To receive the necessary information from the suspected, "false" defenders are often appointed. Refusals of investigators and inspectors to deliver copies of the documents concerning the client after performance of investigatory actions with participation of an appointed lawyer can take place. Lawyers are overheard and watched via video devices in chambers of imprisonment before trail on criminal cases, they are searched and the materials of the lawyer files are seized from them when they are leaving the isolation ward of temporary custody, the pre-trial detention centre.

Quite often the lawyer is forced leave their portfolios, mobile phones and other personal things which can be suspicious from the point of view of the officers of the isolation ward of temporary custody or the pre-trial detention center in the check-room despite the numerous personal inspections with the help of modern devices.

In conformity with Article 18 of the Federal Law of the Russian Federation "On Holding in Custody of the Suspected and Accused" of July 15, 1995 (in the edition of December 8, 2003) "appointments are given to the defender after presentation of the certificate of the lawyer and the warrant. Demand of other documents is forbidden".

For this reason actions of some heads of isolation wards of temporary custody and pre-trial detention centers who frequently demand from the lawyer (defender) a written sanction for appointment with of the suspect or accused are illegal. In this connection Clause 149 of the Regulations of Investigatory Cells of the Criminal-Executive System, ordering their chiefs to allow the suspected and accused appointment with the defender "with the presence of the document proving their admission to participation in the criminal case, given out by a person or body in whose proceeding the case is", is not subject to use as obviously contradicting the abovementioned Federal Law, which, according to the Constitution of the Russian Federation, has superiority over any departmental statutory act.

In the part, stating that appointments of the suspected and accused with the lawyer participating in the case as a defender are possible after the lawyer has presented the document proving their admission to participation in the criminal case, given out by a person or body in whose proceeding the case is, Clause 149 of the Regulations of Investigatory Cells of the Criminal-Executive System of the Ministry of Justice of the Russian Federation approved by the Order № 148 of the Ministry of Justice of the Russian Federation of May 12, 2000 (in the edition of the Order № 55 of the Ministry of Justice of the Russian Federation of February 21, 2002) is also recognized by the Presidium of the Supreme Court of the Russian Federation of October 2, 2002 as Illegal and not current from the date of the introduction of the decision into reality.[26]

Operative services listen to personal telephone conversations of lawyers without the corresponding authorization. Attempts to incline the lawyer to private cooperation with the bodies carrying out the operative-search activity take place.

Ungrounded appeals are sent to advocatory boards of investigators, public prosecutors, judges and Administration of Justice officers to compromise the objectionable lawyers defending provisions of principle in the case.

Contrary to the law the principle of equality and competitiveness of the sides, recorded in Article 123 of the Constitution and Article 15 of the Code of Criminal Procedure of the Russian Federation is broken. In particular, it is reflected in refusal of inspectors, public prosecutors and judges to recognize objects and documents collected by the lawyer as established by the legislation of the Russian Federation, as proofs.

Another infringement of requirements of Article 6 of the Federal Law "On Advocacy and Legal Profession in the Russian Federation" is refusal to deliver the required data from various state authorities.

The reasons of crisis of legal profession are analyzed in modern legal literature. Among those reasons is the fact that the lawyer case has proved unprepared to economic reforms which have been taking place in our country in the last years.

The incipient mafia capitalism did not require the help of qualified lawyers. Legal reforms, a rough change of the legislation, arbitrariness of officials, strengthening of corruption, growth of criminality – all these factors have required reorganization of advocacy which is happening in rather unhealthy forms and leads to serious failures in the sphere of realization of the Human Right to Legal Defense.

"Qualified legal aid, as V.I. Sergeev writes, is not an explanation of the law, writing of a petition and a statement in the interests of the principal. It is much more complicated. It is a struggle for your principal. It is a methodical, intellectual, multiechelon fight led according to the rules of legal art. With the opponents surpassing you twice, three times, ten times – the state and its corrupted officials. A fight for the rights – this is the basis that distinguishes advocacy from all the other kinds of activity.

Moreover, it is not a fight of single persons, but that of the whole corporation. One lawyer cannot teach the whole system to execute the law, but the lawyer corporation in aggregate with other measures and levers used in a civil society can do it. Modern lawyers, a whole lot of them, with all their previous activity, are ready for such battles for the rights"[27].

It seems that advocacy will manage to fulfill these tasks is they observe some essential conditions.

Among those conditions we would name democratization of legal profession, strengthening of its independence of authority, clarification from corrupt members and increase of the professional level, overcoming of legal nihilism in the consciousness of judges, law machinery officers, bringing to account of the officials encroaching upon the rights of lawyers.

Notes

1. This tendency also exists in the modern Russian society. The work of counselors rendering legal help free of charge is exceptionally well received by the society. The attitude of the majority to those rendering the same services for payment is rather ambiguous.

2. See: D.V. Dozhdiov Roman Private Law: University textbook / Editor: V.S.Nersesiants. Moscow: 1997, P. 93 / Дождев Д. В. Римское частное право: Учебник для вузов / Под ред. В. С. Нерсесянца. М., 1997. С. 93.

3. See: Modern Foreign Constitutions: Collected documents on constitutional right of foreign countries. M., 1996. P. 237./ Современные зарубежные конституции: Сб. документов по конституционному праву зарубежных стран. М., 1996. С. 237.

4. See: M.A. Cheltsov. Soviet Criminal Process. Moscow, 1975. P. 772. / Чельцов М. А. Советский уголовный процесс. М., 1975. С. 772.

5. See: A Textbook on History of the Russian State and Law. M., 1994. P. 17. / Хрестоматия по истории отечественного государства и права: Учеб. пособие. М., 1994. С. 17.

6. See: Ibidem, P. 234.

7. See: Ibidem, P. 434.

8. See: Supreme Soviet of USSR Bulletin 1979. № 49. P. 846. /Ведомости Верховного Совета СССР. 1979. № 49. Ст. 846.

9. See: L.B. Alekseeva, V.M. Zhuikov, I.I. Lukashuk. International Regulations of Human Rights and Their Application in Court. Practice Book. M., 1996. P. 264 / Алексеева Л. Б., Жуйков В. М., Лукашук И. И. Международные нормы о правах человека и применение их судами Российской Федерации: Практ. пособие. М., 1996. С. 264.

10. See: A Collection of Standards and Regulations of the United Nations Organization in the Field of Crime Prevention and Criminal Law. UNO. New York, 1992. P.118. / Сборник стандартов и норм Организации Объединенных Наций в области предупреждения преступности и уголовного правосудия. ООН. Нью-Йорк, 1992. С. 118.

11. See: Ibidem, P.178.

12. See: L.B. Alekseeva, V.M. Zhuikov, I.I.Lukashuk. Ibidem, P. 328.

13. See: A.V. Kozhevnikov. The Lawyer – A Representative of the Victim, the Civil Plaintiff, the Civil Defendant in the Soviet Criminal Procedure. An abstract of the dissertation of the candidate of jurisprudence. Sverdlovsk, 1974. P. 5-6. / Кожевников А. В. Адвокат – представитель потерпевшего, гражданского истца, гражданского ответчика в советском уголовном процессе: Автореф. дис. ... канд. юрид. наук. Свердловск, 1974. С. 5-6.

14. L.K. Merenkova Representation According to the Soviet Civil Law. Tomsk, 1980. P.9 / Меренкова Л. К. Представительство по советскому гражданскому праву. Томск, 1980. С. 9.

15. S.N.Bratus. Object and System of Soviet Civil Right. M., 1963. P. 184 Братусь С. Н. Предмет и система советского гражданского права. М., 1963. С. 184.

16. See: L.K. Merenkova, Ibidem, P.7 / Меренкова Л. К. Указ. соч. С. 7.

17. See: Resolution of the Constitutional Court of the Russian Federation of January 28, 1997 on the case of the check for constitutionality of Part 4 of Article 47 of the Code of Criminal Procedure of the Russian Federation in connection with complaints received from B.V. Antipov, R.L. Gitis, S.V. Abramov. / По делу о проверке конституционности части четвертой статьи 47 Уголовно-процессуального кодекса РСФСР в связи с жалобами граждан Б. В. Антипова, Р. Л. Гитиса и С. В. Абрамова: Постановление Конституционного Суда Российской Федерации от 28 января 1997 г.

18. See: Comparative Constitutional Law. Moscow, 1996. P. 282. / Сравнительное конституционное право. М., 1996. С. 282.

19. See: Y.N. Umanski. Soviet State and Law. Moscow, 1970. P. 159. / Уманский Я. Н. Советское государство и право. М., 1970. С. 159.

20. See: A.V. Mitskevich. Subjects of Soviet Law. Moscow, 1970. P. 52. / Мицкевич А. В. Субъекты советского права. М., 1970. С. 52.

21. L.D. Voevodin. Legal Status of a Person in Russia. Textbook. Moscow, 1997. P. 222. / Воеводин Л. Д. Юридический статус личности в России: Учеб. пособие. М., 1997. С. 222.

22. M.V. Baglay, B.N. Gabrichidze. Constitutional Right in the Russian Federation. University textbook. Moscow, 1996. P. 225. / Баглай М. В., Габричидзе Б. Н. Конституционное право Российской Федерации: Учебник для вузов. М., 1996. С. 225.

23. See: The Bulletin of Federal Chamber of Lawyers of the Russian Federation 2003. № 3 (3). P. 124–125 / Вестник Федеральной палаты адвокатов РФ. 2003. № 3 (3). С. 124–125.

24. Protection of Rights, Freedoms and Legitimate Interests of Citizens in Criminal Legal Proceedings and crisis of legal profession// The Legal Expert 2003. № 4. P. 57. / Защита прав, свобод и законных интересов граждан в уголовном судопроизводстве и кризис адвокатуры // Правозащитник. 2003. № 4. С. 57.

25. See: Ibidem P. 57.

26. See: The Lawyer Bulletin 2002. № 12 / Адвокатские вести. 2002. № 12.

27. V.I. Sergeev. Will the Syndrom of Kashtanka Overcome Legal Profession? // Modern Advocacy. 2004. Jan.28 P. 2–3. / Сергеев В. И. Одолеет ли адвокатуру синдром Каштанки? // Современная адвокатура. 2004. 28 янв. С. 2–3.

Chapter 17. NONGOVERNMENTAL HUMAN RIGHTS
ORGANIZATIONS' ACTIVITIES IN THE
PROTECTION OF CIVIL RIGHTS: MODERN
TENDENCIES IN THE SOCIAL LIFE OF RUSSIA

To ensure human rights efforts of each citizen are necessary as well as activity of nongovernmental human rights organizations that are to restore the infringed rights by their methods and to control the state of affairs in connection with human rights.

Nongovernmental human rights organizations occupy one of the key places in the system of protection of the rights and freedoms of a person, In the Russian Federation public amateur performance of citizens is regulated by Article 30 of the Constitution of the Russian Federation, Article 116-123 §5 Ch. 4 of the Civil Code of the Russian Federation (Part 1)[1], the Federal Law of the Russian Federation "On Public Associations " of May 19, 1995 (the edition of July 19, 1998) which ascribes to them all organizations created under the initiative of citizens, except for religious and commercial, including political parties and trade unions[2]. Besides, separate types of human rights organizations can be formed on the basis of the following laws: the Federal Law of the Russian Federation of January 12, 1996 "On Noncommercial Organizations"[3], the Federal Law of the Russian Federation of June 28, 1995 "On the State Support of Youth and Children's Public Associations"[4], the Federal Law of the Russian Federation of August 11, 1995 "On Charities and Charitable Organizations"[5].

For a historically short period since the moment of declaration of the state independence of the Russian Federation a wide network of nongovernmental human rights organizations has appeared in the country.

Development of nongovernmental human rights organizations reflects the basic tendencies in development of democracy and structurization of interests of the society.

In the present work *the nongovernmental human rights organization is understood as a kind of a public association the purpose of with is to protect the rights and freedoms of a person and which operates ir-*

respective of the state bodies and other political structures, carries out the activity on the basis of the national and international legislation, does not aim to get benefit and has its own sources of financing. Besides, human rights organizations can be national and international; can represent themselves as representatives of persons, whose rights have been infringed within the limits of national and international procedures of human rights protection.

Human rights organizations carry out a number of important functions both in the field of human rights protection and their propagation. Studying the practical activities of the nongovernmental organizations in the field of human rights protection, it is possible to single out the following forms of activity:

1) activity to gather information and (or) supervision over observance of human rights; 2) participation in lawmaking in the field of human rights; 3) assistance on ensuring of restoration of the infringed human rights and (or) humanitarian help to victims of infringement of human rights; 4) activity in human rights education; 5) granting of services in the sphere of the civil, political, economic, cultural and social rights.

The purpose of the present work is research of forms of activity of nongovernmental human rights organizations in civil rights protection.

In the modern world human rights organizations represent an appreciable economic, social and cultural phenomenon which has become a reality in the Russian society, too.

Human rights organizations have occupied a worthy niche in the infrastructure of protection of the rights and freedoms of a person. It is already impossible to imagine functioning of the system of protection of human rights without such instrument as human rights organizations. They "have become a buffer between the state and the person so that observance of human rights became valid in the present reality"[6]; nongovernmental human rights organizations "have become the "eyes and ears" of the official governments; a kind of a barometer of a status of the society"[7].

Human rights organizations give a word to those who otherwise could not express their point of view. They aspire to affect the state policy on behalf of those layers of the population which without this influence would not have any influence in the society; they work so that no group of the population having financial resources, power or a high social status, could use their advantage in mercenary interests.

One of forms of human rights organizations activity in protection of civil rights is monitoring of observance of human rights. The information received as a result of such monitoring reflects a serious state of affairs in certain segments of the society[8]. Practically most of the nongovernmental human rights organizations have arisen in reply to certain specific situation. For example, prosecution of citizens for their political convictions and also torture by investigatory bodies in many countries became the reason of establishment of "Amnesty International"[9]; incessant confrontations and thereof occurrence of their numerous victims became the reason of creation remedial to the organization "Medecins Sans Frontieres" ("Doctors without Borders").

For more effective protection of civil rights human rights organizations use nonconventional forms and methods which, at first sight, can seem inadequate to the purposes of their activity. One of the basic methods used by human rights organizations, is their purposeful influence on representatives of executive, legislative and judicial authority with the purpose of acceptance of socially significant decisions in the field of human rights, or as the mentioned influence is called in political science, "lobbyism"; with reference to an the studied problem it would be more exact to call it "public influence in the sphere of upholding of observance of the rights and freedoms of a person". In this connection it is possible to ascertain that human rights organizations are potential interested participants of the lobbyist activity. It is necessary to admit that only few authors mark close connection of high-grade lobbyist activity with the activity of the civil society. It is necessary to mention N.A. Zakharov who remarks that if in "authoritative and the more so totalitarian societies only a limited circle of politicians having access to the ruling elite is engaged in lobbying... then in conditions of a democratic society lobbyism... becomes simultaneously both an element of political activity and a form of manifestation of the civil society, testifying its vital force and ability to self-organizing"[10].

In this connection it is necessary to say that human rights organizations can exert double influence on acceptance and realization of the law: firstly, they act as public representatives who have the right to know how and in what direction the legislation will develop and to influence this development in a certain way; and secondly, they are interested in participation in legislative activity if it is conducted according to the principles of professionalism, mutual respect, "game rules" common for all. In fact, to make this influence, "pressure", really legitimate, it is necessary to involve new social forces which represent the broad audience of public interests but had no direct access to authority before because plurality of those participating in lobbying of the organizations authority, equal opportunities of participation for everyone transform lobbyism into an institution of democratic politics[11].

To confirm the last thesis it is necessary to say that existence of lobbyism, in fact, supplements the constitutional system of democratic representation, allowing participating in acceptance and realization of political decisions to those groups which have no other opportunities. As it is known, under the Russian selective legislation not all public associations have the right to put forward their representatives on elections to the bodies of the government and some human rights organizations have directly recorded interdiction on participation in any political activity in the charters[12].

Thus, the system and practice of the civilized influence on authority practically remains the only opportunity for human rights organizations to influence the decisions accepted by the bodies of the government in some way. In these terms lobbyism complies with the spirit of democratic politics.

It is necessary to note that influence on authority acts as a kind of instrument of self-organizing of the civil society by means of which public support or opposition to any bill will be mobilized; it serves as means of struggle against bureaucratism, isolation of the state machinery. Various ways of influence on the authority promote development of the civil society, protection of interests of social groups and layers, increases their interest in the events which are taking place.

These processes are included in all human rights organizations. Success of formation of a lawful state in many respects depends on how effectively human rights organizations as one of the institutions of the civil society can protect civil rights and freedoms, because priority of human rights and freedoms is one of its major principles

Objects of influence of human rights organizations are bodies of executive, legislative and judicial authority.

According to Clause 1 of Article 104 of the Constitution of the Russian Federation among the representatives of the legislative branch of authority the Council of Federation; members of Council of Federation and deputies of the State Duma have the right of the legislative initiative[13].

At Soviet time public associations had the right of legislative initiative: on behalf of the all-Union bodies they had the right to introduce bills in the Supreme Soviet of the USSR. Unfortunately, nowadays public associations have no opportunity to introduce the bills in regulatory bodies.

These days human rights organizations as a kind of public associations have the only real opportunity of participation in lawmaking -that is by influence on the legislative mechanism "from inside". Human rights organizations haven't yet mastered modern methods of work with deputies of the State Duma by participation as experts in working groups on bills, in parliamentary hearings and other actions, organized by the State Duma and Council of Federation machinery.

Relations between human rights organizations and the bodies of the government on the whole have an obviously asymmetric character. The bodies of the government, with rare exception, do not address remedial organizations with the request to state their position on the problem which interests legal experts. In most cases the initiative comes from human rights organizations which try, using channels accessible to them, to transmit their point of view to the bodies of the government. As a rule, it comes as a (usually overdue) reaction to certain bills, drafts of decrees, decisions, which in the opinion of leaders of human rights organizations restrain public interests, civil rights and freedoms. So far the authority recognizes human rights organizations neither as an "expert" resource, nor as a full participant of lawmaking.

However, there's a different situation as far as it concerns the nongovernmental organizations which have appeared with direct or indirect assistance of the state. To them belong branches of international nongovernmental organizations - the international committee of the Red Cross (Russian Red Cross), the Green Cross and also public organizations that consist of "people of authority" or which have developed from authorities, for example, many female public associations, trade unions and others.

From the point of view of their organization, such quasi-human rights organizations re, in fact, "joined" with the "profile" state structure which has generated them.

The problems connected with access to authorities, which usually lobbyist groups face; simply do not exist for such associations by virtue of their specific status. Civilized "pressure" of the organization in fact, merges with efforts of the corresponding executive (or legislative) body and becomes a component of "departmental lobbyism". The associations concerning this category as a matter of fact represent institutionalized channels constantly current in connection with authorities.

Lobbyist coalitions of human rights organizations with the state bodies do not necessarily assume institutionalization of connections; they can also be formed on an informal basis. As an example can serve the constantly working interaction between the Remedial Committee "For Civil Rights" (Moscow) and organizations of execution of punishment of the Moscow and Kaluga areas; realization of joint partner projects between the Moscow branch of "Penal Reform International" and "International Prison Reform" (London, Great Britain), regional Managements of Execution of Punishment of the Ministry of Justice of Russia (the Samara, Ryazan, Tomsk areas and others) and also with Central Administrative Board of Execution of Punishment of the Ministry of Justice of the Russian Federation; teamwork of regional public organization of assistance to democratic reforms "Information. Consultation. Assistance." (Moscow) and Management of Administration of the President of Russia concerning appeals for pardon.

Other forms of interaction with authorities and (or) official bodies have not received any significant distribution.

Steady connections of human rights organizations with some state bodies (the Ministries of Defense, Educations, Home Affairs and others) of the majority of associations with prestigious but powerless advisory bodies (the Commission of Human Rights under the President of Russia, the regional Commissions of Human Rights, various public councils under authorities, etc.) adjoin with fragmentary and casual interaction with other structures.

The best example of the organization carrying out close interaction with bodies of the government is the Unions of Soldier's Mothers (USM)[14]. Firstly, human rights organizations as those already have solid operational experience – most of them were created more than eight years ago and it is a significant period for current human rights organizations. Secondly, the structure of the Unions of Soldier's Mothers is rather flexible: these unions are not incorporated in the centralized Russian association with the general charter, they have a different level of development and their aims are not quite identical. They depend on activity of their members also caused by general political conditions in regions (traditionally it is considered that associations as such should be engaged first of all in protection of the rights of military men). Thirdly (and it is, probably, the main thing), apart from authorities, soldier's mothers should also deal with such closed independent interstate public structure as the armed forces.

The Unions of Soldier's Mothers were created on the wave of reorganization and publicity in Russia when the information on events in the intra-army life began to spread widely. Then they actively proved in the course of confrontations, in particular during the Chechen war, being engaged in search of missing persons and returning from captivity both officers and soldiers of fixed period service. Now these directions of activity are still developing. Nevertheless, not all the regional Unions of

Soldier's Mothers consider this their priority. As the basic purpose many of them see control of order in military units in which serve recruits from certain region, and observance of the rights of military men.

In the course of acquaintance with the activity of the regional Unions of Soldier's Mothers, an interesting picture, both typical and a little bit non-standard in comparison with other nongovernmental organizations, starts to appear.

Typicalness lies in dependence of activity of the USM on their regional origin. It should be said that in areas and republics with rigid methods of management they have the same range of problems as other noncommercial public organizations do. That is, they either carry out policy of local authorities, directly putting themselves in dependence on them, or do not show any activity at all. The Union of Soldier's Mothers of the Republic of Kalmykia can serve as an illustration. In spite of the fact that it was created in 1995, no practical results of its activity are visible. However, probably if government officials of Kalmykia have a necessity for new demonstration of displays of the social policy, the Kalmyk USM will help to present it at a necessary level.

Direct dependence on state bodies is also observed in Kursk. Despite the initiative partially shown by the regional organization of USM which was expressed, for example, in carrying out in June-July 1999 of a charitable marathon to help soldiers serving in the "hot regions" such as Tajikistan, Afghanistan, the Chechen Republic, and their families, its other activity is outside the field of vision of the public. The Kursk USM has rather close connections with the local authorities and consequently there's no talking about its opposition to their arbitrariness. About the status and the real purposes of this association eloquently says even the fact that its representatives are on a regular basis involved in carrying out of the draft campaign in the region.

A non-trivial way of self-expression was selected by the members of the Tambov USM. Generally this organization incurs the functions traditionally executed from the organizations of the Russian Defense Sports Technical Organization (POCTO), namely pre-conscription military training of youth. Thus, members of the Tambov USM in every possible way support carrying out of military training at schools of the area. As to other sides of their activity, practically nothing is known about them.

As it has already been noted, despite the breadth and diffusion of the spectrum of activity of the USM, some of them are engaged into practical work which has rather serious results. Among such organizations known for their real affairs, it is possible to mention the Union of

Soldier's Mothers of the Chuvash Republic and also the Saratov Union of Soldier's Mothers (not to confuse with the Saratov Committee of Soldier's Mothers).

The activity of these organizations there embraces practically all functions which, owing to mass media, are known in the work of the capital USM. They carry out big work, first of all, ensuring observance of the legislation in the field of military service.

One of the most acute problems solved by the USM is the care of the military men of fixed period service who are called from corresponding regions and participating in military actions. For example, in August 1998 Dagestan was visited by a delegation of the Saransk Soldier's Mothers for definition of the exact number of the Mordovian military men who were taking part in military operations in the Chechen Republic, and distribution of medicines.

In the Bashkortostan Republic the functions inherent to the USM are carried out by the republican committee on protection of the rights of military men and members of their families. Among its achievements, for example, regular sending of the humanitarian help to the areas of confrontation and resolution of problems of the military men in trouble, first of all those called from Bashkortostan (for example, their returning from captivity).

Big work is carried out by the members of the Committee of Soldier's Mothers of the Chuvash Republic. On a regular basis they manage to carry out such actions as sending of humanitarian cargoes for the soldiers participating in operations in the Northern Caucasus; inspection trips to those parts of the country, visits to the soldier who serve there will also be organized. They are carried out basically with support of charitable donations of private persons and enterprises of Chuvashiya. There is also one-time financial help from the governments. For getting means to carry out such actions members of the committee use such forms of work as, for example, carrying out of charitable marathons.

Perhaps, one of most successfully current Unions of Soldier's Mothers can be considered that of Saratov the headquarters of which are in Balakovo. This organization has been acting for more than eight years, practically without help of the state structures frequently and simply overcoming obstacles coming from authorities. There is no precise information about the number of its members, however, it is known that in 1996 there were more than 4 000 people in it from the whole area (according to the charter, mothers of the future recruits not less than one year prior to recruitment become members of the Union). Without the financial support of the state, the Balakovo USM managed to generate its structure rather rationally due to charitable donations and membership fees which make approximately 15 roubles a month.

Having started with education of recruits in the field of their rights and duties, soldier's mothers seriously attended to the control over the conditions in which their sons serve. The active members of the Union led by its permanent leader Lydia Sviridova (a journalist and legal expert) started to visit the military units where sons of the USM members serve and to initiate contact with the management. Only owing to their persistence and personal qualities contact with the militaries was found. The first step on the way to cooperation was recruitment of Saratov soldiers only into one of the military units in the Samara region. This work led to the fact that in May 1998 in the course of consideration of the problem of the "Reform of Armed Forces of the Russian Federation Deployed in the Saratov Region" there was worked out an agreement between the Command of the District and the Regional Management on assigning of the Saratov recruits, first of all, to the units deployed on the territory of the region and only in process of recruitment - to other units of the Privolzhsky military district

Representatives of the Union also carry out traditional actions, such as fund raising for the Saratov military men and for rendering assistance to mothers who lost their sons during military actions or searching for missing persons. There is constant help to those who serve in so-called "safe" units: they are supplied with food, hygienic accessories, books, audio-and video equipment, etc. got with the support of the Union. The USM members regularly report to public representatives about all the collected means.

The Union also addressed the Ministry of Defence of Russia with the request to send a special commission to study the catastrophic situation around endowment of the soldiers in the Shihansky military garrison of the Privolzhsky military district.

It is remarkable that with the progress in achievement of new success by the Saratov USM the sphere of its activity gradually extends, too. Thus, now its members also carry out protection of the rights of recruits by means of representation of their interests in judicial bodies. In particular, owing to the USM help the process under the claim of Roman Annenkov (Balakovo) and Ivan Volika (Saratov) to the local military commissariats which carry out recruitment for fixed period service in the Armed forces of Russia was won. Both of the recruits were probably the first in the regions to have decided to use the constitutional law on replacement of military service with alternative civil service. Roman Annenkov was guided by the religious beliefs (he is a member of the community of Witnesses of Jehovah) and Ivan Volik was guided by his personal views, based on unwillingness to oppose other people with firearms in hands. However, the draft commissions of all levels refused to satisfy their demands offering Annenkov to serve in a building battalion or railway armies and Volik to serve in signal troops. The recruits appealed to court with the requirement to cancel the decision of the commissions.

Later the Saratov USM experience of litigation on the case of the denied persons, who eventually defended their right to alternative civil service in May 1998 in the Frunze Regional Court of Saratov, was analyzed at the federal level. The Perm legal experts published the collection "Alternative Civil Service" in which the mentioned process was covered. Notwithstanding the complexities with ensuring of attendance of the defendants - representatives of the draft boards in court, the case was won so that the lost party did not appeal the decision of the Frunze court in the Regional Court. The process was recognized exemplary and in the future the Saratov USM experience is supposed to be used widely in such situations.

According to the recruit's lawyer Lydia Sviridova, despite the fact that participation in such processes is not a direct aim of the USM, the latter, being interested in consecutive carrying out of the military reform, should insist on observance of the rights of recruits to be granted the right for alternative civil service.

The Saratov Union of Soldier's Mothers also publishes their own small circulation newspaper "The Kamerton" («Камертон») distributed in military units where young men called from the Saratov region serve. Besides, the information on the USM activity is regularly published in the Balakovo newspaper "The Kroug" («Круг»).

Reasoning from the abovementioned, it is possible to draw a conclusion that the Saratov USM is doing a serious work on many problems. However, right at the beginning of their activity members of the Union repeatedly had to face great problems in the organization of work. Firstly local authorities did not show any interest to the Union, trying to counteract carrying out of some actions. So it was, for example, in April 1997 when members of the Union collected means for mothers who had lost their sons in the Chechen war, to render assistance to the soldiers who were still there. Then the authorities were ordered to detain the participants of the action. The problem was partially solved by Lydia Sviridova's appeal for help to the first vice-president of the regional government Leonid Vashchenkov, yet the action was partially disrupted.

Experience of the USM brings us to the idea that bodies of the government do not show any active interest in cooperation with human rights organizations except for the cases when during pre-election campaigns their representatives seek support of nongovernmental human rights organizations which are popular with the citizens. The reason is that the authorities do not see the necessity of such interaction - the authorities do not see in real force in human rights organizations which could support them. Such approach is unjustified as a number of human rights organizations could help and in fact, under their own initiative do help authorities to solve many social problems assisting development of the democratic principles of the society. It is necessary to mention that, despite general encouragement of human rights organizations by the population, it does not cover all its layers. In the given example it is especially obvious as even the interested layer is instable - as a rule, after young men return from the Arm Forces units their relatives leave the USM, considering their problem solved.

Independence of the state bodies of the Unions of Soldier's Mothers, the opportunity to equally cooperate with representatives of the authorities are proved by the fact that actively working human rights organizations which actually assist authorities in solving their problems practically do not receive any financial and other help. The tradition of gathering funds for their purposes by human rights organizations by carrying out public charitable actions is obvious for the authorities. Though help from the state which could be expressed in granting a preferential tax regime for organizations rendering different sorts of assistance to military men and those military units where they serve is possible.

For remedial organizations in such conditions a unique opportunity to find a way of interaction with authorities is consolidation of their own authority by expansion of the sphere of the activity in certain region. An ultimate goal of such activity can be influence on the process of law-making or even entering regulatory authorities. Besides, it is impossible to underestimate the personal qualities of the leaders of human rights organizations as their personal characteristics allow creating a positive image of the organization, to represent it on the regional and in some cases federal level and also to realize the opportunity of election of their representatives into the regional and federal deputy case.

In recent years there has been rise in activity of human rights organizations in those areas in which scale infringement of human rights is observed: infringement of human rights by national (ethnic) identity; infringement of provisions of the International Humanitarian Right concerning civilians in zones of military actions; infringement of the rights of refugees and compelled immigrants, the rights of military men, the social and economic rights; trouble in the penitentiary system, etc. A number of nongovernmental human rights organizations have started paying special attention to problems of protection of the religious minorities which do not fall under the new law "On Freedom of Conscience and On Religious Associations".

The growth of the human rights movement demands attention and support from the state. The Decree №864 of the President of Russia of June 13, 1996 "Some Measures of the State Support of Human Rights Movements in the Russian Federation" was regarded by this movement as comprehension by the state bodies of the importance of human rights organizations in ensuring of the rights and freedoms of a person. Nevertheless now nongovernmental human rights organizations are not satisfied by such support, regarding it as obviously insufficient: they have no neither the strong legislative status, nor economic base and material aid.

However, there is no sufficient unity and coordination among human rights organizations on a number of questions of principle of protection of the rights and freedoms of a person.

It is especially important to develop close interaction of human rights organizations with the Commissions of Human Rights which according to the mentioned Decree of the President of Russia are created in the overwhelming majority of subjects of the Russian Federation. The structure of many of these commissions includes leaders of human rights organizations and some Commissions of Human Rights are headed by well-known legal experts (the Saratov, Irkutsk regions).

The struggle for ensuring of human rights is a problem of all democratic powers of the Russian society. Their association will assist strengthening of guarantees of human rights, solidarity of the society, and increase of its moral potential. Coordination and strengthening of interaction of nongovernmental human rights organizations, the Commissions of Human Rights, Human Rights Commissioner in the Russian Federation and regions are necessary.

Continuing the military subject, it is necessary to say that, despite of the acts accepted in the last six years strengthening of legal protection of military men and members of their families as well as recruits, till now bodies of the government have not managed to liquidate mass infringement of practically all social guarantees stipulated by the current legislation and privileges for military men and members of their families; rights to health protection, honour and personal dignity.

According to the Commission of Human Rights at the President of the Russian Federation, only martial courts in 1998 considered 43,609 complaints of military men about illegal actions (decision) of bodies of military management and military officials that is twice more, than in 1997 88.8% of the general number of the complaints considered by courts are recognized well grounded and satisfied. The overwhelming majority of complaints to be satisfied (over two thirds) is connected with the fact that military men are not provided with many sorts of allowance, with infringement of their housing rights and order of dismissal from military service.

The greatest alarm is still caused by cases of death and a traumatism of military men as a result of unauthorized mutual relations, assault and other infringement of disciplinary practice. According to the Commission of Human Rights under the President of Russia, with reduction of general destruction of military men by 8.7% counting for 1000 people the level of their destruction as a whole, has increased by 3.7%. Among deaths 22.4% cases refer to suicides caused by unsolved social problems, hard service conditions, mockeries and humiliation of human dignity and at times being morally and psychologically unprepared for military service.

The unsatisfactory situation in the Russian army and braking of processes of carrying out of the military reform have created conditions for formation of a whole group of human rights organizations, whose sphere of interests is in this way or another connected with the Russian Armed Forces. Their environment is very heterogeneous, the three dominating directions of activity are *struggle for transition of the army to the voluntary principle of recruitment, protection of the rights of the soldiers doing fixed period service and protection of the rights of professional military men* (also when they are transferred to the reserve).

The first direction is carried out *by the Antimilitaristic Radical Association (ARA),* which is now concentrating most of its efforts on ensuring of realization of the Constitutional Law of Russian young men to replacement of military service with civil alternative service, but the ultimate goal is nevertheless assistance to transition to the professional army. Nowadays almost all ARA activity is connected with conducting numerous litigations of the members refusing to serve in connection with the character of their belief and demanding to replace military service to alternative (the Federal Law "On Alternative Civil Service" in Russia does not actually exist, despite existence of the Constitutional Guarantee in Clause 3 of Article 59 of the Constitution of Russia). However, this organization which is actively current in Moscow and St. Petersburg is almost unknown in other Russian regions. Probably, it is connected with the fact that its access to mass media is rather limited and it can freely cover its activity mostly in electronic computer networks still not really accessible in a common Russian region. ARA members outside the two cities mentioned above are only estimated in tens and in the capital their radical position frightens off the majority of the youth who simply prefer not to come to the military commissariats when summoned. Estimating success of the ARA tactics, only one thing can be said: as it is known, any of its members is not yet in prison for attempt to realize the Constitutional Law though proceedings far not always develop in their favour.

Another organization or, more likely, a network of organizations which also gives a lot of attention to protection of the rights of recruits is much better known outside Moscow but does not limit its activity only to this problem. We are talking about *the Committees and Unions of Soldier's Mothers (USM)*, which are now widely spread and have huge authority not only among the population but also among the representatives of regional management and the army officer case now. The activity of the Unions/Committees of Soldier's Mothers was earlier discussed in more detail.

The problem of observance and protection of human rights in corrective organizations, investigatory cells, prisons and educational colonies continues to remain an exclusively serious problem for Russia.

Despite certain steps undertaken by the Government of Russia, in particular transfer of the criminal executive system under the jurisdiction of the Ministry of Justice, as before, this system is not only incapable of carrying out correction of the convicts but also frequently deprives of moral and physical health both the citizens kept in it and its employees.

In the conditions which have actually developed in the penitentiary system, the state does not provide protection of dignity of a person, protection of a person against torture, cruel and humiliating treatment. In this system rough human rights to health and life protection are frequently grossly violated.

The distress with the rights of prisoners as one of the most serious problems in the Russian society has caused appearance of human rights organizations specializing on rendering assistance to the given category of the population.

The best known remedial organization working in this sphere is the Regional Public Organization "The Center of Assistance to the Reform of Criminal Justice" ("The Center of Assistance") (Moscow, director of

the Center is Valery Fedorovich Abramkin, a former political prisoner).
"The Center of Assistance" is one of the early human rights organizations
in Russia, the history of which started in the beginning of the 1990s.

The basic purpose of the Center is all possible assistance to the reform
of criminal justice. The purposes of the Center are: assistance to studying
of the existing penal policy and practice, degrees of security of life, health
and personality of convicts, social and psychological consequences of
punishment in the form of imprisonment; carrying out of independent
public examination of the criminal and criminal executive legislation
and also new legislative offers and projects on the subjects of the Center;
assistance to creation of a fair and effective system of criminal justice in
Russia alternative to justice, effective mechanisms of control over jails;
realization of public control over observance of legality and human rights
in jails, studying the facts of investigatory and judicial arbitrariness and
also administrative arbitrariness in places of imprisonment, informing of
the public on these facts and treatment in connection with the revealed
facts in the corresponding state bodies and also in national and international human rights organizations; gathering, processing, storage and
distribution of the information and the documents connected with the
subject of activity of the Center; rendering of material aid to prisoners,
their families, the released and victims of crimes; creation of a databank
on the subjects of the Center etc..

Unfortunately, some of the problems of the Center now remain not
realized in full as there is no necessary legislative base. For example,
realization of public control in penal organizations is hampered by absence of the Federal Law "On Public Control over Enforcement of the
Rights of Prisoners".

Other directions of the "Center of Assistance" are brought into life.
Thus, since 1999 "The Center of Assistance" with financial support of
the Moscow branch of Penal Reform International has been carrying
out projects on rehabilitation of women-prisoners, pregnant women and
minor prisoners in colonies of the Republic Mordovia, the Vladimir,
Moscow, Oryol regions and the city of Moscow (projects "Women in
Prisons" and "Rehabilitation of the Most Vulnerable Groups of the Prison
Population - from Practice to Theory").

Considering the fact that about 350,000 prisoners are released from
prisons every year and also in connection with absence of an current
system of support of the given category of persons, in Russia for a long
time there has been a need for realization of socially significant projects
on rehabilitation of the prisoners preparing to discharge and former

prisoners. This need has recently been aggravated in connection with the resolutions on amnesty concerning minors and women accepted by the State Duma in the end of May 2000 and also in the end of 2001. Besides, the reform of the legislation which will potentially lower the number of prison population by 350,000 people is now being discussed.

Considering the reasons set forth above, human rights organizations (including those representing Russian regions) realize projects, the purpose of which is rehabilitation of former prisoners ("Attendance for the Released" of the public organization "Committee "For civil rights" (Moscow); "The Center of Social Adaptation of Former Prisoners" of the Tchaikovsky branch of the Perm regional human rights center; "Pomoga" («Помога») (Rehabilitation service for former convicts and members of their families) of the Krasnodar regional public organization "Convict "); the projects on rehabilitation of persons serving time (including their education, vocational training and training of the prison personnel on use of humane and constructive methods of rehabilitation): "Training of Personnel of the Kolpinsk Educational Colony to Transformation of Process of Rehabilitation of the Teenager to Joint Activity – Dialogue Equal in Rights" of the St.-Petersburg historical and educational remedial public organization "Memorial "; "Sociolabor rehabilitation of the Teenagers Preparing for Discharge in the Arzamas Educational Colony" (the Nizhniy Novgorod region) of the public organization "Sretenie " («Сретенье»).

Constant overcrowdedness of investigatory cells is a subject of projects in two Russian regions – that is, Nizhniy Novgorod and Rostov, realized in 2000-2001 by the organizations: "The Right to Life" (Nizhni Novgorod) and regional public organization of invalids "The Center of Human Rights" (Taganrog, the Rostov region).

Special concern is caused by the situation which has developed around the rights of minor prisoners. According to the Commission of Human Rights under the President of Russia, among more than 20,000 teenagers those in colonies are 82.2% including 15.5% of teenagers under 16.9.6% of pupils are orphans or children deprived of parental care.

It is more and more difficult for administrations of educational colonies to ensure provision of all of the convicts with food, clothes, articles of prime necessity, medicines, textbooks and school writing materials, to prepare them for returning to independent life.

In such conditions sometimes only human rights organizations assist educational colonies. The teenagers who got into institutions for execution of punishment, regularly help the Committee "For civil rights"

(Moscow), the Dzerzhinsk Human Rights Centre (the Nizhniy Novgorod region), public organization "Sretenie" (the Nizhniy Novgorod region), the public " Center of Assistance to the Reform of Criminal Justice" (Moscow), etc.

Continuation of the "teenage problem" is work of human rights organizations on programs of regenerative justice. One of the leading nongovernmental human rights organizations of Russia in this sphere is the Center "Judicial Legal Reform" (Moscow). Their numerous projects provide influence on the legislation, considering wider use of experience of regenerative justice for resolution of criminal cases and for the first time in Russia use practice of regenerative justice concerning adults. Experience of the Moscow Center is also approved by regional human rights organizations, among them: the Novorossisk city welfare fund "School of the World" (Krasnodar territory), the Karagaisk branch of the Perm Regional Human Rights Center, the Irkutsk crisis center "Angara", the regional charitable public fund on work with minors belonging to the group of social risk "Response" (Moscow), the Novgorod regional public fund "Healthy Family", the Novgorod regional public fund "Protection", etc.

Another problem demanding urgent resolution is the escalating number of appeals to the President of Russia for pardon. The regional public organization of assistance to democratic reforms "Information. Consultation. Assistance." (Moscow) in interaction with the Management of Administration of the President of Russia concerning pardon in 2000-2001 carried out the joint project "Organization" of: Service of Assistance" under the Management of the President of the Russian Federation Concerning Pardon" in which they acted as partners equal in rights. Efficiency of joint actions results has been proved – though the number of appeals to the Commission Concerning Pardon under the President of Russia is not decreasing, however, the time used to answer the appeals and for considerations of clemency applications by the Commission has been considerably reduced.

Another example of positive experience is the project the aim of which is granting of regular legal consultations to prisoners in the colonies of the Tomsk region to ensure protection of their rights (the project "Legal Clinic in Places of Imprisonment"). In the "Legal Clinic" students of the Legal Institute of the Tomsk State University work under the teachers' control. It is a new, unusual project for Russia which promotes close and constructive interaction between the organizations which execute punishment and the civil high school; they can become an example for possible distribution in other regions of Russia, too.

By expert estimations of the Central Administration of Penal Execution, in organizations of the criminal executive system of the Ministry of Justice of Russia a number of convicts suffering from AIDS and HIV-infected in 2000 will exceed 17,000 people. However, the state actions for prevention of the approaching catastrophe are practically not taken; as always, the problem remains for the lack of the necessary state financing. Only few human rights organizations work to help those prisoners who are sick with AIDS and HIV-infected. The small number of human rights organizations working in the given direction, can be explained by the justified risk of infection, expensiveness of actions, presence of qualified personnel in the organization. Most successfully in the given direction work the Nizhniy Novgorod organization "The Right to Life" (chairman of the organization is E.E. Beliaeva), the independent noncommercial organization "Anti AIDS Center" (Voronezh).

In Russia, according to all available information, there are about 2.5 million displaced persons (basically of the Russian nationality). Up to 400,000 persons have left their houses, escaping from war in the Chechen Republic; by efforts of the government many of them have been settled in various areas of Russia but not less than 70,000 still live in temporary dwellings in Ingushetia and Dagestan.

In this connection there is a necessity for legal resolution of the problems of citizenship, refugee status, the problem of indemnification, etc. The State Duma has accepted two basic laws: the Federal Law of the Russian Federation of February 19, 1993 (in edition of June 28, 1997) "Refugees"[16] and the Law of the Russian Federation of February 19, 1993 (in edition of December 20, 1995) "Compelled Immigrants"[17]. The same year Russia signed the Convention of the United Nations "The Status of Refugees" of 1951 and the Report to it of 1967. All this was made with the purpose of creation of legislative base for activity of the Federal Migratory Service formed in 1992.

However, from the very beginning the use of these statutory acts in practice was inconsistent which created serious problems for migrants and for all those who tried to help them. Realization of the laws was extremely complicated because of the limited financing which does not allow even to register all displaced persons and to give them even temporary material support.

Before creation of the Federal Migratory Service the problems of the compelled immigrants were solved off and on, sometimes by groups of interested citizens. The first remedial organization created specially for rendering assistance to refugees, was the nongovernmental "Civil Assistance" committee in Moscow. Founded in 1990, when the first refugees (Armenians from Azerbaijan) appeared in Moscow, the Committee has worked for seven years in the building where the office of "The Literary Newspaper" was situated.

The Committee is continuing its work now, spending the funds received from sponsors to ensure the provision of refugees and the compelled immigrants with financial assets and clothes. Owing to financial support of the Management of the Supreme Commissioner of the United Nations on Affairs of Refugees, the Committee organizes free legal consultations for migrants; if necessary it represents their interests in court. The Committee is also helped by volunteers from the Muscovites; students-volunteers have created a school for children-refugees from the Chechen Republic.

The committee is intensely cocurrent with other human rights organizations engaged in refugee problems and those of compelled immigrants, in particular, with the remedial Center "Memorial", "Human Rights Watch", Russian-American Human Rights Bureau and the Quaker Group. All these human rights organizations actively cooperate with members of parliament.

The refugee and compelled immigrants problems are also being solved by universal human rights organizations such as the Committee of Soldier's Mothers and the Russian Human Rights Research Center. In this direction work international nongovernmental organizations, rendering medical aid to refugees is "Doctors without Borders" (MSF), "Karitas".

Some Russian human rights organizations which have reached higher level of professional development, offer to their employees working in the sphere various courses, render methodical and organizational help. Among such organizations it is necessary to mention the Center of Support of Nongovernmental Organizations "Golubka", where there are only five employees who spend 80% of time outside Moscow, organizing seminars concerning organizational development of human rights organizations and their management. The "Golubka" has also organized a number of seminars on prevention of conflicts and reconciliation, has published a Russian translation of the anthology of texts about principles of nonviolence.

Among organizations of the kind working in the sphere it is necessary to point out the "Rainbow" and the Welfare Fund of Help, too.

It is also important to say that the majority of the mentioned human rights organizations are located in Moscow where the group can be registered, open a bank account rather easily and even influence political decision making.

As an encouraging circumstance it is necessary to recognize the formation of self-help organizations among migrants: They create small enterprises, get land and try to create accommodation for themselves. Now in Russian regions there are seventeen such self-help groups (In the Voronezh, Kursk regions, Tataria, etc.).

However, these migrant human rights organizations face serious problems. Firstly, they are physically isolated one from another, being located in the countryside in different parts of Russia. The second difficulty for the migrant human rights organizations consists in resistance which they often meet from local administrations and the population. Because of the lack of experience, many migrant groups are unable to determine the initial and long-term needs and cannot state them to their potential sponsors.

In the long-term prospect such migrant groups as well as other Russian human rights organizations, require training in methods of influence on acceptance of new bills regulating the legal status of migrants and they should learn the ways, allowing achieving realization of the official laws.

Lack of financial security also causes inefficiency of the laws regulating position of migrants.

Thousands of people who according to the Law of 1993 "Compelled Immigrants" fall under the definition "compelled immigrants", experience difficulties getting this status; tens of thousands of Russians who have come back from former union republics, do not address organizations of the Federal Migratory Service and try to integrate into the Russian reality themselves. These people, however, face such Soviet heritage as the problem of registration. Though according to the Law of June 25, 1993 "On the Right of Citizens of the Russian Federation to Freedom of Movement, the Choice of a Place of Stay and Residence within the Borders of the Russian Federation" residence permit is replaced by registration which should have a notifying rather than allowing character, in fact, the rigid registration system remains: in many cities and villages registration is forbidden to migrants even if they already have Russian citizenship (the given problem was a subject of consideration in the Constitutional Court of Russia, however, even after the decision of Constitutional Court of the situation remains the same (this especially concerns Moscow and the regions bordering about the Chechen Republic).

Despite obvious difficulties, human rights organizations continue to work in the sphere of protection of the rights of refugees and compelled immigrants and it is possible to say that they remain islands of hope for those who have lost all hope for aid and support of the authorities.

According to the results of the research carried out in 1998-2001, the number of children who have been recognized as those "without parental care", makes 625,000. For the last two more years than 113,000 children a year have stayed without parents which catastrophically exceeds the level of the year 1992 when the number of orphans made 67,286. 30,000 more children escape from unhappy families and settle at railway stations and underground stations; some them get to orphanages and children's homes.

After the 1991 economic changes in Russia these children became unnecessary ballast. Such children, whose parents are needy, unemployed, invalids or criminals, make a dramatically growing class of neglected, which has received the name of "social orphans" as it is meant that one of the parents of 95% of them is alive[18].

The statistics on neglected children is extensive and the figures received from various official sources often do not coincide. Children's homes of different types submit to three various departments, that is to the Ministry of Education, Ministry of Health, the Ministry of Work and their statistical categories either meet or are so uncertain that it is extremely difficult to receive exact figures on each of the categories[19].

According to the UNICEF information, published in 1997, in Russia 611,034 children live "without parental care ". 337,527 of them are in orphanages, children's homes and boarding schools for children-invalids[20].

According to official statistics, other children are placed under alternative trusteeship, including so-called "children's homes of family type" the legal status of which is not yet certain[21], and into foster homes. In some statistical documents foster homes are indicated as an alternative form of accommodation for children, however, other data testify that only a few hundred children live in families consisting of a relatively small number of members, and in so-called "children's homes of family type" groups of children are more numerous, than in an average family. Since 1996 in Russia several pilot programs of children accommodation in foster homes as an alternative to large children's homes have been carried out. The given direction in Russia has been recognized as one of the best forms of children accommodation[22]. However, in practice, according to the Ministry of Education of Russia, in 1998 there were only 3,000 children (including the children of parents-tutors) in foster homes that makes only 0.48% of the general number of the registered orphans.

A positive consequence of the transition period of the 90th was that for the first time nongovernmental human rights organizations and independent experts giving the help and the information got access to organizations for orphans. Most obvious improvements of material conditions are observed in children's homes to which international agencies on adoption render considerable aid.

However, some weakening of the centralized control has also had a negative side. Though many cases of abuse in children's organizations have been revealed, an even greater number of them, according to the children's rights defenders, remain unrevealed. This can be explained by the fact that those organizations of the local level are not accountable to the central ones.

As the research in orphan organizations in Moscow, Republic Tatarstan, the Altay territory, the Belgorod, Kursk and Moscow regions has shown, the result of departmental monopolism in management and control over the given organizations is legal vulnerability of teenagers, an opportunity of the diversified abuse (injection of psychotropic medications as punishment, sexual exploitation, uncontrollable expenditures distinguished drafted from the budget funds for the children's needs, frauds with orphan benefits for accommodation, etc.)[23]. All the mentioned facts have been received not only from nongovernmental sources and from pupils of children's homes and boarding schools but also from official data as a result of a random inspection of orphan organizations in several regions of Russia carried out by the State Office of Public Prosecutor of Russia in 1998. Till now orphan organizations remain closed institutions. We also had to face this fact as some heads of the given organizations refused to be interviewed and to give any data without the official sanction of higher instances.

Such state of affairs forces nongovernmental human rights organizations to conduct the work aimed at improvement of the position of neglected children.

In the new social and economic conditions new nongovernmental organizations specializing in protection of the rights of neglected children and orphans began to appear as a result of destruction of a traditional system of social protection of the population and redirection of the society to market mechanisms. Such organizations work to defend the lawful privileges of pupils and graduates of children's homes and (or) boarding schools; they are engaged in legal education of orphans, informing them about their rights and means of their protection. Occurrence of human rights organizations working with such groups of the population was promoted by decrease in efficiency of activity of the state structures current in the sphere of protection of the rights of children. Nongovernmental human rights organizations in the given sphere try to weaken the social tension but we must admit that so far these attempts have not brought about any meaningful result. The activity of nongovernmental human rights organizations is quite busy as nongovernmental human rights organizations realize new projects of social help by means of their own initiative and support of various welfare funds, mostly foreign.

At present there are not more than twenty organizations that exist, really work and help to defend the rights of neglected children and orphans. Most of them are concentrated in Moscow. Unfortunately, Muscovites are poorly informed on the kinds of help and services which are rendered by these organizations (let alone the situation in the Russian provinces).

Organizations on protection of the rights of neglected children and orphans also exist in St.-Petersburg, Kazan, Kursk, Belgorod, Petrozavodsk, Stavropol and other cities. Unfortunately, children who find themselves in a difficult situation practically do not know about their activity. As a consequence, there appear nongovernmental human rights organizations founded by orphans, graduates of orphanages. Among the most stably developing ones we should mention the Committee of Protection of the Rights of Pupils of Children's Homes, the Russian Association of Orphan Organizations. The latter supports the idea of Russian and international adoption. However, the Association concentrates its main efforts on rendering help to hundreds of thousands children who are still in orphan organizations and will probably stay there till their full age. The Committee of Protection of the Rights of Pupils of Children's Homes carries out regular monitoring of the rights of pupils of orphan organizations. Many times the employees of Committee revealed the facts of infringement of the rights of pupils of the Moscow boarding schools (in the form of refusal to render qualified medical aid, sexual mockeries, fraud concerning living quarters of pupils of boarding schools).

One of the well-known nongovernmental human rights associations is the Regional Public Organization (RPO) of Assistance to Protection of Child's Rights "The Right of the Child" of the Russian Human Rights Research Center which has occupied a niche in development of the legal problems of protection of the rights of children and, in particular, protection of the rights of orphans. Work with the bodies of the government and lobbying of interests of the rights of children, first of all, through deputies of the State Duma, allows, though in an insignificant degree, to guarantee at the legislative level the complex of rights which would allow realizing the rights of children as fully as possible. Besides, "The Right of the Child" acts as a kind of an opponent of the Government of Russia on the international level, giving alternative reports on observance of the Convention on the Rights of the Child by the Government of Russia to the Committee of the Rights of the Child of the United Nations.

"The Right of the Child" has developed a project of the Federal Law "On Public-Parliamentary Control over Enforcement of the Rights of Minors in the Russian Federation" which deserves attention. Adoption of the Law provides establishment of public inspectors who will have control powers and the right to come into any children's establishment of Russia at any time without prevention and to communicate with the children without witnesses.

Besides, the new "Public Center of Assistance to the Reform of Criminal Justice" (Moscow) together with common with the experts of the Committee "For Civil Rights" (Moscow) is preparing the bill "On Justice for Minors" where the mechanism of reconciliatory procedures is provided. The publishing house "A Lawyer to Oneself ", current under the aegis of the Committee "For Civil Rights" has published a book by I.V. Babushkin about the history of juvenile justice in Russia from the beginning of the 20th century.

Experience of the Committee "For Civil Rights" is also worth attention - the given Committee was registered in the form of a charitable public remedial organization in 1996. Its founders were 10 participants of the human rights movement. During its existence the Committee has assisted more than 800 orphans in the form of legal consultations, in person and by correspondence, representation of interests of orphans in courts and in the bodies of the Office of Public Prosecutor; visiting of the convicted orphans in the organizations of execution of punishment; in bringing parcels to colonies and investigatory cells; in publishing of remedial literature in their own publishing house "A Lawyer to Oneself "; legal education of orphans and other categories of citizens who have found themselves in especially difficult situations by means of lecturing conducted by the experts of the Committee in various organizations and at the educational seminar "Human Rights Monday".

In 1999 the Committee created a so-called Service of Probation. "It is pedagogical, legal, psychological rehabilitation of orphans for persons on probation. Educational work, games, how to behave when being employed, how to behave in the family, how to resolve conflicts, how to calm down, how to work in the library, that is the practical skills used in the game form. Adaptive social rehabilitation"[24].

The given direction on which the Committee "For Civil Rights" is going to work is rehabilitation and preparation of orphans for the future life after they leave the children's home and (or) boarding schools – which is a new direction of activity for Russian human rights organizations.

It is necessary to mention the work of the Center of Past-Orphanage Adaptation of Pupils of Children's Homes (Moscow) (chairman S.A. Levin) which works in a little bit different sphere but the pursued purposes are the same as those of Babushkin's Service of Probation. The difference between the two services is as follows: while the first Service nongovernmental and exists either on private donations or with the support of foreign welfare funds, the second one is municipal and works at the expense of the budget of the city of Moscow and is supervised by the Moscow Committee of Education.

At the regional level there are not more than ten human rights organizations defending the rights of children - and this is in the whole of Russia. That is why any positive regional experience of creation of such organizations is worth mentioning. Thus, in 1999 on the territory of the Kursk region by forces of the Kursk city public organization "Civil Initiative" preparation for realization of the project on the organization of Service of Legal Aid to Children and their Parents started. At the given stage there is only preparatory work (edition of the bulletin "The Side of the Society" which tells about the rights of children, with a weekly column "Legal Children's Consultation" conducted by the lawyer on the pages of the regional weekly newspaper "The Kursk week").

Experience of the Central Black Earth Human Rights Research Center is also worth mentioning. Thus, the lawyer of the Center N.G. Migunova gives lectures on procedural rights of children and their practical realization in children's organizations in the city of Kursk. However, this does not happen on a regular basis. Apart from lecturing, N.G. Migunova participated in litigations on upholding the rights of orphans.

However, unfortunately, on a more global scale it is impossible to say that these organizations worked effectively at the regional level. Though in the report "On the Situation around Human Rights in the Kursk Region of the Russian Federation in 1998".[25] The state of affairs around the rights of children is mentioned as satisfactory as well as observance of the legislation on protection of motherhood and childhood, the real situation is different. As the research carried out in 1999-2001 in the Kursk region, among others, has shown, the legislation, the real state of affairs in the field of protection of the rights of motherhood, childhood and especially the situation around the rights of orphans leave much to be desired. The employees of the Office of Public Prosecutor, the Committee of Education of the Government of the Kursk region, heads of children's homes and boarding schools of the Kursk region mentioned in conversations that legal protection of children in the Kursk region is on a low level.

It is necessary to say about such disturbing facts as when organizations clearing illegally earned money are founded or a buffer to avoid taxation is created as a kind of nongovernmental remedial organization ostensibly protecting the rights of orphans. According to the tax laws, noncommercial organizations have a number of tax privileges, which unfair people use. Such actions cast a shadow on the remedial as a whole, which anyway does not find due support of the population in Russia.

Despite all these difficulties, the remedial movement is developing. If the state cannot ensure provision of protection of the rights of orphans up to the mark, human rights organizations point to this state duty; and while they work becoming "eyes and ears of the government" there is hope that they can help at least a part of orphans and neglected children, allowing them to stop being deprived of civil rights.

Thus, it is possible to draw a conclusion that human rights organizations are starting to play a more and more active and effective role upholding civil rights, not limiting themselves with national frameworks. Activity of human rights organizations as expert institutions equalizes opportunities of citizens in protecting their rights when they are facing the powerful state machinery. Unfortunately, it is necessary to admit that nowadays in Russia human rights organizations are not so strong, especially this concerns regional organizations, however, gradually the best known human rights organizations, for example the Moscow Helsinki Group, the Center of Assistance to International Protection, the Center of Assistance to the Reform of Criminal Justice, are becoming a kind of resource centers helping to found human rights organizations in the regions. Thus, with developing of the network of nongovernmental human rights organizations, it is possible to say that efficiency of protection of civil rights will increase and the state will see them not as opponents but as partners in protection and observance of civil rights.

Notes

1. See: The Code of Legislation of the Russian Federation. 1994. № 32. Article 3301; 1996. № 9. Article 773; № 34. Article 4026 / Собрание законодательства РФ. 1994. № 32. Ст. 3301; 1996. № 9. Ст. 773; № 34. Ст. 4026.

2. See: The same work. 1995. № 21. Article 1930; 1997. № 20. Article 2231; 1998. № 30. Article 3608.

3. See: The same work. 1996. № 3. Article 145; 1998. № 48. Article. 5849; The Russian Paper. 14 July 1999 / Российская газета. 1999. 14 июля.

4. See: The same work. № 33. Article 3340.

5. See: The same work. № 33. Article 3340.

6. T.D. Matveyeva. International and National Instruments and Mechanisms of Protection of Human Rights. Moscow, 1995 / Матвеева Т. Д. Международные и национальные инструменты и механизмы защиты прав человека. М., 1995.

7. R.Y. Shulga, N.G. Migunova. Nongovernmental Human Rights Organizations as a Mirror of the Society // Human Rights in the Context of Development of a Civil Society: International conference papers (Kursk, 15-16 May, 1997) – Kursk, 1997. P. 123 / Шульга Р. Ю., Мигунова Н. Г. Неправительственные правозащитные организации – зеркало общества // Права человека в условиях становления гражданского общества: Материалы междунар. науч.-практ. конф. (г. Курск, 15–16 мая 1997 г.). Курск, 1997. С. 123.

8. More about monitoring: See: Human Rights Monitoring. Warsaw, 1997. P. 30–78. / Подробнее о проведении мониторинга См.: Мониторинг прав человека // Заметки о правах человека и мониторинге прав человека. Варшава, 1997. С. 30–78.

9. See: L. Yelin. Let Us Compare the Data: "Amnesty International" In Moscow // The New Time 1989. № 16. P. 37–38; S.V. Polubinskaya. The Representatives of "Amnesty International" In Moscow // The Soviet Country and Law. 1989. № 9. P. 143–145 / Елин Л. Сверим данные: «Международная амнистия» в Москве // Новое время. 1989. № 16. С. 37–38; Полубинская С. В. Представители «Amnesty International» в Москве // Советское государство и право. 1989. № 9. С. 143–145.

10. N.A. Sakharov. Lobbyism as a Factor of Political Life // Business and Politics. 1994. № 1. P. 30–31 / Сахаров Н. А. Лоббизм как фактор политической жизни // Бизнес и политика. 1994. № 1. С. 30–31.

11. See: N.G. Zabluk. Lobbying Practice in the USA. Moscow. 1994. P. 5. / Зяблюк Н. Г. Практика лоббистской деятельности в США. М., 1994. С. 5.

12. Look in, for example, Clause 1.1 of the Regulation of the Black-Soil Human Rights Research Center; the Regulation of the Russian Human Rights Research Center (Moscow); the Regulations of the Association "The Right to Life and Civil Dignity" (Moscow) and others / on например: Пункт 1.1 Устава Центрально-Черноземного исследовательского Центра по правам человека; Устав Российского исследовательского Центра по правам человека (Москва); Устав общества «Право на жизнь и гражданское достоинство» (Москва) и другие.

13. This list does not include the Sate Duma and the Federal Assembly as a whole.

14. Since Organizations of Soldier's Mothers exist independently of each other and of the capital organization, they are called differently. Normally the organizations as mentioned in this work are called Unions or Committees of Soldier's Mothers (USM and CSM) having similar functions. We have chosen USM as a conventional term. However when talking about specific examples of their work the authors of this work use the original names.

15. See: The Regulation of the Regional Public Organization "The Center of Assistance to the Reform of Criminal Justice". Approved by the Constituent Assembly of the Public Center of Assistance to the Reform of Criminal Justice 12 July 1993, registered by the Administration of Justice of the city of Moscow 2 August 1993 (with amendments of 18 May 1999). Moscow, 1999 / Устав региональной общественной организации «Центр содействия реформе уголовного правосудия». Утвержден Учредительным собранием Общественного центра содействия реформе уголовного правосудия 12 июля 1993 г., зарегистрирован Управлением юстиции города Москвы 2 августа 1993 г. (с изм. и доп. от 28 мая 1999 г.). М., 1999.

16. See: The Russian Paper 3 July 1977. / Российская газета. 1997. 3 июля.

17. See: The Code of Legislation of the Russian Federation 1995. № 52. Article 5110 / Собрание законодательства РФ. 1995. № 52. Ст. 5110.

18. UNICEF: Children at Risk in Central and Eastern Europe: Perils and Promises, Regional Monitoring Report № 4. Florence, 1997 / ЮНИСЕФ: «Социально незащищенные дети в Центральной и Восточной Европе: проблемы и перспективы»: Отчет регионального

19. The establishments called boarding schools where children live constantly appear in official reports on children's establishments of various sorts. One must not consider these establishments analogue of the educational boards existing in other countries. The Russian boarding schools can be additionally defined as "auxiliary" or "specialized"; they are intended for children who suffer from various diseases or experience difficulties with studies. In some boarding schools children both live and study; sometimes some children in a boarding school have no parents, and some children are taken home for weekends by their parents. In daily use the word "boarding school" is used in any meaning. In charge of the Ministry of Education there are boarding schools for orphans of the age of 5-11 recognized as capable of studying.

20. UNICEF: "Children at Risk". P. 67. / ЮНИСЕФ: «Социально незащищенные дети». С. 67. In the UNICEF report difficulties in reception of authentic statistical data about children in official bodies are emphasized: "Instead of reflecting the problem-focused approach to satisfaction of needs of these children, statistical data are collected and published only by administrative categories though there are significant crossings and variations in functions of various establishments. For example, children with a small degree of physical inability can be placed in children's home; houses for invalids can have practically healthy children. However in most cases there are no summary data that would give information about needs of all children-invalids placed under alternative trusteeship … Insufficiency and inadequacy of statistical data is actually the main obstacle of the effective decision on the national level of numerous problems of children who are being in the charge of the state. There is a sharp need for the coordinated actions on improvement of system of the administrative reporting and development of the researches focused on illumination of a concrete problem at the international level. Without them children will remain « left in the charge of the state".

The same work. P. 68. On complexities of statistical study of the given category of children see also: R.Y. Shulga. A Study of The Situation around Orphans and Methods of Resolution of the Problem: a report on the project carried out within the framework of the Interdisciplinary Academic Center of Social Studies "Intercenter" in 1998. / О трудностях статистического учета данной категории детей см. также: Шульга Р. Ю. Исследование положения с безнадзорными детьми на примере Курской области и правовые методы решения данной проблемы: Отчет по проекту, реализованному в рамках Междисциплинарного академического центра социальных наук «Интерцентр» в 1998 г.);

R.Y. Shulga. Problems of Modern Neglect: Social-Legal Aspect (with the Example of the Kursk Region): a manuscript. 1998 / Он же: Проблемы современной безнадзорности: социолого-правовой аспект (на примере Курской области): Рукопись. 1998.

R.Y. Shulga Neglected Children as a Legal Category: Tendencies of Development and a Way of Resolution of the Problem: a Report at the All-Russia Conference " Juvenile Studies as a Science: Problems of Formation and Prospects » Kazan, 1999 /Он же. Безнадзорные дети как правовая категория: тенденции развития и пути решения проблемы сиротства: Доклад на Всероссийской науч.-практ. конф. «Ювенология – как наука: проблемы становления и перспективы». Казань, 1999.

21. See: An Alternative Report of the Russian Nongovernmental Organizations to the UNO Children's Rights Committee/ Commentaries to the Periodical State Report on Realization of the Convention on Children's Rights in the Russian Federation in 1993-1997 //http://www.openweb.ru/p_z/Ku/main.htm /.

Альтернативный доклад российских неправительственных организаций в Комитет ООН по правам ребенка: Комментарии к Государственному периодическому докладу о реализации Российской Федерацией Конвенции о правах ребенка в 1993–1997 гг. // http://www.openweb.ru/p_z/Ku/main.htm.

22. See: Part 1 Clause 1 Article 123 of the Family Code of the Russian Federation (edition of January 2, 2000) // the Legal Reference System "Consultant Plus" / Часть 1 п. 1 ст. 123 Семейного кодекса Российской Федерации (в редакции от 2 января 2000 г.). // Справочно-правовая система (СПС) «Консультант-Плюс».

23. The research "Adaptation and Possible Models of Orphan Mobility: Social and Legal Aspects" was carried out in 1999–2000 with financial assistance of the Moscow Education Fund and the Ford Fund (Grant № SP-99-1-11/2) / Исследование «Адаптация и возможные модели мобильности сирот: социально-правовой аспект» проводилось в 1999–2000 гг. при финансовой поддержке Московского общественного научного фонда и Фонда Форда (грант № SP-99-1-11/2).

24. Taken from the interview with A.V. Babushkin, President of the Committee "For Civil Rights" (Moscow, 1999), given to the author in the course of the research "Adaptation and Possible Models of Orphan Mobility: Social and Legal Aspects" / Из интервью председателя правления комитета «За гражданские права» А. В. Бабушкина (Москва, 1999 г.), данного автору во время проведения исследования «Адаптация и возможные модели мобильности сирот: социально-правовой аспект».

25. The report was given to the author by the Black-Soil Human Rights Research Center (Kursk)

Chapter 18. DEVELOPMENT OF HUMAN RIGHTS CULTURE AS A GUARANTEE OF REALIZATION OF CIVIL RIGHTS AND FREEDOMS

The recognition of rights and freedoms of a person as the maximum value is the major achievement of civilization. Human rights play the essential role in understanding of current processes in a modern society and a state, especially in conditions of globalization. Foreign and domestic researchers have said a lot about the fact that the given category deserves a special attention of science. However, many questions till now have been theoretically un-grounded, therefore, detailed studying and development of the basic concepts has an important theoretical-methodological and practical value. One of them is the **culture of human rights** which occupies a special position in the system of categories of various social studies: philosophy, cultural science, jurisprudence, etc.

Culture of human rights is a component of spiritual culture. This concept appeared for the first time on the pages of information materials of the United Nations in 1989. But it was not an object of research in a science, in the legal literature till now there is no definition of this category though concept "the culture of human rights" follows from the idea of humanization of rights. Therefore, the definition of the content of the given concept and allocation of the basic structural elements represent special scientific interest.

The term "culture" (from Latin *cultura* - cultivation) designated in the beginning the function connected with purchase of knowledge, experience. In Middle Ages there appeared a notion of a spiritual, intellectual culture (on Cicero - culture of a soul). The 14th-16th centuries began a "humanitarian" culture, not only turned to a person but also proceeding from him. In Russia this term for the first time was found out in "The Pocket Dictionary of Foreign Words" by N. Kirillov in 1846 and characterized the activity for prompting forces dozing in a person[1].

The scientific understanding of the given category is not at all unequivocal in connection with that it reflects an unusually wide, complex and many-sided public phenomenon describing a person, social group, and a society. According to V.M. Mezhuev, "any concept of social study does not cause such divergence in views, such variety in opinions and definitions as the concept of "culture"[2]. According to the estimation of researchers there are more than five hundred of such definitions, thus, it is absolutely clear that neither the essence of culture, nor various shades of it can be fully expressed in one definition.

In the widest meaning culture quite is often understood as all achievements of mankind, everything created by a person. The culture in that case appears as "the second nature", created by a person, forming the human world, unlike the wild nature. Supporters of the given approach usually subdivide culture onto material and spiritual. The material culture covers first of all the sphere of production of goods and its products - technical equipment, technology, means of communication, buildings and constructions, transport and roads, dwellings, everyday goods, clothes, etc. The spiritual culture includes the sphere of cultural production and its results: religion, philosophy, moral, art, science, etc. The spiritual culture in its turn also consists of various elements: moral culture, art, religious, political, legal and, certainly, culture of human rights.

Thus, the culture of human rights is the component of spiritual culture representing the system of knowledge, valuable orientations and views, psychological feelings based on respect of dignity of a person, his rights and freedoms and also practical skills on their realization and protection.

As a matter of fact, culture of human rights is a very complex, many-sided and complex phenomenon. Its uniqueness consists in close connection of its basic parts. As such elements or attributes of the given category it is possible to mark out the following: knowledge, world outlook aims or views, emotional elements, skills which are being system interaction.

For formation of a high level of culture of human rights in a society it is necessary that citizens realized the rights and freedoms, had certain knowledge in the given sphere, respected the rights and dignity of other people and also had skills in the field of protection of rights and freedoms. It is expedient to consider the given elements in more detail.

Firstly, there is the knowledge. Awareness of a person on rights and duties is, undoubtedly, the major element of culture of human rights. Knowledge is the result of knowledge of the reality checked up by practice, its correct reflection in consciousness of a person. Knowledge is got on the basis of comparison of the received information. Therefore, it is not enough to receive data and to have access to certain information on the rights and freedoms of a person, it is necessary that there was a practical experience of knowledge and opinion, often for a long time. According to the researcher A.A. Trebkov, "an overall objective of training should become the formation of general culture of human rights, in which basis there is an acquaintance, first of all, with the content of international standards on human rights"[3]. However, it is impossible to know only the content of international documents in the field of human rights, it is necessary to know in general about the concept and essence of the category of "human rights", its genesis, about historical-philosophical views and approaches, about structure and classification, about universal and national mechanisms of realization and protection of rights and freedoms. Knowledge of human rights gives an opportunity of their effective legal protection both on national and on international level. Besides, they form a necessary condition of ensuring of a due understanding and respect of rights and freedoms of other people.

Secondly, there are world outlook aims. The important role in the progress of culture of human rights in a society development of moral values, the belief defending the rights and freedoms and also formation in a person of corresponding world outlook aims that relates to processes of social development. It is possible to refer a priority of a person to such world outlook aims in relation to the state, respect of dignity inherent in all members of human family, respect of the right to life, inadmissibility of discrimination, tolerance, etc.

We have approached the verge of millennia which demands from people new views, a new structure of values, and a change of consciousness. Fruitful interaction of national cultures, their rapprochement association of people before a person of global dangers are possible only on the basis of basic values which are immanently inherent in all cultures: moral standards, value of a human life, individual freedom and dignity, equality and respect of human rights, mutual understanding and tolerance, a concept of polychromic and multidimensionality of world, refusal of violence and etc. According to Professor A.N. Arinin, "until … the idea of rights and freedoms of a person does not become a moral need, the national idea, capable to unite all society, advance them on new legal, political, social, economic and cultural creation, the procedures and institutions of enforcement of human rights and freedoms will not be realized in practice"[4].

Thirdly, there are emotional elements. Psychological feelings as an element of culture of human rights are also very important. Experience, comprehension, perception of rights and freedoms scientifically influence the development of a world outlook orientation of a person and regulation of people's behaviour, the formation of feeling of security and responsibility. That is the process of knowledge formation of world outlook aims, views, believes is impossible without psychological moments. Thus, experience and emotions of negative character, backwardness of feelings can cause a nihilistic attitude to rights and freedoms, disbelief in ideas of human rights, tolerance, nonviolence, and cultures of the world. Therefore, not denying the huge value of the cognitive side of culture of human rights, it is impossible to reduce to it the whole system of human rights' culture. The process of rights and freedoms realization and the more so a degree of activity of a person in this process appreciably depend on that as far as they are realized and estimated by a person.

Fourthly, there are skills. It is possible to speak about culture of rights of a separate person as far as he knows, understands, comprehends, estimates the rights and freedoms and also as really uses them in practical activities. Therefore, during formation of culture of human rights the major role is played by presence of a practical component of experience are skills on protection and restoration of the infringed rights and freedoms. Certainly, only an educated person can realize rights and also protect and restore the infringed rights and freedoms of other persons. Having a sufficient level of knowledge and practical skills, a person can involve all potential mechanisms of protection of rights at a national level and in the case of need and exhaustion of interstate means of protection is to address to international mechanisms. Besides, during development of culture of human rights skills of constructive cooperation are developed.

The basic components, elements of culture of human rights are the following.

It is necessary to pay attention to the point of view widespread in science about identity of the given category and the concept of "legal culture" or about it as of a part of legal culture. Thus, I.V. Rostovschikov approves that "it is possible to speak about such independent part of legal culture as culture of human rights which high level is one of bases of becoming democracy in Russia and the mortgage of hardening of the public consent"[5]. The concept of "legal culture" is studied well enough in science, for the first time by lawyers in 1960s of the 20th century. There are different approaches to the definition of the given category. The legal culture is, obviously, a legal and wide concept which includes a complex of legal life phenomena.

Certainly, the culture of human rights, on the one hand, represents a component of spiritual culture of a society and on the other, penetrates its other parts, including legal culture. Thus, for example. V. Agranovskaya writes, "Consideration of legal culture through a prism of rights, freedom and duties emphasizes the feature of legal culture as one of ways of a person's activity in the legal sphere"[6]. In her opinion, standards of behaviour in a society, which a person follows, are generated in the form of rights and duties, i.e. legal rights and duties serve in a society as a system of reference points regulating the behaviour of citizens, their mutual relations with each other, with the state, with a society. To choose the variant of behaviour responding to internal belief and interests and also interests and requirements of a society, a person should have sufficient cultural potential. With reference to legal area it is a question of legal culture. The high level of legal culture of a person serves as an indispensable condition of an appropriate realization of rights and freedoms[7].

Thus, the culture of human rights represents a reflection in categories of spiritual culture of a society, in this case in legal culture, the concepts of "human rights".

But "legal culture" and "culture of human rights" are not identical concepts though they consist in complex organic unity as the components of spiritual culture of a society. Thus, the culture of human rights has a major value for formation of legal culture. Thus, the right in itself is the essential factor and way of realization of rights and freedoms of a person, therefore, humanistic character of legal culture promotes more real and effective realization of human rights during life. And the culture of human rights is the factor concerning guarantees of human rights.

It is important to note also that in the basis of the content of legal culture there is, obviously, a legal aspect, while in the basis of culture of human rights the idea of dignity of a human being, certainly lays, and it is a moral category, therefore, at the characteristic of the given concept the moral aspect prevails.

As it has already been said, human rights in the modern world are a powerful layer of universal culture and a high level of culture of human rights is one of guarantees of their realization. Special value in a society gets the formation of culture of human rights as a cultural guarantee of realization of civil rights and freedoms.

Civil rights and freedoms is a special group of rights in which interests of persons as individualities are embodied, i.e. of a person having unique features. These rights are called to ensure the provision of freedom and an autonomy of an individual as a member of a society, his security from any interventions from the outside, including the state. They guarantee an opportunity of self-realization of a person. Rights of a person are directed on ensuring of a priority of individual, internal reference points of development of each person. The indicated rights have non-property character; they are not directly connected with using of material benefits and realized in the sphere of the moral relations embodying cultural and moral values[8].

Realization of civil rights and freedoms allows a person to use the values of individual freedom, such as inviolability of life and value of a human being, personal freedom and an opportunity to dispose of oneself, personal safety and etc. In essence, "this block of rights covers fundamental aspects of a personal freedom, expressing humanistic principles of everyone in a democratic society"[9]. Values of individual freedom and dignity of a human being, first of all, underlie a world outlook element of culture of human rights.

Such fundamental rights of a person as a right to life and the right to dignity, freedom from slavery, the right to security of a person and freedom from torture, cruel treatment and degrading and punishment, Freedom of thought, conscience and religion, freedom from discrimination, etc., cannot be to the full realized if there are no enormous changes in the public consciousness, directed on their humanization.

Thus, for example, within the limits of the United Nations the states, considering that the abolition of the death penalty promotes strengthening of human dignity and progressive development of human rights and that all measures on abolition of death penalty should be considered as a progress in enforcement of the right to life, accepted on December, 15, 1989 the Second Optional Protocol to International Covenant on Civil and Political Rights, directed on abolition of death penalty. Now it has been ratified already by 104 states. Certainly, in any society there always will be supporters of use of death penalty, however, events of last time testify that people began to perceive more seriously the problems of human rights, intolerance to their infringement all over world has considerably amplified, ideas of value of a human life and dignity extend, i.e. gradually there happens humanization of consciousnesses of world community, including by way of a cancelling or moratorium on death penalty. It is impossible to disagree with the opinion of V. Kalchenko who remarks that, unfortunately, ideas of sanctity and inviolability of human life are not prevailing in public consciousness. The modern Russian society experiences the crisis of culture, accompanied reassessment of moral values. And he, in turn, inevitably attracts the crisis of sense of justice expressed in the skeptical attitude to the right as means of protection of life from illegal encroachment and to the state as to the subject putting a legal mechanism in action. "The state, writes V. Kalchenko, should promote the formation in public consciousness of humanistic ideology Thus, it is necessary to actively realize one of the basic duties: protection of the constitutional recorded rights and freedoms"[10].

Formation of humanistic ideology is a reflection of realization of cultural or, in other words, ideological guarantees of rights and freedoms.

The last represents the major and especial kind of guarantees of rights and freedoms as a reflection of aspiration to generate such status in a modern society when minds and feelings of people, their lives and souls are penetrated by the idea of high dignity of a person, respect for a person, value of individual freedom and his inalienable rights. That is, otherwise, such status is the high level of culture of human rights in a society.

Special value for the analysis of the role of formation of culture of human rights in a modern society has the right of cultural guarantee of their realization to dignity. The many-sided concept "dignity" represents also a philosophically-ethical and constitutionally-legal category. So Article 21 of the Constitution of the Russian Federation records the provision according to standards of international law that "dignity of a person is protected by the state. Nothing can be the basis for its belittling". In this case it is a question of dignity of a person in general, though it is possible to consider dignity of a person as a representative of certain group or a community (for example, problems of national dignity of minority) or from the point of view of individual dignity of a separate person.

The doctrine of human rights is based on this value as a matter of fact; the right to dignity is the basic purpose of other human rights, according to E.A. Lukasheva, "a consolidating principle of moral and legal orientation of a society"[11]. Certainly, the given category is a core of all other personal (civil) rights and freedoms without exception. Dignity is guaranteed and protected by such rights as a right to freedom and security of a person, the right of defence of honour and reputation, freedom from torture, etc. This moral concept is the original precondition of rights and freedoms, therefore, respect of self-respect and human dignity, in general, is, perhaps, one of the main problems and the states and public structures. In this regard V. Belinsky who in the Letter to Gogol argued as follows: "Russia needs neither sermons ... nor prays but awakening in people of feeling of human dignity that has been lost in dirt and rubbish for so many centuries".

Besides, general cultural guarantees of civil rights for each certain personal right or freedom special cultural guarantees are characteristic.

The culture of human rights is based on uniform base principles and provisions but it is not single-layered formation and it is not deprived of contradictions. It is most vividly shown at collision of various civil (personal) rights. As an example it is possible to remember the realization of human rights to personal immunity.

The feature of the given right means that it is directed mainly on ensuring and protection of a personal safety of a citizen. Personal safety is a social value, an acute status of an individual at which he is guaranteed against any illegal encroachment on his corporal, moral and cultural inviolability. However, if it is a question, for example, of realization of the right to personal immunity of the accused it should not contradict the rights of a victim. Here it is not only legal but also the major cultural dilemma (who is necessary to be protected), connected with formation of culture of human rights.

Unfortunately, in consciousness of a simple person who is poorly familiar with jurisprudence and does not have a sufficient level of legal culture and culture of human rights the necessity of protection of rights of a suffered person and protection of rights of such people as the accused or the defendant is not perceived as a rule. Reality of the made decision is estimated by them from moral positions. Often from the point of view of a person the categories a "suspected" and a "criminal" are equal. But it is only one aspect of the problem connected with formation of culture of human rights in public.

On the other hand, the purpose of any lawyer to protect human rights is to prevent injustice of punishment of an innocent person. However, in the modern situation in Russia when growth of criminality is being observed, the strong social differentiation of a society, realization of the major principle of presumptions of innocence is at times perceived in a society as an approach to rights of a victim. In terms of it the problem consists in opposition, the contradiction of the whole complex of civil rights of the accused person (presumption of innocence, the right of the accused to defense, personal immunity, etc.), on the one hand, and rights of a victim, on the other. In this connection the formation of culture of human rights in public and in various officials and employees of law enforcement bodies becomes very important.

Cultural guarantees of the right to personal immunity should be provided, including, educational process in various educational institutions and organizations for lawyers bringing up the respect for rights of the imprisoned, detained, accused and condemned, intolerance to infringement of the given right.

The major question of the role of education of professional sense of justice, legal culture in the lawyers assuming the internal realized attitude to rights and freedoms and through them by all legal life of a society, repeatedly has been raised in the literature. It becomes really acute at the analysis of cultural guarantees of such civil rights and freedoms as freedom from torture, cruel and degrading treatment and punishment, inviolability of dwelling, the right to freedom of residence, procedural rights. It is necessary to note that the scornful attitude to human rights of the imprisoned and accused from many lawyers is the usual phenomenon in modern Russia.

The formation of culture of human rights as guarantees of observance of civil rights and freedoms by representatives of separate trades is the major question not only for future lawyers-experts or law enforcement bodies officers but also for workers of other spheres. Thus, realization of a personal right to privacy of correspondence, telephone and cable messages directly depends on the respect of the concept "secrecy" at workers of a communication system and personal privacy of a person from formation of a feeling of delicacy, respect for especially private, individual moments of life, for example, at employees of mass-media.

The world outlook element of human rights culture means not only the development of belief, moral aims directed on respect for rights and basic freedoms of other people as to universal democratic values and formation of a feeling of human dignity but also assistance to mutual understanding, equality of sexes and friendship between all nations, eradication of inequality between racial, national, ethnic, religious and language groups. Among such valuable aims and orientations special role plays the formation in people of a feeling of tolerance that is, certainly, also a cultural guarantee of realization of many civil (personal) rights and freedoms.

In the 17th century the concept "tolerance" was new enough. Modern concepts of tolerance or, more precisely, its concept as a factor strengthening the world, giving protection from injustice, being base for formation of culture of human rights, in many respects was prepared by researches of philosophers of 16th-17th centuries. One of such philosophers who rose against "patience of intolerance" and cruel religious collisions, was, for example, Voltaire, the author of a well-known "Treatise about Toleration" (1763).

Owing to the efforts of UNESCO in last decades the concept "tolerance" has become an international term, the major keyword in problems of human rights. On November, 16, 1995 in Paris 185 states-members of UNESCO, including and Russia, had been accepted the major document of the present is the Declaration of principles of tolerance. According to the definition given in Article 1 of the Declaration, tolerance means "respect, acceptance and correct understanding of rich variety of cultures of our world, our forms of self-expression and ways of displays of human individuality". This definition means the tolerant attitude to other nationalities, races, color of skin, sex, sexual orientation, age, physical inability, language, religion, political or other opinions, national or to a social origin, the property, etc.

It is important to note that "tolerance" in the given context is not used in value of Russian verb "to bear", which, as a rule, has a negative connotation. In Article 1 of the Declaration it is said that "tolerance is not a concession or indulgence ... it is, first of all, an active attitude formed on the basis of a concept of universal rights and basic freedoms of a person. Under no circumstances tolerance cannot excuse encroachment on these basic values ..."

Thus, it is necessary to consider tolerance, first of all, as a respect and a concept of equality, refusal of domination and violence, a concept of multidimensionality and variety of human culture, views, beliefs and refusal of data of this variety for uniformity or to prevalence of any one point of view. Tolerance presupposes readiness to accept others such what they are and to cooperate with them on the basis of the consent.

Modern researchers come to the conclusion that "tolerance is the important component of a vital position of the mature person having the values and interests and ready if it is required, them to protect but simultaneously yours faithfully concerning provisions and values of other people"[12]. Therefore, in our country it is necessary to form such understanding of tolerance, especially at youth; to aspire to that it became habitual. The declaration in Article 4 pays attention to that fact that "education in the spirit of tolerance begins with training people in what their general rights and freedoms consist of, to ensure the provision of realization of these rights and from encouragement of aspiration to protection of rights of others". In other words, such concepts as "the culture of human rights" and "tolerance" are closely interconnected and interdependent. Tolerance is an original basis for formation of general culture of human rights and a cultural guarantee of realization of the major civil (personal) rights and freedoms: Freedom of conscience, the rights to determine and specify the national identity, the rights to using the native language, etc.

The process of achieving of a high level of human rights culture in Russia, certainly, will be long and complex. It is impossible to disagree with E.A. Lukasheva saying that "the most difficult in modern Russia is overcoming of the stereotypes formed by the century connected with belittling of the role of a person, neglecting his rights, freedoms, and dignity. These stereotypes, first of all, determine immorality of a modern Russian society. It is necessary to use all means and, first of all, the constitutional institutions and mechanisms to gradually, step by step, overcome this immorality"[13]. It is thought that on this hard way it is necessary to coordinate, first of all, joint actions of the state with organizations of a civil society on continuous informing and education in the field of human rights, culture of world and tolerance of all layers of the population.

Notes

1. See: Agranovskaya E.V. Legal Culture and Enforcement of Human Rights. Moscow, 1988. P. 8. / См.: Аграновская Е. В. Правовая культура и обеспечение прав личности. М., 1988. С. 8.

2. Mezhuev V.M. Culture and History: Problems of Culture in the Philosophical-Historical Theory of Marxism. Moscow, 1977. P. 3. / Межуев В. М. Культура и история: проблемы культуры в философско-исторической теории марксизма. М., 1977. С. 3.

3. Trebkov A.A. To Know International Standards of Human Rights // State and Law. 1993. # 10. P. 143. / Требков А. А. Знать международные стандарты прав человека // Государство и право. 1993. № 10. С. 143.

4. Human Rights and Freedoms in Program Documents of Political Parties and Associations of Russia. 20th century / Edited by A.N. Arinin. Moscow, 2002. P. 17. / Права и свободы человека в программных документах политических партий и объединений России. XX век / Под ред. А. Н. Аринина. М., 2002. С. 17.

5. Legal Culture in Russia on a Boundary of Centuries: The Review of All-Russia Scientific Conference // State and Law. 2001. # 10; Law and Politics. 2001. # 6; Juridical Education and Science. 2001. # 2. / Правовая культура в России на рубеже столетий: Обзор Всероссийской науч. конф. // Государство и право. 2001. № 10; Право и политика. 2001. № 6; Юридическое образование и наука. 2001. № 2.

6. Agranovskaya E.V. Specified work. P. 18. / Аграновская Е. В. Указ. соч. С. 18.

7. See: Ibidem. P. 20.

8. See in more detail Chapter 1.

9. Human Rights / Edited by E.A. Lukasheva. Moscow, 2002. P. 143. / Права человека / Под ред. Е. А. Лукашевой. М., 2002. С. 143.

10. Kalchenko N.V. Human right for Life (Questions of theory and practice). Volgograd, 2003. P. 13-14. / Кальченко Н. В. Право человека на жизнь (вопросы теории и практики). Волгоград, 2003. С. 13–14.

11. Human rights / Edited by E.A. Lukasheva. Moscow, 2002. P. 260. / Права человека / Под ред. Е. А. Лукашевой. М., 2002. С. 260.

12. Soldatova G.U., Shaigerova L.A., Sharova O.D. To Live in Piece with Oneself and with Others: Training of Tolerance for Teenagers. Moscow, 2000. P. 7-8. / Солдатова Г. У., Шайгерова Л. А., Шарова О. Д. Жить в мире с собой и другими: тренинг толерантности для подростков. М., 2000. С. 7–8.

13. Human Rights / Edited by E.A. Lukasheva. Moscow, 2002. P. 265. / Права человека / Под ред. Е. А. Лукашевой. М., 2002. С. 265.

Conclusion

Let's sum up our research.

Individual freedom is a component of a personal freedom, essential aspect of a civil society. Realized outside of state limits, this freedom mediates that is also shown in the system of social bonds and the relations expressing such important values integral with a person as inviolability of life, dignity, conscience, personal safety of a person. A specific feature of individual freedom (unlike political, economic, social, cultural) is that it embodies individually unique abilities of a person and provides opportunities of self-determination of a person. Genuine individual freedom means interdiction of illegal state intervention into private life of citizens, denying of the totalitarian control over an individual.

Civil human rights is a group of rights embodying individual freedom that are recorded in the International Bill of Rights, in many internationally-legal declarations, conventions and implemented in Constitutions of the majority of the countries of the world, including the Constitution of the Russian Federation (1993). The indicated rights refer to the first generation of human rights. They have a non-property character and are realized in the sphere of moral relations embodying moral and cultural wealth. Being also the legal form of ensuring of a personal safety, they make the major bases of legality as well as law and order.

Civil human rights have properties concerning independent human rights of a subsystem existing within the limits of the general system which center are the rights to life, to dignity, and to freedom.

Being a version of legal rights, they have legal properties inherent in all human rights and the specific qualities peculiar only for them. Thesis formulated in Article 1 of the Universal Declaration of Human Rights: "All human beings are born free and equal in dignity and rights", refers to all rights and freedoms of a person, first of all, to civil ones. Forms of their realization, the system of the guarantees, called to ensure the provision of their realization form the specific structure of each of civil rights. Legal guarantees are especially important for realization of these rights.

In conditions of globalization all over world there were serious contradictions in realization of all human rights, including civil ones. On the one hand, in the 20th century the law of human rights which recorded civil rights was generated. International mechanism of the control over their observance was also created, including world and regional international organizations, legal procedures, etc. In world public opinion the idea of respect for human rights is very firm. Numerous human rights organizations have been created. The tendencies aimed at humanization of legal systems, in particular abolition of death penalty in many countries of world amplify. There are countries though very few which have achieved a high level of observance of human rights, including civil rights.

However, as a whole, the period of globalism is accompanied by strengthening of the negative phenomena in the sphere of realization of civil rights: growth of terrorism, increase in number of murders, kidnappings, arbitrary imprisonment, androlepsy and trade in people, strengthening of international criminality, racial, religious intolerance, growth of number of refugees.

The reasons of mass infringement of civil rights roots in the main conflicts of the modern world. The following refer to their number. On the one hand, huge nationalization of means of production, rapid development of productive forces. It has led to that such wealth are saved up by means of which it is possible to ensure the provision of well-being of all mankind. On the other hand, unfair ways of distribution of this wealth have generated the split on the countries of the North and the South, to rich minority and the poor majority. The struggle for world power resources threatening by ecocatastrophes has amplified. Financial contradictions between the various economic centers are developing. Conflicts between accelerated scientific and technical progress and backlog of moral development of a society, between internationalization of all social life and growth of nationalism, between the various church organizations, including activity of religious fundamentalism forces resisting them have become aggravated. The powerful states, first of all, the USA, have saved up enormous means of mass destruction by means of which it is possible to destroy everything alive on the planet. And it causes aversion of all world mankind. After collapse of the USSR, the USA has achieved political domination in world that has led to strengthening of instability.

All the indicated circumstances promote strengthening of illegal, violent ways of the decision of arising problems and illegal violence (the state arbitrariness, actions of mafia groups, terror, etc.) is an antipode of civil human rights, legality and the law and order.

Ensuring of civil human rights demands democratization of the whole system of international relations, strengthening of their stability with a view of realization of the right of people to peace, the right to life. It presupposes the activization of efforts of the states, international organizations, and public in elimination of firearms of mass destruction, elimination of danger of nuclear conflicts. It is expedient to restore the role and value of the United Nations in ensuring of peace and safety, in its functions of human rights realization.

Especially important is the struggle against international criminality, strengthening of measures of punishment and ensuring of inevitability of the responsibility for such grave crimes against a person as get murders, terrorism, extrajudicial executions, violent and not voluntary disappearances of people, any imprisonment and the conclusions, trade in people, racism. The solution of these problems is probably on the basis of cooperation of the states, in particular their law-enforcement services.

The situation with realization of civil human rights in Russia is unsatisfactory. The given research has revealed serious problems in this sphere. It seems that real ensuring of the given group of rights is inseparable from the problems connected with ensuring of the whole system of human rights in our country. First of all, this creation of reliable material guarantees of rights to a worthy standard of living, on protection from unemployment, on social security, on health protection and medical aid, called to liquidate poverty of a significant part of the population, generating a social stress in a society.

Enforcement of civil rights demands development of legal, organizational and cultural guarantees. First of all it is a question of the further humanization, democratization of the legislation and ensuring of stability of the accepted laws. In particular, it is necessary to solve the problem on exception of death penalty from criminal sentences.

It is expedient to expand the rights of victims of crimes, having provided a principle of equality of the parties in criminal trial. The most serious problem in struggle against crimes against a person is realization of a principle of inevitability of the responsibility of the criminals encroaching on civil rights. Its decision is impossible without serious reform of all state remedial systems. It, in particular, presupposes the development of guarantees of independence of court, struggle against corruption among judges and law enforcement body's officers, increase of efficiency of activity of the Office of Public Prosecutor, investigatory services.

It would be expedient to expand powers of Human Rights Commissioner in the Russian Federation and also to create a system of human rights commissioners in all subjects of the Federation as well as specialized ombudsmen (on the rights of the child, etc.).

The careful analysis and the complex approach are necessary for real ensuring of civil human rights to the system of special guarantees of each of these rights. Thus, encroachment on the right to life is not only murders of citizens by criminals but also death of people in accidents, on production, etc. Therefore, it is necessary to ensure the provision of the system of the legal, organizational, economic and other measures making system of guarantees of this right.

For ensuring of human rights to honour and dignity it is expedient to improve and approve the bill brought in Russian parliament of protection of this right and also to develop a complex of the measures connected with formation at civil servants and the population of culture of human rights.

It is possible to ensure the reality of the provision about the right to freedom from torture and other cruel, inhuman treatment or punishment by means of improvement of conditions of maintenance of the imprisoned and condemned according to international standards and also by means of the real departmental control and public prosecutor's supervision of observance of rights of these citizens. Besides, the wide control from nongovernmental human rights organizations is necessary.

Aiming at ensuring of human rights to freedom of movement in the country the necessity of elimination of illegal limitations of this freedom for many subjects of the Russian Federation has become imminent.

The freedom of conscience and freedom of creeds requires special protection. It would be necessary to make essential changes which would guarantee equality in the rights of believers and atheists, to the current Federal law on freedom of conscience equality of all churches and religious associations. Clerical tendencies shown last years in our country create threat to genuine freedom of conscience.

Finally, a special problem is the development of culture of human rights, increase of a level of sense of justice of citizens and employees of state machinery. It is necessary to introduce teaching of a course of "Human rights" into all educational institutions.

Real ensuring of civil human rights is a component of formation of a democratic and a lawful state.

Bibliography

Monographies and proceedings

1. Azarov A., Roiter V., Hufner K. Human Rights. International and Russian Mechanisms of Protection., Moscow, 2003.

2. Basik V.P. Personal Rights and Freedom of people and Citizens n the Russian Federation. Moscow, 2003.

3. Belomestnyh L.L. Human Rights and their Protection: in 3 vol. Moscow, 2003.

4. Bondar N.S. Constitutional Measurement of equality of citizens of the Russian Federation / N.S. Bondar. U.V. Kapranova. Rostov on Don, 2002.

5. Cheremnykh G.G. Freedom of Conscience in the Russian Federation / Edited by J.A. Dmitriev. Moscow, 1996.

6. Constitutional Rights and Freedoms of a Person and a Citizen in the Russian Federation./ Edited by O.I. Tiunov, Moscow, 2005.

7. Davidovich V. E. Problems of Human Freedom. Lvov, 1967.

8. Davidovich V.E. Verges of Freedom. Moscow, 1969.

9. Ebzeev B.S. Constitution. Democracy. Human rights. Cherkessk, 1992.

10. Ebzeev B.S. Constitutional Personal Freedom in the USSR. Saratov, 1982.

11. Ebzeev B.S. The Soviet State and Human Rights. Saratov, 1986.

12. Ekstein K. Basic Rights and Freedoms: under Russian Constitution and the European Convention. Moscow, 2004.

13. Farber I.E. Freedom and Human Rights in the Soviet State. Saratov: Publishing house of Saratov University. 1974.

14. Freedom of Conscience and Freedom of Speech in an Electronic Epoch: Russia and International Experience: Compilation of works / Edited by B.M. Firsov. S.-Petersburg, 2003.

15. Geldibaev M.H. Human Rights and Custody in Criminal Trial: Theory, History, Practice. S.-Petersburg, 2001.

16. Gomien Donna. The Guidebook of the European Convention on Protection of Human Rights. Strasbourg. The Council of Europe, 1994.

17. Gordeyuk D.V. Realization of the Right of a Child on Residence. Vladimir, 2003.

18. Gorshenev I.P. Theoretical Questions of a personal Constitutional Rights of the Soviet Citizens. Saratov, 1972.

19. Gorshkova S.A. Standards of the Council of Europe of Human Rights and Russian Legislation. Moscow, 2001.

20. Grigoryan L.A. Inviolability of a Dwelling, Secrecy of Correspondence and Telephone Conversations. Moscow, 1980.

21. Guliev V.E., Rudinsky F.M. Democracy and Dignity of a Person /Responsible editor Prof. B.N. Topornin. Moscow, 1983.

22. Guliev V.E., Rudinsky F.M. Socialist Democracy and Rights of a Person. Moscow, 1984.

23. Gluhareva L.I. Human Rights in the Contemporary World, Moscow, 2003.

24. Glushkova S.I. Human Rights in Russia. Theory, History, Practice, Moscow, 2004.

25. Human rights / Chief editor E.A. Lukasheva. Moscow, 1999.

26. Ivanov V.N. Criminally-Legal Protection of Basic Civil Rights. Moscow, 1967.

27. Ivliev G.P. Remedial Guarantees of a personal Immunity at Imprisonment // Questions of the State and the Law in the Developed Socialism / Edited by O.E. Kutafin. Moscow, 1984.

28. Karpov A.I. The Influence of Legal Doctrines about Death Penalty on the Development of Law Enforcement Practice (Historically-legal aspect). Oryol, 2003.

29. Korotky N.N. Procedural Guarantees of a personal Immunity of the Suspected and Accused on a Stage of Preliminary Investigation. Moscow, 1981.

30. Kuchinsky V.A. A Person, Freedom, Law. Moscow, 1978.

31. Kutsova E.F. Guarantees of Rights of a person in Soviet Criminal Trial. Moscow, 1972.

32. Legal Guarantees of Constitutional Rights and Freedoms in a Socialist Society /Edited by L.D. Voevodin. Moscow, 1987.

33. Lukasheva E.A. Socialist Law and a Person. Moscow, 1987.

34. Lyublinsky P.I. Personal Freedom in Criminal Trial. Moscow, 1906.

35. Lyusher F. Constitutional Protection of a personal Rights and Freedoms. Moscow, 1993.

36. Maltsev G.V. Socialist Law and Personal Freedom. Moscow, 1968.

37. Martynchik E.G., Redjkov V.P., Yurchenko V.E. Protection of Rights and Legitimate Interests of a person in Criminal Legal Proceedings /Edited by T.I. Karpov. Kishinev, 1982.

38. Mezyaev A.B. Death Penalty in the Russian Federation: Mutual Understanding of International and National Law. Kazan, 2002.

39. Mironov O.O., Parfyonov V.P. The Right to Defence / Edited by E.A. Lukasheva. Saratov, 1988.

40. Mullerson R.A., Human Rights, Ideas, Provisions, Reality. Moscow, 1991.

41. Nurkaeva T.N. Personal (Civil) Rights and Freedoms of a Person and their Protection by Criminal Means: Questions of Theory and Practice. S.-Petersburg, 2003.

42. Petruhin I.A. Personal Freedom and Criminally-Remedial Compulsion (General Concept of a personal Immunity) /Chief editor I.B. Mihailovskaya. Moscow, 1985.

43. Petruhin I.A. Personal Immunity and Compulsion in Criminal Trial / Chief editor I.B. Mihajlovskaja. Moscow, 1989.

44. Petruhin I.A. Personal Secret (A Person and Authority). Institution of the State and Law of Russian Academy of Science. Moscow, 1998.

45. Rechitsky V.V. Freedom and State. Kharkov, 1998.

46. Revival of Freedom of Conscience and its Protection: Manual on Protection of Human Rights. Moscow, 1999.

47. Romanovsky G.B. Gnoseology of the Right to Life. S. - Petersburg, 2003.

48. Romanovsky G.B. Right to Life. Arkhangelsk; 2002.

49. Romanovsky G.B. Right to Personal Privacy. Moscow, 2001.

50. Rostovschikov I.V. Personal Rights in Russia: their Ensuring and Protection by Law-Enforcement Bodies / Scientific editor N.V. Vitruk. Volgograd, 1997.

51. Rudinsky F.M. A Person and Socialist Legality: Studies. Volgograd, 1976.

52. Rudinsky F.M. Personal Rights and Freedoms of Citizens of the USSR // Constitutional Status of a Person in the USSR. Moscow, 1980.

53. Selihova O.G. The Right to Freedom and Security of a Person. Ekaterinburg, 2003.

54. Serebrennikov I.V. Ensuring of Freedom of Conscience, Religious and World Outlook Belief under the Legislation of Germany. Moscow, 2004.

452   Civil Human Rights in Russia

55. *Sergeev A.P.* The Right to Defence of Reputation. Moscow, 1989.

56. *Shadrin V. S.* Ensuring of Human Rights at Investigation of Crimes. Moscow, 2000.

57. *Shimanovsky V.V.* Observance of Legality at Choosing of the Preventive Punishment at Preliminary Investigation. S. - Petersburg, 1992.

58. *Simorot S.U.* Legal Regulation of Realization of Freedom of Conscience in the Russian Federation. Khabarovsk, 2001.

59. *Smirnov S.A.* Privacy. Moscow, 2002.

60. *Smolkova I.V.* Private Life of Citizens: Bases and Limits of Criminally-Remedial Intervention. Moscow, 1997.

61. *Stetsovsky J.I* Right to Freedom and Security of a Person: Provisions and Reality. Moscow, 2000.

62. *Stetsovsky J.I., Larin I.M.* Constitutional Principle of Ensuring of the Right to Protection of the Accused. Moscow, 1988.

63. *Strogovich M.S.* the Right of the Accused to Defense and Presumption of Innocence /Edited by Prof. V.M. Savitsky. Moscow, 1984.

64. The Law on Freedom of Conscience (1992): International Provisions and Russian Traditions / Chief editor S.B. Filatov. Moscow, 1998.

65. *Tolkachev K.B.* Methodological and Legal Grounds of Realization of a personal Constitutional Rights and Freedoms of a Person and a Citizen and Participation in Law-Enforcement Bodies of the Ministry of Internal Affairs of the Russian Federation. S. - Petersburg. Moscow, 1997.

66. *Tolkachev K.B., Habibulin A.G.* Law-Enforcement Bodies in the Mechanism of Ensuring of a personal Constitutional Rights and Freedoms of Citizens. Ufa, 1991.

67. *Ulitsky S.J.* Political and Legal Problems of Death Penalty. Vladivostok, 2004.

68. *Utyashev M.M., Utyasheva L.M.* Human rights in the Modern Russia, Ufa, 2003.

69. *Voevodin L.D.* Constitutional Rights and Duties of the Soviet Citizens. Moscow, 1972.

70. *Voevodin L.D.* The Legal Status of a Person in Russia: A study-book. Moscow, 1997.

71. *Volodina L.M.* Organizational-Legal Aspects of Mutual Relations of the State and Religious Organizations in Modern Russia. Vladimir, 2000.

72. Volodina L.M. The Mechanism of Protection of Human Rights in Criminal Trial. Tyumen, 1999.

73. Zhuikov V.M. Judicial Protection of Rights of Citizens and Legal Persons. Moscow, Gorodets, 1997.

Dissertations and author's abstracts of dissertations

1. Antipova G.V. The System of a personal Human Rights (Constitutionally-Legal Aspect): Dissertation of...Candidate of Jurisprudence, 2002.

2. Astrakhan A.A. Guarantees and Limits of Realization of Constitutional Rights and Freedoms of the Soviet Citizens: Abstract of Dissertation of...Candidate of Jurisprudence, 1986.

3. Baranova S.G. The Constitutional Law of a Person and a Citizen on Legal Protection: Dissertation of...Candidate of Jurisprudence Ekaterinburg, 2004.

4. Barbin V.V. Constitutionally-Legal Grounds of Limitations of Basic Rights and Freedoms of a Person and a Citizen and their Realization in Activity of Law-enforcement Bodies: Dissertation of...Candidate of Jurisprudence, 2003.

5. Bezlepkin I.V. The Constitutional Bases of Activity of Office of Public Prosecutor on Protection of Rights and Freedoms of a Person and a Citizen in the Russian Federation: Dissertation of...Candidate of Jurisprudence Saratov, 2002.

6. Blotsky V.N. Constitutional Ensuring of Human Rights to Personal Privacy in the Russian Federation: Dissertation of...Candidate of Jurisprudence, 2001.

7. Dolgorukov C.V. The Principle of a personal Immunity in Criminal Legal Proceedings: Abstract of Dissertation of...Candidate of Jurisprudence, Minsk, 1985.

8. Dolzhikov I.V. The Constitutional Criteria of Admissibility of Limitation of Basic Human Civil Rights in the Russian Federation: Dissertation of...Candidate of Jurisprudence, Tyumen, 2003.

9. Ertevtsian M.R. Effectiveness of Realization of the Constitutional Principle of Ensuring of the Right to Protection of the Suspected: Dissertation of...Candidate of Jurisprudence, Kazan, 2002.

10. Fashutdinova N.R. Criminally-Legal Protection of Security of a person and an Obviously False Imprisonment, Detention and Holding in Custody: Abstract of Dissertation of...Candidate of Jurisprudence, Rostov on Don, 1999.

11. Fomichenko. T.M. Constitutionally-Legal Problems of Ensuring of the Right to Life in the Russian Federation in a View of Legal Standards of the Council of Europe: Abstract of Dissertation of...Candidate of Jurisprudence, 2004.

12. Gavrilov B.J. Realization by Bodies of Preliminary Investigation of Provisions about Protection of Constitutional Rights and Freedoms of a Person and a Citizen: Abstract of Dissertation of...Candidate of Jurisprudence, 2001.

13. Gluschenko P.P. Constitutional Rights and Freedoms of Citizens of the Russian Federation: Theoretical and Organizational-Practical Questions of Socially-Legal Protection: Dissertation of ...Doctor of Jurisprudence, S.-Petersburg, 1998.

14. Goncharenko V.D. Human Right to Freedom from Torture and other Cruel, Inhuman or Degrading Treatment or Punishment (Theoretical-Legal Aspects): Dissertation of...Candidate of Jurisprudence, Volgograd, 1999.

15. Gruditsyna L.Y. Features of the Constitutional Guarantees of Realization of Human Rights in Russia (On the example of civil legal proceedings): Dissertation of...Candidate of Jurisprudence, 2004.

16. Homenko N.N. Problems of Constitutionally-Legal Regulation of Death Penalty in the Russian Federation: Dissertation of...Candidate of Jurisprudence, 2001.

17. Kirov A.A. Legal Regulation of Freedom of Movement: Historical Experience and Russian Reality: Dissertation of...Candidate of Jurisprudence, 2003.

18. Komkova G.N. Constitutional Principle of Equality of Rights and Freedoms of a person and a citizen in Russia (Concept, Content, Mechanism of protection): Dissertation of ...Doctor of Jurisprudence, Saratov, 2002.

19. Krasnov I.V. The Constitutional Right on the Qualified Legal Aid and its Ensuring in the Russian Federation: Dissertation of...Candidate of Jurisprudence, Penza, 2003.

20. Kulikov V.A. Personal Inviolability as a Human Right and a Principle of Criminal Trial: Abstract of Dissertation of...Candidate of Jurisprudence, Saratov, 2001.

21. Lebedev V. Judicial Authority on Protection of Constitutional Rights of Citizens on Freedom and Security of a person in Criminal Trial: Abstract of Dissertation of ... Doctor of Jurisprudence. Moscow, 1998.

22. Mamicheva C.V. Rights of Victims of Crimes and Abuse of Power and their Guarantees in the Russian Federation: Dissertation of...Candidate of Jurisprudence, Volgograd, 1998.

23. Manafov A.G. The Constitutional Right of Citizens on the Qualified Legal Aid in the Russian Federation: Dissertation of...Candidate of Jurisprudence, 2002.

24. Melnichenko R.G. The Constitutional Right on Legal Aid: Dissertation of...Candidate of Jurisprudence, Volgograd, 2001.

25. Melnikov N.V. Office of Public Prosecutor of Russia and its Role in Ensuring of Constitutional Rights and Freedoms of Citizens: Dissertation of ...Doctor of Jurisprudence. Rostov on Don, 2001.

26. Morozov I.P. The Constitutional Right of a Person and a Citizen on Freedom and Security of a Person in the Russian Federation: Abstract of Dissertation of...Candidate of Jurisprudence, Saratov, 2002.

27. Ponomarev A.A. Constitutional Basis of Limitation of Rights and Freedoms of a Person and a Citizen in the Russian Federation: Abstract of Dissertation of...Candidate of Jurisprudence, Saratov, 2001.

28. Romanovsky G.B. Constitutional Regulation of the Right to Personal Privacy: Dissertation of...Candidate of Jurisprudence, S.-Petersburg, 1997.

29. Rostovschikova O.V. Freedom of Movement and Freedom of Residence and a Guarantee of its Ensuring and Protection in Russia: Dissertation of...Candidate of Jurisprudence, Volgograd, 2001.

30. Schwarz O.A. Organizational and Remedial Guarantees of the Human Right to Judicial Protection (comparative-legal analysis): Dissertation of...Candidate of Jurisprudence, 1999.

31. Selihova O.G. Constitutionally-Legal Problems of Realization of Rights of Individuals on Freedom and Security of a Person: Abstract of Dissertation of...Candidate of Jurisprudence, Ekaterinburg, 2002.

32. Sergeev A.I. Guarantees of a personal Immunity Connected with Detention and Imprisonment before Trail in the Soviet Criminal Trial: Abstract of Dissertation of...Candidate of Jurisprudence, 1970.

33. Shaimardanov K.D. Constitutionally-Legal Mechanism of Protection of Basic Rights of a Person and a Citizen in the Russian Federation and its Subjects (On the example of Republic Tatarstan): Dissertation of...Candidate of Jurisprudence, Kazan, 2003.

34. Simorot S.U. Legal Regulation of Realization of Freedom of Conscience in the Russian Federation: Dissertation of...Candidate of Jurisprudence, Khabarovsk, 2000.

35. Sinyukova T.V. Legal Guarantees of Realization of Rights and Duties of the Soviet Citizens: Abstract of Dissertation of...Candidate of Jurisprudence, Sverdlovsk, 1986.

36. Snezhko O.A. Constitutional Basis of the State Protection of Rights and Freedoms of a Person and a Citizen in the Russian Federation: Dissertation of...Candidate of Jurisprudence, Saratov, 1999.

37. Solomatin I.V. Problems of Ensuring of Freedom of Conscience in the Russian Federation: Dissertation of...Candidate of Jurisprudence, Surgut, 2003.

38. Strauning E.L. Self-defense of Civil Rights: Dissertation of... Candidate of Jurisprudence, 1999.

39. Tolkachyov C.V. Development of Constitutional Right of Citizens on Entrance and Departure the Russian Federation during Becoming of the Democratic State: Dissertation of...Candidate of Jurisprudence, 2001.

40. Torkunova E.A. Legal Basis of Realization of a Constitutional Right of Russian Citizens on Judicial Protection in the European Court: Dissertation of...Candidate of Jurisprudence, 2002.

41. Tyurin P.U. Constitutional Right of a Person and a Citizen on Inviolability of Dwelling in the Russian Federation: Dissertation of... Candidate of Jurisprudence, Saratov, 2002.

42. Vasilieva E.G .Problems of Limitation of a personal Immunity in Criminal Trial: Abstract of Dissertation of...Candidate of Jurisprudence, Ufa, 2002.

43. Vasin A.L. The Rights of a Person in Russian Political Science: Pre-revolutionary Period: Dissertation of...Candidate of Jurisprudence, Kazan, 1999.

44. Vishniakova I.N. Constitutionally-Legal Regulation of Freedom of Conscience: Dissertation of...Candidate of Jurisprudence, 2000.

45. Volkov S.A. Constitutional Means of Protection of Rights and Freedoms of a Person and a Citizen: Dissertation of...Candidate of Jurisprudence, Rostov on Don, 1999.

46. Vorobiev S.M. The Constitutional Bases of Limitations of a personal Non-property Rights in Activity of Law-enforcement Bodies: Dissertation of...Candidate of Jurisprudence, Ekaterinburg, 2001.

List of Authors

Anisimov, Pavel Viktorovich
Doctor of Jurisprudence, professor (Volgograd)   Chapter 14

Burjanov, Sergey Anatolevich
Lawyer, legal expert (Moscow)   Chapter 9

Glebov, Vasily Gerasimovich
Candidate of Jurisprudence, senior lecturer (Volgograd) Chapter 10

Goncharenko, Vyacheslav Dmitrievich
Candidate of Jurisprudence, senior lecturer (Volgograd) Chapter 6

Hutorskaya, Natalia Borisovna
Candidate of Jurisprudence, senior lecturer (Moscow)   Chapter 12

Kalchenko, Natalia Viktorovna
Candidate of Jurisprudence, senior lecturer (Volgograd) Chapter 3

Kolosovich, Sergey Aleksandrovich
Candidate of Jurisprudence, senior lecturer (Volgograd) Chapter 10

Manafov, Aga Gadirovich
Candidate of Jurisprudence, lawyer (Moscow)   § 2 Chapters 16

Mamicheva, Svetlana Vladimirovna
Candidate of Jurisprudence, lawyer (Volgograd)   Chapter 11

Melnichenko, Roman Grigoryevich
Candidate of Jurisprudence (Volgograd)   § 1 Chapter 16

Menshutina, Elena Ljvovna
Federal judge (Moscow)   Chapter 15

Pavlenko, Evgenie Mihajlovna
Lawyer, post-graduate student (Moscow)   Chapter 18

Ponomarenko, Sergey Ivanovich
Lawyer (Rostov-on-Don)   Chapter 10

Romanovsky, George Borisovich
Candidate of Jurisprudence, senior lecturer   Chapter 8
(Severodvinsk)

Rostovshchikov, Igor Viktorovich
Doctor of Jurisprudence, professor (Volgograd)   Chapter 13

Rostovshchikova, Olga Vasilievna
Candidate of Jurisprudence, senior lecturer (Volgograd) Chapter 7

Rudinsky, Felix Mihajlovich
Doctor of Jurisprudence, professor (Moscow)
Introduction, Conclusion, Chapters 1, 2, 4, 5, 15

Shishenina, Irina Vladimirovna
Lawyer, post-graduate student (Moscow)   § 5 Chapter 1,
                                                     § 3 Chapter 4

Shulga, Ruslan Jurevich
Candidate of Jurisprudence (Moscow)   Chapter 17